# The Elementary School Teacher

# THE
# ELEMENTARY SCHOOL TEACHER

VOLUME XI

SEPTEMBER, 1910—JUNE, 1911

The University of Chicago Press
CHICAGO, ILLINOIS

Published
September, October, November, December, 1910
January, February, March, April, May, June, 1911

Composed and Printed By
The University of Chicago Press
Chicago, Illinois, U.S.A.

# INDEX TO VOLUME XI

## INDEX TO ARTICLES



*Names marked with an asterisk indicate authors of books reviewed.

---

## INDEX TO AUTHORS



*** Names marked with an asterisk indicate authors of books reviewed.**

VOLUME XI NUMBER I

# THE ELEMENTARY SCHOOL TEACHER

SEPTEMBER, 1910

## NATURAL HISTORY IN THE GRADES

OTIS W. CALDWELL
The University of Chicago

### VI. SIXTH GRADE

Pupils of the sixth grade usually are at a stage of development which makes possible and desirable a more prolonged and more intensive study of a few topics as compared with the rather large number that have been outlined in the work of the first five grades. The garden work that was begun during the spring of the preceding school year is used as the basis for part of the sixth-grade work; the other part deals with hygiene and elementary human physiology.

In the preceding spring this grade planted numerous vegetables and flowering plants, some of which have been cared for through the summer. At the opening of school in the autumn the seeds of these plants are available for collection and use in a study of some of the special topics to be considered by the class. In case of plants that mature early and would lose all their seeds during the summer, the entire plants are collected and kept in order that they may be available for school use. The collection of seeds from plants planted by the pupil is in itself a valuable piece of work. Pupils have been studying how plants grow from seeds, how plants must be cared for in order that they may thrive, how pollination is effected, and now the collection and a brief study of seeds completes these general facts of the plant life-cycle. Collection of seeds should be made, carefully labeled and given to the new fifth grade. This supply cannot be entirely depended upon for all needed seeds for the next year's work of the fifth grade, but will be of some value. It is of great educational value, however, to have the sixth and fifth grades co-operate in this way.

The difference in form, size, color, and number of seeds produced by different kinds of well-known plants is always interesting. Various seed-bearing structures (fruits) are well shown by a good collection of garden plants. Comparison may be made between such fruits as those of the radish, cress, shepherd's purse, sunflower, poppy, geranium, pansy, rose, abutilon, evening primrose, wild lettuce, milkweed, and catalpa. Class or individual trips to vacant lots for the purpose of collecting seeds and fruits will result in augmenting the collection and the interest therein. These fruits should be mounted on large cardboard, being grouped according to their source, to their form, or to the persons collecting them.

How many seeds does a plant produce is the next problem that is presented. Here is begun a definite study of the average number of seeds produced by each of a few kinds of plants, the forms selected for this work being those easily handled as the sunflower, radish, evening primrose, jimson-weed, or catalpa. Careful counts are made of the seeds actually found within a number of fruits (pods or heads), and then the average number of those counted is calculated. In one case of seeds which were very small, one class found how many teaspoons of seeds they had, then by arranging in a row on a sheet of paper one teaspoonful they made their estimate. Since, in most cases, the number varies and since there is danger of error the number of fruits from which seeds are counted should be rather large. It is a good plan to have each member of the grade count seeds from at least one fruit of each kind of plant, then have all calculate the average number. The next step is to determine the average number of fruits borne upon one plant. Sometimes as in the case of the catalpa or rose the material available makes this calculation possible for but one plant. By use of the number of seeds in a fruit and the number of fruits on a plant the total seed-production of one plant is approximated. This total number produced from a single plant, presents to children in a striking way the large possibilities for reproduction that are constantly occurring.

The next problem is to determine the area of ground that would be required if all seeds produced should grow next year and produce plants similar to the one that produced these seeds. This is estimated by measuring the area of ground covered by one adult plant of the kind under consideration. As before, several are measured in order that a fairly dependable average may be made. Pupils show much difference of opinion regarding what should be considered as the area covered by one plant, and it has been agreed that the space shaded shall be counted as the space belonging to a plant. This is so considered regardless of the fact that other plants may grow in this shaded area. It is best to estimate a length and breadth of the area covered and thus secure an approximation of the number of square feet, since more complicated arithmetical processes would be entangling. In order to make certain that the significance of the rate of possible increase of space covered is seen, this calculation should be made with more than one plant, or with a plant and an animal (robin, fish, toad), an additional calculation that is helpful is had by calculating the amount of space occupied or the number of offspring produced by the third or fifth generation. It is only by carefully calculated concrete cases that any real significance comes from this work.

The next problem is found in the pupil's statements already frequently made, such as: "It does not happen so"; "Not so many new plants really are produced"; "How does it come that the earth isn't covered by this plant?" "Why do not more plants grow?" "What becomes of all the seeds that do not grow?" "Why do not more individuals of this kind of plant grow?" The fact that not all grow is at once seen by pupils when they have finished the last problem, and they almost immediately begin to suggest some of the reasons that occur to them in explanation of this fact. Observation, study, and consultation produce many aspects of the situation some of which are: there is not space (room) for all to grow and some are stifled after they have begun to grow; some places are too dry for these plants to grow and some too wet; not all can secure adequate light, air, and soil; many seeds fall upon unfavorable places and do not germinate; many seeds decay; many seeds are eaten by birds (refer to fifth-grade work upon the food of birds); many plants are devoured by animals, or killed by plant or animal diseases; but a few survive as compared with all that are possible. These are the ones that grow where they can have space, light, air, water, proper temperature, and that are not destroyed by crowding from other plants or by attacks from herbivorous animals or parasites.

At this point reference should be made to seed distribution which was studied in the fifth grade. Some additional study of structures that serve to carry seeds proves valuable in the new light of these studies, there being apparent now more of the real meaning of having a seed germinate in a relatively unoccupied and favorable place. Also it will prove helpful to bring into the room a square foot of vacant lot soil taken four inches deep, and keep it in a box under favorable conditions so that all seeds in it may grow. Once a week count and remove all seedlings and finally determine how many seeds began to grow in this area.

It is not wise to attempt to carry a study of the struggle for existence into further details in the grades. The concrete data, with some of the relatively evident interpretations, are all that should be sought. This, it is hoped, will furnish a concrete basis upon which some years later a more searching study will be made. It is hoped that an interest will be developed which will cause these pupils always to be observant of the abundant illustrations that relate to this problem.

The reader will find that the fulness of the preceding outline suggests the use of more time than will really be needed to accomplish this work. Some classes will require more time than others but six or seven weeks should be ample.

The major part of this year's work is upon hygiene and elementary human physiology. The forthcoming adolescent period, intensified interest in themselves physiologically, socially, and intellectually, an interest in the industrial and social factors of the environment make this an excellent period for a formal study of this topic. In preceding grades there has been constant admonition by the teacher upon detailed matters pertaining to schoolroom and personal cleanliness, health, and proper positions, exercise, and habits. Indeed, development of habits in proper hygiene must begin as early as does education and continue until their efficiency no longer depends upon constant external stimulus. But at this age it is thought best to give attention to development of an understanding of some of the reasons for proper practices. This should intellectualize some of the previous admonitions, thus giving basis for more faithful performance and extension of habits, and should prepare an intelligent foundation for proper response to the many situations incident to youth.

The preceding elementary-science work leads logically to this work in hygiene. In each grade some study has been made of the life of plants and animals. In schoolroom and garden experiments, in field observations, and in reading there has been a constant study of how plants and animals live; their food, their air and water supply, their relation to one another, the development of young into adults, the diseases that may attack them, pollination, seed-formation, and the new plant, all give in study of both structure and function a background which is believed to furnish the most logical approach to an elementary understanding of the pupil's own body and its needs.

Obviously the amount of experimentation that was used with plants and animals cannot now be made, though much valuable experimentation is possible and necessary. Pupils must look upon their bodily actions from the point of view of experiment; sometimes they must really perform experiments; and often they must interpret their own function in terms of what they know of plants and animals. Good topics for introductory experiments are circulation, respiration, and muscular activity. All know something of each of these functions and each pupil can be interested at once in comparing his condition with that of his fellows. For example, two boys were at the opening of this work called before the class and their pulses taken (a process with which all are familiar). These boys were then told to run around the block in which the school building stands and return immediately to the room. The pulses were again taken. An explanation of the difference in readings was called for, and this furnished a basis for beginning work upon the circulatory system. The same sort of an experiment is good for introducing respiration and for relating it to circulation. The nature of some of the leading bones and their relation to one another in muscular work may be introduced by a study of several gymnastic feats with which all children are familiar.

Organs and the processes that are performed by means of them are studied not anatomically or from the point of view of physics and chemistry, but from the point of view of their proper efficient working. How the parts of a healthy human animal work when highest efficiency is secured must be made clear. Then to secure constantly this high efficiency attention must be given to things that interfere with it. Improper posture is not wrong primarily because it may lead to crooked bones, though that is bad, but primarily because crooked bones reduce efficiency. Good heart-action, respiration, sight, hearing, digestion, etc., enable us to do more bodily and intellectual work. Abuse of the body resulting in reduction of vitality simply involves disposing of part of our native capital by means of which we might accomplish things. Ventilation, cleanliness, proper bodily temperature, proper sleep, etc., are the conditions under which bodily parts may work properly.

Infection and disease also have a place in this course. By reference again to diseases of plants and animals and to what is already known of human disease a fairly clear notion of the nature of bacterial disease may be given. Some simple demonstrations in growth of bacteria in test tubes, this being elaborated by careful and concrete discussion, proves helpful. The distribution of bacteria, especially disease-producing bacteria, means of infection in case of some of the common diseases, proper water, milk, and food supply are topics for demonstration and discussion.

The influence of alcohol and narcotics is one of the topics that must be considered in connection with highest efficiency of the human body. This topic, as some others, must be kept free from foolish emotionalism and kept upon the basis of individual and social efficiency. That it is an ethical question is obvious; also bodily efficiency is an ethical question. The best reaction from instruction upon dangers from alcohol and narcotics will doubtless come from a clear and abiding understanding of the relation they bear to the normal work of the human body.

This grade should study the city regulations regarding public health—water and milk supply, garbage and sewage disposal, street-cleaning, the city health department. The school and home garden and the general movement relative to beautifying home grounds should be emphasized in its bearing upon public health.

Such a course in hygiene as here outlined is greatly benefited if a simple, direct, readable, and appropriate book can be used as a pupil's reader. A series of books for different grades has been prepared by Dr. Luther Halsey Gulick. Of this series one well suited to the sixth grade is *The Body and Its Defenses.*

# AN EXPERIMENT IN INDUSTRIAL EDUCATION

ALFRED P. FLETCHER
Director of Industrial Training, Public Schools of Rochester, N.Y.

A quarter of a century ago educators of the United States saw clearly the need for industrial education. Their addresses and magazine articles on that subject make interesting and timely reading today. The arguments which we are using were used by them.

As the leaders in educational work were looking about for some plan of handwork which could be brought into the curricula of the schools, two carefully worked-out systems were discovered. These were the Russian system of manual training with its abstract exercises, and the Swedish sloyd system with its perfectly graded series of models.

These forms of handwork with various modifications have been gradually introduced into our schools until today the city system which does not include manual training from its primary grades through the high school is considered unprogressive.

Few will deny that manual training has had a great and beneficial influence upon our education. That it is, however, inadequate as a system of industrial training is evidenced by the great demand for vocational training now arising in all parts of the country. Some of the existing conditions that show the necessity of such training may be briefly stated in the following paragraphs.

The skilled labor of the country is largely foreign born. The supply of skilled workers is far below the demand and our American boys are not being trained to fill the positions. For years we have been saying, "Every boy ought to learn a trade," but we have provided no opportunities for him to learn that trade. As a helper under a journeyman mechanic he has had a chance to pick up a little of the practice but practically nothing of the theory of the trade.

Our schools are failing to hold the boys until they reach the age when the industries want them, and as a result the years of fourteen to sixteen have come to be known as the "wasted years."

Our education is characterized as undemocratic in that it is planned for the small number who are being prepared for higher education. Where our schools do train for the industries the aim is to turn out captains of industry rather than privates in the industrial army.

These and many other equally valid arguments are today presented to us. As a result our manual-training high schools are changing their names to technical high schools; trade schools are being established, and many experiments are being tried in the field of elementary education. The purpose of this article is to describe one such experiment.

In December, 1907, one of the leaders of industrial educational work in this country said to a Rochester teacher, "The way to start a vocational school is not to read books on the subject nor to examine the courses of study of schools already established, but to make an investigation of the needs of the local industries and a study of the 'boy' problem in a given community. The data thus obtained will point the way to the kind of school which your locality requires."

Following this bit of advice an investigation was made by the writer into the conditions and future prospects of the boys in the sixth, seventh, and eighth grades of the grammar schools.

It was found that 14 per cent of the boys of these grades were fourteen years of age or over, were not expecting to enter high school, and were on the point of dropping out to go to work. It was evident, therefore, that any form of instruction which would keep such boys in school for a year or two longer would be of real value. Visits to many of the local factories gave much help as to the kinds of instruction which would best fit boys to get a position quickly and to make rapid advancement after entering the industry. Some of the points mentioned by factory superintendents and foremen were: practice in the use of mathematical principles in actual shop problems; a general knowledge of materials, their kinds, methods of preparation for market, etc.; a clear and accurate working knowledge of the most common tools of the industry and skill in their use, and lastly, the ability to use time to the best advantage.

Following this investigation circular letters were sent to the principals of the grammar schools and to the parents of those boys who might be expected to enter. These letters explained the purpose of the school, the courses to be offered, and the proposed method of instruction. As a result, one hundred boys applied for admission.

During the past eighteen months three vocational schools, two for boys and one for girls, have been established. A brief description is here given of one of these, known as Rochester Shop School No. 34, which was the first school to be established in New York State under the new industrial education law.

The school was organized in an old eight-room school building not otherwise needed for school purposes. Teachers were obtained from various places, i.e., an all-around cabinet maker was secured from a local furniture factory, one teacher with normal and college training was secured for the book work, and an electrical engineer with practical experience was put in charge of the electrical shop.

The school at the present time has four departments: Cabinet-making, Carpentry, Electrical, and Plumbing, with 26 boys in each department—13 in the first-year class and 13 in the advanced or second-year class. This means that not more than 13 boys will be graduated from each department yearly.

The faculty includes a principal, who spends part of his time in teaching, four shop instructors, a classroom teacher, and an instructor in drawing.

The Cabinet-making Department is a complete little factory with its glueing-room, machine-room, assembly room, and finishing-room. In this department there is division of labor, the boys being promoted from one branch of the work to another as soon as a reasonable degree of efficiency has been acquired. Following is a list of articles now being manufactured:

## LINE OF PRODUCTS FOR 1910

ELEMENTARY

25 large drawing-boards
100 primary looms
25 pillow looms, with heddles
100 drawing-kits
25 sawhorses
50 sewing-boxes
36 manual-training benches
12 umbrella racks

ADVANCED

50 bookcases, 2 designs
120 desk chairs
20 teacher's sanitary desks
12 music cabinets
Sample line for the following year

Any article to be included in the "line" of products must meet two conditions: (1) it must be something needed in the schools and which the Board of Education would otherwise purchase; (2) it must have educative value for the pupil. Many needed articles are rejected because the making of them would teach the boys little or nothing. The instructor of this department personally directs the work of the machine-room and supervises the work of the other rooms largely through boy foremen. The

### COST OF ROCHESTER SHOP SCHOOL
DECEMBER 1, 1908 TO JANUARY 1, 1910
(Including the Summer Session)

| | General | Cabinet-making Department | Electrical Department | Total |
|---|---|---|---|---|
| Equipment | 442.76 | 2,132.62 | 335.21 | 2,910.59 |
| Sinking fund (10 per cent of equipment) | 44.28 | 213.26 | 33.52 | 291.06 |
| Salaries | 1,954.00* | 1,965.00 | 1,250.00 | 5,169.00 |
| Material | 1,078.12 | 1,746.48 | 486.97 | 3,311.57 |
| Drawing supplies | 74.95 | ....... | ....... | 74.95 |
| Repairs | 257.44† | ....... | ....... | 257.44 |
| | | 3,924.74 | 1,770.49 | 9,104.02 |
| Totals | 3,408.79 | (1,859.35) | (1,549.44) | |
| Grand totals | ....... | 5,784.09‡ | 3,319.93§ | 9,104.02 |
| Credits¶ | ....... | 2,631.50 | 308.14 | 2,939.64 |
| Net totals | ....... | 3,152.59 | 3,011.79 | 6,164.38 |
| Average cost per pupil | ....... | 63.05 | 60.24 | 61.64 |
| Average cost per pupil (10 months) | ....... | 52.54 | 60.24 | 56.39 |

* Includes cost of lighting and heating.

† The general expense is apportioned between the Cabinet-making and the Electrical departments.

‡ Includes the product of the Cabinet-making Department. This department was on a productive basis for nine of the twelve months.

¶ The item of credits gives the value of the work performed by the pupils.

§ Covers the 63 jobs of electrical work in the various school buildings of the city. The Electrical Department was on a productive basis only three of the ten months (October 1 to December 21).

cost accounts of each department of the school are kept separately. The table shows a statement which has recently been prepared for the Board of Education and which shows the cost of two of the departments for the first year.

ARTICLES MADE

| | |
|---|---|
| 200 Bookcases | 25 drawing-tables |
| 18 kindergarten tables | 62 sawhorses |
| 32 saw boxes | 25 bench rests |
| 25 drawing-boards | 15 miscellaneous articles |
| 12 sewing-boxes | 200 looms |
| 100 toy knitters | 700 panels |

The following are typical examples of the work done:

October 1—Replacing telephones, School No. 23.
October 15—Installing buzzer, Board of Education office.
November 2—Repairing gongs, School No. 4.
November 9—Installing lights, East High School.
November 17—Repairing fire alarms, School 27.
December 15—Installing spot light, School No. 14.
December 20—Repairing stereopticon, School No. 26.

The Carpentry and Plumbing departments have been in operation less than a year and the expense of maintenance cannot be given. The cost of equipment for these departments would not exceed $300 each.

The carpentry, plumbing, and electrical shopwork taught in the school is much the same as would be taught in any trade school in these branches. The really valuable and vital shopwork however, is the installation and repair work which is being done in the various school buildings of the city by the groups of boys sent out from the shop school. It is often said that no trade can be taught in a school, yet, when the school shopwork is supplemented by the doing of all kinds of real work under the varying conditions which constantly arise, the opportunities for a thorough grounding in the craft are immeasurably increased. This outside work is much more interesting to the pupils than any work which would be constructed merely for the sake of construction and which would have to be torn down. The confidence gained by the boys in attempting and mastering these varying problems plays no small part in their progress. Since the materials used in the outside work are not wasted and the labor performed by the boys has a real value and results in a considerable saving to the city, the cost of instruction in the school is brought down to a very conservative figure.

A concrete example of the outside work may perhaps be interesting. On Monday morning a call comes from a grammar school that the fire alarm system is out of order. That afternoon a group of boys visits the school and locates the trouble. The next morning they make out a bill of materials needed for the repair work. If the job is at all complicated they also make the necessary drawings. As soon as the materials are delivered the same group of boys returns to the school and makes the proper repairs. In many cases this work is carried out under a boy foreman and only inspected by the instructor when completed.

At this moment of writing (March 15, 2:30 P.M.) one group of boys from the Electrical Department is at school No. 33 putting guards on the lights for basket-ball, a second group is at school No. 23 repairing the lighting circuit, and a third group with an instructor is at school No. 13 repairing the intercommunicating telephone system. A group of boys from the Plumbing Department is setting and connecting a sink at No. 34. A group from the Carpentry Department is building teachers' lockers for school No. 25, and a second group is erecting a portable schoolhouse in the rear of the shop school.

In the drafting-room the boys make the designs, working-drawings, tracings, and blueprints of the articles to be constructed in the shops and of the work called for in the various school buildings.

The courses in drawing and mathematics are outlined by the shop instructors to meet the demands of the shopwork. The ideal toward which we are working is this: today the need of some formula is met in the shop; during the next period in the classroom the pupil will have an opportunity to work out this formula. How completely this ideal can be realized is as yet a problem. The effect of this correlation is that the incentives for book work are direct and vital rather than indirect and unappreciated, as is often the case in ordinary school work.

The work of the classroom is largely individual. Since boys are admitted at any time during the year it follows that general class work in some subjects (i.e., drawing and mathematics) is impossible. Pupils will also be graduated at any time in the year at which the course will be finished. The average length of time for the completion of any course will be two years.

This individual rather than class graduation will decidedly simplify the matter of finding positions for the boys as they leave the school. Textbooks to fit the various courses are at present being worked out by the instructors. The time given for the various subjects is as follows:

Shopwork, 15 hours weekly.
Mathematics, 4 hours weekly.
English, 3½ hours weekly.
Drawing, 5 hours weekly.
Spelling and industrial history, 2½ hours weekly.

The school day is six hours in length, except for the groups who go in the afternoon to outside work. For these the working day would probably average 7½ hours.

The question is often asked regarding the attitude of the labor unions toward the school. So far the most friendly spirit has been maintained on both sides. Every effort is made to keep the local unions fully informed regarding the plans and methods of the school.

While it is altogether too early to make any predictions regarding the future of the school or its real value to the boy or the community, it is certain that a school of this type will reach and holds many boys for whom the grammar or high school has no attractions. To such boys a shop course gives a new interest and a new sense of successful accomplishment. The real test of the value of the training, however, will come when the boys graduate and enter the industries.

A careful following of the boy after he begins his life-work and a study of the defects in his preparation will afford most valuable data for the improvement of the courses.

# AGRICULTURAL EDUCATION: EDUCATIONAL PERIODICALS

BENJAMIN MARSHALL DAVIS
Miami University

The number of educational periodicals published in the United States probably exceeds that on any other subject. Most of these publications are in the library of the United States Bureau of Education. In 1906 they numbered one hundred and fifty-six (64).[1]

For purposes of classification the periodicals included in this number may be considered fairly representative of all such publications in the United States. They naturally fall into three groups: (1) general, including those devoted to subjects of general interest or to various general problems in education, and whose circulation is not limited to any particular section of the country or class of readers; (2) special, including those devoted to some single phase of education, as, for example, orthography, penmanship, phonetics, geography, school art, manual training, science, etc.; (3) local, including those whose main circulation is confined to a single state or group of states.

The bibliography alone of contributions and references to agricultural education in these periodicals would occupy several times the space allotted to a single article of this journal. It will therefore be necessary to confine the discussion of this subject, as represented in various educational periodicals, to some references of historical interest in Barnard's *Journal of Education,* and to a brief account of each of the above three groups.

No investigation of an educational movement would be complete without consulting Barnard's *Journal of Education.* "Wherever libraries of education are now gathered his encyclopedic journal has a place of honor. Whoever will found such a

[1] The references are to the bibliography at the end of this article or to bibliographies in other articles of this series.

library must look first to secure a set of this great work. Because he saw so far, the contents of that great work will not soon grow out of date." (65). In this work are many references to agricultural education. Three are worthy of special interest: early agricultural schools; agriculture in schools for homeless children and in schools for delinquent children; and agricultural education in foreign countries.

An account is given of probably the first agricultural school in the United States. It was founded in 1797 at Lethe, S.C., by Dr. John de la Howe. He left a will which provided for the endowment of "an agricultural or farm school in conformity, as near as can be, to a plan proposed in the *Columbian Magazine* for the month of April, 1787, for educating, boarding, and clothing twelve poor boys and twelve poor girls of the Abbeville District." The endowment consisted of 500 acres of farm land and 1,000 acres of forest (66).

An account of another early school is of interest because it anticipated some of the present notions of industrial education. The following is a quotation from a letter of a Mr. Coe to the son of Josiah Holbrook, the founder of the school:

> He [Josiah Holbrook] had long cherished the idea of endeavoring to found an institution in which the course of instruction should be plain and practical; an agricultural school, where the science of chemistry and mechanics and land surveying should be thoroughly drilled into the minds of the pupils by practice. With these views the agricultural seminary was commenced in Derby (Conn.) in 1824, and continued to the fall of 1825, under the direction of your father and myself; and, as far as I know, was the first educational movement of the kind in all that region. . . . . We did what we could to train the students in the *analysis of soils* and in the application of the mechanical powers to all farming operations, and took out our young men often into the field and country for practical surveying, geological excursions, road making, and the labors of the farm; but not being able at that time to place the school on an eligible foundation, it was abandoned (67).

Josiah Holbrook after giving up his school turned his attention to adult instruction which was somewhat like our present agricultural extension among farmers.

Our present organization of agricultural colleges is very

similar to a plan for such schools proposed in Barnard's *Journal of Education* in 1856 by Professor John A. Porter of Yale. This was the year after the act establishing the first agricultural college (Michigan) was passed and the year before it was formally opened. He deplored the lack of agricultural instruction in this country and suggested that such instruction might be supplied by having a demonstration farm, an experiment farm, and means of instruction in all sciences connected with culture of the soil. He says:

> What a center of light would such a school as here described be to the whole agricultural community. All purported discoveries in agriculture would come to be tested, and important truths developed by experiment would go forth from it into the world. . . . . Through its pupils it would disseminate widely the varied practical information which its courses would furnish, and beyond this, it might be made a means of eliciting the experimental labor of hundreds of intelligent farmers throughout the country, for the decision of the important agricultural questions which are still unsettled (68).

In a footnote at the end of the article the editor calls attention to an account in his *National Education in Europe* of the system of agricultural education established in France as it was in 1854, and also to the Institute of Agriculture and Forestry in Würtemburg, and the system of agricultural education in Ireland.

Pestalozzi and his work, particularly his influence on our own school practices, receive much consideration in the journal under discussion. For example, we find the historical beginning of nature-study in this country in the object-teaching at Oswego. This attempt to put his doctrine into practice is described in great detail (69). In another place Pestalozzi is quoted as saying with reference to objective teaching that "agricultural labor offers a wider field than any other employment for this means." This statement should be contrasted with the absurd efforts made in some schools to apply these principles. It would be interesting in this connection to trace the influence of these early object-lessons on nature-study teaching and to discover to what extent it is responsible for the struggle which nature-study has had to find a legitimate place in our schools.

The agricultural school of De Fellenburg and Wehrli was a

school for the poor at Hopwyl, and many of the pupils were juvenile offenders of various sorts (70). Several Fellenburg schools were established in this country in the early part of the last century. The *Journal* brought the work of these schools in this country and in Europe into notice again. About the same time there seems to have been a revival of these methods in certain schools and institutions in this country. Practically all of the reform schools for boys in the United States are now provided with farms, and agriculture is an important part of their work. How much influence, if any, the *Journal* had in bringing this about we do not know. But we find it giving, on the one hand, details of such work as in the agricultural school just referred to, and on the other, accounts and discussions of reform schools and institutions for homeless children in this country (71).

Education in foreign countries occupied a prominent place in the *Journal*. From time to time accounts of agricultural education in various countries appeared. A good example of these accounts is to be found in one devoted to agricultural education in France and about twenty different parts of the world. This is a part of an exhaustive study of scientific instruction applied to national industries in different countries (72).

The first group of educational periodicals—those mainly devoted to general problems of education or to publication of educational research—is quite small in number compared with the other two groups. Their circulation is also much less than most of those of the third group. Notwithstanding their small number and limited circulation these periodicals contain some of our most valuable educational literature, and are, on the whole, a source of high authority in educational matters. The attention given to agricultural education is much less than would seem to be warranted in view of the great public interest in the subject and of the fact of its rapid introduction into schools of various sections of the country. Compared with other sources the literature on this subject as found in the leading periodicals of this group is very meager (Barnard's *Journal* excepted). A few of the earlier articles discuss how agricultural education might be gradually developed in the elementary and secondary schools. Some work of an extension character was regarded at that time (1900–1) as the most feasible and practicable, nature-study, reading courses, itinerant schools, and short courses being suggested as the best means of creating an interest in the subject (73, 74).

A little later the place of agriculture in our public-school system is carefully considered with conclusions favorable to its introduction (75). In the meantime the subject is being rapidly introduced in our schools, and certain tendencies are arising that are viewed with some alarm because they are not in harmony with the national policy in school matters. An editorial in one periodical calls attention to some of the dangers arising from the establishment of agricultural high schools:

> If the new type of work means the establishment of a *separate* system of high schools, the existing high schools will be sapped of the very means of their existence. . . . . There is one other and more urgent reason why a separate class of high schools must not be allowed to spring up. Just as sure as they do they will breed social distinctions and cause stratifications in society. It has been our boast that children of all nationalities, occupations, and creeds enter our schoolroom doors and emerge together as American citizens. The American public school is the greatest factor in developing American citizenship that we possess, and its function in developing American citizenship is greater than teaching arithmetic, Latin, or trades. Social efficiency is much more needed just now than business efficiency. But alas, too many are thinking only of business acumen. . . . . The one who argues for the establishment of a separate system of agricultural high schools or separate industrial high schools is wittingly or unwittingly an enemy to our present high schools and to true democracy (76, pp. 57–59).

The implication in this editorial that existing high schools furnish all that is really needed in secondary education is open to question, and soon brings a rejoinder:

> I am afraid that the distinctions are here or have got to come, and that the high schools which are nothing more than college preparatory schools will have to sink into relative insignificance compared with schools which will teach the masses how to make a living as well as how to live. . . . . We need as never before many-sided men and women, but men and women who will put how to live and how to make a living first, and how to use one's leisure second (77, p. 199).

At present the importance of the problem suggested in the foregoing discussion is being appreciated, and all the more because agricultural high schools continue to be established. Besides general discussions of the whole question of industrial education as related to elementary and secondary schools two plans for agricultural education in existing high schools are proposed and are being considered. For example, one writer believes in the correlation of high-school science and agriculture and gives numerous illustrations to show that "the benefit of correlation inures as well to the fundamental sciences as to their application in agriculture" (78). Another thinks that agriculture should be taught as a separate science. He says:

"Educators are coming to see more and more clearly that agriculture is both a science and an art, and as a result it is being taught in ways which are not strictly applicable to the teaching of other sciences." He sums up fifty-six replies to a questionnaire sent out to secondary-school men and college professors and concludes that a "majority who have had actual experience in teaching the subject advocate its being taught separately (79)."

Among the periodicals of the second group two are devoted to special phases of education that include agriculture. One is *School Science and Mathematics* and the other is the *Nature-Study Review*. The former is published in the interest of secondary education and the latter of elementary education. The editors and associate editors of both periodicals are well-known schoolmen who are actively interested in the various problems of education of their own special lines of work.

In a recent number of *School Science and Mathematics* we find among the introductory sentences of an article on biologic science in secondary schools the following:

> This is pre-eminently an age of applied science; it is an intensely practical age; the average individual comes in daily contact with problems of science as never before. It is self-evident that science work in elementary schools should play an important part in the education of our youth who go into life—as a vast majority do—with no further fitting than that received in the elementary school or secondary school. It was with this thought in mind that the writer began the following preliminary investigation which aims in the first place to present some statistics bearing upon

the teaching of science, and especially of biologic science, in the secondary schools, and in the second place to suggest possible modifications in our present courses in biologic science that will make such courses a better preparation for the kind of life into which most of our young people are launching, the active life of the thinking, doing citizen (80).

This somewhat lengthy quotation with respect to one secondary-school subject is given because it represents very well the general attitude of the recent contributors to this journal. Agriculture is closely allied to all of the fundamental sciences and any such modifications of science teaching as indicated in the above reference will have an important bearing on agricultural education in the secondary schools. These contributors are already teaching particular branches of science, and their writings have to do with their own subjects in relation to agriculture rather than with agriculture as a separate subject.

The general field covered by the *Nature-Study Review* includes, as is stated in the introduction to the first number, "school gardening and the closely allied elementary agriculture" (81). This magazine is now in its sixth volume and has published numerous articles on agriculture as adapted to the elementary schools. For awhile, from September to December, 1909, a special department of school agriculture was conducted. But it was abandoned, the policy now being to devote certain numbers exclusively to this subject, as in the May number of the present volume.

The third group includes about one hundred periodicals in which every section of the country is represented. It is through these that the masses of the teachers are reached. In many states some educational periodical becomes a sort of official organ for the state department of education. Practically all whose subscribers are teachers in the rural schools give considerable attention to agriculture, mainly in the way of suggestions and helps to teachers. The effect of these periodicals on the actual teaching of agriculture in the public schools has been, up to the present, far greater than of any of the first or second group. One periodical, the *School News* (Illinois), has been referred to in a previous article of this series (42). It was one of the first to take up elementary agriculture in response to the new demand upon the rural teachers. In 1900 it began to publish short articles on various phases of agriculture adapted to the elementary schools. The practical efforts of this magazine to help the rural teachers is further shown in connection with the new course of study for the state of Illinois. This course includes agriculture. The department of the magazine devoted to school work in agriculture expands the course of study in agriculture into descriptive details and gives specific directions to teachers as to how to present the new work (82).

The *Nebraska Teacher,* besides publishing special articles on various phases of agriculture, is now publishing a series of articles by Superintendent E. C. Bishop on "Agriculture and Home Economics" (83). These articles are intended to assist teachers in their work with the boys' and girls' clubs of the state.

Many similar examples might be given but these two are typical of the work that is now being done by many if not most of the periodicals of the third group. They are close to the teachers and seem to know what they need, or at least what they want, and give it to them in a simple and concrete way.

## BIBLIOGRAPHY

Only references cited by number in the text are included.

64. "Educational Periodicals." U.S. Bureau of Education. *Report* of the Commissioner (1906), pp. 257–59.

This is a list of educational periodicals in the United States in 1906 that are in the library of the Bureau of Education.

65. "Henry Barnard," C. H. THURBER, *School Review,* VIII (1900), 505–6.

A tribute to the life and work of Henry Barnard.

66. "Fellenburg and Manual Labor Schools," HENRY BARNARD, Barnard's *Journal of Education,* XV (1865), 232–34.

An account of the influence of Fellenburg's Agricultural School at Hofwyl on the establishment of similar schools in this country.

67. "Josiah Holbrook," HENRY BARNARD, *ibid.,* VII (1860), 229–47.

68. "Plan of an Agricultural School," JOHN A. PORTER, *ibid.,* I (1856), 329–35.

69. "Primary Instruction by Object Lessons," *ibid.,* XII (1862), 605–45.

This is a report of a committee selected by the Board of Education of the city of Oswego, N.Y., to attend an examination of the primary schools of that city with special reference to an investigation of the system of object-teaching recently introduced into these schools.

70. "Pestalozzi, De Fallenburg and Wehrli, and Industrial Training," *ibid.*, X (1876), 81–92.

Republished from the *Transactions of the National Association for the Promotion of Social Science,* 1858.

71. "Preventive and Reformatory Education," HENRY BARNARD, *ibid.*, III (1858), 561–818.

A very complete discussion of the subject including the work in foreign countries as well as in our own country.

72. "Scientific Instruction," HENRY BARNARD, *ibid.*, XXI (1871), 807.

73. "Newer Ideas in Agricultural Education," L. H. BAILEY, *Educational Review,* XX (1900), 377–82.

74. "A Significant Factor in Agricultural Education," KENYON L. BUTTERFIELD, *Educational Review,* XXI (1901), pp. 301–9.

Extension work advocated.

75. "Place of Nature-Study, School Gardens and Elementary Agriculture in Our School System," J. R. JEWELL, *Pedagogical Seminary,* XIII (1906), pp. 273–292.

This is preliminary to a more complete presentation of the same subject (21).

76. "Agricultural High Schools," FREDERICK E. BOLTON, *School Review,* XVI (1908), 56–58.

An editorial note.

77. "The Agricultural High School," ARTHUR D. CROMWELL, *ibid.*, 198–200.

A rejoinder to (76).

78. "The Correlation of High-School Science and Agriculture," JOSIAH MAIN, *Education,* XXX (1909), 135–45.

79. "Shall Secondary Agriculture Be Taught as a Separate Science?" G. A. BRICKER, *ibid.*, 352–56.

A view directly opposite to that expressed in (78) is presented.

80. "The Methods, Content and Purpose of Biologic Science in the Secondary Schools of the United States," G. W. HUNTER, *School Science and Mathematics,* X (1910), pp. 1–10, 103–11.

81. "Introduction" (to first number), M. A. BIGELOW, *Nature Study Review,* I (1905), 1–2.

82. "School Work in Agriculture," D. O. BARTO (Taylorville, Ill.), *School News,* XXI (1907).

A department of this magazine for aiding teachers to make use of the prescribed state course of study in elementary agriculture.

83. "Lessons in Agriculture and Home Economics," E. C. BISHOP (Lincoln, Neb.), *Nebraska Teacher,* XII (1910).

A series of articles to aid teachers in their work with the Nebraska boys' and girls' clubs.

# THE TEACHING OF MORALS IN GUATEMALA[1]

ROY TEMPLE HOUSE
Weatherford, Okla.

At least one of the little Central American states is making an earnest and consistent effort to prove her title to serious consideration. The government of Guatemala is now sending her official publications to educational institutions in the United States. Guatemalan documents run somewhat to poetry and rhetoric, but statistics and real information are not lacking, and the series furnishes valuable data for a study of the ambitious little state which issues them.

The treatise on morals to which the present article calls attention has been in print for ten years, but it was sent out as a government bulletin only a few weeks ago, and has probably been hitherto quite unknown to American educators. The fashion is so nearly universal with us of tabooing formal instruction in morals, that the title of the volume may discourage examination of it. But read the compiler's preface before passing adverse judgment; and ponder especially that part of it which gives specific instructions for its use. You will meet a frank admission that a class in morals, devoting a definite period to the study of that excellent but somewhat dreary subject, would accomplish considerably less than nothing; but it does not follow that a text like the one we have before us (says the estimable Latin educator) cannot be productive of untold good. Let every teacher in the school, no matter what his subject, master this volume's content and arrangement and lay it on his desk as a weapon to be used when occasion arises.

Suppose now that while a mathematics class is in progress, the master, furtively watching the conduct of his audience while ostensibly intent on the current demonstration, should notice

[1] Rafael Spínola, *Moral razonada.* Primer Curso. Guatemala, Tipografia Nacional, 1900.

that a certain hard-hearted youth on the back seat is torturing a fly; he must interrupt his demonstration and warn the children that cruelty to animals is a mistake and a sin; and to complete his lessons in morals, he should call the offender forward and force him to read aloud to the class the chapter which deals with our duties toward the other members of the animate world. Or again, suppose a child appears in the grammar class with soiled hands or clothing; it is advisable that the teacher suspend his discussion of the parts of speech till the offender has read to his fellow-grammarians a few paragraphs from that section of the ever-ready reference volume which deals with the care of the person and clothing. Latin grandiloquence is always somewhat amusing to an Anglo-Saxon; but the constant binding of general principles to individual cases of application is the only effective method of teaching morals, as it is the only effective method of teaching anything else.

We are told that the volume before us is for the use of the primary schools only; that the same author has compiled a *Tratado de Moral Filosófica y Pedagógica* for study in the secondary schools for boys, and another for the schools for girls, in addition to a companion volume to the one we are now discussing, which is to be read by and to the smaller girls. For the audience to which our book is addressed a large part of it seems to handle questions in a manner that has a trifle too much of subtlety; and such subjects as the moral basis of matrimony, for example, seem a little out of place in a book intended for the use of small boys; but the second criticism, at least, is met and faced by the author in his preface. It is unfortunately true, he reminds us, that the majority of boys never reach the advanced schools at all, hence it is necessary to give them at this time advice with regard to all the problems of later life, or they will never receive it at all. One might retort that several eminently useful branches of study which are reserved for the higher schools might on the same ground be given to small children; but such a retort is scarcely an argument, and there is something to be said for Señor Spínola's inclusion.

The book is a large one. There are nearly six hundred

pages, of which perhaps one-fourth is the author's own discussion of manners and morals, and the remaining three-fourths a selection of appropriate reading material from classic sources. It flatters an Anglo-Saxon reader to find that the author who is perhaps most generally quoted is the English moralist Samuel Smiles. The selection is surprisingly varied, and on the whole is an extremely good one. There is no school reader published in the United States which draws its material from so wide a field. An English translation of the *Moral Razonada* would furnish the child such a collection of classic discussion with an ethical bent as is scarcely accessible to him at present.

A very practical section of the book is formed by thirty pages of social "don'ts," as to whose origin we are furnished the somewhat hazy information that "The author of this excellent Compendium of Urbanity is anonymous, and it is translated into Spanish by the young Don Enrique Díaz Durán." One wonders a little concerning the practicability or advisability of warning the ten-year-old boy who perhaps owns just one suit of clothes and one pair of trousers at a time, "Do not wear black clothing in the morning, or at least do not wear black trousers with an ordinary sack coat; wear them only in the evening;" and there is a charming naïveté that an Anglo-Saxon can only admire but never emulate, in the injunction, "Do not whistle in the street, in a public vehicle, in church, at the theater, the circus or any public gathering, or in any place where whistling might annoy anyone. I might better say: Do not whistle anywhere." It is a little puzzling, again, to read on p. 115 a moving picture of the evils that inevitably follow the use of tobacco, and on pp. 370 and 379 a set of careful directions to be observed by smokers. In general, the rules here given are the rules observed in polite society north of the Rio Grande, and it is probable that drilling them into the hard head of a ten-year-old youth will make him more of a gentleman, even if he does struggle a little at the time of injection.

Though two of his most frequently cited authorities are Samuel Smiles and Benjamin Franklin, Señor Spínola is no utilitarian. Let us translate a part of one of his earlier paragraphs, retaining the typography that gives the book one element of its quaint charm:

> *A very essential quality of virtue.*—In order that virtue be GENUINE and not a FALSE virtue, it is necessary that he who practices it have not sordid self-interest in view, and that he do not practice it either from FEAR OF PUNISHMENT or HOPE OF REWARD; such motives degrade the reason of a man, which is what constitutes his DIGNITY AND SOVEREIGNTY. Virtue should be practiced for VIRTUE'S SAKE ONLY. . . . .

And may this earnest treatise inspire the young Guatemalans to a love of the right that will save their country from the errors that have retarded neighboring states!

# THE SCHOOL AND THE LIBRARY [1]

CHARLES H. JUDD
The University of Chicago

It gives me great pleasure to appear before this gathering as the representative of the National Education Association. I do not know what qualifications are ordinarily sought in such a representative, but I judge that two are at least permitted. First, one must be unable to attend the meetings of the National Education Association itself, because it is so far away; and second, one must be supplied with a liberal lack of knowledge of library science. Whatever the qualifications of the representative it is an easy task to say to the Library Association that there is a close bond connection and sympathy between the two associations. We who teach cannot do the work of the schools without recognizing our dependence on the work that is being done in the community by the library; and I venture to assume that you feel the reciprocal relations yourselves and recognize the importance of a good school in a city where you conduct a good library.

If I make an effort to comment in any wise upon library matters I shall have to confine myself to those aspects of library work which have to do directly with school organization. I am not competent to speak on your larger problems of the library and the community. But certain it is that we are developing within the schools themselves more work of the type in which you are interested.

There are two general lines of discussion and interest which it seems to me proper for one who is interested primarily in the school to present to those of you who are interested primarily in libraries. First, let me say that we are coming to see that the study period in the school is more and more the

[1] Address before the American Library Association, July 2, 1910, at Mackinac Island, Mich.

place where the kind of work that you do in the libraries can very properly be introduced and enlarged. All of you know from your own personal experiences as students if not from your experiences as teachers—and I am sure many of you have had this latter form of experience—that the period when students are supposed to study has heretofore been a period when they have been separated from everything except a single textbook or possibly the small supply of books that they could have in their desks, and then they have been called upon to be extremely quiet while they studied. They have been called upon to obey the directions of someone in charge of the study room and the function of that person in charge of the study room has been a rather trying function; it has been the function of keeping order in the room, not the function of contributing in any lively way to the actual educational progress of the school. The study-room period has been a time when the teacher has been allowed to catch up with her reports or to catch up with some needed work and perhaps at times to catch up with her personal correspondence. At all events, it has been an occasion when the intellectual contact between the school and the children has been somewhat curtailed and the school is not supposed to be wholly responsible for anything except order. It has been a partial substitute for home study, the assumption being that the home study would not be done so vigorously because nobody at home would be delegated to watch with equal care over the reluctant studier. Today we are modifying all this and many of us are interested in seeing it further modified. I am sure that it is appropriate for me to enlist if I can the sympathies of this association for the modification of that sort of a study hour in the schools. I think the ideal study hour is a study hour in a room filled with books exactly as any reference library is filled with books. I think the kind of order which should prevail in that room is the kind of order that prevails in any well-organized library; the student should have the opportunity to leave his individual desk and refer to the books which give him enlarged information; he ought indeed to be encouraged to leave his own desk with its meager supply of books and he ought to go from shelf to shelf within any limits of reasonable attack upon the subject in hand. It seems to me there is the finest kind of an opportunity for training of a type of study that is not common in the individual recitation room. As a matter of fact we are doing more and more of this sort of thing in the individual recitation room; we are asking children to bring into the elementary schools and we are asking the older students to bring into their high-school classes reports of what they have looked up in the libraries, and we are encouraging them to go in a larger way to the shelves; but if we could give them definite training in how to do this, if we could have the teacher who goes about the study room engaged not merely in keeping order but in helping the students to refer to books, giving them a kind of training which we all of us recommend as important, giving them a kind of training for which heretofore no individual officer of the school has been set apart,—I say if we could make these study periods genuine periods of training in the use of books, in the use of a library, it seems to me we should add, without encumbering the course of study, a very important line of training. We should thus reduce watching and keeping order to their proper place of minor importance and elevate to its proper place of major importance the function of using many books. In other words, we should carry over, if you please, a portion of your domain into our domain. We should not only have the schools made the depositories for the books from the public library, but we should have the study period itself transformed into a period of library study or training in library methods.

If this transformation of the study period seems as important to you as it does to me, let me urge upon you the responsibility for contributing to this movement. We cannot work this out merely from the side of the schools; we must have the co-operation of the technical librarian who comes into the school with an idea that is perhaps specialized, perhaps different from the ideas of the ordinary teacher who is acquainted with the ordinary study period. We must have the contribution, from the side of the librarian, of enthusiasm for this kind of work. We have such a study room as this in one of the schools with which I am connected. It was suggested by our librarian and is being worked out with her co-operation, and we regard it as one of our most progressive lines of organization.

Perhaps you cannot bring about the change suddenly, but you could easily begin to introduce it on a small scale, especially if you are situated near the schools or if you have branches in any of the schools. You might very properly encourage the school authorities themselves to delegate to you the authority to conduct one of these study periods. I know you are busy like the rest of us, and just as soon as I make the proposition that you take over this new task I have no doubt that my suggestion will be received with enthusiasm by school authorities and with corresponding reserve by librarians. My function however is to represent the school authorities. I see, therefore, very clearly how you might make a beginning in some such fashion as this: you might make the proposition that you would take care each day of ten such students for one or two periods. Ten students, you know, are very simple to handle. Students get difficult to handle only when there are fifty of them together and then the accumulated momentum of fifty devices for making a disturbance is so great that you have a disciplinary problem; but the accumulated momentum of ten devices for making a disturbance is relatively very small and any able-bodied librarian, with sufficient self-assurance, can put a check to those ten devices without great difficulty. I should say that it might be well for you to get the school authorities to arrange the program. You can make your period with them very attractive to the children. Suppose you get the school authorities to make the program on a given afternoon that the children should be deliberately let out of a certain school to the number of ten and be allowed to go to the library. Of course children go to the libraries now, but let us arrange this as a deliberate substitute for the old-fashioned study period and let us make this new study period an opportunity for training in the methods of the use of books. If we do this I feel sure we shall bring together our two institutions in a very productive fashion.

There is another line of interest which I am here to suggest to you. We cannot co-operate intelligently unless we recognize some differentiation of our functions. I do not think it is at all fair to say that the school and the library are doing the same thing. We differ in the first place in the fact that you reach a very much larger community than we can reach in any given year; you reach an older and maturer reading constituency and thereby your function is differentiated from ours in the school. There is another way in which your function differs from ours. Perhaps you have thought this out more clearly than I, perhaps I am bringing coals to Newcastle in suggesting it—but it has always impressed me that you have the advantage of us who teach in the schools in the fact that you use books as wholes and we use books in very small sections. Have you ever been impressed with the fact that when a book is used by a class in a school it takes a year or half a year to read it, and students get notions about the difficulty of going through a book which are altogether distorted; they get the idea that a book must be read in small doses; that when you have finished up one reading you should set that particular reading entirely aside, put it out of your mind as soon as possible so as not to be impeded by any memory which you may have accumulated out of that small section as you pass on to the next? If we have bad habits of this kind in the schools you who work in libraries see the opposite vice. You see people who come in and read a book in fifteen or twenty minutes. Furthermore, you have people among your readers who are mature enough and well trained enough to make rapid reading of a book a virtue. They know how to select. They read the book at the important point and then decide whether they should read the other parts of the book. The art of rapid use of books is one of the arts which we have been learning in the schools very gradually. We are just beginning to see that children can be taught to deal with books as wholes, that they can take up books, not those that we use merely as textbooks, not those that are marked off by heavy headlines so as to impede progress, but all books containing relevant matter. Children should learn that some books are made for rapid use. Many books ought to be looked over and a large part of the contents, for the moment at any rate, neglected or even discarded. That is, the use of a book as a whole for the purpose of extracting from it some information or for the purpose of getting a broad general view is just as legitimate as the dull grinding over a textbook. We can change the attitude of the next generation toward books, provided we can have some help, and the help which we ought to have, you are in a position to give us. If you would help these students when they come to you to pick out those portions of a book which are of advantage and if you would make it your business, or if you would encourage the teachers in the schools with which you are connected to make it the business of those schools in co-operation with you, to help children to learn the methods of using whole books and extracting the valuable part from books, then we should have a very large addition to our pedagogical machinery. You know what I mean. You ought to have special card catalogues, it seems to me, prepared by teachers and by yourselves which will refer in detail to a number of different books citing chapter and verse, helping out a faulty index or supplementing a good table of contents.

Again, I realize that I am unloading on the Library Association a duty, which if your representative were speaking this morning before the National Education Association he would be unloading on the teacher. Such preaching of new duties is, however, the privilege of a prophet who is far away from his home constituency and in the presence of others who have nothing to do but spend their time on beautiful islands holding conventions. To charge you with any remissness in your duties is certainly not my function this morning, but think of the great catalogues that might have been made up this morning if this whole body had set itself about the business of telling where all of the information could be had about certain phases of fifth-grade geography or history! The trouble with the children when we turn them loose in a general library is that they have not the machinery for the use of that library; and then—frankly apologizing for that great body which I represent and which is absent today—many of us who teach have not the machinery inside of ourselves, if we wanted to give it to the children. A library is very formidable to a newcomer. Even the material equipment impedes one's progress. I have long wished for an opportunity to tell the makers of card catalogues that they ought to invent an automatic device for turning cards, especially where there are one hundred and fifty on the same subject. Your spiritual equipment I have never doubted, but your material equipment is very difficult to handle and it gets more and more difficult when you offer it to a child in the grades. When you see somebody who is just four feet high confronting a bureau of information that is six feet high, with the top drawers of A's just out of reach, you can realize how that saps the enthusiasm for the use of a library as a source of material related to fourth-grade geography. What we need is material worked over in such a way that pupils will be encouraged from the beginning to realize that the book which is given to them in the classroom is nothing more nor less than a sample and very frequently a meager sample, a sample that raises a great many questions and answers very few. He ought to learn that if the questions thus raised are to be answered they must be answered in the larger book shelves accessible in the libraries. Our duty, and if I may venture to preach, your duty, is to make that path, especially for the early students, very much smoother than it is at the present moment. For my own part I am not at all persuaded that the path hasn't got to be worked out in very much greater detail even for older students. Parents come to us in our schools very frequently asking for lists of books that should be read, lists of books that shall be specifically appropriate to the needs of the boy and the girl in the sixth, seventh, and the eighth grade. This kind of specific preparation of a library to introduce the student to whole books without throwing the whole library at him; to give him the machinery by which he shall be able to extract certain portions of your shelved wisdom; to encourage him little by little to expand upon the way in which we use the books in the school—that is someone's general problem. I think we who teach have made the mistake, which I confess very frankly, of tying ourselves down too closely to the single book. We are breaking away from that somewhat. We are trying to get children to use books as wholes, and if you would come at it from your end of the problem, where you deal with the library as a whole, and if you will begin to narrow somewhat the total view, we shall meet each other half way. We shall get our pupils to raise a certain number of questions and then shall push them out into the library to get their questions answered. Thus we shall develop the kind of co-operation which is at all worth cultivation—that co-operation which permits of the differentiation of function. I do not believe libraries are going to swallow up the schools, at least for some time, nor will the schools swallow up the growing institutions which you represent. The school is very hospitable to the movement of introducing into the schools branch libraries; indeed, the school is eager for all possible reciprocity between our two great educational institutions. You reach a larger constituency than we do; you reach your constituency in a somewhat different way. We are trying to prepare the future constituency for the use of these storehouses of knowledge and art of which you are the custodians. If you will give us a little help in working out some of the methods, of which I think we are relatively ignorant; if you will help the students whom we send to you, then we shall be forgiven for meeting apart each year and merely sending representatives back and forth.

The collection which your executive officers have helped to prepare for the National Education Association is, I am sure, highly appreciated by those who are at the other meeting in Boston, and I have the message from the executive officers of the National Education Association extending to you their very hearty and cordial greetings and their hope for future co-operation of the type which has been possible in the past. Long may there be the warmest sympathy between our two great branches of the public educational system.

# EDITORIAL NOTES

One of the educational problems which a summer vacation brings vividly to the consciousness of the community is the problem of determining how much schooling should be provided in a year. Many a parent is fully persuaded on the first of September that school ought to be kept open eleven or twelve months. After a struggle to keep a restless boy properly occupied, after a contest with cheap and unprofitable forms of amusement, many a mother looks forward to the opening of school with relief. The teacher, on the other hand, dreads the task of undoing the ill effects of two or three months of idleness or worse. The slow process of getting a grade under way is a familiar discouragement to all who teach.

**Vacation Viewed as an Interruption**

Many who note these facts on the first of September will forget them by the first of November and will accept as before the familiar dogma that vacation is necessary because everyone is worn out at the end of the school year. The summer months, furthermore, are impossible months for intellectual work. One should be idle; one has no energy; one may do himself permanent injury by not relaxing during these months!

**Vacation as a Physical and Climatic Necessity**

To be sure, there is abundant evidence that many children suffer more from climatic conditions during the rigorous months of the winter and early spring than during the warm months. Furthermore, if we were put to the definite test we should all assert that the ideal educational system is one which so mixes effort and relaxation that exhaustion never appears. We should therefore find it difficult to defend certain of the common statements about the necessity of a long summer vacation. Yet so fixed has the custom of such vacations become that—except on the

**Why Not in Winter, or Every Day?**

first of September—we are likely to ask no questions that shall disturb our practices and beliefs about these vacations. The problem will not down, however. We must deal with it, fully recognizing the facts which at this time in the year are before us. Indeed, there are practical activities now well under way which indicate the direction which our thinking must follow.

**Safeguard Against Exhaustion**

First, all school activity must be so organized as to furnish its own safeguard against exhaustion. If the older school left the pupil worn out at the end of the day or the year, the new school has prevented this by introducing activity and relaxation and variety.

**Training in Recreation**

Second, amusement should be mixed with serious work and both should be intelligently guided. The public must learn to play as well as to read serious books and do sums in addition. One of the great discoveries of our social workers is that modern men and women are as clumsy about recreation as they are in other forms of organized activity. We must teach men and women to enjoy themselves and we can best do this by teaching the children in the schools.

**Individual Vacations**

Third, we should recognize that periods of delay in individual development do not obey any law of the calendar. One child is interrupted in his development at one date, another child at another. If in addition to these individual interruptions we impose a general interruption, the sum for a given child may be very great in a single twelvemonth. Why not provide for continuity in the institution and allow individual needs to dictate the interruptions? This is not so difficult as it seems when stated in this form. The fact is that we are providing now for all kinds of individual interruptions. Children are sick, or families move from one place to another, or parents are negligent until the active truant officer terminates a vacation which does not limit itself to the conventional dates. Whenever a child suffers from one or the other of these irregularities we feel the urgent demand that our school system become more flexible and more complete in its provision of opportunity.

Fourth, economic and social necessity will force us to make a radical change in our present practice. The community has invested in the schoolhouse and ground a sum of money which it will not permit to lie idle during a sixth or a quarter of the year. The plant must be kept open if it can be profitably used. That it can be profitably used is being demonstrated in all of our great cities today. Our vacation school has not only come to stay, it has come to modify the whole conception of public right to use the school. Those who can afford to go away to the country or seashore are in no wise hindered from doing so by the program here outlined. Many of these seek even now the advantages of training camps or schools in the woods. Let those who can afford them out of private means have these advantages of variety in surroundings and instruction. The parallel demand is that those who cannot go to mountain or shore should have for their development the same opportunity that we have always recognized as necessary during the fall, winter, and spring.

**Change a Social Necessity**

Finally, what will come to the teacher through the adoption of this program? Nothing but advantage. Many a young woman goes into a store or office now because she can there earn wages twelve months in the year. She simply cannot afford the present school vacation. Furthermore, in a well-organized system the teacher, like the pupil, could have some option as to absence from the school. The better school systems are even now providing leaves of absences for teachers and officers. This system of vacation for a reason will doubtless develop. When it becomes an established practice we shall have a more efficient school and a better adjusted staff of instructors.

**Vacation for a Reason**

# BOOK REVIEWS

*The Principles of Education.* By WILLIAM CARL RUEDIGER, PH.D. Houghton Mifflin Co., 1910. Pp. xii+305.

This is one of the two or three most useful books that have appeared as texts or outlines for courses in the principles of education in colleges and normal schools. In general it is excellent in its selection and organization of material. Most of it can be understood by students who have not had courses in philosophy; in fact, there is little or no metaphysics in it. While necessarily theoretical in character, the practical bearing of the principles discussed is usually obvious and important.

The subject-matter selected for treatment corresponds to part of that very commonly given in the non-metaphysical courses in the principles of education in American universities. "The standpoint of no particular philosophical system is adopted, but the material is presented from the point of view of inductive science."

The relative emphasis on larger topics may be gathered from the following: there are four chapters or one-fourth of the book devoted to the curriculum, its values and administration; three chapters, or about one-sixth to educational aims; the same amount to elemental educational values; two chapters or about one-eighth to the psychological basis of education; one chapter each for the professional training of teachers, biological bases of education, formal discipline, the agencies that educate.

The central thought of the book is implied in Mr. Ruediger's definition of the aim of education "from the biological standpoint as the adjustment of the individual to the life in which he must participate." A chapter is devoted to the interpretation of this statement and separate chapters to other content aims and formal aims which are criticized and compared with the author's statement.

The chapters on the elemental educational value which are classified as instrumental, cultural, and formal repeat to a certain extent some of the points contained under aims.

The discussion of the curriculum includes a systematic classification of subjects, chapters on the value of the humanities and of the sciences and philosophy. In the organization of the subjects into the curricula of the elementary and secondary schools, Mr. Ruediger makes this distinction which some might question: "Just as the distinctive function of elementary education is to impart the tools, conventions, and basal concepts of knowledge, so that of secondary education is general culture" (p. 228).

The author's general point of view might be characterized as eclectic, as not dominated by any one individual or school. Nevertheless, it is evident that Professor Thorndike's influence is a large factor, particularly in the biological and psychological parts of the book. The two psychological chapters summarize the fundamentals of the dynamic part of Thorndike's *Elements of Psychology* and certain phases of the *Principles of Teaching.* The biological chapter reflects the influence of the *Educational Psychology.*

Many of the chapters are followed by exercises for reflection and discussion. Each chapter is followed by a brief select list of reference readings from books which will be found in every normal-school library. Citations to authorities, instead of being made in footnotes, are made by key numbers incorporated in the text to the works named in a list at the end of the book. Mechanically the book possesses the attractive qualities of the rapidly growing Houghton Mifflin series of pedagogical texts.

I have no fundamental adverse criticisms to offer. Some teachers would prefer to see a more adequate treatment of correlation, concentration, and the culture-epochs theory. Others would prefer more of an account of the larger administrative problems of American education and some introduction to their statistical discussion. The college course in the principles of education, when it has been freed from metaphysical tendencies, is sure to become the most fundamental of the professional courses. I imagine it will become the one course that practically all students will take, to be supplemented by educational psychology or methods or the history of education. If this is true, some of the topics mentioned above should certainly be included. But Mr. Ruediger has not conceived his book in exactly this way, and as it stands it contains a wealth of topics all of which should be included in such a course.

I have already alluded to the "comprehensibility" of the book, a virtue which is strikingly absent in many recent texts. It is difficult to find sentences in this book which a normal-school student would fail to understand. There are a few, however, such as "The primordial variation toward differentiated nerve tissue in the multicellular hydroids proved to be a variation in the right direction" (p. 22).

S. Chester Parker

---

*A Comparative Study of the Play Activities of Adult Savages and Civilized Children.* By L. Estelle Appleton, Ph.D. Chicago: The University of Chicago Press, 1910. Pp. 94.

Miss Appleton has made a study of the play of children and of adult savages in order to determine to what extent they display similar characteristics. The results then bear upon the validity of the culture-epoch theory, so far as play is concerned. The author first examined reports of the play of five tribes which stand lowest in civilization, the Veddahs, Australians, Bushmen, Yahgans, and Eskimos, and tabulated the characteristics so as to indicate the type of bodily activity used, the type and degree of organization involved, and the psychological processes manifested. A similar analysis was then made of the play of five groups of civilized children on the basis of studies made by different persons in different cities. This analysis was carried further by distinguishing the characteristics of the play of children in five different periods.

The author finds, besides certain similarities, marked differences between savages and civilized children which at least greatly modify the parallelism between them. With regard to the bodily characteristics she says: "With the children's group, however, there are in addition to such plays, finger plays, vocal plays, visual, tactual, auditory, and perceptual plays, having almost nothing to correspond to them among the non-civilized adults, but which are indulged in by quite young children among civilized peoples. . . . . These facts *suggest*, at least, a keener sensitivity and somewhat more specialized muscular control on the part of civilized children." In organization the play of savages most nearly corresponds to that of civilized children from the ages of seven to fifteen. "The parallelism is not complete however, for long before the end of this period civilized children are showing a considerable tendency to organize themselves into societies, both spontaneous and formal." They have, moreover, long since dropped many childish plays retained by adult savages.

"In the psychological characteristics, however, we find the greatest disparity between the two groups. The difference in complexity is very great and beyond this civilized children have many plays in which purely intellectual activity is the attractive element—guessing games, charades, puzzles, geographical games, etc.—a class finding no representation whatever among the tribes here studied."

The results of the study indicate to the mind of the author that evolutionary development has affected not only the civilized adult but also every stage of development of the civilized individual, so that the child does not correspond in his bodily characteristics even, and still less in his mental characteristics, to any stage in the development of the race. "A process of differentiation has been going on throughout the cultural period which has profoundly modified not only the final product, i.e., the product found in civilization, but also all the intervening stages."

The author has collected a large amount of illustrative material in regard to the play of both savages and civilized children, and her monograph is valuable for this as well as for its discussion of the relation between the two types of play.

Frank N. Freeman

---

*Agriculture and Its Needs.* By Andrew Sloan Draper. Syracuse, N.Y.: C. W. Bardeen, 1909. Cloth. 16mo, pp. 92. 50 cents.

This book is a clear and vigorous statement of the present condition and needs of agricultural education in the state of New York. "New York has 226,000 farms averaging 100 acres each, 200,000 of them operated by their owners." An educated farmer rather than a good farm is the direct aim of agricultural education, though the former is scarcely securable without the latter. To give an efficient education to the farmer he must be induced to study his farm. The farm is the laboratory in which the farmer must get a good deal of his education. In New York agriculture is worse off than it was a half-century ago, and the people have not yet fully learned that they not only have not kept pace in modern agricultural development, but have become less efficient than they used to be. Commissioner Draper sets forth with his characteristic vigor New York's present agricultural conditions, her natural advantages, the attractiveness of rural life, ways of increasing earnings, what can be done in the rural schools, the place of the agricultural college, the general dignity of agricultural education in a democracy, and the demand upon agricultural colleges to prepare teachers of agriculture as well as agriculturists.

Otis W. Caldwell

# BOOKS RECEIVED

## AMERICAN BOOK COMPANY, NEW YORK

*Champion Spelling Book.* By WARREN E. HICKS. Cloth. Pp. 40. $0.25.

*A Manual of Debate.* By RALPH W. THOMAS. Cloth. Pp. 224. $0.80.

*Picture Primer.* By ELLA M. BEEBE. With Introduction by CHARLES L. SPAIN. Cloth. Illustrated. Pp. 112. $0.25.

*The Adventures of Pathfinder.* Adapted from J. Fennimore Cooper's *Pathfinder.* By MARGARET N. HAIGHT. Cloth. Illustrated. $0.35.

## C. W. BARDEEN, SYRACUSE, NEW YORK

*Fifty Fables for Teachers.* By C. W. BARDEEN. Syracuse: C. W. Bardeen, 1910. Pp. 164. Illustrated. $1.00.

## A. S. BARNES COMPANY, NEW YORK

*Voice Training for School Children.* By FRANK R. RIX. Cloth. Pp. 77.

*The Song Series, Book II.* By ALYS E. BENTLEY. Cloth. Illustrated. Pp. 142. $0.42.

*Swedish Folk Dances.* By NILS W. BERQUIST. With Introduction by C. WARD CRAMPTON. Cloth. Illustrated. Pp. 53.

## P. BLAKISTON'S SON & CO., PHILADELPHIA

*Text-Book of Elementary Zoölogy.* By THOMAS WALTON GALLOWAY. Cloth. Illustrated. Pp. 418.

*A Text-Book of Field Zoölogy.* By LOTTIE E. CRARY. Cloth. Illustrated. Pp. 364.

## THE CENTURY COMPANY, NEW YORK

*A History of the United States.* By S. E. FORMAN. Cloth and Half-Leather. Illustrated. Pp. 419+lxxi. $1.00.

## CHARITIES PUBLICATION COMMITTEE, NEW YORK

*Among School Gardens.* By M. LOUISE GREENE. Cloth. Illustrated. Pp. 388. $1.25.

## DOUBLEDAY PAGE & CO.

*Open Air Schools.* By LEONARD P. AYRES. Cloth. Illustrated. Pp. 171. $1.20.

## E. P. DUTTON & CO., NEW YORK

*The Most Beautiful Thing in the World.* By FLETCHER HARPER SWIFT. New York: E. P. Dutton & Co., 1905. Pp. v+57. With illustrations by George Alfred Williams. $0.30.

## GINN & CO., BOSTON

*Oral Arithmetic.* By GEORGE WENTWORTH AND DAVID EUGENE SMITH. Cloth. Pp. 216. $0.35.

*Page, Esquire, and Knight.* By MARION FLORENCE LANSING. Illustrated by CHARLES COPELAND. Cloth. Pp. 182. $0. 35.

*A Practical English Grammar for Upper Grades.* By JOHN T. PRINCE. Cloth. Pp. 256. $0.60.

*Handbook of Parliamentary Law.* By F. M. GREGG. Boston: Ginn & Co., 1910. Pp. xii+112. $0.50.

*A Fifth Reader.* By FRANCES E. BLODGETT AND ANDREW B. BLODGETT. Cloth. Illustrated. Pp. 481. $0.75.

*The Body and Its Defenses.* By FRANCES GULICK JEWETT. Cloth. Illustrated. Pp. 342. $0.65.

GOVERNMENT PRINTING OFFICE, WASHINGTON

*State School Systems:* III. By EDWARD C. ELLIOTT. Paper Covers. Pp. 305.

*The Movement for Reform in the Teaching of Religion in the Public Schools of Saxony.* By ARLEY BARTHLOW SHOW. Paper covers. Pp. 44.

HARPER & BROS., NEW YORK

*Little Miss Fales.* By EMILIE BENSON KNIPE AND ALDEN ARTHUR KNIPE. Cloth. Pp. 226. $1.25.

*Travels at Home by Mark Twain.* Selected by PERCIVAL CHUBB. Cloth. Illustrated. Pp. 143. $0.50.

*Making Good: Stores of Golf and Other Outdoor Sports.* By F. H. SPEARMAN, VAN TASSEL SUTPHEN, POULTNEY BIGELOW, AND OTHERS. Cloth. Illustrated. Pp. 213. $0.60.

HINDS, NOBLE & ELDREDGE, NEW YORK

*The Howell Primer.* By LOGAN DOUGLASS HOWELL. Cloth. Illustrated. Pp. 127. $0.25.

HOUGHTON MIFFLIN CO., BOSTON

*Old Ballads in Prose.* By EVA MARCH TAPPAN. Illustrated by FANNY Y. CORY. Cloth. Pp. 164. $0.40.

LONGMANS, GREEN & CO., NEW YORK

*A Bibliography of History for Schools and Libraries.* By CHARLES M. ANDREWS, J. MONTGOMERY GAMBRILL AND LIDA LEE TALL. Cloth. Pp. 224. $0.60.

THE MACMILLAN CO., NEW YORK

*Elements of United States History.* By EDWARD CHANNING, in consultation with SUSAN J. GINN. Cloth. Illustrated. Pp. 349+lx. $0.90.

*Elements of Algebra.* By ARTHUR SCHULTZE. Cloth. Pp. 309. $0.85.

*American Government and Politics.* By CHARLES A. BEARD. Cloth. Pp. 772. $2.10.

*Selected Essays and Addresses of Thomas Henry Huxley.* Edited with Notes and an Introduction by PHILO MELVYN BUCK, JR. Cloth. Pp. 340. $0.25.

*Tillers of the Ground.* By MARION I. NEWBIGIN. Illustrated. Cloth. Pp. 224. $0.50.

*The Building and Care of the Body.* By COLUMBUS N. MILLARD. Cloth. Illustrated. Pp. 235. $0.40.

CHARLES E. MERRILL CO., NEW YORK

*Mother Goose Primer.* By BELLE WILEY. Cloth. Illustrated. Pp. 128. $0.32.

CHARLES SCRIBNER'S SONS, NEW YORK

*Ben, the Black Bear.* By WILLIAM H. WRIGHT. New York: Scribner, 1910. Pp. iv+121. Illustrated from photographs by the author and J. B. Kerfoot.

*All around Asia.* By JACQUES W. REDWAY. ("Redway's Geographical Readers.") New York: Scribner, 1910. Pp. xiv+313. Illustrated.

SMALL, MAYNARD & CO., BOSTON.

*The Achievements of Luther Trant.* By EDWIN BALMER AND WILLIAM MACHARG. Illustrated by WILLIAM OBERHARDT. Pp. 365.

STURGIS & WALTON CO., NEW YORK

*Children's Gardens for Pleasure, Health and Educaion.* By HENRY GRISCOM PARSONS. Cloth. Illustrated. Pp. 226.

TYP. A VAP. DA EMPRESA LITTERARIA E TYPOGRAPHICA, PORTO, PORTUGAL

*Annuario das Escolas Normaes do Porto.* II, 1909–10. Paper covers. Pp. 282.

THE UNIVERSITY OF CHICAGO PRESS, CHICAGO

*A Critical Study of Current Theories of Moral Education.* By JOSEPH KINMONT HART. Paper Covers. Pp. 48. $0.53 postpaid.

# CURRENT EDUCATIONAL LITERATURE IN THE PERIODICALS [1]

IRENE WARREN
Librarian, School of Education, The University of Chicago

ALLINE, ANNA L. State supervision of training schools for nurses. Teach. Coll. Rec. 11:41–44. (My. '10.)

(The) American library and museum. Print. Art. 15:189–94. (My. '10.)

ARMSTRONG, J. E. The advantages of limited sex segregation in the high school. School R. 18:339–50. (My. '10.)

ASHLEY, M. L. Experiment as educational method. Educa. Bi-mo. 4: 351–61. (Je. '10.)

BACHMAN, FRANK P. Elimination and repetition. Educa. R. 40:48–50. (Je. '10.)

BAYLISS, CLARA KERN. The development of education. Educa. 30:561–70. (My. '10.)

BEARD, RICHARD OLDING. The university education of the nurse. Teach. Coll. Rec. 11:27–40. (My. '10.)

BEECHING, CANON. Shakespeare as a teacher. Liv. Age. 47:391–402. (14 My. '10.)

BINGHAM, W. VAN DYKE. The use of experiment in teaching educational psychology. Journ. of Educa. Psychol. 1:287–92. (My. '10.)

BLAN, LOUIS B. Retardation of elementary school pupils. Educa. R. 40: 51–64. (Je. '10.)

BLOW, SUSAN E. The service of Dr. Harris to the kindergarten. Kind. R. 20:589–603. (Je. '10.)

BRUNCKEN, ERNEST. The new county library system of California. Pub. Lib. 15:226–29. (Je. '10.)

BUCHNER, E. F. The evaluation of higher education by means of the unit system. Educa. R. 39:511–21. (My. '10.)

[1] Abbreviations.—Atlan., Atlantic Monthly; Cent., Century Magazine; Chaut., Chautauquan; Educa., Education; Educa. Bi-mo., Educational Bi-monthly; Educa. R., Educational Review; Ind. Educa., Indian Education; Journ. of Educa. (Lond.), Journal of Education (London); Journ. of Educa. Psychol., Journal of Educational Psychology; Journ. of Geog., Journal of Geography; Kind. R., Kindergarten Review; Liv. Age, Living Age; Out., Outlook; Pop. Educa., Popular Educator; Pop. Sci. Mo., Popular Science Monthly; Print. Art, The Printing Art; Pub. Lib., Public Libraries; School R., School Review; Sci. Amer., Scientific American; Scrib. M., Scribner's Magazine; Teach. Coll. Rec., Teachers College Record.

CAMP, WALTER. Track athletics. Cent. 80:269–79. (Je. '10.)

CATTELL, J. MCKEEN. The achievements and shortcomings of the American college. School R. 18:369–83. (Je. '10.)

———. The case of Harvard College. Pop. Sci. Mo. 76:604–14. (Je. '10.)

COBURN, LOUISE H. The reader and the library. Pub. Lib. 15:219–23. (Je. '10.)

(The) decline of the university in scientific research. Sci. Amer. 102:370. (7 My. '10.)

DODGE, RICHARD ELWOOD. Geography in rural schools. Journ. of Geog. 8: 202–9. (My. '10.)

DOWNEY, JAMES E. Educational progress in 1909. School R. 18:400–23. (Je. '10.)

ELSON, WILLIAM H., AND BACHMAN, FRANK P. The old vs. the new three R's. Educa. 30:571–81. (My. '10.)

FLEXNER, ABRAHAM. Medical education in America. Atlan. 105:797–804. (Je. '10.)

FREEMAN, VIRGINIA WINCHESTER. The proposed movement for treating stammering in the public schools. Educa. Bi-mo. 4:408–14. (Je. '10.)

GORDON, KATE. Esthetic experience and education. Educa. Bi-mo. 4: 346–50. (Je. '10.)

HALE, WM. GARDNER. Latin composition in the high school. School R. 18: 297–318. (My. '10.)

HARRIS, HERBERT, AND REED, EDWIN C. The fifth annual International Esperanto Congress. School R. 18:395–99. (Je. '10.)

Harvard University course in printing. Print. Art. 15:186. (My. '10.)

HEPBURN, W. M. Public and school libraries of Nova Scotia. Pub. Lib. 15:229–33. (Je. '10.)

HORNADAY, W. T. The right way to teach zoölogy. Out. 95:256–63. (4 Je '10.)

IN-YOUNG. The duties of a Chinese student. Out. 95:125–28. (21 My. '10.)

JOHNSON, DOUGLAS WILSON. The college student's knowledge of geography. Pop. Educa. 27:205–8. (Je. '10.)

KENT, ERNEST B. The elementary curriculum and the industries. Educa. 30:582–90. (My. '10.)

KENT, HENRY W. Art museums and schools. Educa. R. 40:78–81. (Je. '10.)

KING, IRVING. Measurements of the physical growth of two children. Journ. of Educa. Psychol. 1:279–86. (My. '10.)

Library publicity through the press. Pub. Lib. 15:223–25. (Je. '10.)

LOOMIS, H. N. State normal schools and the rural-school problem. Educa. R. 39:484–99. (My. '10.)

MACLAURIN, RICHARD C. Science and education. School R. 18:319–25. (My. '10.)

MANN, C. R. Physics in the college course. Educa. R. 39:472–83. (My. '10.)

MANNY, FRANK A. The process of Americanization in the kindergarten and the school. Kind. R. 20:612–16. (Je. '10.)

MCFARLAND, J. HORACE. University training for printers. Print. Art. 15: 181–85. (My. '10.)

MCILVAINE, CAROLINE M. Chicago historical society library. Educa. Bi-mo. 4:415–18. (Je. '10.)

MILLER, E. A. Moral conditions in Ohio colleges. Educa. R. 39:500–10. (My. '10.)

MINER, J. B. The college laggard. Journ. of Educa. Psychol. 1:263–71. (My. '10.)

NUTTING, ADELAIDE. A brief account of the course in hospital economics. Teach. Coll. Rec. 11:1–6. (My. '10.)

O'SHEA, M. V. Education and the changing social order. Educa. Bi-mo. 4:331–40. (Je. '10.)

PACKARD, JOHN C. A proposed reform in mathematics. Educa. R. 39: 455–58. (My. '10.)

PORTER, MARGARET LOVE. The educational use of dramatic instinct in grammar grade reading. Educa. 30:550–53. (My. '10.)

PRITCHETT, HENRY S. The spirit of the state universities. Atlan. 105: 741–53. (Je. '10.)

REPPLIER, AGNES. The girl graduate. Cent. 80:227–30. (Je. '10.)

ROBINSON, JAMES HARVEY. The significance of history in industrial education. Educa. Bi-mo. 4:376–89. (Je. '10.)

ROUNDS, C. R. The varying systems of nomenclature in use in our texts in English grammar. Educa. R. 40:82–88. (Je. '10.)

RUEDIGER, WILLIAM CARL, AND STAYER, GEORGE DRAYTON. The qualities of merit in teachers. Journ. of Educa. Psychol. 1:272–78. (My. '10.)

RUHL, ARTHUR. Some American preparatory schools. Scrib. M. 47:681–700. (Je. '10.)

RYNEARSON, EDWARD. Co-operation of the business men of Pittsburg with the commercial department of its high school. School R. 18:333–38. (My. '10.)

SADLER, M. E. Education in England. Ind. Educa. 8:437–39. (My. '10.)

SALMON, DAVID. The monitorial system in France. Educa. R. 40:30–47. (Je. '10.)

SHEPHERD, JOHN WILKES. The school garden in large cities. Educa. Bi-mo. 4:390–95. (Je. '10.)

SNEDDEN, DAVID. The achievements and short-comings of the American college. School R. 18:384–94. (Je. '10.)

———. Centralized vs. localized administration of public education. Educa. 30:537–49. (My. '10.)

———. The new scheme for the training of teachers in Scotland. Educa. R. 39:433–54. (My. '10.)

SPANHOOFD, EDWARD. What we might learn from German schools. Educa. R. 40:65–77. (Je. '10.)

STEWART, ISABEL M. Problems of nursing education. Teach. Coll. Rec. 11:7–26. (My. '10.)

THOMAS, JOHN M. The teacher and the community. Educa. R. 39:459–71. (My. '10.)

TIRRELL, HENRY A. The Norwich tests, 1862–1909. School R. 18:326–32. (My. '10.)

WASHINGTON, BOOKER T. Educational engineers. Out. 95:266–67. (4 Je. '10.)

WEBB, E. A. M. Nature study as a means of culture. Journ. of Educa. (Lond.) 41:303–4, 306. (My. '10.)

WHEELOCK, LUCY. The changing and the permanent elements in the kindergarten. Kind. R. 20:603–11. (Je. '10.)

WHITE, FRANK MARSHALL. The epoch of the child. Out. 95:214–25. (28 My. '10.)

WOOD, MARY I. The woman's club movement. Chaut. 59:13–64. (Je. '10.)

VOLUME XI NUMBER 2

# THE ELEMENTARY SCHOOL TEACHER

OCTOBER, 1910

## NATURAL HISTORY IN THE GRADES

OTIS W. CALDWELL
The University of Chicago

### VII AND VIII. SEVENTH AND EIGHTH GRADES

Pupils of the ages usually found in the seventh and eighth grades are much interested in those aspects of elementary science which appear in the home and community. Evidence of this attitude is seen in frequent inquiry as to how certain common phenomena occur and as to how the pupil's constructive ability may be applied to bringing about results with these common materials. This is not a new attitude. It is the inquiring and investigative attitude of the previous grades intensified by a larger outlook, and made more real to the pupil by his demand for a rational interpretation of common things. In the sixth grade all the previous experiences with plants and animals were used as the basis for an elementary study of the human body, its proper use and care. This was the elementary science of physiology and hygiene—of bodily efficiency. The same background is now used for consideration of the elementary science of the home and community. The sixth-grade elementary hygiene and the elementary-science topics of the seventh and eighth grades are educationally closely related.

Topics that are appropriate for study in these grades vary with the region. In an agricultural community emphasis may well be placed upon elementary agricultural science, while in other communities other industries and interests furnish vital problems. Some of the essential elementary problems, however, are almost universal. Topics of importance that are not readily divisible into agricultural and manufacturing groups are: the phenomena of boiling, refrigeration, distillation, solution, crystallization, water supplies, steam and its applications, heating and heating systems, heat measurements, the atmosphere, chlorophyll work of plants, the most important plants in the world's food supply, the domestication of plants and animals, energy and the machines by means of which work is done. They are of universal importance, and if studied in an experimental and investigative manner and not didactically they have universal educational value.

There are at least three factors that must be kept in mind as essential for work in these grades. They are: first, the possibility of experimentation which may be performed in such a way that accurate observation and inference may be required; second, the constructive and inventive capacity of pupils must be called forth, preferably by actually demanding that they devise some apparatus, and at the least by demanding interpretation of processes and apparatus devised by others; third, the topics must involve knowledge that appeals to the pupils as being worth while. On this last point it must be recalled that pupils of this age are not so much interested in a scientific arrangement of facts as they are in learning about the scientific import of common matters. Facts as children see them are not classified into the different grooves that we choose to call the different sciences, but they see the topics of interest and desire an interpretation of the phenomena that are involved regardless of the particular science that is needed for the explanation. It may be questioned whether some of the topics suggested allow all three of these factors to be used. Certainly the proportionate use will vary. In such a topic, however, as the history of the domestication of plants and animals, printed matter must be looked upon as the records of the experiments of others; and illustrative material—charts, pictures, etc.—must be secured therefrom so that a connected story of any given plant or animal may be constructed. One seventh-grade boy in his work collected a large stack of pamphlets, made lantern slides, and presented to his fellows several highly interesting discussions upon the sugar-producing plants of the world, thus showing that printed statements may be very real things and may become the basis of new constructive effort in the form of a graphic report.

It is important throughout this work that the pupils keep carefully made notes upon experiments and observations. A notebook specially for the elementary science should be kept. This will not only be of great advantage in securing careful attention and accurate observation but should give at this early period methods of recording things in brief, pointed, and well-written notes. This book should also contain, in every possible case, sketches of apparatus used. Oftentimes carefully prepared sketches are much more valuable than notes, since one can often write something that while not wrong does not tell all the truth, but in making sketches lines will not go together properly unless accurate seeing has preceded. Both notes and sketches should be brief but accurate.

The general plan of work that is here presented has been used with variations for three years. Further experience will doubtless necessitate other changes. The topics that have received major attention in one year have not always been the ones to receive such attention the next year. During the past year the teaching in these grades of the Elementary School of the School of Education was done largely by Mr. H. R. Halsey.

The following outlines are partly the outcome of Mr. Halsey's experience, and partly the outcome of observation and experience of others in the same and preceding years.

## SEVENTH GRADE

The general topics used in the seventh grade include an elementary study of the meaning of chlorophyll to plants; the nature of different soils in their relation to plant life; some of the processes by means of which a plant lives—root and leaf absorption, conduction through the stem, evaporation and transpiration, and the elementary chemistry of food-manufacture by means of chlorophyll; surplus food, food-storage and its significance to other living things; the special growth and food-storage habits of man's domestic plants; the history of domestication of domesticated plants and animals, and the present methods of their improvement through cultivation, transplantation, and breeding. A study is made of the forms of energy that are used in the industries with electricity as a type; an experimental study of electricity and electrical apparatus; manufacture and use by pupils of simple electrical apparatus.

The work may begin by a study of the nature of a plant—its roots, stems, and leaves—or by a study of the leaf of a plant, or by use of plant-responses, as wilting, transpiration, root-pressure, or by a study of the soil in its relation to plant-activities. If we begin with the soil the first experiments to be performed are those with the structure and water-holding capacity of soils. Qualitative experiments with reasonable approximation of quantitative results are employed. One series of experiments relates to water-holding power and the other to water-lifting power. Secure a given quantity—e.g., one quart—each of sand, loam, and clay and weigh carefully. Place where they will dry rapidly, and weigh from day to day. (If artificial heat can be used in drying, more accurate results may be had in a short time.) Each pupil should note the amount of water evaporated from each kind of soil. In closing this experiment pour upon each kind of soil the amount of water that was found to be evaporated from it and observe the amount again absorbed and the relative rate of this absorption. After having prepared thoroughly dried samples of each kind of soil, place each in a glass tube that is at least an inch in diameter, tying cloth over one end to hold the soil. Stand the three tubes in a dish of water and determine the rate at which each lifts water. A similar set of tubes is used to investigate the rapidity with which water passes downward by pouring water into the tops of the tubes. The observations and inferences from these experiments demand careful observation and discussion and constant reference to the life of plants in these soils. Mixed soils and organic matter in the soils should receive attention, but to be studied in detail require too prolonged work for pupils of this grade. Explanation of the significance of surface cultivation of soils both in garden and field as well as the significance of dry-land farming is based upon these experiments, and should be given in this connection.

How plants take up soil water and the things that are in solution in it cannot be answered fully by experiment at this time, but two or three simple experiments form the basis for interpretation of what is known of the process. First a stem and leaf lifting experiment (Fig. 1) is performed by cutting off, under water, the top of a potted plant. It should be cut so as to

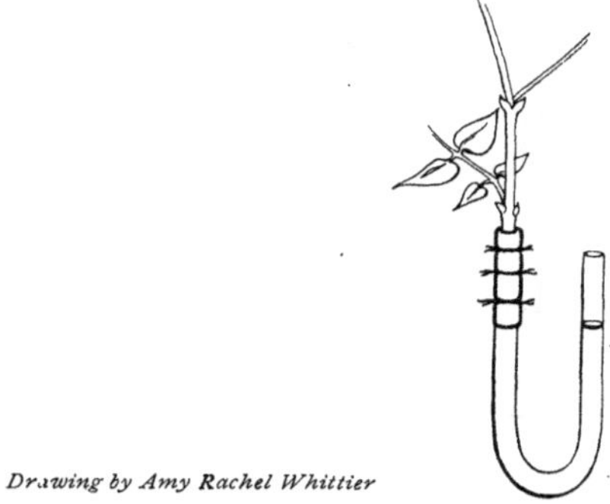


FIG. 1.—A simple device to test the power of a stem to lift water

leave about one and one-half inches of the stump. A relatively hard-stemmed plant, as the geranium, Indian corn, or a woody plant, is best. Then by handling the plant and tubing under water so as to avoid getting air into the plant or tubing, attach the stem by means of rubber tubing to one arm of a U-shaped glass tube, making certain that the glass and rubber tubes are entirely filled with water. The connection should be made air-tight by carefully tying the rubber-tube collar about the base of the stem and the top of the tube. Remove the plant and tube and support them carefully upon a ring-stand and observe whether the water in the tube disappears. Secondly, attach in the same way to the stump of the plant, not necessarily under water, a straight piece of tubing (Fig. 2), keep the roots watered, and note results. By means of these experiments it will be found that roots force water upward and that leaves and stems lift water.

Several other demonstration experiments may be made. Chlorophyll may be dissolved from the leaf by alcohol. Chlorophyll containing cells of a leaf or of algae should be shown the class. Starch food may be demonstrated, if present, by use of an iodine test, first having treated ordinary starch with iodine to show the characteristic color reaction.

These experiments form the basis for a discussion of the work of chlorophyll. Pupils of this grade greatly enjoy learn-

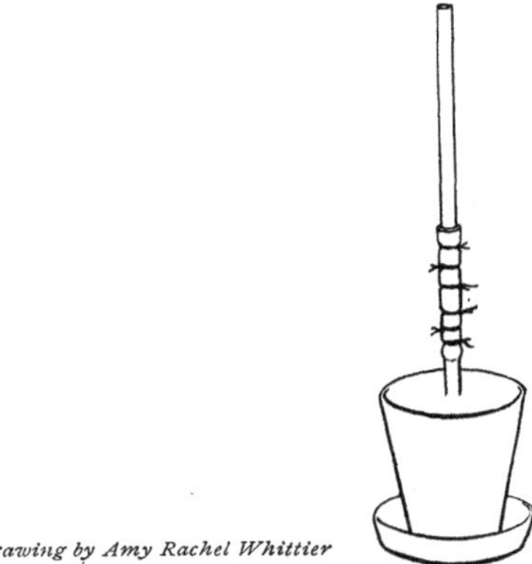

*Drawing by Amy Rachel Whittier*

FIG. 2.—Apparatus for testing the ability of plant roots to force water upward

ing the simple chemistry that may be used in this connection. The chemical formulae for water, carbon dioxide, cane sugar or glucose, and starch are introduced. It is clearly stated that many intermediate chemical changes occur before sugar and starch are made, but that these are too difficult for our study. We deal with the initial materials and final results in order to make a basis for a general interpretation of the significance of plant work. Electrolysis and synthesis of water have twice been used as a demonstration of chemical change, and if the apparatus is set up before the class and the pupils are called upon to observe and explain phenomena, an intensely interesting exercise is had.

The relation of surplus food of plants to dependent plants (toad-stools and mushrooms, plant parasites, etc.), to animals, and to the world's food supply in general is given brief attention. The book by Carpenter on *How the World Is Fed,* published by the American Book Company, offers valuable reading material upon this topic. This readily leads to a brief study of the history of domestication of plants and animals. It is not intended that this should be a study of the biological evolution of domesticated plants and animals, but a study of whence and how came these forms in man's experience with them. This study should be associated with an investigation of the regions and methods now employed in best production of domesticated plants and animals. Different aspects of this topic should be assigned to different pupils, making certain that there is available source material for each topic assigned. First in class discussion there is prepared a list of the most important domesticated animals and plants—horse, cow, pig, poultry, corn, wheat, potato, apple, tulip, rose, etc. (The fifth-grade course includes a study of the use of these to men, therefore that aspect may now be reviewed as a basis for further work.) The problem of ascertaining whence and how they came, where and how they are now being grown and improved, must be clearly defined. Then each pupil is assigned one topic, and each is given definite direction as to how he may begin his work. To most pupils should be handed but one or two references upon which they should report to the class. Some should write to experiment stations or commercial firms for their data. In some cases interesting work is done by having pupils correspond with pupils in regions where work upon some of these topics is going on. As in the case of the nature of the growing cotton plant, valuable co-operation with a southern schoolboy might readily be arranged and letters and samples of importance and interest thus secured.

If possible, schoolroom or garden experiments in cross pollination should be made, though with our facilities not much can be done. Experimental horticultural work in this connection would doubtless be highly valuable. In previous garden work, however, a study of pollination and seed-formation was made and the facts then gained are now used as a basis for an understanding of how cross breeding of plants is effected. Some of the results of plant and animal breeding will have been developed in the special studies but the general topic should be discussed. One or two of the conspicuous triumphs of plant-breeders, such as in increasing the oil or starch content of corn and in production of hardy oranges, should be studied.

It is desirable that there be prepared for reading simple accounts of the domestication, present conditions, and methods of improvement of plants and animals of universal importance. Such accounts if made available would enhance the efficiency of this phase of elementary science.

The study of chlorophyll and its utilization of part of the sun's energy in food-making should in this grade be accompanied by a study of a form of energy which has wide mechanical possibilities and which offers opportunity for use of the pupil's inventiveness. For this the topic of electricity is used. It has seemed necessary to have most of the experiments performed before the class, these being performed by a group of pupils or by the teacher. Demand for explanations should always be preceded by an experiment or demonstration. There are few appliances so well known that their previously observed working can be recalled with sufficient accuracy to serve as a basis for discussion. Most of the children have access to some electrical apparatus at home, and several have purchased apparatus. Any who wish are allowed to go into the elementary-science room after school hours and try experiments, and several have often availed themselves of this opportunity.

Various initial experiments have been used with different classes. The study of magnets or of the dynamo offers excellent beginning topics. In the past year an explanation of electrical appliances was called for with the incandescent carbon-filament lamp as the first instrument that was used. Most of the class had handled the lamps and thought they could explain how they work. A few minutes occupied in attempts to explain, however, convinced the children that they needed to understand several things before they could give a satisfactory explanation. Electric bulbs were passed to the class and the plan of construction called for. The pupils were exacting in their demand for clear explanations from one another and few statements were allowed to pass unchallenged. Experiments with the socket and use of the key were made at school and at home. Drawings illustrating the mechanism and the course of the electric current through the filament were finally made by the children and much interest was shown in explaining these drawings.

The arc lamp was next investigated and gave little difficulty, although there was needed help from the teacher in explaining the flow of current when the carbons were separated. The automatic regulating device was left until later when electromagnets were considered.

Magnets were next taken up. Different articles were tested for magnetism. Individual experiments were made with the usual compass and iron filings apparatus. Various magnets were tested to determine their polarity. A broken magnet compelled most of the children to rethink their conclusions already formed. An electromagnet was then examined and the relation of polarity and direction of current discussed. So far the current used had been taken from the light mains in the classroom. At this point experiments with batteries as sources of curents were taken up. The dry, Daniel, and storage forms were used. Each type was studied both from the point of what it does and of how it is made. Many of the pupils constructed wet cells of various types. Then followed applications of the electromagnet—the telegraph, electric bell, motor, dynamo, telephone, automatic clutch for the arc lamp, etc. In case of the first three the pupils were given the problem of devising a piece of apparatus to accomplish the end stated. The solution of the telegraph came promptly. The electric bell was more difficult. Plans were presented by means of board drawings, and criticisms from the class uncovered the faults until several quite different but acceptable plans were developed. Some of these were very original. The keen and pointed criticism of the class indicated insight into the factors involved (Plate I, Fig. 1).

Devising a motor was the most difficult problem. Some suggestions were given, but the keen interest of the boys especially served to bring out a large number of suggestions so that several types of motors were planned. Finally a half-dozen different types of motors were brought into the class and studied. More than one-half the pupils bought the parts of the small Ajax motors and wound and assembled them, thus constructing working motors. A small hand dynamo was used in running the motors.

Some of the pupils suggested that a motor might run a dynamo which in turn might run the motor. This occasioned vigorous argument and presentation of evidence and the claim was of course disproven.

Telephones were brought into the room and studied, but not all the pupils got a good understanding of the instrument. Different types of lamps were used—the mercury lamp (for which an original plan for an automatic tilting device was devised by one of the boys), the Tungsten, Nernst, and flaming arc, and their cost of operation was compared with that of the carbon-filament lamp. This work of course involved calculations and the use of the units, ampere, volt, and watt, in which the pupils took great interest. Numerous problems involving cost of currents for various instruments were given and solved with readiness and accuracy.

The wireless telegraph appealed to some of the boys more than did any topic. Two weeks were spent on the instrument, at the end of which time at least a dozen boys had outfits in operation at their homes. Some succeeded in passing and receiving messages over a distance of two miles. Higgins' *Elementary Science*, published by Ginn & Company, contains many valuable suggestions for the elementary physics of the seventh and eighth grades.

## EIGHTH GRADE

The topics in elementary science that have been found useful in this grade are: The phenomena of boiling, condensation, the distillation of water, expansion and contraction; steam and its uses; heat energy, the sources from which, in the industries, heat is derived; manufacture of gas from coal, wood, paper, etc.; combustion and oxidation (rusting); temperature measure-

## PLATE I

FIG. 1.—ELECTRICAL APPARATUS MADE BY PUPILS IN THE SEVENTH GRADE

FIG. 2—EIGHTH-GRADE BOYS CONSTRUCTING APPARATUS WITH WHICH TO DISTILL WATER

The apparatus is in focus which throws the pupils slightly out of focus

## PLATE II

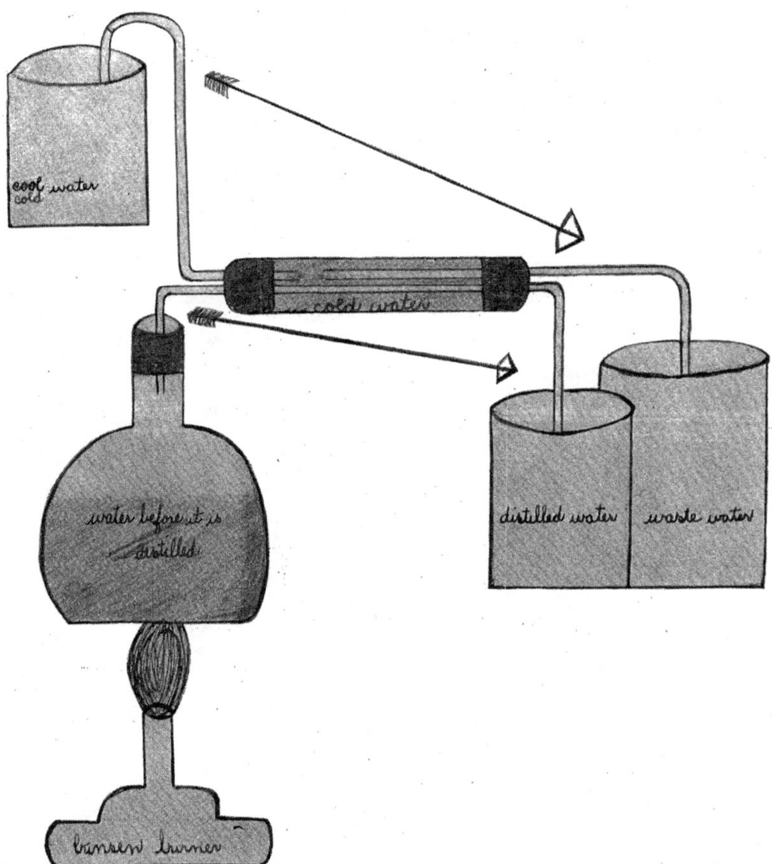


A Boy's Diagram of His Distilling Device, Made After the Apparatus Was Constructed

This is one of the best of the diagrams received in this work. Below is a copy of a calculation that was made and turned in as part of the report of one pupil. The part of the report given is only that which relates to the use of the apparatus in determining the cost of using the pupil's apparatus:

I burn gas at the rate of 1 cent every 2 hours. I distill 4 oz. every 15 minutes or 1 pint every hour, or a quart every 2 hours, therefore costing 1 cent a quart.

Distill 4 oz. in 15 minutes.
16 oz. or 1 quart in 60 minutes.
1 quart in 2 hours.
1 gallon in 8 hours.

It cost 1 cent every 2 hours. Then it cost 1 cent for every distilled quart, or it cost 4 cents for every distilled gallon.

Hydrox costing $0.10 per gallon.
My way costing $0.04 per gallon.
I make $0.06 per gallon.

ments and construction of thermometers. The atmosphere, its elementary physical and meteorological phenomena; precipitation; the barometer; wind energy; pumps; light, its relation to food and energy of the world as already shown in chlorophyll work, and some of its phenomena and reactions as shown in a study of photography. The elementary science of some of the materials of the industries, as fibers, paper, glass, rubber, paint, etc. An elementary study of forests and forest influences upon soils, waters, climate, health, animal and plant life; the timber industries (topic opened in the fifth grade), the regions of the world's leading forests, methods and reasons for extending forests.

The study of heat may well begin either with an experiment in boiling or one in expansion of solids. In the first case a tea-kettle and an open pan operated in boiling water before the entire class afford excellent beginnings. In expansion of solids the ball and ring experiment is good. In studying the phenomena of boiling it is best to use a standard thermometer, simply stating in case questions arise that later the working of the instrument will be considered. It is helpful, however, to record temperatures of water in different stages of experiments. First boil the water in the tea-kettle and secure as complete observation and interpretation as the pupils can make. Close the spout of the tea-kettle and repeat the experiment. In the open pan slowly bring the water to the boiling point and ask pupils particularly to study the occurrences at the surface of the water. Accompany these observations with an experiment in weighing a pan of water before and after boiling. By collecting steam in a cold tube and noting the resulting condensation of water the problem of distillation is introduced. Plans for the manufacture of a miniature still from common laboratory materials are called for. Drawings of proposed plans have been required in some cases before experimentation and in some cases after building an apparatus (Plate I, Fig. 2). Better thinking and more efficient experiments seemed to come from first devising a plan on paper, although in amost every case the plans had to be changed before a working apparatus could be built. Some of the stills were built so well that it was possible to distill water and by means of a gas meter to determine the cost of distillation by means of this apparatus (Plate II).

During the past year instead of experiments in distillation more attention was given to the use of steam engines. Most of the pupils knew a little about engines, but rational explanations were absent. The cylinder and piston of a steam pump were first assigned and were readily explained. The stride valve, thus making locomotion possible, was added by several who doubtless had numerous observations from which to draw. Models and drawings were then placed before the class. A large model of the chest valve, valve cylinder, and revolving mechanism was borrowed and proved of much interest and value. The construction of the boiler was explained and discussed in its relation to the other parts of the engine. Pupils then made drawings illustrating the construction and action of various parts of the steam engine, and carefully written statements in explanation were prepared. In connection with the experiments made by one class upon distillation, the construction of thermometers was taken up. The principles involved and methods of gradation were discussed and different types of thermometers were constructed. Some of these were graded in the Fahrenheit system, some in Centigrade, and some in systems devised by the pupil. In all cases the pupils transferred the value of units in their readings into terms of other units. The accuracy with which these thermometers were made is shown by the fact that although some of the thermometers were several degrees away from standard readings the average taken from all the instruments made by the class was less than one degree from the standard reading.

In the manufacture of gas from various substances further illustration is had of the method of study. Ordinary clay pipes were filled, some with soft coal, some with wood, and some with paper. The bowls of the pipes were cemented with ordinary cement or with potter's clay. When dry these were fastened upon ring stands and the bowls slowly heated by a gas flame. From some of the pipe stems there soon appeared a jet of smoky gas. To this a lighted match was applied, when it began to burn. If the flame under the bowl is removed the gas soon ceases to be formed, and if reapplied it begins again and continues until the gas-forming properties of the material are exhausted. The pipe bowls are then opened and the charred contents examined. An explanation of these materials and occurrences is thought-stimulating and provides a basis for an understanding of other gas-forming materials and processes.

The nature of combustion and oxidation follows. During the past year three weeks were given to laboratory work with oxygen, the meaning of oxidation, and methods of aiding and preventing it. Carbon dioxide followed and as in the case of oxygen was studied in experiment and in discussion of the place of this gas in nature and industry. There are taken up various experiments with the atmosphere relating to its reality, weight, pressure, expansion, and contraction, pumps, water-carrying power, and currents. Previous work in geographic aspects of the atmosphere is called for. The construction and reading of weather maps are studied. As suggested above, photography is used as a means of studying light, this topic also receiving more time during the past year than previously. Some general discussion of photography leads to the pinhole-camera experiment. Each pupil constructed a pinhole camera, securing therefor a starch box or a similar box. The nature of light action through prisms and through lenses was discussed. The action of light upon a sensitized emulsion and the mechanical and chemical processes involved in developing and printing were discussed. Each pupil took a picture and carried it through each requisite process to the final print. Most of the pinhole cameras leaked light, but a few good pictures were secured. Several of the pupils secured notions of the fundamentals involved in photography which, in addition to being instructive, will in the use of their own cameras prove useful to them.

A list of the important industries in and about Chicago is prepared by the class, and each pupil or group of pupils is assigned one industry and is asked to prepare a brief report concerning the raw materials used, the processes and machinery involved, and the final and by-products made in the industry. The lumber industry is omitted from these assignments and is made the topic for a more extensive study. Five weeks were spent last year in a study of elementary forestry in this country and in Europe. A review of local native trees, and of local lumber supplies (discussed in geography course), and of how a tree grows, is followed by assignment of readings from pamphlets and library books. Much of the study must be entirely classroom work contributed largely by the teacher, since experience of pupils and reading material for pupils of this age are not abundant. There are, however, available discussions of forest needs and influences, photographs, and descriptions of what is being done in various parts of the country in forest extension and in withstanding forest enemies. Forest fires, predatory insects, and unnecessary commercial destruction are of interest to all. *The Primer of Forestry,* by Gifford Pinchot, U.S. Department of Agriculture, is valuable for this work. The U.S. Forest Service also publish a list, in a bulletin which cites many available helps in such work. And *Care of Trees,* by B. E. Fernow, published by Henry Holt & Co., 1910, is full of authentic practical suggestions.

# A COMPARATIVE STUDY OF THE GRADES OF PUPILS FROM DIFFERENT ELEMENTARY SCHOOLS IN THE SUBJECTS OF THE FIRST YEAR IN HIGH SCHOOL

FRANKLIN W. JOHNSON
Principal of the University High School, Chicago, Illinois

[Editorial Note.—The editors of this *Journal* are the officers of the Elementary School of the University of Chicago. They present with very great satisfaction the following article as a full, concrete illustration of the application of impersonal scientific methods to elementary-school problems. In the near future other studies of larger school systems will be presented, and it is hoped that the significance of this method will be widely recognized. If studies of this type could be made in every school system, supervision and administration of schools would rise to a level never attained in any educational system.

Attention is not unlikely to be drawn to those parts of the report which seem to show defects in the work of the University Elementary School. In later years similar reports will be made, and it is hoped that concrete evidence can then be presented of the advantages of knowing one's own weaker points. This study is the basis of the present administration of the school. The officers of the school are clear also that their problem is not merely to prepare for high school. The Elementary School does many types of work not touched on in this report. The aim of the school, however, is to do the conventional types of work in such a way as to achieve equal efficiency with other schools and at the same time to work out problems not taken up by these other schools.

Finally, the significance of these results will not be fully appreciated by any reader who fails to recognize that the high school is studied by these tables quite as much as the elementary school. Is the relation here discovered in history due to the training in the elementary school or to the methods employed in the high school? The practical answer to this question is to be found in the fact that the history instructors in these two schools have been organized since the preparation of these tables into a single department. They have their problem set before them in impersonal and yet very emphatic form.—The Editors.]

This study was undertaken for the purpose of testing the efficiency of the University Elementary School on the basis of the grades received in the first year of the University High

School. The pupils under consideration entered the High School in the autumn of 1909. The class contained 128 members of whom 44 came from the University Elementary School and 84 from other elementary schools, these being with a few exceptions the public schools of the city of Chicago.

In Diagrams 1–7, representing the grades of the Autumn Quarter, each number represents the same pupil throughout, those from the University Elementary School being indicated by bold-faced type (e.g., **19**), all other pupils by numbers in plain roman (e.g., 30). The numbers were assigned without reference to the schools from which the pupils came in the order in which the names occurred in the class lists of the various classes in English in the Autumn Quarter. The grades in the University High School are reported by teachers in multiples of five, passing grades ranging from 60 to 100. In the diagrams the grades are given at the bottom and the numbers in each column represent the pupils receiving these grades. For the purpose of comparison each diagram is divided into quintiles or groups comprising one-fifth of the class. The method adopted for the division into quintiles places in the lower quintile those pupils at the top of the column necessary to fill out the number. It will be noted that in the diagram for the Autumn Quarter in English this method happens to place an undue number of pupils from the University Elementary School in the two lowest quintiles and removes from the highest quintile to the next lower all the elementary-school pupils who received a grade of 75. The comparative standing in English of the pupils of the University Elementary School for the Autumn Quarter is thus less favorable than it should properly be and the standing in this subject is made somewhat less favorable for the entire year. An equitable redistribution would change the result as indicated in the broken line in Diagram 8. Chance seems to have played no similar part in any other portion of the comparison.

The diagrams are of interest not only because they exhibit the relation of pupils from the Elementary School to others, but also because of the light which they throw on the practices of different departments in the High School. Thus it will be seen at once that the English department differs radically from the Latin Department in its use of the higher marks. The Science Departments distribute their students in a manner altogether different from the English Department.

Furthermore the diagrams make it possible to trace the individual variations of each pupil. Thus pupil number one stands in the highest quintile in English, Latin, Mathematics, and Design, but takes his place in the third quintile in French and German. Pupil number 2 stands in the highest quintile in all subjects which he takes. Number 5 stands well in English, Mathematics, and History, fair in Latin and Design, and far down the scale in Science. Number 102 shows the widest single variation, standing low in all subjects except Mathematics, in which he is one of the three to receive the highest grade.

DIAGRAMS 1–7

UNIVERSITY HIGH SCHOOL

Freshman Class, 128 pupils, *Autumn Quarter*, 1909

DIAGRAM 1.—ENGLISH

| Fail. | 60 | 65 | 70 | 75 | 80 | 85 | 90 | 95 |
|---|---|---|---|---|---|---|---|---|
| 130 | **118** | 110 | **65** | 47 | 20 | **11** | **1** | |
| 129 | **117** | 108 | **64** | **46** | **19** | **10** | | |
| **128** | **116** | **88** | **63** | 45 | 18 | **9** | | |
| **127** | **115** | **87** | 62 | **44** | 17 | **8** | | |
| 126 | **113** | **86** | 61 | **43** | 16 | 7 | | |
| 125 | **112** | **85** | 60 | **42** | 15 | 5 | | |
| 124 | **111** | **84** | 59 | **41** | 14 | 4 | | |
| 123 | 109 | **83** | 58 | **40** | 13 | 3 | | |
| 122 | 107 | **82** | 57 | **39** | 12 | 2 | | |
| 121 | 106 | 81 | 56 | **38** | | | | |
| 120 | 103 | **80** | 55 | **37** | | | | |
| 119 | **102** | **79** | 54 | **36** | | | | |
| 114 | **101** | **78** | 53 | **35** | | | | |
| 105 | **100** | 77 | 52 | 34 | | | | |
| 104 | 99 | 76 | 51 | 33 | | | | |
| | 98 | 75 | 50 | 32 | | | | |
| | 97 | 74 | 49 | 30 | | | | |
| | 96 | 73 | 48 | 29 | | | | |
| | 95 | 72 | | 28 | | | | |
| | 94 | 71 | | 27 | | | | |
| | 93 | **70** | | 26 | | | | |
| | 92 | 69 | | 25 | | | | |
| | 91 | **68** | | 24 | | | | |
| | 90 | 67 | | 23 | | | | |
| | 89 | 66 | | 22 | | | | |
| | | | | 21 | | | | |

128 pupils

| | | |
|---|---|---|
| 1st | Quintile | 26 |
| 2d | " | 26 |
| 3d | " | 26 |
| 4th | " | 25 |
| 5th | " | 25 |

## Diagram 2.—Latin

101 pupils

| | | |
|---|---|---|
| 1st Quintile | | 21 |
| 2d | " | 20 |
| 3d | " | 20 |
| 4th | " | 20 |
| 5th | " | 20 |

| Grade | Pupils (top to bottom) |
|---|---|
| Fail. | 130, 129, **128**, 125, 124, 123, 121, **117**, 114, 99, **84**, 66, 60, 51, 48, 3 |
| 60 | 126, **118**, **115**, 103, 75, 73, **65**, 58 |
| 65 | 120, **112**, **102**, 97, 91, **88**, **78**, 30, 26 |
| 70 | 110, 109, 106, 96, **85**, 77, 61, 59, 56, 50, 32, 25 |
| 75 | **127**, **116**, **113**, 107, 98, 53, 28, 17, 14 |
| 80 | **101**, 90, **83**, **79**, 62, 55, 54, **43**, **35**, 33 |
| 85 | 119, **100**, 95, **86**, **82**, 72, **63**, 49, **46**, **41**, **36**, 23, 15, 5 |
| 90 | **87**, 81, **64**, **40**, **39**, **38**, **37**, 20, **19**, 18, 13, **11**, **8**, 7, **1** |
| 95 | 47, **44**, **42**, 12, **10**, **9**, 4, 2 |

## Diagram 3.—Mathematics

127 pupils

| | | |
|---|---|---|
| 1st Quintile | | 26 |
| 2d | " | 26 |
| 3d | " | 25 |
| 4th | " | 25 |
| 5th | " | 25 |

| Grade | Pupils (top to bottom) |
|---|---|
| Fail. | 130, 129, 125, 123, 121, **117**, **115**, 99, 98, 96, 81, 75, **65**, 34, 29 |
| 60 | **128**, **127**, 122, **113**, 109, 107, 106, 104, 97, **88**, **82**, **80**, **79**, 77, **70**, 69, 66, 17, **9** |
| 65 | 124, 120, 119, 114, 108, 105, 94, 92, 89, **78**, 62, 57, 54, 52, 50, 49 |
| 70 | **116**, **112**, **111**, 95, **85**, **83**, 74, 73, 72, 61, 58, 56, **37**, 18, 16, 14, **8** |
| 75 | 126, 110, 103, **100**, 91, 90, 76, 67, **63**, 55, 51, 48, **41**, **38**, **35**, 27, 25, 24, 22, 21, 20, 13, 12 |
| 80 | **101**, 93, 71, **68**, 59, 45, **43**, **40**, **39**, **36**, 32, 30, 28, 23, 15, **11**, **10**, 7, 5, 3 |
| 85 | **87**, **86**, 60, **46**, 33, 26 |
| 90 | **118**, **64**, 53, **44**, **42**, **19**, 4, **1** |
| 95 | **102**, 47, 2 |

DIAGRAM 4.—SCIENCE

84 pupils
1st Quintile 17
2d " 17
3d " 17
4th " 17
5th " 16

| Fail. | 60 | 65 | 70 | 75 | 80 | 85 | 90 | 95 |
|---|---|---|---|---|---|---|---|---|
| | | | | | **111** | | | |
| | | | | | 109 | | | |
| | | | | | 106 | | | |
| | | | | | 97 | | | |
| | | | | | 92 | 107 | | |
| | **127** | | | | 90 | 91 | | |
| | 125 | | | 119 | **88** | **79** | | 74 |
| | 105 | 124 | | **115** | 66 | 73 | 103 | 33 |
| 123 | **70** | **113** | **128** | 110 | **64** | 72 | 95 | 22 |
| **117** | 69 | 99 | **116** | 96 | 52 | 67 | 89 | 21 |
| 108 | **68** | 98 | **78** | 59 | 26 | 61 | 71 | 15 |
| 104 | **65** | 94 | 58 | 56 | 25 | 51 | 32 | 13 |
| 77 | 54 | **80** | 55 | 53 | 17 | 50 | 23 | 7 |
| 57 | 49 | 75 | **38** | 28 | **9** | 48 | 18 | 4 |
| 29 | 34 | 5 | 27 | 14 | **8** | **10** | 12 | 2 |

DIAGRAM 5.—HISTORY

97 pupils
1st Quintile 20
2d " 20
3d " 19
4th " 19
5th " 19

| Fail. | 60 | 65 | 70 | 75 | 80 | 85 | 90 | 95 |
|---|---|---|---|---|---|---|---|---|
| | | | | 123 | | | | |
| | | | | **115** | 107 | | | |
| | | | 110 | **111** | **64** | | | |
| | **127** | | 98 | 103 | 61 | | | |
| | 119 | | 95 | 76 | 56 | | | |
| 129 | 114 | | **88** | 74 | 53 | | | |
| **128** | 108 | | 81 | 60 | 52 | | | |
| 125 | 104 | **116** | 75 | 54 | 48 | | | |
| 124 | 99 | 106 | 71 | 50 | 47 | | | |
| 121 | 96 | 92 | 67 | 49 | 45 | | | |
| 120 | **80** | 91 | 66 | **44** | **39** | 59 | | |
| 105 | **78** | 90 | **65** | **42** | 33 | 30 | 18 | |
| **102** | 77 | **82** | 58 | 26 | 25 | 21 | 13 | |
| 97 | 72 | **79** | 55 | 22 | 24 | 15 | 12 | |
| 94 | 69 | 73 | 51 | 17 | 23 | **10** | 7 | |
| 93 | **68** | 57 | 34 | 16 | 14 | **8** | 4 | |
| **70** | 32 | **38** | 27 | 3 | **9** | 5 | 2 | |

DIAGRAM 6.—FRENCH AND GERMAN

38 pupils
1st Quintile 8
2d " 8
3d " 8
4th " 7
5th " 7

| Fail. | 60 | 65 | 70 | 75 | 80 | 85 | 90 | 95 |
|---|---|---|---|---|---|---|---|---|
| 122<br>**112**<br>108<br>**80** | 94<br>89<br>22 | **118**<br>**102**<br>24 | **111**<br>**101**<br>**100**<br>**85**<br>**83**<br>**68**<br>62<br>**42**<br>**1** | 74<br>**70**<br>67<br>**63**<br>**41**<br>**36**<br>20 | **87**<br>**43**<br>**40**<br>**39**<br>**35** | 76<br>**46**<br>45<br>**11** | **86**<br>**19** | 21 |

DIAGRAM 7.—DESIGN

119 pupils
1st Quintile 24
2d " 24
3d " 24
4th " 24
5th " 23

| Fail. | 60 | 65 | 70 | 75 | 80 | 85 | 90 | 95 |
|---|---|---|---|---|---|---|---|---|
| 130<br>77 | **102**<br>**8** | 119<br>**82**<br>48<br>**42** | 124<br>123<br>121<br>120<br>105<br>96<br>91<br>89<br>81<br>**80**<br>**78**<br>76<br>74<br>66<br>62<br>53<br>49<br>**44**<br>**41**<br>32<br>23<br>17 | 129<br>125<br>122<br>109<br>108<br>107<br>106<br>104<br>103<br>99<br>94<br>92<br>**88**<br>**83**<br>**79**<br>**70**<br>69<br>**68**<br>**63**<br>57<br>50<br>**43**<br>**38**<br>**36**<br>34<br>26<br>21<br>**19**<br>13 | **127**<br>**118**<br>**117**<br>**116**<br>**112**<br>110<br>**101**<br>97<br>95<br>**64**<br>60<br>59<br>55<br>**46**<br>**37**<br>20<br>18<br>14<br>**11**<br>**10**<br>**9**<br>5 | **128**<br>**115**<br>**113**<br>**111**<br>**85**<br>75<br>73<br>**65**<br>61<br>58<br>56<br>47<br>45<br>**40**<br>**35**<br>22<br>16<br>15<br>12<br>7<br>3<br>**1** | **100**<br>98<br>**87**<br>**84**<br>72<br>71<br>51<br>30<br>29<br>28<br>27<br>25<br>4 | **86**<br>33<br>2 |

Turning from these considerations to the main problem of comparison it is obvious that if the pupils from the Elementary School were in all respects like those from other schools a certain percentage of them should be distributed through each quintile in each of the subjects. Thus since there are 128 taking English and 44 of them come from the Elementary School, we might expect 34.4 per cent of each quintile to be from the Elementary School. Table I shows in detail how far the facts depart from this expectation. In the first column of figures at the left of Table I is recorded the total registration in each subject. In the second column the number of pupils from the Elementary School is recorded. In the third column is shown the percentage of University Elementary School pupils in each subject; in the other columns appear the percentage of University Elementary School pupils in each quintile and the variations in each subject from the normal or expected percentage. In the first and second quintiles an excess (+) represents an unfavorable showing for the University Elementary School, while a deficiency (—) represents a corresponding favorable showing; in the fourth and fifth quintiles an excess represents a favorable and a deficiency an unfavorable showing.

Tables II, III, and IV set forth similarly the facts for the Winter and Spring Quarters and for the entire year.

The matter can be exhibited graphically on the basis of Table IV by means of Diagrams 8–14. In each of these diagrams the horizonal line marked "o" indicates the level at which the Elementary School representatives should stand. The position which they take in each quintile is shown by the curve which crosses this horizontal line. Thus in Latin the real distribution is below the normal line for the three lowest quintiles and above for the two highest. By way of contrast the History curve is above the normal in the lowest quintile and below in all others.

From Diagrams 8-14 it appears that the pupils of the University Elementary School are greatly superior in Latin, Mathematics, French and German, and Design; in English they are somewhat inferior but stand in large proportion in mediocre

TABLE I

EXCESS OR DEFICIENCY IN GRADES OF UNIVERSITY ELEMENTARY SCHOOL PUPILS IN EACH QUINTILE FOR THE AUTUMN QUARTER

| Subject | Number Pupils | Number U. Ele. School Pupils | Percentage U. Ele. School Pupils | 1st or Lowest Quintile | | 2d Quintile | | 3d Quintile | | 4th Quintile | | 5th or Highest Quintile | |
|---|---|---|---|---|---|---|---|---|---|---|---|---|---|
| | | | | Percentage U. Ele. School Pupils | Variation from Normal | Percentage U. Ele. School Pupils | Variation from Normal | Percentage U. Ele. School Pupils | Variation from Normal | Percentage U. Ele. School Pupils | Variation from Normal | Percentage U. Ele. School Pupils | Variation from Normal |
| English | 128 | 44 | 34.4 | 34.6 | + 0.2 | 46.2 | +11.8 | 23.1 | −11.3 | 44.0 | + 9.6 | 24.0 | −10.4 |
| Latin | 101 | 40 | 39.6 | 23.8 | −15.8 | 30.0 | − 9.6 | 30.0 | − 9.6 | 55.0 | +15.4 | 60.0 | +20.4 |
| Mathematics | 127 | 43 | 33.9 | 30.8 | − 3.1 | 26.9 | − 7.0 | 28.0 | − 5.9 | 36.0 | + 2.1 | 48.0 | +14.1 |
| Science | 84 | 19 | 22.6 | 29.4 | + 6.8 | 41.2 | +18.6 | 17.7 | − 4.9 | 23.5 | + 0.9 | 0.0 | −22.6 |
| History | 97 | 22 | 22.7 | 25.0 | + 2.3 | 35.0 | +12.3 | 15.8 | − 6.9 | 21.1 | − 1.6 | 15.8 | − 6.9 |
| French and German | 38 | 24 | 63.2 | 37.5 | −25.7 | 87.5 | +24.3 | 50.0 | −13.2 | 85.7 | +22.5 | 57.1 | − 6.1 |
| Design | 119 | 43 | 36.1 | 25.0 | −11.1 | 29.2 | − 6.9 | 50.0 | +13.9 | 54.2 | +18.1 | 21.7 | −14.4 |
| Total | 694 | 235 | 33.9 | 28.9 | − 5.0 | 37.6 | + 3.7 | 29.5 | − 4.4 | 42.3 | + 8.4 | 31.1 | − 2.8 |

TABLE II

EXCESS OR DEFICIENCY IN GRADES OF UNIVERSITY ELEMENTARY SCHOOL PUPILS IN EACH QUINTILE FOR THE WINTER QUARTER

| Subject | Number Pupils | Number U. Ele. School Pupils | Percentage U. Ele. School Pupils | 1st Quintile | | 2d Quintile | | 3d Quintile | | 4th Quintile | | 5th Quintile | |
|---|---|---|---|---|---|---|---|---|---|---|---|---|---|
| | | | | Per-centage U. Ele. School Pupils | Variation from Normal | Per-centage U. Ele. School Pupils | Variation from Normal | Per-centage U. Ele. School Pupils | Variation from Normal | Per-centage U. Ele. School Pupils | Variation from Normal | Per-centage U. Ele. School Pupils | Variation from Normal |
| English | 108 | 42 | 38.9 | 50.0 | +11.1 | 45.5 | + 6.6 | 22.7 | −16.2 | 38.1 | − 0.8 | 38.1 | − 0.8 |
| Latin | 74 | 33 | 44.6 | 33.3 | −11.3 | 53.3 | + 8.7 | 26.7 | −17.9 | 60.0 | +15.4 | 50.0 | + 5.4 |
| Mathematics | 105 | 39 | 37.1 | 28.6 | − 8.5 | 28.6 | − 8.5 | 42.9 | + 5.8 | 28.6 | − 8.5 | 57.1 | +20.0 |
| Science | 75 | 18 | 24.0 | 33.3 | + 9.3 | 33.3 | + 9.3 | 13.3 | −10.7 | 26.7 | + 2.7 | 13.3 | −10.7 |
| History | 80 | 19 | 23.8 | 43.8 | +20.0 | 12.5 | −11.3 | 25.0 | + 1.2 | 25.0 | + 1.2 | 12.5 | −11.3 |
| French and German | 32 | 21 | 65.6 | 85.7 | +20.1 | 14.3 | −51.3 | 100.0 | +34.4 | 50.0 | −15.6 | 83.3 | +17.7 |
| Design | 104 | 43 | 41.3 | 23.8 | −17.5 | 42.9 | + 1.6 | 47.6 | + 6.3 | 61.9 | +20.6 | 30.0 | −11.3 |
| Total | 578 | 215 | 37.2 | 38.5 | + 1.3 | 35.0 | − 2.2 | 34.5 | − 2.7 | 40.9 | + 3.7 | 37.2 | 0.0 |

TABLE III

EXCESS OR DEFICIENCY IN GRADES OF UNIVERSITY ELEMENTARY SCHOOL PUPILS IN EACH QUINTILE FOR THE SPRING QUARTER

| Subject | Number Pupils | Number U. Ele. School Pupils | Percentage U. Ele. School Pupils | 1st Quintile | | 2d Quintile | | 3d Quintile | | 4th Quintile | | 5th Quintile | |
|---|---|---|---|---|---|---|---|---|---|---|---|---|---|
| | | | | Percentage U. Ele. School Pupils | Variation from Normal | Percentage U. Ele. School Pupils | Variation from Normal | Percentage U. Ele. School Pupils | Variation from Normal | Percentage U. Ele. School Pupils | Variation from Normal | Percentage U. Ele. School Pupils | Variation from Normal |
| English | 106 | 42 | 39.6 | 50.0 | +10.4 | 28.6 | −11.0 | 33.3 | − 6.3 | 38.1 | − 1.5 | 42.9 | + 3.3 |
| Latin | 63 | 34 | 53.9 | 76.9 | +23.0 | 46.2 | − 7.7 | 38.5 | −15.4 | 58.3 | + 4.4 | 50.0 | − 3.9 |
| Mathematics | 91 | 37 | 40.7 | 42.1 | + 1.4 | 33.3 | − 7.4 | 22.2 | −18.5 | 50.0 | + 9.3 | 55.6 | +14.9 |
| Science | 66 | 14 | 21.2 | 21.4 | + 0.2 | 15.4 | − 5.8 | 30.8 | + 9.6 | 23.1 | + 1.9 | 15.4 | − 5.8 |
| History | 71 | 17 | 23.9 | 46.7 | +22.8 | 14.3 | − 9.6 | 28.6 | + 4.7 | 14.3 | − 9.6 | 14.3 | − 9.6 |
| French and German | 30 | 20 | 66.7 | 66.7 | 0.0 | 50.0 | −16.7 | 66.7 | 0.0 | 66.7 | 0.0 | 83.3 | +16.6 |
| Design | 105 | 41 | 39.0 | 19.0 | −20.0 | 28.6 | −10.4 | 52.4 | +13.4 | 33.3 | − 5.7 | 61.9 | +22.9 |
| **Total** | 532 | 205 | 38.7 | 42.7 | + 4.0 | 30.2 | − 8.5 | 36.8 | − 1.9 | 38.1 | − 0.6 | 44.8 | + 6.1 |

TABLE IV

EXCESS OR DEFICIENCY IN GRADES OF UNIVERSITY ELEMENTARY SCHOOL PUPILS IN EACH QUINTILE FOR THE ENTIRE YEAR

| Subject | Number Pupils | Number U. Ele. School Pupils | Percentage U. Ele. School Pupils | 1st Quintile | | 2d Quintile | | 3d Quintile | | 4th Quintile | | 5th Quintile | |
|---|---|---|---|---|---|---|---|---|---|---|---|---|---|
| | | | | Percentage U. Ele. School Pupils | Variation from Normal | Percentage U. Ele. School Pupils | Variation from Normal | Percentage U. Ele. School Pupils | Variation from Normal | Percentage U. Ele. School Pupils | Variation from Normal | Percentage U. Ele. School Pupils | Variation from Normal |
| English | 342 | 128 | 37.4 | 44.3 | + 6.9 | 40.6 | + 3.2 | 26.1 | −11.3 | 40.3 | + 2.9 | 34.3 | − 3.1 |
| Latin | 238 | 107 | 45.0 | 40.8 | − 4.2 | 41.7 | − 3.3 | 31.3 | −13.7 | 57.4 | +12.4 | 54.3 | + 9.3 |
| Mathematics | 323 | 119 | 36.8 | 33.3 | − 3.5 | 29.2 | − 7.6 | 31.3 | − 5.5 | 37.5 | − 0.7 | 53.1 | +16.3 |
| Science | 225 | 51 | 22.7 | 28.3 | + 5.6 | 31.1 | + 8.4 | 20.0 | − 2.7 | 24.4 | + 1.7 | 9.1 | −13.6 |
| History | 248 | 58 | 23.4 | 37.3 | +13.9 | 22.2 | − 1.2 | 22.4 | − 1.0 | 20.4 | − 3.0 | 14.3 | − 9.1 |
| French and German | 100 | 65 | 65.0 | 61.9 | − 3.1 | 52.4 | −12.6 | 70.0 | + 5.0 | 68.4 | + 3.4 | 73.7 | + 8.7 |
| Design | 328 | 127 | 38.7 | 22.7 | −16.0 | 33.3 | − 5.4 | 50.0 | +11.3 | 50.0 | +11.3 | 37.5 | − 1.2 |
| Total | 1,804 | 655 | 36.3 | 36.0 | − 0.2 | 34.6 | − 1.7 | 33.2 | − 3.1 | 40.6 | + 4.3 | 37.1 | +0.8 |

position; while in History and Science they are decidedly inferior. The inferiority in English is partially accounted for by the chance grouping in the Autumn Quarter referred to above. An equitable distribution gives the results indicated in the broken line in Diagram 8, showing that there is but a slight inferiority. For the inferiority in Science and History

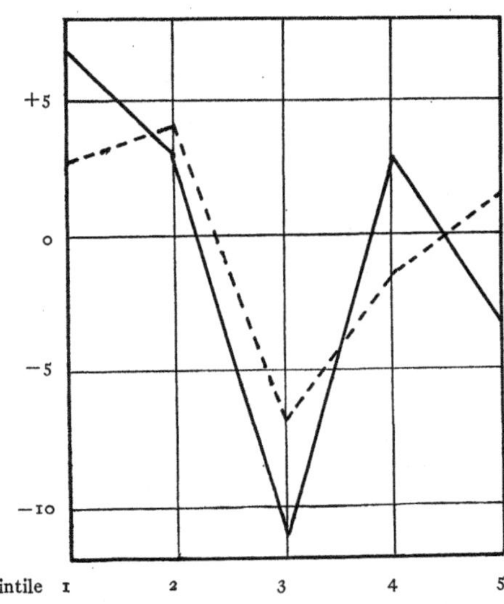


DIAGRAM 8.—Excess and deficiency in grades in English of pupils of Universit Elementary School. (Broken line shows correction in Autumn Quarter.)

another explanation must be sought. This may be found, in part at least, in the fact that 16 pupils of the University Elementary School omit History and Science and take French and German in their place. A comparison of the standing of these pupils with the 28 others from the school indicates that the work of those not taking History and Science is in general of very much superior grade. Table 5 and Diagram 14 exhibit this fact. This table is exhibited graphically in Diagram 14.

The problems which are suggested by this study are numerous. It is not the purpose of this report to enter into detailed discussion of these problems. The paper is offered rather as an exhibition of the kind of study which should in every case accompany supervisory inspection. How one department com-

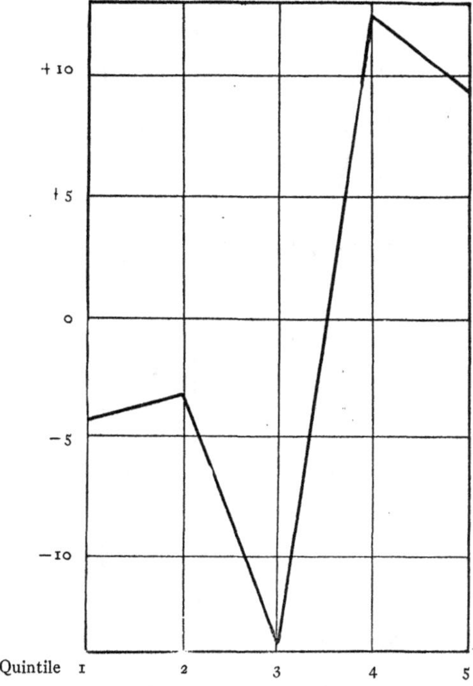


DIAGRAM 9.—Excess and deficiency in grades in Latin of pupils of the University Elementary School.

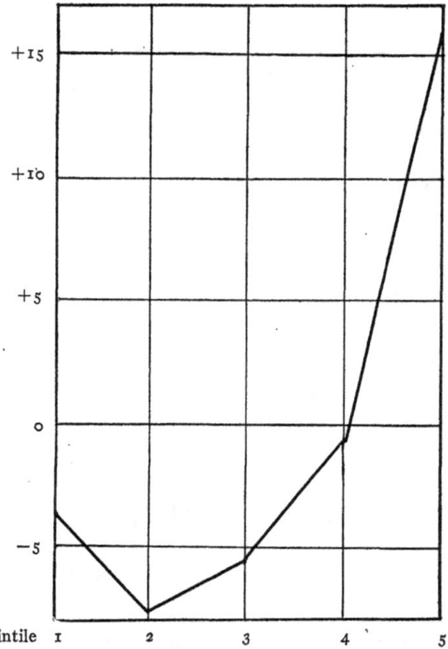


DIAGRAM 10.—Excess and deficiency in grades in Mathematics of pupils of the University Elementary School.

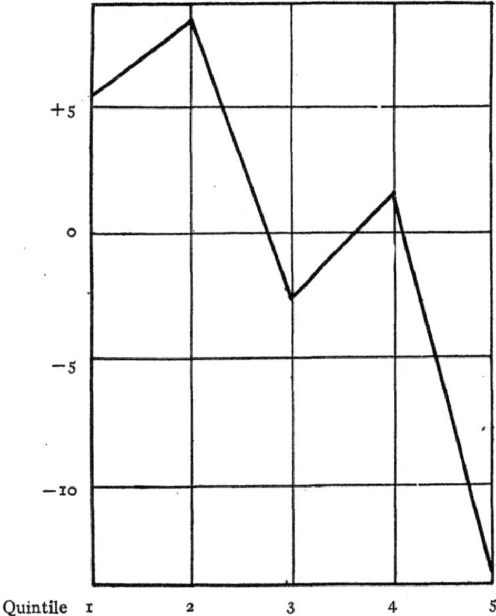


DIAGRAM 11.—Excess and deficiency in grades in Science of pupils of the University Elementary School.

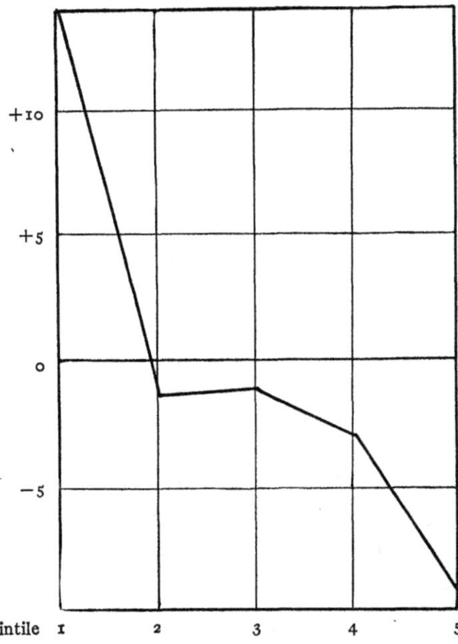


DIAGRAM 12.—Excess and deficiency in grades in History of pupils of the University Elementary School.

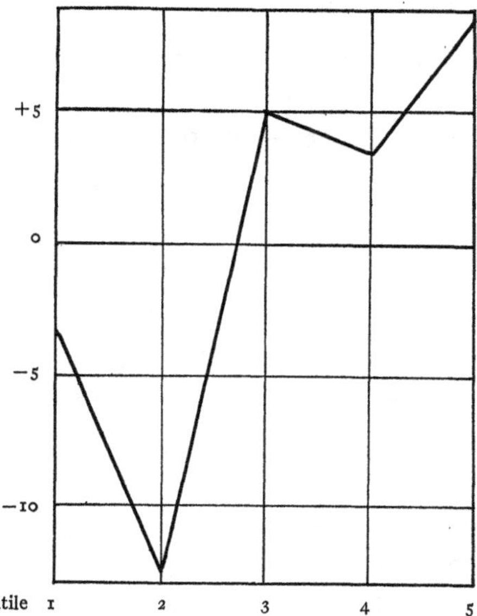


Diagram 13.—Excess and deficiency in grades in French and German of pupils of the University Elementary School.

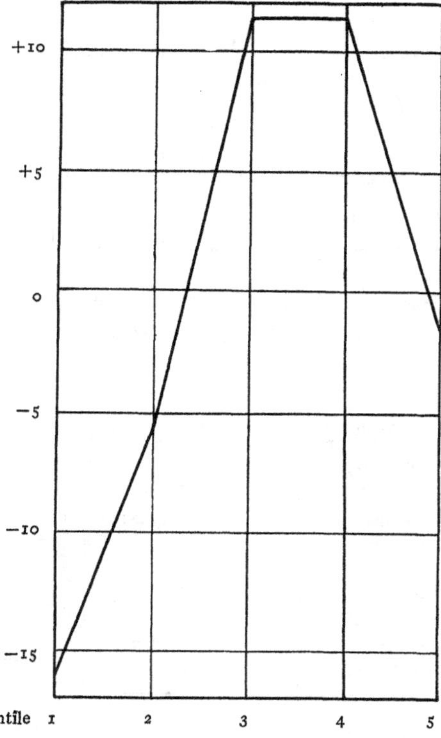


Diagram 14.—Excess and deficiency in grades in Design of pupils of the University Elementary School.

pares with another, how one school compares with another, and ultimately how one teacher compares with another can be discovered by minute and exact comparisons of the products.

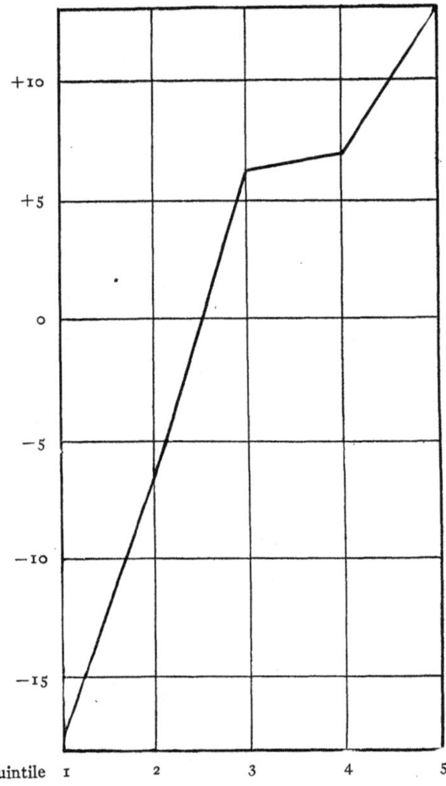


DIAGRAM 15.—Excess and deficiency in grades of pupils from the University Elementary School not taking Science and History compared with grades of other pupils from school.

TABLE V

COMPARISON OF THE GRADES OF THE 16 UNIVERSITY ELEMENTARY SCHOOL PUPILS NOT TAKING SCIENCE AND HISTORY WITH THOSE OF THE OTHER 28 FROM THE SAME SCHOOL

| Total Number of Grades U. E. S. | Number Grades of 16 | Percentage of Grades of 16 | 1st Quintile | | 2d Quintile | | 3d Quintile | | 4th Quintile | | 5th Quintile | |
|---|---|---|---|---|---|---|---|---|---|---|---|---|
| | | | Percentage of 16 | Variation | Percentage of 16 | Variation | Percentage of 16 | Variation | Percentage of 16 | Variation | Percentage of 16 | Variation |
| 481.... | 189 | 39.3 | 21.8 | −17.5 | 33.0 | −6.3 | 45.4 | +6.1 | 46.2 | +6.9 | 52.2 | +12.9 |

# AGRICULTURAL EDUCATION: PERIODICAL LITERATURE[1]

BENJAMIN MARSHALL DAVIS
Miami University

Popular periodicals have become an important factor in education. They reach thousands of people. Several have a circulation of more than 100,000, and a few claim to reach a million readers. Every subject of popular interest is exploited. This popular interest determines in a large measure the choice of subject-matter, but not always. Interest in new things is often stimulated by well-written articles. Indeed there is a keen search for new things or the beginnings of new movements that may seem to have elements of popular interest. The importance of rural education, the inefficiency of the present system, and the need of redirecting rural education are new things from the standpoint of the popular periodical.

An educational system which originated in pioneer days, and which served its purpose well in those days, persists today with less modification than has taken place in any other feature of rural life. The few changes that have taken place were brought about largely through imitation, either voluntarily or impressed by law, of urban schools, and were not the changes of an adaptive growth. This static condition of rural education until a few years ago, and in most communities at the present time, was looked upon with complacency and satisfaction. Patrons who were not satisfied quietly moved to some town or city where their children might have better educational advantages, but little or no criticism of the rural school was ventured and little or no effort made to improve it.

With this situation in mind, it is easy to see why any departure from the established routine in rural-school manage-

[1] A discussion of "Agricultural Education in Educational Periodicals" appeared as the preceding article of this series, in this magazine, September, 1910.

ment or any effort to make its work better adapted to rural conditions would be regarded by editors of popular periodicals as something new and worthy of wide publicity.

Consolidation of rural schools began in the early nineties. Various periodicals gave accounts of the schools of Kingsville Township, Ohio, which in 1892 instituted a plan of consolidation for rural schools. This movement soon attracted much attention, and many visits were made to Ohio for the purpose of seeing the plan in actual operation. In a few years the plan was not only extended to other parts of Ohio but was introduced in many other states. It has worked so successfully as to be considered one of the most important features of any general scheme for improving rural schools.

The work of Kingsville Township was not the historical beginning of the consolidated-school movement, but it was the potential beginning, largely due to the public notice it received through newspapers and periodicals.

Superintendent O. J. Kern, of Winnebago County, Ill., had barely demonstrated the success of his Farmer Boys' Experiment Club which he had organized in February, 1902, among the schoolboys of his county, when he was asked to give an account of it in one of our leading popular magazines. This work of his was something new in a county system of schools, and furthermore it had begun at once to interest farmers and to change their attitude toward the rural schools. Winnebago County was a typical county with large agricultural interests. Its problems and interests were like those of hundreds of other counties. Superintendent Kern had found something that looked toward making the school life of the country boys more worth while, but he had much more in mind than his Boys' Experiment Club. He believed that the whole rural-school system needed readjustment and that it might be slowly brought about.

Here was a chance for the magazine to be of service by giving publicity to successful work, and for the writer to get others interested in his plans, and to get them to work along similar lines. The article appeared under the title of "Learning by Doing for the Farmer Boy" and was illustrated by five good pictures with the "boy" prominently in the foreground of each. The title and the pictures were attractive and were likely to cause the reader to pause in turning through the pages of the magazine long enough at least to read the introductory paragraph. This was an expression of an ideal for rural education which up to that time (1903) had not come much into public notice:

It is not the belief or wish of the writer that we should educate country boys to be farmers merely, any more than that we should educate boys to be blacksmiths, carpenters, or electricians. We should aim to train boys to be men in the highest sense of the term. But why not a course of training in the country school for the country boy which shall teach him more about country life around him? Along with his study of the kangaroo, the bamboo, and the cockatoo, why not study the animals on the farm and a proper feeding-standard for them, the care and composition of the soil on the farm, the improvement of types of grains and vegetables, and the protection of birds beneficial to the farmer? Instead of all the boys' arithmetic being devoted to problems, more or less theoretical, on banking, stocks, exchange, brokerage, alligation, and partnership, why not some practical problems with reference to farm economics? For the boys who will remain on the farm (and 85 per cent perhaps will) the course of instruction should be such as will be an inspiration and a help in their future life-work (84).[a]

A year later under the title of "Common-Sense Country Schools" a description of Mr. Kern's work appeared in another magazine (85). Other references to his work have been published from time to time.

Boys' clubs for carrying on agricultural experiments have been organized in all of the agricultural states. Accounts of their work are attractive reading, and no doubt not only stimulate the boys in other localities to form similar clubs but help to educate adult farmers to be more appreciative of expert opinion. But the most important contribution made by periodicals to agricultural education through boys' clubs has been in making the way easier for agricultural colleges and public-school officers to carry on the work in various parts of the country.

In the same number of the magazine in which Mr. Kern's article appeared is another dealing with the problem of rural

[a] The references are to the bibliography at the end of this article or to bibliographies in other articles of this series.

education (86). The need of a school system adapted to rural conditions is set forth. Special emphasis is placed upon the value of agricultural high schools and of consolidated rural schools. At that time there were twelve agricultural high schools in the United States. There are now seventy-five.

Another account of important work in agricultural education was published in the same year (1903) with the title "Teaching Farmers' Children on the Ground" (87). It is of interest to compare the opinion of Superintendent Kern as to the needs of the rural school with that of the writer of this article who was not professionally engaged in education. The following is taken from his description of a rural school:

> But there is more the matter with the ordinary country school than its smallness of scale. . . . . Yet that these children come from homes where the livelihood is earned out of the ground is ignored in the lessons. The instruction as far as it goes is good: it is staple reading, writing, and arithmetic, with a little grammar, geography, and history. This is all. It might do well enough if the boys and girls were all going to be clerks or traders; or if, in the fulness of their ambition, they were to strike out for professional careers. But of sowing and reaping there is never a word; nothing about planting and tending of trees, the production of milk, butter, and cheese. Never, even remotely, does a lesson touch on building and drainage, on the composition of foods or chemistry of fuel, or light up for so much as a moment the drama of struggle and survival of which every clover patch is a theater. It is well that children should learn at school useful lessons they can learn nowhere else, but should not the children of the farm be led to see somewhat of the inexhaustible scope for brains which offers itself to the farmer? The fact is, that rural instruction has been largely devised in cities with a view to city conditions. And the courses in city schools are faulty enough, ridden as they are by clerky traditions which permit the word to usurp the place of the act, instead of being merely its symbol and aid. The second evil in rural education throughout America is the stress laid upon verbal studies, the blinking the actual world of duty and joy for which country children should be informed and trained.

This is followed by a description of the proposed scheme for the improvement of rural education in Canada planned on a scale to include the whole Dominion. Not only is this description accurate but it includes a good historical and economic background. This account of the "Macdonald Movement" before it was carried out in actual practice prepared the public mind for the numerous reports of the work that have appeared since.

Mention should be made of one more popular article on rural education appearing in 1903, entitled "Farmer Children Need Farmer Studies" (88). The title indicates the general nature of the discussion. That the writer is in full accord with the views already noted of other contributors is shown by the following statements:

> Our educational system has been made for city people, and the country school finds it second hand and ill-fitting and unattractive. To this fact more than any other, perhaps, is due the backwardness of education in agricultural states.

Quoted from a private letter:

> Statistics show that in this state each year sixty young men take up ministry, sixty-six law, and seventy-two medicine, while 13,000 annually take up agriculture as a gainful pursuit. But our school books are written for the few not the many. . . . . At present the entire curriculum leads away from the farm. . . . . Pick up any high-grade arithmetic in use in the rural schools and you will find no lack of attention to banking and commissions and foreign exchange and commercial affairs generally. But agriculture arises to no such dignity—not even in schools that will find five times as many recruits for the farm as for the city. The same applies to other texts.

The typical examples above presented of popular periodical literature on rural education appeared in 1903. This year was chosen because it seemed to mark the beginning of a somewhat general public interest in the subject, and partly because most of the development of agricultural education in elementary and secondary schools has taken place since that time.

During the period from 1904 to the present the subject of rural education has continued to receive notice in popular periodicals (85, 89, 90, 91, 92). The public has been kept informed concerning various phases of its development, agricultural and other industrial work in schools receiving especial attention.

One magazine addressed the following question to a number of prominent educators: "What new subject or new method or new direction of effort or new tendency in educational work is of most value and significance and now needs most emphasis and encouragement?" (93). Nineteen replies were received. As most of the writers were college presidents various college problems were mentioned as of greatest importance but no two proposed the same problem. The only subject that was mentioned by more than three was practical education, summed up as follows: Trade work in public schools; interest in rural schools; practical studies; agriculture for rural schools; reaching all the people; teaching every man his job.

A good account of the present status of agricultural education in elementary and secondary schools appeared under the title "Catching Them Young" (94). After describing some recent progress in farming methods the author adds:

> Of what value is this knowledge if the sons and daughters are to quit the farm, leaving corn-belt prosperity to the haphazard agriculture of the city-born and of transplanting foreigners who find conditions and climate vastly different from those of the fatherland? Therefore the corn-belt has at last set itself to raising that greater and more valuable crop of farm boys and farm girls who find material comforts and ample financial recompense on the farm. The greatest factor in the raising of this new crop is education. . . . . But the farm boys and girls in order to be interested must be caught young. Before they are old enough to enter the land-grant colleges the lure of the city has entered their minds and the mischief is done. Raising bumper crops of corn and oats, the typically agricultural states of America have heretofore failed to raise satisfactory crops of stay-at-home boys and girls.

An editorial in another magazine revives the criticism which appeared against rural schools a few years before. It is entitled "The Martian and the Farm" (95) and makes the remarks of the supposed Martian who is represented as visiting an ordinary country school the basis of some pointed comments on the rural schools:

> I notice that these Americans seem to think the raising of crops to be quite unnecessary; and that they are applying their remarkable intelligence to the task of depopulating their rural regions. They have acuteness to see that if they are to drive people out of the country, they cannot begin with the adult population. Life in the open country is so alluring and so natural that even when it has not been made as complete as it might be, it holds people fast. So these far-reaching Americans, in order to crowd people back

into the cities, where they obviously want them to be, have devised a campaign of education directed toward the children. They have planned all their rural schools on city models. Even in such details as arithmetic problems, they see to it that the children's minds should be directed toward urban life. . . . . If this visitor were told what he interpreted as an astute campaign was a mere matter of stupidity and tradition, and that the American People were really wondering how they could check the congestion of cities, he would be forced, out of decent respect for the people he was visiting, to be incredulous.

How can a child born and reared in the country respect the life of the farmer when the community in which he lives does not regard the farmer's occupation worthy of study? How can he be expected to look with ambition toward agriculture as a vocation when he finds that training for it is regarded as less important than preparation for a clerkship? How can he think of village and rural life as anything more than a makeshift when he finds that in the schools he attends there is not a word taught concerning crops or cattle or roads?

The situation in this country is then contrasted with the national policy of rural education recently inaugurated in Canada and the importance of a similar movement in this country suggested. The criticism of the condition in rural schools as to their indifference to rural life does not go unchallenged. In a later number of the same magazine appears a reply in which the editor is brought to task for making implications that were not warranted by the facts in the case. The work in agricultural education of the Middle West is cited as a refutation. The writer in a five months' visit in Canada had been unable to see any reason for holding up the Canadian scheme for rural education as a model for this country (96).

Another letter of reply is published from a farmer who could see no more reason why "a country child should be taught how to run a farm than a city child should be taught how to run a bank."

It seems plain to me [he says] that the public schools are intended to give the young a practical education to prepare them for life, not to prepare them for any particular work in life. . . . . Why tax the community in general to instruct its children for work and life on the farm, when many of the patrons and many of the children themselves would prefer general education? (97).

The above editorial and its sequel, the two letters of reply, give some insight into the present situation. No doubt the condition referred to in the editorial does not apply to all rural schools but in general it is not much overdrawn. The writer of the first letter unduly magnifies the work of agricultural education in this country, for it has not had time to modify the ordinary rural schools to any considerable extent, even in the favored Middle West. On the other hand, his five months' visit in Canada failed to show him that the efforts of the Canadian educators are aimed directly at the rural schools. The second letter reveals an attitude which is familiar to those who have undertaken to hold up the chief interest of a rural community as a motive for better schols.

In reviewing the relation of popular periodicals to agricultural education only typical examples have been given. No attempt has been made to have the references complete. Sufficient citations have been given to indicate the character and scope of the discussions of the subject as they have appeared in these periodicals, and to show the service rendered by keeping the subject before the public, and by helping to secure a favorable attitude toward the improvement of rural schools.

Brief reference should be made also to periodicals whose circulation is limited to smaller groups of readers. There is a large number published in the interest of farmers. Most of them are local, being chiefly confined in circulation to a single state. Many are of doubtful value and are about as useful to the farmers as gold bricks. Those that are really sincere in their efforts to improve farm life have exerted considerable influence for the betterment of rural schools and for the introduction of agriculture. Special articles as well as letters from subscribers are published. The most important of these are reviewed from time to time in the *Experiment Station Record* of the United States Department of Agriculture (13) and need not be mentioned here except in this general way. On the whole, agricultural periodicals have maintained too conservative an attitude toward agricultural education, both as to colleges and elementary and secondary schools. One cannot avoid the suspicion that this attitude on the part of some of these publications is not wholly disinterested. Agricultural education would, among other things, most certainly develop more critical readers, and this would soon react upon the circulation or upon the character of the matter published. Again, the fear of offending some of their readers, thus affecting circulation, makes the publishers cautious in giving space to views that might unsettle the faith of the fathers in the little one-room school.

Occasionally a well-written article on agricultural education appears in the more special periodicals. For example in a magazine "devoted to the philosophy of science" we find a discussion of "Agriculture the Basis of Education" (98). The writer regards the two primal contacts of the child, with nature and with parents, as more fundamental than all questions of subject-matter and methods of formal education. "The mental conditions of agriculture are just as essential to normal development of the human mind as air, food, and exercise for the development of the human body." He refers to the education of the early Greeks in support of his views: "The young Greek of the Homeric age appears to have had much more intimate and adequate contacts with nature and with his elders than our modern education provides, or even permits."

A similar conclusion as to the educational influence of agriculture, though discussed from an entirely different standpoint, is found in an article on "Farm Life as a Basis of Practical Education" (99). The subject for another discussion is the "Need for Agricultural Education" (100). The economic importance of this kind of education is urged. Another point of view is set forth under the title "Rural Education" (101).

> Rural education is but a section of the general school question; agricultural education is a branch of technical training. These two phases of education of the farm population meet at many points, they must work in harmony, and together they form a distinct educational problem.

Three difficulties are mentioned: (1) To secure a modern school equal to the city school; (2) to enrich and expand the curriculum so as to make it a vital and coherent part of rural-community life; (3) to provide adequate high-school facilities in the rural community.

## BIBLIOGRAPHY

Only references cited by number in the text are included.

84. "Learning by Doing for the Farmer Boy." O. J. KERN. *Review of Reviews,* XXVIII (1903), 456–61.

A description of the Farmer Boys' Club organized in Winnebago County, Ill., February 22, 1902. It includes method of organization, educational excursions, experimental work of the boys, local meetings of the club, the club and the farmers' institute, future outlook of the club. There is also a short account of the first consolidated school in Illinois.

85. "Common-Sense Country Schools." ADELE MARIE SHAW. *World's Work,* VIII (1904), 4881–94.

An illustrated account of O. J. Kern's work among the rural schools of Winnebago County, Ill. It contains a good account of the Farmer Boys' Club.

86. "The New Education for Farm Children." WILLET M. HAYS. *Review of Reviews,* XXVIII (1903), 449–55.

The article is introduced by a general discussion of the educational situation, concluding that there should be a school system adapted to rural conditions. A scheme is presented for an articulated system of education adapted to rural needs: (1) consolidated rural school; (2) agricultural high school; (3) agricultural college. This is one of the first publications of the author's views on a system of rural education. His present views on this subject have been reviewed at some length in a previous article of this series (15).

87. "Teaching Farmers' Children on the Ground." GEORGE ILES. *World's Work,* VI (1903), 3415–20.

After a general discussion of rural education, its needs and shortcomings, the author gives an account of the program for rural educational reform, known as the Macdonald Consolidated Rural School Movement, which was to take effect in Canada the following September. A large number of interesting facts are given not only concerning this proposed reform but also concerning the agricultural work in general in Canada.

88. "Farmer Children Need Farmer Studies." CLARENCE H. POE. *World's Work,* VI (1903), 3760–62.

Reviewed in text.

89. "Agricultural High Schools" (Editorial). *Independent,* LVIII (1905), 334–36.

90. "Two Clear Aims in Education" (Editorial). *World's Work,* XII (1906), 7706–7.

These aims are (1) training for practical purposes, the machinery of which has been perfected only for the professions; (2) training for culture where public good is put before personal aims.

91. "Agricultural Education in the United States." J. C. MEAD. *Nineteenth Century,* LX (1906), 299–306.

A popular historical account dealing mainly with agricultural colleges.

92. "Agriculture in the Common Schools" (Editorial). *Independent,* LXIII (1907), 1508–9.

Two questions are raised: (1) Are the sciences underlying agriculture to be taught? (2) Where will teachers be found to give adequate instruction along such lines? Both questions are answered, the first by making use of pupils' everyday experiences, the second through training schools for teachers.

93. "New Work in Education." *World's Work,* XVI (1908), 10453–62.

Reviewed in text.

94. "Catching Them Young." F. G. Moorhead. *Technical World,* XI (1909), 612–18.

Reviewed in text.

95. "The Martian and the Farm" (Editorial). *Outlook,* XXIX (1909), 433–34

Reviewed in text.

96. "Training for Farm Life." D. H. Smalley. *Outlook,* XXIX (1909), 811–12.

A reply to (95).

97. "The Automatic Farm." Wm. Halstead. *Outlook,* XXIX (1909), 812–13.

A reply to (95).

98. "Agriculture the Basis of Education." O. F. Cook. *Monist,* XVII (1907), 347–64.

Reviewed in text.

99. "Farm Life as a Basis of Practical Education." *Craftsman,* XVI (1909), 243–45.

Some of the plans of the Craftsman Farms are set forth. Active farm operation is regarded as the first step in creating an ideal school environment. "To use the idea of education seems as big and interesting as the whole of life itself. And the farm work which is necessary to make the land productive for our own maintenance and also to make the ground attractive to the eye seems to us to afford a series of experiments, the educational value of which no scientific laboratory could equal."

100. "Need for Agricultural Education." D. Y. Thomas. *Annals of the American Academy,* XXXV (1910), 150–55.

The purpose of this paper is to "emphasize the advisability" of extending the work in agricultural education. "Education must be democratized and made to subserve the economic interest of man. This will not kill the cultural school but foster it. The man who wants to be a lawyer or a doctor or a teacher or a journalist will have a hundred opportunities where he now has one."

101. "Social Problems of American Farmers: Rural Education." Kenyon L. Butterfield. *American Journal of Sociology,* X (1905), 615–19.

Reviewed in text.

# DENTAL EXAMINATION OF SCHOOL CHILDREN

W. C. REAVIS
Oakland City, Indiana

The movement for dental examination of school children that has long been a matter of great concern in many European countries has come largely from two sources in America. First, public-health officials in their effort to cope with the problem of public sanitation have found that the schools, on account of the unhygienic condition of the mouths of many children, are centers for the spread of contagious diseases. Second, educators in their effort to make the school a more efficient institution for the conservation of everything that might influence the welfare of the largest number of children have found that one of the greatest factors in mental and moral development is the status of the child's physical condition. Hence, with a different end in view, both professions have been led to seize the same means, and as a result the hygienic condition and environment of the child are receiving more attention than ever before.

The attitude of the American public toward the care of teeth —especially children's teeth—has been one of gross neglect. Until recent years, the subject has not received a just amount of attention from professional men; neither has it received sufficient emphasis in the teaching of physiology and hygiene in the public schools. For these reasons, ignorance of the proper care of teeth is widespread. For example, an idea has seemed to prevail that teeth need no attention until they begin to ache. This common notion has resulted in the loss of millions of teeth that could have been saved by adequate dental care at the proper time.

The real seriousness of the situation forces itself upon us as a national problem when we look into the condition of children's teeth over the country at large, and examine a sufficient number of statistics to permit of definite conclusions

An examination of 172,000 school children of New York City[1] has revealed the startling fact that 95 per cent need the attention of a dentist; 75 per cent had never visited a dental office. Detailed examination of 7,608 children from a selected school district showed the following results by grades:

| Grade | Number Examined | Number with Defective Teeth | Percentage with Teeth Defective |
|---|---|---|---|
| 1A | 678 | 427 | 62.9 |
| 1B | 1,115 | 749 | 67.2 |
| 2A | 951 | 660 | 69.4 |
| 2B | 788 | 416 | 52.8 |
| 3A | 663 | 358 | 54.0 |
| 3B | 620 | 350 | 56.4 |
| 4A | 533 | 227 | 42.6 |
| 4B | 531 | 209 | 39.4 |
| 5A | 338 | 101 | 29.9 |
| 5B | 299 | 97 | 32.4 |
| 6A | 314 | 91 | 29.0 |
| 6B | 367 | 64 | 38.3 |
| 7A | 212 | 76 | 35.8 |
| 7B | 159 | 17 | 10.6 |
| 8A | 134 | 64 | 47.7 |
| 8B | 70 | 7 | 10.0 |
| Total | 7,608 | 3,913 | 51.4 |

At Brookline, Massachusetts, the wealthiest town in America, 75 per cent of the school children examined needed dental service. This clearly indicates that the ravages upon the teeth are by no means confined to the poorer class of people.

A recent dental examination of the children of Sidney and the country districts of New South Wales revealed the following conditions:

| | Boys | Girls |
|---|---|---|
| Number examined | 4,433 | 3,216 |
| Permanent teeth decayed | 14% | 16% |
| Milk teeth decayed | 30% | 35% |
| Dirty mouths | 15% | 11.7% |
| Decayed teeth per pupil | 4.2 | 4.8 |

Dental inspection in four representative schools of Cleveland showed 92.83 per cent, 97.1 per cent, 95.31 per cent, and

[1] For references for this and subsequent statements of statistics see bibliography at end of paper.

98.43 per cent defective mouths respectively, and 15,061 dental cavities out of a total of 2,677 children, or an average of 5.6 decays per pupil.

In Germany, of 20,000 children between the age of six and sixteen, 95 per cent had dental caries.

Free dental service in the public schools of Mexico showed that the entire school enrolment suffered from the propagation of dental defects. Dr. Maximo Silva, chief physician of the school of primary instruction, reports that all of the children have bad teeth. Irregularities are very common, mastication is bad, and most of the children suffer from gastric and intestinal catarrh.

Dr. Ottofy reports, after giving much time to the study of teeth among different nations, that the Filipino children have only five sound teeth out of every hundred, the American children have seven, the Chinese twelve.

These alarming proportions serve as only a few examples of actual conditions. Dr. Osler says:

> There is not any one single thing more important to the public in the whole range of hygiene than the hygiene of the mouth. If I were asked whether more physical deterioration was produced by alcohol or defective teeth, I should unhesitatingly say defective teeth.

Recruiting officers in the United States Army and Navy have long recognized the fact that a man with defective teeth makes an unreliable soldier or sailor. During the year 1906, out of the 18,000 young men rejected, 1,000 were refused enlistment on account of bad teeth alone; and in the British army out of 23,000 men refused enlistment for all causes, in one year, 5,000 of these were rejected for either loss of teeth or on account of decayed teeth.

The French sub-minister of war recently issued a circular regarding dental hygiene of the army, in which he shows that dental lesions have been responsible for much sickness. In 1903, on account of teeth alone, 1,845 soldiers entered the hospital for treatment amounting to 18,639 days. Now, recruits are examined before entrance and regularly every three months after, in order that habits of hygiene may be established and maintained.

Experiments conducted on nine men for a period of four and one-half months to ascertain the value of proper mastication and enjoyment of food showed at the end of the experiment that the men were able to do double the amount of work. In the light of this fact, we must inevitably conclude that there is a great waste in vitality to the child who is compelled to masticate his food with a set of grinders that cannot half perform their work.

There is no time in life when good digestion and assimilation are of such vital importance as in the public-school period in which examinations reveal the teeth to be most seriously impaired. If the teeth are allowed to rot during this lapse of time between the loss of the temporary set and the eruption of the permanent set, when the tissues of the body are calling for a large amount of building material, a great waste in body and mind is sure to result.

If the decaying deciduous teeth do not receive proper treatment, they often become sensitive and so tender to the touch of food that the process of mastication is slighted and the child forms the habit of bolting his food, a habit that insures indigestion with its retinue of ills. In addition to a decrease in weight that is sure to follow, Leonard P. Ayres has conclusively shown that the average number of grades completed is .29 per cent less than by those having no physical defects, and that school progress is 5.9 per cent slower.

Dental caries if allowed to exist become receptacles for the culture of disease-producing germs that not only drain into the alimentary canal, endangering the health of the particular individual, but also are scattered through the air by coughing and sneezing, thus spreading contagion to those around. One child with a very bad mouth may inoculate a number of others, regardless of how careful or clean they may be.

Dr. Christian Greve in his work on the *Prevention of Disease* declares that good care must be taken of the milk teeth, if the cutting of the permanent set is to be regular.

The first teeth must not be destroyed before their time, because inflammation and abscesses of these may injure the germ of the permanent tooth, and because by early extraction abnormalities in position may arise. When a milk tooth is removed and the permanent tooth does not quickly fill up the gap, this becomes smaller by the approximation of the neighboring teeth, and the permanent tooth which subsequently appears must take an inclined position, i.e., forward or backward to the alveolar arch. On the other hand the milk teeth or their remnants must not remain too long in the mouth, but be removed in time to prevent similar ill effects.

Irregularities and abnormalities in shape and position not only injure the looks of an individual, but also are conducive to early decay. Particles of food lodge among the irregularities and are difficult to dislodge, and as a result decay is permitted to set in earlier and to go on more rapidly.

Dr. Holmes of the University of Pennsylvania reports a case where impacted dentition was found to be the cause of an extreme peripheral irritation that resulted in the moral delinquency of a boy, who speedily recovered after the extraction of the disturbing teeth. This clearly indicates that physiological activities going on in the jaws as a result of the exchange of deciduous and permanent dentures may be fruitful causes of serious reflex disturbances.

The common practice of parents has been to disregard the first set of teeth, thinking that, because they were short-lived, the sooner they were destroyed, the sooner they would be replaced by a sound permanent set. To see the fallacy of this notion, one needs only observe the conditions of decay of the first permanent molars that erupt between the sixth and seventh year, commonly called the sixth-year molars.

The following chart showing the results of an examination of the sixth-year molars of 400 school children at Oakland City, Indiana, last February, ought to convince the most skeptical that neglect of the temporary teeth means the rapid and early decay of the permanent set.

While the exact causes of decay in its larger aspects are not definitely known beyond the fact that certain sugar-splitting enzymes produce lactic acid that decalcifies the tooth structure, thus affording entrance for bacteria, a study of the above curves leads us to believe that decay is largely a matter of local infection, for 13.5 per cent of the sixth-year molars became affected before they were a year old. The rapid decline in decay after the fourteenth year is due to the greater care exercised by the older pupils in regard to the sanitary conditions of the mouth and more frequent dental care. The importance of timely inspection and antiseptic treatment is imperative, for the removal of

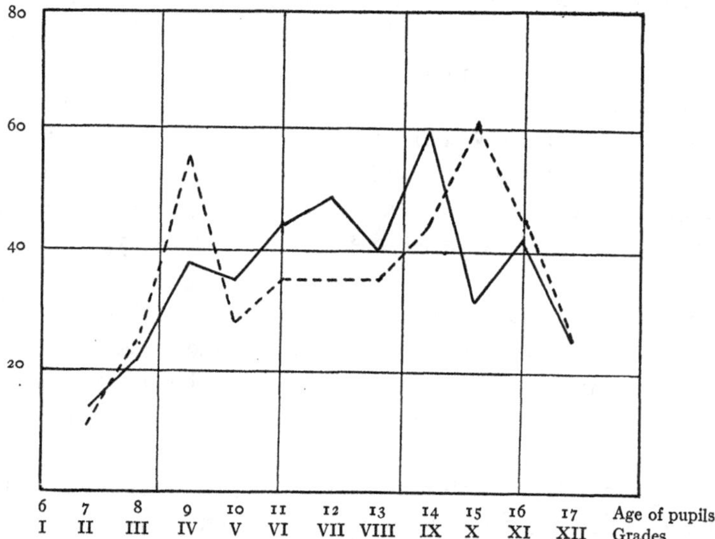


An Examination of the Sixth-Year Molars of 400 Children at Oakland City, Ind.

The unbroken line represents the percentage of defective sixth-year molars according to age of children examined.

The broken line represents the percentage of defective sixth-year molars according to the grade.

74 children had at least one molar decayed.
60 children had at least two molars decayed:
62 children had at least three molars decayed.
44 children had the four molars decayed.
147 children had molars in good condition, i.e., either sound or filled.

bacteria and decomposing food particles from the mouth prevents both decay and the spread of many diseases.

Until public sentiment crystallizes on this important question, the professional dentists must give of their time in cooperation with school officials to the hygienic education of the children and the public. Free dental examination of school children and the circulation of good literature on the nature and care of the teeth ought to hasten the day when a free dental clinic will become a department of every city school system. Free infirmaries for the treatment of children's teeth have already been established in several American cities, and for several years they have been regarded as indispensable in many cities of Russia, Germany, Belgium, Sweden, Denmark, Italy, France, England, and Japan.

Because school boards are not yet ready to provide for the establishment of these clinics is no reason why dentists and school officials should do nothing to alleviate present conditions. With proper co-operation between these professions the public can be aroused and educated to a higher sense of hygienic betterment.

At Oakland City, Indiana, the question was brought before the teachers' and parents' association by the superintendent of schools and the local dentists, and a demand was at once made upon the Board of Education to permit the dentists to make an examination of the school children. Blanks were prepared showing the cuts of both temporary and permanent sets of teeth and the following facts were recorded: name and age of pupil, name of parent, name of teacher, number and location of decayed teeth, condition of mouth and remarks by the examiner in regard to the particular needs of the pupil. The blanks were printed in red ink and the secretary who recorded the observations of the dentist marked with a pencil X, O, or F to denote whether the tooth was decayed, out, or filled. The duplicates that were sent to the parents thus showed the location and condition of each defective tooth. A sample box of tooth paste with directions for the best use of a brush was given to each pupil examined.

In brief, the results of the examination were as follows: 407 children were examined, 53 had teeth in good condition, 210 had from one to four teeth decayed, 133 had from five to ten teeth needing attention, 1,616 defective teeth were found, 87 per cent of the pupils had bad teeth, with an average of 3.97 decays per pupil.

During the following three months 15 per cent of the children received dental attention and a great many who had previously neglected to care for their teeth formed regular habits of using the brush. The examination proved to be a great education to the children in hygiene, as well as the means of awakening the parents to a greater sense of responsibility in the physical condition of the child.

## Free Dental Examination

Name of pupil ______________________ Age______

Name of parent ______________________

Name of teacher ______________________

Has the pupil ever had any dental work done? ____________

CONDITION OF TEETH

FIRST SET

Decay — Extracted

SECOND SET

Filled

Remarks: Teeth marked need attention X ____________

______________________

Examined by Dr. ______________________

______________________ Date______________191__

With this mass of data at hand in regard to the prevalence of defective teeth and their known effects upon the individual child and the possibilities of endangering the health of associates, it seems that a fruitful field is open to all who are interested in social and hygienic betterment.

## BIBLIOGRAPHY

MACKENZIE. *Medical Inspection of School Children,* 26–27, 255–65.

GREVE. *Prevention of Disease,* 267–97.

AYRES. *Laggards in Our Schools,* 97–100, 231–32, 192–99.

JOHNSON. "Condition of Teeth of School Children," *Ped. Sem.,* 8:45–58.

BURNHAM. "Hygiene of Teeth," *Ped Sem.,* 13:293–306.

CORNELL. "Physical Condition of School Children," *Psych. Clinic,* 3:134–35.

ROUTZAHN. "A City-School Clinic," *Chautauquan,* 40:571–72.

WEEKS. "Care of Teeth of Children," *Dental Cosmos,* 52:738–44. 1910.

"Condition of Teeth of School Children, New South Wales," *Dental Cosmos,* 52:755–58. 1910.

Editorial: "What Next?" *Dental Cosmos,* 52:798–801. 1910.

RUSHTON. "Abstract of Gov. Report," *Dental Register,* 64:68–75. 1910.

WHEELER. "Care of N.Y. Children's Teeth," *Dental Register,* 64:254–57. 1910.

Editorial, *Dental Review,* 24:70–73. 1910.

TALBOT. "Care of Mouths of School Children," *Dental Summary,* 30:517–18. 1910.

BARNES. "Dental Inspection in Public Schools," *Dental Summary,* 30:518–27. 1910.

MEINHART. "Lectures on Oral Hygiene in Schools," *Dental Summary,* 30:267–69. 1910.

EBERSOLE. "Report on Proposed Dental Education and Hygiene in Cleveland," *Dental Summary,* 30:234–41. 1910.

HOLMES. "Can Impacted Teeth Cause Moral Delinquency?" *Psych. Clinic,* 4:19–23. 1910.

"Early Care of Teeth-Deformity," *Dental Register,* 63:390–410. 1909.

Editorial, *Dental Register,* 61:485–86.

"Dental Hygiene in French Army," *Dental Cosmos,* 50:433.

"Dental Service in Public Schools of Mexico," *Dental Cosmos,* 50:604–5.

FERRIS. "Is Your Child's Face Beautiful?" *Dental Cosmos,* 50:1347–49.

WHITE. "Instruction in Oral Hygiene," *Dental Cosmos,* 50:313–16.

OTTOFY. "Teeth of Igrots," *Dental Cosmos,* 50:669–95.

WOODBURY. "The People's Disease," *Boston Med. Jr.,* 158:405–10.

BAKER. "Dental Caries as Factors in the Etiology of Other Diseases," *Boston Med. Jr.,* 158:401–5.

BELL. *Popular Essays upon the Care of the Teeth,* 131.

GULICK AND AYRES. *Medical Inspection of Schools,* 97–100, 231–32, 192–99.

## EDITORIAL NOTES

One freqently hears complaints regarding the home study which is required of the pupils of our present-day schools.

**Overwork at Home**

These complaints come from parents or appear in the newspapers in the form of interviews with some physician or nerve specialist. All sorts of evil consequences are laid at the door of overstudy, ranging in gravity from the breakdown of individual children to the general moral decay of the nation. In the meantime, the teacher is literally at his or her wits' end to find time for the various types of education which the modern school is expected to give. One cannot omit the work given in arithmetic in order to make room for the courses in drawing, or the parent who a moment ago objected that his child was doing too much will come forward with a complaint to the effect that his child is doing too little.

**Errors at Home**

The school should record its counter-complaint that parents consume too much of the time of children in frivolous doings which seriously disturb the routine of school. Too much social life, too much music, too much demand for assistance, too much neglect where watchful helpfulness would promote intellectual and physical development—these are the faults of parents. Many a child comes to school heavy-eyed and unable to pay attention to work because of the excess of engagements that have nothing to do with school. Here again there is another side, for the parent, anxious to give his child a well-rounded education, is at his wits' end to find time for the many very proper and beneficial types of social activity which offer themselves as possible.

**The Problem of the Child's Program**

The problem can never be solved so long as the teacher and the parent approach it from opposite points of view and throw accusations of usurpation back and forth in a spirit of enmity and distrust. The fact is that the problem is a general one. It is the problem of so conserving the child's time and energy as to give him the best that school and home can offer him. The child has a right to expect wise elders to guide him to the organization of a program that will systematize his whole day. There is too much to be acquired in the present-day world for the child to throw away two-thirds of his time. He ought to be guided in his recreations so that he shall get the most out of them. He ought to have the opportunity for social life just as much as he has the opportunity for the use of books. He can have all these good things only by conserving himself. The analogy suggested by the word conserving is very strong. There was a time when as a nation we could afford to waste raw material. But our life has grown more strenuous and complex; the demands upon us are heavier and we find that we must systematize where formerly we proceeded without plan; we must save everything and turn it to use. So also with the time and energy of children. Where the school program was meager and the community so sparse that social life was less developed there was much time to throw away. Now, there is more than anyone can absorb, and he who uses the most is the master of the rest.

**Is System Opposed to Spontaneity?**

Someone will object that these suggestions promise to take all the spontaneity out of child life. Let the children be free and do not hang about their necks the millstone of a set program! If we must have a set program during part of the day let there be relaxation during the rest of the hours! These outcries are ill advised. The picture of children bursting out of a school where they have been repressed during a few hours of formal anguish is not just to our modern school. The child in school today has the relaxations of music, constructive work, and physical exercise. The old-fashioned delirium of recess was not a natural expression of child nature. The absorption of a modern boy in the interests aroused by school is not unnatural. There is such a method of organizing interests so as to set the individual at work and at play in a reasonably self-controlled manner. Variety can be introduced and the whole life so ordered that there shall be no demand for riotous outbreaks.

The school recognizes this now. Parents do not always realize to what an extent the regular school program is devoted to organized recreation. There is much in every school today which reaches over into the domain that used to be conceded to the home. The home has given up some of its duties to the school. All this readjustment means increased uniformity in the child's day and life. If he plays at ten o'clock in the morning it is fair that he should study at seven-thirty in the evening. If he studies hygiene at nine-thirty in the school it is consistent that he shall have a domestic program that will permit no breach of hygienic principles at the corresponding hour in the evening. A program does not mean sitting in a fixed position. It means an orderly arrangement of all one's duties and pleasures.

**Concession in Both School and Home Engagements**

Where then will flexibility come in? It ought to come in more than it does. The child who cannot carry a heavy program should have a light one for the whole day. The child who can carry more work ought to have the opportunity. Much of our trouble at the present time is due to our effort to make all individual programs alike. We ought to let one child work at one rate, another at a wholly different rate. The intelligent arrangement of individual programs is the largest problem of our modern education. The instructors in physical education have realized that school gymnastics must be fitted to individual needs and to the other activities of the individual. When will parents and teachers reach the same intelligent view regarding the intellectual and social life of children?

**Individual Programs**

# BOOK REVIEWS

*Education in Sexual Physiology and Hygiene.* By PHILIP ZENNER, M.D. Cincinnati: Robert Clarke Co., 1910. 16 mo., pp. 128. $1.00 net.

Among the many subjects consideration of which is being forced upon teachers by social conditions is that of instruction in sexual physiology and hygiene. Dr. Zenner's book is entitled to be called a contribution toward a solution of the problem. It reports a series of lessons on the subject in an elementary school and also gives an account of the effect produced by these lessons.

There are also printed several talks to college boys, filled with the kind of information that a physician can best bring home to young men. There is, however, no indication as to the results of this instruction.

The last forty pages contain what might be termed a physician's message to teachers and parents. The author insists upon the necessity of instruction with regard to matters of sex, points out the possibility of doing injury as well as good, makes some suggestions about methods, and insists upon the need of proper preparation on the part of the instructor, whether parent, teacher, or physician.

The book makes no pretention to completeness; it recognizes the tentative character of the undertaking. Its suggestions are valuable.

W. L. EIKENBERRY

---

*A Holiday with the Birds.* By JEANNETTE MARKS AND JULIA WOODS. With Illustrations by CHESTER A. REED. New York: Harper & Bros., 1910. Pp. 211. 75 cents.

*A Holiday with the Birds* is a reader in the natural history of birds. The book is appropriate to be read by children in the intermediate grades. The first five chapters deal with general facts such as relate to feathers, preening, moulting, special senses, digestive and circulatory systems. Nine chapters deal with different characteristics and habits of members of the families of birds. Four closing chapters deal with the egg and the making of a bird; aunts, uncles, and cousins of the bird family; bird migration; and bird protection.

The entire book is in the nature of a conversation between three children, the summer tutor and companion, and other occasional members of their parties. The book suffers somewhat from the inconsequentialities and meaningless foreign frivolities that usually appear when attempt is made to manufacture conversation in order to present facts regarding nature. Nevertheless a large amount of dependable, valuable, and interesting bird lore is presented, and it is possible that the conversational style may increase the book's attractiveness to younger children. Teachers will certainly find the book stimulating and helpful as a nature reader for occasional use, and the story form doubtless will carry the interest of some children directly through the entire book.

O. W. C.

# CURRENT EDUCATIONAL LITERATURE IN THE PERIODICALS[1]

IRENE WARREN
Librarian, School of Education, The University of Chicago

AYRES, LEONARD P. Relation between physical defects and school progress. Amer. Phys. Educa. Rev. 15:389–95. (Je. '10.)

BURNHAM, W. H. School hygiene in the children's institute. Pedagog. Sem. 17:183–88. (Je. '10.)

CHASE, HARRY W. Work with the backward and subnormal in the children's institute. Pedagog. Sem. 17:189–203. (Je. '10.)

ELLIS, DAVID A. Decade of school administration in Boston. New Eng. Mag. 42:521–24. (Jl. '10.)

FAIRMAN, CHARLES G. College trained immigrants. New Eng. Mag. 42: 577–84. (Jl. '10.)

GRINNELL, JOSEPH. Methods and uses of a research museum. Pop. Sci. Mo. 77:163–68. (Ag. '10.)

GULICK, LUTHER H. Report of the committee on the status of physical education in public normal schools and public high schools in the U.S. Amer. Phys. Educa. Rev. 15:453–54. (Je. '10.)

HALL, G. STANLEY. General outline of the new child study work at Clark University. Pedagog. Sem. 17:160–65. (Je. '10.)

HARRINGTON, THOMAS F. Health and education. Amer. Phys. Educa. Rev. 15:373–88. (Je. '10.)

Home science in the rural districts. Good Housekeep. 51:143–44. (Ag. '10.)

HOPKINS, MARY D. An American schoolgirl in Germany. Atlan. 106: 359–67. (S. '10.)

HORNE, HERMAN H. Principle underlying modern physical education. Amer. Phys. Educa. Rev. 15:433–39. (Je. '10.)

KARPINSKI, LOUIS. A unique collection of arithmetics. Pop. Sci. Mo. 77: 226–35. (S. '10.)

LIBBY, WALTER, COWLES, HELEN, AND OTHERS. Contents of children's minds. Pedagog. Sem. 17:242–72. (Je. '10.)

MCKEEVER, WILLIAM A. The moving picture. Good Housekeep. 51:184–85. (Ag. '10.)

[1] Abbreviations.—Amer. Phys. Educa. Rev., American Physical Educational Review; Atlan., Atlantic Monthly; Good Housekeep., Good Housekeeping; New Eng. Mag., New England Magazine; Pedagog. Sem., Pedogogical Seminary; Pop. Sci. Mo., Popular Science Monthly.

MAGNI, JOHN A. Department of child linguistics. Pedagog. Sem. 17: 213–18. (Je. '10.)

MEYLAN, GEORGE L. Effects of smoking on college students. Pop. Sci. Mo. 77:169–77. (Ag. '10.)

———. Report of the committee on the status of hygiene in colleges and universities in the U.S. Amer. Phys. Educa. Rev. 15:446–52. (Je. '10.)

(The) modern schoolhouse. Good Housekeep. 51:268–70. (S. '10.)

NIDA, WILLIAM L. The lighting of schoolrooms. Good Housekeep. 51: 263–67. (S. '10.)

ROTCH, THOMAS MORGAN. Roentgen ray methods applied to the grading of early life. Amer. Phys. Educa. Rev. 15:396–420. (Je. '10.)

SCHMIDT, CLARA. Teaching of the facts of sex in the public schools. Pedagog. Sem. 17:229–41. (Je. '10.)

SMITH, LEWIS WORTHINGTON. Literature and the pedagogue. Poet Lore 21:311–21. (Jl.–Ag. '10.)

SMITH, THEODATE L. Correspondence department of the children's institute. Pedagog. Sem. 17:176–82. (Je. '10.)

Special child surveys in Worcester by Clark students. Pedagog. Sem. 17: 219–28. (Je. '10.)

STECHER, WILLIAM A. Extension work in physical training in public elementary schools. Amer. Phys. Educa. Rev. 15:440–45. (Je. '10.)

TANNER, AMY E. Experimental didactics in the children's institute. Pedagog. Sem. 17:204–12. (Je. '10.)

WALLIN, J. E. WALLACE. The moving picture in relation to education, health, delinquency and crime. Pedagog. Sem. 17:129–42. (Je. '10.)

WELD, HARRY P. The mechanism of the voice and its hygiene. Pedagog. Sem. 17:143–59. (Je. '10.)

WILSON, LOUIS N. Library facilities for the work of the children's institute and the new building for this work. Pedagog. Sem. 17:166–75. (Je. '10.)

VOLUME XI NUMBER 3

THE ELEMENTARY SCHOOL TEACHER

NOVEMBER, 1910

# A GRADED COURSE IN SCHOOLROOM GYMNASTICS

JULIA ANNA NORRIS
School of Education, The University of Chicago

Among the conditions to be dealt with in arranging a course in schoolroom gymnastics the one which stands out most prominently is the faulty posture in sitting and standing which is so characteristic of the untrained school child. Less to be noticed in the lowest grades, except in children whose strength has been depleted by illness, it becomes more and more frequent as the grades advance, until in the highest it is not unusual to find children whose rapid growth and lack of proper development has led to a condition of narrow chest and stooping shoulders which has gone too far ever to be entirely corrected. Besides the menace to health thus endured, these individuals must go through life lacking that advantage in all relations with others which goes with good physical presence. Improvement of posture and carriage then may be considered the prime object of schoolroom gymnastics.

Next to posture in importance comes the relief of congestions in the large abdominal veins where the blood gradually settles during sedentary occupations. Vigorous exercise is the only agency that can be depended on to relieve these congestions, through its call of the blood out into the working muscles and its pumping action on the great veins themselves. All of this effects, moreover, a quickened rhythm of heart, a deeper, fuller respiration, and a generally fresher feeling due to the more rapid movement of lymph and removal of waste material from the tissues of the body.

Among other results to be accomplished by this work are the training in prompt and accurate response to direction, skill in handling the body through the development of the great neuro-muscular mechanism, and the subordination of the unit to the whole gained through concerted action.

Among these objects the one which differentiates gymnastics from other forms of exercise is the postural one. The physiological changes, the skill in handling the body, and, among adolescent children, the subordination of the individual for the good of the whole, may be reached more easily through games than gymnastics, and certain forms of dancing will accomplish the first two of these results as readily as games. But in neither games nor dancing is much thought given to the training of erect carriage with heads held high and chests full and active. Hence in gymnastic work this is a consideration which should never be lost sight of by the teacher. Her own carriage before the children, if she sets them a good example, will go a long way in helping her to secure results, and many a teacher has attested to the benefits which she herself has received in improved posture and proportions through having felt the necessity of living up to her teachings.

Three principles are most useful to hold in mind when working for correction of posture:

1. Overcorrection of the fault, in order to stretch short muscles and tighten relaxed ones. For instance in the frequent cases of narrow chests the muscles of the front of the chest need to be stretched while those between the shoulder blades should have a tuck taken in them. The children should assume this strongly corrected position before each movement in the lesson, after the few seconds of relaxation which should succeed each movement.

2. The retention of this strongly corrected position during an entire movement, because every exercise tends to make permanent the relations of the body which are held during its performance. An essentially good exercise can have only a bad

effect if taken with poor posture, for it will strengthen the muscles which hold that posture and thus make it even harder to overcome.

3. The education of the sense of posture. If a child stands in incorrect attitude when he makes conscientious effort to straighten up it shows that he does not recognize his own position. Admonition and explanation under these circumstances will do very little good. What is necessary is to mold him into the proper position and let him feel it. This manual correction may need to be done many times before the child will be able to interpret his muscle sensations correctly, but it is the only way in which he can adequately be taught to recognize what he is striving for, and it will finally bring results.

The teacher should carry in her mind a clear picture of the effect she wishes to accomplish by any direction or command, so that deviations from the desirable will strike her attention immediately. According to the prevalence or nature of the error the whole class may receive a few words of suggestion, or while they are standing in the rest position an explanation and illustration may be made, or the manual method may be used in individual cases. All faults cannot be corrected at once, and it should be recognized that the most important ones are those which detract from good carriage in any way—drooping heads and shoulders, flat chests, sway backs, etc. Details of exact direction or extent of movement or relations of hands and feet may properly take a secondary place in favor of the vital importance of posture.

It should also be remembered that the same general objects will be worked for in lesson after lesson, and though perfection may not be gained in any one set of exercises, that is no reason for discouragement or for drilling overtime on those exercises. Succeeding lessons, working for the same results through varied movements, will secure improvement without sacrificing it to monotony. Two weeks is a good period of time for the development of a lesson, introducing part of it at a time.

The manner of giving directions and commands is of great importance. There is a distinct art in modifying the tone of the voice and its inflections so as to evoke the kind of response desired—brisk movements of the small segments of the body, slow movements of the trunk, quick preliminary action, vigorous muscular work, delicate control of balance, etc. This variety and flexibility in conducting a lesson make it a living thing, and call out the interest and co-operation of the child.

Fresh, cool air should always be freely admitted to the room at the time of the gymnastic lesson. This can best be done by opening windows, with due regard for cold drafts. In buildings with ventilating systems the objections of the janitor can usually be overcome by opening all the windows at once.

In this course the method of work will vary for different ages. For children under eight years, or roughly for the first and second grades, the method recommended is the gymnastic story play, with its appeal to the dramatic interest, its absence of abstract terms, its mingling of spontaneity with directed work. In the other grades gymnastic exercises by command will be used, with their appeal to the interest in military uniformity and precision in the younger children, and to self-improvement among the older ones, where the introduction of simple dance steps will also bring in an aesthetic interest.

In all grades a short drill in sitting posture should preface the lesson. At the direction, "Straight sitting position!" for the little people, and the command, "Attention!" for those who have reached the dignity of gymnastics, an erect posture is assumed, the feet flat on the floor, the hips pushed well back against the chair back, the upper part of the trunk poised sufficiently far forward so that it is easy to hold the required posture of active chest, straight neck, and high head. The arms should hang straight down at the sides. At "Rest!" the children lean back against the chairbacks and relax. This alternation of position should be repeated several times, with care to get really good posture.

The story play and the gymnastics by command are so different in method of development that they will be considered separately.

### THE GYMNASTIC STORY PLAY

The gymnastic story play may be considered as an informal method of dealing with formal material—gymnastics—or a formal method of dealing with informal material—the story. Briefly, it consists of a series of something like six exercises grouped about a simple story of childish activities. The story must be one which will appeal to the fundamental interest of the child in order to be enjoyed by him during a series of lessons, and it must be capable of dramatization through exercises which conform to the requirements of a good gymnastic lesson.

As far as possible the themes of the stories may well be chosen with relation to the season of the year, as "The Picnic" in May, or to the holidays which are approaching, as in the case of "Christmas Morning" in December and the "Soldier Play," which comes in the same month as Memorial Day. The interest in the "Christmas Morning" grows more and more lively throughout the month of December, although it will fail to call forth more than passive interest after the first of January. In the same way the "Valentine's Day" story will be the center of great enthusiasm for the two or three weeks ending February 14, after which it falls flat.

The set of story plays which will be suggested in this outline are adapted to children who live in a temperate climate and who know something of both the city and the country. If there are winter stories which will not appeal to southern children or country stories which will not appeal to city children there is abundant opportunity for teachers to work out new story plays to fit such conditions, always remembering the two main requirements—a story which shall be simple and fundamental in its interest and exercises which make up a good gymnastic lesson.

The exercises should be about six in number, and should always give representation to the following classes of movements: postural correction, arm and shoulder girdle, trunk, leg, respiratory, and running or jumping. Two classes of movements are not infrequently found combined in the same exercise, as in kneeling and picking flowers, where the leg and trunk muscles are used, or in rowing a boat, in which trunk and arm muscles are used and a strong corrective element introduced, or in climbing a ladder, where arms and legs work together. There is a decided advantage in these combination movements for they give opportunity for more vigorous and widespread exercise than is obtained when pure types of movements are used of such simplicity that they are suitable for little children, and they make possible the use of perfectly natural neuro-muscular co-ordinations. The combination of leg and trunk exercises with other classes is especially desirable since this is the age at which the development of the large fundamental groups of leg and trunk muscles is going on rapidly and locomotion for its own enjoyment forms a large part of all play.

The order of the exercises must largely be determined by the story, though it is usually possible so to arrange a story that the more vigorous exercises come toward the end, and usually it will be found that the respiratory exercise occurs at or near the end, following a more vigorous exercise. It will be noticed that the respiratory movements are always taken with inhalation through the nose and exhalation through the mouth. This is for the purpose of avoiding confusion on the part of the child, who at this age finds it difficult to discriminate between the two acts if the mouth is kept closed. With the aid of this little device the teacher can be sure of her results.

The method of presenting and conducting the story play must be carefully considered, for it must be very gently and skilfully guided between the Scylla of a formal gymnastic lesson on the one hand and the Charybdis of mere entertainment for the children on the other. There must be a delicate balance which will permit careful correction of posture without focusing the child's attention on his anatomy, concerted response to direction without rigidity, acquirement of the habit of rhythm without conscious drill, and on the other hand spontaneity of suggestion without waste of time, freedom of expression without loss of attention to the teacher's directions, and enjoyment without disorder.

It must always be remembered that the gymnastic story play is fitted to secure postural correction and improvement just as surely as is a gymnastic lesson, and to this end a strong posture must be called for before each movement and must prevail during its performance. It is well to use the word, "Position!" immediately before each movement. The response should be the quick assumption of the erect standing position, which should mean essentially for little children heads high, chests active, and weight evenly balanced on the feet. A little child usually gives his chest credit for occupying the entire front of his body, and abdomen as well as chest is likely to become round and prominent in his efforts for good posture. The suggestion, "Big up here" (with teacher's hand on chest), and "Little down here" (with her hand on abdomen) is helpful in correcting this error in anatomical conception. "Tall heads" and "Stand tall" are good admonitions to swear by. The recognition of a fine round chest by a friendly tap upon it will often result in a large crop of them.

There will be children who are not reached by any of these suggestions, however, children with cramped, weak chests and prominent shoulder blades who are unable of their own volition to assume the proper attitude. These the teacher must help by laying her hands on the shoulders, and with her thumbs on the prominent shoulder blades and fingers over the front of the shoulder joints she must roll the offending shoulders up and off the chest, at the same time forcing the chest forward with her thumbs into its proper place. Gradually a child so helped acquires through the training of his muscle sense the ability to correct himself.

These more or less anatomical methods of correction are necessary in obtaining good starting posture, but during the performance of the exercises abstract suggestions are usually out of place. Almost always a suggestion in line with the dramatization of the story will bring the desired result. If in pushing a baby carriage the children lean forward and cramp the chest it is well to remind them that this is a full-sized baby carriage, and that they may even have to reach up to grasp the handle, or that surely only strong-looking children would be allowed by the mother to take the baby out riding. If in coasting down hill the children's backs show a tendency to hump it is only necessary to pretend that a race is going on and that the children with the straightest backs will reach the foot of the hill first, and every child will immediately make an effort to have that straightest back. And so on, *ad infinitum.*

In the same way unnecessary noise in running or jumping can usually be controlled by dramatic suggestion. If we find that the feet are heavy in the hopping in the story "Birds Learning to Fly" we do not try to see how lightly the *children* can hop, but we remember that little birds *never* make a noise hopping on the limb of a tree, and straightway most concentrated effort is made for light feet. The suggestion that the running is being done on the grass or the snow conduces to easy elimination of noise in that exercise. In many plays the exhalation effort in the respiratory exercise is accompanied by a tone, or a whistle, or a hissing sound, and, being rather fascinating, the sound tends to be prolonged, but suggestions correlating the sound with the story will serve to control this exuberance.

It is well to take two lessons for the introduction of a new gymnastic story play, so that the children may not become tired by being given so much new material in so short a time. Every teacher's individuality will show in her method of introducing the lesson, but certain suggestions are appropriate. After setting a background in which to place the story it is well to take up at one time only that part of it which refers to one movement. Telling the whole story at once is likely to result in too much talking and too little exercise, and often tires the children. It should be unnecessary to emphasize the need of a strong, vigorous posture on the part of the teacher throughout the lesson (not to speak of the rest of the session), for admonition without example does not sink in very deeply. She should study out the possibilities for correction of posture and for vigor of exercise in each movement and should be careful to illustrate it accurately to the children. Large arm and leg movements with free use of shoulder and hip joints should be encouraged; small hand and foot exercises have little value.

At first the teacher will find it necessary to take the movements with the children. As they know the play better, however, she should work toward developing an independent response from them both for their own sake and because it will give her a better opportunity to move among them making corrections.

Between the movements there should be relaxation. If the child naturally relaxes, as is usually the case, nothing need be said about it, but if the movement has keyed him up to military erectness a direction for resting will be necessary. "Rest position" is convenient, and means that the child stands at ease with feet in the stride position, thus usually insuring an even distribution of weight between them.

It goes without saying that a childlike spirit should pervade the giving of the lesson, both its story and its action. The teacher's voice, by its brightness and the use of the staccato in directions which call for swift response will bring out the quickness of motion which is characteristic of children. Rising from a squatting or a bending to an erect standing position should always be done briskly, both because it brings better posture than a slow action and because it usually also brings a smile to the face of the child; the bright staccato use of the direction "Up!" will usually accomplish this result.

If the children are performing their movements vigorously, using large motions and getting a corrective effect, it is not necessary that there should be uniformity in the small details of exact direction, or exact extent, of motion, or position of feet, or of an arm which is perhaps not being used at the time. Such details are better passed by lightly. In rhythmic exercises such as running in place, the teacher should set the time for the class, and this should be done before the direction is given at all in order that the children may feel the rhythm before starting to express it. A few seconds spent in preliminary beating of time will often save confusion later. The fact that the child's natural rhythm is faster than the adult's should always be remembered.

It is not worth while to spend much time in training little children to discriminate between left and right. It is such a difficult mental process for them that it makes the action of the play unwarrantably slow. On the other hand much may be done toward educating them in the appreciation of left and right by using the terms and indicating by a gesture which side is meant.

The length of time a lesson should occupy is about ten minutes. Less will make it difficult to obtain results in both posture and vigor of exercise; more may result in a loss of fresh, concentrated attention. Ten minutes wisely used is sufficient to give the child a strong impulse in the direction of better carriage, so that he is proud to have it and glad to respond to suggestions concerning it which will of course be necessary at other times of day.

There are usually several good opportunities in each story for the children to make suggestions which will help keep the whole plot vital for them. They like to tell what kinds of flowers they are picking, or what the birds see on the ground, or what the firemen save from the burning building. Since there is only ten minutes' time for everything these contributions must be sought and given without wasting time, an error which it would be easy to fall into. It serves the double purpose of saving time and emphasizing posture to call on particular children for suggestions because they look so tall and strong that you think they would give good ones. Tall and strong posture thus comes to take the place of the wild waving of hands if children wish to voice their ideas. The question, "How many" have accomplished this or that will usually bring response from the whole class, to their own satisfaction and with very little expenditure of time.

Most of the story plays may be used with advantage for about a month, especially if on one day of the week, preferably Wednesday, a game be substituted for the story play. In this way a story play is not repeated on consecutive days sufficiently to risk monotony, and, which is quite as important, a regular period of supervised play is insured of sufficient length for a real game. Thus the children are given occasion for the freedom of expression of developing tendencies and characteristics which is best afforded by play and the teacher has a valuable opportunity for studying and guiding those tendencies and characteristics. Shorter game periods, by the way, should be introduced between lessons at other times of day.

During September and June I would not use anything even so little formal as the gymnastic story play. In September the children are having difficulty in adapting themselves to the confinement of indoor life after the vacation, and the gymnastic period is best used for supervised *outdoor* games. In June the strain of the long indoor year is showing in increasing restlessness and drooping, and it is good practice to drop gymnastic stories and to return again to outdoor games.

Following are two gymnastic story plays suggested for autumn:

### Autumn in the Woods

#### FOR FIRST GRADE

(Adapted from *Gymnastic Stories and Plays*, by Rebecca Stoneroad, M.D.; D. C. Heath & Co.)

*Story.*—The children go out to play in the woods. First they sit down and pretend that they are the little flowers that go to sleep every night and are awakened by the sunlight in the morning, or perhaps that Jack Frost has nipped them and made them close their eyes. The leaves are falling gently and the children catch great basketfuls and throw them over their heads. They reach high for especially pretty leaves and then scatter them, making a leaf-carpet about their feet. Now they kneel, gather great armfuls of the leaves, rise, and toss them in this direction or that. Now they are ready for a run. And they follow their leader in and out among the trees, and they pant breathlessly afterward.

*Exercises:*

1. Going to sleep like sleepy flowers.
   Purpose: Practice in straight sitting position.
   Starting position: Straight sitting position.
   Signals: A. Go to sleep, or Jack Frost comes.
   Child assumes rest sitting position with head relaxed and dropped on chest, eyes shut.
   B. Morning! or Wake up! or Sunshine!
   Child instantly assumes straight sitting position with eyes open.
2. Catching leaves in baskets and throwing them over the head.
   Purpose: Correction of chest and upper spine.
   Starting position: Standing position.

Signals: A. Make your baskets.
Clasp hands in front.

B. Catch.
Raise arms to height of shoulders, bending elbows so that arms circumscribe a circular opening.

C. Toss.
Swing arms overhead without unclasping hands.

3. Reaching up and making the leaves fall.
Purpose: Correction of chest and upper spine.
Signals: A. Reach.
Swing arms high over head and look up.

B. Scatter.
Pretend to scatter leaves softly on ground.

4. Gathering armfuls of fallen leaves and throwing them about.
Purpose: Back and leg exercise.
Signals: A. On left (right) knee—down.
Kneel with body erect.

B. Gather.
Bend forward and sweep arms through imaginary leaves, gathering a quantity.

C. Straight up.
Straight kneeling position, arms still clasped about leaves.

D. Stand.
Quickly regain straight standing position.

E. Throw.
Pretend to toss leaves in any direction suggested.

5. Running among trees.
Purpose: General exercise.
Signal: Run.
One row follows another around room.

6. Panting after the run.
Purpose: Deep breathing.
Signals: A. Breathe in.
Through the nose.

B. Breathe out.
Through the mouth.

*Suggestions for holding interest:*

Mention of a recent frost.

Get full baskets before throwing leaves.

Ask for colors and kinds of leaves. The children who look up the straightest will probably see the prettiest ones.

Ask for suggestions as to where they shall throw leaves—through a window, to the teacher, to each other, etc.

## An Automobile Ride

### FOR SECOND GRADE

*Story.*—The uncle of one of the children takes the whole class out to the country in his automobile for a ride. They help him crank the automobile and when they reach the country they climb a high rail fence to get into a field where they see a pump. There they pump water for each other, and later they push each other in a rope swing in one of the trees, going high up in the air. In the grass they find thistledown and blow it far and wide. As it begins to grow dark they see fireflies twinkling, and running back to the automobile they try to catch them.

*Exercises:*

1. Cranking the automobile.

   Purpose: Trunk and arm exercise.

   Signals: A. With left (right) hand take hold of crank.
   Bend forward at hip joint, spine straight, and grasp imaginary crank.

   B. Crank it.
   Pull up strongly with arm, shoulder, and back, swinging arm in outward circle.

2. Climbing the fence.

   Purpose: Leg and arm exercise.

   Signals: A. Left.
   Lift left hand high and bend up left knee.

   B. Right.
   Same on right side.

   C. Left.

   D. Right.

   E. Jump.
   Jump forward, landing softly on toes.

3. Pumping water.

   Purpose: Trunk and arm exercise.

   Signals: A. Hands on pump handle.
   Raise bent elbows to shoulder height, hands in front of chest.

   B. Push.
   Bend trunk forward at hip joint, spine straight, arms pushed straight down.

   C. Pull.
   Raise body to erect position and bend arms up again.

4. Swinging each other.

   Purpose: Arms and correction of chest.

Signals: A. Pull.
Raise both arms well back overhead, holding imaginary swing seat.
B. Push.
Push arms vigorously forward and upward, at the same time stepping forward with one (either) foot.

5. Blowing thistledown.
Purpose: Deep breathing.
Signals: A. Toss up the thistledown.
Make a tossing motion.
B. Breathe.
Inhale.
C. Blow.
Exhale, blowing breath upward.

6. Catching fireflies.
Purpose: General exercise.
Signal: Ready—run.
Each row runs round the room catching imaginary fireflies with hands.

*Suggestions for holding interest:*
Whose uncle, whose field, whose turn to swing?

# RETARDATION IN THE SCHOOLS AND SOME OF THE CAUSES

OWEN J. NEIGHBOURS
Petersburg, Indiana

The following material is the result of a careful study of the first eight grades in the schools of a town having a population of about 2,200.

There are enrolled in these grades 557 pupils, a number of whom have recently moved into the town, while others moved away from the town before this investigation was made. It was, however, possible to obtain accurate data concerning about 500 of the pupils enrolled during the year. These 500 were studied with a view of obtaining the number of years each was retarded, the particular grade or grades in which the retardation occurred, and some of the causes of the retardation.

In determining causes, only home conditions and attendance were considered.

## METHOD

I. Lists of all pupils in each grade were prepared, together with the age last September and the age when first entering school.

Using Ayres's method of supposing a child retarded who has not been promoted each year, the number of years of retardation was determined by subtracting the age at which the pupil entered school from the age in September.

The figures showing the number of years of retardation for each pupil were corrected at the end of the school year, for those who were not promoted at the close of school.

The pupils who were shown by the above method to be retarded were asked to name the grades in which they had spent more than one year.

The results obtained proving untrustworthy, it was necessary to seek additional information in order to discover in what grades the retardation occurred.

As nearly all of the grade teachers have been teaching in the town as long as their pupils have been in school, the teachers were able to correct the data given by the pupils. In doubtful cases the records were also consulted. Nearly all of the cases of retardation and the grades in which they occurred were accounted for in this way.

II. The percentage of attendance of each child during the whole number of years he has been in school was determined by taking the average of his percentages of attendance for the several years.

On account of a large floating school population in the town, the number of pupils for whom the attendance figures could be determined was less than the number for whom retardation figures were determined.

III. In studying home conditions three determining factors were considered: (1) financial advantages of the home; (2) educational advantages of the home; (3) moral atmosphere of the home.

In studying these conditions the following grading was used:

*Financial:*

A=considerable property
B=moderate means
C=poor

*Educational:*

A=special school advantages
B=common school education with limited advantages gained from reading and travel
C=educational advantages limited to ability to read and write

*Moral:*

A=all that could be expected
B=fair—not all that could be expected
C=influence not for good

Two lists of the pupils in each room were prepared: one was given to the teacher now in charge of these pupils and the other to the teacher who had the same pupils last year. Each of these teachers was requested to grade the home conditions of each pupil according to the above-named system of grading. In this way two opinions concerning the home conditions of each child were secured. In this grading scheme one teacher did not know the opinions of the other teacher who was grading the same list of pupils.

The opinions of the two teachers in each case coincided to rather a surprising degree. Out of 1,212 judgments, not counting the first grade, for which only one list was prepared, there were 113 judgments which differed by one point and 6 judgments which differed by two points from the corresponding judgments of the same lists. Where these opinions were much at variance and in doubtful cases, outside information was sought.

The opinions of the teachers seemed even more trustworthy on account of the fact that most of them are teaching in their home town, where they have lived since childhood.

## RESULTS

Table I shows the number of years of retardation for the pupils in the different grades, and the grades in which the retardation occurred. By dividing the total years of retardation in each grade by the number of pupils in the grade for which this total of years of retardation is determined, the average number of years of retardation is determined.

The curve in Chart 1 is a graphical representation of the average number of years of retardation for the pupils in the different grades. The general direction of the curve is upward, with two sudden drops in Grade 3A and the sixth grade. This may mean that these two grades are composed of pupils of more than ordinary ability. It may also mean that the fifth grade is the point at which most of the retarded pupils leave school. There is then a sudden rise in the eighth grade to be accounted for.

The facts in the case are, Grade 3A is an unusually good grade, while this cannot be said of the eighth grade. The eighth grade contains a number of retarded pupils who did not drop out at the usual place. It is also noticeable from the table that most pupils who are retarded in the lower grades leave school before reaching the higher grades.

Before explaining Table II, it may be well to explain the significance of Grades 3A and 3B. Except during the past year, it has been customary for most pupils to spend two years in the third grade. With the exception of a few of the very brightest, the second-grade pupils have been promoted to Grade 3B, and after

## TABLE I

DISTRIBUTION OF YEARS OF RETARDATION WHILE PUPILS WERE IN DIFFERENT GRADES

| Grade | While in Grade | | | | | | | | | | Total Years of Retardation | Number of Pupils in Grade | Average Number of Years of Retardation |
|---|---|---|---|---|---|---|---|---|---|---|---|---|---|
| | 1 | 2 | 3B | 3A | 4 | 5 | 6 | 7 | 8 | Unknown | | | |
| 1.......... | 47 | | | | | | | | | 0 | 47 | 95 | .49½ |
| 2.......... | 27 | 6 | | | | | | | | 0 | 33 | 53 | .62 |
| 3B......... | 28 | 15 | 39 | | | | | | | 0 | 82 | 55 | 1.49 |
| 3A......... | 22½ | 2 | 41 | 2 | | | | | | 0 | 67½ | 59 | 1.14 |
| 4.......... | 13 | 11 | 34 | 10 | 23 | | | | | 13 | 104 | 65 | 1.6 |
| 5.......... | 13 | 6 | 37 | 6 | 6 | 21 | | | | 9 | 98 | 61 | 1.6 |
| 6.......... | 6 | 5 | 18 | 6 | 3 | 1 | 2 | | | 4 | 45 | 43 | 1.05 |
| 7.......... | 1 | 4 | 9 | 7 | 5 | 4 | 3 | 11 | | 4 | 48 | 43 | 1.11 |
| 8.......... | 1 | 0 | 8 | 1 | 0 | 1 | 11 | 4 | 11 | 4 | 41 | 24 | 1.71 |
| Total..... | 158½ | 49 | 186 | 32 | 37 | 27 | 16 | 15 | 11 | 34 | 565½ | 498 | 1.13 |

This table counts 1 year in Grade 3B as retardation.

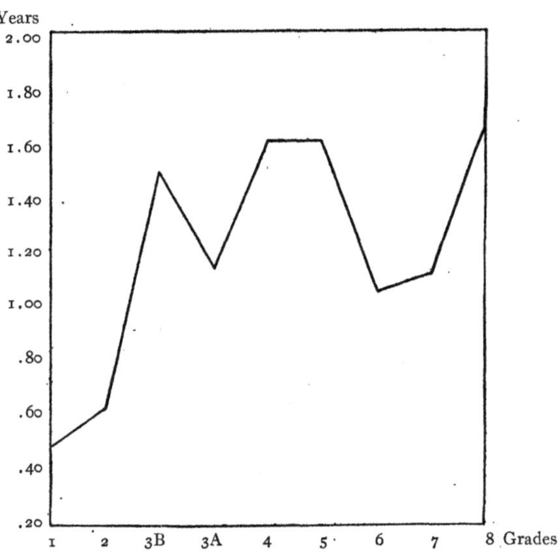


CHART 1.—Curve showing average number of years' retardation by pupils in different grades, counting 1 year in Grade 3B as retardation.

spending a full year in this grade they have been promoted to Grade 3A. In consequence, most of the pupils in the school above Grade 3B have spent nine years in the eight grades.

TABLE II

DISTRIBUTION OF YEARS OF RETARDATION WHILE PUPILS WERE IN DIFFERENT GRADES

| Grade | While in Grade | | | | | | | | | Total Years of Retardation | Number of Pupils in Grade | Average Number of Years of Retardation for Each Grade |
|---|---|---|---|---|---|---|---|---|---|---|---|---|
| | 1 | 2 | 3B | 3A | 4 | 5 | 6 | 7 | 8 | | | |
| 1 | 47 | | | | | | | | | 47 | 95 | .494 |
| 2 | 27 | 6 | | | | | | | | 33 | 53 | .622 |
| 3B | 28 | 15 | 5 | | | | | | | 48 | 55 | .872 |
| 3A | 22½ | 2 | 2 | 2 | | | | | | 28½ | 59 | .483 |
| 4 | 13 | 11 | 0 | 9 | 22 | | | | | 55 | 65 | .846 |
| 5 | 13 | 6 | 2 | 6 | 6 | 17 | | | | 50 | 61 | .819 |
| 6 | 6 | 5 | 0 | 6 | 3 | 1 | 2 | | | 23 | 43 | .534 |
| 7 | 1 | 4 | 0 | 8 | 5 | 4 | 3 | 11 | | 36 | 43 | .837 |
| 8 | 1 | 0 | 0 | 1 | 0 | 1 | 11 | 4 | 7 | 25 | 24 | 1.04 |
| Total | 158½ | 49 | 9 | 32 | 36 | 23 | 16 | 15 | 7 | 345½ | 498 | .609 |

This table does not count 1 year in Grade 3B as retardation.

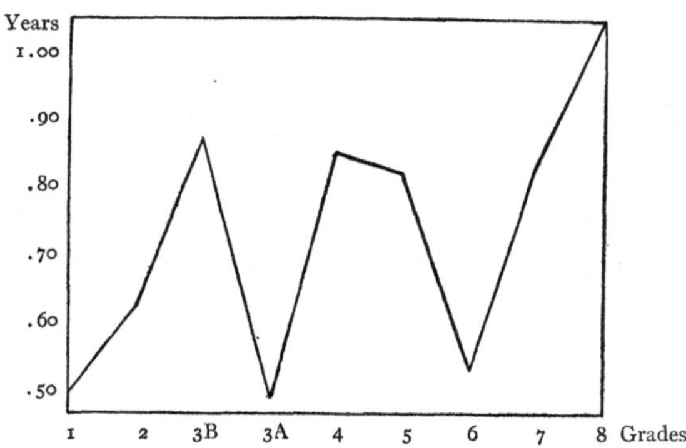


CHART 2.—Curve showing relation between grades and average number of years' retardation of pupils. This curve does not count 1 year in Grade 3B as retardation.

Table II shows the same relations as Table I except that in Table II one year spent in grade 3B is not counted as retardation, as is the case in Table I. Since most children, regardless of ability, were required to spend two years in the third grade, it is evident that Table II, with the accompanying Chart 2, gives a nearer just representation of the average number of years pupils in the different grades are retarded.

### TABLES III AND IV

DISTRIBUTION OF PUPILS BY GRADES AND AGES

| Age | Grades | | | | | | | | | Total | |
|---|---|---|---|---|---|---|---|---|---|---|---|
| | 1 | 2 | 3B | 3A | 4 | 5 | 6 | 7 | 8 | | |
| 6 | 79 | 6 | 0 | 0 | 0 | 0 | 0 | 0 | 0 | 85 | |
| 7 | 21 | 15 | 5 | 7 | 0 | 0 | 0 | 0 | 0 | 48 | |
| 8 | 11 | 13 | 13 | 16 | 5 | 0 | 0 | 0 | 0 | 58 | |
| 9 | 3 | 10 | 12 | 22 | 14 | 1 | 0 | 0 | 0 | 62 | |
| 10 | 1 | 3 | 9 | 12 | 15 | 11 | 4 | 0 | 0 | 55 | |
| 11 | 0 | 1 | 3 | 6 | 12 | 17 | 13 | 3 | 0 | 55 | |
| 12 | 0 | 0 | 2 | 0 | 9 | 15 | 11 | 9 | 0 | 46 | |
| 13 | 0 | 0 | 5 | 2 | 6 | 10 | 8 | 15 | 4 | 50 | |
| 14 | 0 | 1 | 0 | 0 | 3 | 5 | 7 | 12 | 13 | 41 | |
| 15 | 0 | 0 | 0 | 0 | 1 | 0 | 1 | 5 | 4 | 11 | |
| 16 | 0 | 0 | 0 | 0 | 0 | 0 | 0 | 1 | 5 | 6 | |
| 17 | 0 | 0 | 0 | 0 | 0 | 0 | 0 | 0 | 1 | 1 | |
| 18 | 0 | 0 | 0 | 0 | 0 | 0 | 0 | 0 | 0 | 0 | |
| Total | 115 | 49 | 49 | 65 | 65 | 59 | 44 | 45 | 27 | 518 | |
| Above normal age | 36 | 28 | 31 | 42 | 46 | 47 | 27 | 33 | 23 | 313 | Table III figures for light line |
| Percentage above normal | 31.3 | 57.1 | 63.2 | 64.6 | 70.7 | 79.6 | 61.3 | 73.3 | 85.1 | 60.4 | |
| Above normal age | 36 | 28 | 31 | 20 | 31 | 30 | 16 | 18 | 10 | 220 | Table IV figures for heavy line |
| Percentage above normal | 31.3 | 57.1 | 63.2 | 30.7 | 47.6 | 50.8 | 36.3 | 40 | 37 | 40.2 | |

The light rule considers Grade 3B as retardation; the heavy rule does not consider Grade 3B as retardation.

Tables III and IV show the distribution of pupils in the grades according to age. Inasmuch as most pupils in this school enter at the age of six, the following would be the minimum age for pupils not retarded:

Grade 1 .................. 6 years
Grade 2 .................. 7 years
Grade 3B ................. 8 years
Grade 3A ................. 9 years
Grade 4 .................. 10 years
Grade 5 .................. 11 years
Grade 6 .................. 12 years
Grade 7 .................. 13 years
Grade 8 .................. 14 years

If one year spent in grade 3B is to be counted as retardation, the following becomes the list of ages for the different grades:

Grade 1 .................. 6 years
Grade 2 .................. 7 years
Grade 3 .................. 8 years
Grade 4 .................. 9 years
Grade 5 .................. 10 years
Grade 6 .................. 11 years
Grade 7 .................. 12 years
Grade 8 .................. 13 years

In Tables III and IV the light line would be the mark below which retardation is counted if the latter table is taken as a guide. The heavy line would be the mark of retardation if the former table is taken as the standard. Figures showing the percentage of retardation in each grade are given in the lower part of the table.

These results are further illustrated in Charts 3 and 4. The full light columns represent the number of pupils in each grade, the shaded portion represents the number who are retarded.

It is thus shown that, with the exception of the first grade, the percentage of retardation increases until the fifth grade is reached. From this point the percentage of retardation does not increase until the eighth grade is reached. This would show again that pupils retarded early in the grades drop out of school about the time they reach the fifth grade. The eighth grade exception has already been noted.

Tables V and VI show the percentages of retardation in the different grades as determined independently of the method used by Ayres in his "Laggards in Our Schools." The figures in these tables were determined by questioning the pupils and the teachers, and searching what records could be found in order to discover how much each individual child had been retarded. In the main, this was done by subtracting the age on entering school from the age last September. The results are believed to be correct because practically all of the years represented by the differences in ages in September and at the time when the child starts to school were

TABLE V

TABLE SHOWING TOTAL ENROLMENT AND RETARDATION IN DIFFERENT GRADES, COUNTING GRADE 3B AS RETARDATION

| Grade | Number Enrolled | Number Retarded | Percentage of Retardation |
|---|---|---|---|
| 1 | 95 | 49 | 51 |
| 2 | 53 | 21 | 40 |
| 3B | 55 | 40 | 73 |
| 3A | 59 | 45 | 76 |
| 4 | 65 | 49 | 75 |
| 5 | 61 | 50 | 82 |
| 6 | 43 | 28 | 65 |
| 7 | 43 | 28 | 65 |
| 8 | 24 | 20 | 83 |
| Total | 498 | 330 | 66.2 |

TABLE VI

TABLE SHOWING TOTAL ENROLMENT AND RETARDATION IN DIFFERENT GRADES, NOT COUNTING 3B AS RETARDATION

| Grade | Number Enrolled | Number Retarded | Percentage of Retardation |
|---|---|---|---|
| 1 | 95 | 49 | 51 |
| 2 | 53 | 21 | 40 |
| 3B | 55 | 22 | 40 |
| 3A | 59 | 25 | 42 |
| 4 | 65 | 34 | 52 |
| 5 | 61 | 35 | 57 |
| 6 | 43 | 18 | 42 |
| 7 | 43 | 23 | 53 |
| 8 | 24 | 16 | 67 |
| Total | 498 | 243 | 48.7 |

accounted for by the pupils, the teacher, or the records. Following is a comparison between the two methods.

| By Ayres's Method | Percentage of Retardation for Whole School |
|---|---|
| Counting 1 year in 3B as retardation | 60.4 |
| Not counting 1 year in 3B as retardation | 40.2 |

| By Actual Determination of Individual Cases | Percentage of Retardation for Whole School |
|---|---|
| Counting 1 year in 3B as retardation | 66.2 |
| Not counting 1 year in 3B as retardation | 48.7 |

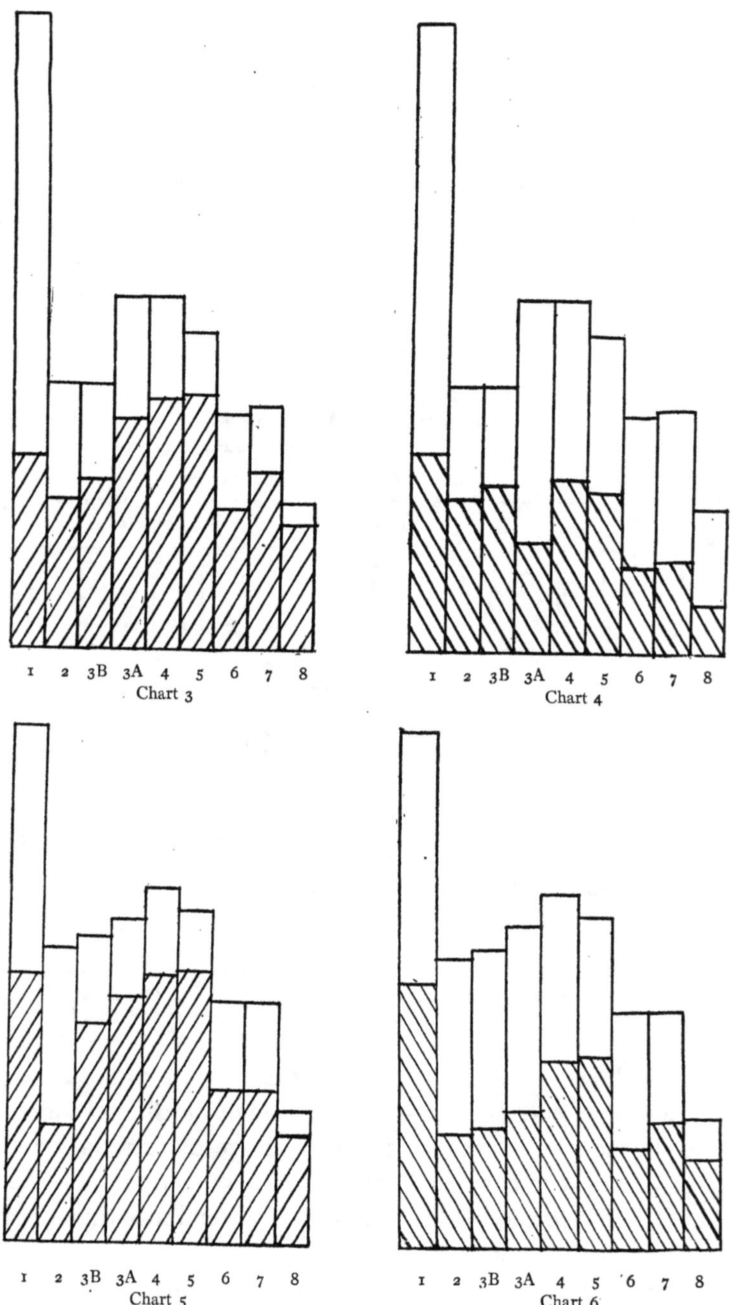

Chart 3

Chart 4

Chart 5

Chart 6

Charts 3 and 5 count 1 year spent in Grade 3B as retardation.
Charts 4 and 6 do not count 1 year in Grade 3B as retardation.
Charts 3 and 4 are based on Ayres's method.
Charts 5 and 6 are based on the method of individual study.

Charts 3, 4, 5, 6 represent the proportion of pupils in the different grades who have been retarded. The full-height columns represent the number of pupils in the different grades. The cross-hatched portions represent the number of pupils who have been retarded.

Ayres's method is thus shown to give approximately the same results as the method of studying individual cases.

Table VII shows the relation between retardation and the percentages of attendance for the whole time pupils have been in school.

In Chart 7 the abscissa represents the percentages of attendance, while the ordinate represents the percentages of retardation. Beginning with the level between 90 and 100 per cent on the left,

TABLE VII

TABLE SHOWING THE NUMBER OF CASES OF RETARDATION FOR DIFFERENT PERCENTAGES OF ATTENDANCE

| Grade | Percentage of Attendance and Retardation | | | | | | | | | | | | Below 50 | |
|---|---|---|---|---|---|---|---|---|---|---|---|---|---|---|
| | 95–100 | | 100–90 | | 90–80 | | 80–70 | | 70–60 | | 60–50 | | | |
| | Total | Retarded | Total | Retarded | Total | Retarded | Total | Retarded | Total | Retarded | Total | Retarded | Total | Retarded |
| 1........... | 9 | 3 | 25 | 11 | 22 | 13 | 17 | 6 | 6 | 6 | 5 | 2 | 11 | 9 |
| 2........... | 7 | 2 | 16 | 3 | 10 | 3 | 7 | 4 | 3 | 3 | 1 | 1 | 1 | 1 |
| 3B......... | 10 | 9 | 19 | 17 | 11 | 7 | 9 | 8 | 4 | 4 | 1 | 1 | 1 | 1 |
| 3A......... | 15 | 13 | 28 | 21 | 17 | 14 | 5 | 4 | 3 | 3 | 1 | 1 | 0 | 0 |
| 4........... | 18 | 12 | 33 | 25 | 8 | 7 | 7 | 7 | 3 | 3 | 0 | 0 | 0 | 0 |
| 5........... | 16 | 12 | 32 | 25 | 7 | 7 | 8 | 8 | 0 | 0 | 0 | 0 | 0 | 0 |
| 6........... | 16 | 9 | 27 | 17 | 9 | 6 | 0 | 0 | 0 | 0 | 0 | 0 | 0 | 0 |
| 7........... | 11 | 4 | 24 | 12 | 9 | 9 | 2 | 2 | 0 | 0 | 0 | 0 | 0 | 0 |
| 8........... | 11 | 9 | 16 | 13 | 5 | 4 | 2 | 2 | 0 | 0 | 0 | 0 | 0 | 0 |
| Total....... | 113 | 73 | 220 | 144 | 98 | 70 | 57 | 41 | 19 | 19 | 8 | 5 | 13 | 11 |
| Percentage of retardation | | 64½ | | 65½ | | 71½ | | 72 | | 100 | | 62½ | | 84½ |

In tables VII, IX, X, XI, XII, in the double columns of figures the first column contains the total number of pupils having the condition named as the heading of the double column. The second column in each double column contains the number of such pupils who have been retarded.

the curve shows an increase in percentage of retardation as the percentage of attendance decreases. Through the different intervals 90–100, 80–90, 70–80, 60–70, the percentage of retardation rises. Strange to say, the curve is lower between 50 per cent and 60 per cent of attendance and below 50 per cent of attendance than between 60 per cent and 70 per cent.

By carefully examining Table VII, it is seen that all of the cases of attendance below 60 per cent occur in the first three grades. All of these pupils except five in the first grade are retarded. These five were promoted from the first grade to the second grade in spite of low attendance. There being few cases showing a percentage of attendance below 60 per cent, these five not retarded make the percentage of retardation low. However, with the exception of the interval 60 per cent to 70 per cent, the curve remains at about the same level from 100 per cent back to 50 per cent of attendance. This would mean that the percentage of retardation

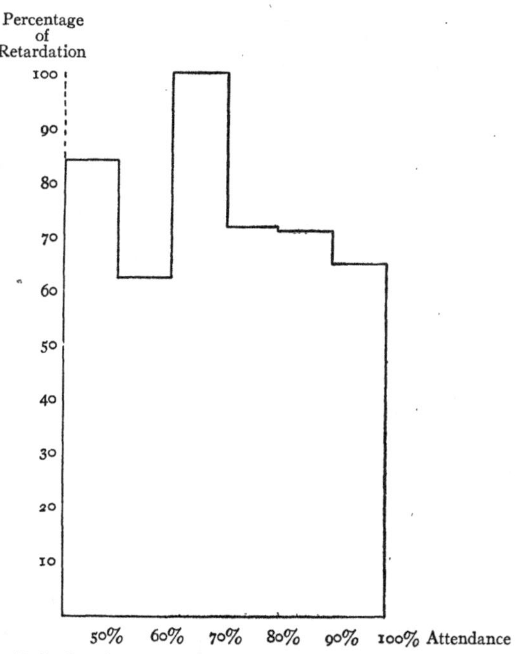


CHART 7.—Relation between retardation and attendance, based on number of cases of retardation.

is about the same for all pupils whose attendance is irregular. This curve deals only with cases of retardation and not with the number of years of retardation. The pupils whose percentage of attendance is between 90 per cent and 100 per cent may have an average of only one year of retardation, while those between 50 per cent and 60 per cent may have an average retardation of several years.

Table VIII and the accompanying Chart 8 show this to be true. In this table the average number of years of retardation for the

## TABLE VIII

TOTAL NUMBER OF YEARS OF RETARDATION IN EACH GRADE FOR THE FOLLOWING PERCENTAGES OF ATTENDANCE

Total Years Retardation

| Grade | 90-100% | 80-90% | 70-80% | 60-70% | 50-60% | Below 50% |
|---|---|---|---|---|---|---|
| 1 | 11 | 10 | 5½ | 9 | 2 | 11 |
| 2 | 11 | 7 | 7 | 3 | 2 | 1 |
| 3B | 23 | 12 | 21 | 8 | 6 | 3 |
| 3A | 29 | 23 | 8 | 5 | 2 | 0 |
| 4 | 45 | 8 | 20 | 11 | 0 | 0 |
| 5 | 33 | 22 | 21 | 0 | 0 | 0 |
| 6 | 27 | 11 | 0 | 0 | 0 | 0 |
| 7 | 17 | 21 | 3 | 0 | 0 | 0 |
| 8 | 26 | 9 | 6 | 0 | 0 | 0 |
| Total retardation in years | 222 | 123 | 91½ | 36 | 12 | 15 |
| Total number having attendance indicated | 220 | 98 | 57 | 19 | 8 | 13 |
| Average years of retardation | 1.00† | 1.25 | 1.60 | 1.89 | 1.50 | 1.15 |

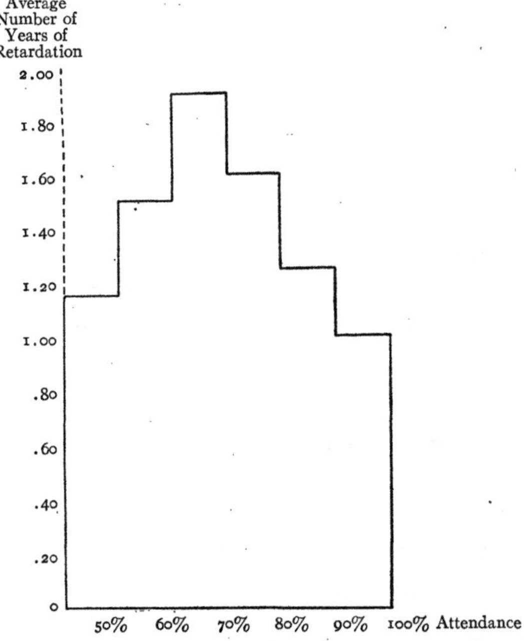


CHART 8.—Relation between retardation and attendance, based on number of years of retardation.

different percentages of attendance is calculated. In Chart 8 the curve shows a gradual uniform rise from 100 per cent of attendance back to 60 per cent. The decline from this point is accounted for as in Chart 7.

Tables IX, X, and XI show the relation between home conditions and retardation. In the letter combinations, the letter standing in the first place represents the financial conditions of the home; in the second place, the intellectual conditions of the home; in

TABLE IX

NUMBER OF CASES OF RETARDATION CONSIDERING HOME CONDITIONS

| Grade | AAA | | AAB | | AAC | | ABA | | ABB | | ABC | | ACA | | ACB | | ACC | |
|---|---|---|---|---|---|---|---|---|---|---|---|---|---|---|---|---|---|---|
| | Total | Retarded | Total | Retarded | Total | Retarded | Total | Retarded | Total | Retarded | Total | Retarded | Total | Retarded | Total | Retarded | Total | Retarded |
| 1........... | 2 | 0 | 1 | 0 | 0 | 0 | 3 | 0 | 4 | 0 | 0 | 0 | 0 | 0 | 0 | 0 | 0 | 0 |
| 2........... | 2 | 0 | 0 | 0 | 0 | 0 | 1 | 0 | 0 | 0 | 0 | 0 | 0 | 0 | 0 | 0 | 1 | 0 |
| 3B......... | 0 | 0 | 0 | 0 | 0 | 0 | 1 | 0 | 0 | 0 | 0 | 0 | 0 | 0 | 0 | 0 | 0 | 0 |
| 3A......... | 0 | 0 | 0 | 0 | 0 | 0 | 4 | 0 | 2 | 1 | 0 | 0 | 0 | 0 | 0 | 0 | 0 | 0 |
| 4........... | 1 | 0 | 0 | 0 | 0 | 0 | 2 | 1 | 0 | 0 | 0 | 0 | 0 | 0 | 0 | 0 | 0 | 0 |
| 5........... | 1 | 0 | 0 | 0 | 0 | 0 | 5 | 1 | 0 | 0 | 0 | 0 | 0 | 0 | 0 | 0 | 0 | 0 |
| 6........... | 0 | 0 | 0 | 0 | 0 | 0 | 3 | 0 | 0 | 0 | 0 | 0 | 0 | 0 | 0 | 0 | 0 | 0 |
| 7........... | 0 | 0 | 0 | 0 | 0 | 0 | 3 | 0 | 1 | 1 | 0 | 0 | 0 | 0 | 0 | 0 | 2 | 1 |
| 8........... | 0 | 0 | 0 | 0 | 0 | 0 | 3 | 2 | 0 | 0 | 0 | 0 | 0 | 0 | 0 | 0 | 0 | 0 |
| Total....... | 6 | 0 | 1 | 0 | 0 | 0 | 25 | 4 | 7 | 2 | 0 | 0 | 0 | 0 | 0 | 0 | 3 | 1 |
| Percentage of retardation | | | | | | | | 16 | | 29 | | | | | | | | 33⅓ |

the third place, the moral conditions of the home; e.g., BCA would mean the home conditions of the pupils in question have been rated as follows: financially, B; intellectually, C; morally, A.

Twenty-seven combinations of home conditions are possible. For each of these is determined the number of pupils having such a combination of home conditions and the number of such pupils who are retarded. From these figures the percentage of retardation for each individual combination is calculated. In general, where there is a preponderance of A's and B's, the percentage of retardation is lower, while where there is a preponderance of B's and C's, the percentage of retardation is higher.

## TABLE X

NUMBER OF CASES OF RETARDATION CONSIDERING HOME CONDITIONS

| Grade | BAA | | BAB | | BAC | | BBA | | BBB | | BBC | | BCA | | BCB | | BCC | |
|---|---|---|---|---|---|---|---|---|---|---|---|---|---|---|---|---|---|---|
| | Total | Retarded | Total | Retarded | Total | Retarded | Total | Retarded | Total | Retarded | Total | Retarded | Total | Retarded | Total | Retarded | Total | Retarded |
| 1 | 1 | 0 | 0 | 0 | 0 | 0 | 15 | 7 | 8 | 2 | 2 | 0 | 3 | 3 | 6 | 4 | 6 | 2 |
| 2 | 0 | 0 | 0 | 0 | 0 | 0 | 5 | 1 | 2 | 0 | 0 | 0 | 1 | 0 | 2 | 0 | 0 | 0 |
| 3B | 0 | 0 | 1 | 0 | 0 | 0 | 3 | 0 | 3 | 2 | 1 | 1 | 0 | 0 | 0 | 0 | 0 | 0 |
| 3A | 1 | 0 | 0 | 0 | 0 | 0 | 9 | 3 | 2 | 0 | 0 | 0 | 0 | 0 | 0 | 0 | 0 | 0 |
| 4 | 1 | 0 | 0 | 0 | 0 | 0 | 13 | 1 | 1 | 0 | 1 | 1 | 0 | 0 | 3 | 2 | 0 | 0 |
| 5 | 1 | 1 | 0 | 0 | 0 | 0 | 5 | 3 | 10 | 4 | 0 | 0 | 0 | 0 | 5 | 4 | 0 | 0 |
| 6 | 3 | 0 | 0 | 0 | 0 | 0 | 8 | 3 | 1 | 0 | 0 | 0 | 0 | 0 | 1 | 1 | 2 | 2 |
| 7 | 1 | 0 | 0 | 0 | 0 | 0 | 7 | 3 | 2 | 1 | 3 | 2 | 2 | 1 | 2 | 2 | 1 | 0 |
| 8 | 0 | 0 | 0 | 0 | 0 | 0 | 4 | 3 | 3 | 1 | 0 | 0 | 1 | 1 | 1 | 1 | 1 | 0 |
| Total | 8 | 1 | 1 | 0 | 0 | 0 | 69 | 24 | 32 | 10 | 7 | 4 | 7 | 5 | 20 | 14 | 10 | 4 |
| Percentage of retardation | | 12½ | | | | | | 35 | | 31¼ | | 57 | | 71½ | | 70 | | 40 |

## TABLE XI

NUMBER OF CASES OF RETARDATION CONSIDERING HOME CONDITIONS

| Grade | CAA | | CAB | | CAC | | CBA | | CBB | | CBC | | CCA | | CCB | | CCC | |
|---|---|---|---|---|---|---|---|---|---|---|---|---|---|---|---|---|---|---|
| | Total | Retarded | Total. | Retarded | Total | Retarded | Total | Retarded | Total | Retarded | Total | Retarded | Total | Retarded | Total | Retarded | Total | Retarded |
| 1 | 0 | 0 | 0 | 0 | 0 | 0 | 0 | 0 | 2 | 1 | 2 | 0 | 1 | 1 | 17 | 11 | 22 | 16 |
| 2 | 0 | 0 | 0 | 0 | 0 | 0 | 2 | 0 | 3 | 0 | 1 | 1 | 0 | 0 | 17 | 10 | 10 | 9 |
| 3B | 0 | 0 | 0 | 0 | 0 | 0 | 6 | 3 | 6 | 2 | 2 | 1 | 1 | 1 | 13 | 12 | 12 | 8 |
| 3A | 0 | 0 | 0 | 0 | 0 | 0 | 0 | 0 | 8 | 4 | 2 | 2 | 0 | 0 | 12 | 12 | 10 | 5 |
| 4 | 0 | 0 | 1 | 0 | 0 | 0 | 3 | 1 | 6 | 1 | 0 | 0 | 0 | 0 | 8 | 8 | 23 | 19 |
| 5 | 0 | 0 | 1 | 0 | 0 | 0 | 0 | 0 | 4 | 3 | 0 | 0 | 0 | 0 | 13 | 13 | 8 | 8 |
| 6 | 0 | 0 | 0 | 0 | 0 | 0 | 2 | 2 | 3 | 0 | 4 | 3 | 3 | 2 | 0 | 0 | 6 | 4 |
| 7 | 0 | 0 | 0 | 0 | 0 | 0 | 4 | 3 | 1 | 1 | 0 | 0 | 0 | 0 | 7 | 4 | 6 | 6 |
| 8 | 0 | 0 | 0 | 0 | 0 | 0 | 0 | 0 | 3 | 2 | 0 | 0 | 2 | 2 | 2 | 2 | 3 | 3 |
| Total | 0 | 0 | 2 | 0 | 0 | 0 | 17 | 9 | 36 | 14 | 11 | 7 | 7 | 6 | 89 | 72 | 100 | 78 |
| P'c't'ge of retardat' | | | | | | | | 53 | | 39 | | 64– | | 86– | | 89– | | 78 |

Following is a list of combinations of home conditions, giving in order the percentages of retardation. Those showing no retardation are omitted.

| Financial | Educat onal | Moral | |
|---|---|---|---|
| B | A | A | ...........12½ |
| A | B | A | ...........16 |
| A | B | B | ...........29 |
| B | B | B | ...........31¼ |
| A | C | C | ...........33⅓ |
| B | B | A | ...........35 |
| C | B | B | ...........39 |
| B | C | C | ...........40 |
| C | B | A | ...........53 |
| B | B | C | ...........57 |
| C | B | C | ...........64 |
| B | C | B | ...........70 |
| B | C | A | ...........71½ |
| C | C | C | ...........78 |
| C | C | A | ...........86 |
| C | C | B | ...........89 |

All percentages of retardation above 50 per cent accompany combinations in which B's or C's occupy first and second positions. Of the eight combinations giving percentages above 50 per cent, seven contain C in the middle or second position; five contain C in the first position. In the third positions are found 3 A's, 2 B's, and 3 C's. These observations would show that financial and intellectual conditions are larger factors in determining retardation than are moral conditions, and also, that intellectual conditions are the most prominent factors of all, while moral conditions seem to be least prominent.

These conclusions are more clearly shown from Table XII and the accompanying figure. The table shows an increase in retardation with the descending scale, A to B to C, in each of the three general classes—financial, educational, and moral.

The curves in Chart 12 give a graphical comparison of the whole field of retardation and home conditions considered in Table XII. Here we find the highest educational condition accompanied by the lowest percentage of retardation and the lowest educational condition accompanied by the highest percentage of retardation.

The reverse is true with moral conditions. The best moral conditions are accompanied by higher percentages of retardation than are the best financial and educational conditions, while the

TABLE XII

RETARDATION AND HOME CONDITIONS

| Grade | Financial | | | | | | Educational | | | | | | Moral | | | | | |
|---|---|---|---|---|---|---|---|---|---|---|---|---|---|---|---|---|---|---|
| | A | | B | | C | | A | | B | | C | | A | | B | | C | |
| | Total | Retarded | Total | Retarded | Total | Retarded | Total | Retarded | Total | Retarded | Total | Retarded | Total | Retarded | Total | Retarded | Total | Retarded |
| 1 | 10 | 0 | 41 | 18 | 44 | 29 | 4 | 0 | 36 | 10 | 55 | 37 | 25 | 11 | 38 | 18 | 32 | 18 |
| 2 | 4 | 0 | 10 | 1 | 33 | 20 | 2 | 0 | 14 | 2 | 31 | 19 | 11 | 1 | 24 | 10 | 15 | 9 |
| 3B | 1 | 0 | 8 | 3 | 40 | 27 | 1 | 0 | 22 | 9 | 26 | 21 | 11 | 4 | 23 | 16 | 15 | 10 |
| 3A | 6 | 1 | 12 | 3 | 32 | 23 | 1 | 0 | 27 | 10 | 22 | 17 | 21 | 2 | 24 | 17 | 12 | 7 |
| 4 | 3 | 1 | 19 | 4 | 41 | 29 | 3 | 0 | 26 | 5 | 31 | 29 | 22 | 3 | 19 | 11 | 24 | 20 |
| 5 | 6 | 1 | 21 | 12 | 26 | 24 | 3 | 1 | 24 | 11 | 26 | 25 | 12 | 5 | 33 | 24 | 8 | 8 |
| 6 | 3 | 0 | 15 | 6 | 18 | 11 | 3 | 0 | 21 | 8 | 12 | 9 | 19 | 7 | 5 | 1 | 12 | 9 |
| 7 | 6 | 2 | 18 | 9 | 18 | 14 | 1 | 0 | 21 | 11 | 15 | 11 | 17 | 7 | 13 | 9 | 12 | 9 |
| 8 | 3 | 2 | 10 | 6 | 10 | 9 | 0 | 0 | 13 | 8 | 10 | 9 | 10 | 8 | 9 | 6 | 4 | 3 |
| Total | 42 | 7 | 154 | 62 | 262 | 186 | 18 | 1 | 204 | 74 | 228 | 177 | 148 | 48 | 188 | 112 | 134 | 93 |
| Percentage of retardation | | 16⅔ | | 42½ | | 71 | | 5 5/9 | | 36 | | 77½ | | 32½ | | 59½ | | 69† |

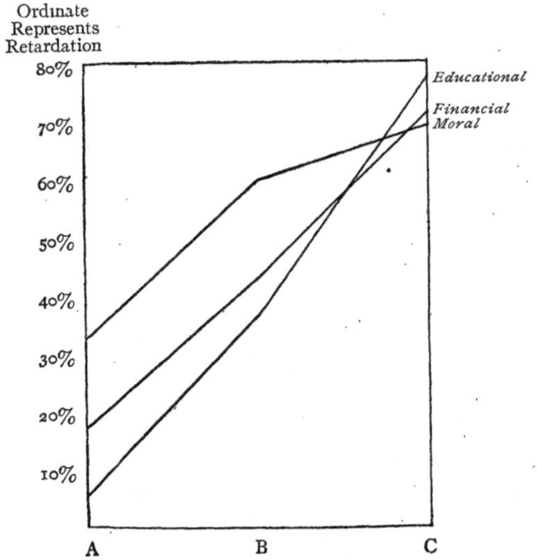


CHART 12.—Comparison of retardation and home conditions.

worst moral conditions are accompanied by a lower percentage of retardation than either the worst financial conditions or the worst intellectual conditions. At both extremes of the scale the curve for financial conditions occupies a position between the other two curves.

In the order of accompanying percentages of retardation, home conditions may be arranged as follows:

| | |
|---|---|
| A educationally | $5\frac{5}{9}$ per cent retardation |
| A financially | $16\frac{2}{3}$ per cent retardation |
| A morally | $32\frac{1}{2}$ per cent retardation |
| B educationally | 36 per cent retardation |
| B financially | $42\frac{1}{2}$ per cent retardation |
| B morally | $59\frac{1}{2}$ per cent retardation |
| C morally | 69 per cent retardation |
| C financially | 71 per cent retardation |
| C educationally | $77\frac{1}{2}$ per cent retardation |

## GENERAL CONCLUSIONS

1. Taking the mean of results obtained by Ayres's method of determining retardation by distribution of ages in grades, and the results obtained by studying individual cases, about 44 per cent of the pupils considered in this discussion have failed to complete one grade each year.

2. Most of the pupils who are retarded in the lower grades are eliminated before reaching the higher grades.

3. The fifth grade marks the point of greatest elimination.

4. In general, the average number of years a child spends in each grade varies inversely as his percentage of attendance.

5. If the financial, educational, and moral conditions of the home are rated in the descending order, A to C, the A conditions in each case are accompanied by the lowest percentages of retardation, while the C conditions are accompanied by the highest percentages of retardation.

Of these three, the educational condition constitutes the greatest factor, and the moral condition the least factor, in determining retardation.

# AGRICULTURAL EDUCATION: STATE ORGANIZATIONS FOR AGRICULTURE AND FARMERS' INSTITUTES

BENJAMIN MARSHALL DAVIS
Miami University

Perhaps no other offices concerned with the public business of various states include so wide a range of activities, duties, aims, and methods as do the state organizations for agriculture. One state commissioner of agriculture says of his department:

> If I were asked to supply a name, it would be called the Dumping Ground for a Legislature to place all subject-matter that body finds necessary to frame into law.

The justice of this observation will be more readily appreciated by reference to the following constitutional provisions for his office:

> He shall perform such duties in relation to agriculture as may be prescribed by law, shall have supervision of all matters pertaining to the public lands under regulations prescribed by law, and shall keep the Bureau of Immigration. He shall also have supervision of the State Prison, and shall perform such other duties as may be prescribed by law.

Some state organizations for agriculture have even a wider range of duties. On the other hand, there are some in which the duties of this office are limited to the supervision of the state agricultural college, or to the management of the state fair.

There are five forms of organization. The first includes those organizations known as "Departments" and consists of a commissioner and one or more assistants. The second form comprises the boards, which are composed of a varying number of members, some appointed by the governor and others being members of the board by virtue of their official position in the state. The third includes bureaus which are essentially the same as the boards. The fourth form is a combination of the first and second; the regular department is supervised by a board of agriculture. The fifth and final form is that known as the Michigan organization, under which the state board of agriculture is merely a board of trustees for the state agricultural college (102, p. 328).[1]

In about half the states the administrative officer is chosen by popular vote; in the rest he is appointed by the governor or chosen by the members of the board. Being thus a political office in some instances, the position as secretary or commissioner of agriculture is more or less on a political basis, and therefore fails properly to fulfil the purpose for which it was intended, viz., to promote the agricultural interests of the state. It is the purpose of this article to sum up the work now being done by the various state departments, and by the state farmers' institutes in promoting agricultural education, particularly in elementary and secondary schools.

In one-half of the states the farmers' institutes are conducted under the direct or indirect control of the state organizations for agriculture; in the other half they are conducted by the state agricultural colleges. Since the methods and aims of all farmers' institutes are essentially the same in both groups, those under state supervision and those under state agricultural college supervision will be considered in the second part of this discussion. As might be expected, the attitude of the various state organizations for agriculture is favorable toward agricultural education in the public schools. In many reports of secretaries or commissioners of agriculture much emphasis is placed upon the importance of recognizing agriculture as a school subject. The following extract is typical:

The Department has continued its efforts to impress upon the people of the state the importance and necessity of agricultural and industrial instruction in the public schools. These schools should fit for vocation. The population of this and other states is continually increasing, and in order for the farms to meet this increase there must be a more intelligent system of agriculture. This can best be brought about by teaching the principles of agriculture in the public schools. The farmer has a business to be studied and learned. It needs a trained mind as much as any other occupation. Let us educate our boys who are to be farmers of the future, for that work. Specific training of a practical kind is a necessity for the

[1] The references are to the bibliography at the end of this article or to bibliographies in other articles of this series.

coming occupants of our farms, as well as those engaged in mechanical industries. The most valuable asset of the state is her children. They should be trained to high ideals of every day living and to high efficiency in their respective vocations (103, p. 11).

At the annual meetings of boards of agriculture of several states agricultural education receives attention, special addresses being given on this subject and published in the proceedings (104, 105, 106, 107).

Special bulletins or leaflets are published and distributed by a few state offices of agriculture. The Massachusetts State Board of Agriculture has issued from time to time leaflets on elementary agriculture and nature-study. The New York State Department of Agriculture publishes annual reports of the state Experiment Station at Cornell University. These contain reprints of various nature-study, rural school, and teachers' leaflets sent out from Cornell University, and also accounts of the extension work in agriculture and nature-study conducted by the university among the schools of the state. The Missouri State Board has recently published a bulletin on elementary agriculture meant to be used "only as the first year's work," and "written on the supposition that neither teacher nor pupils know much of scientific agriculture" (108).

About half of the states hold annual state fairs under the management of the state offices of agriculture. In nearly all, there is a department of education in which prizes are offered for school exhibits. Some give special encouragement to agricultural subjects. The prizes aggregate a few dollars in some fairs to several hundred in others.

The Nebraska State Fair offered "to the Nebraska boy under eighteen years of age, growing the largest yield of corn from one acre of ground, in the year 1910, $50; second, $25; third, $20; fourth, $15; fifth, $10; and to the sixth, seventh, eighth, ninth, tenth, and eleventh, $5 each."

The South Dakota State Fair made the boys' and girls' contests a special feature at its recent meeting. Three hundred and fifty dollars were offered in cash prizes, the largest first prize being one hundred dollars. The contest was announced in a special bulletin containing instructions as to the details of preparation for the contests (109).

One of the most popular buildings at the last Minnesota State Fair was the Agricultural Hall Annex which was devoted entirely to the exhibits in agriculture, household arts, and manual training of the ten high schools receiving state aid for teaching these subjects.

The Oklahoma State Fair of 1910 has arranged for a school of agriculture to be held on its grounds. Each county is entitled to two delegates, one hundred and fifty-four boys being provided for. "This work will be done at the fair grounds. The boys and instructors will sleep in a large tent." A portion of each day is to be devoted to instruction, lectures in the mornings and object-teaching or laboratory work in the afternoons (110). A similar school for boys is conducted by the Illinois State Fair.

Contests, for example, corn contests, are held in some states under the direction of the state office of agriculture. Such contests are being held in Missouri this year all over the state, and a Farm Boys' Encampment is conducted under the same management. In South Carolina contests have been held throughout the state under the joint direction of the State Department of Agriculture and the United States Demonstration Work. In the state contest which is soon to take place over three thousand boys are enrolled. The winner of last year's contest, Bascomb Usher, raised on one acre one hundred and fifty-two and one-half bushels of corn. The average production of corn per acre for the entire state was about eighteen bushels. A number of other southern states are conducting similar co-operative contests.

South Carolina, through its Department of Agriculture, has been aiding the practical teaching of agriculture in a few high schools by maintaining a skilled teacher and operating a farm and practice garden in connection with the school (111). The commissioner says:

> This has been in the nature of an experiment, but we have gone far enough in the matter to see that admirable results may be obtained, and

at a very minimum of cost. The only cost, in fact, to us is the salary of the man nine months in the year. The land is furnished by the patrons of the school, as are also the work animals, implements, fertilizers, etc., and the school is given the profits from the farm.[2]

These are typical examples of the work of various state offices of agriculture in promoting an interest in agriculture and rural life among boys and girls. Many others might have been given. It is a new field of activity for these offices, and promises much if organized and extended so as to co-operate with other educational efforts. Perhaps the greatest value of such work for agricultural education to the public schools lies in placing the stamp of official approval upon this kind of education.

In many states practically nothing has been done by these offices, and in none more than a beginning of what might be done. The state fair, for example offers unusual educational opportunities. If the same energy now expended in managing and controlling amusement-park features of these fairs (which are of doubtful value at best) were directed toward helping the schools of rural communities there might be a great educational gain for the state.

## STATE FARMERS' INSTITUTES

The farmers' institute movement in the United States has now reached a degree of importance and development that places it along side of the leading institutions of the country organized in the interest of industrial education. Forty-five states and territories held institutes in 1905, aggregating 10,555 half-day sessions, which were attended by 995,192 persons, chiefly adults (112, p. 7).

The growth of this movement may be seen by comparing the above summary for 1905 with the following summary for 1908: number of institutes 4,643; half-day sessions 13,056; attendance 2,098,268. In addition to the regular institutes included in the above a number of special institutes were held with an attendance of 340,414, which, added to the attendance at the regular institutes, make a total of 2,438,682. There is

[2] Quoted from private letter.

no record of attendance of 732 meetings of women's institutes, of 174 meetings of boys' institutes, or of several other meetings which might be regarded as farmers' institutes (113).

The function of the farmers' institute is to educate the people on their own ground. It is a phase of extension work that carries education directly to the localities in which the people live. It deals less with individual men on their farms than with small communities or groups of men; it therefore has the opportunity to exert great influence in developing the social life of rural neighborhoods (102, p. 462).

With these aims on the one hand, and with an attendance of over two million on the other, farmers' institutes become a factor in rural education second only to the public schools. Although the institutes are intended for adults it must be remembered that adults are patrons of the rural schools, and wherever the farmers' institute arouses the adult population to a realization of a need for better schools, improvement in these schools is likely to follow.

In 1896 the American Association of Farmers' Institute Workers was organized and has held annual meetings ever since. This association is a sort of clearing-house for exchange of ideas and methods, and is intended also to secure a more or less uniform type of institute in the several states. In 1898 the association requested the secretary of the Department of Agriculture at Washington to arrange for a division in connection with the department to be known as the Division of Farmers' Institutes. This request was subsequently granted by establishing the office of Farmers' Institute Specialist.[3]

The general policy of farmers' institutes is influenced greatly by the association and by the office of Farmers' Institute Specialist. At the meeting for 1908, the

subjects for discussion in the general program were mainly directed toward defining the status of the farmers' institute in its relation to other forms of agricultural education. The points brought out were that the farmers' institute occupies the position of field agent for agricultural education; that it provides a most efficient channel for carrying agricultural information directly to the farmer who is unable to leave his occupation to go to school;

[3] The work of this office was referred to in the first article of this series, *Elementary School Teacher,* November, 1909, pp. 101–9.

and that it should broaden its work until it embraces other more advanced forms of educational work and extend its efforts until all rural people have full opportunity to enjoy its benefits (113, p. 293).

Farmers' institute workers are further assisted by state meetings where they gather together to plan the year's work. Here the policy for the work of the whole state is determined. In many of these meetings the relation of the institute to the public schools receives attention, and methods for assisting the introduction of agriculture and other rural-life subjects into the rural schools are discussed.

The following extracts of letters from some state directors or superintendents of farmers' institutes will indicate more definitely what these institutes are doing in this matter:

In connection with the Farmers' Demonstration Train we always send preliminary notice to the schools where the train is scheduled to stop, inviting them to have their pupils visit the train (Cal.).

At our annual conference of institute workers, the question of the relation of the school and church to the farm and rural life receives due consideration. The result is that an atmosphere favorable to the development of the schools along practical lines is pretty generally diffused (Ind.).

The farmers' institute lecturers have encouraged institute patrons to insist in their respective counties that agriculture be taught in the public schools (Md.).

Not only is this subject discussed by many of the lecturers, but at a large number of the institutes special speakers upon this and allied subjects are provided (Mich.).

For two years we have been giving lectures in agriculture and allied subjects in the high schools of the state; last year to the extent of eighty. Plans are nearly perfected for increasing this line of work the coming season, giving lecture courses consisting of four lectures in each of such schools as apply for them (Mont.).

We have several speakers who lecture before evening sessions of farmers' institutes on such subjects as: agriculture in the rural schools, domestic science in the rural schools, value of agricultural education, etc. (Neb.).

Each of the four corps of institute lecturers is accompanied by a representative of the Educational Department who arranges for special sessions in the public schools in connection with institutes where he can secure cooperation of the local school authorities. At these special sessions the farmers' institute lecturers give talks on elementary agriculture and nature-study. The total attendance at these special sessions held during the school periods amounted to 22,697 (N.Y.).

When we are holding an institute in a town we very often send the lecturers to the schools to speak to the school children on certain phases of farm life (N.D.).

No instructions are given institute lecturers regarding this work; however, at many institutes teachers and pupils are called to the meeting and special lectures are given them (Okla.).

We are trying to give a good deal of attention to the introduction of agricultural education in the public schools. I have attended ten teachers' institutes during the summer with this object in view, speaking at some of them three times, and I think the subject has been discussed by some person in every institute in the state (S.D.).

Our farmers' institute instructors do what they can to promote and encourage the teaching of agriculture in the rural schools. Many of them have lectures upon this subject (W.Va.).

For the last twenty-four years a great deal of attention has been given to the discussion of agricultural education in the public schools of Wisconsin by the farmers' institute workers of this state; in fact, we feel that public sentiment among farmers has been developed by these discussions until Wisconsin has, we think, a little more practical agriculture in her schools, from the rural district up through the county agricultural schools and the agricultural college, than has any other state in the Union (Wis.).

In most states where the farmers' institute is conducted by the agricultural college there is a close correlation between this department and that of agricultural extension. In some colleges they are practically identical. As has been indicated in a previous article of this series special provision has been made by several colleges for extension work among the schools.[4] Where this arrangement obtains, the farmers' institute workers merely co-operate with those engaged in the work among the schools, and do not initiate any work themselves.

From what has been presented concerning the organization and work of the farmers' institutes it will be seen that they have been a considerable factor in the movement for agricultural education in the public schools, first, by arousing favorable sentiment among the farmers, and second, by direct help to teacher and pupils.

[4] *Elementary School Teacher,* February, 1910, pp. 277–86.

While these institutes will doubtless continue to encourage the introduction of agriculture into the public schools and emphasize the importance of re-directing rural schools, in many states, and soon in all the agricultural states, the demands of the rural schools for help along industrial lines will require some special attention not now provided.

## BIBLIOGRAPHY

The facts of the text have been obtained chiefly from reports of state offices of agriculture, and from letters of secretaries or commissioners of agriculture and state directors of farmers' institutes. Only references made by number in text are included in bibliography.

102. "State Organizations for Agriculture," *Encyclopedia of American Agriculture*, IV (1909), 328–39.

A brief general account is given, followed by short sketches of the various state organizations.

103. "Agricultural Education," A. W. GILMAN, *Seventh Annual Report of the Commissioner of Agriculture of the State of Maine* (1908), 11–12.

Reviewed in text.

104. An Address—no title, P. G. HOLDEN, *Annual Report of the Nebraska State Board of Agriculture* (1909), 112–37.

A stenographic report of an address supposed to be upon corn but a considerable portion of it relates to rural education, and offers many valuable suggestions on this subject.

105. "Some Rural Problems," WALLACE, *ibid.* (1910), 124–39.

Four problems are discussed: maintenance of soil fertility, farm labor, education, and socialization of farm life. Mr. Wallace was a member of the Country Life Commission. His discussion of rural education, therefore, is of more than ordinary interest.

106. "Rural Education," A. C. TRUE, *Annual Report of the Pennsylvania Department of Agriculture* (1907), 231–36.

General improvement of rural schools is regarded as necessary and certain to be brought about. Better teaching, consolidation, attention given to nature-study and agriculture in public schools are suggested as means of improvement.

107. "The Most Useful School in the Country," D. J. CROSBY, *ibid.* (1909), 257–63.

Two small country schools are described in considerable detail as illustrating the possibilities of a rural school: one at Calvert Center, Md., the other at Waterford, Pa.

108 "Steps in Agriculture," S. M. JORDON, *Monthly Bulletin, Missouri State Board of Agriculture,* VIII, No. 8 (1910), 136.

This contains simple studies to help "teachers interest our boys and girls in better farming" as follows: the stand of corn, leaves or blades, roots, flowers and blossoms, yield, corn judging, score card, seed selection, weeds, insects, flies, grafting and budding, crossing, diseases of plants, wheat and oats, clovers and cowpeas.

109. "Boys' and Girls' Contests," A. E. CHAMBERLAIN, South Dakota State Board of Agriculture, *Special Bulletin* (1910), 1–15.

Reviewed in text.

110. "The School of Agriculture at the State Fair," S. E. ANDREWS, Oklahoma State Board of Agriculture, *Monthly Press Bulletin*, Series 1910, No. 7 (September), 8–9.

An account in detail of how the school is to be conducted.

111. "Agricultural Schools," E. J. MARTIN, Office of Commissioner of Agriculture, Commerce and Industries of South Carolina, *Sixth Annual Report* (1909), 93–94.

An account of agricultural demonstration work in connection with certain high schools.

112. "History of Farmers' Institutes in the United States," JOHN HAMILTON, U.S. Department of Agriculture, Office of Experiment Stations, *Bulletin* 174 (1906), 1–96.

As the name indicates, it is a historical account of farmers' institutes in the United States. It is divided into five parts: introduction, historians, government aid to institutes, American Association of Farmers' Institute Workers, institutes in the several states and territories.

113. "The Farmers' Institutes in the United States, 1908," JOHN HAMILTON, U.S. Department of Agriculture, Office of Experiment Stations, *Annual Report of the Office of Experiment Stations* (1908), 289–335.

A summary of the work of farmers' institutes for 1908 giving institutes held, sessions, attendance, appropriations, and other data concerning the year's work.

# OUR INHERITED PRACTICE IN ELEMENTARY SCHOOLS

S. CHESTER PARKER
The University of Chicago

## V. PESTALOZZIAN OBJECT-TEACHING AND ORAL INSTRUCTION

This is the fifth of a series of articles intended to emphasize a method of teaching the history of education in which special attention is paid to educational practice in its relation to social conditions. This method can be illustrated to advantage in the work of Pestalozzi. The relation of this great reformer to general social movements can best be shown in connection with the Swiss Revolution of 1798 and with what might be called "Pestalozzian industrial training." His great influence on the actual practice of elementary schools can be illustrated in connection with "Pestalozzian object-teaching and oral instruction" and "Pestalozzian formalism." The former will be treated in this paper.

Pestalozzi protested vigorously against teaching children words and phrases that they did not understand, and insisted upon the substitution of real experience with natural objects as the fundamental starting-point of instruction. In this he was following Rousseau in "psychologizing instruction," and he himself considered it his most important reform. He said,

> If I look back and ask myself what I have really done toward the improvement of the methods of elementary instruction, I find that in recognizing observation as the absolute basis of all knowledge, I have established the first and most important principle of instruction.

We have seen how the influence of the Reformation and the invention of printing tended to make learning to read and memorizing the catechism the fundamentals in elementary education. Calling attention to this, Pestalozzi said,

> In Europe the culture of the people has ended by becoming an empty chattering, fatal alike to real faith and real knowledge; an instruction of

mere words and outward show, unsubstantial as a dream, and not only absolutely incapable of giving us the quiet wisdom of faith and love, but bound, sooner or later, to lead us into incredulity and superstition, egotism and hardness of heart. . . . . Everything confirms me in my opinion that the only way of escaping a civil, moral, and religious degradation, is to have done with the superficiality, narrowness and other errors of our popular instruction, and recognize sense impression as the real foundation of our knowledge.

If we study a few examples of object-teaching as they occurred in Pestalozzi's experience we will get a concrete notion of what he meant by the "necessity of basing instruction on sense perception" and will see the relation to arithmetic, language, geography, and other studies.

In the *Journal* in which he described the education of his own child in 1774 he said,

I tried to make him understand the meaning of numbers. At present he knows only their names without attaching any precise meaning to them. The child has been in the habit of associating no difference of meaning with the various names of numbers he pronounces. . . . . Why have I been so foolish as to let him pronounce important words without taking care at the same time to give him a clear idea of their meaning?

In *Leonard and Gertrude* (1781) we get examples of how he followed up this theory with the spinning children at Neuhof.

The instruction [Gertrude] gave them in the rudiments of arithmetic was intimately connected with the realities of life. She taught them to count the number of steps from one end of the room to the other, and two of the rows of five panes each, in one of the windows, gave her an opportunity to unfold the decimal relations of numbers. She also made them count their threads while spinning, and the number of turns on the reel, when they wound the yarn into skeins. Above all, in every occupation of life she taught them an accurate and intelligent observation of common objects and the forces of nature.

From the third class that Pestalozzi taught at Burgdorf (1800) we have one of the clearest examples of his object-teaching. One of his pupils there wrote,

The language exercises were the best thing we had, especially those on the wall-paper of the school room, which were real practice in sense impression. We spent hours before this old and torn paper, occupied in examining the number, form, position, and color of the different designs, holes, and rents, and expressing our ideas in more and more enlarged sentences. Thus he would ask: "Boys, what do you see?" (He never addressed the girls.)

*Answer:* "A hole in the paper."

Pestalozzi: "Very well, say after me:

"I see a hole in the paper.

"I see a long hole in the paper.

"Through the hole I see the wall.

"Through the long narrow hole I see the wall.

"I see figures on the paper.

"I see black figures on the paper.

"I see round black figures on the paper.

"I see a square yellow figure on the paper.

"By the side of the square yellow figure I see a round black one.

"The square figure is joined to the round figure by a large black stripe, etc."

At Burgdorf natural history materials, chiefly minerals and plants, were collected by the children on their walks, and examined and described, but the teachers were ignorant of any scientific classifications.

From Yverdon (1805) we have a good example of a sense-perception geography lesson, as described by a pupil.

The first elements of geography were taught us from the land itself. We were first taken to a narrow valley not far from Yverdon, where the river Buron runs. After taking a general view of the valley, we were made to examine the details, until we had obtained an exact and complete idea of it. We were then told to take some of the clay which lay in beds on one side of the valley, and fill the baskets which we had brought for the purpose. On our return to the Castle, we took our places at the long tables, and reproduced in relief the valley we had just studied, each one doing the part that had been allotted to him. In the course of the next few days more walks and more explorations, each day on higher ground, and each time with a further extension of our work. Only when our relief was finished were we shown the map, which by this means we did not see until we were in a position to understand it.

These examples are representative of the methods of sense-perception or object-teaching used by Pestalozzi in various stages of his experimentation.

*Object-teaching and oral speech.*—The primary purpose in teaching through observation and real experience was to have the children get real and clear ideas instead of mere words or hazy notions. This led to a subordination or elimination of book study which had two important effects on practice: (1) the teacher became an active instructor of groups of children, instead of a hearer of individual recitation; (2) children were given training in oral speech which had practically no place in the elementary schools before.

We have seen (in an earlier article) how the Christian Brethren and the Lancasterian schools substituted group recitations for individual recitations, but with them teaching continued to be primarily hearing children recite from books. With oral instruction based on object-teaching the schoolroom activity took on an entirely different character. In the first place a single objective center of attention usually became the center of interest, such as the hole in the wall paper at Burgdorf or the valley at Yverdon. In connection with some such center of attention, e.g., in studying beans, the teacher raised questions intended to set the children to thinking actively for the answer to a problem which they felt in common, such as "How many beans are on the table?" "What is the color of the beans?" In the absence of books, any information which the children did not possess or could not discover had to be given by the teacher, hence the teacher's knowledge of the objective world became important. This change in the emphasis from "what the book said," to what the children had experienced or were experiencing and what the teacher knew, led to an elaborate development of the technique of instruction during the nineteenth century. The teacher was now confronted with such questions as, What objective experiences to select for children? How arrange to give them these experiences? How keep children actively attentive and thinking about the object? What kind of questions to ask in order to bring out unnoticed characteristics? How systematize and arrange the child's experiences and ideas? How provide for repetition and fixing them since simply rereading in a book was no longer possible? How much should the children be told, how much should they discover themselves? In telling them, what form of expression should be used?

These oral methods assumed two extreme forms: (1) the teacher simply questioned the children about their experience and told them nothing; (2) the teacher told them everything, his words being substituted for those of the textbook. The evil consequence of both these extremes was that children did not learn how to use books, which Pestalozzi sanctioned by his statement that he had not read a book for years. The influence of these extremes on the training of teachers is important. With the extreme of all questioning, it was assumed that the teacher's knowledge was unimportant, a proper method of questioning being the sole requisite. Inasmuch as some people are naturally good questioners, it was assumed that they were skilled teachers. This was especially characteristic of the early work of Pestalozzi and his assistant Krusi, who through ignorance could only question children about holes in the wall paper, or have them describe natural objects. The extreme of lecturing by the teacher tended to emphasize the teacher's knowledge, and made for the development of academic subject-matter in courses for training teachers.

With Pestalozzi himself, oral instruction usually took the form of concert recitation, the children repeating after him a series of statements. This was perhaps the poorest form that the oral instruction assumed, inasmuch as it involved neither useful knowledge in the teacher nor active thought by the children, but merely imitative shouting.

The second large influence of oral objective teaching was to give children training in oral speech, sometimes oral composition. In *Leonard and Gertrude,* the latter was in no haste for the children to "learn to read and write. But she took pains to teach them early how to speak; for, as she said, 'Of what use is it for a person to know how to read and write, if he cannot speak? since reading and writing are only an artificial sort of speech.'" Thus the aim of teaching children to speak was an important element in Pestalozzian object-teaching. While there were many crudities in Pestalozzi's methods of language training, the following valuable points characterized the methods as developed by his more intelligent followers: (1) the child should have clear ideas to be expressed, these to be based on real experiences; (2) his vocabulary should be systematically enlarged in expressing these ideas; (3) he should be trained to keep in mind an increasing series of ideas and express them in order.

Good examples of this training in expression based on observation are to be found in the reports on Prussian Pestalozzian schools. In that of Calvin E. Stowe (1839) a number of concrete cases are given in the form of descriptions of lessons which he observed in his travels in Prussia. One of these descriptions concerning children from six to eight years of age stated that,

for six months or a year, the children are taught to study things, to use their own powers of observation, and speak with readiness and accuracy, before books are put into their hands at all. A few specimens will make the nature and utility of this mode of teaching obvious.

In a school in Berlin, a boy has assigned him for a lesson a description of the remarkable objects in certain directions from the school house, which is situated in Little Cathedral street. He proceeds as follows:

When I come out of the school-house into Little Cathedral street, and turn to the right, I soon pass on my left hand the Maria Place, the Gymnasium and the Anklam Gate. When I come out of Little Cathedral street, etc.

Horace Mann also described such lessons as he had observed them in Prussia and commented on their value for training in speaking, at the same time contrasting with them in a very unfavorable light the mechanical methods which prevailed in American schools. He said,

Again, the method I have described necessarily leads to conversation, and conversation with an intelligent teacher secures several important objects. It communicates information. It brightens ideas before only dimly apprehended. It addresses itself to the various faculties of the mind, so that no one of them ever tires or is cloyed. It teaches the child to use language, to frame sentences, to select words which convey his whole meaning, to avoid those which convey either more or less than he intends to express; in fine, it teaches him to seek for thoughts upon a subject, and then to find appropriate language in which to clothe them.

An American example of these Pestalozzian objective-language methods, taken from the *Oswego Methods* of 1862, is the following for children 9 to 10 years of age:

The children were to give any term which may be used in describing a face, and the teacher wrote them on the board as mentioned. They gave *pretty, homely, white, rosy, freckled, wrinkled, blushing, happy, bashful, sad, pale, cheerful, thin, sorrowful, sour, ugly.*

When a sufficient number of words had been written upon the board, the teacher called up a pupil to mark each word that may be used to describe one face. The first pupil marked words making the following description: "Happy, thin, wrinkled, pleasant, pale, pretty, white, cheerful face," etc.

*Transition from systematic object-teaching to natural science.*—The object-teaching described so far has been of a rather informal nature, the teacher utilizing the common objects in the children's immediate environment to enlarge their knowledge and train them in a command of language. In some cases, however, the object-teaching was highly systematized and collections of materials used in physics, chemistry, mineralogy, botany, and zoölogy were placed before the children, who were required to learn to describe them in scientific terms. This was characteristic of the Oswego lessons as described by the investigating committee in 1862. Systematic training for children from 6 to 8 was provided in assorting and naming the colors of yarns and colored cards. In the next highest class (9-10) children were taught the scientific nomenclature of colors, to classify them as primary, secondary, and tertiary. Older children were taught the sensory qualities of certain chemicals as in the following lesson intended to teach children to distinguish acids from alkalies.

A class of boys and girls were arranged upon the stage so that they could observe the vials of liquids and solids upon the table in the center. . . . . The children were each given some cream of tartar to taste; they pronounced the taste *sour.* The name of the substance was written on the blackboard. Then they were given some sal soda to taste, and they said it tasted "bitter and burning." The name of this was written on another part of the board. The teacher then told the children that we called those substances which taste sour *acids,* and wrote the word *acids* over cream of tartar. She then told them that the name for those substances which have a "bitter, burning taste," is *alkalies*. This word was written over sal soda. Then the children were given some vinegar to taste, etc.

These Oswego examples were considered by some as lessons in elementary science because they used some of the materials of the natural sciences and introduced their nomenclature and classifications. But the phrase "object-teaching" was the name by which this work was ordinarily known, the phrase "nature-study" coming into general use later.

As a consequence of the general attention attracted by the Oswego experiment, "object-teaching" became the great topic of discussion at teachers' meetings during the sixties. The *Proceedings of the National Teachers' Association* for this decade show the same interest in object-teaching as is manifested today in industrial education or variation of instruction to meet individual needs. The consideration of oral instruction was generally linked with object-teaching and the values and dangers of the various methods of oral instruction were argued pro and con.

The transition from object-teaching to elementary science or nature-study, taught by oral methods, appears clearly in the development of the curriculum in the St. Louis schools about 1870. William T. Harris, later United States Commissioner of Education, was then superintendent in St. Louis, and his reports contain complete statements of the character and justification of his innovations. While a conservative innovator, Superintendent Harris was thoroughly in touch with European educational thought and practice. and under his management the St. Louis schools proved the practical possibilities and values of many innovations which other cities introduced many years later.

The transition mentioned above was concisely stated by Superintendent Harris in his report for 1870-71 as follows:

For several years "object lessons" have been used to some extent by our teachers. Last year oral lessons in physiology were given in all the grades. Upon the adoption of the course of study in Natural Science these lessons have been confined to the hour given to that course and brought in as one of the means of giving zest and interest.

Mr. Harris said that in previous reports he had argued at length for the fundamental subjects, reading, writing, arithmetic, and geography as more important than any of the new "special subjects" demanding admission to the curriculum, but that this year he had to report and justify the introduction of natural science. The social justification stated was "the importance of natural science as furnishing the theoretical basis of productive industry and the consequent elevation of the masses of all the people by means of the wealth created thereby."

The difference between "object-teaching" and "natural science" seemed to be in the degree of classification. Science was conceived "as completely classified knowledge," hence the important thing in instruction was to see that the children learned the classifications. The "syllabus of lessons in natural science" was most formidable, embracing almost everything in "nature inorganic"—mathematics, physics, chemistry, astronomy; and "nature organic"—botany, zoölogy, physiology. The technical phrases of these sciences were to be introduced, though not so rapidly as to burden the pupils. Good "types" or representative examples of the general classes were to be studied. The objective method was ordered in these words:

> Every lesson should be given in such a way as to draw out the perceptive powers of the pupil by leading him to reflect on what he sees or to analyse the object before him. It is at first thought strange—although it is true—that powers of observation are to be strengthened only by teaching the pupil to *think* upon what he sees.

Analysis, classification, and cause and effect were emphasized.

The values of oral instruction not only for the pupil but also in developing the teacher were emphasized by Mr. Harris. He said,

> It seems to me this phase of the subject—its value to the teacher—is worth quite as much as the immediate value of these lessons to the pupil. . . . . The teacher is led to study and thoroughly prepare herself, and then in [the] lesson, she is led to probe in a freer manner than ordinary, the miscellaneous fund of experience possessed by the individuals of her class; thus she cannot fail to find herself getting more and more emancipated from the slavish use of the text book and able to stand before her class with a consciousness of her strength and ability to draw out the resources of each and all her pupils and combine the same into one result.

The extensive influence of Pestalozzian objective teaching on oral instruction and the study of natural objects has been shown by this brief discussion. The influence on the teaching of geography was described in recent numbers of the *Elementary School Teacher*. The influence on the teaching of arithmetic was probably greater than on any other subject, resulting in the great vogue of "mental" or "intellectual arithmetic" in the nineteenth century. This was the first phase of Pestalozzianism to secure a strong hold on American schools, through the general adoption of Warren Colburn's *First Lessons* published in 1821. Nearly all of the important improvements in American elementary-school methods between 1820 and 1870 were Pestalozzian in their origin.

# EDITORIAL NOTES

The paper which Mr. Johnson published in the October number of the *Elementary School Teacher* has attracted the attention of many school superintendents. Material of the type which Mr. Johnson there brought together exists in the records of every school system. This material needs only to be promulgated in tables and graphs to become a very important factor in the supervision of the school system.

Every supervisor recognizes the necessity of defending his judgments of the efficiency or inefficiency of a school or teacher by facts which cannot be treated as purely matters of opinion.

When it is shown that a student in an elementary school has been prepared to carry on efficiently the work of a higher school there is no longer ground for argument with regard to the efficiency of the lower school, at least within that sphere of its activity.

When, on the other hand, a school does not qualify its students to go forward with their later studies, there must be some defect in the lower school which ought to be remedied. Mr. Johnson's article is an example which undoubtedly will be widely imitated by supervisors who are preparing to subject their systems to a careful study.

There may be at first a prejudice against the kind of comparison which is there illustrated. Teachers are sometimes afraid to have their work subjected to this kind of study. It will very shortly be seen, even by those who are now timid and skeptical, that such a frank and objective statement of results is of very great advantage even to the teacher or school which is subjected to adverse criticism as a result of the investigation.

It is possible to correct faults only when these faults are clearly recognized. When one has no means of comparing the work which he does day by day with the work done by others engaged in the same type of educational work, there is likely to be a great deal of indefiniteness in the standards set up. This indefiniteness of standard leads to a great variety of unfortunate consequences. The teacher is uncertain even though she may do good work. Some investigation of the type illustrated in Mr. Johnson's paper would relieve the uncertainty of such a situation. On the other hand, it would stimulate many a teacher, who is not aware of defects, to improve and eliminate these defects.

A second very great virtue of such investigations is that they leave behind a permanent record which records in writing the history of any school or any school system.

A new official coming to a school system usually goes through a period of readjustment on his own part and on the part of the schools, which is very expensive to the system as a whole. He finds it impossible to compare a school which he is disposed to criticize, with its own history, since he has no statement of this history. He is very likely, therefore, to make the mistake of attempting to reform a school which is at the present moment on the road to improvement.

He has, on the other hand, no means of determining when a school is gradually deteriorating. The biologists long ago learned the lesson that exact measurements and records form the only means of studying changes in animal organisms. All groups of animals are gradually modifying their characteristics, and we overlook these changes because we do not have some record of the immediately preceding generation. The biologists have, therefore, begun to take careful measurements of each succeeding generation for the purpose of detecting changes. When they find a progressive change going forward, they have one of the most important facts in their science. We should have the same kind of material in education. A school which is bad in its discipline, but is rapidly improving, is, on the whole, in much better condition than a school which is fairly good in its discipline, but is gradually deteriorating.

Finally, objective material of this type, if clearly presented, would answer many of the criticisms made by business men and others who are at the present time very doubtful with regard to the efficiency of our schools. One of the reasons why the school work of the present day is regarded by laymen as inefficient is to be found in the fact that there is no measurement of the efficiency of this work. When an opinion gains circulation that a certain school is efficient or inefficient, that opinion cannot be met by educators with any facts which would either sustain or overthrow the opinion. The best that the educational expert can do in most cases is to assert his own opinion, and reiterate this opinion in opposition to the criticism of the community. An exchange of opinions of this sort between educational experts and the community aways results in the defeat of the single expert. If, on the other hand, the expert could present facts which would appeal to the community and would make clear the efficiency of the school, without reference to his own opinions, support for the schools and respect for their work would increase in very large measure.

# BOOK REVIEWS

*The Body and Its Defences.* By LUTHER HALSEY GULICK AND FRANCES GULICK JEWETT. Boston: Ginn & Co., 1910. Pp. vii+342. 65 cents.

The Gulick Hygiene Series has been opportune and effective in giving a wholesome turn to this aspect of elementary school work. The two-book series is now completed with the subject of this review. This book is elementary physiology and hygiene combined, but combined in such a way that both are constantly presented. The ordinary topics of the physiologies—bones, muscles, circulation, etc.—are fully treated, but their structure and proper use are constantly made parts of the same discussion.

Photographic illustrations and text examples, both abundant in number, are taken largely from the activities of the home, playground, and industries in which boys and girls are interested. Almost all the text cuts are free from the mass of confusing details sometimes found in elementary physiologies.

The text is direct and simple. Terms that may be new to children are given in a glossary and key to pronunciation. The anecdote method of discussion is used so constantly that the book is well calculated to prove an interesting reader for the pupil.

Effects of alcohol upon the various parts of the body receive attention out of all proportion to that given to other related injurious substances. This doubtless is done in order to meet certain uneducational though worthily conceived laws which relate to this one phase of temperance education. With the statutes as they are in some of the states, probably this phase of the book necessarily is what it is, and it should be said that no one has handled the subject in a better way.

The book and the others of the two sets constitute an excellent series and if faithfully used should help greatly in raising the efficiency of a subject which has often fallen short of its possibilities.

O. W. C.

# CURRENT EDUCATIONAL LITERATURE IN THE PERIODICALS[1]

IRENE WARREN
Librarian, School of Education, The University of Chicago

AYRES, LEONARD P. The John F. Slater Fund for the education of freedmen. Journ. of Educa. 72:229–30. (15 S. '10.)

BAGLEY, W. C. The scientific method in educational research. Nat. Study R. 6:172–78. (S. '10.)

BAILEY, H. T. Reasons for teaching drawing. School Arts Book 10:19–27. (S. '10.)

BLAYNEY, T. L. The history of art as a college discipline. Educa. 31:21–31. (S. '10.)

BROWN, J. F. Impressions of the German system of training teachers for the higher schools. School R. 18:471–80. (S. '10.)

BURSTALL, SARA A. Variant types of curricula in secondary schools. School W. 12:323–25. (S. '10.)

CALDWELL, O. W. Natural history in the grades: Sixth grade (6.) El. School T. 11:1–7. (S. '10.)

CHARLES, FRED L. Certain proposed lines of advance in agricultural nature study. School and Home Educa. 30:13–17. (S. '10.)

Children's lives sacrificed to ignorance. Lit. Digest 41:380. (10 S. '10.)

CLOYD, D. E. Student organization in city high schools. Educa. 31:17–20. (S. '10.)

COOK, JOHN W. History of Education (2). School and Home Educa. 30:9–13. (S. '10.)

———. Some of the effects of music in the public schools. School and Home Educa. 30:17–21. (S. '10.)

DAVIS, B. M. Agricultural education: educational periodicals. El. School T. 11:15–23. (S. '10.)

DEARBORN, W. F. Experiments in learning. Journ. of Educa. Psychol. 1:373–88. (S. '10.)

[1] *Abbreviations.*—Educa., Education; Educa. R., Educational Review; El. School T., Elementary School Teacher; Journ. of Educa., Journal of Education; Journ. of Educa. Psychol., Journal of Educational Psychology; Kind. R., Kindergarten Review; Lib. Journ., Library Journal; Lit. Digest, Literary Digest; Nat. Study R., Nature Study Review; R. of Rs., Review of Reviews; School and Home Educa., School and Home Education; School R., School Review; School W., School World; Sci. Amer., Scientific American.

VOLUME XI NUMBER 4

THE ELEMENTARY SCHOOL TEACHER

DECEMBER, 1910

# A COMPARATIVE STUDY OF THE GRADES OF THE PUPILS FROM THE DIFFERENT WARD SCHOOLS BASED UPON THE FIRST YEAR IN HIGH SCHOOL

H. L. MILLER
Principal of the High School, Kansas City, Kansas

The investigation which is described in part in this paper was undertaken for the purpose of presenting to the principals and teachers of the elementary school an impersonal statement of the position which the pupils promoted from the different ward schools occupied in the high school. The record of some pupil—very good, or very poor—has not infrequently given currency to a general impression of the efficiency of a particular center in the elementary school. The method pursued in this study was intended to correct any such traditional and inadequate conceptions as might grow up by chance remarks, by a careful analysis which would portray the facts with reference to all the pupils of a given center. A comparative account of the grades of the pupils who entered the high school in September, 1909, was prepared. At the close of the first semester, 190 pupils from an entering class of 230 were in school, and it was the record of these pupils which formed the basis of this study. (The practice in Kansas City is to promote pupils twice a year. The class entering in January, 1910, was studied in the same manner. Approximately 20 ward schools carry the work of the entire course of the elementary school.)

The material was arranged so that the results could be exhibited graphically. In order that comparisons might be easily made, tables and diagrams were provided for each principal. Each diagram contains a series of three graphic representations of the grades in English, algebra, and Latin respectively. English and algebra are prescribed for all pupils the first year in high school. Of this class 70 per cent chose Latin. These three subjects are used in presenting this study. Four grades are employed in ranking pupils. They are the Arabic numerals 1, 2, 3, and 4; 3 is the lowest passing mark; 4 is a failure. The abscissal line in each diagram is divided into four parts, each part representing a grade. The first in order is the highest grade given. The number of pupils receiving the respective grades is tabulated below the grades in the diagrams, and following this tabulation there will be found the percentage of grades. The percentage of grades, i.e., the 1's, 2's, 3's, and 4's, is represented on the ordinate lines. For example, in Diagram I, in English, 61 pupils received a grade of 1; 70, a grade of 2; 26, a grade of 3; and 25, a grade of 4. Reducing to a percentage basis, we have 34 per cent, 38 per cent, 14 per cent, and 13 per cent respectively. These facts are exhibited graphically under the subject of English.

The general averages for the 190 pupils who finished the first semester (18 weeks) of high-school work are presented in Diagram I. This diagram is the basis of comparison in each of the following cases. Incidentally, this diagram was the occasion for a productive line of discussion among the teachers of the high school. The percentage of failures in English and algebra, the character of the curve in algebra, the large number of 1's in English as contrasted with the 1's in algebra, the ability of the pupils who take Latin were topics suggested and discussed. Are pupils better prepared to take up English than algebra? Is algebra a suitable subject for first-year mathematics in the high school? What is the relation between the Latin and English work? Who are the failures, i.e., do pupils fail in one, two, or more subjects, or is there any correspondence existing between failures in English and Latin? These and similar questions were raised, and there were evidences of a desire to approach the study of the problems presented in a scientific manner. Any hasty verbal statement of explanation was challenged at once. Many of the same questions were raised by the principals and teachers of the elementary school. Is there any evidence of poor work in arithmetic in the grades from the report in algebra in the high school? was a question discussed with enthusiasm. The main line of interest, however, centered around the comparative study of the respective ward schools.

Diagrams II–VII inclusive represent six of the ward schools and illustrate the method of comparison which was adopted in this study. The grades of the pupils from the different ele-

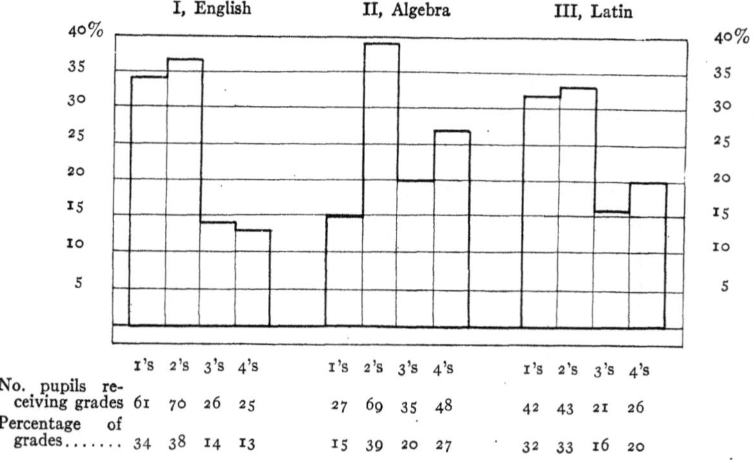


| | I, English | | | | II, Algebra | | | | III, Latin | | | |
|---|---|---|---|---|---|---|---|---|---|---|---|---|
| | 1's | 2's | 3's | 4's | 1's | 2's | 3's | 4's | 1's | 2's | 3's | 4's |
| No. pupils receiving grades | 61 | 70 | 26 | 25 | 27 | 69 | 35 | 48 | 42 | 43 | 21 | 26 |
| Percentage of grades....... | 34 | 38 | 14 | 13 | 15 | 39 | 20 | 27 | 32 | 33 | 16 | 20 |

DIAGRAM I.—Freshman class, 190 pupils of the 230 who entered September 1909, High School, Kansas City, Kan.

mentary-school centers are graphically exhibited in the three subjects pursued in the first year of the high school. In each instance, the number of pupils who entered from the particular ward school is given. The tables are made up for those who remained in the high school one-half year. Diagram II indicates that the pupils from Ward School A rank with the average of the Freshman class with a high degree of consistency. In algebra, there is a striking similarity. The failures are practically the same in all three subjects.

Diagram III presents marked deviations from II. The pupils did remarkably well in English. This fact suggested that the

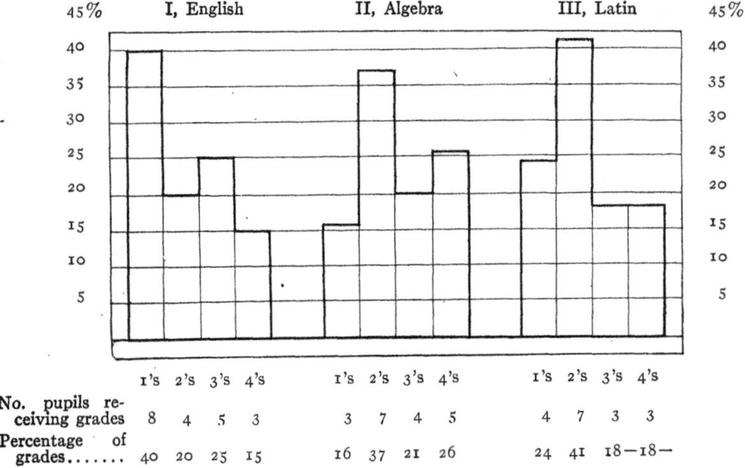


| | I, English 1's | 2's | 3's | 4's | II, Algebra 1's | 2's | 3's | 4's | III, Latin 1's | 2's | 3's | 4's |
|---|---|---|---|---|---|---|---|---|---|---|---|---|
| No. pupils receiving grades | 8 | 4 | 5 | 3 | 3 | 7 | 4 | 5 | 4 | 7 | 3 | 3 |
| Percentage of grades....... | 40 | 20 | 25 | 15 | 16 | 37 | 21 | 26 | 24 | 41 | 18— | 18— |

DIAGRAM 2.—Freshman class, 19 pupils of the 23 who entered from Ward School A.

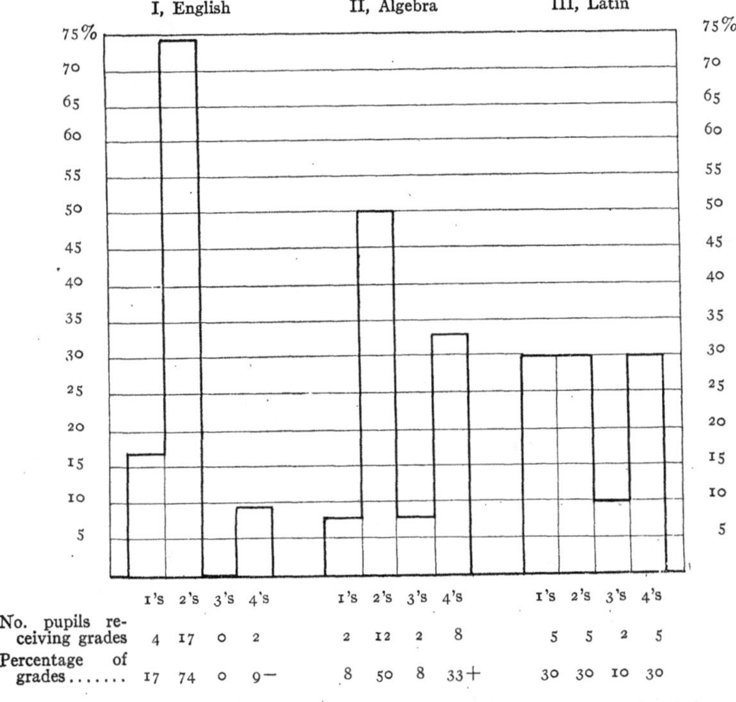


| | I, English 1's | 2's | 3's | 4's | II, Algebra 1's | 2's | 3's | 4's | III, Latin 1's | 2's | 3's | 4's |
|---|---|---|---|---|---|---|---|---|---|---|---|---|
| No. pupils receiving grades | 4 | 17 | 0 | 2 | 2 | 12 | 2 | 8 | 5 | 5 | 2 | 5 |
| Percentage of grades....... | 17 | 74 | 0 | 9— | 8 | 50 | 8 | 33+ | 30 | 30 | 10 | 30 |

DIAGRAM 3.—Freshman class, 24 pupils of the 28 who entered from Ward School B.

language work in this center was strong. An examination of the grades in algebra and Latin would indicate that School B sends to the high school two classes of pupils—one group fairly good and the other not thoroughly prepared to take up the advanced grade of work. The lowest passing grade, 3, has a low percentage and marks clearly the dividing line between the two groups from this ward school.

Diagram IV indicates that the pupils from School C maintained a standing above the average, especially in English and Latin. In algebra 65 per cent of the grades fall within the high

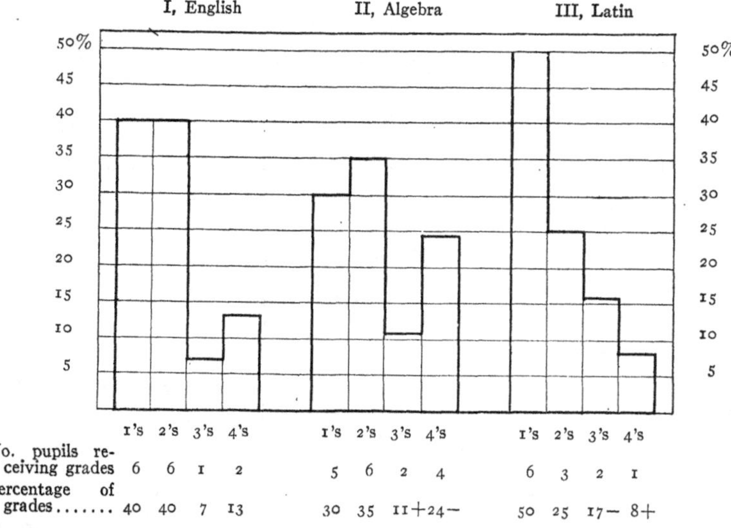


DIAGRAM 4.—Freshman class, 17 pupils of the 19 who entered from Ward School C.

grades, 1's and 2's. This school is located in a district where it would be expected that a better grade of pupils would be found than in B.

Diagram V represents a school still more favorably situated. The record in English is high. No low grades are recorded against these pupils. There is a low percentage of failure in algebra and none in Latin. In all cases where a splendid showing of this character was made, there were clear indications of self-congratulations upon the excellent work the teachers of these ward buildings were doing.

Diagram VI stands in sharp contrast. There were no grades in any subjects in the highest order. The percentages of failures were high. The number dropped out during the term was 6 out of an enrolment of 16. The condition of this school can be accounted for in part from the location. The community is made up of a large number of people who work at manual

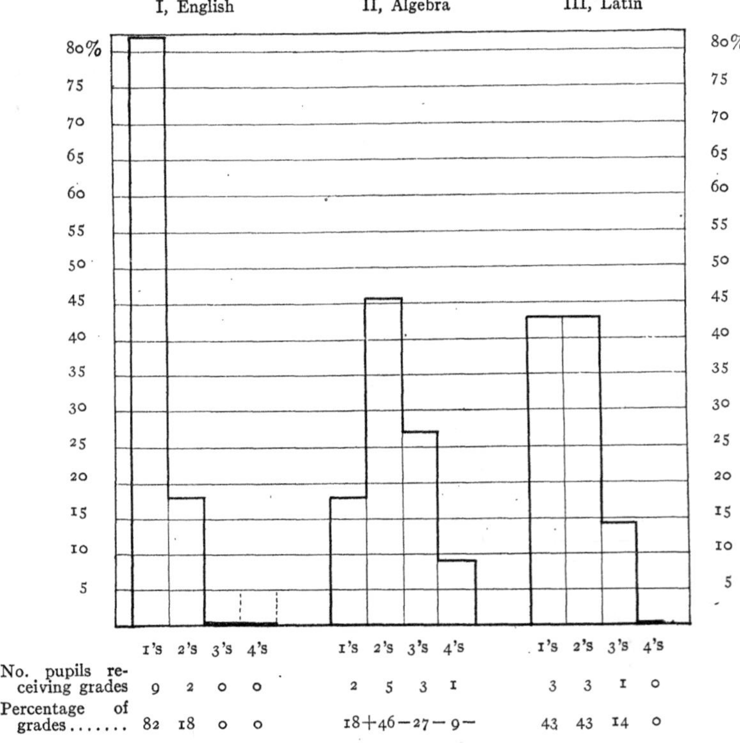


DIAGRAM 5.—Freshman class, 11 pupils of the 11 who entered from Ward School D.

labor. The foreign element predominates. The principal and teachers of this ward school did not resent a showing of this kind. They felt that it was complimentary that as many pupils as there were made the effort to attend high school.

Diagram VII suggests that there was a selection of pupils taking Latin. In fact, a careful analysis of any curve raises numerous questions relating to the efficiency of the elementary school, the selection of studies in the high school, and the standards in both the elementary and high schools in the different subjects.

Diagram VIII is given for the purpose of indicating the fallacy of mere verbal statement in the attempt to account for school conditions. This school was located outside the city limits when this study was made. There were 5 pupils who entered high school and remained throughout the year. This

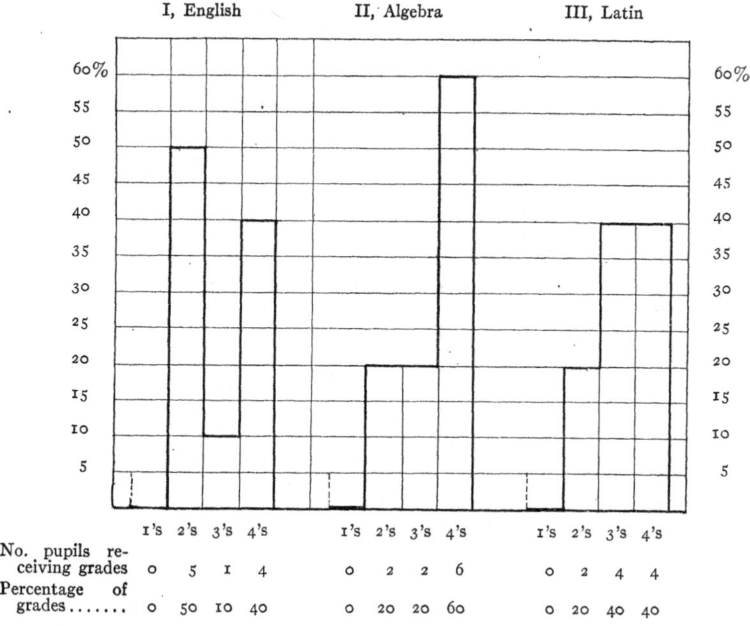


DIAGRAM 6.—Freshman class, 10 pupils of the 16 who entered from Ward School E.

remarkable showing is exhibited graphically. No 3's or failures were found. There is a preponderance of 1's in all the subjects. There was another school similarly situated which made exactly the opposite showing. A large percentage dropped out of high school; those who remained made low grades; and in two subjects there was 100 per cent of failures. To set up the claim that the latter school made a poor record because there was no supervision, such as the city afforded its elementary school, is a poor argument when the former school as represented in Diagram VIII is under consideration. The conditions were the same in respect to lack of close supervision. It is not clear which of these two schools is to be regarded as the exception. A further analysis of these schools was at once suggested.

The statement is often made in teachers' meetings that pupils from the rural schools and other towns do or do not rank favorably with the pupils promoted directly from the elementary

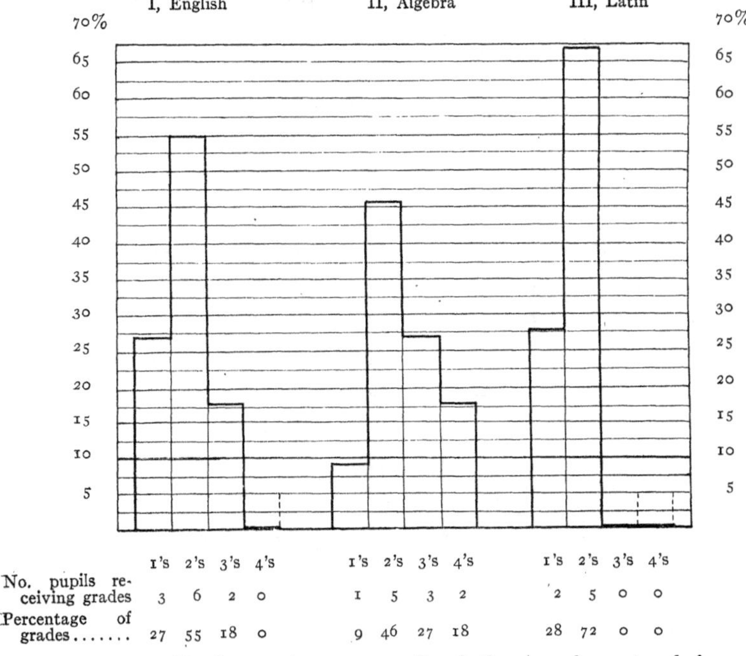


| | I's | 2's | 3's | 4's | I's | 2's | 3's | 4's | I's | 2's | 3's | 4's |
|---|---|---|---|---|---|---|---|---|---|---|---|---|
| No. pupils receiving grades | 3 | 6 | 2 | 0 | 1 | 5 | 3 | 2 | 2 | 5 | 0 | 0 |
| Percentage of grades....... | 27 | 55 | 18 | 0 | 9 | 46 | 27 | 18 | 28 | 72 | 0 | 0 |

DIAGRAM 7.—Freshman class, 11 pupils of the 11 who entered from Ward School F.

school to the high school in a city system. Diagram IX compared with Diagram I reveals a striking similarity in many details. One of the surprising facts is the ranking of this miscellaneous group in English. Pupils from the rural schools are usually considered below the average in ability in language and above the average in ability in mathematics. When the attention of the language teachers in the high school was called to the facts as portrayed in Diagram IX, the explanation was offered that the pupils of the rural schools have a better knowl-

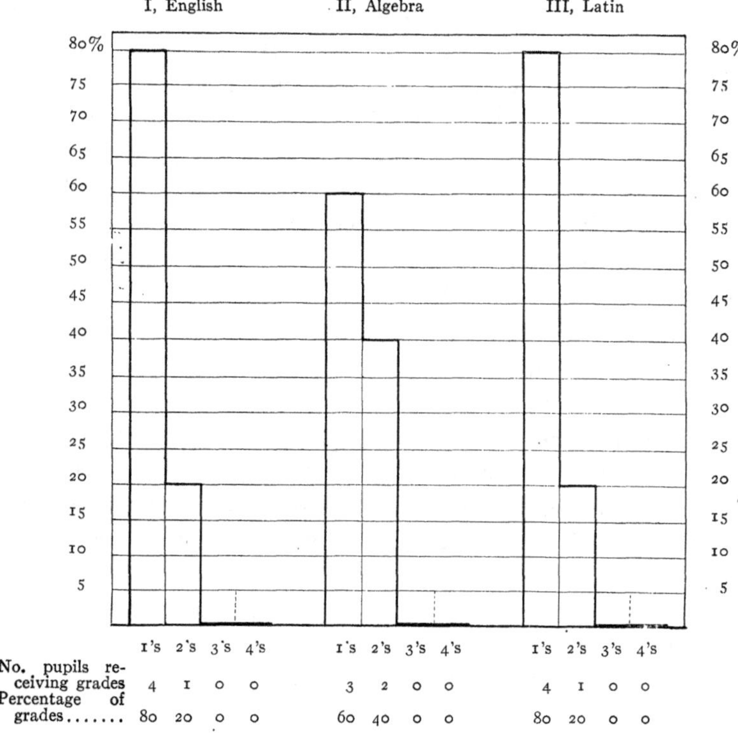


DIAGRAM 8.—Freshman class, 5 pupils who entered from Ward School G.

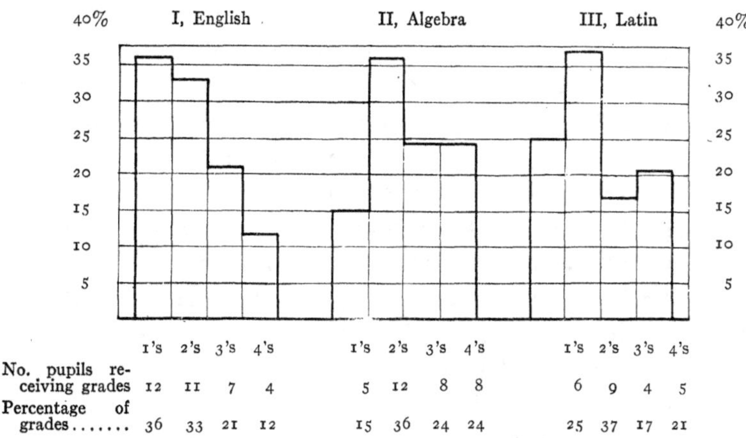


DIAGRAM 9.—Freshman class, 33 pupils of 39 who entered from rural schools and other cities.

edge of technical English grammar than the city pupils and that this fact enabled them to keep step with the pupils of the city who might have a more varied training in the classics.

No attempt has been made in this presentation to exhaust the discussion which these simple graphic representations aroused. Only a few characteristic curves have been reproduced in this paper. The method it is hoped has been adequately suggested in the meager discussion of a few typical examples. It should be remembered that this type of investigation and report proved quite as stimulating to high-school teachers as to the elementary teachers and principals. The effect of such an impartial presentation of the facts was on the whole very satisfactory. The professional spirit in which the principals of the ward schools received the report gave evidence of the value of this kind of study of elementary-school problems. It is believed that comparisons of this character each year will tend to establish a scientific attitude in the administration of school systems. Instead of relying upon chance remarks here and there concerning the efficiency of a ward school, the method suggested in this study enables principals to make accurate comparisons, and by filing each year a convenient graphic report of this sort there would be no difficulty in determining the position which the various ward schools maintain in the high school. Fluctuations from term to term could be investigated more intelligently in the light of such facts. This is a concrete illustration of the use which can be made of office records in stimulating a productive type of study of school problems. Moreover records reduced to the form suggested in this paper afford a convenient means of reference and comparison from year to year within the high school itself. It is not improbable that the character of the graph would be modified materially on account of the personnel of the teaching corps or changes in the course of study. Teachers and principals of the elementary school are encouraged to study the work of the high school quite as freely as their work is studied by the high-school teacher. Such impersonal methods as suggested above may become the means of stimulating investigation of problems of mutual interest in our school systems.

# MEASUREMENT OF GROWTH AND EFFICIENCY IN ARITHMETIC (*Continued*)

## A YEAR'S PROGRESS

S. A. COURTIS
Home and Day School, Detroit

In a previous article[1] the writer described an attempt made by the Detroit Home and Day School, a private school for girls, to measure the growth of ability in arithmetic through the school by giving the "Stone" tests under identical conditions to every grade from the third to the thirteenth inclusive. Although the experiment was largely a product of chance conditions, the knowledge gained, both of the condition of arithmetic in the school and of the possibilities of the method, seemed to warrant a further experimental study of the same problem by the same means. After due consideration of the various tempting lines of investigation opened, it was decided to try to measure the change produced by a year's regular work under existing conditions in order to have some standard by which to measure the effect of future changes in method. Accordingly, new tests were devised and given at the beginning of the school year, September, 1909, and again at its close, June, 1910. The present article, therefore, will be a brief summary of the results obtained together with some account of the development of the method. As far as possible repetition of previous conclusions will be avoided, and the discussion limited to points of general interest.

In planning the work for the year, the first point to be settled was the scope of the tests themselves. From the work of the previous year it was evident that, as Dr. Stone concludes, ability in arithmetic is no simple thing, but a complex of many separate abilities, and as there was little evidence of transfer from one to another, it seemed necessary to test for

[1] *Elementary School Teacher,* X (No. 4), 177.

each of the separate elements as well as for the general complex. A preliminary study of the specific abilities involved in the Stone tests revealed such a bewildering array that it was decided to limit the new work strictly to the four operations with whole numbers. The specific elements of such work from the standpoint of the classroom were judged to be (1) ability to give a ready response in the case of any of the elementary combinations in the four operations, (2) ability to recognize a situation in a problem as calling for the use of a certain operation, (3) ability to borrow and carry, and (4) the ability to copy correctly the figures of a given example or problem. Accordingly provision was made for the testing of each of these as well as the general abilities involved in working abstract examples and concrete problems.

To test the first ability, four speed tests were devised, one for each operation, consisting of the 81 fundamental combinations (zero combinations omitted), so arranged that the results only were to be written by the children. Fig. 1 shows a part of

SPEED TEST—Addition

Write on this paper as many answers to these simple addition examples as you can in the time allowed.

| 5 | 4 | 2 | 4 | 2 | 2 | 9 | 1 | 2 | 1 | 6 | 7 | 1 | 5 | 1 | 7 | 1 | 2 | 8 | 8 | 3 | 1 | 4 |
|---|---|---|---|---|---|---|---|---|---|---|---|---|---|---|---|---|---|---|---|---|---|---|
| 7 | 7 | 6 | 4 | 7 | 9 | 9 | 2 | 3 | 8 | 8 | 7 | 4 | 6 | 6 | 8 | 5 | 3 | 8 | 9 | 5 | 3 | 9 |

Fig. 1

the test in addition. These tests will be known hereafter as Speed Tests, Fundamentals. Emphasis was put upon "speed," because the thing to be tested was *readiness* of response. From the fourth grade on every child, if allowed sufficient time, could give the correct answer to every one of the problems in the four tests. Nevertheless, individual children and adults have been found to differ widely in the number of answers written in a given time. The tests measure, therefore, not only *what* is known but *how well* it is known. The time allowance set for these tests was 90 seconds.

In the construction of the tests no attention was paid to the question of the relative difficulty of the combinations, or to that of the amount of writing to be done. Consequently the tests are very uneven and the data obtained from their use unreliable. Particularly is this true of the test in subtraction, which from a score of 40 on was very much more difficult than the other tests. This fact must be remembered in considering the scores of the various grades shown in the graphs and tables. However, the use of the tests made evident the necessity for a very careful determination of the value of the different units in each test and the need of extreme caution in making inferences from tests whose components are selected by chance.

Similarly a speed test in reasoning was used to test the ability to recognize a situation as calling for the use of a certain operation. Part of the text is shown in Fig. 2. It consisted of a miscellaneous collection of many simple one-step problems. It will be noted that the children were not asked to work the problems, but to indicate the operation to be used by writing its name in the blank space after an example. The thing tested, however, is again a complex, the ability named being merely its arithmetical phase. Speed in this test was probably determined as much by ability to read quickly and understandingly as by control of knowledge of the operation to be used in the different situations. Here, too, the varying

ARITHMETIC TEST—Reasoning—Speed Test

Do not work the following examples. Read each example through, make up your mind what operation you would use if you were going to work it, then write "add," "subtract," "multiply," or "divide," as the case may be, in the blank space after the example.

1. A pile of fruit contained 89 apples; 27 apples were added to it. How many apples were there in the pile then? .............

2. A girl who had 17 dolls gave away three. How many had she left? ................

3. A thermometer rose 27 degrees in the morning and five times as much in the afternoon. How many degrees did it rise in the afternoon? ..........

4. A man worth $60,000 divided his property equally among his 7 children. How much did each one receive? ...............

Fig. 2

length of the problems gave units of varying value. The time allowance for this test was two minutes.

The name given to the third ability needs discussion as well as the method by which it was tested. The child is learning to "borrow and carry" all through the 2d, 3d, and 4th grades at least, but a little consideration will show that the ability thus named is not the same in the four operations. In subtraction the number borrowed or carried is always 1, and the procedure is comparatively simple. In addition the number carried varies from 0 to 9 and must be retained a longer time. In multiplication the situation is still more complex owing to the larger numbers involved, the additions that must be performed, and the greater time interval during which the number carried must be retained. Division, the combination of all the other operations, has the difficulties of all, and the added strain due to the constantly varying procedure. There is a common element throughout—the memory factor—but there may well be four abilities instead of one. However, the term "borrowing and carrying" will be used of all as expressing roughly the significance of what is tested in every case.

Provision was made for the testing of this ability by so choosing the figures of the first four examples of the test on Fundamentals (see Fig. 3), that no borrowing or carrying was required. In a comparison of the scores for the first four examples with those for the remaining examples, the increase in the number of mistakes per example is due partly, if not almost wholly, to the effect of this factor. The effect is twofold: actual mistakes in borrowing and carrying may occur or there may be an increase in the mistakes in the combinations used, due to the added strain. Here, however, as in all the tests, the results are not wholly reliable because of the inequalities in the units of which the test is composed.

The ability to copy the figures of the examples and problems correctly was also tested indirectly. A blank piece of paper was supplied, and the instructions directed that examples and problems be copied and worked on this paper. Mistakes in copying were then detected in the scoring.

In addition to these special tests, the two from the previous year were retained but were limited to the four operations (Figs. 3 and 4). In the test on Fundamentals it will be

ARITHMETIC TEST—Fundamentals

Copy the following examples on the sheet of blank paper and work as many as you can in the time allowed. Work them in order, and put down on the paper you hand in all the work you do not do in your head.

1. Add: a. 2, 3, 4, 1 b. 234, 851

2. Subtract: 898456, 297125

3. Multiply 231322 by 3.

4. Divide 1243284 by 4.

5. Add: a. 37, 76, 89 b. 276, 749

6. Subtract: 923, 789

7. Multiply 89 by 37.

8. Divide 85666 by 29.

9. Add: a. 345, 684, 983, 27, 405 b. 695797, 6926895

10. Subtract: 8749367, 5639598

11. Multiply 6789 by 768.

12. Divide 706654443 by 7841.

Fig. 3

ARITHMETIC TEST—Reasoning

Work the following examples on the blank paper, putting down there all the work you do not do in your head.

1. A thermometer stood at 57 degrees at 8 o'clock in the morning. It rose 22 degrees during the morning, and fell 47 degrees during the afternoon. What was the temperature at 6 o'clock?

2. A train-boy made $7.50 on books, magazines, etc., and $8.25 on candy, fruit, etc., each day, for 7 days. What were his total earnings for the week?

3. A man had $2700 in one bank, $1650 in another. If at his death he left his money to his three sons, giving each an equal share, how much did each receive?

4. A man bought 17 old books for 75c apiece and sold them for $1.37 apiece. How much did he make?

Fig. 4

noted that the examples in addition are in two parts. The purpose of this was to test out a conclusion of the previous work, reached also by Dr. Stone, that column addition of several figures is performed as correctly as the shorter two-figure additions which are constantly occurring in multiplications. The two parts of the addition examples, as far as was possible, are composed of such numbers that the additions to be performed are the same. In the test of Reasoning the examples contained the various combinations of operations in two- three- and four-step problems. In both tests the inequalities in the units make comparison of scores of doubtful value. The time allowance for the test in Fundamentals was ten minutes; for Reasoning eight minutes.

During the year it became evident that still another component of the general ability must be tested for—the rate of motor activity in writing figures. Accordingly, after some preliminary work to determine the relative effort involved in writing the different figures, a speed test in copying figures was constructed (Fig. 5). This ability is not to be confused with

SPEED TEST—Copying Figures

Copy as many of these figures as possible in the time allowed. Write as rapidly as possible, but form the figures as carefully as in working examples:

| | | | | | | |
|---|---|---|---|---|---|---|
| 24967 | 42976 | 62947 | 72964 | 24967 | 42967 | 62974 |
| 72946 | 26974 | 46927 | 64972 | 74926 | 26947 | 46972 |
| 64927 | 74962 | 27946 | 47962 | 67924 | 76942 | 27964 |

FIG. 5

the ability mentioned above, as in this test all the elements of perception and attention, which in the former test play the major part, have been so reduced to a minimum that the thing tested is largely the rate of motor activity. The time allowance for this test was one minute.

All the tests (except the last) were given, under as nearly identical conditions as possible, both in September, during the second week of school, and in June, the week before the close. The tests were printed and a copy of each, together with the necessary blank paper, was given each child. The testing was conducted in the four assembly rooms of the school and the tests were taken by all grades from the 3d to the 13th inclusive. The same person acted as examiner in both tests (except in grades 3, 4, and 13 in June), and the same time allowances, paper, and arrangements held for all from the lowest to the highest. The papers were scored by the teachers and assistants of the mathematics department in accordance with a very definite printed system in which provision was made for the classification of every mistake. In June the scoring was done by one person.

In addition to the above, the speed tests in Fundamentals and in Copying Figures were given in the classrooms by the teachers of the various grades from 4–9 inclusive at intervals during the year—at the end of the first six weeks, before and after the Christmas and Easter vacations, and every week during the last ten weeks of school. The schedule of the tests and the dates at which they were taken was not the same for all grades, but more detailed information on these points can be had, where necessary, from the tables. At least two tests were taken in any one week and often all five.

The purpose of the test at the end of the first six weeks' work was to eliminate the effects of familiarity with the tests and of the recovery in knowledge and ability due to the first weeks of school. During these weeks no specific drill was given in the various tables other than that incidental to the regular work in arithmetic (except in grade 5), but from that time on, the first five minutes (approximately) of each lesson, (three recitations a week) were devoted to specific drill on the combinations. The results as a whole, therefore, give a more or less complete record of the effects of the different phases of school work in arithmetic upon the knowledge of the tables in the four operations.

In scoring the results a record was kept of the work attempted (Ats.) and the part right (Rts.) for each individual. In both these records each combination (figures in the copying test), and each whole example counted one point, the records for the different tests being kept separately. No credit was given for part of an example, the work of the previous year having shown that gross scores by whole examples express the relative ability of grades as well as exact scores where allowance is made for every figure, and at a great saving in time. In the speed tests in Fundamentals, although a record was kept, the results for "Rights" are not given. The errors made were so few as to be negligible. Ignorance of the combinations was shown, not by errors, but by reduction in the number attempted.

Table 1 and Figs. 6 and 7 give for each grade the average gross score in the various tests both in September and in June. A discussion of the distribution of ability within the grades will be found below. The difference between the two averages in each case, or the growth for the year, is also given.

Before taking up the discussion of these results, however, there are one or two points that need special comment.

The time set for the speed tests in Fundamentals proved awkward to control. During the year several mistakes in timing occurred which were corrected at the time either by repeating the test or by discarding the results. From other measurements made of the ability of the 9th grade in subtraction during the year, it is probable that such a mistake was made in the test for subtraction in September in the case of the assembly room of the 9th, 10th, 11th, and 12th grades. Accordingly, the results have been corrected by computing what they would have been in a minute and a half assuming that the actual time allowed was two minutes. The actual values obtained are given by the light dotted lines in the graph. In the case of the test of the 13th grade in Copying Figures, a similar mistake has probably occurred, the corrected and actual results being indicated as before. These mistakes but serve to emphasize the necessity for *identical conditions* in comparative testing where the achievement of one group is to be compared with that of another. They also make it probable that next to the construction of the tests themselves, no other factor within the

TABLE 1

SEPTEMBER AND **June** RESULTS IN ALL TESTS. GRADE AVERAGES AND GROWTHS

| Grade | Addition | | Subtraction | | Multiplication | | Division | | Copying Figures | |
|---|---|---|---|---|---|---|---|---|---|---|
| | Average | Growth | Average | Growth | Average | Growth | Average | Growth | Average | Growth |
| 3 | 12<br>**27** | **15** | 9<br>**28** | **19** | . .<br>. . | . . | . .<br>. . | . . | **57** | |
| 4 | 23<br>**39** | **16** | 19<br>**37** | **18** | 6<br>**22** | **16** | 8<br>**26** | **18** | **78** | |
| 5 | 35<br>**64** | **29** | 30<br>**54** | **24** | 24<br>**56** | **32** | 19<br>**50** | **31** | **107** | |
| 6 | 43<br>**63** | **20** | 33<br>**53** | **20** | 30<br>**47** | **17** | 26<br>**48** | **22** | **117** | |
| 7 | 53<br>**85** | **32** | 36<br>**64** | **28** | 41<br>**74** | **33** | 34<br>**70** | **36** | **113** | |
| 8 | 56<br>**84** | **28** | 42<br>**69** | **27** | 49<br>**72** | **23** | 41<br>**77** | **36** | **116** | |
| 9 | 67<br>**81** | **14** | 45 (60)<br>**54** | **9** | 56<br>**69** | **13** | 46<br>**64** | **18** | **118** | |
| 10 | 72<br>**79** | **7** | 47 (63)<br>**54** | **7** | 59<br>**69** | **10** | 52<br>**66** | **14** | **117** | |
| 11 | 76<br>**82** | **6** | 51 (69)<br>**54** | **3** | 62<br>**68** | **6** | 57<br>**63** | **6** | **116** | |
| 12 | 74<br>**79** | **5** | 50 (67)<br>**57** | **7** | 56<br>**63** | **7** | 53<br>**62** | **9** | **111** | |
| 13 | 77<br>**85** | **8** | 57<br>**62** | **5** | 59<br>**76** | **17** | 56<br>**54** | **−2** | **106**<br>**(141)** | |

| Grade | Speed Reasoning | | | | Fundamentals | | | | Reasoning | | | |
|---|---|---|---|---|---|---|---|---|---|---|---|---|
| | Ats. | | Rts. | | Ats. | | Rts. | | Ats. | | Rts. | |
| | Ave. | Gth. | Ave. | Gth. | Ave | Gth. | Ave. | Gth. | Ave. | Gth. | Ave. | Gth. |
| 3 | 2.6 | . . . | 2.4 | . . . | 1.8<br>**3.4** | **1.6** | 1.0<br>**1.6** | **0.6** | . . . | . . . | . . . | . . . |
| 4 | 5.8<br>**7.5** | **1.7** | 4.2<br>**4.7** | **0.5** | 3.6<br>**5.5** | **1.9** | 2.4<br>**4.0** | **1.6** | 1.1<br>**4.7** | **3.6** | 0.6<br>**2.6** | **2.0** |
| 5 | 8.3<br>**14.6** | **6.3** | 7.2<br>**11.1** | **3.9** | 7.0<br>**9.0** | **2.0** | 5.0<br>**6.3** | **1.3** | 4.1<br>**7.8** | **3.7** | 3.4<br>**5.2** | **1.8** |
| 6 | 9.2<br>**13.7** | **4.5** | 8.1<br>**11.5** | **3.4** | 8.2<br>**9.3** | **1.1** | 6.2<br>**6.2** | **0.0** | 6.1<br>**7.7** | **1.6** | 3.3<br>**4.3** | **1.0** |
| 7 | 9.9<br>**15.6** | **5.7** | 9.0<br>**13.7** | **4.7** | 8.9<br>**10.9** | **2.0** | 6.8<br>**9.4** | **2.6** | 7.2<br>**8.2** | **1.0** | 4.6<br>**6.3** | **1.7** |
| 8 | 12.3<br>**15.4** | **3.1** | 11.2<br>**14.2** | **3.0** | 9.9<br>**11.1** | **1.2** | 9.8<br>**9.1** | **−0.7** | 8.0<br>**8.7** | **0.7** | 6.8<br>**6.7** | **−0.1** |
| 9 | 11.4<br>**15.3** | **3.9** | 10.4<br>**13.2** | **2.8** | 10.3<br>**11.0** | **0.7** | 7.0<br>**6.8** | **−0.2** | 8.1<br>**8.8** | **0.7** | 6.2<br>**6.7** | **0.5** |
| 10 | 14.7<br>**16.5** | **1.8** | 12.6<br>**14.6** | **2.0** | 10.5<br>**11.2** | **0.7** | 7.7<br>**8.5** | **0.8** | 8.8<br>**8.9** | **0.1** | 6.5<br>**6.8** | **0.3** |
| 11 | 14.7<br>**16.7** | **2.0** | 13.3<br>**14.7** | **1.4** | 10.8<br>**11.4** | **0.6** | 8.8<br>**8.2** | **−0.6** | 9.0<br>**8.9** | **−0.1** | 6.6<br>**7.0** | **0.4** |
| 12 | 15.4<br>**16.9** | **1.4** | 14.2<br>**15.3** | **1.1** | 10.6<br>**11.2** | **0.6** | 8.1<br>**8.5** | **0.4** | 9.4<br>**9.0** | **−0.4** | 7.1<br>**7.3** | **0.2** |
| 13 | 14.0<br>**15.5** | **1.5** | 12.8<br>**13.6** | **0.8** | 10.5<br>**11.2** | **0.7** | 8.7<br>**8.6** | **−0.1** | 9.0<br>**9.1** | **0.1** | 6.9<br>**7.0** | **−0.1** |

control of the examiner is so important as the time. The tests for the next year will have a time allowance of even minutes, and some simple mechanical timing device will be adopted.

Interesting as is the record of the year's work to one whose

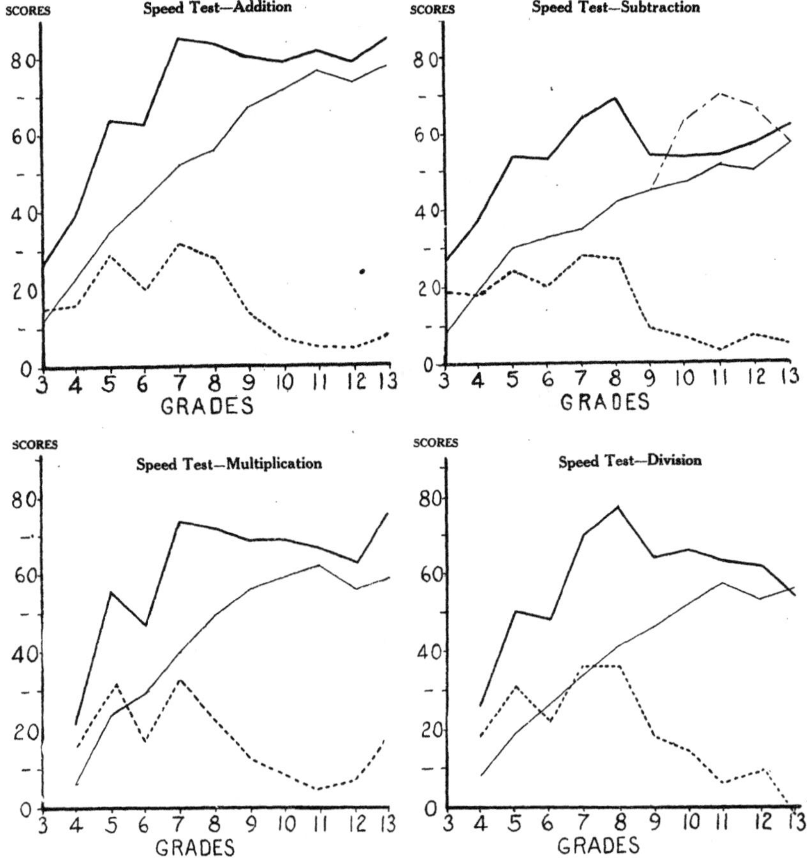


FIG. 6.—September (light lines) and June (heavy lines) grade averages and growths for the year (dotted lines) in tests of knowledge of the tables in each of the four operations.

success or failure it discloses, there is space here to discuss only the more general features. Chief among these is the confirmation of the fact shown in the previous work, that there are marked variations of ability, both of different grades in the same test and of the same grade in different tests. The differences in the amounts of growth for the year show such variations *in the making.* Compare, for instance, the growth of the 8th grade in knowledge of the fundamental combina-

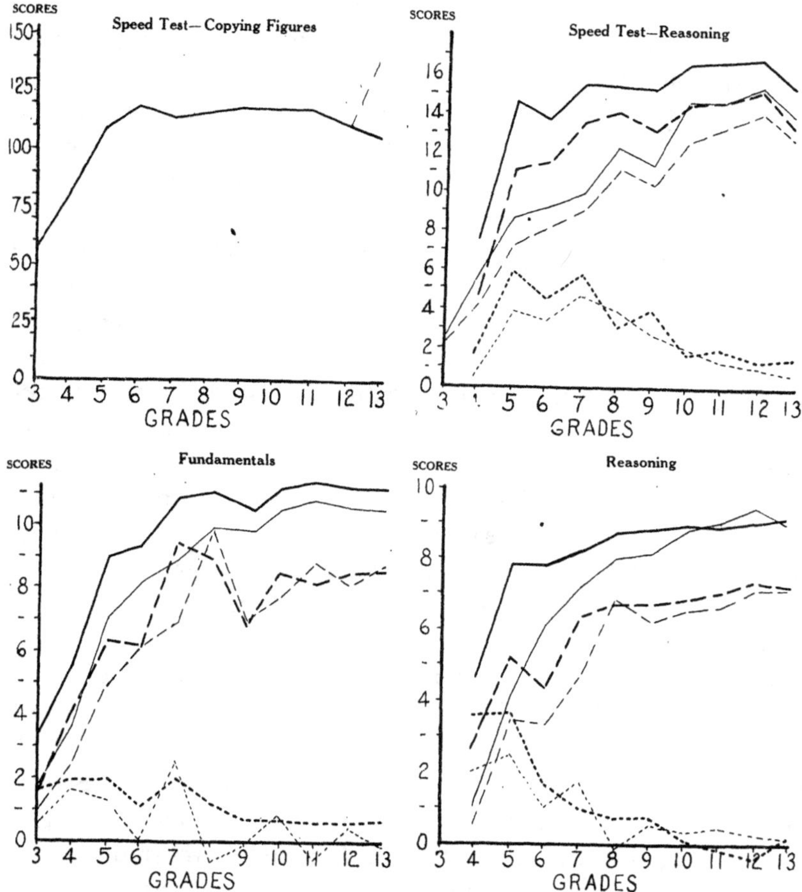


FIG. 7.—September (light lines) and June (heavy lines) grade averages and growths for the year (dotted lines) in the tests shown. The examples attempted are indicated by unbroken lines, those right by broken lines. The growths in examples attempted are shown by the heavy dotted lines, in examples right by the light dotted lines.

tions in the four operations. The absolute growths are respectively 28, 27, 23, 36. The deviations from the average are − 4 for multiplication and +9 for division, with an extreme difference between the largest and the smallest growths of 13. Translated into weeks this means that nearly six weeks' more work in multiplication and 11 weeks' less work in division was needed to give uniform growths in the four abilities. The percentages of growths are 50, 64, 47, and 88, so that relatively the results are even worse. In September the lowest score was 41 (in division), the highest 56 (in addition), a difference of 15. In June the lowest was 69 (in subtraction), the highest 84 (in addition), the difference, 15, being the same as before. From this point of view, therefore, the year's work has tended slightly to make the scores more uniform. However, it is very evident that the product of "a year's work in arithmetic" is by no means the standard article that our grade system and our courses of study sometimes assume it to be. In other words, each statistical study of educational problems but serves to emphasize the necessity for the constant use of scientific standards and measurements in the schoolroom if there is to be uniformity in the product or efficiency in the teaching effort.

So far as the variations noted above are constant with class after class at the same grade, they point to the operation of causes which ought at least to be accurately and fully determined, if not removed. The defect of the sixth grade is a case in point. This is notoriously a difficult grade. In Dr. Rice's study of the comparative abilities in arithmetic and in spelling of school children in different cities, the scores of the 6th grades are in very many cases below those of the 5th and 7th grades. In the test in arithmetic reported in Scott's *Social Education,* the same drop at the 6th grade is found. Further, the present sixth grade had a high 5th-grade standing last year, while conversely, the poor 6th of last year has made high scores in the present tests. The writer believes the cause to be physical and hopes to be able to prove it so from the data of these tests in connection with the physical measurements taken by the school. Whatever the cause, if it were known, a more efficient adjustment of time and work might be possible.

A similar cause may be operative in grades 8, 9, and 10. The low 9th of the present year was an exceptional 8th-grade class, while the present 10th grade has risen from its previous low position. Further, the present 8th grade shows symptoms of disorganization, as will be seen from the loss in accuracy both in Fundamentals and in Reasoning. The relatively large growth of the 9th grade, greater than that of any other class not studying arithmetic, may be due to a partial recovery of previous loss. So far as these apparent constant variations are really due to general causes, they are likely to affect all subjects alike, and the explanation, when found, may be of general value.

A simple explanation of the eccentric variations shown will at once occur to everyone: namely, that the results of such tests are not to be depended upon. However, repeated measurements during the year, both of grades and of individuals, make it certain that the results obtained do accurately represent the true conditions. A full discussion of this point will be found below.

During the past few years, many radical changes have been made in the methods and texts of the various courses in mathematics through the school, and the results of the testing work are of interest as measures of the effect of such changes. In general, it may be said that the June records of every grade have exceeded the September records of the next higher grade, so that unless the summer vacation causes a great loss of ability at least no harm has been done by the changes. The coming September tests will be needed before the final word can be said on this point. However, as the scores of the 7th and 8th grades in many cases largely exceed those of the high-school grades, the writer is hopeful for the future. On the other hand, it is only fair to call attention to the fact that the September record in all tests is more regular in general form than either the present, or previous, June records. It may be that there is a maximum capacity and an optimum growth for each grade, and that all work in excess of these natural limits is waste effort. The final solution of all such problems must await the cumulative evidence of similar tests through many years.

In this connection a few words must be said in regard to the tendency of the curves for all tests to approach a maximum. This is plainly shown in the graph for the speed test in Copying Figures, where the score for the 6th grade is probably not exceeded by any other grade in the school. The average age of the 6th grade is twelve years, and the general result would seem to mean that complete mastery of such motor control as is essential to speed in writing figures is acquired by this age. Opposed to this is the fact that the range of individual variation in all the classes of the school is very great, and that the range of adult variation is even greater. One thing is certain. In the little remedial work that has been done with individuals up to the present time, no difficulty has been experienced in producing marked increases in scores and no signs of any approach to an upper limit of ability have been seen. The writer believes that the present maxima merely mark the average achievement under present conditions, and that the future will see an increase of from 10 to 50 per cent in the final ability reached. The plans for the coming year include the setting of a standard score for each grade and the effort to bring all below the standard up to grade by special individual work.

The tendency of the scores in the upper grades to approach a maximum has also a bearing on the question of "transfer" of ability, a question of interest to the psychologist and educator alike. The mathematical courses beyond the 8th grade are algebra (grades 9, 10, 13) and geometry (grades 11, 13). No arithmetic is taught in the high-school years. Consequently the growth during the year in these grades is due either to (1) familiarity with the tests and the procedure, i.e., "practice effects"; (2) incidental growth in arithmetic due to its use in the courses in science and mathematics, or in daily life; (3) the effects of maturity, or (4) transfer of ability from the work in other school subjects. It is evident from the small amount of the gains during the year that the part due to "transfer" must be very small, while the slight differences in the scores of these grades make it probable that the "gain" of the year will be offset by the "loss" during the summer. In other words, the present results confirm the conclusion of the previous year that the degree of ability in arithmetic attained by the average child in the grades is not materially increased by this high-school work. Consequently methods which insure completeness and thoroughness in the early training become of very great importance.

# A GRADED COURSE IN SCHOOLROOM GYMNASTICS

JULIA ANNA NORRIS
School of Education, The University of Chicago

## GYMNASTICS BY COMMAND

This branch of schoolroom work is much more formal than the gymnastic story play; it is indeed characterized by military precision and control. It is to be introduced at the time when the child is getting beyond his delight in make-believe and dramatization and is entering upon his enjoyment of drill of all sorts. In general it is a good rule to drop the gymnastic story play at the end of the second year, and to use the more formal work from the third grade on.

The command itself consists of three parts: a preliminary, explanatory phrase in which the movement to be performed is indicated, a pause which gives the child time to go over quickly in his mind what he is to do, and the word of execution, which is the signal for the doing. For example, in the command "Hips firm and feet sideways—place!" "hips firm and feet sideways" explains to the child what the form of the movement is to be, the pause gives him time to apprehend it, and the word "Place!" is the signal for the performance of it.

The explanatory portion should be spoken distinctly and not too rapidly. It may consist of from one to several words, and its complexity or newness will largely govern the length of the following pause. Even a simple and often-used command, however, like "Hips—firm!" will be followed by better response if some short opportunity is given for grasping its import, in order that the slower children may be ready to join with the quicker ones in uniform action.

Skilful shading of the word of execution goes far in evoking the kind of response desired. Shot at the class in a snappy syllable it will bring action that is quick without being strong. Used more deliberately and forcefully it will rouse the muscles to stronger action. Drawn out encouragingly it will often steady the class in holding its balance. A use of the staccato with rising inflection in counting will help to produce light, clean-cut foot work. Voice and manner should always show that the teacher recognizes the fundamental pleasure which every normal child takes in muscular exercise.

The command has a decided advantage over music in the gaining of corrective results. One has a natural repugnance for interrupting a musical accompaniment every minute or oftener to inject stimulating suggestions into a lesson, and much faulty performance is therefore allowed to slip by uncorrected. But with the command an exercise can be stopped at any point and the correction made at the moment it is needed. Moreover, when performed with musical accompaniment all movements must conform to the same rhythm, and all tend toward the same rather limited expenditure of muscular exertion. Each exercise should have its own rhythm, one quick, another slow, variations easily controlled by commands, as also are the variations in muscular energy proper to different exercises.

The command is good training for concentrated attention. The inattentive child stands out self-detected because of doing the wrong thing, and the shock brings his scattered wits to focus on the work in hand. In order to get the best effect the commands should never grow to be mere forms which the children learn the order of; it should be understood by the class that any variation may occur, and that their part is to be on the alert to comprehend and to act quickly. The children should not be allowed to anticipate the executive word by premature action, as the result will be a lack of uniformity.

Gymnastics must never be expected to perform the function of recreation, and therefore should not take the place of recess periods. By some authorities a gymnastic lesson is ranked next to mathematics in the degree of mental fatigue which follows it, and although it would not be safe to accept this as applying to all gymnastics, nevertheless it is good evidence that they do not at all remove the necessity for free play periods.

If possible the teacher should memorize the lesson so that

she may not lose her opportunity to inspire through having to make frequent reference to notes. A few memoranda on a rear blackboard, however, may relieve her mind of care without drawing attention to her dependence on them. But a memorandum carried about in the hand will often stand in the way of needed manual corrections. The fact that the order of movements is practically the same in all lessons affords a basis for memorizing which relieves the necessity of much of its burden.

The order of movements is generally as follows: (1) introductory, (2) leg, (3) arch, (4) arm, (5) balance, (6) abdominal, (7) back, (8) jump, (9) respiratory. A poise step may be introduced into the lesson, in which case the leg, balance, and jump classes are omitted.

The introductory class consists of brisk small movements for the purpose of gaining the attention of the class. Facings, march steps, and quick hand placings, used without preconcerted order, will call for keen concentration on the part of the pupil.

The leg class consists of movements which start the blood flowing rapidly through the large groups of leg muscles and pump along the venous circulation by alternate flexion and extension of ankle, knee, and hip joints.

The arch movements straighten the neck and upper spine into erectness and raise the chest. They are usually taken slowly and strongly.

The arm movements use the large groups of arm, shoulder blade, and chest muscles in such wise as to promote still further an erect posture.

The balance class is for the gaining of good poise, either through rhythmic poise steps, or by standing exercises in which the base of support is diminished, as by standing on one foot.

The abdominal class includes slow side twistings and side bendings of the trunk for the front and side abdominal muscles. Backward bending at the waist will be found to be omitted entirely; most people already have the sway-back tendency sufficiently well developed.

The back class includes all forward bendings, in which position gravity forces all posterior spinal muscles into action.

The jump class includes jumping, running, and dancing steps, and insures quickened heart rhythm and breathing.

The breathing movements are accompanied by arm movements which are always simple in character, in order that the attention of teacher and class may be given to the breathing rather than to the technique of arm work. The tempo of the arm movements should bear a direct relation to the natural rhythm of breathing.

The lessons progress in difficulty from week to week in various ways. The essential movement may be increased in difficulty, as in the progression from heel raising through heel raising and knee bending to heel raising and deep knee bending. The starting position of hands or feet may be increased in difficulty, e.g., a certain movement of the trunk may be easy if taken with the hands on the hips and much more difficult if taken with the hands stretched above the head. The length of time during which a gymnastic position is held may be increased by the introduction of accessory movements, e.g., trunk bending forward is simple, but it may become a difficult or a much more vigorous exercise if the position is maintained while certain arm movements are being performed. Closely related to this mode of progression is the combining and performing in a series of movements which may be simple in themselves, as arm and leg movements, arm and trunk movements, etc.

A short daily drill in sitting posture, alternating the erect and the resting position, should precede the standing exercises. In the resting position the back should rest against the back of the chair, but a caved-in chest is not necessary. In the erect position the weight should be balanced so far forward that there will be no strain in maintaining the posture. A little experimenting will show the difference between the conscious effort needed to hold an erect sitting attitude in which the body is tilted slightly backward and the ease with which a broad-chested, flat-shouldered position can be held if the balance is sufficiently far forward.

Every exercise should be preceded by the command, "Attention!" and followed by the command, "Left (or right) in place—

rest!" Thus the children are given frequent relaxation intervals two or three seconds in length, and on being called to attention again they make greater efforts for energetic attitude than would be the case if they knew there was going to be no respite from it. The rest position should be an orderly one, the child standing with one foot in front of the other, and sufficiently on the alert to give quick response to the command for attention.

In addition to this regular short period of relaxation the rest position should always be given if a new movement is to be explained. It is particularly important that the class should not be left to hold fatiguing attitudes while the teacher talks to them of faults to be overcome.

The illustration of new movements should be technically correct. If the teacher doubts her ability to show a complicated exercise in good form she should teach it to some child who may then act as a model, performing the movement at her command.

In general it is better for the teacher to refrain from performing movements with the class. The freedom she thus gains to move about the room observing and correcting is very valuable; the children on the other hand get a much better training for independence of action if they have no model to watch.

Occasionally, however, certain ends may be most quickly reached if the teacher takes a movement with the class. If the children are lagging, for instance, a quick response can usually be regained if they are given the chance to "race with" the teacher in some simple hand placing.

The position of the gymnastic lesson in the daily program should be such that it will facilitate other work. In general it should come between two lessons which are sedentary in nature, thus improving the children's power to grasp the second one. To put it at the beginning or the close of a session is to waste an opportunity. An arrangement which has worked excellently in upper grades places gymnastics at ten o'clock and recess at eleven, dividing the morning into three approximately equal periods. In the afternoon a break of five minutes for recreation in the middle of the session helps the children to do good work during the last hour.

The length of time given to the lesson should be fifteen minutes, except in the third and fourth grades where ten minutes proves long enough.

The costumes of the girls in the upper grades call for a few words. They must needs take their schoolroom gymnastics in whatever clothing they wear to school, and their enjoyment of and benefit from the work will depend largely on their being properly dressed. If the teacher can interest them or their mothers early in the year, before their arrangements for the winter are made, in having sensible dresses the advantage will be felt all the year. Loose waists and sleeves and the absence of a corset are the essentials. The girl should be able to stretch her arms high above her head without pulling apart or tearing her waist, and she should be free to bend and twist the trunk without restriction, which is impossible if she is corseted.

The boys should prepare for the lesson by removing their coats when they stand. Some boys object on the ground of convention, but the practice adds so much to the value of the lesson that it should be insisted upon.

In the following gymnastic lessons the term "fundamental position" means the erect standing position: heels together, weight poised forward, head high, chest high and round, shoulder blades flat, arms and fingers straight down at sides, eyes to the front.

The commands printed in italics indicate the preparatory and finishing positions. Those printed in ordinary type represent the essential movement, and should be repeated four or five times.

## GYMNASTIC STORY PLAY FOR GRADE I

### CHRISTMAS MORNING

(Adapted from *Gymnastic Stories and Plays*, by Rebecca Stoneroad, M.D.; D. C. Heath & Co.)

*Story*—The children have been sleeping all night and dreaming of the pretty toys they expect to find in the morning. It begins to grow light and they stretch their arms and try to wake up, but find it hard to get their eyes open so early. When they get up they find a Jack-in-the-box in their stockings and they try him to see how he works. They find a whip with a long lash for snapping, a doll that can make a bow, a Jumping-Jack that hops merrily when his string is pulled, and, way down in the toe of the stocking, a whistle.

*Exercises*

1. Sleeping and Stretching
   Purpose: Arms and correction of chest.
   Signals: A. Go to sleep.
   Rest sitting position, with heads falling on chests and eyes shut.
   B. Stretch.
   Sit up straight, stretching arms upward and backward, eyes still closed. Repeat A and B three or four times.
   C. Wake up.
   Spring to straight sitting position with eyes open.

2. Jack-in-the Box
   Purpose: Leg exercise and straight back.
   Starting position: Standing position.
   Signals: A. Down.
   Bend knees strongly, keeping body erect.
   B. Up.
   Pop up to standing position quickly.

3. Snapping the Whip
   Purpose: Correction of chest and shoulders.
   Signals: A. Take whip in left (right) hand.
   B. Snap. Make a large, sweeping outward circle with arm, ending with a quick jerk.

4. Jointed Doll
   Purpose: Back exercise, straight back.
   Signals: A. Bow.
   Bend forward at hip joint, spine straight, finger tips pointing backward.
   B. Up.
   Straight standing position.

5. Jumping-Jack
   Purpose: General exercise.
   Signals: A. Up on toes.
   B. Hop—hop, etc.
   In the first hop land on toes with feet apart; in the second, with feet together.
   At first give a separate signal for each hop; later let the children count rhythmically at the signal "Ready—hop!"

6. Blowing the Whistle
   Purpose: Deep breathing.

Signals: A. Take up the whistle.
B. Breathe.
C. Whistle.
Blow through circular opening between thumb and index finger, making whistling sound.

*Miscellaneous Suggestions:*

Children may bring to school the toys mentioned and the teacher may use them as models or in various ways at her pleasure.

Children may suggest the next toy to be found, varying the order of exercise.

## GYMNASTIC STORY PLAY FOR GRADE II

### Santa Claus's Visit

(Adapted from *Gymnastic Stories and Plays*, by Rebecca Stoneroad, M.D.; D. C. Heath & Co.)

*Story*—On Christmas eve Santa Claus comes driving over the house tops with his reindeer to leave Christmas presents, and he finds that it takes a hard pull to make his galloping steeds stop at the chimneys. It is a cold night, and after descending the chimney he jumps from one foot to the other to get warm, but very softly so as not to waken the children. After getting his breath again he bends over and reads the names on the stockings, and he puts a Christmas present into every one from the pack on his back. Then he climbs up the chimney on his rope and drives off to the next house.

*Exercises:*

1. Pulling in the Reindeer
Purpose: Arm exercise and correction of chest.
Taken in straight sitting position.
Signals: A. Hands on reins.
Stretch arms out in front.
B. Pull.
With elbows bent pull hands back to shoulders, with strong outward rotation of shoulder joint.
C. Let them go.
Same as A.

2. Warming Feet
Purpose: General exercise.
Signals: A. Hands on hips.
B. Up on toes.
C. Ready—run.
Run in the place, springing lightly from one foot to the other. At first give a signal (count) for each spring, later let them take it rhythmically.

3. Panting
   Purpose: Full Breathing.
   Signals: A. Breathe in.
   Inhale through nose.
   B. Breathe out—
   Exhale through mouth.
4. Reading Names on Stockings
   Purpose: Trunk exercise.
   Signals: A. Hands on hips.
   B. Bend forward.
   Bend forward at hip joint, spine straight, eyes up.
   C. Count (or, Read).
   Count up to about six, turning head gradually from left to right. Or use names instead of numbers.
   D. Straight up.
   Spring into erect standing position.
5. Placing Presents in Stockings
   Purpose: Leg and trunk exercise.
   Signals: A. Reach.
   Left hand on right shoulder (or the reverse).
   B. Put it in.
   Bend knees and bend body forward, reaching out to deposit presents.
   C. Straight up.
   Spring into erect standing position.
6. Climbing Rope up the Chimney
   Purpose: Correction of chest and upper spine.
   Signals: A. Hands on rope.
   Left hand high up, right in front of chest.
   B. Pull.
   Bring upper hand strongly down till it rests on lower.
   C. Move lower hand up as high as it will reach.

*Miscellaneous Suggestions:*

Drive the reindeer over different streets that the children know, and stop at definite children's houses. Let the child whose house is visited name the members of his family; Santa Claus then reads these names from the stockings. Let children suggest what presents shall be given to various members of the family.

## GYMNASTICS, GRADE III

### Lesson I

Atten—tion!

Children assume the erect sitting position, lower portion of spine against chair back, upper portion poised well forward, chest active, head high, arms and fingers straight down at sides, feet flat on floor.

Rest!

Rest sitting position, spine supported by chair back, general relaxation without "slumping."

Alternate the above commands several times.

Atten—tion! Standing position—One!

One foot is stretched halfway across aisle.

Two!

Children rise to fundamental standing position with the most direct movement possible.

Change Places!

Children vacate every third aisle and stand in the remaining aisles according to height, shorter ones in front.

Ready—run!

Children run rhythmically, row by row, around room and back to places.

1. Introductory. Atten—tion! Left (or right) in place—rest!
   Atten—tion! Fundamental standing position: heels together, weight poised forward, head high, chest high and round, shoulder blades flat, arms and fingers straight down at sides, eyes to the front.
   Left in place—rest! Foot mentioned in command is placed diagonally forward, weight on backward foot, general relaxation without "slumping." Alternate left and right foot.
   The "in-place-rest" position should follow every exercise and should itself be followed by "Attention!" before any other command is given.
2. Leg. Feet—close! Feet—open! Feet—close and open!
   Foot closing and opening counting to six (or more)—start!
   Feet—close! Bring inner edges of feet close together lifting toes and turning on heels.
   Feet—open! Return to starting position.
3. Arch. Head to left—twist! Forward—twist! To right, etc.
   Head twisting in four counts—1!—2!—3!—4!
   1! To left. 2! Forward. 3! To right. 4! Forward.
4. Arm. Hips—firm! Po—sition!
   Hands on hips, fingers in front, straight line from finger tips to elbows.
5. Leg. Alternate toe raising, counting to six (or more)—go!
   Toe of one foot moves up while other is moving down, knees and hips straight.
6. Breathing. Arm sideways—raise!—sink!
   Inhale while raising extended arms to height of shoulders in side plane. Exhale while lowering them.

Ready—run!

Children run around room and back to their own seats, sitting down without command.

N. B. The directions for opening and closing this lesson apply to all the lessons for the third grade.

### Lesson II

1. Leg. Foot placing sideways—1!—2! Together—1!—2!
   Feet sideways—place! Together—place!
   Foot placing sideways—1! Place left foot one foot-length's distance to left. 2! Place right foot one foot-length's distance to right. Together—1! Replace left foot. 2! Replace right foot.
   Feet sideways—place! Children count "1! 2!" while placing the feet.
2. Arch. Head to left—bend! Upward—raise! To right, etc.
   Head bending in four counts—1!—2!—3!—4!
   Eyes are kept to front during the bending.
3. Arm. Shoulders—firm! Po—sition!
   Forearm bent up sharply bringing hands to shoulders as far back as possible, so as to broaden chest and pinch shoulder blades together.
4. Trunk. Trunk forward—bend! Upward—raise!
   Bend in hip joint only, spine straight, eyes up, finger tips pointing backward; finish with horizontal position of back, or sooner if back begins to curve.
5. General exercise. Mark time—march! Class—halt!
   Mark time—march! Swing feet forward alternately beginning with left, and bring heels again together at each count. Keep shoulders steady. Class—halt! Two mark-time steps follow the word "halt," the children counting aloud, "1! 2!" The word "halt" may fall on either left or right foot.
6. Breathing. Arms forward—raise!—sink!
   Inhale while raising extended arms to height of shoulders in front plane.

## GYMNASTICS, GRADE IV

The direction for opening the lessons for the fourth grade are the same as for the third, but the run at the end of the lesson is omitted and an extra movement introduced.

Italicized commands indicate preparatory and finishing positions, not the essential exercise.

### Lesson I

1. Introductory. One step forward (or backward)—march!
   Taken in two counts, children counting aloud. Step forward or backward with left foot, on "one" bring right foot up beside left with a click of the heels on "two."
2. Leg. *Hips—firm!* Alternate toe raising, counting to eight (or more)—start! *Po—sition!*
   See Grade III, Lesson I, movements 4 and 5.

3. Arch. *Hips—firm!* Head to left—twist! Forward—twist! To right, etc.
   The same in four counts—1!—2!—3!—4!
   The same, class counting—"go! *Po—sition!*"
   1! To left. 2! Forward. 3! To right. 4! Forward.
4. Arm. Shoulders—firm! Po—sition!
   See Grade III, Lesson II.
5. Trunk. *Hips—firm!* Trunk forward—bend! Upward—raise! *Po—sition!*
   See Grade III, Lesson II.
6. General exercise. Mark time—march! Class—halt!
   See Grade III, Lesson II.
7. Breathing. Arm raising sideways—1!—2!
   See Grade III, Lesson I.

### Lesson II

1. Introductory. Two steps forward (or backward)—march!
   Two steps forward and backward—march!
   Two steps are taken in three counts. On "one" step forward with left foot, on "two" take full step forward with right foot, passing beyond left, on "three" bring left up to right with a click of the heels.
   In the combination of forward and backward steps class counts, 1—2—3! 1—2—3!
2. Leg. *Hips—firm!* Feet sideways—place! Feet together—place! *Po—sition!*
   See Grade III, Lesson II.
   *Hips—firm!* Foot placing sideways, and together—start! *Po—sition!*
   Class counts—1!—2!—3!—4!
3. Arch. *Hips—firm!* Head to left—bend! Upward—raise! To right, etc.
   Head bending in four counts, 1—2—3—4!
   The same, class counting, start! *Po—sition!*
   Eyes are kept to front during bending.
4. Arm. Chest—firm! Po—sition!
   Each arm makes a horizontal shelf, elbow at height of shoulder in side plane, forearm bent forward, hand in front of chest touching it, palm down, hands as far apart as possible, elbows pulled well back.
5. Trunk. *Hips—firm!* Trunk to left—bend! Upward—raise! To right, etc.
   A deep inhalation should accompany the bending, an exhalation the raising. Shoulders squarely to front.
6. Jump. *Hips—firm! Heels—raise!* Spring jump with feet apart counting to eight—start! *Heels—sink! Po—sition!*

Children count aloud. They jump landing on toes with feet apart on the odd numbers and together again on the even numbers.

7. Breathing. Arm raising forward—raise!—sink!
See Grade III, Lesson II.

## GYMNASTICS, GRADE V.

The directions for opening the lessons for the fifth grade are the same as for the third with the exception of the run, which is omitted.

### Lesson I

1. Introductory. One step forward—march! One step backward—march! One step forward and backward—march!
See Grade IV, Lesson I.

2. Arch. *Hips—firm!* Head forward—bend! Upward—raise! *Po—sition!*
Head forward—bend! Neck relaxes and head drops forward on active chest.
Upward—raise! Raise head slowly and strongly with chin in and neck back; inhale deeply and lift chest strongly.

3. Arm. Arm stretching sideways—1!—2! Stretching downward—1!—2!
Arm stretching sideways—1! "Shoulders firm" position (see Grade III, Lesson II). 2! Extend arms forcibly in side plane at height of shoulders, palms down, fingers straight.
Stretching downward—1! "Shoulders firm" position. 2! Fundamental position with forcible extension.

4. Back. Shoulders—firm! Trunk forward—bend! Upward—raise! Po—sition!
The same in four counts—1!—2!—3!—4!
See Grade III, Lesson II.

5. General exercise. Mark time—march! Class—halt!
See Grade III, Lesson II.

6. Breathing. *Arms forward—raise!* Arm moving sideways—1!—2! *Arms—sink!*
Arms forward—raise! See Grade III, Lesson II.
Arm moving sideways, 1! With thumbs up move extended arms sideways as far as they will go, inhaling meanwhile.
2! Return arms to front plane, exhaling.

### Lesson II

1. Introductory. Left—face! Right—face!
Left facing four times—go!
Left—face! Taken in two counts. On "one" turn 90° to left, pivoting on heel of left foot and pushing with toe of right foot. On "two" bring right heel against left with a click.

2. Leg. *Hips firm and left foot forward—place!* Feet—change! Foot changing, counting to eight—go! *In one count, po—sition!* Hips firm and left foot forward—place! Hands and foot move simultaneously. Foot is placed directly forward, two foot-lengths distance, weight evenly distributed between feet.
Feet—change! Taken in two counts. On "one" left foot is brought back to fundamental position. On "two" right foot is placed forward.

3. Arch. Neck backward—bend! Upward—raise!
Neck backward—bend! Bend head and neck backward with chin in and shoulders steady till the eyes look directly upward at ceiling. Upward—raise! Raise head with chin closely held in, at the same time pressing neck forcibly back against collar, making an effort to arch neck.

4. Arm. Chest—firm! Arms sideways—fling! Arms—bend! Po—sition! *Chest—firm!* Arm flinging sideways—1!—2! *Po—sition!*
Chest—firm! See Grade IV, Lesson II. Arms sideways—fling! Quick and forcible extension of arms sideways. Arms—bend! "Chest firm" position.

5. Balance. Left leg forward—raise! Foot re—place!
Leg is raised in front plane 45° or more, with knee straight and toe extended.

6. Abdominal. *Hips—firm!* Trunk to left—bend! Upward—raise! To right, etc.
Trunk to left—bend! During a deep inhalation bend trunk to left curving from waist to top of head, stopping before there is any feeling of strain.

7. Back. *Hips—firm!* Trunk forward—bend! Head twisting—1!—2!—3!—4! Upward—raise! *Po—sition!*

8. General exercise. *Hips—firm!* Heel raising and knee bending—1!—!2—3!—4! *Po—sition!*
1! Raise heels. 2! Bend knees to right angle, turning them well out to side. 3! Straighten knees again. 4! Lower heels.

9. Breathing. Arm raising forward and upward—raise!—sink!
Inhale while raising extended arms through the front plane to their full height above head.

## GYMNASTICS, GRADE VI

The directions for opening the lessons for the sixth grade are the same as for the third with the exception of the run, which is omitted.

### Lesson I

1. Introductory. One step forward (or backward)—march!
Two steps forward and backward—march!
Two steps backward and forward—march!
See Grade IV, Lessons I and II.

2. Leg. *Hips—firm!* Foot placing forward and backward with change of feet —go! *Po—sition!*
   Class counts to four twice. 1! Place left foot forward one foot-length's distance. 2! Replace it. 3! Place it backward one foot-length's distance. 4! Replace it. Repeat with right foot.

3. Arch. Neck backward—bend! Upward—raise!
   See Grade V, Lesson II.

4. Arm. Arm stretching sideways—1!—2! Arm stretching downward—1!—2!
   See Grade V, Lesson 1.

5. Back. *Neck firm and feet sideways—place!* Trunk forward—bend! Upward—raise! *In one count po–sition!*
   Neck—firm! Tips of fingers meet on back of neck, elbows back, wrists straight, neck pressed back against fingers.
   Feet sideways—place! See Grade III, Lesson II.
   In combining the two above movements the left foot moves on first count, the hands and right foot on second count.
   Trunk forward—bend! See Grade III, Lesson II.
   In one count, po—sition! Bring heels together with a little jump, at same time bringing arms to fundamental position.

6. General exercise. Mark time—march! Class—halt!
   See Grade III, Lesson II.

7. Breathing. Arm raising sideways upward in two counts—1!—2!
   1! Raise extended arms through side plane to full height above head, turning hands at level of shoulders. 2! Return through side plane.

### Lesson II

1. Introductory. Left—face! Right—face!
   Left about—face! Right about—face!
   Left—face! See Grade V, Lesson II.
   Left about—face! The same technique as above, facing 180°.

2. Leg. *Hips firm and left foot forward—place!* Left knee—bend! Knee—stretch! Feet—change! Right knee, etc. *Po—sition!*
   Or, *Hips firm and left foot forward—place!* Knee bending and stretching counting to eight—go! Etc.
   Left knee—bend! Bend left knee to right angle, at the same time inclining trunk forward so as to maintain a straight line from backward heel up to shoulder.
   Feet—change! See Grade V, Lesson II.

3. Arch. *Hips firm and feet sideways—place!* Chest—raise! Re—turn! *Po—sition!*
   Chest—raise! With a full breath lift chest, carry head and neck backward

with chin in till eyes look at ceiling, and finally pinch shoulder blades together. Do not bend backward at waist.
Re—turn! Fundamental position.

4. Arm. *Shoulders—firm!* Left arm sideways—stretch! Arms—change! *Po—sition!* Shoulders—firm! See Grade III, Lesson II.
Left arm sideways—stretch! Full forcible extension in side plane at height of shoulder, palm down.

5. Balance. *Hips—firm!* Heels—raise! Knees—bend! Deep—bend! Knees —stretch! Heels—sink! *Po—sition!*
Knees—bend! To right angle with knees turned well apart.
Deep—bend! Bend till almost sitting on heels.

6. Abdominal. *Left hip, right neck—firm!* Trunk to left—bend! Upward —raise! Arms—change! to right, etc.
To left—bend! See Grade V, Lesson II.

7. Back. *Hips—firm.* Trunk forward—bend! Neck—firm! Hips—firm! Trunk—raise. *Po—sition!*
Or, Change between neck and hips firm—1!—2!

8. Jump. *Hips—firm!* Jump in place in six counts—1!—2!—3, 4!—5!—6! *Po—sition!*
1! Raise heels. 2! Bend knees to right angle. 3, 4! Jump up with straight knees landing on toes softly with knees bent again. 5! Straighten knees. 6! Lower heels.

9. Breathing. Arm raising sideways with heel raising: raise!—sink! Inhale while combining heel raising with arm raising to height of shoulder in side plane.

## GYMNASTICS, GRADE VII

The directions for opening the lessons are the same as those for third grade with the exception of the run, which is omitted.

### Lesson I

1. Introductory. Left—face! Side step to left—march!
Side step to right—march! Right—face!
See Grade V, Lesson II, for facings.
Side step to left—march! Taken in two counts: 1! Step to left with left foot. 2! Bring right heel up to left with a click.

2. Leg. *Neck—firm!* Heels—raise! Knees—bend! Knees—stretched! Heels—sink! *Po—sition!*
Neck—firm! See Grade VI, Lesson I, movement 5.
Heels raise, etc. See Grade V, Lesson II, exercise 8.

3. Arch. *Hips—firm!* Neck backward—bend! Upward—raise! *Po—sition!*
See Grade V, Lesson II.

4. Arm. Arm stretching upward—1!—2!
Arm stretching downward—1!—2!
Arm stretching upward—1! "Shoulders firm" position. See Grade III, Lesson II. 2! Arms extended forcibly upward as high as stretched fingers can reach.
Arm stretching downward, 1! "Shoulders firm" position. 2! Fundamental position.

5. Abdominal. *Neck firm and feet sideways—place!* Trunk to left—bend! Upward—raise! To right, etc. *Po—sition!*
Feet sideways—place! See Grade III, Lesson II.
In combining neck firm with feet sideways place the left foot moves on first count, the hands and right foot on second count.
Trunk to left—bend! See Grade V, Lesson II.
Po—sition! Taken in one count. With a little jump bring heels together and arms to fundamental position.

6. Jump. *Hips—firm!* Jump in place in six counts, 1!—2!—3, 4!—5!—6! *Po—sition!*
See Grade VI, Lesson II.

7. Breathing. *Hips—firm!* Arm moving backward, 1!—2! *Po—sition!*
1! Inhale while drawing elbows back as far as possible. 2! Exhale while elbows move passively to starting position.

### Lesson II

1. Introductory. Review left and right, left about and right about facings, and march steps forward and backward, one step and two steps.
See Introductory movements in all lower grades.

2. Leg. *Hips—firm!* Left forward fall—out! Feet—change! *Po—sition!*
Left forward fall—out! Taken in one count. Left foot is placed three foot-lengths' distance forward with weight on it and knee bent to right angles. At the same time trunk is inclined forward so that there is a straight line from backward heel up through knee, hip, and spine to head. Both heels flat on floor.
Feet—change! Taken in two counts: 1! Replace left foot with a spring from the toe. 2! Fall forward on right foot.

3. Arch. *Arms sideways stretch and feet sideways—place!* Chest—raise! Re—turn! *Po—sition!*
Arms sideways stretch, etc. Taken in two counts: 1! Take "shoulders firm" position and place left foot sideways. On two extend arms sideways forcibly, palms down, and place right foot sideways.
Chest—raise! See Grade VI, Lesson II.

4. Arm. *Shoulders—firm! Left arm sideways—stretch!* Arms—change! *Po—sition!*

Arms—change! Change with a very forcible bending of one arm and stretching of the other.

5. Balance. *Arms sideways—raise!* Left leg forward—raise! Feet—change! Re—place! *Po—sition!*
Left leg forward—raise! See Grade V, Lesson II.
Feet—change! Taken in two counts: 1! Replace left foot. 2! Raise right. Class counts.

6. Abdominal. *Sitting on desks—place! Hips—firm!* Trunk to left—twist! Forward—twist! To right, etc. *Standing position—place!*
Sitting on desks—place! In the quietest quickest way take seats on desks, facing back of room, with toes braced under front edge of chairs.
Trunk to left—twist! Twist shoulders as far as possible with erect position.
Standing position—place! Quickly and quietly resume fundamental standing position facing front of room.

7. Back. *Chest—firm!* Trunk forward—bend! Arm flinging sideways, —1!—2! Trunk—raise! *Po—sition!*
Chest—firm! See Grade IV, Lesson II.
Trunk forward—bend! See Grade III, Lesson II.
Arm flinging sideways, 1! Fling arms forcibly into side plane, well up to shoulder height. 2! Chest firm.
This movement may be taken in rhythmic series at the command: The same in six counts—go!

8. Jump. *Hips—firm!* Jump forward—1!—2!—3, 4!—5!—6! *Po—sition!*
Land on toes with knees bent about a foot in front of starting position.

9. Breathing. Arm raising forward, upward, and sinking sideways downward —raise!—sink!
Raise! Inhale while carrying arms up to full height through the front plane. Sink! Exhale while bringing arms down through side plane, turning palms naturally on the way down.

## GYMNASTICS, GRADE VIII

The directions for opening the lessons are the same as for third grade except the run, which is omitted.

### Lesson I

The same as for Grade VII.

### Lesson II

1. Introductory. Review left and right and left about and right about facings, and one and two march steps forward and backward.
See Introductory movements in lower grades.

2. Leg. *Hips—firm!* Foot placing forward, sideways, and backward—start! *Po—sition!*
Six counts with left foot, six with right. 1! Place left foot two foot-length's

distance forward carrying half the weight forward on it. 2! Replace. 3! Same sideways. 4! Replace. 5! Same backward. 6! Replace.

3. Arch. *Arms sideways stretch and feet sideways—place!* Chest—raise! Re—turn! *Po—sition!*
See Grade VII, Lesson II.

4. Arm. Left arm sideways, right arm upward stretching—1!—2! Arm changing—1!—2! Downward stretching—1!—2!
1! Always means, "shoulders firm" position.
2! Extend arms forcibly with fingers straight in the direction indicated by command.

5. Balance. *Arms half sideways—bend!* Left (right) leg sideways—raise! Re—place! *Po—sition!*
Arms half sideways—bend! Form a letter E lying on its back by raising arms in side plane to height of shoulders with forearms bent to right angles and hands pointing upward. Head makes middle stroke of letter E.
Left leg sideways—raise! Raise leg about 45° in side plane with knee straight and toe pointed.

6. Abdominal. *Sitting on desks—place! Hips—firm!* Trunk backward—bend! Upward—raise! *Standing position—place!*
Sitting on desks—place! In the quickest, quietest way take seats on desks, facing back of room, with toes braced under front edge of chairs.
Trunk backward—bend! Bend backward about 45° in hip joint only, keeping chest active and head back.
Standing position—place! Quickly and quietly resume fundamental standing position facing front of room.

7. Back. *Chest—firm!* Trunk forward—bend! Arm flinging sideways—1!—2! Trunk—raise! *Po—sition!*
See Grade VII, Lesson II.

8. Jump. *Hips—firm!* Jump forward—1! 2!—3! 4!—5!—6!
See Grade VII, Lesson II.
The jumping counts "3, 4!" may be repeated several times, before finishing with "5!—6!"

9. Breathing. Arm rotation and deep breathing—1!—2!
Inhale while arms are rotated outward until thumbs point backward, exhale while returning to starting position.

# THE EVOLUTION OF AIM AND METHOD IN THE TEACHING OF NATURE-STUDY IN THE COMMON SCHOOLS OF THE UNITED STATES

IRA BENTON MEYERS
School of Education, The University of Chicago

The following sketch on the teaching of nature-study in the common or elementary schools of the United States is a summary of the various efforts of the schools during the past to direct the attention of children to a study of their nature environment in such a way as to render the results educative. It includes studies known at different periods as natural history, natural science, object-lessons, lessons on common things, nature-study, elementary science, and frequently as one of the specialized sciences, botany or zoölogy.

The aim in the study has been to get the various reasons offered, by the advocates of this work, for introducing it into the common schools; the aim or purpose of the study as stated at different periods and stages of its existence; the ways in which it was taught; the various modifications which it has undergone; the degree of success or failure attending the teaching, as evidenced by the praise or criticisms of the times; and the bearing which this past experience may have upon giving direction to our present-day outlook into the teaching of nature-study.

The paper also touches, in a very general way, upon the attitude of the people, during these several stages, toward elementary education as a whole in so far as it gives some insight into those phases of aim and procedure which have influenced the nature-study movement.

In following the evolution of aim in the teaching of nature-study it may aid the story, if we sketch briefly the general condition of the people and their attitude toward elementary education at the time nature-study was first introduced into the common schools.

At the end of the first quarter of the past century, the period when nature-study was first seriously introduced into the schools 7 per cent of the people lived in cities while 93 per cent lived in the country and were occupied, to a very large extent, with work which brought them into direct daily contact with a wide range of their nature environment. For two-thirds of the year the boys were kept at home hard at work plowing, planting, hoeing, haying, harvesting, and caring for live stock. The girls were busy in homes with cooking, washing, house-cleaning, mending, knitting, sewing, and gardening; while both boys and girls roamed freely and widely in fields and woods seeking wild fruits, nuts, berries, and flowers, or fishing and hunting. Their methods of living kept them in direct contact with the common natural objects and phenomena about them. Quite the whole of their time was spent in some useful and essential activity; their moments of leisure were limited.

At the close of the century 40 per cent of the people lived in cities engaged in occupations dominated by a social environment and commercial influences, divorcing children from this direct, familiarizing contact with nature, and surrounding them with a home and vocational life so complex, or with a social organization and attitude such, as to give children little or no chance to take part in any of the ministering-to-family-needs activities. A large portion of the time of the children was unoccupied, and they were left more or less to their own devices, in an environment offering but little in the way of stimulating content and wholesome activity. The time spent by the country child with things and situations is spent by the city child in social play and sightseeing. It is true that just in proportion as leisure time increased, the school term increased; but, as we shall show later, it did not put back into the lives of the children that which the city took out.

Our common schools, at this period, did not take into account the educational values of this childhood experience and activity. It was not their aim to promote individual development, and to aid the child to acquire that knowledge and power essential to the demands of everyday life. Their aim was to place the child in possession of the tools for acquiring knowledge and it was held that these tools were spelling, reading, writing, and arithmetic, along with some incidental training in behavior, morals, and religion. People believed that once in possession of these tools of learning the whole world of knowledge could be brought to the foot of man. This one idea dominated the schools of the time; parents with a firm faith in it kept it constantly before their children stimulating them to effort. The total spirit of the period is well illustrated in the autobiographical statement of Edmund Stone in his reply to an inquiry as to how he acquired his education:

> I first learned to read; the masons were at work at your home. I approached them one day and observed that the architect used a rule and compass, and I was informed that there was a science called arithmetic. I purchased a book and I learned it. I was told that there was another science called geometry. I bought the necessary books and I learned geometry. By reading I learned that there were good books of the kind in Latin. I bought a dictionary and I learned Latin. I learned also that there were good books of the kind in French. I bought a dictionary and I learned French. And this, my lord, is what I have done. It seems to me that we may learn everything when we know the twenty-six letters of the alphabet.

It is plainly evident that the spirit abroad in the land was that of aggressiveness, of industry, of using leisure moments to acquire something which daily living did not immediately demand. When, in about 1827, it was recommended that geography be added to the common-school curriculum, it was strenuously objected to on the plea that it had to do with acquiring information, and that imparting information was not a function of the common schools. Later, however, the imparting of information became a dominant passion in teaching.

By 1830, the period at which nature-study began to gain some headway in the common schools, the school curriculum had been enriched, in many places, especially in New England, by adding grammar, geography, and occasionally United States history. The atmosphere of the schoolroom is well summed up by Swett:

It was the office of the teacher to keep order and hear recitations. It was the duty of the pupils to memorize the textbook lessons and recite them without comment, or question. The end aimed at was the memorization of the textbook; in arithmetic sums were worked out by rule, and this was supposed to be the highest kind of discipline.

This represents in a fair way the school atmosphere when nature-study entered. It did not enter as part of the system but as a thing aside; it got into the clutches of the system, however, later on. At this period there was abroad in the land a strong sentiment for training children in behavior and developing their religious feelings. The people recognized the instinctive interest of children in natural objects and phenomena; they were fully aware of their insatiable curiosity, and of the ease, wonder, and delight with which they formed acquaintanceship with each new thing. The dominant conception of the people, in their interpretation of nature, was that of special creation, and in this conception they found motive for the study of nature in the elementary schools. They contended that, by taking advantage of the spontaneous interests and pleasure which a child takes in his nature environment, he might be led the better to appreciate the wonders of creation and thus be led: "to more fully and reverently love and admire a Being who could and did create such wonderful things for the children of man."

All natural history in the common schools was taught with this end in view, but none, unless it was astronomy, was calculated to accomplish this purpose so effectively as that which treated of life. Most of the natural history lessons were in the form of stories to be read, and were mostly blendings of natural history, morals, and religion. The following from Lovell's *Young People's Second Book* (1836) is a fair example:

**THE HEN**

Of all the feathered animals, there is none more useful than the common hen. Her eggs supply us with food during her life, and her flesh affords us delicate meat after her death. What a motherly care does she take of her young! How closely and tenderly does she watch over them and cover them with her wings; and how bravely does she defend them from every enemy, from which she would fly away in terror, if she had not them to protect.

While this sight reminds you of the wisdom and goodness of the Creator, let it also remind you of the care which your own mother took of you during your helpless years, and of the gratitude and duty which you owe to her for all her kindness.

Nature stood as a source from which to draw great moral and religious truths, and recognizing, as the people of the period did, childhood as the time for impressing these truths upon the race, it was but a logical result of their reasoning that the study of nature should find favor in the elementary schools. At the same time they contended that the students of the female seminaries, as mothers, would exert a controlling influence upon child life, and that with a knowledge of nature, and of the lessons to be drawn from her, they would be the better prepared to guide the pupils during the impressionable years of their childhood. They argued that:

The study of nature is a source of instruction and enjoyment from which no mind should be excluded, and least of all the minds which usually give direction to the propensities of early childhood, and which ought to be supplied with means for attaining ascendency over the dawn of character.

In addition to the idea of leading children: "more fully to appreciate the Creator through an acquaintance with his wonderful works," popular sentiment considered the study of nature essential for children because of its pleasing and stimulating influence. "It is an inexhaustible source of innocent amusement." "It satisfies childish curiosity." "It caters to the natural tendency of the mind to observe, compare, examine, classify, anything submitted to it." "It breaks up tendencies toward sedentary habits by inviting us to walk and breathe the pure air of field and hills." Yet these things were so far from their ideas of real education that the work was not to be looked upon as an *essential* part of school study. "The matter of natural history being one of gratification rather than an essential; the study should be looked upon as a matter of recreation."

The total attitude of the advocates for natural history, during the period, is well summed up by Gould:

Everything formed by the hand of the All-Wise Creator is worthy of our consideration, and we may derive from the contemplation of such objects something to excite our wonder. But since man's necessities may all be supplied by a superficial knowledge of the history and qualities of a few articles, it has happened that the study of natural history, which embraces in its survey, every created thing, has never formed a branch of elementary education, and is found to have been cultivated only in the midst of prosperity, and a state of advanced civilization. . . . . Through the study of natural history we learn the use of created things. . . . . I feel that I may safely recommend its study not only as a source of pure rational enjoyment, but as one of high moral power, and that no study is more likely to purify the affections, and to direct them to the great Author of nature, he only being worthy of adoration. . . . . The study is largely a matter of relaxation and gratification rather than one essential to supply the necessities of life; no one will be compelled to engage in it, and when pursued it will be done voluntarily and eagerly.

It is difficult to catch more than a glimpse of what is actually passing between teachers and pupils in the schoolroom, but we soon meet the complaint that:

The study is regarded as an accomplishment, like the study of the fine arts, too inapplicable to the sterner duties of ordinary study. . . . . The system of utility and selfish views of immediate practical use comes into action.

With the gradual rise of natural history in the common schools and in turning to the female seminaries to train the girls to carry on the work, as teachers and mothers, the study was wholly confined to botany on account of its being: "by far the most attractive, elegant, and precise study; so well adapted to the refinement of female education; and the subject of its study so universally admired." With this specialized turn given to the study in the upper schools, it not only became a study of botany, but people came to look upon this phase of natural history as especially adapted to the temperament of girls. This attitude is well expressed in the words of the period:

Botany is peculiarly fitted for introduction into girls' schools; it is admirably adapted to the tastes, feelings, and capacities of females, as is well demonstrated by the fact that the majority of botanists are females. Boys are less easily interested in it, more apt to be careless and harsh in their treatment of specimens and too much attached to rude and boisterous sport. . . . . Botany should be considered as a science of amusement; but with this strong recommendation, that it be acquired without stealing a single hour from more important studies.

It is easy to see that the general attitude, in both the lower and upper schools, as to the real educational value of the study was practically the same; a wholesome pastime but not a serious and essential study. The introduction of the study into the schools gave rise to a demand for textbooks. This demand was met in 1836 by two books, Mrs. Lincoln's *Botany,* and *Botany for Beginners.* This last book was written in an attractive style, so far as relates to the purpose for which intended; being designed chiefly "for use of primary schools and for the younger pupils in the higher schools and seminaries." The author states in her preface:

So much has, of late, been urged by those who take an interest in the subject of education, in favor of introducing the natural sciences in the common schools, that it is to be hoped that the time is not far distant when plants and minerals will be as familiar objects in our district schoolhouses as the spelling book now is.

Turning to the schoolrooms to note the actual teaching of natural history we find the range of study extremely limited. This does not seem to be so much the result of the feeling of inutility as from a feeling on the part of teachers of lack of proper facility for carrying on the work. The few books that existed, especially on animal life, were defective in that they were untruthful, fanciful, and were for the most part translations of foreign books treating of objects outside of the pupil's environment, and did not serve to give him any introduction to the nature world about him. To add to the difficulties teachers looked upon the textbook as something to be memorized by the students. After about 15 years of struggle the work, of both types, where carried on at all, settled to a sort of a mechanical routine. In botany the work took on the form of plant analysis and classification. This type of work rendered the study too difficult for elementary schools, so that in the end the method of work excluded the study from the school which gave it initiative.

It will be of interest to note as we go on how frequently it has happened that a study, introduced into the schools for the purpose of ministering to the normal needs of children, has been turned about and used as an end instead of a means. The tone in educational discussion soon begins to change. Instead of telling of the realization of the purposes which lead to the introduction of nature teaching we find people declaring:

> From too great a want of elementary textbooks, and a greater want of proper instruction, the entrance to the domain of natural history is rendered disagreeable. The student is disgusted with its technicalities before his zeal is awakened to its curious facts. He attempts to study its theory and its theory is considered the end and aim of pursuit. . . . . Take, for instance, the single branch of botany, as pursued in our schools it is usually a task. The student commits to memory page after page of some textbook so as to be able to tell the correct term of each organ of a plant without a single idea as to its economy. A specimen is put into his hands, and after being able to count the stamens, to determine without much hesitancy the size and form of the leaves, and by much trouble to discover through the manual the name—the mighty work is done. Pupils are now as wise as the instructor, their labors and investigations must cease.

As has been noted, the study took its initiative in the common schools because of what it promised in the way of wholesome physical, mental, and religious training. That direct contact of children with their nature environment would lead to a knowledge of the facts of nature was taken for granted. The work ended in an attempt to teach an organized fund of knowledge for its own sake. Although the study still led a desultory existence the cycle was in reality completed; its stages being: a recognition of the fact that children are instinctively interested in their nature environment; that their reactions to these interests exert on them a strong growth influence—physically, mentally, spiritually; the school attempts to utilize this interest; knowledge is systematized; a textbook is written, teachers are trained through a textbook, they attempt to teach children by the same method, contact with nature is lost, spontaneous interests vanish from the schoolroom, the study becomes a mere matter of memorizing the system, public protest, exit the study either by neglect or expulsion.

To say that this study was a complete failure would be contrary to the testimony of some of the people who passed through and survived, and contended that they were greatly benefited by the work.

It is fair to say that it reached a few and not the masses, and that in its main purpose of utilizing and developing the intelligent interest of children in their nature environment it was a failure. The one thing which remains constant in each succeeding generation of children is that same restless interest in their nature environment; their desire to know plants, animals, minerals, and all objects and phenomena about them; to roam the fields and woods, to pry about streams and ponds, and to ask questions about these things. The presence of this spirit is sufficient to insure a return of the schools to this same viewpoint regardless of the number of its failures. It is sufficient to insure our return in the present and the future until that time when we are able to grasp the elements which will bring about a blending of these instinctive interests with the aims, demands, and organization of the school.

[*To be continued*]

# EDITORIAL NOTES

In 1908, Mr. Kilpatrick, a principal of one of the public schools of New York City, published a volume setting forth the advantages of departmental teaching in elementary schools. In his preface, he calls attention to the fact that the development of departmental teaching is in keeping with the principles advocated by ex-President Eliot, Superintendent Maxwell, and others who are interested in the improvement of school methods.

**Departmental Teaching**

It is the experience of the present writer that the tendency in American schools is in the direction indicated by Mr. Kilpatrick's book. On several occasions groups of teachers and supervisors have been asked whether in the schools from which they came there is an increasing tendency toward departmental teaching, or a disposition to move backward toward the method of allowing a single teacher to treat all of the subjects. The testimony in all cases has been that the movement in an overwhelming majority of cases is toward departmental teaching.

**Recent Movement Everywhere in Its Favor**

The fact that so many schools are moving in this direction is itself sufficient evidence that there is much to be said in favor of this method of organizing the elementary schools. It is not necessary, therefore, to enter here into the various arguments in favor of departmental teaching. The purpose of the present discussion is to call attention to certain radical defects in this method of organizing schools, and to point out the fact that if schools are to continue to develop in the present direction, there must be explicit effort on the administrative side to counteract the evil effects of departmental teaching.

**There Should Be a Pause for Consideration**

One grave disadvantage of departmental teaching is the general confusion which comes into the life of the pupil through contact with different teachers who hold entirely different ideals of instruction, and who aim to promote the interests of different subjects with too little regard for the combination of all subjects.

**Lack of Organization in Work of Pupils**

This confusion is increased by the demands which are made

by separate teachers for special devotion to the subjects which they represent. When the child finds that he has been called upon by four special teachers to prepare for the work of the next day outside of school, he will certainly be undecided as to which subject he should neglect, and which he should emphasize. The school does not help him to adjust his work so as to select that which is most important.

**Correlation of Programs as Well as of Subjects**

If these various demands on the part of teachers are to be helpful rather than confusing to the pupils, it will be necessary for the various subjects to be represented at some one point where they can be correlated. This correlation must consist not merely in the relating of subject-matter in different subjects, but there must be some balancing of the effort of the students so as to make up a reasonable daily program, and some adjustment of home study so that there may be a reasonable distribution of the pupil's energy.

**New Demands not Centralized**

Another way of setting forth this disadvantage of the present system may be stated as follows. There is no one who realizes the congestion of the program, because the teacher's program does not represent the full difficulty that confronts the individual pupil.

**Teachers Will not Take up Subjects**

We are very eager as teachers to introduce into the program of elementary-school children some work in nature-study, some hand-work, music, and physical education, little realizing that the demands which are ultimately made upon the child's time and attention pass very much beyond the comprehension of anyone who gives only a single subject.

If we turn back from the departmental system and ask any individual teacher to conduct all of these various subjects, we realize instantly the burden that is placed upon the pupils. It is a very striking fact that the grade teacher who is unwilling to teach nature-study, is entirely willing to have the children called upon to pursue this line of work. If the grade teacher were called upon to teach the subject, there would be perhaps undue conservatism in the introduction of new subjects. There would, however, be a complete realization of the demand made upon the pupil when the subject is introduced.

Here again, some corrective method must be found. The faculty should bring together the programs of the individual children in such a way as to take note of all of the engagements which the children have. There should then be some redistribution of time, involving a full recognition of the fact that the program is not only administered by teachers but is followed by pupils.

**Greater Centralization Needed**

Up to this point the discussion has merely suggested some of the difficulties in our present tendency. Is it not proper for us to go further and to raise seriously the whole question of the advantage of this type of organization? Certainly the demands for more individual attention to the pupils which are being made at the present time cannot properly be met under any system which removes the teacher from personal acquaintance with the children. Certainly the need of rearranging subject-matter so as to fit it to the maturity of the students is not being adequately met by those who are interested primarily in subject-matter rather than in the general program of the students.

**Can Departmental Teaching Survive?**

Our schools are profiting by the specialized training of teachers who are equipped in their various departments, but we are losing the advantage of intimate personal contact with the students. This is especially true in the larger schools where departmental teaching has been most largely introduced.

**Need of Personal Attention to Pupils**

# BOOK REVIEWS

*Among School Gardens.* By M. Louise Green. New York: Charities Publication Committee, 1910. Illustrated. Pp. xv+388. $1.25.

One of the excellent pieces of work that has been made possible by the Russell Sage Foundation is a painstaking investigation of the purpose and method of the school-garden movement. The results of this investigation have taken the form of a book. Dr. Greene, to whom this work was assigned, has covered all sorts and conditions of garden work—school gardens, home gardens and window boxes, community, civic, and industrial gardens. The United States and Canada are fully treated and there are numerous important references to European gardens. In the first chapter, which is upon "The Evolution of the School Garden," the remarkably extensive and intensive growth of the movement in the United States is shown. Less than twenty years (nineteen years according to the records) have passed since through the assistance of the Massachusetts Horticultural Society and under the direction of Mr. Henry Lincoln Clapp the first school garden was established at Roxbury, Mass. It was rapidly and generally recognized that gardens afforded splendid opportunities for many-sided development of boys and girls, and the idea which was at first called a "fad" soon secured practical recognition in every state. The school and home have been brought closer together. School and home gardens both serve as excellent laboratories for the study of elementary science and economics. Better and more purposeful education is secured and the possible good reaction on the home is indicated when we note the claim that in Cleveland, Ohio, due to the school-garden influence, over 50,000 home gardens have come into existence. Almost equally striking results are reported from other cities and in the country the home garden has received a new stimulus.

Other chapters deal with: "Different Kinds of Gardens," "Soil Fertility," "Cost of Equipment," "Planning and Planting the Gardens," "After Planting, What?" "Some Garden Weeds," and "The School Garden in Vacation and in Term Time."

Throughout the entire book the discussions and abundant illustrations present in a concrete and authoritative way the many things that both experienced and inexperienced teachers want to know in order to secure the best educative results. Some of the features of the lengthy and valuable appendix are: an outline in garden study showing the relation between garden work and the other subjects of the primary school (Grade 2), transplanting, potting, and resetting, insecticides, tables giving data for planting of vegetables and flowering plants, testimony from adults regarding the value of garden work, and a garden bibliography consisting of thirty-one pages.

O. W. C.

*Education through Music*. By CHARLES HUBERT FARNSWORTH, Adjunct Professor of Music, Teachers College, Columbia University. American Book Co. Pp. 208.

Mr. Farnsworth occupies nineteen chapters with the theory and practice of music-teaching through the primary and grammar grades. He refutes the charge that his theory is too idealistic by following its utterance with detailed suggestions for putting it into practice. He contends that the study of music in elementary schools should give the child much more than an expert ability to name tones on the staff. It would seem that he is willing to sacrifice some of that expertness to the intellectual strength which his broader treatment of the subject aims to give. He seems to have found the tortuous channel between the Scylla of unbalanced emotionality and the Charybdis of inhibited aesthetic impulse, reaching with his eighth-grade class the high seas of general musical appreciation founded on discrimination and analysis.

The inexperienced teacher might find difficulty in following his lead all the way, but for the musician who meets his students often enough to follow a logical sequence in his lessons, the complete course is fascinating and practical. Suggestions abound as to the treatment of problems psychologically suited to the successive school years, and though these sometimes make serious breaks in the time-honored scheme of progression dear to the heart of educators in music, they appeal to common-sense.

It might be well to read the closing chapter of the book, "The Broad and the Narrow View of Education in Relation to Music," as a stimulus to open-mindedness, before undertaking its perusal as a whole. But in whatever spirit it is approached, no one interested in the progressive teaching of music in the schools can afford to pass it by.

M. R. KERN

# CURRENT EDUCATIONAL LITERATURE IN THE PERIODICALS[1]

IRENE WARREN
Librarian, School of Education, The University of Chicago

EDITOR'S NOTE.—Owing to pressure on space in the November number, a portion of Miss Warren's material was omitted. It is here published, preceding the regular and new contribution for December, in order that our readers may lose none of the continuity of the work.

DOANE, W. C. Contributions to the history of American teaching (6). Educa. R. 40:109–12. (S. '10.)

EDSON, A. W. Instruction of exceptional children in the New York City public schools. Educa. 31:1–10. (S. '10.)

———. Observation and practice teaching in the New York City training schools. Educa. R. 40:138–44. (S. '10.)

FLETCHER, A. P. An experiment in industrial education. El. School T. 11: 8–14. (S. '10.)

FRODSHAM, M. G. The students' careers association. School W. 12:331–34. (S. '10.)

GREENWOOD, J. M. William Torrey Harris—the man. Educa. R. 40:173–83. (S. '10.)

GRUENBERG, BENJAMIN. William James. Sci. Amer. 103:198–99. (10 S. '10.)

HAWKES, H. E. Mathematics in the college course. Educa. R. 40:145–56. (S. '10.)

HAYS, W. M. How schools and the Department of Agriculture can co-operate (2). Journ. of Educa. 72:175–76. (1 S. '10.)

HOWERTH, IRA WOODS. Instruction by correspondence. School and Home Educa. 30:22–27. (S. '10.)

Is Europe taking religion out of its schools? R. of Rs. 42:350. (S. '10.)

[1] *Abbreviations.*—Chau., Chautauquan; Col. Univ. Q., Columbia University Quarterly; Educa., Education; Educa. R., Educational Review; El. School T., Elementary School Teacher; Geographical T., Geographical Teacher; Journ. of Educa., Journal of Education; Journ. of Educa. Psychol., Journal of Educational Psychology; Liv. Age, Living Age; Man. Train. Mag., Manual Training Magazine; Pedagog. Sem., Pedagogical Seminary; Pop. Sci. Mo., Popular Science Monthly; Primary Educa., Primary Education; Psychol. Clinic, Psychological Clinic; R. of Rs., Review of Reviews; Relig. Educa., Religious Education; School R., School Review; School W., School World; Teach. College Rec., Teachers College Record.

JOHNSON, G. E. The renaissance of play. Kind. R. 21:65–74. (O. '10.)

JUDD, C. H. On the comparison of grading systems in high schools and colleges. School R. 18:460–70. (S. '10.)

———. (The) school and the library. El. School T. 11:28–35. (S. '10.)

MARION, G. E. The library as an adjunct to industrial laboratories. Lib. Journ. 35:400–4. (S. '10.)

MAURER, A. H. Football in the high school. Educa. R. 40:132–37. (S. '10.)

MIERS, H. A. Relations between university and school education. School. W. 12:341–46. (S. '10.)

MOORE, ANNIE C. Report on storytelling. Lib. Journ. 35:404–12. (S. '10.)

(The) moving picture and the national character. R. of Rs. 42:315–20. (S. '10.)

PALMER, F. H. Correspondence schools. Educa. 31:47–52. (S. '10.)

PATON, J. L. Testing intelligence. School W. 12:321–23. (S. '10.)

Popular appeal of the library. Lit. Digest 41:446. (17 S. '10.)

POULSSON, EMILIE. History of the story in the kindergarten. Kind. R. 21:85–91. (O. '10.)

Professor William James. Lit. Digest 41:384. (10 S. '10.)

RAND, E. K. A symposium on the value of humanistic, particularly classical, studies: The classics and the new education. I, The classics in European education. School R. 18:441–59. (S. '10.)

SHELDON, W. D. A neglected cause of retardation. Educa. R. 40:121–31. (S. '10.)

SIES, R. W. Scientific methods in education. Educa. R. 40:157–72. (S. '10.)

SMITH, T. F. A. German schools—A national system. School W. 13:325–29. (S. '10.)

TANNER, AMY E. The child as the center of correlation in the kindergarten. Kind. R. 31:75–80. (O. '10.)

Temptations of a college president. Educa. R. 40:113–20. (S. '10.)

(The) third international congress of school hygiene. School W. 12:329–31. (S. '10.)

VATTIER, G. Experimental pedagogy in France. Journ. of Educa. Psychol. 1:389–403. (S. '10.)

---

ALDEN, PERCY. The British child and the state (2). Chaut. 60:183–202. (O. '10.)

ANDREWS, BENJAMIN R. The schools of household and industrial arts—Teachers College. Col. Univ. Q. 12:397–407. (S. '10.)

BATTEN, S. Z. Methods of training for social service. Relig. Educa. 5:390–98. (O. '10.)

BENNETT, CHARLES A. Visiting manual training schools in Europe—VI. Man. Train. Mag. 12:28–46. (O. '10.)

BICKNELL, PERCY F. A child of the Orient in the turmoil of London. Dial 49:226–27. (1 O. '10.)

Björkman, Edwin. William James: builder of American ideals. R. of Rs. 42:463–67. (O. '10.)

Blair, R. The relation of science to industry and commerce. School W. 12: 390–91. (O. '10.)

Botkin, Alice Sinclair. The relation of outside subjects to major subjects in the high school. Educa. 31:103–7. (O. '10.)

Bourne, Henry E. Reminiscences of an English teacher. Dial 49:232–33. (1 O. '10.)

Brown, Daisy R. Young people's ideas of the value of Bible study. Pedagog. Sem. 17:370–86. (S. '10.)

Brownson, Carleton L. The relations between colleges and secondary schools: tendencies and possibilities. School R. 18:548–59. (O. '10.)

Caldwell, Otis W. Natural history in the grades: Seventh and eighth grades. El. School T. 11:49–62. (O. '10.)

Chase, Harry Woodburn. Psychoanalysis and the unconscious. Pedagog. Sem. 17:281–323. (S. '10.)

Children in English poetry. Liv. Age 49:108–11. (8 O. '10.)

Coe, George A. Responsibility of the college for the student. Relig. Educa. 5:302–6. (O. '10.)

Davis, Benjamin Marshall. Agricultural education: Periodical literature. El. School T. 11:79–89. (O. '10.)

Feasey, J. Eaton. Outdoor work for schools of normal type. School W 12:392–93. (O. '10.)

Felmley, David. The educational value of manual training. Man. Train. Mag. 12:1–8. (O. '10.)

Fiske, G. Walter. Student self-government in colleges. Relig. Educa. 5: 307–15. (O. '10.)

Fleming, Walter L. General William T. Sherman as a history teacher. Educa. R. 40:235–38. (O. '10.)

Fullerton, H. B. The educational value of experimental farms. Craftsman 19:38–43. (O. '10.)

Gates, Herbert W. The Christian Association and the college. Relig. Educa. 5:346–50. (O. '10.)

Goddard, Henry H. Four hundred feeble-minded children classified by the Binet method. Pedagog. Sem. 17:387–97. (S. '10.)

———. What can the public school do for sub-normal children? Training School 7:242–48. (S. '10.)

Goode, J. Paul. Some fundamental principles of Japanese education. School R. 18:634–36. (N. '10.)

Harries, A. H. Some faults in the teaching of geography in secondary schools, and some remedies. Geographical T. 5:271–75. (Summer '10.)

Huber, John B. Infantile paralysis: a menace. R. of Rs. 42:597–600. (N. '10.)

HUEY, EDMUND B. The Binet scale for measuring intelligence and retardation. Journ. of Educa. Psychol. 1:435–44. (O. '10.)

HUGHES, PERCY. The distinction between the liberal and technical in education. Pop. Sci. Mo. 77:379–85. (O. '10.)

ILIFFE, J. W. Education at the British Association. School W. 12:377–79. (O. '10.)

JOHNSON, FRANKLIN W. A comparative study of the grades of pupils from different elementary schools in the subjects of the first year in high school. El. School T. 11:63–78. (O. '10.)

JOHNSTON, KATHARINE L. M. Binet's method for the measurement of intelligence. School W. 12:391–92. (O. '10.)

KEPPEL, FREDERICK P. The administrative organization of the university. Educa. R. 40:293–99. (O. '10.)

KYLE, EMILY E. The home and education congress at Brussels. School W. 12:376–77. (O. '10.)

LEGGE, J. G. The teaching of handicraft and elementary science in elementary schools. School W. 12:361–66. (O. '10.)

LIPMANN, OTTO. The examination of intelligence in children. School W. 12:366–69. (O. '10.)

LOVEJOY, OWEN R. Six years' battle for the working child. R. of Rs. 42:593–96. (N. '10.)

LYNCH, ELLA FRANCES. The bright child. Psychol. Clinic 4:141–44. (O. '10.)

MACDONALD, J. B. The Binet tests in a hospital for the insane. Training School 7:250–51. (S. '10.)

MCKEAG, ANNA J. The use of illustrative experiments in classes in education. Journ. of Educa. Psychol. 1:467–72. (O. '10.)

MCMURRY, OSCAR L. AND EGGERS, GEORGE W. Bookbinding in the school. Man. Train. Mag. 12:9–27. (O. '10.)

MABIE, HAMILTON W. A French circulating library. Outlook 96:316–20. (8 O. '10.)

MAIN, JOHN H. T. The personal element in education. Relig. Educa. 5:326–33. (O. '10.)

MANN, CHARLES RIBORG. Physics and education. School R. 18:541–47. (O. '10.)

MATLOCK, WILLIAM H. Instruction in religion in state universities. Educa. R. 40:256–65. (O. '10.)

MERIAM, J. L. Recitation and study. School R. 18:627–33. (N. '10.)

MITCHELL, H. B. A new system of honor courses in Columbia College. Educa. R. 40:217–28. (O. '10.)

(The) modern child. Liv. Age 49:58–60. (1 O. '10.)

MUIRHEAD, JOHN H. The religious basis of education. Relig. Educa. 5:281–95. (O. '10.)

MUSSEY, H. R. Economics in the college course. Educa. R. 40:239–49. (O. '10.)

NISHIYAMA, SEKIJI. Japanese secondary education. Educa. 31:99–102. (O. '10.)

O'SHEA, M. V. Readings in great educators: A message from ancient Rome. Prim. Educa. 18:485–86. (N. '10.)

PELSMA, JOHN R. A child's vocabulary and its development. Pedagog. Sem. 17:328–69. (S. '10.)

REAVIS, W. C. Dental examination of school children. El. School T. 11: 90–98. (O. '10.)

RICHARDS, CHARLES R. The place of industries in public education. Man. Train. Mag. 12:47–51. (O. '10.)

RUEDIGER, WILLIAM C. The Sunday-school curriculum. Educa. 31:117–23. (O. '10.)

SARGENT, D. A. Physical education in its various phases. Mind and Body 17:201–5. (O. '10.)

SHEFFIELD, ALFRED DWIGHT. The rational study of English grammar. School R. 18:618–26. (N. '10.)

SHOREY, PAUL. A symposium on the value of humanistic, particularly classical studies: The classics and the new education: III. The case for the classics. School R. 18:585–617. (N. '10.)

SIMONS, MAY WOOD. Industrial education in Chicago. Pedagog. Sem. 17: 398–418. (S. '10.)

SMITH, JESSIE FRANCES. Report on English in secondary schools in England and Scotland. Educa. R. 40:266–92. (O. '10.)

Social work for children in the United States. Chaut. 60:256–66. (O. '10.)

STARBUCK, EDWIN D. Authority and democracy in colleges. Relig. Educa. 5:315–26. (O. '10.)

STEVENS, ROMIETT. Stenographic reports of high-school lessons. Teach. College Rec. 11:1–66. (S. '10.)

SUTHERLAND, ALEXANDER. School gardening. School W. 12:393. (O. '10.)

TAYLOR, CHARLES KEEN. The boy in the private school. Psychol. Clinic 4: 132–35. (O. '10.)

TAYLOR, GRAHAM. The church and civic education. Relig. Educa. 5:385–90. (O. '10.)

TERRY, H. L. Physics in the high school. Educa. R. 40:250–55. (O. '10.)

THOMAS, CHARLES SWAIN. Essential principles in teaching English. Educa. 31:82–98. (O. '10.)

THOMPSON, W. O. The Christian Association and the college. Relig. Educa. 5:339–45. (O. '10.)

TOWN, CLARA HARRISON. The training of a case of infantile stammer. Psychol. Clinic 4:136–40. (O. '10.)

VOTAW, CLYDE W. College course in morality and religion. Relig. Educa. 5: 295–302. (O. '10.)

WALLIN, J. E. WALLACE. The rationale of promotion and elimination of waste in the elementary and secondary schools. Journ. of Educa. Psychol. 1:445–66. (O. '10.)

WALTON, GEORGE A. Teaching the Bible in private schools. Relig. Educa. 5:351–54. (O. '10.)

WEEKS, ARLAND D. Ways in which the higher institutions may serve rural communities. Educa. R. 40:229–34. (O. '10.)

WENLEY, R. M. A symposium on the value of humanistic, particularly classical studies: The classics and the new education: II. The classics and the elective system. School R. 18:513–29. (O. '10.)

WHITBECK, R. H. Where shall we lay the emphasis in teaching geography? Educa. 31:108–16. (O. '10.)

WHITE, E. M. The real religious difficulty: With special reference to secondary schools. Journ. of Educa. 42:657–59. (O. '10.)

WILLETT, HERBERT L. Religious journalism. Relig. Educa. 5:355–59. (O. '10.)

WILSON, JAMES. The new regulations for technical schools. School W. 12: 373–76. (O. '10.)

WITMER, LIGHTNER. What is meant by retardation? Psychol. Clinic 4: 121–31. (O. '10.)

WORKS, GEORGE A. A high-school course in applied chemistry. School R. 18:560–64. (O. '10.)

WRIGHT, MARK R. A training college under canvas. School W. 12: 369–73. (O. '10.)

ZEHRING, BLANCHE. Mechanizing our higher institutions. Relig. Educa. 5: 334–38. (O. '10.)

VOLUME XI NUMBER 5

# THE ELEMENTARY SCHOOL TEACHER

JANUARY, 1911

## THE SOCIAL SERVICE OF PUBLIC SCHOOLS AS INDICATED BY THE RESULTS OF A STUDY OF A TYPICAL COMMUNITY

JAMES H. RISLEY
Owensboro, Ky.

Much has been said and written of late on the alleged defects prevalent in our public schools which prevent them from being of the greatest possible usefulness to the social groups which they are designed to serve. It has been claimed that they are undemocratic, furnishing, especially in their higher courses, a training fitted only for a few, and that the greater number of students drop out before they have finished their courses and begin work for which they have had little direct preparation.

This study was undertaken with a view of finding out, if possible, just how much schooling a typical body of citizens have had and what correlation, if any, exists between the number of years they have attended school and their financial success. It was the further design of the study to see whether these people had any well-defined idea concerning the value of their own training and its efficiency in helping them to adjust themselves to their environment.

### METHOD OF THE INVESTIGATION

The city studied was Owensboro, Kentucky, a manufacturing city of 20,000 inhabitants and surrounded by a fine agricultural community. A questionnaire was prepared, and sent out by school children so that it fell into the hands of citizens in all parts of the city and surrounding country districts.

The following form was used:

Name.......... Address.......... Occupation..........

How long did you attend school?.......... When?..........

Are you a college graduate?.......... High-school graduate?..........

What subjects did you study in school?..........

Which of these do you think have been of most real value to you? (mention others besides the three R's).......... Why?..........

Are there any subjects that have been of little or no value to you? .......... Why?..........

If you could begin your school work over again, what changes would you like to have made in school courses or methods?..........

This questionnaire was supplemented by personal interviews, and altogether answers were secured from a thousand people representative of all classes, trades, and professions, and may be considered as coming from sources which will fairly represent the entire citizenship.

After gathering in the material, an attempt was made to classify the respondents according to their salaries or incomes from labor. This was accomplished, in the case of some six hundred individuals, with a fair degree of accuracy, with the help of a number of different persons well acquainted in the community and competent to form estimates of the earning capacity of the people. Inquiry was also made of merchants, foremen, and managers about the wages of employees.

Table 1 affords a complete summary of the facts relative to this six hundred people with regard both to years of schooling and to salaries received. The numbers on the left of the table represent the years of school attendance, those on the right the total number attending. Figures at the top represent salaries or incomes from work, while those at the bottom represent the numbers receiving such salaries, and the percentage of the whole number each group represents. A perusal of this table alone will indicate a correlation between school attendance and amount received as salary or income, and it becomes more apparent by a study of the accompanying charts.

Chart 1 shows the distribution of the entire 1,000 according to years of school attendance. It appears that .8 per cent of the whole number attended school one year; 1.2 per cent 2 years;

## TABLE I

### Showing Relation between School Attendance and Earning Capacity

| Period of School Attendance | 100 | 200 | 300 | 400 | 500 | 600 | 700 | 800 | 900 | 1000 | 1100 | 1200 | 1300 | 1400 | 1500 | 1600 | 1700 | 1800 | 1900 | 2000 | 2500 | 3000 | 4000 | 5000 | 6000 | 8000 | Total |
|---|---|---|---|---|---|---|---|---|---|---|---|---|---|---|---|---|---|---|---|---|---|---|---|---|---|---|---|
| 1 | 3 | 2 | ... | ... | ... | ... | ... | ... | ... | ... | ... | ... | ... | ... | ... | ... | ... | ... | ... | ... | ... | ... | ... | ... | ... | ... | 5 |
| 2 | 2 | 2 | ... | 6 | ... | ... | ... | ... | ... | ... | ... | ... | ... | ... | ... | ... | ... | ... | ... | ... | ... | ... | ... | ... | ... | ... | 10 |
| 3 | 3 | 2 | 2 | 7 | ... | ... | 6 | ... | ... | ... | ... | ... | ... | ... | ... | ... | ... | ... | ... | ... | ... | ... | ... | ... | ... | ... | 20 |
| 4 | ... | 2 | 1 | 15 | 17 | 2 | 5 | 2 | ... | ... | 4 | ... | ... | ... | 3 | ... | ... | 2 | ... | ... | ... | ... | ... | ... | ... | ... | 53 |
| 5 | ... | 6 | 9 | 12 | 18 | 10 | 5 | 15 | 4 | 4 | 4 | ... | 3 | ... | 2 | ... | ... | ... | ... | ... | ... | ... | ... | ... | ... | ... | 92 |
| 6 | ... | 5 | 4 | 10 | 20 | 6 | 2 | 14 | 11 | 2 | 4 | 5 | ... | ... | ... | ... | ... | ... | ... | ... | ... | 2 | ... | ... | ... | ... | 85 |
| 7 | ... | 1 | 7 | 1 | 20 | 4 | ... | 9 | ... | ... | 2 | ... | 2 | 4 | ... | 1 | ... | ... | ... | ... | ... | ... | 1 | ... | ... | ... | 52 |
| 8 | ... | ... | ... | 7 | 12 | 14 | ... | 9 | ... | 12 | 4 | 8 | ... | 2 | ... | 1 | 1 | 2 | ... | 3 | 2 | 1 | 1 | ... | 2 | 1 | 82 |
| 9 | ... | ... | ... | ... | 3 | 1 | 2 | 7 | ... | 6 | ... | 6 | ... | 4 | 9 | 2 | ... | ... | ... | 2 | ... | 1 | 2 | ... | ... | ... | 45 |
| 10 | ... | ... | 2 | ... | ... | 3 | ... | ... | 7 | 2 | 1 | 4 | 4 | 1 | 3 | ... | 3 | 2 | 1 | 2 | 1 | ... | 1 | ... | ... | ... | 37 |
| 11 | ... | ... | 1 | ... | ... | 4 | ... | ... | 4 | ... | ... | ... | 3 | 3 | 5 | 2 | 2 | ... | 1 | ... | ... | ... | ... | 2 | ... | ... | 27 |
| 12 | ... | ... | ... | 14 | ... | ... | 4 | ... | ... | 1 | ... | 8 | ... | 4 | ... | ... | 2 | ... | 1 | 2 | 3 | 2 | 2 | ... | 2 | ... | 45 |
| 13 | ... | ... | ... | 8 | ... | ... | ... | ... | 2 | ... | ... | 2 | ... | ... | 2 | 1 | ... | ... | ... | ... | ... | 1 | ... | ... | ... | ... | 16 |
| 14 | ... | ... | 1 | ... | ... | ... | ... | 2 | ... | ... | 2 | ... | ... | ... | 1 | ... | ... | 3 | 1 | 1 | 2 | ... | ... | 2 | ... | ... | 15 |
| 15 | ... | ... | ... | ... | ... | 2 | ... | ... | ... | ... | ... | ... | 1 | ... | 1 | 1 | ... | ... | ... | ... | ... | 2 | ... | ... | ... | ... | 7 |
| 16 | ... | ... | ... | ... | ... | ... | ... | ... | ... | ... | ... | ... | ... | ... | ... | ... | ... | 1 | ... | ... | ... | ... | 2 | ... | ... | ... | 3 |
| 17 | ... | ... | ... | ... | ... | ... | ... | ... | ... | ... | ... | ... | ... | ... | ... | ... | ... | 2 | ... | ... | ... | ... | ... | ... | ... | ... | 2 |
| 18 | ... | ... | ... | ... | ... | ... | ... | ... | ... | ... | ... | ... | ... | ... | ... | ... | ... | ... | ... | 2 | ... | ... | ... | ... | ... | ... | 2 |
| 19 | ... | ... | ... | ... | ... | ... | ... | ... | ... | ... | ... | ... | ... | ... | ... | ... | ... | ... | ... | ... | ... | ... | ... | ... | ... | ... | ... |
| 20 | ... | ... | ... | ... | ... | ... | ... | ... | ... | ... | ... | ... | ... | ... | 2 | ... | ... | ... | ... | ... | ... | ... | ... | ... | ... | ... | 2 |
| Total | 8 | 20 | 27 | 80 | 90 | 46 | 24 | 58 | 28 | 27 | 21 | 33 | 13 | 18 | 28 | 8 | 8 | 12 | 4 | 12 | 8 | 9 | 9 | 4 | 4 | 1 | |
| Percentage | 1.3 | 3.3 | 4.5 | 13.3 | 15 | 7.7 | 4 | 9.7 | 4.7 | 4.5 | 3.5 | 5.5 | 2.2 | 3 | 4.7 | 1.3 | 1.3 | 2 | .6 | 2 | 1.3 | 1.5 | 1.5 | .6 | .6 | .1 | |

3 per cent 3 years; 10.5 per cent 4 years; 17.5 per cent 5 years; 12.6 per cent 6 years, etc., the number gradually decreasing to 20 years, where we find only 2 per cent. The highest point in

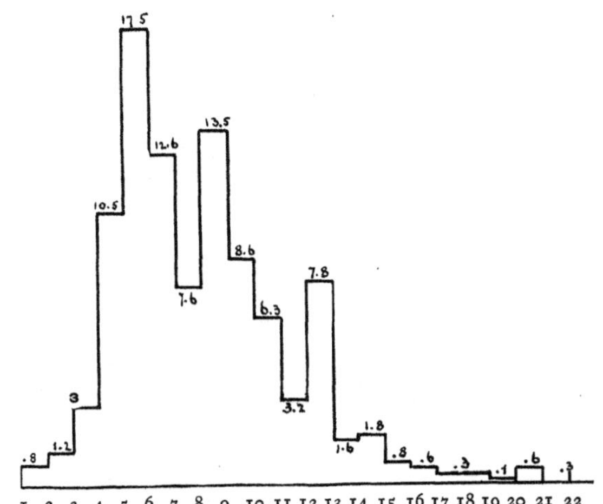

CHART 1.—Distribution of 1,000 according to years' attendance

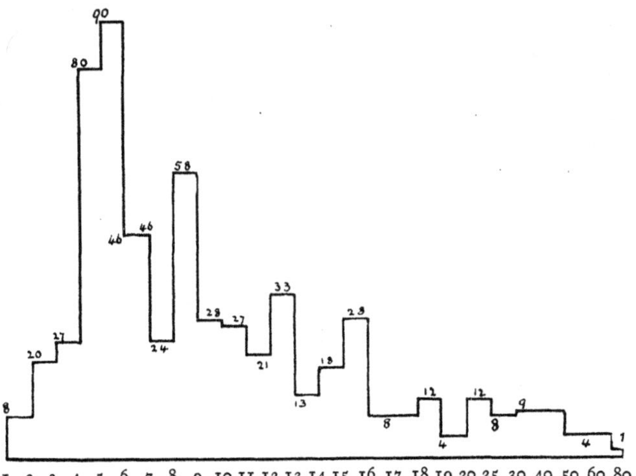

CHART 2.—Distribution of 600 according to salaries or incomes

the curve is at 5 years, which probably represents the average amount of schooling a majority of people have had.

Chart 2 shows the distribution of the 600 of whom estimates could be made according to salaries or incomes. Here the curve reaches its highest point at $500. The chart divided into thirds would show the first third receiving $500 or less, the second, from $500 to $1,000, the third over $1,000.

Chart 3 shows the distribution of the 600 of Chart 2 according to years of schooling, and the general similarity of outline is at once apparent. Dividing it into thirds we find the first group to be composed of those who have attended school five

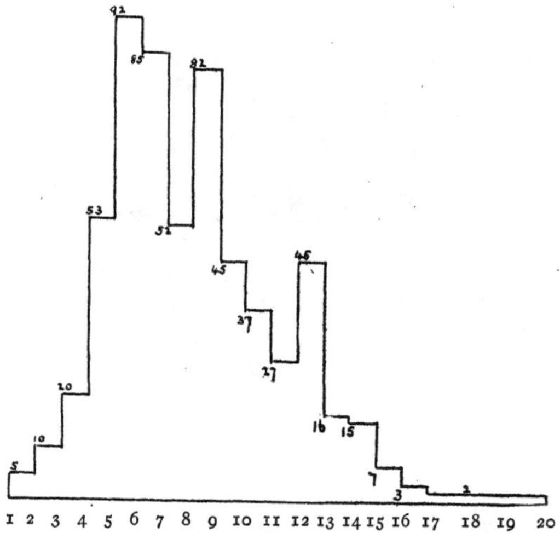


CHART 3.—Distribution (600 of Chart 2) according to years in school

years or less, the second from five to eight, and the third more than eight years.

In Chart 4 the correlation between salaries and years of attendance is set forth still more plainly. The figures at the base represent the years of school attendance, while the blocks represent salaries or incomes. Lines from upper left to lower right represent the groups receiving $500 or less; lines from upper right to lower left, those receiving from $500 to $1,000; anl blank spaces, those who earn over $1,000. Dividing the chart into thirds we find that of all those in the first group, only 18 make over $1,000 as compared with 49 in the middle group and 123 in the third group. Of those making from $500 to $1,000, the first third of the chart contains 53, the second, 83, the third, 47. This shows a preponderance of those who are of the middle group in attendance to belong to the middle group in salaries also. By actual count we find

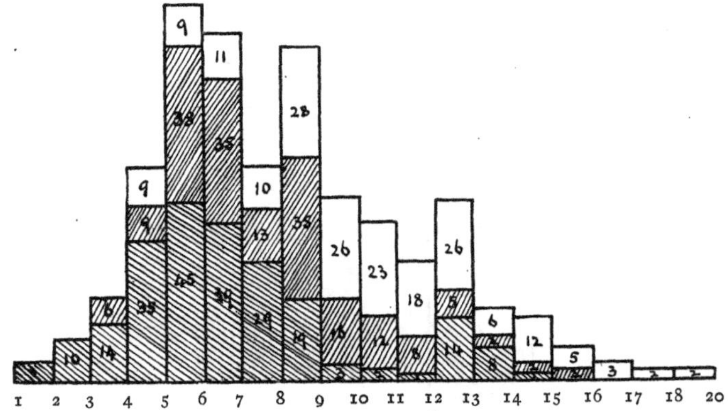


CHART 4.—Oblique lines from upper left to lower right indicate the number receiving $500 or less; lines from upper right to lower left, those receiving from $500 to $1,000; the blank space, those receiving over $1,000.

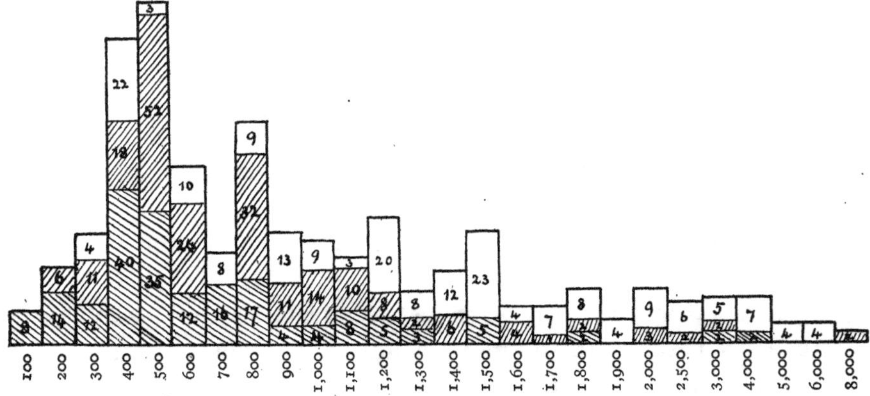


CHART 5.—Oblique lines from upper left to lower right indicate the number attending school five years or less; lines from upper right to lower left, those attending from five to eight years; the blank spaces, those who attended over eight years.

that 317 of the whole number fall into the same groups or divisions in salaries as in years of school attendance.

This same co-ordination is brought out in Chart 5, where the numbers at the bast line represent salaries, while the blocks represent years of schooling. Here in the first group 29 have gone to school over 8 years, while in the second group there are 49, and in the third group 125.

There is a noticeably large number of those who attended school from ten to twelve years in the first group with those who earn $400 or $500. This lack of correlation comes from the fact that there were a number of grade teachers in the list, a class of public servants the most shamefully underpaid of all trades or professions, when the amount of preparation expected of them is taken into consideration. Some further lack of correlation may be explained by the fact that there are numbers of young men just out of college or high school who have not yet had an opportunity to get themselves properly adjusted and make their value known to the world. Some young men start out with financial backing or the influence of prominent relatives and their success comes early; while others who have even better preparation must secure recognition by slow and laborious process extending through many years. Thus in order to explain fully the lack of co-ordination which these charts show, we would have to enter into the history of the individuals of the non-co-ordinating groups and study them in relation to age, family, environment, and all other hindrances or helps to human progress. This would clearly be an impossible task. It is sufficient for our study that our statistics represent some general degree of correlation. The facts set forth in this study agree in the main with the conclusion of Mr. Staples, who made a similar study at Lake Geneva, Wisconsin (see *Elementary School Teacher,* February, 1910).

As to the value these people themselves place upon the training they have received, the relative value of subjects pursued, and what changes they think should be made, the summaries of answers will show. The two questions as to the relative value of subjects brought out a great diversity of opinion. The following table gives the list of subjects occurring with greatest frequency in the answers, the first column of figures being the number of respondents considering them of most value, the second column being the number who have found the same subject of no value to them:

| Subject | Most Value | No Value |
|---|---|---|
| English | 25 | — |
| Literature | 36 | — |
| English grammar | 90 | 2 |
| Rhetoric | 15 | 1 |
| Spelling | 86 | — |
| Commercial branches | 55 | 1 |
| Algebra | 20 | 23 |
| Geometry | 25 | 10 |
| Language | 13 | — |
| Latin | 24 | 20 |
| History | 51 | 9 |
| Physiology and hygiene | 17 | 9 |
| Geography | 28 | 4 |
| Psychology | 11 | — |

In addition the following subjects were mentioned, none more frequently than six times: Greek, German, chemistry, botany, geology, natural philosophy, elocution, vocal music, pedagogy, drawing, ethics, and civics.

The following additional subjects were voted of little or no value by six or less of the respondents: German, Hebrew, French, Greek, trigonometry, physics, chemistry, botany, zoölogy, astronomy, geology, political economy, civics, music, and drawing.

When it comes to the question as to what change the respondents would like to see made, the opinions vary still more widely. Ten say that they prefer the courses and methods of the past, while fifty think that present courses and methods are good enough. The other respondents fall into several groups.

1. Those who think more stress should be placed upon certain subjects. There is little agreement as to what subjects these should be, the following being the chief subjects mentioned, with the number of votes for each:

|  |  |
|---|---|
| Laboratory work in science | 15 |
| Drawing | 15 |
| Music | 12 |
| Latin | 9 |
| Spelling | 9 |
| English | 9 |

The rest of the respondents mention a variety of subjects. none of which are mentioned more than six times. They are as follows: Penmanship, mathematics, arithmetic, reading, literature, debating, grammar, elocution, physiology, chemistry, botany, zoölogy, geography, social science, German, Greek, French, and history.

2. A second group would make certain eliminations, the most frequent suggestion being the elimination of examinations. Others mention "fairy tales," frequent textbook changes, and school amusements, while a few select certain subjects for elimination, the chief being Latin, Greek, and algebra.

3. Certain subjects not yet introduced into these schools are demanded by a third group. Here we find something on which there is more agreement. The chief suggestions are as follows: Introduce thorough courses in

| | |
|---|---|
| Domestic science | 75 |
| Manual training | 69 |
| Physical culture | 40 |
| Agriculture | 15 |
| Vocational training | 30 |
| The Bible, religious and moral instruction | 21 |

4. Another group confines answers to miscellaneous suggestions, the following being the suggestions of greatest frequency:

| | |
|---|---|
| More intensive work in fundamental subjects | 35 |
| Better training for teachers | 20 |
| Longer lunch period | 30 |
| Smaller classes | 10 |
| More study in school | 9 |
| Shorter school hours | 8 |
| Smaller classes | 10 |
| Begin language in lower grades | 8 |
| Have better libraries | 10 |
| Give more attention to individual pupils | 12 |

In addition, the following suggestions occurred, none of which were mentioned by more than six respondents: More extensive work, better grading, better facilities for college preparation, stricter discipline, better understanding between teachers and pupils, two years in eighth grade, more home study, separate courses for boys and girls, better training of memory, better training of the senses, more election in the high school, stricter attendance laws, longer recess periods, uniform dress for students, open school with prayer, more male teachers, concrete methods, less expensive high schools and more money for the grades, separate classes for dull students.

The above summaries speak for themselves and need very little comment. Of the subjects regarded as of greatest value, the English group is the favorite with a total of 254 votes; 44 favor language, and it is noticeable that Latin, which a number of modern educators would have us eliminate from the curriculum, is still a favorite among those who have studied it. Two reasons are expressed for this preference, one the formal discipline idea and the other the more practical one of greater facility in the use of the mother tongue. One man, who is an expert accountant, affirmed the formal discipline doctrine in most emphatic terms. He affirmed that Latin and Greek had given him greater strength for the accomplishment of the intricate and puzzling tasks which fell to him than all other subjects combined.

Then 55 place commercial subjects first on the list, giving direct utility as the reason for their preference. In fact, the notion of utility is prevalent in all answers as to relative values. The fact that knowledge of a subject can actually be made to accomplish something which will aid them to master the difficulties of their work is the criterion of value in the minds of a very large majority of these people.

When it comes to opinions as to which subjects were of little or no value, we find many answers tending to neutralize the statements of greatest value, a proof that a subject may appear to be of very great value to one person but worthless to another. There are reasons for this. A subject may have been studied so short a time as to preclude any positive measure of value, and this fact will explain a great many statements found in these answers. Again, the subject may have been so poorly taught that the student has failed to get anything of value from it.

Two hundred and fifty-six, or about one-third of the respondents, express the belief that every subject pursued has been of value to them. Of the rest, 37 place little value on the language group, the largest number naming Latin as the subject of least value. Thus it appears that no school system or curriculum could be established by popular vote if it depended on a large number of people agreeing on any one subject. The votes tend rather to neutralize each other.

When we come to the question as to changes in subject-matter or curriculum, we find the same variance of opinion. Ten of the respondents would advocate a return to the system of the past as it existed when they were in school. Fifty express themselves as being well satisfied with the schools as they exist at present. Many would like more intensive work on fundamental subjects, a few would have more extensive work. Some would like more work or better work in a variety of different subjects. Others would eliminate those same subjects from the curriculum. There was the greatest unanimity in the desire for courses in manual training and domestic economy, 69 mentioning the former and 75 the latter. Fifteen would have courses in agriculture, 21 some sort of religious instruction, 30 vocational training, and 40 physical training. Thus, while it has been shown that people who have made any considerable study of Latin and Greek and other subjects of the traditional curriculum have still a preference for those subjects, it is true that there is a decided leaning toward the newer groups of subjects which aim at a more immediate adjustment to the affairs of ordinary life. People have not stopped to think very seriously as yet what has been of most service to them in the education of the past, but in this turning toward the practical we see evidence of the awakening of a universal popular demand that education shall be for service and that there shall be a closer correlation than ever between the amount of school training and the social efficiency and economic success of the individual.

To sum up the conclusions of this discussion: Approximately one-third of the people have attended school five years or less, one-third from five to eight, one-third over eight years.

A correlation has been shown to exist between the number

of years spent in school and the earning power of the individuals. Where this correlation does not appear, it is often due to exceptionally low rates of wages paid to certain well-educated classes. Eliminate these classes from the study and the correlation would appear to be very much closer.

There is no well-defined general opinion among the people as to the relative value of the subjects they have pursued. Such opinions as are given base their claims on the doctrine of formal discipline or direct utility, chiefly the latter. On the whole, the opinions are so much at variance as to make it clear that public opinion could not be taken as a safe guide in making a school curriculum.

The one subject on which there is the greatest agreement is the demand for more attention to the newer groups of subjects which aim at a closer correlation between the work of the school and the practical life of the individual in his social environment.

# THE EVOLUTION OF AIM AND METHOD IN THE TEACHING OF NATURE-STUDY IN THE COMMON SCHOOLS OF THE UNITED STATES (*Concluded*)

IRA BENTON MEYERS
School of Education, The University of Chicago

In 1845, in the higher schools the idea of study for the sake of discipline became a prominent factor in the work, and science, especially botany, held its place because of its disciplinary value. In the elementary schools all organized attempts to teach natural history practically died out. In the meantime geography had gained considerable headway and the description of landscape, plants, and animals as incorporated in this study was considered ample natural history for the elementary schools. School work settled down to a study routine in which anyone who could handle the system, diagram, work all of the sums, and keep order was ready to teach. Against the character and content of this type of work in elementary schools people soon began to complain. Both Gray and Agassiz, the recognized leaders of their respective sciences, raised their voices in protest. Gray said:

> I do not suppose that the mere treasuring up of facts will effect the object of education. . . . . I venture the assertion that, if the truth were known, the child acquires a greater number of useful ideas, more real development and strength of mind, during his play hours with his rabbits, his kites, from his story books, than from the lessons assigned him during his hours of study; he is really educated more out of school than in school.

By the early fifties a new movement was attempted and a strong plea made for a return to a freer out-of-door study of nature from the standpoint of the child's interests. The movement in America seems to have been stimulated by the work of the Prussian schools and its spirit is fairly stated by Raumer:

> I will state the method which the student should follow: He should first examine in all directions the neighborhood of his residence and should make himself so thoroughly familiar with it that he can call up before his

mind whatever he chooses. Such an acquaintance is the result of the unconscious and fresh pleasures which youth, joyful and free from scientific anxieties, will find for itself in such an examination, obtaining in this artless way a simple, general impression of the vicinity not forced by the teacher. He is not teased while rejoicing in the blue heavens and the rapid motion of the clouds, in the oak woods, and flowery meadows, where the butterflies play, by a professor with a kianometer to measure the blue of the sky, nor by recommendations not to stare in the woods but rather to ascertain whether the oaks are *Quercus rubra* or *alba;* or, not to look at the flowers all at once as if they were a yellow carpet but to take his Linnaeus and determine the species of *Ranunculus.* No entomologist is setting him to chase butterflies and to impale them. . . . . In this paradisaic pleasure is planted the seed of the perception of an intellectual world, whose secrets will not be fully ascertained and understood even after the longest and most active life of scientific effort. But most teachers, by the dispersion of these simple impressions of nature, destroy these earlier impressions of children and the brightness of the imaginary world which they see.

This second movement for a return to nature from the standpoint of children's interest had made but little headway when it was intercepted by another and stronger movement. Two ideas had grown up in school work, both at home and abroad, and become associated with nature teaching. One was that of mental discipline, already prominent in the science work of the higher schools; the other, that of acquiring practical or useful information, some knowledge of the natural and manufactured objects met and used in everyday life. The first idea gave rise to a type of teaching termed "object-lessons," the primary purpose of which was sense-training, mental exercise, and discipline. It called for a complete and detailed analysis of an object to insure complete observation and accurate judgment. Its advocates believed that the end, mental discipline, could be most effectively attained through an intensive study of a few type objects. The second idea gave rise to a type of instruction termed, "Lessons on Common Things," and was intended to give children information on common materials and phenomena about them from the standpoint of meaning, their use to man, and something of the processes by which they are rendered useful. So far as relates to any natural history in the common schools these two types of work held and dominated the field during the succeeding thirty years (1860–90).

The conflict brought on by the growth of the idea of organic evolution was a strong factor in silencing any plea for a return to pure natural-history study in the common schools. "Its enemies are those who are sneering at 'bugology' or who lift their hands in pious horror because some bold speculator or lover of notoriety thinks geology contradicts the Bible." It was only when organic evolution had gained a stronghold in the minds of the more liberal thinking public that a return to a study of nature, from the standpoint of the child's interests in nature, could be attempted. Taking a glimpse at the higher schools and academies during this period, botany in the form of plant analysis and textbook memorization still held sway. A little before the middle of the period, under the masterful guidance and leadership of Huxley and his followers, as well as on account of the rapid growth in biological knowledge, zoölogy began to gain prominence in the more progressive schools. Up to this period the school work in zoölogy was of the strictly natural-history type.

In 1872 Huxley remarked:

> Certain broad laws of biology have a general application throughout the animal and plant world, but the ground common to these kingdoms of nature is not of very wide extent, and the multiplicity of details so great that the student of living beings finds himself obliged to devote his attention to one or the other.

This marks the first distinct step toward specialized study. To this Huxley added the remark which gave direction to this work for the succeeding sixteen years:

> My own impression is that the best model for all kinds of training in physical science is that afforded by the methods of the study of anatomy in the medical schools.

It is not necessary to point out that the study has made a direct shift in the schools from the viewpoint of the educator to that of the specialist in a particular subject. The pupil is now treated in his class work exactly as he would be if he were preparing himself as a specialist in zoölogy, except that he shall stop the study with the job half completed. On the other hand it was assumed that under the influence of this work, as carried on, the aims of the educator, interest, discipline, character, moral culture, would follow as a matter of course; and educational discussions turned to a discussion of the relations of science to "discipline," to "moral culture," to "character-building," etc. Natural-history types of work quite wholly disappeared from the schools and specialized types of work took their place. Pupils analyzed, observed, dissected, not from any impulse of intense individual interest but because the laboratory manual so directed. This work reached its culmination in Huxley and Martin's *Practical Biology*.

In the beginning stages of the work classification was the foundation upon which the work was based; later morphological work became the prominent factor, especially in zoölogy, and classification was transferred to the back of the book, the argument being that children should first have something to classify. The work in the sciences, as well as the "object-lessons" and "lessons on common things," in the elementary schools had just reached perfection in organization of subject-matter, perfect text-books had been written, and the schools were well settled to their routine work, when the complaint began again to grow that "science and object-lessons as taught are becoming a grind and destroying the children's instinctive interests in natural objects and phenomena."

The late seventies and early eighties stand out as a transition period during which elementary science and object-lessons made up the bulk of the nature-teaching in the schools, but enthusiasm was on the wane, there was a growing remonstrance against the type of work carried on in both schools, and centers of work of a new character were forming in various localities. Under the influence of the teachings of Pestalozzi and his followers the feeling that the child's education should deal more with things, from the standpoint of his interest, and less with books, had been kept alive and gained considerable headway, notwithstanding that object-lesson teaching had proved that the study of things could become as formal a process in learning as the textbook when things were not considered from the standpoint of the pupils' interests. From the other side had come the growing influence of science, convincing the people that it held something better than routine analysis and classification.

As might be expected the better elements of both took a prominent part in the movement now in its formative stage. This movement was distinctly an American movement, brought on by American school conditions; whereas previous movements were made up largely of elements borrowed from foreign countries and applied to American conditions. Three of the centers in this new movement are cited as typical of the influences which entered into it.

One of these centers is represented by the work of Alpheus Hyatt and Lucretia Crocker around Boston. Professor Hyatt was a student and follower of Agassiz and his work partook of the point of view of science. The character of this work is well represented in his *Guides for Science Teaching* (1878). I am inclined to believe that had the elementary schools, during this earlier period held to the spirit of Agassiz' teachings they would have accomplished far more in their work.

At about this same time (1877–78) Dr. W. T. Harris was trying out a course in elementary science in the schools of St. Louis. In his introductory remarks to the teacher he says: "The course is arranged with reference to method rather than quantity and exhaustiveness." He thought out the course as progressing spirally: plant life in the first grade, animal life in the second grade, physical elements and mechanical powers in the third grade, coming around to botany again in the fourth grade. Referring to botany he says:

> If only one topic is thoroughly discussed in each quarter of the year some very important ideas will be gained of the science of botany. In the fourth year the student will come round to the subject again and can deepen his insight into the methods of studying the world of plants, learn the general outline of classification, and train his observing powers.

It is evident that Dr. Harris had in mind, as the aim in the work, discipline and preparation for science. At the third level of the rounding of the spiral these more general topics merge into the more general elementary sciences: in the sixth grade, into elementary physics and astronomy; in the seventh grade, physical geography; and in the eighth grade, natural philosophy.

In the meantime Professor H. H. Straight was developing a type of work in the Oswego normal school (1878–82).[1] Professor Straight was a student under Agassiz and was well grounded in the sciences. On the other side he had become greatly influenced by the teachings of Pestalozzi, and in his work he blended in an admirable way these two points of view. I consider that this work, more than any other, represented in spirit and practice this new nature-study movement. Similar types of work were advocated and carried on in other localities, among which may be mentioned the work of Boyden in Plymouth Co., Mass., Payne in Pennsylvania, Ford at Kirksville, Mo., Howe at Chicago, etc. But, so far as I have been able to analyze the situation, no new elements entered into any of these other centers.

During the late eighties Professor Wilbur S. Jackman had been studying the science-teaching problem as related to high-school work; he had outlined a course of study which he asked, and was granted, permission to carry out in the Central High School of Pittsburgh. Before the course went into effect he was called to the Cook County Normal School to take up the work interrupted by the death of Professor Straight. With the work of Professor Straight to open the way, under the leadership of Colonel Parker and with a broad, sympathetic, liberal, thinking mind of his own, the outlook was for strong and effective work.

Up to this period (1891) the thing lacking to fuse this new work into one great movement was a good textbook or guide for teachers. Numerous outlines had appeared in educational journals and in pamphlet form, but they were scattered and showed little unity of opinion. In the latter part of the year Mr. Jackman issued his *Nature-Study*. The time for a book was never more ripe; no book ever met so directly the spirit of the

[1] He was called to Cook County Normal School, 1883–85.

movement which it represented, and yet it proved a sore disappointment to teachers. It met the teachers unprepared, it treated of outlook, of purpose, of methods of setting to work with the children, of what was best to do and how to do it; but alas, it failed to tell the teacher what the results would be after she had done the work, it failed to give the answer to the questions asked. For a quarter of a century the schools had preached "study things and not books," had handled and taught from objects in both science and object-lessons, under the impression that they were studying things, and when the students of the system were put to the test it was found, *en masse,* to have been dead formalism. That the proper doing of a thing would furnish the answer, that if it did not it was because the method of the doing was wrong, and needed correction, did not occur to the school world. It made little difference what the nature of the activity was, or the incentive under which carried on, it was *an* answer that was wanted and as stated by a supervisor of nature-study, "I don't need a book that asks questions, I want one that contains answers." The book indicated a direct return to the original and ever-recurring idea of bringing children into direct contact with the whole of their nature environment from the standpoint of their own interests in nature. The underlying idea was no longer that of the "Wonders of Creation," but the writer states:

> The spirit of nature-study demands that children shall be intelligently directed in an investigation of their nature environment; that there shall be, under the natural stimulus of the desire to know, a constant effort at a rational interpretation of the common things observed.

Mr. Jackman doubtless believed that the work adequately carried out would usher the grade pupil, well prepared in spirit, subject-matter, and methods of work, into the sciences of the high school. The movement during the next fifteen years (1890–1905) affords an interesting study in which to trace out the influences which have side-tracked true ideals in elementary education, in order to make room for special interests.

The absence of information in Mr. Jackman's book was remedied two years later (1894) by Howe's *Systematic Science Teaching.* In method this book should have preceded Mr. Jackman's, since it shows clearly a direct transition from object-teaching; in another respect that it should follow was the proper procedure. It covers the whole range of the nature environment, starts from the standpoint of children's interests, tells the teacher what to do and how to do it, but gives sufficient running information to relieve the teacher of the necessity to find out anything for herself in the way of original observation and inference.

In the meantime there grew up a general feeling that—

> Nothing appeals so strongly to the young child as life, and when associated with color and movement the appeal is almost irresistible. Change in weather, the formation and nature of soil, minerals and rocks, the effects of erosion and a host of other phenomena of great interest makes no such an appeal, does not enter so apparently and directly into child life, and can be left with safety until a later school period.

Suiting the book to the occasion we have (1898) Lange's *Handbook of Nature-Study*. It treats of plant and animal life only, reduces directions to the teacher to a minimum, except a few fine-print directions on securing materials, and fills the body of the book with a more or less complete description of individual plants and animals. The book doubtless met the demands of teachers, but that the trend is toward dead formalism is clearly indicated.

With the trend of teaching toward a study of plant and animal life, teachers found that they could secure better attention, more interest, if the work in hand assumed story form, and made an appeal to the emotional, rather than the intellectual, side of child life. At the same time there grew up a feeling that nature-study of a more primitive type, myth, folklore, as well as story, was what the child needed; and the movement took a turn in this direction. At the same time numerous excellent stories, attractive to children and adults alike, appeared and a period of story reading and telling was established. The situation was somewhat saved by the timely appearance of Hodge's *Nature-Study and Life* (1901). This book held to the plant and animal phase and recognized feelings and sentiments as powerful factors in elementary education, and approached the study from a humanistic and economic standpoint. The book is too recent and well known to require description. Its great strength was in influencing teachers to develop the personal-interest-in-nature side of the child. To have pets, grow plants, make gardens, encourage wild bird life, use aquarium and insect houses in study of animal life, and to encourage children, and to give them opportunity to put more of themselves into the work. He did not make the mistake of Mr. Jackman in believing that the teacher should be able to go it alone, but filled in ample, excellent text as well as furnished liberally excellent references.

It is of interest to note how, in all of these movements, the popular teaching mind seizes upon some one prominent factor, pampers it, nourishes it, accentuates it until it completely dominates and distorts the situation; whereas had it been treated in a normal way, held in proper association with other equally important ideas, the whole would have exerted a pleasant, wholesome, broadening educational influence upon child life. But in the present instance the emotional stood in the forefront, caught the attention of teachers, and animal stories became the rage of the season. We were getting children into sympathetic touch with nature with a vengeance, but it was a world of nature as revealed through human fancy and not through observation and scientific research. Had we stuck to animals, observed them to see whether they verified the stories, the results might have been most profitable, but such observation spoiled the story. We had so far outstripped nature that the story was more interesting to the child than the living animal itself. Further, because of the reaction due to the overdoing of a good thing, I found parents and teachers asking whether children should be allowed to read books like Thompson-Seton's and Long's. Should a child be allowed occasionally to have a lump of sugar?

The work on the whole was beginning to generate doubt in the minds of people, and a feeling was developing that all of this work, if carried on at all in the elementary schools, should be grouped under the head of elementary science and taught in harmony with scientific method. This feeling was furthered by numerous criticisms on results as observed in nature-study teaching of which the criticism of Professor Armstrong in the *Moseley Educational Commission Report* (1904) is typical:

> The Nature-Study lessons I witnessed, when not specifically botanical or zoölogical and scientific in character, were eminently superficial and worthless.[2]

Up to this date there had been no co-operative effort on the part of advocates of nature-study and little attempt to define, in any broad and comprehensive way, the fundamentals of nature-study; to determine what it really is, its scope, and the character of the work which it should attempt to do. At this crisis in the situation, when people began to say that the work was "in bad repute," when eminent educators contended that it was "a dangerous fad," Professor M. A. Bigelow came to its rescue in founding the *Nature-Study Review*, secured, from various parts of the United States and Canada, through a symposium, the opinion of various people as to the nature, aim, scope, and purpose of the study, thus placing it again squarely before the teaching public and setting up anew a starting-point in nature-study. The outlook into this present epoch is so clearly defined in the editor's introduction of the *Nature-Study Review* and in his editorial to the symposium[3] that there is no need of a restatement here. It is sufficient to say that it represented a return to the idea of an approach to the whole of the nature environment, biological and physical, industrial as well as pure science, from the standpoint of the child's interest in nature.

## SUMMARY

In reviewing the history of nature-study teaching in the schools, from the standpoint of aim and method, some interesting facts were revealed. One of these facts was the constant shift in point of view. It was perfectly clear, throughout the entire period covered, that the main cause of the shift in viewpoint was due to a lack of any definite goal toward which the teacher felt the work was headed; and of any definite standards

[2] See McMurry, "Advisable Omissions from the Elementary Curriculum," *Educational Review*, XXVII, 478–93 (May, 1904).

[3] *Nature-Study Review*, I, No. 1 (January, 1905).

except the most artificial, by which they could measure the degree of their success in the same manner as can the contractor, the merchant, the lawyer, the doctor, and other business and professional people of the world.

Again, it was made plain that the educational point of view of the elementary teacher and the point of view of the specialist in subject-matter are entirely different in type and content. The textbooks used in the schools were written by specialists in subject-matter and from the specialist's viewpoint in which the fundamental aim was that of mastering the subject. In every instance, regardless of the educational outlook of the teacher, her aim came under the dominating influence of the specialist, and this meant a shift from using the subject as a means to that of making it an end.

A still more striking fact which was clearly revealed in each movement was that in every period when the movement was in its formative stage the real educational results were of better quality than at any later stage in the period. In the beginning stages the subject-matter was poorly organized and looked upon with deep distrust by the specialist. On the other hand, as the period advanced subject-matter became better organized, more easily available to the teacher, more complete textbooks appeared, and the subject grew into the good graces of the specialists only to receive the condemnation of the educator. In other words, though it sounds like a paradox, the educational results were always most satisfactory at that stage when the work seemed jumbled and undefined, and least satisfactory when worked out into a well-organized system. At the unorganized, bookless stage the teacher was thrown upon her own resources, and although the work was frequently crude, it bore the stamp of personal effort, and contained an element of personality which is always needed to impart freshness to school work, whereas in the later stages where the teacher relied upon a textbook, this personal effort, and the vigor and freshness which goes with it were almost wholly lacking—the teacher and the work both were lifeless.

Again it was perfectly clear that teachers have little or no notion of the special need of having children linger and loiter, without lagging, in an interesting way, for a considerable time with various objects and situations before attempting to use them in class discussion. It is this element of lingering with things that makes pets, potted plants, insect cages, aquaria, school gardens, and a host of other types of work interesting and profitable if rightly conducted.

Again, it was perfectly clear that people failed to appreciate, and fail to appreciate the fact at the present day, that it is impossible to train teachers in our normals and universities through a system of textbooks and libraries and expect them to go forth and do strong, vigorous, active, original work with children; working from the standpoint of children's interest when they have never worked from the standpoint of their own instinctive interests.

Again, one could not escape the fact, in searching out the story of nature-study teaching, that in all stages there were in various nooks and corners, working seemingly apart, attracting little or no attention, numerous quiet, self-sufficient, clear-sighted, sympathetic teachers, in touch with the children, generating and absorbing into the school work the interests of the children, and gaining from them vigorous and intelligent response. It is perfectly clear that the central ideas embodied in nature-teaching from the beginning, and which have rejuvenated it from time to time, namely an approach to the whole of the nature environment from the standpoint of the children's interests in nature, is as strong at the present day as at any past period, and that failure to realize the purpose, during a century of struggle, has been due to a misconception of the real aim of education and of the normal processes in learning.

# A COMPARATIVE STUDY OF THE RESULTS OBTAINED IN INSTRUCTION IN THE "SINGLE TEACHER" RURAL SCHOOLS AND THE GRADED TOWN SCHOOLS[1]

W. S. SMILEY
State University of Iowa

In the rural sections of this country there has recently been considerable agitation for the consolidation of a number of the smaller school districts into one large district. With one commodious schoolhouse, several teachers, and a large number of children transported at public expense to a central school, it has been possible to adopt the grade system. This method of organization is considered an advantage by some, but by others it is held to be a detriment to successful learning. This study is an effort to gather data which will measure the contribution of grade organization to elementary education. No amount of opinion can solve the problem, and even this investigation can hope only to point out a method by which material may be gathered and presented. Aside from its contribution to the methods and results of "experimental education," this study indicates some of the weaknesses of our school organization and thus suggests a departure from the conventional form of organization for our consolidated rural schools.

The method used is a comparison of the "single teacher" rural schools with a number of graded town schools. This method was feasible because in the two systems there was only one factor that was not common to both, and that was the

[1] The writer is indebted to County Superintendents D. E. Brainard, F. L. Hoffman, G. E. Farrell, A. M. Deyoe, C. H. Miller, Estelle Coon, A. L. Heminger, and H. McVicker; to City Superintendents C. R. Golly, A. C. Grubb, W. R. Merriss, F. P. Reed, F. W. Malke, H. S. Dewelle, E. M. Carson, C. M. Parker, Margaret Buchanan, Thomas Smiley, H. E. Dow, W. R. Sandy, Alfred Williams, A. J. Quigg, and H. E. Blackmar; and to Professors F. E. Bolton, C. E. Seashore, and C. H. Judd.

grade system. Examinations were given to eighth-grade pupils in arithmetic, geography, grammar, history, and spelling. The same questions were submitted, at the same time, with the same instructions, to pupils of the same age, who had studied the same textbooks. These pupils came from the same class of people, and had teachers of about equal preparation.

In selecting the questions for the tests in each subject the following principles were observed. The questions were to cover all of the subject-matter expected below high school. No catch questions should be admitted. The questions should emphasize both the mechanical and reasoning elements and should be so classified. No questions should be selected that would emphasize one method of instruction more than another. Previous eighth-grade examination lists in both city and county examinations, questions mentioned in textbooks, and the studies of Drs. Stone and Cornman were used. The arithmetic questions were selected directly from the set prepared by Dr. Stone, "Some Arithmetical Abilities of 6A Children." The questions in spelling were adopted from Dr. Cornman's study, "Spelling in the Elementary Schools, an Experimental and Statistical Investigation." Questions in other subjects were prepared as follows. After about forty questions had been selected they were submitted to the pupils of the eighth grade of the Iowa City schools and to the pupils of the rural-school District No. 1, West Lucas Township, Johnson County, Iowa. The answer papers were all gone over carefully and the value of the answers was estimated. If the answer was perfect, it was marked 1. An answer that was entirely wrong was marked 0, and those that were considered partly right were given a fractional grade. The results were all tabulated and each question ranked in the order of the number of times that it had been answered correctly.[2] The best twenty questions were then adopted for the tests.

## METHOD OF GATHERING DATA

Ten county superintendents and fourteen town superintendents signified their willingness to co-operate with us. To these

[2] Thorndike, *Educational Psychology*, 169.

we sent the lists of questions accompanied by the following directions:

It seems that the best way to choose the schools is for you to pick out enough schools so that the tests can be given to from 20 to 30 eighth-grade pupils in your county. Your acquaintance with your schools will enable you to choose those in average communities, with teachers of average ability. The schools near towns, from which the brightest pupils go to the town schools before the age of fifteen, should not be chosen. We are sending all the questions to you in the hope that you will send them to teachers who will take an interest in the work, and who will be honest in living up to the "directions." If you send them out next week the tests could be given beginning Monday, February 14, 1910.

The only directions sent to the town superintendents were that they require the teachers to give the tests, and that they live up to all directions.

The following directions were sent to each teacher:

Have all the pupils in the eighth grade take the tests. By eighth grade we mean those who will finish the common school branches this year and be ready for the high school next year.

Do not give any explanations, suggestions, corrections, intimations, or any other help to any pupils, and do not have them make any preparations for the tests. (This is important. To make the work of any scientific value you must consider yourself responsible for the fairness of the examinations. Be on your guard against cheating in any form by the pupils.) The object of the examination is to compare school systems, not to test individual schools, therefore the conditions should be the same.

If possible give the tests in the forenoon immediately after the school has been called together. A good order might be to give arithmetic Monday, history Tuesday, geography Wednesday, grammar Thursday, and spelling Friday. Dictate the directions to the pupils for spelling.

Record on each paper the time required for the completion of the examination. Tell the pupils that you are going to do this before the tests begin. Please see to it that the questions to be answered by the pupil are answered correctly. Do not allow them to ask questions about anything.

QUESTIONNAIRE TO THE TEACHER

How many classes have you daily? ..........
How many pupils under your charge? ..........
How many grades? ..........
What textbooks do you use in each subject? ..........
About what is the daily attendance? ..........
How long have you held your present position? ..........

The following questionnaire and directions were given to each pupil:

Give the year,.......... month,.......... and day.......... of your birth. Boy or girl..........? Name or number of your school.......... Twp..........? Co...........? Date..........?

What work have you done in this subject, giving books studied, and time spent upon it? ..................................................

Do not copy the questions. Write on both sides of the paper. Do not ask any questions. Do not waste time, because you should finish these tests as soon as possible without hurrying. Your teacher records the time required.

## METHOD OF HANDLING DATA

Reports were received from 213 town children and 176 country children. The papers in each subject were arranged and numbered. The towns and counties were each given a Roman numeral, and the country schools a letter, and the pupils were assigned Arabic numerals. (Thus in referring to No. 9, New Albany Twp., Story Co., as an illustration, we call the county, XIV; school, *a;* pupil, No. 3, 2, 1.) This method of numbering the papers enables one to go to any paper at any time and verify the results in the tables. It also makes it possible to withhold the name of the school from the public, and at the same time give out the results.

In marking the papers all answers were marked 0, when wrong or only partially correct; and 1, when correct. All papers in one subject were marked before another subject was begun. If the papers from the rural schools were marked first in arithmetic, the papers from the graded schools were marked first in the next subject. This was done to shift the effect of any unconscious change in the method of marking. In all cases where there was doubt as to what the ruling should be in any situation, a written memorandum was kept of the ruling, as a guide for similar cases. All of the papers except a few in spelling were marked by the writer; during the marking of these spelling papers he was present to supervise.

## ARITHMETIC

Dr. Stone's lists which were prepared for 6A children contained twelve questions each. Since we were to deal only with eighth-grade pupils we felt that it was not necessary to use so many and therefore selected the more difficult questions as better for our purpose. Only the last seven problems in "fundamentals" and the last eight in "reasoning" were used. Dr. Stone listed in his group of "fundamentals" the questions that were designed to test the operations in addition, multiplication, division, and subtraction.

The questions submitted in the fundamentals follow:

1. Add 4695, 872, 6786, 567, 858, 9447, 7499.
2. Multiply 976 by 87.
3. Divide 278254 by 678.
4. Multiply 5489 by 9876.
5. Divide 5099941 by 740.
6. Multiply 876 by 749.
7. Divide 62693256 by 859.

Papers were received from 60 "single teacher" and 14 graded schools. The results are tabulated in Tables 1, 2, 3, and 4. In calculating the results in the "fundamental" operations each problem was divided into a number of parts. The following method of division was used. Question 1=4*a*; 2=3*a*, 2*m*; 3=4*m*, 4*d*, 2*s*; 4=6*a*, 4*m*; 5=4*m*, 4*d*, 4*s*; 6=4*a*, 3*m*; 7=5*m*, 5*d*, 4*s*. In this table *a* means addition; *m*, multiplication; *d*, division; and *s*, subtraction; the numbers before the sign of equality designate the number of the problem. This table was developed as a fairer means of interpreting the results than the use of answers.[3] Dr. Stone[4] says that there was little difference in the mistakes made when adding a short or a long column of figures. This being true it seems fair to arrange the problems on the above basis. Another method was considered but rejected because of its greater length. In it each separate opera-

[3] Curtis, *Elementary School Teacher*, October, 1910.

[4] Stone, "Some Arithmetical Abilities of 6A Children."

tion constitutes a problem. The seventh problem is used to illustrate the method used.

```
859) 62693256 (72984
     6013
     ----
      2563
      1718
      ----
       8452
       7731
       ----
        7215
        6872
        ----
         3436
         3436
         ----
```

In the first place there are five divisions. If there were two mistakes in the quotient, 2 was subtracted from the number 5, leaving 3 the mark for division. In solving this problem the divisor was multiplied by each number in the quotient, making five separate operations. Each operation was considered an operation in multiplication, and if no mistakes were made the answer was given the mark 5*m*. There were only four operations of subtraction if no mistakes were made, because there should be no remainder. If there was no mistake in the solution of the seventh problem, the mark would be 5*m*, 5*d*, 4*s*. The results of all of the operations are arranged in the tables and the comparisons made from the tables. The Roman numerals in the horizontal column at the top of the tables indicate the school if it is graded, and the county if it is of the "one teacher" rural system. There are in this column fourteen graded schools and eight counties. The fundamental operations are arranged in order. The vertical column at the left of the page indicates the problem in which the operation is found. The same problem may occur under three different heads, multiplication, division, and substraction. The horizontal columns contain the results for each school in each operation. The vertical column marked T contains the totals for the horizontal columns. The column marked P indicates what the total should be if there were no

# TABLE I. ARITHMETIC

## Boys, Graded Schools, Fundamentals

| Grades and Number of Pupils | | | | | | | | | | | | | | | P | Percentage |
|---|---|---|---|---|---|---|---|---|---|---|---|---|---|---|---|---|
| I 7 | II 16 | III 10 | IV 5 | V 0 | VI 11 | VII 6 | VIII 7 | IX 5 | X 7 | XI 10 | XII 8 | XIII 14 | XIV 8 | T 114 | | |
| ADDITION | | | | | | | | | | | | | | | | |
| 28 | 57 | 40 | 20 | 39 | 22 | 28 | 20 | 28 | 40 | 28 | 51 | 29 | .. | 430 | 456 | |
| 21 | 49 | 29 | 15 | 33 | 18 | 21 | 15 | 20 | 30 | 24 | 42 | 24 | .. | 341 | 342 | |
| 42 | 91 | 58 | 30 | 66 | 34 | 42 | 30 | 42 | 60 | 44 | 83 | 48 | .. | 670 | 684 | |
| 28 | 64 | 40 | 19 | 44 | 23 | 28 | 20 | 27 | 40 | 32 | 54 | 31 | .. | 450 | 456 | |
| | | | | | | | | | | | | | | 1,891 | 1,938 | 98 |
| MULTIPLICATION | | | | | | | | | | | | | | | | |
| 13 | 22 | 30 | 9 | 15 | 10 | 14 | 10 | 14 | 20 | 15 | 28 | 15 | .. | 221 | 226 | |
| 28 | 64 | 34 | 20 | 38 | 24 | 27 | 20 | 27 | 39 | 30 | 56 | 32 | .. | 439 | 456 | |
| 28 | 55 | 28 | 12 | 43 | 18 | 17 | 16 | 27 | 40 | 31 | 55 | 29 | .. | 399 | 456 | |
| 26 | 63 | 46 | 20 | 38 | 22 | 24 | 18 | 28 | 40 | 32 | 56 | 25 | .. | 438 | 456 | |
| 20 | 46 | 29 | 13 | 31 | 17 | 20 | 15 | 21 | 27 | 37 | 42 | 22 | .. | 340 | 342 | |
| 32 | 68 | 48 | 25 | 48 | 24 | 32 | 25 | 35 | 47 | 53 | 70 | 39 | .. | 546 | 570 | |
| | | | | | | | | | | | | | | 2,383 | 2,506 | 95 |
| DIVISION | | | | | | | | | | | | | | | | |
| 27 | 63 | 36 | 20 | 33 | 24 | 26 | 20 | 27 | 39 | 27 | 55 | 30 | .. | 427 | 456 | |
| 27 | 57 | 32 | 19 | 31 | 22 | 24 | 17 | 24 | 32 | 32 | 52 | 24 | .. | 393 | 456 | |
| 32 | 60 | 40 | 23 | 45 | 23 | 32 | 24 | 33 | 49 | 39 | 68 | 30 | .. | 498 | 570 | |
| | | | | | | | | | | | | | | 1,318 | 1,482 | 89 |
| SUBTRACTION | | | | | | | | | | | | | | | | |
| 13 | 32 | 20 | 10 | 19 | 12 | 12 | 10 | 14 | 18 | 14 | 28 | 16 | .. | 218 | 228 | |
| 28 | 63 | 39 | 19 | 38 | 23 | 27 | 20 | 27 | 28 | 32 | 52 | 28 | .. | 425 | 456 | |
| 26 | 59 | 38 | 20 | 37 | 19 | 26 | 19 | 28 | 40 | 32 | 55 | 30 | .. | 432 | 456 | |
| | | | | | | | | | | | | | | 1,075 | 1,140 | 94 |

## TABLE II. ARITHMETIC

### Girls, Graded Schools, Fundamentals

| Grades and Number of Pupils | | | | | | | | | | | | | | | P | Percentage |
|---|---|---|---|---|---|---|---|---|---|---|---|---|---|---|---|---|
| I<br>7 | II<br>5 | III<br>15 | IV<br>6 | V<br>8 | VI<br>6 | VII<br>2 | VIII<br>5 | IX<br>0 | X<br>7 | XI<br>7 | XII<br>14 | XIII<br>12 | XIV<br>3 | T<br>97 | | |
| ADDITION | | | | | | | | | | | | | | | | |
| 26 | 20 | 48 | 22 | 32 | 23 | 4 | 24 | .. | 28 | 27 | 56 | 45 | 11 | 366 | 378 | |
| 21 | 15 | 44 | 18 | 23 | 18 | 6 | 15 | .. | 20 | 20 | 42 | 36 | 9 | 287 | 291 | |
| 41 | 29 | 81 | 36 | 47 | 36 | 12 | 30 | .. | 41 | 42 | 84 | 72 | 18 | 569 | 582 | |
| 27 | 20 | 55 | 24 | 31 | 24 | 8 | 20 | .. | 27 | 28 | 56 | 48 | 12 | 368 | 378 | |
| | | | | | | | | | | | | | | 1,590 | 1,629 | 95 |
| MULTIPLICATION | | | | | | | | | | | | | | | | |
| 13 | 10 | 26 | 12 | 13 | 12 | 4 | 9 | .. | 14 | 14 | 28 | 24 | 6 | 185 | 189 | |
| 26 | 20 | 52 | 24 | 32 | 24 | 8 | 20 | .. | 28 | 27 | 56 | 47 | 11 | 375 | 378 | |
| 27 | 20 | 41 | 18 | 23 | 21 | 6 | 15 | .. | 27 | 27 | 54 | 48 | 9 | 336 | 378 | |
| 28 | 20 | 50 | 24 | 32 | 24 | 8 | 20 | .. | 28 | 28 | 55 | 48 | 12 | 377 | 378 | |
| 21 | 15 | 40 | 18 | 24 | 17 | 6 | 14 | .. | 21 | 21 | 28 | 35 | 8 | 268 | 291 | |
| 34 | 25 | 69 | 30 | 38 | 25 | 10 | 24 | .. | 35 | 33 | 55 | 55 | 15 | 448 | 485 | |
| | | | | | | | | | | | | | | 1,989 | 2,099 | 94 |
| DIVISION | | | | | | | | | | | | | | | | |
| 21 | 20 | 49 | 24 | 32 | 24 | 8 | 20 | .. | 28 | 24 | 56 | 47 | 10 | 363 | 378 | |
| 26 | 18 | 50 | 24 | 32 | 24 | 8 | 20 | .. | 28 | 25 | 56 | 46 | 12 | 369 | 378 | |
| 28 | 25 | 60 | 30 | 35 | 25 | 10 | 20 | .. | 33 | 28 | 63 | 51 | 14 | 422 | 485 | |
| | | | | | | | | | | | | | | 1,154 | 1,241 | 91 |
| SUBTRACTION | | | | | | | | | | | | | | | | |
| 14 | 10 | 25 | 12 | 16 | 12 | 4 | 10 | .. | 14 | 14 | 28 | 24 | 6 | 189 | 189 | |
| 27 | 19 | 53 | 24 | 32 | 24 | 8 | 20 | .. | 28 | 18 | 55 | 47 | 12 | 367 | 378 | |
| 26 | 20 | 51 | 24 | 32 | 20 | 8 | 20 | .. | 28 | 28 | 54 | 42 | 12 | 365 | 378 | |
| | | | | | | | | | | | | | | 921 | 945 | 95 |

## TABLE III. ARITHMETIC

Boys, "One Teacher" Schools, Fundamentals

| Grades and Number of Pupils | | | | | | | | | P | Percentage |
|---|---|---|---|---|---|---|---|---|---|---|
| I<br>12 | II<br>5 | III<br>9 | IV<br>2 | V<br>6 | VI<br>10 | VII<br>9 | VIII<br>4 | T<br>57 | | |
| | | | | ADDITION | | | | | | |
| 46 | 20 | 35 | 8 | 24 | 36 | 35 | 16 | 220 | 228 | |
| 36 | 15 | 27 | 6 | 18 | 30 | 27 | 12 | 171 | 171 | |
| 71 | 30 | 54 | 12 | 36 | 60 | 53 | 24 | 340 | 342 | |
| 48 | 20 | 36 | 8 | 24 | 40 | 35 | 16 | 227 | 228 | |
| | | | | | | | | 958 | 969 | 99 |
| | | | | MULTIPLICATION | | | | | | |
| 21 | 10 | 18 | 4 | 13 | 48 | 16 | 8 | 138 | 114 | |
| 48 | 20 | 36 | 8 | 24 | 33 | 36 | 16 | 221 | 228 | |
| 42 | 19 | 36 | 8 | 24 | 36 | 34 | 16 | 215 | 228 | |
| 44 | 20 | 34 | 8 | 24 | 33 | 32 | 16 | 151 | 228 | |
| 34 | 15 | 25 | 6 | 18 | 26 | 26 | 12 | 162 | 171 | |
| 59 | 25 | 42 | 10 | 29 | 48 | 45 | 15 | 273 | 285 | |
| | | | | | | | | 1,160 | 1,254 | 93 |
| | | | | DIVISION | | | | | | |
| 48 | 20 | 36 | 8 | 24 | 39 | 36 | 16 | 227 | 228 | |
| 44 | 20 | 31 | 8 | 26 | 24 | 29 | 16 | 198 | 228 | |
| 51 | 13 | 42 | 9 | 29 | 43 | 50 | 20 | 257 | 285 | |
| | | | | | | | | 682 | 741 | 92 |
| | | | | SUBTRACTION | | | | | | |
| 23 | 15 | 18 | 4 | 12 | 20 | 18 | 8 | 118 | 114 | |
| 47 | 20 | 39 | 8 | 24 | 34 | 36 | 16 | 224 | 228 | |
| 47 | 19 | 35 | 8 | 24 | 39 | 35 | 16 | 223 | 228 | |
| | | | | | | | | 565 | 570 | 99 |

## TABLE IV. ARITHMETIC

GIRLS, "ONE TEACHER" SCHOOLS, FUNDAMENTALS

| GRADES AND NUMBER OF PUPILS | | | | | | | | | P | PERCENTAGE |
|---|---|---|---|---|---|---|---|---|---|---|
| I 13 | II 15 | III 20 | IV 11 | V 15 | VI 5 | VII 18 | VIII 14 | T 111 | | |
| ADDITION | | | | | | | | | | |
| 50 | 59 | 76 | 44 | 60 | 20 | 68 | 52 | 431 | 444 | |
| 39 | 45 | 60 | 33 | 45 | 15 | 54 | 42 | 333 | 333 | |
| 78 | 90 | 118 | 66 | 90 | 30 | 103 | 84 | 659 | 666 | |
| 52 | 59 | 80 | 43 | 60 | 20 | 72 | 56 | 442 | 444 | |
| | | | | | | | | 1,865 | 1,887 | 98 |
| MULTIPLICATION | | | | | | | | | | |
| 25 | 30 | 40 | 20 | 29 | 10 | 35 | 28 | 217 | 222 | |
| 51 | 60 | 79 | 41 | 59 | 18 | 71 | 56 | 435 | 444 | |
| 48 | 59 | 78 | 44 | 60 | 15 | 69 | 55 | 426 | 444 | |
| 51 | 60 | 80 | 40 | 56 | 19 | 63 | 54 | 423 | 444 | |
| 39 | 45 | 60 | 31 | 45 | 15 | 54 | 40 | 329 | 333 | |
| 65 | 74 | 99 | 51 | 69 | 23 | 76 | 70 | 527 | 555 | |
| | | | | | | | | 2,357 | 2,442 | 97 |
| DIVISION | | | | | | | | | | |
| 48 | 60 | 78 | 41 | 60 | 18 | 69 | 56 | 430 | 444 | |
| 41 | 60 | 78 | 41 | 50 | 13 | 60 | 49 | 492 | 444 | |
| 56 | 75 | 98 | 49 | 67 | 23 | 75 | 70 | 513 | 555 | |
| | | | | | | | | 1,435 | 1,443 | 99 |
| SUBTRACTION | | | | | | | | | | |
| 26 | 30 | 40 | 22 | 30 | 10 | 36 | 28 | 222 | 222 | |
| 52 | 60 | 75 | 44 | 60 | 20 | 65 | 55 | 431 | 444 | |
| 51 | 60 | 79 | 44 | 60 | 20 | 60 | 56 | 430 | 444 | |
| | | | | | | | | 1,083 | 1,110 | 98 |

mistakes. And the column marked Percentage indicates the percentage which is the result obtained by dividing the quantity in Column T, by the quantity in Column P. There are two tables for each subject, one containing the results from the boys' papers, and the other from the girls' papers.

ARITHMETIC

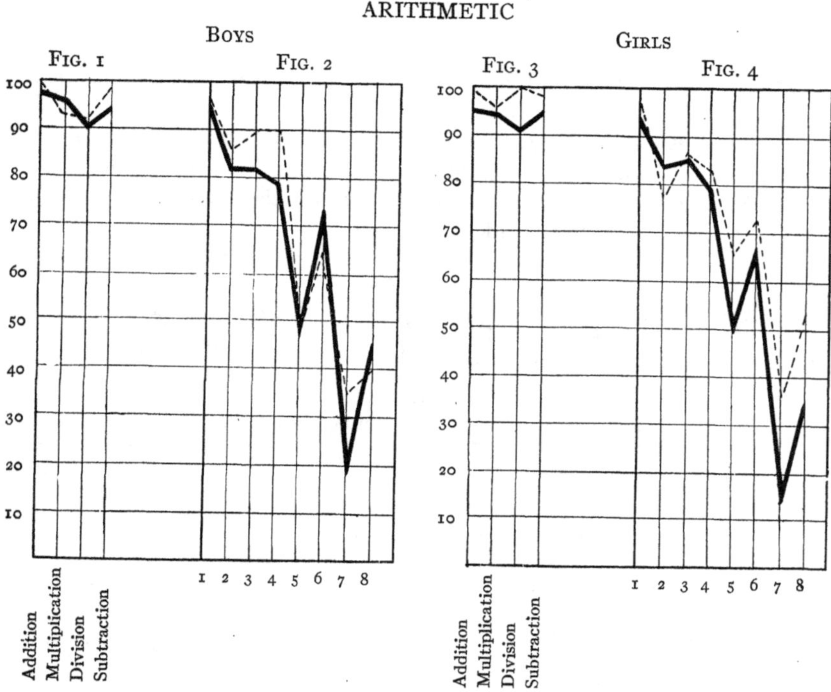


In the curves based upon these tables the broken lines indicate the results from the "one teacher" and the full lines the results from the graded schools. Figures 1 and 2 are comparisons of the boys for fundamentals and reasoning respectively. Figures 3 and 4 show results for the girls.

REASONING PROBLEMS

1. The uniforms for a baseball nine cost $2.50 each. The shoes cost $2.00 a pair. What was the total cost of the uniforms and shoes for the nine?

2. In the schools of a certain city there are 2,200 pupils; one-half are in the primary grade, one-eighth in the high school, and the rest in the night school. How many pupils are there in the night school?

3. If $3\frac{1}{2}$ tons of coal cost $21.00, what will $5\frac{1}{2}$ tons cost?

4. A news dealer bought some magazines for $1.00. He sold them for $1.20, gaining 5 cents on each magazine. How many magazines were there?

5. A girl spent one-eighth of her money for carfare, and three times as much for clothes. Half of what she had left was 80 cents. How much money did she have at first?

6. Two girls received $2.10 for making button-holes. One made 42, the other 28. How should they divide the money?

7. Mr. Brown paid one-third of the cost of a building; Mr. Johnson paid one-half the cost. Mr. Johnson received $500.00 more annual rent than Mr. Brown. How much did he receive?

8. A freight train left Albany for New York at 6 o'clock. An express left on the same track at 8 o'clock. It went at the rate of 40 miles an hour. At what time of the day would it overtake the freight train if the freight train stopped after it had gone 56 miles?

## REASONING

In the reasoning problems the numbers in the vertical column at the left are the numbers of the problems. The horizontal

### TABLE V. ARITHMETIC

BOYS, GRADED SCHOOLS, REASONING PROBLEMS

| | I | II | III | IV | V | VI | VII | VIII | IX | X | XI | XII | XIII | XIV | T | P | Percentage |
|---|---|---|---|---|---|---|---|---|---|---|---|---|---|---|---|---|---|
| 1 | 6 | 16 | 10 | 5 | ... | 9 | 6 | 7 | 5 | 7 | 10 | 8 | 12 | 7 | 108 | 114 | 95 |
| 2 | 6 | 15 | 9 | 4 | ... | 8 | 6 | 6 | 5 | 4 | 8 | 8 | 10 | 5 | 94 | 114 | 82 |
| 3 | 5 | 15 | 7 | 5 | ... | 9 | 4 | 6 | 5 | 6 | 8 | 8 | 14 | 6 | 98 | 114 | 82 |
| 4 | 3 | 12 | 10 | 5 | ... | 6 | 5 | 7 | 5 | 7 | 7 | 8 | 12 | 5 | 102 | 114 | 79 |
| 5 | 3 | 9 | 4 | 4 | ... | 5 | 1 | 5 | 5 | 6 | 2 | 4 | 6 | 1 | 55 | 114 | 46 |
| 6 | 6 | 13 | 7 | 4 | ... | 7 | 5 | 7 | 4 | 6 | 3 | 7 | 10 | 4 | 83 | 114 | 73 |
| 7 | 0 | 3 | 0 | 1 | ... | 3 | 1 | 3 | 4 | 1 | 1 | 3 | 1 | 0 | 21 | 114 | 18 |
| 8 | 4 | 3 | 3 | 4 | ... | 7 | 2 | 3 | 4 | 7 | 3 | 1 | 7 | 3 | 51 | 114 | 45 |
| Number of pupils | 7 | 16 | 10 | 5 | 0 | 11 | 6 | 7 | 5 | 7 | 10 | 8 | 14 | 8 | 114 | | |

"ONE TEACHER" SCHOOLS, REASONING PROBLEMS

| | I | II | III | IV | V | VI | VII | VIII | IX | X | XI | XII | XIII | XIV | T | P | Percentage |
|---|---|---|---|---|---|---|---|---|---|---|---|---|---|---|---|---|---|
| 1 | 12 | 5 | 9 | 2 | 5 | 10 | 8 | 4 | ... | ... | ... | ... | ... | ... | 55 | 57 | 97 |
| 2 | 11 | 5 | 8 | 2 | 6 | 8 | 5 | 4 | ... | ... | ... | ... | ... | ... | 49 | 57 | 86 |
| 3 | 9 | 5 | 8 | 2 | 6 | 9 | 8 | 4 | ... | ... | ... | ... | ... | ... | 51 | 57 | 90 |
| 4 | 11 | 5 | 8 | 2 | 5 | 10 | 7 | 3 | ... | ... | ... | ... | ... | ... | 51 | 57 | 90 |
| 5 | 8 | 3 | 5 | 1 | 4 | 5 | 4 | 3 | ... | ... | ... | ... | ... | ... | 33 | 57 | 50 |
| 6 | 6 | 6 | 7 | 2 | 5 | 5 | 6 | 3 | ... | ... | ... | ... | ... | ... | 37 | 57 | 65 |
| 7 | 2 | 5 | 5 | 2 | 0 | 2 | 4 | 0 | ... | ... | ... | ... | ... | ... | 20 | 57 | 35 |
| 8 | 4 | 5 | 3 | 1 | 4 | 2 | 2 | 2 | ... | ... | ... | ... | ... | ... | 23 | 67 | 40 |
| Number of pupils | 12 | 5 | 9 | 2 | 6 | 10 | 9 | 4 | ... | ... | ... | ... | ... | ... | 57 | 57 | |

## TABLE VI. ARITHMETIC

GIRLS, GRADED SCHOOLS, REASONING PROBLEMS

| | I | II | III | IV | V | VI | VII | VIII | IX | X | XI | XII | XIII | XIV | T | P | Percentage |
|---|---|---|---|---|---|---|---|---|---|---|---|---|---|---|---|---|---|
| 1 | 7 | 4 | 15 | 6 | 7 | 6 | 2 | 5 | ... | 7 | 6 | 14 | 10 | 3 | 92 | 97 | 95 |
| 2 | 6 | 5 | 13 | 5 | 4 | 4 | 2 | 5 | ... | 6 | 7 | 11 | 10 | 3 | 81 | 97 | 83 |
| 3 | 5 | 5 | 10 | 6 | 8 | 6 | 2 | 4 | ... | 7 | 5 | 13 | 10 | 3 | 86 | 97 | 76 |
| 4 | 4 | 4 | 13 | 6 | 6 | 3 | 2 | 5 | ... | 6 | 5 | 13 | 8 | 2 | 77 | 97 | 88 |
| 5 | 1 | 5 | 2 | 5 | 3 | 1 | 2 | 3 | ... | 4 | 2 | 12 | 5 | 2 | 47 | 97 | 48 |
| 6 | 3 | 5 | 7 | 5 | 4 | 3 | 1 | 4 | ... | 4 | 5 | 13 | 8 | 3 | 62 | 97 | 67 |
| 7 | 1 | 0 | 0 | 0 | 1 | 0 | 1 | 1 | ... | 0 | 0 | 6 | 1 | 2 | 13 | 97 | 13 |
| 8 | 1 | 4 | 2 | | 4 | 1 | 1 | 0 | ... | 3 | 2 | 5 | 5 | 2 | 33 | 97 | 34 |
| Number of pupils | 7 | 5 | 15 | 6 | 7 | 6 | 2 | 5 | 0 | 7 | 7 | 14 | 12 | 3 | 97 | 97 | |
| "ONE TEACHER" SCHOOLS, REASONING PROBLEMS | | | | | | | | | | | | | | | | | |
| 1 | 12 | 15 | 19 | 11 | 15 | 5 | 18 | 14 | ... | ... | ... | ... | ... | ... | 109 | 111 | 99 |
| 2 | 12 | 10 | 13 | 10 | 13 | 2 | 14 | 11 | ... | ... | ... | ... | ... | ... | 85 | 111 | 77 |
| 3 | 11 | 15 | 20 | 7 | 14 | 5 | 11 | 13 | ... | ... | ... | ... | ... | ... | 6 | 111 | 86 |
| 4 | 8 | 14 | 18 | 9 | 13 | 3 | 14 | 14 | ... | ... | ... | ... | ... | ... | 93 | 111 | 84 |
| 5 | 6 | 13 | 16 | 8 | 11 | 1 | 5 | 13 | ... | ... | ... | ... | ... | ... | 73 | 111 | 65 |
| 6 | 6 | 12 | 19 | 9 | 14 | 2 | 11 | 13 | ... | ... | ... | ... | ... | ... | 86 | 111 | 72 |
| 7 | 3 | 11 | 5 | 4 | 7 | 0 | 6 | 4 | ... | ... | ... | ... | ... | ... | 40 | 111 | 36 |
| 8 | 4 | 14 | 9 | 8 | 6 | 1 | 5 | 12 | ... | ... | ... | ... | ... | ... | 59 | 111 | 53 |
| Number of pupils | 13 | 15 | 20 | 11 | 15 | 5 | 18 | 14 | ... | ... | ... | ... | ... | ... | | 111 | |

columns contain the number of correct answers for each school or county. The vertical columns marked T, Percentage, and P contain the sum of correct answers, the percentage of correct answers, and the sum of the answers had there been no errors. The percentage is obtained by dividing the sum of the correct answers by the sum of the answers if no mistakes were made.

### GEOGRAPHY QUESTIONS

1. Name and locate five important cities in Iowa.
2. In what state is each of the following cities: St. Louis, New Orleans, Cleveland, Davenport, Omaha, Minneapolis, Pittsburgh, Boston, Seattle, San Francisco?
3. What parts of the earth have four seasons?
4. Locate the Isthmus of Panama.
5. Name and locate three mountain ranges in the United States.
6. What is the climate of Porto Rico?
7. Into what zones is the earth's surface divided?
8. What are five important minerals of the United States?

9. Name three commercial advantages of Chicago, and explain how they have affected the growth of that city.

10. The Mississippi River forms the eastern boundary of what states?

11. Locate Oxford, Berlin, Rome, St. Petersburg, Copenhagen, the Hague, Geneva, Venice, Athens, Manila.

12. How did the United States gain possession of the Philippines?

13. Name five important pork-packing cities.

14. Name three reasons why the eastern part of our country is so thickly settled.

15. In what states and territories are the gold mines of the United States?

16. What country of South America is likely to become an important rival of the United States in cattle and wheat raising? Why?

17. To what country do we export most of our cattle products? Why?

18. In what three parts of Europe are the principal mountain ranges?

19. How do you account for the difference in climate between Oregon and New England?

20. What are the three things that mainly affect climate?

21. What are the three movements of the waters of the ocean?

22. Name the capitals of England, France, Brazil, Japan, Chili.

## GEOGRAPHY

According to our general plan we have divided these questions into two groups, "mechanical" and "reasoning." Questions 1, 2, 3, 4, 5, 7, 8, 10, 11, 12, 15, 18, 20, 21, and 22 are called "mechanical," and 6, 9, 13, 14, 16, 17, and 19 are called "reasoning" questions. This classification is of course only a rough attempt at analyzing the mental processes used in answering the questions, but in general seems justifiable. Under "mechanical" are classed those questions that seem to require little more than mere memory. There are however under this classification questions that range from mere visual imagery to problems of reasoning. Question 10 is an example of the first, and Question 11 of the second sort. In either case the process used in answering the question may be only memory, but again it may be that the child recalls the location of the place by means of his power to reason.

In marking the papers no more definite location was required than the assignment of cities to their proper country. In this subject the same method of tabulation was used as has been previously described as being used in arithmetic, but to save space only the percentage results are here presented.

TABLE VII. GEOGRAPHY
PERCENTAGES

| "One Teacher" Schools | | Graded Schools | |
|---|---|---|---|
| 57 Boys | 115 Girls | 106 Boys | 97 Girls |
| 89 | 81 | 85 | 82 |
| 91 | 92 | 95 | 77 |
| 51 | 48 | 50 | 49 |
| 99 | 46 | 88 | 84 |
| 76 | 71 | 69 | 73 |
| 91 | 88 | 76 | 66 |
| 92 | 86 | 73 | 78 |
| 100 | 97 | 99 | 89 |
| 51 | 59 | 51 | 41 |
| 43 | 48 | 35 | 31 |
| 76 | 71 | 62 | 69 |
| 92 | 89 | 86 | 70 |
| 77 | 65 | 64 | 43 |
| 51 | 51 | 39 | 43 |
| 48 | 49 | 32 | 29 |
| 65 | 53 | 53 | 53 |
| 36 | 35 | 49 | 59 |
| 61 | 69 | 64 | 63 |
| 13 | 28 | 21 | 12 |
| 8 | 16 | 10 | 5 |
| 11 | 40 | 15 | 11 |
| 50 | 45 | 21 | 30 |

RESULTS

In comparing the curves representing the boys in Fig. 5, it is observed that the full line goes above the broken line five times—on Questions 2, 17, 18, 19, and 20. In Fig. 6, in which the girls are compared, the full line is above on Questions 3, 4, and 17. In the "one teacher" schools the "range" is 80 per cent from 18–98 per cent, and for the graded schools it is 89 per cent from 6–96 per cent. The two curves have the same general tendency, at no time running counter to one another, indicating that the questions were satisfactory. If they had not run so nearly in the same direction it would have been thought that for one system the questions were not as fair as for the other, that the results depended on method of instruction rather than subject-matter. The curves are higher when the questions bore upon subjects connected with our own state and country, than when they bore upon other states and foreign countries.

GEOGRAPHY

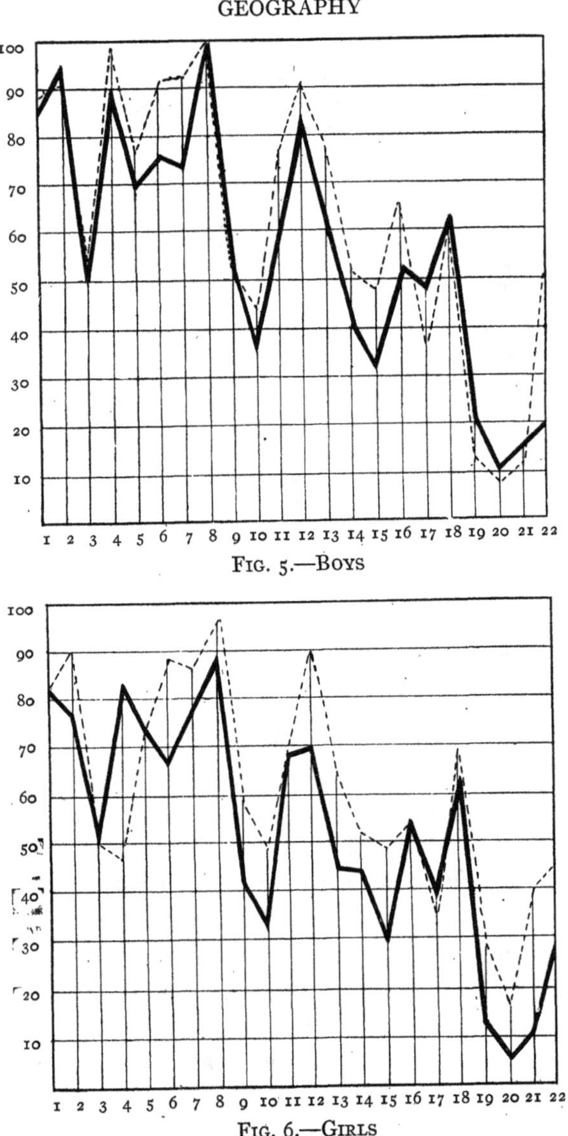


FIG. 5.—BOYS



FIG. 6.—GIRLS

In comparing the results in the different groups, the average percentages were arranged in a table according to the group in which it was classified.

REASONING GROUP

| Q | Percentages | | |
|---|---|---|---|
| | G | O. T. | D |
| 6 | 71 | 89 | 18 |
| 9 | 45 | 62 | 17 |
| 13 | 51 | 68 | 17 |
| 14 | 43 | 52 | 9 |
| 16 | 53 | 59 | 6 |
| 17 | 42 | 35 | −7 |
| COMMERCIAL | | | |
| 8 | 97 | 98 | 1 |
| 9 | 45 | 62 | 17 |
| 13 | 51 | 68 | 17 |
| 14 | 43 | 53 | 9 |
| 15 | 31 | 58 | 27 |
| 16 | 53 | 59 | 6 |
| 17 | 42 | 35 | −7 |
| LOCATION | | | |
| 1 | 80 | 84 | 1 |
| 2 | 76 | 76 | 0 |
| 4 | 90 | 97 | 7 |
| 5 | 72 | 72 | 0 |
| 10 | 33 | 47 | 14 |
| 11 | 24 | 31 | 7 |
| 18 | 64 | 71 | 7 |
| 22 | 12 | 40 | 28 |
| PHYSICAL | | | |
| 3 | 48 | 42 | −6 |
| 5 | 12 | 12 | 0 |
| 6 | 71 | 89 | 18 |
| 7 | 78 | 88 | 10 |
| 15 | 31 | 58 | 27 |
| 16 | 31 | 58 | 27 |
| 19 | 53 | 59 | 6 |
| 20 | 6 | 18 | 12 |
| 21 | 12 | 40 | 28 |
| VISUAL IMAGE | | | |
| 1 | 85 | 85 | 0 |
| 4 | 90 | 97 | 7 |
| 5 | 72 | 72 | 0 |
| 10 | 33 | 47 | 14 |
| 18 | 64 | 71 | 7 |

In the above table, Q, O.T., G, and D, equal, respectively, the number of the question, "one teacher," graded, and difference. When the graded surpasses the "one teacher" system the difference is a negative quantity.

# AGRICULTURAL EDUCATION: AGRICULTURAL SOCIETIES

BENJAMIN MARSHALL DAVIS
Miami University

The development of agricultural societies may be divided into four periods: (1) from 1785 to 1850—the period of beginnings; (2) from 1850 to 1870—the period of agricultural fairs; (3) from 1870 to 1892—the period of great organizations; (4) from 1892 to the present—the period of adjustment (102, p. 291).[1]

## FIRST PERIOD

The first period in its relation to agricultural education is an important one, particularly in its historical significance. The influence of these early societies on agricultural education is perhaps greater than that of any other single factor contributing to its development. The idea of such an education is regarded by some as originating in these societies. That it was much exploited by them is certainly true. The idea persisted and grew, and may be followed from this early period to the establishment of land-grant colleges. The idea persists today, but modified to include elementary and secondary education.

In 1785 the Philadelphia Society for the Promotion of Agriculture was organized, and later in the same year a similar society was formed at Charleston, S.C. Within that decade a number of other societies were organized. Among the members of these societies were many prominent men such as George Washington, Benjamin Franklin, and Timothy Pickering. These men were also interested in education. It is not strange that the two interests should be combined in their minds into the idea of agricultural education.

Benjamin Franklin had given expression to this idea many years before the founding of the first agricultural society. Referring to the education of the youth of Pennsylvania he says:

[1] The references are to the bibliography at the end of this article or to bibliographies in other articles of this series.

> While they are reading natural history might not a little gardening, planting, grafting, inoculating be taught and practiced, and now and then excursions made to the neighboring plantations of the best farms, their methods observed and reasoned upon for the information of youth, the improvement of agriculture being useful to all and skill in it no disparagement to any? (102, p. 361.)

This idea was first put into actual practice in 1792 when agriculture became a subject of instruction in Columbia College. This was brought about chiefly through the agitation of the New York, and other agricultural societies.[2] Another example of the attitude of these early societies toward agricultural education is found in the action of the Philadelphia Society in 1794. The society appointed a committee to outline a plan for establishing a "State Society for the Promotion of Agriculture, connecting with it the Education of Youth in the knowledge of that most important Art while they are acquiring other useful knowledge suitable for the agricultural citizens of the State." The plan which was drawn up and presented to the society includes some very definite references to agricultural education. Agricultural information was to be disseminated in whatever manner the legislature should think best, "whether by endowing professorships to be annexed to the University of Pennsylvania and the College of Carlisle, and other seminaries of learning, or for the purpose of teaching the chemical philosophy and elementary parts of the theory of agriculture." County societies were to be created with "county schoolmasters" as secretaries; and the schoolhouses the places of meeting and the repositories of their transactions, models, etc. "The legislature may enjoin on these schoolmasters the combination of the subject of agriculture with other parts of education. This may easily be effected by introducing, as school books, those on this subject, and thereby making it familiar to their pupils" (102, p. 363). The fact that the plan of the committee was rejected does not alter its significance in its bearing upon subsequent developments in agricultural education. It is especially noteworthy that the plan proposed is in harmony with some present-day practices: the rural school as a community center, correlation of agriculture with other school subjects, and agricultural textbooks.

[2] This *Journal,* X, No. 4 (November, 1909), 101.

During this entire period the subject of agricultural education was much discussed. Various plans were proposed for its development. Some provided that the societies themselves should organize stock companies to establish schools for instruction in agricultural subjects. Several such schools were started, but owing to difficulties (chiefly financial) they were not successful. These attempts were an important stage in the evolution of the agricultural college.

Stock-company plans were succeeded by others involving state or federal support. The agricultural societies representing associated effort were finally able to secure the attention of legislative bodies. In New York State, for example, the New York State Agricultural Society began a campaign for a school of agriculture soon after the date of its organization (1832), and continued it until 1853 when the legislature granted a charter for such an institution. The founding of the Agricultural College of Cornell University was no doubt due in a large measure to the activity of the New York State Agricultural Society, and of other agricultural societies of the state.

The Michigan State Agricultural Society which was formed in 1849 immediately set to work to secure a state agricultural college. Its efforts at once secured the attention of the legislature. The matter was brought up at each session of the legislature until, in 1855, a bill authorizing the establishment of the State Agricultural College of Michigan became a law.

The activities of the agricultural societies of New York and Michigan in promoting agricultural education is typical of what was accomplished by similar societies in Pennsylvania, Connecticut, and other states during this period.

## SECOND PERIOD

In 1858 there were over 900 agricultural and horticultural societies listed at the Patent Office, and in 1868 the Department of Agriculture listed 1,350. All but about 100 of these were organized after 1849 (102, p. 292).

The chief interest of most of these societies was in holding fairs. In many ways these fairs were of considerable educational value, especially in diffusing new ideas, in furnishing an opportunity for social intercourse, and in introducing better farm practice and new types of farm products. Often addresses by prominent speakers were provided as special educational features.

On the whole this period was marked by a great development of organized effort, including associations of many kinds, and ranging from national organizations to mere local farmers' clubs.

### THIRD PERIOD

This period is characterized by large associations, national in scope. It represents a stage in development when agricultural people began to recognize the importance of "getting together," and of using co-operative means for securing better business and educational opportunities and more favorable legislation. This was undertaken through large formal organizations, through co-operative concerns which were intended to do away with the "middleman," through activity in politics, and through education, directly by means of colleges and other schools, and by means of discussions and publications. Several large organizations constituted the machinery of this movement, the most important of which were the Grange and the Farmers' Alliance.

The Grange was founded in 1867, and became a national society in 1873. It is a very complete organization with the lodge as a unit, subordinate to the County Grange which is subordinate to the State Grange, this in turn being subordinate to the National Grange. The purposes are fraternal, social, educational, political, and financial. Educational work is a feature of each meeting, a certain part of the program being devoted to this subject. Sometimes the educational work of the lodges of a whole state is planned definitely by one of the state officers, the state grand lecturer. The meetings of the lodge are often held in schoolhouses, thus making the school property a community center for adults as well as children. The interest of the Grange in the school does not stop with the use of the schoolhouse as a meeting place, but it lends its support to all measures intended for the betterment of rural education, and particularly to those involving a greater use of country-life subjects. The Grange was for a time a very powerful society, but by 1880 its power as a national organization was lost. It declined rapidly both in membership and influence until ten years later when it began to revive again.

The Farmers' Alliance was somewhat similar to the Grange in plan and purpose. Its activity however was chiefly directed toward securing better legislation favorable to rural interests, mainly financial. Soon after the formation of the Populist party little was left of the Farmers' Alliance as an organization.

### FOURTH PERIOD

With more than a century of experience agricultural societies are now being readjusted to secure for all interests of agriculture and rural life advantages that may be secured only through organized effort. They may be classified into three groups: national, state, and local. A large number of each group is devoted to some special agricultural interest, such as bee-keeping, apple production, sheep-breeding, and the like, almost every conceivable phase of agriculture being represented by an organization.

Of the national societies the Grange is perhaps the most important. Since 1890 it has emphasized social and educational features, and has recovered from the decline of the previous decade. Its interest and influence in educational matters are greater than ever before.

There are now over seven hundred state agricultural societies most of which are devoted to special interests. In some states the state society has no connection with local societies, but in others the state organization is made up of representatives from local societies.

The latter plan is well illustrated by the Michigan State Association of Farmers' Clubs. In 1908 the state association included one hundred and twenty clubs from thirty-two counties. In 1908 these clubs had a membership of over seven thousand. The association holds an annual meeting in which a majority of the associated clubs are represented. The program consists of reports of various clubs, several addresses on subjects of general interest to farmers, and reports of committees.

A good example of the work of a local club is shown by the following synopsis of its annual report to the association:

The club is eleven years old, with a membership of 71, and average attendance of 50. Annual dues are ten cents per member; the club holds twelve meetings a year, all-day meetings from October to April. Men's meetings in February, May; temperance meetings in February, March;

young people's meetings in April; ladies' meeting in May; club fair in October; picnic in August. The club publishes a paper called the *Rural Grit* (114, p. 15).

The addresses at the annual meetings are on topics of general interest to farmers, often on agricultural education. The most important committee is the one on resolutions. Some recommendations directed toward legislation are usually found in its reports.

The published proceedings of the various agricultural societies contain important contributions to the literature of agricultural education. The importance lies not so much in the new points of view or new ideas presented as in the fact that these articles indicate the attitude of the most progressive farmers on this question. The *Report of the Proceedings of the New Jersey Horticultural Society* for 1910 contains a discussion of "What Shall We Teach the Farmer's Child?" (115). A scheme is proposed for dividing the school year into more equal periods between farm practice and school work. The difficulty of applying such a plan is found in the present long high-school year and short vacation period, and in the absence of instruction in agricultural subjects. The author may have had in mind some shop work, as is being introduced in Cincinnati, and in other places.

The idea is suggestive of possibilities that might be developed in rural schools to advantage, provided the long vacation period were spent in applying the scientific principles of agriculture to farm practice. The boys of the Baltimore County (Md.) Agricultural High School carry on extensive experiments on their home farms during vacation periods. Their work is inspected from time to time by the teacher of agriculture in the high school, the teacher being employed to give his time during the entire year to school matters. This plan has been in operation only one year, but the results have been very satisfactory. Such an arrangement would do away with some of the objections to the present system of education raised by the above paper, that the

high schools are simply feeding the boys and girls to universities and general colleges, but unfitting them for the practical duties of life. . . . . One great trouble with farming today is the fact that for half a century or more country teachers have worn the label and wire of an education arranged for a town school. The material benefits of education, such as they are in a public way, and the public spirit of it, have been town bred and built. One great reason why farming of late years has become more hopeful and prosperous is because we are at last developing a definite form and spirit of farm education.

There are so many societies publishing proceedings that no further reference will be made except to refer to the fact that the discussions appearing in these proceedings on instruction in agriculture in the public schools usually favor such instruction, but not always. Occasionally views are expressed against it. In the *Proceedings of the Iowa Horticultural Society* for 1909 we find an example of the latter (116). The writer reviews the conditions of the Iowa rural schools. His own county has 208 rural schools. He regards the introduction of agricultural instruction in these schools as impossible, even if desirable. He would improve the teaching of these schools by placing more emphasis on the "three R's." He says, "the most persistent and able advocates of agriculture in the public schools are teachers and professors in our state and other colleges." This is not an isolated example of the conservative attitude of the farmer toward education. Similar views are held in every farming community in the country. The little one-room school is regarded as necessary for any scheme of rural education. If the scheme does not fit into the existing system it is unworthy. Much of the opposition to consolidation is no doubt due to the reluctance of abandoning the single-room school, and to the inability to see how a readjustment of school affairs can be brought about.

The sentence just quoted referring to "teachers and professors" advocating agricultural instruction shows a little of the resentment that has grown up lately in several parts of the country toward the activity of those interested in the promotion of agricultural education in the elementary and secondary schools. A prominent agricultural journal has recently cast some reflection on the motives of some of the men now engaged in agricultural extension among public schools, intimating that the matter is being agitated for the benefit of agricultural colleges. The editor finds some sympathy among his readers, as evidenced by a protest from one subscriber against so much space being given to school matters, and so little being given to the discussion of sheep-killing dogs!

Particular mention should be made of the work of the Massachusetts Horticultural Society in its relation to the school-garden movement (117). Soon after Henry L. Clapp introduced school gardening into the George Putnam School of Boston, the Massachusetts Horticultural Society began to encourage the establishment of school gardens in other places in New England by offering prizes for the best gardens entering competition, and by giving prominence to the subject in its published proceedings. Since 1893, one feature of its annual meeting is the session devoted to hearing reports on school gardens. The growth of the school-garden movement of the United States owes much to this society.

The following are a few extracts from letters written by officers of some agricultural societies in answer to an inquiry as to what their societies are now doing toward promoting agricultural education. These are typical expressions, and are taken at random from a number of replies:

Our meetings are always public and we invite teachers, students, and the general public to attend the sessions. We have not taken any definite steps toward the teaching of agriculture or horticulture in the schools, although whenever occasion offers, we are glad to say a word favoring the movement (Vermont).

We have held sessions at the State Normal Schools and have had addresses that we thought would be of value to prospective teachers (New Jersey).

We think it is an important subject and hope to see more of at least the rudiments of horticulture taught in the schools soon (Kansas).

We have papers and discussions in nearly every volume we publish regarding horticultural subjects, bearing on their relation to the public schools (Illinois).

We have undertaken recently the task of improving in some measure the grounds surrounding the rural schools of the state. We have realized for years the deplorable conditions in this respect; the lack of adequate playgrounds; the lack of order and even common cleanliness, the utter lack of any decoration, and other things too numerous to mention. We are feeling our way carefully and so far have but little to report. We have selected seven districts widely separated and for these schools we furnish landscape plans and trees and shrubs to plant the same. We also furnish expert superintendence and inspection. So far the work has been very discouraging on account of the lack of co-operation or even friendly spirit on the part of school officers and teachers. We hope, however, for better things and intend to keep on (Wisconsin).

The brief account just given of agricultural societies is sufficient to indicate at least some of their most important relations to agricultural education, and to impress upon the student of rural education the value of their influence in any movement affecting the country schools. Being composed of representative members of the very communities that are supposed to be benefited by improved rural education, their point of view in educational matters must be considered in any plans to bring about better rural school conditions and their co-operation is needed for attempt to carry out these plans.

## BIBLIOGRAPHY

The facts of the text were obtained partly from the contributions of Kenyon L. Butterfield and L. H. Bailey in the *Encyclopedia of American Agriculture,* from private letters from secretaries of various state agricultural societies, and from proceedings of these societies. Only the references made by number in the text are included in the bibliography.

114. Michigan State Association of Farmers' Clubs, *Proceedings of the Seventeenth Annual Session* (1909), p. 56.

Besides a report of the proceedings there is included resolutions regarding state and national affairs, and constitution and by-laws of the Association.

115. "What Shall We Teach the Farm Child?" H. W. COLLINWOOD. *Proceedings of the New Jersey State Horticultural Society,* Thirty-fifth Annual Session (1909), 169–74.

Reviewed in text.

116. "Agriculture in Our Public Schools." WILLIAM LANGHAM. *Proceedings of the Iowa State Horticultural Society,* XLIV (1909), 147–54.

Reviewed in text.

117. "Report of Committee on School Gardens and Children's Herbariums of the Massachusetts Horticultural Society," *Transactions of the Massachusetts Horticultural Society.* 1894–1907.

Beginning with 1894 and continuing to 1907 these reports of the committee on children's school gardens appeared in the transactions of the Society. After 1907 the Society discontinued the special school-garden feature of its meetings and of its transactions.

# EDITORIAL NOTES

In his annual report issued in November, 1910, Dean Russell of Teachers College makes some very significant remarks about manual training. He opens his comments by referring to the generous support given to this department from the beginning of Teachers College. "It must be confessed, however," he goes on to say, "that the results have not been commensurate with the expenditures made on account of the department, nor has it realized the expectations of its founders in educational efficiency." This statement is followed by a discussion of the difficulty of getting properly qualified students to take manual-training courses. Finally, there is a statement of the policy of Teachers College in the following promises: "The term manual training will be gradually abandoned and in its place we shall have industrial arts, household arts, fine arts, elementary science and the like, indicative of subjects to be taught rather than of teaching methods or educational discipline. The final outcome is the establishment of a School of Industrial Arts to supplant the department of manual training."

**Dean Russell on Manual Training**

Such an announcement as this will be welcomed in many quarters. Manual training certainly has not articulated itself with the other work in our schools. The teachers who have turned to the manual arts have in general been inferior in training and lacking in breadth of educational view. The criticism of the department is merited. Is the solution offered the necessary outcome of this criticism? First, let it be noted that no subject should be condemned because it is badly taught. There is no subject in the course of study which does not suffer seriously at the hands of untrained teachers. Second, there must be something of value in the industrial arts else they would not be evolved out of the unsuccess of manual training. This kernel of value in sewing and carpentry cannot be merely the skill in that particular trade. The educational institution which uses

**Particular Trades versus General Training**

sewing for educational purposes must see beyond the stitches to something of value in the experience of the student. Suppose that some teacher of sewing fails to teach that subject well. Will there be a further breaking up of sewing into the art of making hems and the art of buttonholing? Can the values of handwork be defined in detail only? Is there no broad general result which can be advocated? Dean Russell seems to believe that there is something general for on the next page he advocates turning young artisans into teachers in these industrial arts by giving them "that background of knowledge in drawing, mathematics, science, and language" which will make them leaders of their fellows. "The training of the teachers," he continues, "requires little more than we are now offering [in the night school]: it means the organization of a special curriculum in which the theory of trade teaching and practice in class instruction shall have a place." What will be taken up in the theory of trade training? Will there be some discussion of tests for the selection of proper candidates for this trade or that? Will there be a separate theory for this industry and that? How can there be any generalization of the teacher's art?

Frankly, the scheme proposed seems too atomic and fragmentary to hold together. There is something worth saving in the general idea of manual training as a broad inclusive educational conception. The concept needs expansion rather than contraction. One trouble in the past has been that industry and art have been divorced. As a result there has grown up in the minds of students a feeling that useful things and beautiful things do not belong in the same class. If we divide art and the arts any further we shall suffer even more. Why not begin to enlarge the conception of manual training or some other conception which can fill the same function so as to include industrial design as well as fine art? When this is done, why not give the general principles of all industrial design to those who are interested in each of the arts? If there is not some general unifying force which will hold together the various types of industrial training, the training will do nothing to create a broad interest in industry as distinguished from trade.

**General Principles Needed**

The same type of consideration arises with reference to the relation of the industries and the other school subjects. Manual training has thus far been outside the "regular" school work. The reason for this is that no one has taken a broad enough view of its function to work it out in a form that makes it as general as arithmetic or geography. The reason why our public schools continue to teach arithmetic is that in arithmetic all the pupils get a kind of training which will be useful to them whatever they take up later in life. When one finds bad teaching in arithmetic he does not break the subject up into the arithmetic of cooking and the arithmetic of plumbing. He goes about the improvement of teaching. Let us take the same attitude a little longer regarding the industrial course in our schools. The experiment of manual training is still young in American schools. The present writer for one is not ready to agree that there is no place for a general department which shall unite all these different activities under one general body of principles.

**Manual Training Must Be Related to Other Subjects**

C. H. J.

# BOOK REVIEWS

*A History of Education during the Middle Ages and the Transition to Modern Times.* By FRANK PIERREPONT GRAVES. New York: Macmillan, 1910. Pp. xv+327. $1.10.

This is the second in a series of textbooks on the history of education, the first, issued in 1909, dealing with the period before the Middle Ages, and the present volume dealing with the period from the beginning of the Middle Ages to the French Revolution. About one hundred pages are devoted to the Middle Ages and two hundred to the Renaissance and the seventeenth and eighteenth centuries. This is about equal in scope and amount of material to the middle third of Monroe's *Text Book in the History of Education.*

The author's point of view is described at length in the preface and first chapter of the earlier volume. There it is stated that he follows Davidson in regarding education as conscious evolution, and uses the same method of approach as Professor Monroe. It is expected that the student will gain from the study of the text an appreciation of the way in which educational systems arise in response to social needs, become stereotyped as social habits or institutions which limit the individual, and are reformed or brought up to date by protesting movements or individuals.

The social background of each movement is discussed, in some cases particularly well, e.g., in the chapter on humanistic education in Italy. A good statement of the varied influences at work is given in such a concrete way as materially to aid the student in appreciating what the Renaissance was.

The book maintains a fair balance between three factors, namely, general social movements, educational theory, and the actual establishment of schools. There are chapters on monasticism, Charlemagne, Alfred, Muhammedan learning, mysticism and scholasticism, feudalism and chivalry, the friars, universities, developments of cities and city schools, the Renaissance, humanistic education in Italy, humanistic education in the North, influence of Protestantism, Catholic education, beginnings of realistic education, sense realism, and on Puritanism, Pietism, and Rationalism.

The language used is simple and adapted to the understanding of the ordinary student; which one would not expect after reading that the author follows Davidson. The only incomprehensible parts are in the chapter on scholasticism, a topic which philosophical-minded writers on the history of education continue to think essential, and which ordinary students will continue to fail to understand.

The following minor criticisms are offered: (1) The book retains some elements of the encyclopedism which the better texts in history are eliminating. Thus in a 21-page chapter on realism there are only 16 pages devoted to a discussion of Rabelais, Montaigne, Mulcaster, Milton, and Locke. On p. 54 we have the half-dozen leading scholastics given with their dates in the same number of lines. Seven followers of Chrysoloras—Niccoli, Bruni, Guarino, Battista Guarino, Poggio, Filelfo, Vergerio—all are described in two pages (119–20) which might better have been devoted to Chrysoloras who receives only a half page. (2) Greater care might have been taken to give the student a comprehension of actual school conditions. On p. 98 it is stated that gild schools were generally elementary in character, but not infrequently secondary, and that "while most of the work was in the vernacular, courses in Latin and other higher subjects were also afforded." Such evidence as Leach gives would seem to indicate just the opposite. Moreover, the impression gained (on p. 198) of the active establishment of elementary schools by Protestant German states, is scarcely borne out by Paulsen's account according to whom Latin schools were the primary interest of the educational leaders and German schools either prohibited (as in Saxony) or were makeshifts as in Würtemburg. Nor is the student given any adequate picture of what horrible makeshifts Protestant elementary schools were down to the nineteenth century. (3) In common with other texts which claim to emphasize the social background of education, little account is given of the development of modern science as a factor in modern social and educational reform. Only one page (262) is devoted to sixteenth- and seventeenth-century science and Newton is not mentioned in it. Yet this is followed by four pages on Francis Bacon. Similarly the discussion of Voltaire and French Rationalism is preceded by a 6-page discussion of Locke, while Newton, the chief inspirer of Voltaire and called by the latter "the greatest man in the world," is not mentioned.

These criticisms are not intended to deny the general value of the book which I think is the best text for the limited period covered that we have in English.

S. Chester Parker

# BOOKS RECEIVED

AMERICAN BOOK CO., NEW YORK

*Stephen of Philadelphia.* By JAMES OTIS. Cloth. Illustrated. Pp. 166. $0.35.

*Peter of New Amsterdam.* By JAMES OTIS. Cloth. Illustrated. Pp. 158. $0.35.

*Stories of American Discoverers for Little Americans.* By ROSE LUCIA. Cloth. Illustrated. Pp. 176. $0.40.

*Dramatic Reader for Grammar Grades.* By MARIETTA KNIGHT. Cloth. Illustrated. Pp. 267. $0.50.

*Nature Myths of Many Lands.* By FLORENCE V. FARMER. Cloth. Illustrated. Pp. 224. $0.45.

*Vocational Education.* By JOHN M. GILLETTE. Cloth. Pp. 303. $1.00.

*The Last of the Mohicans.* Adapted by MARGARET N. HAIGHT. Cloth. Illustrated. Pp. 142. $0.35.

*Easy French Prose Composition.* By H. A. GUERBER. Cloth. Pp. 91. $0.25.

ATKINSON, MENTZER & GROVER, NEW YORK

*The Personal Equation.* By LAWRENCE MCTURAN. With an Introduction by JAMES L. HUGHES. Cloth. Pp. 248.

*The Childhood of Ji-Shib, the Ojibwa.* By ALBERT ERNEST JENKS. With Illustrations and Decorations by STACY H. WOOD. Cloth. Pp. 96.

COLONIAL BOOK CO., CHICAGO

*Elementary Lessons in English.* By GEORGE C. HOWLAND. Cloth. Illustrated. Pp. 207. $0.60.

*Advanced Lessons in English.* By GEORGE C. HOWLAND. Cloth. Illustrated. Pp. 314. $0.40.

COLUMBIA UNIVERSITY PRESS, NEW YORK

*Handwriting.* By EDWARD L. THORNDIKE. Paper covers. Pp. 93. $0.30.

*Equipment for Teaching Domestic Science.* By HELEN KINNE. Paper covers. Illustrated. Pp. 100.

*A Syllabus of a Course on Elementary Bookmaking and Bookbinding.* By SARAH J. FREEMAN, A.B. Paper covers. Illustrated. Pp. 42. $0.30.

DANA ESTES & CO., BOSTON

*Rainy Day Pastimes for Children.* By BARONESS VON PALM. Cloth. Illustrated. Pp. 125. $1.00.

DOUBLEDAY, PAGE & CO., NEW YORK

*Children's Diet in Home and School.* With Classified Recipes and Menus. By LOUISE E. HOGAN. Cloth. Pp. 194.

FORBES & CO., CHICAGO

*Confidences: Talks with a Young Girl concerning Herself.* By EDITH B. LOWRY, M.D., Cloth. Pp. 94. $0.50.

GINN & CO., BOSTON

*Wentworth's Plane Geometry.* Revised by GEORGE WENTWORTH and DAVID EUGENE SMITH. Cloth. Pp. 287. $0.80.

*Song Reader.* By JAMES M. MCLAUGHLIN and W. W. GILCHRIST. Cloth. Pp. 156. $0.45.

*The Blodgett Readers by Grades. Books I, II, and III.* By FRANCES E. BLODGETT and ANDREW B. BLODGETT. Cloth. Illustrated. Book I, pp. 131, \$0.30; Book II, pp. 173, \$0.35; Book III, pp. 221, \$0.40.

*Little Plays for Little People.* By MARION I. NOYES and BLANCHE H. RAY. Cloth. Illustrated. Pp. 122. \$0.35.

HARPER & BROS., NEW YORK

*Travels in History.* By MARK TWAIN. Cloth. Illustrated. Pp. 171. \$0.50.

HOUGHTON MIFFLIN CO., BOSTON

*Ethics for Children.* By ELLA LYMAN CABOT. Cloth. Pp. 254. \$1.25.

*The Basket Woman.* By MARY AUSTIN. Cloth. Illustrated. Pp. 222. \$0.60.

*Captains of Industry.* By JAMES PARTON. Cloth. Illustrated. Pp. 114. \$0.25.

*Little Mr. Thimblefinger Stories.* By JOEL CHANDLER HARRIS. Cloth. Illustrated. Pp. 164. \$0.40.

B. F. JOHNSON PUBLISHING CO., RICHMOND

*School Arithmetic. Elementary Book.* By JOHN M. COLAW, FRANK W. DUKE, and JAMES K. POWERS. Cloth. Illustrated. Pp. 256. \$0.35.

LITTLE, BROWN & CO., BOSTON

*Betty in Canada.* By ETTA BLAISDELL MCDONALD and JULIA DALRYMPLE. Cloth. Illustrated. Pp. 111. \$0.60.

*Boris in Russia.* By ETTA BLAISDELL MCDONALD and JULIA DALRYMPLE. Cloth. Illustrated. Pp. 120. \$0.60.

*Gerda in Sweden.* By ETTA BLAISDELL MCDONALD and JULIA DALRYMPLE. Cloth. Illustrated. Pp. 120. \$0.60.

*Fritz in Germany.* By ELLA BLAISDELL MCDONALD and JULIA DALRYMPLE. Cloth. Illustrated. Pp. 120. \$0.60.

THE MACMILLAN CO., NEW YORK

*The Industrial History of the United States.* By KATHARINE COMAN, PH.B. Cloth. Illustrated. Pp. 461. \$1.50.

*Selections from the Old Testament.* Edited with Introduction and Notes by FRED NEWTON SCOTT. Cloth. Pp. 335. \$0.25.

*The Man without a Country, and Other Stories.* By EDWARD EVERETT HALE. Edited by SAMUEL MARION TUCKER, PH.D. Cloth. Pp. 200. \$0.25.

*An Outline for the Study of American Civil Government.* Prepared for the New England History Teachers' Association by its Committee. Cloth. Pp. 187. \$0.50.

*A First Reader for New American Citizens.* By FRANCES SANKSTONE MINTZ. Cloth. Illustrated. Pp. 188. \$0.50.

*Principles of Secondary Education.* By CHARLES DE GARMO. Cloth. Pp. 213. \$1.00.

*New Geographies: First Book.* By RALPH S. TARR, B.S., F.G.S.A., and FRANK M. MCMURRY, PH.D. Cloth. Illustrated. Pp. 263. \$0.65.

RAND, MCNALLY & CO., CHICAGO

*Old Fashioned Fairy Tales.* By MARION FOSTER WASHBURNE. Cloth. Illustrated. Pp. 115. \$0.45.

*The Lady of the Lake.* Edited by FLORUS A. BARBOUR. Cloth. Illustrated. Pp. 254.

*Little Rhymes for Little Readers.* By WILHELMINA SEEGMILLER. Cloth. Illustrated. Pp. 87.

# CURRENT EDUCATIONAL LITERATURE IN THE PERIODICALS[1]

IRENE WARREN
Librarian, School of Education, The University of Chicago.

AGATHON. The changed spirit of the Sorbonne. Educa. R. 40:387–96. (N. '10.)

BAILEY, L. H. The place of agriculture in higher education. Educa. 31: 249–56. (D. '10.)

BONHAM, MILLEDGE L. The problem of defective pupils in the regular schools, public and private. Educa. 31:211–17. (D. '10.)

CARY, C. P. Some unfortunate tendencies among state universities. Educa. R. 40:325–33. (N. '10.)

CHAMBERS, WILL GRANT. The conversational method: its dangers; its fundamental principles. Educa. 31:169–74. (N. '10.)

COOPER, CHARLES. An American trade school for girls. School W. 12:413–15. (N. '10.)

DAVENPORT, E. The opportunity of the high school. Educa. R. 40:348–55. (N. '10.)

DAVIS, BENJAMIN MARSHALL. Agricultural education: state organizations for agriculture and Farmers' Institutes. El. School T. 11:136–45. (N. '10.)

DAVISON, ELLEN SCOTT. History in German secondary schools. Educa. R. 40:356–68. (N. '10.)

DEARBORN, GEORGE V. N. Attention: certain of its aspects and a few of its relations to physical education. Amer. Phys. Educa. Rev. 15:559–71. (N. '10.)

Educational outlook in England. Educa. R. 40:397–406. (N. '10.)

ERSKINE, JOHN. English in the college course. Educa. R. 40:340–47. (N. '10.)

Gladstone's letters to his children. Outlook 96:777–81. (3 D. '10.)

[1] *Abbreviations.*—Amer. Phys. Educa. Rev., American Physical Education Review; Atlan., Atlantic Monthly; Educa., Education; Educa. R., Educational Review; El. School T., Elementary School Teacher; Journ. of Educa., Journal of Education; Journ. of Educa. Psychol., Journal of Educational Psychology; Kind. R., Kindergarten Review; Lit. D., Literary Digest; Pop. Educator, Popular Educator; Pop. Sci. Mo., Popular Science Monthly; Primary Educa., Primary Education; Psychol. Clinic, Psychological Clinic; R. of Rs., Review of Reviews; School W., School World.

GODDARD, HENRY H. The application of educational psychology to the problems of the special class. Journ. of Educa. Psychol. 1:521–31. (N. '10.)

———. The institution for mentally defective children an unusual opportunity for scientific research. Training School (N.J.) 7:275–78. (N. '10.)

GREENWOOD, J. M. The home and school life. Educa. 31:238–43. (D. '10.)

HARTWELL, CHARLES H. Grading and promotion of pupils. Educa. R. 40:375–86. (N. '10.)

HATCH, WILLIAM E. Industrial education in Massachusetts. Educa. R. 40:369–74. (N. '10.)

HAWKINS, MASON A. Vocational education. Educa. 31:141–50. (N. '10.)

HILL, PATTY SMITH. The history of the kindergarten song in America. Kind. R. 21:193–206. (D. '10.)

HOLMES, ARTHUR. An educational experiment with troublesome adolescent boys. Psychol. Clinic 4:155–78. (N. '10.)

HUNT, CLARA WHITEHILL. Picture books for children. Outlook 96:739–45. (26 N. '10.)

HUSTON, KATHARINE WOODWARD. Elementary school ideals. Educa. 31:160–68. (N. '10.)

JOHNSTON, CHARLES. New intellectual forces at Yale. Harper's Weekly 54:11. (12 N. '10.)

JOHNSTON, CHARLES HUGHES. Naturalizing the educative process. Educa. R. 40:334–39. (N. '10.)

JONES, ERNEST. Psycho-analysis and education. Journ. of Educa. Psychol. 1:497–520. (N. '10.)

LATHROP, JOHN M. College training for business. Educa. 31:244–48. (D. '10.)

LEONARD, MARY H. The religious freedom of the schools. Educa. 31:218–23. (D. '10.)

Mental and physical factors involved in education. School W. 12:418–20. (N. '10.)

MEYERS, JESSIE G. The story of a public school child. Training School (N.J.) 7:278–80. (N.'10.)

MONTMORENCY, J. E. G. de. The medieval education of women. Journ. of Educa. (Lond.) 42:720–22. (N. '10.)

MORRELL, GRACE E. The importance of basketry in the training of defectives. Training School (N.J.) 7:280–81. (N. '10.)

NEIGHBOURS, OWEN J. Retardation in the schools and some of the causes. El. School T. 11:119–35. (N. '10.)

O'GRADY, HARDRESS. The teaching of free composition in modern foreign languages. School W. 12:408–11. (N. '10.)

O'SHEA, M. V. The origin of modern educational ideals. Primary Educa. 18:545–47. (D. '10.)

PARKER, S. CHESTER. Our inherited practice in elementary schools: Pestalozzian object-teaching and oral instruction (4). El. School T. 11: 146–55. (N. '10.)

Playground for little children, A. Outlook 96:783–84. (3 D. '10.)

PUTNAM, JAMES JACKSON. William James. Atlan. 106:835–43. (D. '10.)

ROBERT, JEANNE. A boys' and girls' republic. R. of Rs. 42:705–12. (D. '10.)

STEVENSON, JOHN J. Classics and the college course. Pop. Sci. Mo. 77: 554–60. (D. '10.)

STORR, F. Domestic science in the secondary school. School W. 12:405–8. (N. '10.)

SUPER, CHARLES W. Learning foreign languages. Pop. Sci. Mo. 77:561–69. (D. '10.)

SWETT, HARRY PREBLE. The high school pupil. Educa. 31:224–30. (D. '10.)

Traveling college for farmers. Lit. D. 41:857. (12 N. '10.)

TREUDLY, T. Dr. William T. Harris. Educa. 31:231–37. (D. '10.)

UPTON, HENRY L. Teachers' pensions. Pop. Educator 28:173–75. (D. '10.)

WHITE, FRANK MARSHALL. Making bad boys into good men. Outlook 96:711–20. (26 N. '10.)

VOLUME XI NUMBER 6

THE ELEMENTARY SCHOOL TEACHER

FEBRUARY, 1911

# COMMUNITY ARITHMETIC FOR THE SEVENTH AND EIGHTH GRADES

WALTER W. HART
University of Wisconsin, Madison, Wisconsin

## I. INDEFINITE AIM IN THESE GRADES

The course of study in mathematics for the seventh and eighth grades has been in an unsettled state for a long time. There has been and is little agreement in regard to the content of the curriculum, not to mention methods of instruction. Some courses contain no algebra or generalized arithmetic and no geometry, except the traditional work in the mensuration of certain plane and solid figures; on the other hand, there are courses at the other extreme in which the major portion of the time in the eighth grade is devoted to algebra. The courses have had the catch-all character, consisting of a variety of topics lacking unity. The work has been criticized especially as lacking social meaning; many of the topics commonly given cannot be said to possess much direct or even remote meaning for the pupils, as an example of which may be mentioned cube root which is still taught in some schools; and such a topic as stocks and bonds, which, while relating to current business practice, is usually carried to such length as to lose most of the pupils. It has even been suggested that the instruction in the lower grades is more effective than that in the upper grades because the teachers in these lower grades know better what they are trying to accomplish. Without intending to join in any statement regarding the relative efficiency of the teaching, this may be said, that in the first six grades the dominant mathematical purpose is to put the pupils in possession of the mechanics of the subject, to give them control over the essential number facts and processes and the ordinary tables of denominate numbers, whereas in the two upper grades there is no such clear-cut purpose in evidence.

### II. THE SOCIAL AIM OF EDUCATION

In the meantime the social function of the work of the elementary grades has become a recognized factor in shaping the courses of study of the other studies. It is quite generally agreed that the school should bring the pupils into contact with matters of interest in their own community, always with the reservation that the materials of teaching should come within the scope of the children's power and interest. The term community is to be interpreted here in a broad way, extending gradually from the home to the town and state and then to the country at large.

### III. TWO AIMS FOR UPPER GRADE MATHEMATICS

In view of the foregoing, the following two aims may properly be accorded a prominent place in determining the character of the mathematics work in the seventh and eighth grades: first, to maintain and increase efficiency in the fundamentals of arithmetic as taught in the earlier grades; second, to aid in the effort to give the pupils some insight into the life of the community in which they are to have a part. On the strictly mathematical side, it is important that the power the pupils have gained in the essentials of arithmetic shall be "conserved" and increased through appropriate drill. Whatever else of mathematical product the public may want of their schools, they unite in expecting that the graduates of the grammar grades shall be reasonably rapid and accurate in the fundamental operations of arithmetic, especially with such numbers as occur in daily life. Such skill is the product of persistent, well-directed drill; it is because of the neglect of such drill in the upper grades that much of the criticism of the mathematics work is thoroughly justified. This drill work becomes especially necessary if the children are to retain their acquaintance with and become skilful in the manipulation of fractions. In regard to the second aim, it is beginning to be recognized that the mathematics must contribute its share of "social insight," to use a phrase of Professor Suzzallo's. This statement does not imply that in the earlier work also this should not be one of the aims; but, in the case of the upper grades, this aim seems to afford the unifying principle which has been so noticeably lacking. The pupils have been taught the essentials in the lower grades; they are about to leave school, many of them permanently, and should now have their attention turned toward the social whole of which they form a part. What better principle of selection of material for mathematics work can there be than this?

This doctrine meets with quite general approval; it is the practice of it which causes difficulty, a difficulty which arises from the fact that the character of drill necessary cannot be entirely placed in book form, and secondly, that it is unlikely that publishers will place upon the market a book which is designed to meet the needs of one community.

The purpose of this article is to call attention to an attempt to put this theory into practice. It will become clear that the general plan might be followed in any other community, but that the material used in the classroom would have to be selected to fit the conditions of the particular community served.

## IV. THE PLACE AND CONDITIONS

In the Indianapolis schools, the classes are organized on a half-year basis; thus there is a 7B, a 7A, an 8B, and an 8A grade, in the order indicated. The course of study called for continued drill upon the essentials, as well as for attention to certain new topics. This drill was expected to be both abstract and concrete, but there was no specification as to the material to be used, except that it should be simple, modern, and within the experience of the children. It was likely to be of a miscellaneous sort, a practice which is unwise owing to the tendency to scatter attention. Considerable time was being devoted to algebra. It was decided to systematize the drill work, to give it definite local meaning, and, in order to get additional time for it, to cut down the work in algebra. The modified work was introduced in grade 7A and above.

### V. PLAN FOR GRADE 7A

For this grade the problems were grouped under the general topic "Problems of the Home," with the following subtopics: (*a*) grocery, meat market, and department store problems; (*b*) making change; (*c*) cost of heating and lighting the home; (*d*) cost of furnishing the home.

The set (*a*) consists of the problems which customers and clerks must solve daily. The problems are grouped so as to direct attention for a time toward grocery problems, then toward meat-market problems, etc. The material was collected by a committee of teachers from local tradesmen. The result is a collection of problems involving usual buying quantities under local conditions. Current prices are to be used and the problems are to be solved mentally as a rule. Some examples follow:

#### MEAT MARKET—SET A

1. Find the cost of a chicken weighing 3½ lbs.; 4 lbs.; 4¼ lbs.; 4½ lbs.
2. Find the cost of 1½ lbs. of pork chops; 2 lbs.; 2¼ lbs.; 3 lbs.; 2½ lbs.
3. Find the cost of a piece of bacon weighing 2 lbs.; 2¼ lbs.; 2¾ lbs.
4. Find the cost of a piece of ham weighing 5 lbs.; 6 lbs.; 6¼ lbs.; 6¾ lbs.; 7 lbs.

#### MEAT MARKET—SET B

1. How much lard should be given for 10 cents? 15 cents? 20 cents? 25 cents? 30 cents?
2. How much sirloin steak should be given for 10 cents? 20 cents? 25 cents? 30 cents? etc.
3. How much in weight should be given to a woman asking for a rib roast which will cost 35 cents? 40 cents? 45 cents? 59 cents? etc.
4. How much boiled ham should be given for 10 cents? 15 cents? 20 cents? 25 cents? etc.

#### GROCERY—SET C

1. Find the cost of ½ lb. of American cheese; of cream cheese; of Swiss cheese.

2. Find the cost of ½ pk. potatoes; of a small measure of potatoes.

3. Find the cost of ¼ lb. of tea; of ½ lb.

4. Find the cost of 2 bars of laundry soap; of three bars; of 5 bars.

GROCERY—SET D

1. Find the amount of rice to be given for 15 cents; 20 cents; 25 cents; etc.

2. Find the amount of tea to be given for 15 cents; 20 cents; 25 cents; etc.

3. Find the amount of pepper, allspice, cinnamon, cloves, etc., to be given for 5 cents; 10 cents.

4. Find the amount of shelled almonds, pecans, walnuts, to be given for 5 cents; 10 cents; 15 cents; etc.

GROCERY—SET E

1. Get together a list of supplies such as might be ordered by a family on each of the six days of a week. Have the bills for these made out on slips prepared like those used in the market. Have the total figured up daily and at the end of the week.

2. A woman ordered the following goods over the telephone: 25 cents worth of granulated sugar; 10 cents worth of corn meal; a 35 cent porter-house steak; 10 cents worth of figs; 15 cents worth of cheese. Make out the sale slip for the order, fill in the amount of each article to be given for the money; find the total of the bill and the amount of change which the delivery boy must give the woman if she pays him with a $5.00 bill.

GROCERY—SET F. ECONOMICAL PURCHASING

1. Compare the cost per pound of sugar bought by the pound with the cost when bought by the 25-pound sack.

2. Compare the cost of laundry soap when bought by the bar and when bought by the box; when bought by the quarter's worth.

3. A housekeeper having canned a bushel of peaches, wishes to know the cost per can. Find it if she used a bushel of peaches, 9 lbs. of sugar, 100 ft. of gas, and 15 Mason jars. Compare this cost with the current price for a can of peaches at the store.

The department-store section consists of a list of various kinds of ribbons, laces, silks, embroidery, and trimming materials, with current selling prices and selling quantities. These items were selected because the dealings in them are usually in small quantities, almost always involving computation with fractions. The data was obtained direct from the local stores. The managers were entirely willing to co-operate. They said that the average customer and many otherwise very desirable clerks were unable to obtain with any degree of certainty the cost of such purchases. Incidentally there is no small gain to the school system in having the business men know that the school is making a serious effort to meet such a situation. A few examples follow:

1. Baby ribbon, 2 cents, 3½ cents per yard; 19 cents, 32 cents per bolt.

Hair ribbon, 5″ to 7″ at 10 cents, 19 cents, 25 cents, 35 cents, 59 cents per yd. Quantities usually bought: 1, 1½, 1¼, 1⅜, 2, 2¼ yds.

Shoe ribbon, at 10 cents and 18 cents. Quantity bought: for 3-eyelet shoe 1½ yds.; for 4-eyelet shoe 1¾ yds.; for 5-eyelet shoe 2 yds.

2. Lace—cluny, imitation: ¾-inch at 10 cents; 1½-inch at 12½ cents; 3½-inch at 19 cents and 25 cents; real: ¾-inch at 25 cents; 3½-inch at 50 cents and 59 cents.

And thus for the various items this information is given. It is to be used in the making of problems. Also the following problems were given; they were taken direct from the canceled saleslips in one store:

Find the cost of ⅝ yd. of lace at $19.50 per yard; find the cost of 18¾ yds. of muslin at $1.12½ per yd.; 18¾ yds. of crepe at $1.25 per yd.; 4½ yds. of gingham at 6¾ cents per yd.; 8¾ yds. of gingham at 7½ cents per yd.

For written work the following type of problem is included:

Bought 4 yds. of china silk at 49 cents a yd.; 8 yds. of cluny lace at 59 cents; ⅞ yd. net at 75 cents; and 18 yds. of ribbon at 5 cents for a waist. What did the material for the waist cost?

As to the effect of this sort of work, some may object that while this is good correlation with domestic science it will not prove of interest to the boys; this may be true of the department-store problems. However, for both boys and girls these problems come very near to satisfying the present demand for school material which has vocational value and practical value. It is pertinent to point out that the average problems used in connection with the application of interest to business seem designed to meet the interests of the boys and not so much so those of the girls. In the case of the market problems, it may be objected that the work is too simple; that it belongs in the fifth grade with fractions. Any of us will admit the need of constant review on fractions, and then besides, the pupils are getting more out of it than arithmetical skill. To illustrate, they brought saleslips from home and told of their watchfulness in purchasing for the family; one girl said that she had made the butcher give her another chop when she found him failing to give full weight; one boy told of adding up the weekly bill from the grocer and of finding a mistake on it. The work was real to them.

Under the topic "making change," the pupils are taught the addition method which is now commonly used in the stores. Under the topic "Cost of Heating and Lighting the Home," certain problems are introduced which give drill upon the local rates for coal, gas, and electricity.

### VI. PLAN FOR GRADE 8B

For Grade 8B, the problems are grouped under the topic "Problems Relating to the Industries of the City and State," with the following sub-topics: (*a*) manufacturing interests of Indianapolis; (*b*) manufacturing interests of Indiana; (*c*) problems of certain lines of work; some railroad problems; some foundry problems; buying and selling paper; paying employees.

The first two sets are based upon the United States Census Reports, and the others were gathered in the city. They are designed to give the pupils an idea of these activities of their own community, of the number of employees, of the wages paid. They are expected to appeal to the vocational interest which should be growing at this time, and to show how arithmetic enters into the daily life of some of the workmen. A few examples will be given. Appropriate statistics are given to enable the pupils to solve the following problems:

Find the total number of wage-earners in 1900, and in 1905; find the total amount of wages paid in both years; find the total cost of manufacture in both years; find the total value of the manufactured products; find the total profits in each year and the per cent of profit; find the average wages paid in both years; compare the wages of the city wage-earner with those of the wage-earner in the state at large; what percentage of the manufacturing establishments of Indiana are located in Indianapolis? What percentage of the manufactured products were made in Indianapolis?

It will be noticed that these problems involve about all of the essential processes, so that as review drill-work they are effective.

In a railroad shop running from 6:30 A.M. to 5:15 P.M., with ¾-hour off for lunch, what will a boy earn in one day at 12½ cents per hour?

How many pieces 8 inches long can be cut from an iron bar 29 inches long, if ¼ inch is wasted on each cut? Illustrate by a drawing, assuming that the original bar had the dimensions 1″×1″×29″.

A brass foundry has to make 72 lbs. of castings. If 1½ per cent of the metal is lost in the melting, how much metal must be melted to furnish the required amount?

A certain grade of paper is sold at the rate of 480 sheets for $28.00. How much does this average per sheet? When bought in smaller quantities 10 per cent is added to the list price. Find the cost of 240 sheets; of 160; of 100; of 50.

"Paying employees" proved to be a fruitful source of problems as well as an interesting topic to the pupils. Attention is directed to the fact that in paying employees, it is customary to give each individual his money in as large denominations as possible. For example, suppose that Smith is to receive $18.79; he would be given one $10.00 bill, one $5.00 bill, one $2.00 bill, one $1.00 bill, one 50c piece, one 25c piece and four 1c pieces. In determining the amount of money with which to pay several employees, it is obviously necessary to consider carefully the amount to be drawn from the bank in each denomination; this becomes a good problem from the school point of view.

## VII. PLAN FOR GRADE 8A

For Grade 8A two sets of problems were provided: one set is designed for drill upon the essentials at the beginning of the term, and the other set is designed to give additional drill and to correlate with the civics work toward the end of the term. The former consists of problems based upon certain statistics which give the area, population, and wealth of Indianapolis during a term of years; some Indiana problems; and some based upon the area, population, and wealth of the United States. The second set consists of problems under the following topics: (*a*) cost of the Indianapolis schools; (*b*) cost of the city government of Indianapolis; (*c*) money raised by taxes; (*d*) money raised by the sale of bonds; (*e*) money raised by special assessments.

The statistics upon which these problems are based were obtained from local, state, or national reports. The problems are designed to give the necessary drill in arithmetic, and to do that in a miscellaneous way; at each point, the main point of interest should be the topic being discussed, not the arithmetical work, but it is obvious that the arithmetical work must be of the very best if the results are to have any meaning. This is exactly the way in which arithmetic is usually applied, and it is certainly desirable that the pupils should have some experience of this kind. But the problems are designed also to give the pupils some acquaintance with the various matters being discussed; this will come about as a result of the constant effort to keep up interest in the topic being considered. The idea of average and per capita are taught in connection with this work. Some of the statistics and some of the questions follow:

COST OF IMPROVEMENTS IN INDIANAPOLIS DURING 1891–1908

| | | |
|---|---|---|
| Asphalt streets and alleys ........... | 58.54 miles.... | $3,168,049.94 |
| Brick streets and alleys ............ | 66.23 miles.... | 2,150,242.18 |
| Wooden streets and alleys .......... | 22.93 miles.... | 1,291,318.47 |
| Bitulithic streets ..................... | 7.66 miles.... | 271,085.65 |

PROBLEMS

1. Find the cost per mile of each kind of improvement.
2. Find the cost per front foot of each kind.
3. Find the number of miles of streets and alleys paved.
4. Find percentage paved with each kind of pavement.

Under the cost of government, such questions as the following are raised:

1. Find the total expenditures for all purposes in each year (4 years).
2. Find the per capita cost for each year.
3. Find the percentage spent upon permanent improvements.
4. Find the percentage of increase in the per-capita expense from year to year.

Under the topic "Money Raised by Taxes," an itemized statement of the tax rate for one year is given to show the various funds to which the taxes are distributed, and the portion which each receives. Then additional tables are given to enable the pupils to answer the following questions:

1. Find the total tax rate for city purposes; for state purposes; for city schools; for county purposes.

2. Find the total tax rate for each year in the table.

3. What percentage on the dollar is this?

4. Find the increase in the rate 1900 to 1905; 1905 to 1906; 1906 to 1907; 1907 to 1908.

Under the topic "Money Raised by the Sale of Bonds," it is designed to give the subject of stocks and bonds a local meaning. An itemized statement of the bonded indebtedness of the city is given; attention is called to the limit of indebtedness, and to the margin of legal indebtedness. The bonds issued by the school board are also used as a basis for problems. For example:

1. In 1909 the Board of School Commissioners issued $50,000 worth of bonds, receiving $51,856 for them. What was the amount of premium? What was the premium on each bond? What was the per cent of premium on each bond?

The bonds bear 3½ per cent interest. If you had bought one of these bonds, what would you have paid for it? How much interest would you receive annually? What rate of income would you receive on your investment?

Under the topic "Money Raised by Special Assessments," attention is directed to the manner of computing the sewer assessments in the city, and it is a somewhat complicated problem, involving the computation of the area drained. The manner of computing street assessments also is given. This is a good example of the real purpose of this work; the intention here is that the pupils shall learn how the assessments are computed, not that they shall merely work some arithmetic problems; speaking more generally, the problem material is considered of the maximum importance, the arithmetical work being only a means to the end.

## VIII. PLAN OF COLLECTING AND DISTRIBUTING THE PROBLEMS

The material for this work was gathered by a committee of teachers of mathematics, engaged in the seventh and eighth grades, working under the chairmanship of the writer, who was then connected with one of the local high schools; the work at all times received the interest and direction of the administrative officers of the schools. The problems were used in mimeographed form for one year, and were then printed privately by the Indianapolis Board of School Commissioners for free distribution to the pupils of the schools.

# A STUDY OF A SUBNORMAL CHILD

VINNIE CRANDALL HICKS

Many teachers have had neither training nor experience in the recognition of subnormality among their pupils. They find a certain child failing to comprehend the work given to him, failing to enter into the group life of his classmates, yet they have no comprehension of the special problem which such a child presents. In consequence of this ignorance on their part, the child may be advanced from one grade to another as the years pass by, because his teachers are unwilling to keep him longer and he grows too large to remain among little children. When, at fifteen or sixteen, he may have reached the fifth grade, his instructors and even his parents begin to realize that there is something radically wrong. This realization years before would have saved much misdirected effort.

It is with this lack among our teachers in mind that the following description of a defective child has been written. The child chosen was not one rendered backward by any sense-deprivation, nor was he a case of congenital idiocy, but one whose outward appearance betokened little of his mental incompetence; just such a case, in fact, as might appear in the room of any teacher who reads this.

R. was eleven, rather stocky, and of very low stature, an inheritance from his parents. His head was of decidedly brachiocephalic type, but showed no noticeable asymmetry. The only facial peculiarities evident to the ordinary observer were a peculiar use of the eyes and a lack of expression. Contrary to the rule with many of the mentally defective, his hands were small and very delicate in form. He had the carriage and gait of an old man, though not troubled by either lameness or deformity. He stood habitually with the right knee bent and forward. This had raised the left hip higher than the right. He had a clear, healthy skin, good teeth, good circulation, and seemed well nourished. His voice was low, harsh, and guttural, and he rarely varied from a monotone in speaking or singing. He had a peculiar closed utterance between his teeth, and was inclined to be slovenly in his enunciation.

When I began work with him about four months ago, he had no real knowledge of numbers at all. He could add like numbers up to fives just as he could repeat a Mother Goose rhyme, and he could often add 1 to a number under 10 in very much the same way. His writing was a rather pretty, round back-hand but with little sense of line or proportionate letter heights. Nor did he know all of his capitals. He was as good a speller orally as an ordinary fourth-grade child, with the possible exception that his experience of words was not so large. In reading he knew only the word wholes which had been matters of frequent experience with him. Other words he had to construct orally and yet had little knowledge of phonetics to help him. His method of getting at a strange word was something like this: he would spell the word aloud, cast about in his mind for words familiar to him which began or ended similarly, try these, mentally comparing their spelling with what he saw before him, and so with the help of the context, he often made out the new word. But words which it would take him ten minutes to figure out when he was not interested in the story, he would recognize at once if the story happened to suit. The same phenomenon was noticeable in his reading in general. Only a most interesting and simply constructed story would hold his attention. Even with what *seemed* to be the best will in the world he wandered in his gaze, lost his place, and only with great difficulty concentrated enough to find it again. It might take him three-quarters of an hour to read an ordinary first-reader page, and his gaze would wander to all parts of the open book, or even of the room, a dozen times in a single paragraph.

This gives briefly his ability as a student of books when I began my work with him. He had been sent to public school at eight, but had to be taken out because he did not respond at all to the teacher's efforts and also showed a fear of the other boys and a great sensitiveness to their noise. This auditory hyperaesthesia he displayed most markedly once at the country club, when he was nine I believe. He was dining there with his parents when the band, which happened to be near him, began to play. The first blare sent him flying from his seat and screaming about the room. He was quieted only with much difficulty. The only sign of the persistence of this sensitiveness which I have seen has been his lack of attention to lessons if he hears some unusual sound, with perhaps the phlegmatic remark, "That is an ugly noise." After his public-school experience, he was tried in a private school. Again his lack of responsiveness marked him as different from his fellows, and he was kept only three days.

To the ordinary teacher, a study of the history of this case would not be illuminating. He was an only child, born after eight years of married life. His mother too was an only child, and it is significant that she never played with other children or evinced the slightest interest in them. R. has undoubtedly suffered from too much mother and grandmother since the day he was born. Their constant attentions have removed from his sluggish nerve cells the natural stimulation they needed. The women attribute his apathy, lack of responsiveness, and general slowness to "pure ugliness." Like ugliness in many a more normal child, it is probably due to a definite physiological cause. In his babyhood R. had a severe attack of diphtheria, and from that time until they were removed last year, suffered from adenoids. The diphtheritic poison has seemed to clog the nerve cells so that they react very slowly to any stimuli, and under unfavorable conditions do not react at all. Fear is the chief unfavorable condition. But this is so invariable a characteristic of defective and backward children that I consider it an effect rather than a cause. A child like this one whose muscular co-ordinations are not properly developed and whose faculty of generalization is small, suffers constantly from being unable to cope with his environment physically and mentally. This demand on the nerve cells for work they are unfitted to do results in fear.

I have given R. a considerable number of the so-called psycho-physical tests. Some seventeen of these were my own. I gave him also nos. 5, 6, 11, and 13 of the Norsworthy tests; the 6th of de Sanctis; and several of the Binet tests from the 12th on.

The results of these tests confirmed and amplified the more casual observations and gave me the following facts to work on: All of his senses seemed to be intact. Auditory perception was more acute than visual or tactual. Associations played a relatively small part in his memory images; yet numbers of two digits he remembered best by *visual* form association. Voluntary attention was very weak. Muscular sense was normal. The ability to compare, to appreciate relationships, and to control associations seemed good, and his capacity to reason about things no longer present to the senses was pretty fair. Ability in abstract ideas as shown by mathematical concepts was poor in the extreme; as shown in a knowledge of abstract words, was below grade; and as shown by ideas on everyday subjects, was pretty good. Motor ability was extremely poor. Power of concentration was so poor as to make one almost suspect the possible presence of *petit mal* epilepsy.

With the above record to go on and a history of being unable to stay in any school where he was placed, the question was where to begin. His parents, and parents are often a troublesome factor in these matters, wanted R. to learn the three R's and to do it at high speed. Yet what he needed first of all was training in concentration, in muscular co-ordination, and in visualizing. The lack of these caused all of his defects, or, more properly speaking, was the sum total of his defects. Under the guise of the aforesaid much desired three R's, calisthenics, and music, I have been striving for these qualities. I have engaged a competent teacher to give him calisthenics and dancing steps so that his larger arm and leg muscles might be brought into better co-ordination. In four months under her tutelage he has improved so that he is now in a dancing class which she carries on for normal children. And while he moves through the dances much like an old man in his dotage, he does his steps and arm motions correctly and sometimes keeps fair time to the music. This same teacher has given him piano and voice lessons. Little progress is shown in the latter. He differentiates possibly two or three tones, but only when much urged thereto, and it takes a most lenient ear to hear them. His breathing exercises and study of tone placing do not seem to have had the beneficial influence on his general articulation that I had hoped. The piano work has been valuable for more than one reason. First, it satisfies a real love which the child has for music. Still better, it is a wonderful help in the training of the finer muscles; it increases the power of co-ordination of eye and hand, ear and hand, eye and ear. R. now plays simple scales and exercises from memory, reads a little, and plays in a very simple duet with his trainer. The piano work is increasing his motor ability and will certainly increase his powers of discrimination and comparison.

My own work with R. has been largely confined to reading, writing, spelling, and arithmetic. With a child of his temperament, it takes a long time to win confidence, and he is inclined to be curious or even resentful when any innovations on the regular line of his work are presented. So I have done considerable humdrum work with him which does not show much progress. Taking up the subject of study and methods employed separately, the easiest was:

*a*) Spelling:—When I began with R. he spelled well orally words of first-reader difficulty. His written spelling was poor, even if he had studied the lesson faithfully. This was partly due to his slow writing. He gave so much thought to that, that his memory of the word became confused. Moreover, his memory images were almost entirely auditory and he seemed to distrust the whispered letters which he uttered before writing. We have improved this written spelling by the use of many methods. The first was to give him a little more free writing. Then, though I did not forbid him to say the letters to himself, I encouraged him to write down a letter just as soon as he whispered it, not waiting until lack of self-confidence had made him forget it. In addition we had exercises in word-building and in phonetics. To give a different aspect to this branch of the work and also an added interest, we played two games. One was a kind of anagrams. I gave him, shuffled up, the letters of some word in his day's spelling-lesson which had troubled him, and he rearranged the word. In this he has never yet shown any knowledge of common suffixes or prefixes or any ordinary letter combinations. He can sometimes tell by inspection an utterly impossible combination, but more often has to spell the letters orally before he can pass judgment; and this is true just the same if he has the word correctly spelled. The other game we have played is "hang." I mark off spaces for the letters of some word in his spelling-lesson. He guesses. For every letter which is wrong I put part of the body of a man on the gallows, ending with the rope around his neck. In this game R. finds it very hard to guess letters. He knows his alphabet, yet has no use of it. Almost always he will guess the vowels and then the consonants in order, as a very little child might. But the game helps to whip his flagging interest and to give him a little further insight into word-building.

*b*) Of my work with R.'s writing I can't say much. He has been having the finger, arm, and hand co-ordinations with his other teacher, and I have preferred to give most of our very limited time to other things. I have succeeded, however, in giving him a better idea of line and of letter proportion, though his capitals are still very faulty. His faults are those of backwardness rather than any genuine defect. He needs work on a large board instead of my small one. His writing is at present all finger motion.

*c*) Reading is in some ways the least encouraging of our work. The child knew how to read when I took him. And while he could read more difficult selections than the ordinary pupil in high first, he could not read them so rapidly. I gave him first the Hiawatha Primer, hoping that the Indian story would arouse in him the usual boyish interest. Though we read well over into the story, he entirely failed to exhibit this normal interest. Yet, strangely enough, in spite of this undeveloped group sense, he had enough maturity of taste to criticize the frequent repetition in the story. He never learned to read the longer words like Hiawatha, Nokomis, warriors, etc., with any surety. Any word which began with a capital might be any one of the proper names. But if he made a mistake in reading and I spelled the word for him or had him spell it orally, he gave it correctly at once. It is very seldom indeed that he has come to any word in any of our lessons that he did not recognize when he *heard* its letters. I abandoned the Hiawatha Primer because I saw that it was not serving the purpose for which I had hoped, viz., to rouse him from his apathy. And I may say in passing that this primer is as difficult as most second readers. We next tried the first reader of the Indiana Educational Series, and this went better so far as interest was concerned. The stories were more nearly on the level of R.'s intelligence. Our greatest difficulty in working with both of these books was lack of concentration. Voluntary eye fixation seemed impossible for him. At any slight trouble in reading a word, his gaze would wander over both pages of the book, and perhaps around the room. If I said "R., that word is not on the wall," he would bite his lip, turn his head in proper position for reading, and still look out of the corners of his eyes in any direction but that of the book. If I pointed with a pencil as he read or allowed him to point with his finger, this trouble was greatly minimized. And, by the way, when he points at a word, he places his finger over the word. It remains a mystery to me how he sees the word to read it. I have never told him not to point at the words with his finger, but have gradually got him into the habit of holding his book alone. This takes both of his hands and eliminates his pointing. I myself point for him as little as I can, yet it is often necessary. I start him on his day's reading independently. He may read the first paragraph without wandering, but probably not. Rather than have him wait indefinitely while finding the place, I indicate it for him. His interest must be maintained even at the expense of good methods; for, as his attention weakens, his spells of wandering increase in frequency and in length. His lack of concentration has been much increased since we began to read the second reader of the Indiana Educational Series. The first two books read were arranged primer fashion, a sentence to a line. But this more advanced reader continues the thought from one line to the next in the usual way. When R. reaches the end of a line and feels that there is still more to follow, he is much inclined to rest by looking elsewhere. He has no difficulty in finding the beginning of the next line if his attention is in good working order. Reading a sentence or a paragraph over if he has wandered particularly in it does not help him at all. He is just as likely to show lack of concentration the third time as the first, in fact more so. The feeling that I am not satisfied with him brings that half-fearful state which seems to clog his nerve cells. Moreover, the element of fatigue enters in adversely. It would be well to mention here the entire lack of understanding which parents display toward this fatigue factor. For instance, because this lad is a strong, healthy child, his mother scorns the idea that his lessons may fatigue him. Lazy or ugly is her dictum. She cannot realize that the accomplishment of a seemingly very simple mental task may mean hard labor for him. It is true that he could do many things if he "paid attention," which he does not do now, but that very matter of attention is what lies beyond his control at present. And the teacher who suffers from some consistently inattentive pupil should study all possible causes of this inattention and attempt to remedy them before admitting that the child in question is wilfully bad.

One method which I use to help R. concentrate is to cover both pages where he is reading with a blank sheet of paper, leaving a slit just large enough to show two lines. This device does not keep his attention from wandering, but it does help him to find the place when he has lost it, and so keeps him from feeling discouraged. The fear element has to be considered constantly in his reading. When he is ready to begin his day's reading, he will put off the dreaded moment by questions, suggestions, and much hemming and clearing of his throat. And when at last I have encouraged him to begin, his tones are closed in behind his teeth and only emitted with the greatest seeming difficulty. His mother tells me that he reads much more fluently at home, especially on the first reading of a story when his interest in it is fresh. So I am now trying the scheme of giving him only a little to prepare and taking some time every day for reading new matter. So far I can see little difference. He will not read well until his power of sustained attention is increased, and that I am working on in many different ways. It enters constantly into his work in dancing and music with his other teacher, with the advantage of interest to help it along. It enters too into his work in mathematics, and that is my next topic.

*d*) The attention which is necessary during visual processes is the kind which R. lacks. I have tried to increase this by playing with him a certain game of solitaire. In order to win he must pay the closest attention to every card turned up in my hand as well as to at least nine cards on the board. His improvement in this has been most marked. At first I had to hint and wait whenever one of his cards was turned up, but now he is alert and watchful. In addition to this value of the game, he is learning to associate a figure with the actual number of single things it represents; he is becoming more and more familiar with the simple sequence of numbers; and in adding his cards after each hand and in keeping score, he is learning to perform actual arithmetical processes. His interest in the game makes him forget that he may make a mistake in answering, and he will perform additions which would be impossible for him if asked abstractly.

Aside from this game, I have taken up mathematics with R. according to a logical sequence of the mental processes necessary. First came the actual drill in counting so that he might know the numbers in their proper juxtaposition. This is foundational. He knew how to count to 100 when I took him, but his counting was slow and laborious, and any attempt at retrogression confused him. This of course meant that the idea of subtraction was difficult for him. Practice has caused a marked improvement in the rate and ease of his counting, and has so increased his perception of the propinquity of the numbers that he goes backward with considerably greater ease than at first.

Next came the training in the combination of numbers. He could already add similar numbers, but only as a matter of word memory. It meant no understanding of the process involved. And he was as likely to say 7 plus 1 are 9, and 8 minus 1 are 4 as not. So in addition to his drill in oral counting, I gave him additions of 1's on paper, putting at the bottom of the paper the sequence of numbers from 1 up as far as he would need them. As he did his examples he would place his finger on the large number, then move it one number to the right in order to add one to the number. To subtract one he moved his finger one number to the left of his starting place. This work was valuable in fixing his attention both visually and tactually on one of the numbers. Moreover, it gave him a confidence in his own powers, because by taking pains he could always get the correct results. This practice we carried on for many weeks and covered all additions up to 20, and all subtractions in which the subtrahend was not over 4 and the minuend over 12. His work on paper was almost always correct. This was partly due to help at home, though I had expressly forbidden it. Written work done under my own eye was good enough, however, so that I felt sure that the child understood what he was doing. But the many days spent in this practice seemed to leave no mark on his memory images. He might work out 5 plus 6 on paper correctly day after day, but if I asked him to give me their sum offhand, he would reply almost anything. That the work did have its effect, however, I am sure, for in counting up his score in our solitaire he would give results before he stopped to think what he was doing, and in the majority of cases they were right. This building up of number knowledge does not yet go beyond 10. Along with this visual and auditory drill I gave a little that was tactual. Brightly colored wooden sticks about four inches long I gave to him in bunches of five, with the instruction to separate the bunches in as many different ways as he could. With some help he got all of the six ways, and I had him write down the figures representing these divisions. We worked several days on these component parts of five, and with good results.

My next effort was to begin to wean him away from any sense props for his number work. This sounds like teaching him to use a certain method and then teaching him not to use it. But the weaning process will necessarily be long and slow. I have built up for him a series of number perceptions of various kinds. Now, when the stimulus is presented to him I must try to have his motor reaction to it come in just one instead of in several ways. For instance when I tell him to add 6 and 2, I don't want him to scan a list of numbers for 6 and then look 2 beyond for the correct sum. Nor do I want him to begin to feel of six fingers or sticks or to make six lines on a piece of paper. He may depend on any one of these acts to get his answer, but it must be mentally. This power he has already acquired with 1 and 2 additions. Of the various perception possibilities which I supplied to him, he has chosen the auditory images. Up to 20 he can make his 2 additions correctly, abstractly, though slowly. He is at present working on 1 additions up to 100. His power of abstraction is not yet strong enough to enable him to think 3 beyond a number, but with this start, greater ability will surely come. The worst was over when he acquired his first idea of the quantitative value of numbers. And now every day of drill in these simple number processes is increasing his feeling of familiarity with them, decreasing his fear of making absurd mistakes, rousing his interest in the things that can be done with numbers, and making his memory images of number combinations stronger and stronger.

In closing this report I should say that I have had this child only an hour and a half twice a week, three hours altogether, and his other instructor has had him two hours. Unless one could actually see the unbelievable slowness with which he responds to any stimuli, one could hardly realize how difficult it has been to get results in our brief time together. In addition to the regular drill in the fundamentals described above, I have given him now and then a letter or a composition to write, have had him reproduce in writing a short written story, have done a very little work in geography by having him study the globe, construct statements about it, then write them down, and later copy them in a book in ink. (He had never worked with ink.) For the sake of the general tonic effect, I shall from this time add history, geography, and science to his regular studies.

I am now at work on a list of books which his mother can read to him with benefit. She is very anxious to assist, but is quite without ability. This will illustrate. Recently I let her take a copy of some of Mara Pratt's history stories, telling her to read them to R. as she found time and that I would then question him about them or have him write essays on them. Two days later, at R's next lesson, she returned the book proudly stating that they had read all of the stories. Of course for my purpose or for any other, such cramming was perfectly useless. But I hope in the future to improve this condition of things so that she can give some intelligent help by home reading and bring the body of R.'s information up a little nearer that of the normal child of his age.

The case is one of considerable interest just because it is so puzzling. No ordinary school will keep the child. The public subnormal rooms are not fitting places for him. Private tutelage is all that is left. Yet it is my firm conviction that the boy needs the stimulating influence of school life more than he needs anything else. Moreover, the money which his parents pay for an hour a day of private work would pay for ten times as much tuition in a school like our elementary school. But, unfortunate though this may be, at present the ordinary school is no place for R. or children like him. They only worry their instructors, take a larger percentage of the school time than is their rightful share, often become marks for the ridicule of their playmates, and suffer sadly from their confinement to a school régime absolutely unfitted to their abilities. Every teacher from first grade to fifth should be able to recognize these cases and eliminate them from the schoolroom. For such recognition, studies similar to this one of R. should be helpfully suggestive.

# A COMPARATIVE STUDY OF THE RESULTS OBTAINED IN INSTRUCTION IN THE "SINGLE TEACHER" RURAL SCHOOLS AND THE GRADED TOWN SCHOOLS (*Concluded*)

W. S. SMILEY
State University of Iowa

## GRAMMAR QUESTIONS

2. Write the names of the months of the year in one column and their abbreviations in another.

3. What is a pronoun?

4. Name the different persons in the personal pronouns.

5. Supply the proper form of WHO in the following: A babe was borne to Danae, a smiling boy . . . . she names Perseus. For years she kept him hidden, and not even the women . . . . brought food to the hiding place knew about him.

6. Write correctly: Go very quick. I seen him do it. Them books are mine. Why shouldn't us girls form a club?

7. Compare the adjective "difficult."

8. Compare the adjective "fine."

9. Tell how the following words in capitals are used. This TEST is EASY. I took my TEST this morning.

10. Write a letter to McClurg and Company, Chicago, Illinois, ordering a copy of Tennyson's poems.

11. Tell to what part of speach each of the words in capitals belongs. He ran FAST. He was a FAST runner. They FAST twice a week. The FAST lasted forty days.

12. Fill in the blanks with shall or will.

*a*) We . . . . break through the ice if we are not careful.

*b*) We . . . . try to do our duty.

*c*) He . . . . misspell his words.

*d*) They . . . . be captured if I can help it.

13. Give an illustration of an indirect object.

14. Select the correct word from among those in parentheses and write it over the dash.

*a*) I shall not wait —— you more than five minutes (on, for).

*b*) It is a question between you and —— (me, I).

15. What is a clause?

16. Name the tenses of the verb "learn" in the indicative mood.

17. Write a sentence containing a preposition. Underline the preposition.

18. What is meant by number in verbs?

19. What is meant by voice in verbs?

20. Pick out the transitive verbs in the following sentences.

It rains and the wind is never weary.
Ellen was elected president of her club.
John reads German easily.
Into the valley of death rode the six hundred.

The first of these questions was not evaluated as were the others, because in it the mistakes were counted. There were two common mistakes found in the papers, the spelling of February, and the omission of periods in the abbreviations. In the records no effort was made to keep these two separate, but all are recorded together.

Question 10 was another exception. Both it and Question 2 are omitted from the curve. In marking the results from Question 10 it seemed best to divide the letter into five parts, the "heading," the "recipient's address," the "salutation," the "close," and the "mistakes in punctuation." The following abbreviations were used: H, for heading; RA, for recipient's address; S, for salutation; C, for close; and E, for errors. The errors were mistakes in spelling and punctuation. If there were no mistakes in the letter, it would receive the following set of grades:

H equals 2
RA equals 2
S equals 2
C equals 2
E equals 0

If there was a mistake in the arrangement on the page of any of the above elements, that element was marked 1; if it was omitted, it was marked 0. If there was an extra capital in the "close," the mark was 1. In the other questions the method used in the previous subjects was used. Each part of a question was graded separately and the results recorded in a separate column.

TABLE VIII. GRAMMAR

PERCENTAGES

| Q | "One Teacher" Schools | | Graded Schools | |
|---|---|---|---|---|
| | 57 Boys | 110 Girls | 109 Boys | 95 Girls |
| 2 | 25 | 16 | .. | .. |
| 3 | 96 | 99 | 97 | 97 |
| 4 | 99 | 95 | 93 | 95 |
| 5*a* | 85 | 79 | 82 | 84 |
| 5*b* | 99 | 100 | 95 | 96 |
| 6*a* | 86 | 93 | 80 | 92 |
| 6*b* | 99 | 100 | 98 | 99 |
| 6*c* | 100 | 100 | 94 | 99 |
| 6*d* | 73 | 89 | 90 | 97 |
| 7 | 81 | 84 | 66 | 72 |
| 8 | 86 | 89 | 74 | 77 |
| 9*a* | 76 | 91 | 87 | 92 |
| 9*b* | 65 | 74 | 68 | 69 |
| 9*c* | 61 | 85 | 79 | 85 |
| 10*a* | 1.5 | 1.7 | 1.7 | 1.4 |
| 10*b* | 1.4 | 1.7 | 1.4 | 1.6 |
| 10*c* | 1.4 | 1.3 | 1.4 | 1.2 |
| 10*d* | 1.2 | 1.2 | 2.4 | 1.2 |
| 10*e* | 4.0 | 3.7 | 1.3 | 4.2 |
| 11*a* | 69 | 78 | 64 | 69 |
| 11*b* | 78 | 84 | 75 | 87 |
| 11*c* | 75 | 83 | 79 | 87 |
| 11*d* | 81 | 89 | 85 | 93 |
| 12*a* | 49 | 61 | 55 | 59 |
| 12*b* | 59 | 62 | 60 | 56 |
| 12*c* | 83 | 93 | 86 | 83 |
| 12*d* | 63 | 71 | 73 | 64 |
| 13 | 46 | 56 | 33 | 42 |
| 14*a* | 95 | 94 | 92 | 95 |
| 14*b* | 39 | 49 | 50 | 57 |
| 15 | 59 | 71 | 57 | 68 |
| 16 | 49 | 52 | 55 | 55 |
| 17 | 85 | 89 | 83 | 88 |
| 18 | 38 | 43 | 28 | 42 |
| 19 | 28 | 45 | 33 | 42 |
| 20*a* | 31 | 28 | 17 | 29 |
| 20*b* | 69 | 82 | 52 | 75 |
| 20*c* | 78 | 78 | 57 | 71 |
| 20*d* | 29 | 32 | 19 | 31 |

The "mechanical" and "reasoning" grouping was again used. Questions 2, 3, 4, 15, 18, and 19 are classed as "mechanical," and 5, 6, 7, 8, 9, 10, 11, 13, 14, 17, and 20 are "reasoning."

## RESULTS

The full line is below the broken line for the greater part of the time; in fact it gets above the broken line only on

Questions IX*a*, etc., XI*d*, XIV*a* and *b*. In the use of "shall" and "will" in Question 12, the average for both systems of schools is 66 per cent. The average for the grades is 65 per cent, and for the "one teacher" schools 67 per cent. In the

GRAMMAR

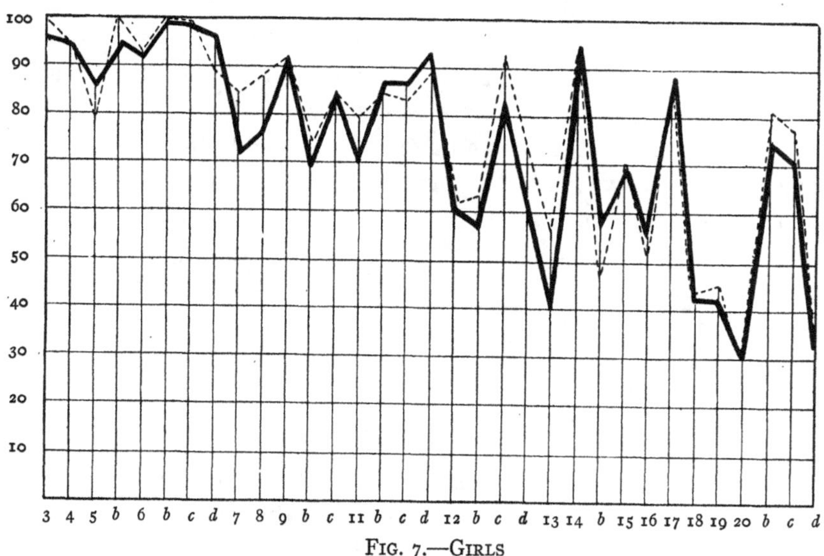


FIG. 7.—GIRLS

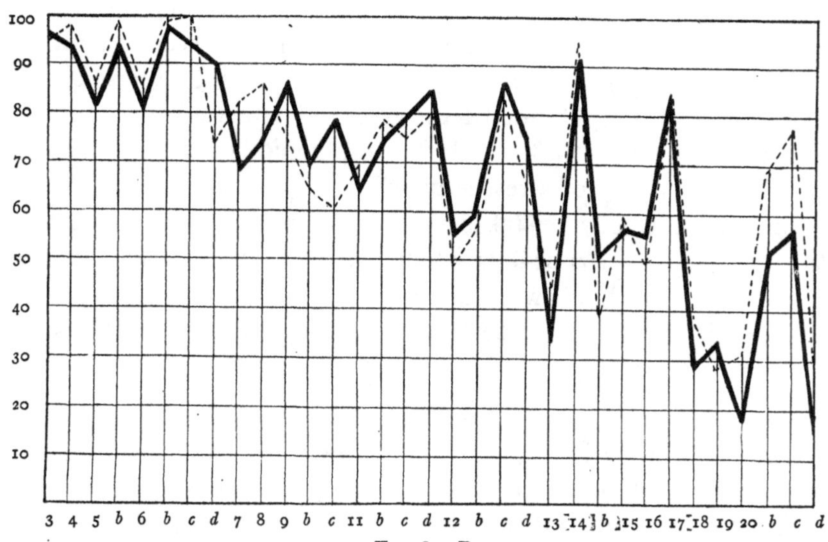


FIG. 8.—BOYS

selection of the transitive verbs in Question 20, 744, or 49 per cent of correct judgments were made. This would seem to indicate that they knew nothing about the use of the term, because by the laws of chance they should have been able to choose 50 per cent correctly if they knew only the meaning of the term "verb." In the returns from the graded schools it was evident that a large number were not even able to pick out the verb. In grading the papers it was often observed that "never" and "easily" were chosen as verbs.

In Question 2 the percentage of mistakes in the "one teacher" schools was one higher than found in the graded schools. Question 10, the letter, received the following grades:

| Q | G | O. T. |
|---|---|---|
| H. | 83 | 89 |
| RA. | 75 | 86 |
| S. | 89 | 69 |
| C. | 63 | 64 |
| E. | 2.47 | 3.98 |

The most frequent mistake made in the "heading" was in its position on the page. It was often placed at the end of the letter. The "recipient's address" was sometimes omitted and sometimes given the position that belonged to the "heading." The "salutation" was sometimes omitted, sometimes placed on the same line with the first line of the "body" of the letter, and sometimes on the right side of the page. There were two mistakes that prevailed in the "close," the capitalization of both words, and the use of "respectively" for "respectfully." The "errors" were chiefly mistakes in punctuation. In this respect the grade pupils surpassed the other group, having on the average about 2.5 mistakes, while the other group had about 4 mistakes per letter. The grade children also excelled in the use of the "salutation."

## HISTORY

Questions in chronology, biography, and geography were included in the list in United States history. This classification was in no way connected with the other attempt at dividing the list into the two groups, "mechanical" and "reasoning." Again it is to be observed that this classification is only suggestive of the general character of the questions, because it was impossible to avoid overlapping in the questions.

HISTORY QUESTIONS

1. Name the nations that made explorations in America in the sixteenth century.

2. Why was the work of Paul Jones beneficial to America during the war for independence?

3. Who is governor of Iowa?

4. Why did the American colonists object to the "Stamp Act"?

5. What happened on the following dates: 1492, 1620, 1776, 1619, 1789, 1803?

6. Who was General Wolfe?

7. Why do we consider Lafayette a great man?

8. Who was president of the Constitutional Convention?

9. What effect did the invention of the cotton gin have upon slavery?

10. Who was the founder of Rhode Island?

11. What remarkable address was given at Gettysburg?

12. What object did Penn have in founding a colony in America?

13. What part of America did each of the countries mentioned in the answer to Question 1 settle?

14. Why was the Boston Tea Party organized?

15. Why was the "Fugitive Slave Law" passed?

16. For what were U. S. Grant, James Fenimore Cooper, William Henry Harrison, and Grover Cleveland noted?

17. Why was the "Monroe Doctrine" good for North and South America?

18. Show how important executive officers (such as ministers, judges, and members of the President's cabinet) are appointed.

19. Why was Grant's campaign against Vicksburg necessary in the Civil War?

20. Why were Forts Duquesne, Crown Point, Ticonderoga, Niagara, Acadia, and Louisburg, Quebec, objective points for the English during the French and Indian war?

In this subject the same method was used as was employed in the other subjects. All questions that were not correct were marked 0, and those that were correct were marked 1. Unless four countries were mentioned as having made explorations in America during the sixteenth century, the answer was considered incorrect. The answer to Question 9 was considered imperfect if it did not mention the reasons why easier seeding of cotton increased the demand for slaves. "William Rogers" was not considered a correct answer to Question 10 and was marked 0. The President alone has not the power to appoint executive officers, and unless the answer mentioned specifically the function of the Senate in that work, the question was marked 0.

TABLE IX. HISTORY

PERCENTAGES

| Q | "One Teacher" Schools | | Graded Schools | |
|---|---|---|---|---|
| | 57 Boys | 106 Girls | 106 Boys | 100 Girls |
| 1 | 65 | 62 | 45 | 51 |
| 2 | 76 | 66 | 67 | 59 |
| 3 | 75 | 73 | 58 | 69 |
| 4 | 41 | 42 | 53 | 56 |
| 5*a* | 97 | 98 | 94 | 99 |
| 5*b* | 83 | 88 | 61 | 64 |
| 5*c* | 79 | 83 | 59 | 63 |
| 5*d* | 41 | 54 | 29 | 36 |
| 5*e* | 48 | 56 | 35 | 39 |
| 5*f* | 57 | 63 | 47 | 60 |
| 6 | 37 | 26 | 40 | 29 |
| 7 | 58 | 52 | 64 | 57 |
| 8 | 50 | 52 | 43 | 42 |
| 9 | 41 | 41 | 51 | 52 |
| 10 | 59 | 57 | 68 | 64 |
| 11 | 74 | 66 | 63 | 68 |
| 12 | 59 | 66 | 75 | 82 |
| 13 | 64 | 53 | 46 | 49 |
| 14 | 64 | 73 | 88 | 82 |
| 15 | 51 | 53 | 60 | 69 |
| 16*a* | 88 | 85 | 73 | 65 |
| 16*b* | 39 | 46 | 34 | 26 |
| 16*c* | 74 | 85 | 63 | 67 |
| 16*d* | 81 | 79 | 51 | 59 |
| 17 | 47 | 43 | 42 | 53 |
| 18 | 9 | 9 | 9 | 6 |
| 19 | 39 | 33 | 27 | 17 |
| 20 | 9 | 10 | 9 | 6 |

The curves in Fig. 9 show the boys from the grades reaching the highest and lowest points. The boys from the "one teacher" schools have a more uniform, and at the same time higher, average curve. The same condition is found to exist in Fig. 10. Other figures show a marked similarity in all points, and indicate a superiority on the part of the children from the "one teacher" schools.

In general the two curves take the same direction, but there are three exceptions. In stating the effect the invention of the cotton gin had on slavery (Question 9) the full curve goes up to 54 per cent and the broken curve down to 41 per cent; on Question 11 (the Gettysburg Address) the full line fell to 64 per cent and the broken line rose to 71 per cent; in stating the reasons for Penn's settlement of Pennsylvania in Question 12

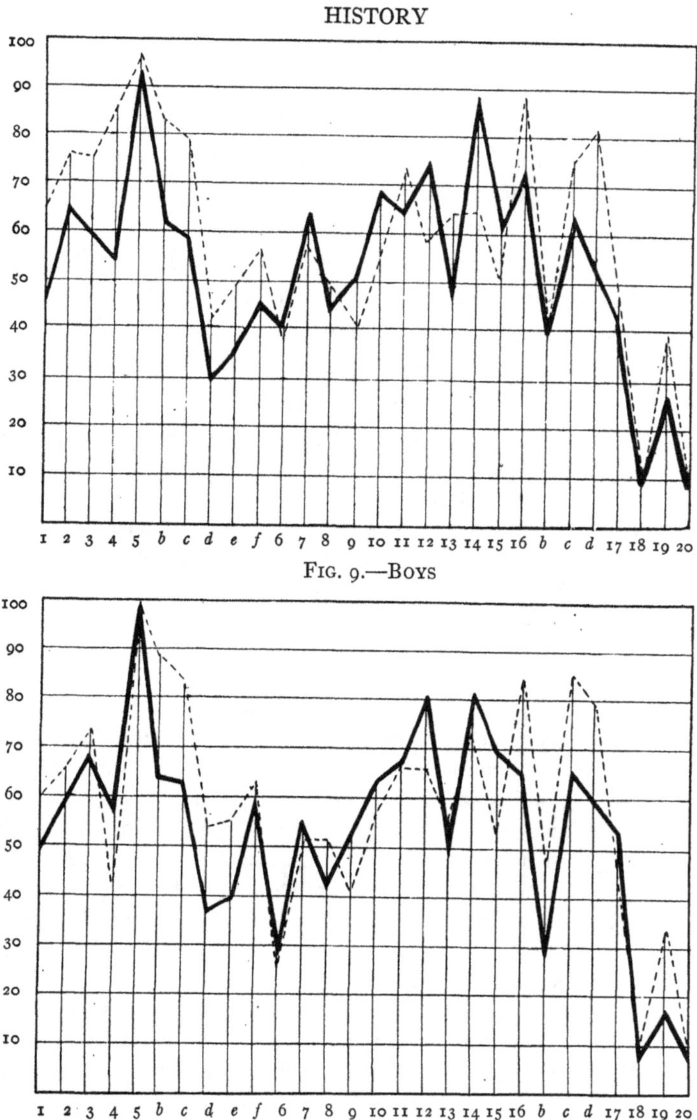


FIG. 9.—BOYS

FIG. 10.—GIRLS

the full curve rises to 77 per cent while the broken curve falls to 63 per cent. The curves reach their highest point on the first part of Question 3 and their lowest point on Question 20.

The "range" for both systems of schools is the same, 84 per cent.

## SPELLING

The spelling examination questions were arranged in three parts, the first being taken from Dr. Cornman's study, p. 95, the second from the same source, p. 92, and the third, a composition on "Coasting." In this examination it was necessary for teacher to pronounce the words and dictate the sentences.

Part one was made up of words that are not often used by children but are all found in spelling-books. In marking the papers no distinction was made between a word that had only one mistake and a word that had more than one. The words were numbered in order, from one to fifty. But two marks were used, 1 and 0. The questions follow:

1. Pronounce the following words to be written by the pupils: anxious, accomplish, acquire, alcohol, ancient, appearance, assistance, auctioneer, brilliant, cashier, character, circular, cologne, conceit, counterfeit, cylinder, diameter, disappoint, divisible, excellent, experience, fashionable, flourish, glazier, guest, idolize, important, innocent, irritate, legible, lieutenant, magnetize, messenger, mischievous, mucilage, obstinacy, orchestra, particular, penitentiary, petroleum, pleasure, poultice, profession, receipt, refrigerator, repetition, sacrifice, secretary, sincere, spectacle.

2. Dictate the following to be written by the pupil: While running he slipped. The weather is changeable. His loud whistling frightened me. He is always changing his mind. His chain was loose. She was baking a cake. I have a piece of it. Did you lose your almanac? I gave it to my neighbor. Was it necessary to keep me waiting so long? Do not disappoint me so often. Do not deceive me. The children are hopping. This is certainly true. If we have patience we shall certainly succeed. He met with a severe accident. Sometimes children are not sensible. You had no business to answer him. The ride was very fatiguing. I appreciate your kindness, I assure you. Intelligent persons learn by experience. He is thoroughly conscientious; therefore I trust him.

3. Write a composition of fifty words on the subject, "Coasting."

To the teacher: Do not allow them to use any books for reference, and do not allow them to get any help in spelling the words they use. The object of this question is to find out how they spell the words they use in everyday life.

## TABLE X. SPELLING

PERCENTAGES

| No. | Question 1 | | | | Question 2 | |
|---|---|---|---|---|---|---|
| | "One Teacher" Schools | | Graded Scaools | | "One Teacher" Schools | Graded Schools |
| | 51 Boys | 74 Girls | 96 Boys | 87 Boys | 166 Boys and Girls | 206 Boys and Girls |
| 1 | 87 | 86 | 81 | 79 | 99 | 99 |
| 2 | 89 | 92 | 83 | 88 | 79 | 70 |
| 3 | 81 | 83 | 74 | 84 | 99 | 97 |
| 4 | 85 | 59 | 68 | 67 | 79 | 71 |
| 5 | 85 | 77 | 74 | 91 | 98 | 99 |
| 6 | 69 | 71 | 58 | 81 | 85 | 87 |
| 7 | 81 | 75 | 75 | 88 | 95 | 92 |
| 8 | 63 | 68 | 67 | 72 | 84 | 88 |
| 9 | 71 | 83 | 81 | 84 | 98 | 99 |
| 10 | 81 | 75 | 83 | 74 | 96 | 94 |
| 11 | 83 | 84 | 66 | 87 | 89 | 88 |
| 12 | 88 | 88 | 93 | 97 | 94 | 95 |
| 13 | 39 | 49 | 44 | 41 | 99 | 96 |
| 14 | 69 | 73 | 65 | 77 | 93 | 89 |
| 15 | 69 | 65 | 57 | 71 | 58 | 55 |
| 16 | 68 | 65 | 60 | 72 | 89 | 80 |
| 17 | 68 | 68 | 80 | 90 | 95 | 91 |
| 18 | 50 | 68 | 37 | 40 | 77 | 73 |
| 19 | 75 | 75 | 63 | 72 | 98 | 98 |
| 20 | 75 | 71 | 58 | 63 | 98 | 96 |
| 21 | 79 | 73 | 63 | 87 | 51 | 42 |
| 22 | 91 | 94 | 83 | 90 | 78 | 78 |
| 23 | 69 | 64 | 58 | 50 | 98 | 91 |
| 24 | 84 | 77 | 71 | 55 | 91 | 89 |
| 25 | 95 | 90 | 86 | 96 | 91 | 89 |
| 26 | 69 | 67 | 52 | 63 | 87 | 77 |
| 27 | 95 | 90 | 88 | 98 | 87 | 78 |
| 28 | 81 | 69 | 64 | 82 | 96 | 90 |
| 29 | 61 | 66 | 57 | 79 | 88 | 83 |
| 30 | 41 | 48 | 43 | 54 | 93 | 91 |
| 31 | 55 | 51 | 39 | 52 | 99 | 100 |
| 32 | 32 | 33 | 28 | 20 | 77 | 67 |
| 33 | 87 | 75 | 80 | 81 | 76 | 70 |
| 34 | 63 | 51 | 61 | 64 | 95 | 98 |
| 35 | 41 | 48 | 39 | 34 | 97 | 100 |
| 36 | 42 | 42 | 45 | 41 | 54 | 52 |
| 37 | 63 | 57 | 58 | 63 | 69 | 65 |
| 38 | 83 | 79 | 78 | 94 | 98 | 94 |
| 39 | 34 | 36 | 32 | 19 | 92 | 93 |
| 40 | 69 | 63 | 49 | 66 | 78 | 67 |
| 41 | 95 | 68 | 84 | 95 | 95 | 98 |
| 42 | 42 | 58 | 34 | 43 | 97 | 99 |
| 43 | 79 | 81 | 71 | 87 | 79 | 78 |
| 44 | 58 | 56 | 49 | 58 | 57 | 56 |
| 45 | 50 | 51 | 53 | 49 | 37 | 32 |
| 46 | 51 | 63 | 45 | 55 | 85 | 83 |
| 47 | 87 | 73 | 69 | 80 | 94 | 99 |
| 48 | 64 | 72 | 65 | 86 | 95 | 100 |
| 49 | 87 | 66 | 74 | 82 | .. | .. |
| 50 | 71 | 58 | 64 | 75 | .. | .. |

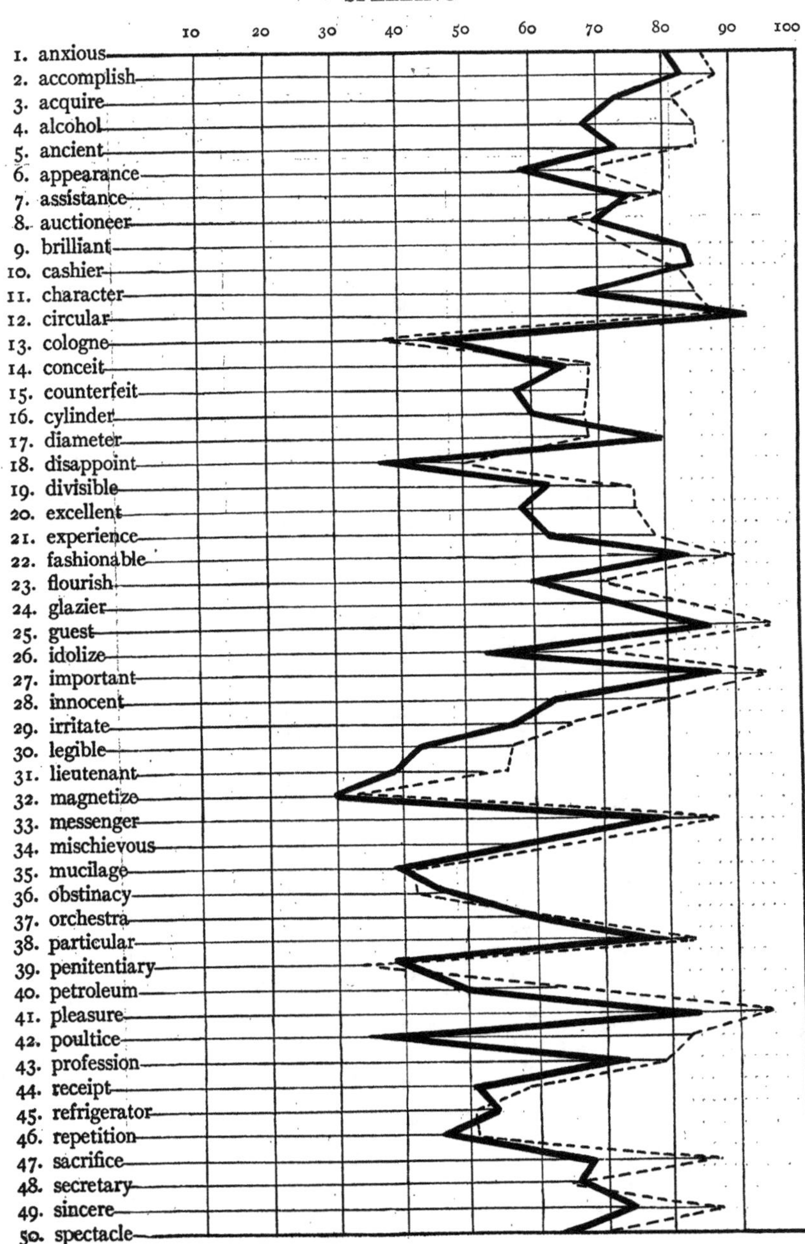


FIG. 11.—PART I—BOYS

SPELLING

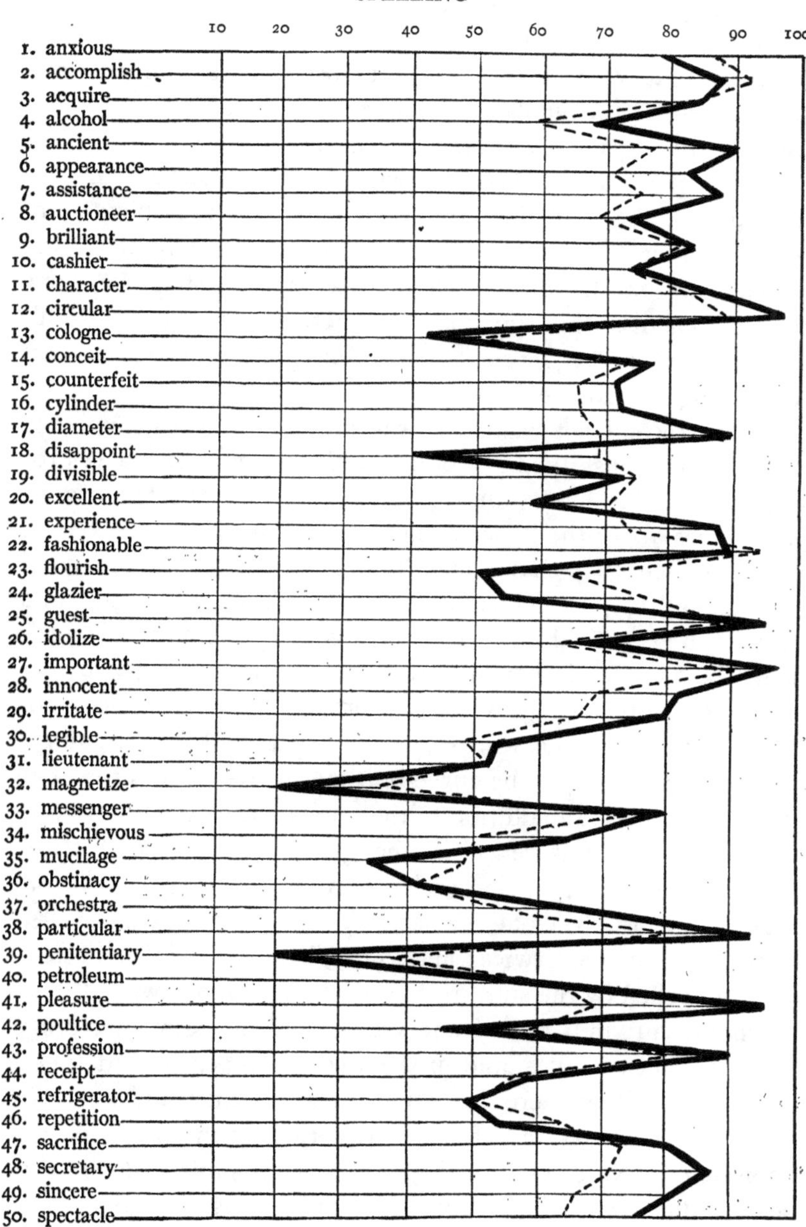


FIG. 12.—PART I—GIRLS

The same method of marking was employed in both the first and second parts. In the second part—the dictation exercise—the words that were most likely to be missed were numbered and a record kept of the number of times each word was missed. The results of the first part are recorded in the curves in Fig. 11. In this curve the graded schools surpass the "one teacher" in only three places, the twelfth, the seventeenth, and the thirty-sixth words—"circular," diameter," and "obstinacy." "Circular" was the easiest for the graded, and "accomplish" for the "one teacher" schools, while for both "magnetize" was the most difficult. The most frequent error in spelling "magnetize" was in substituting "i" for "e."

In the second list "slipped" was the easiest word numbered and "conscientious" the most difficult. Here again the curves for both systems have the same general direction, but the graded system goes above the "one teacher" system twelve times, on the words "whistling," "changing," "mind," "baking," "sometimes," "answer," "ride," "assure," "persons," "learn," "trust," and "him." In none of the above cases was the percentage of words spelled below 85. It would therefore seem that the grade children excel in spelling the simplest words. The most difficult for both systems were the words "lost," "disappoint," "fatiguing," and "conscientious." The curve on these words favors the "one teacher" schools. In addition to the numbered words the following words were misspelled in the grade system: "no," "to," "often," and "very," twice each; "gave," once; and "always," three times. In the "one teacher" system "no" was misspelled four times; "often," twice; and "very," once. "No" and "to" were misspelled by the substitution of "know" and "two." "Disappoint" occurs in both lists and was spelled correctly an average of 52 per cent of times, and in the second, 50 per cent of times. In the composition there did not seem to be much difference in style or in the character of the words used by the pupils of the two systems. No record was kept of the words misspelled in this question, but only of the number. There was a total of 133 missed by the grade children, or an average of .65 of a word for each paper submitted, and 37 missed by the "one teacher" school pupils, or an average of .25 of a word for each.

SPELLING

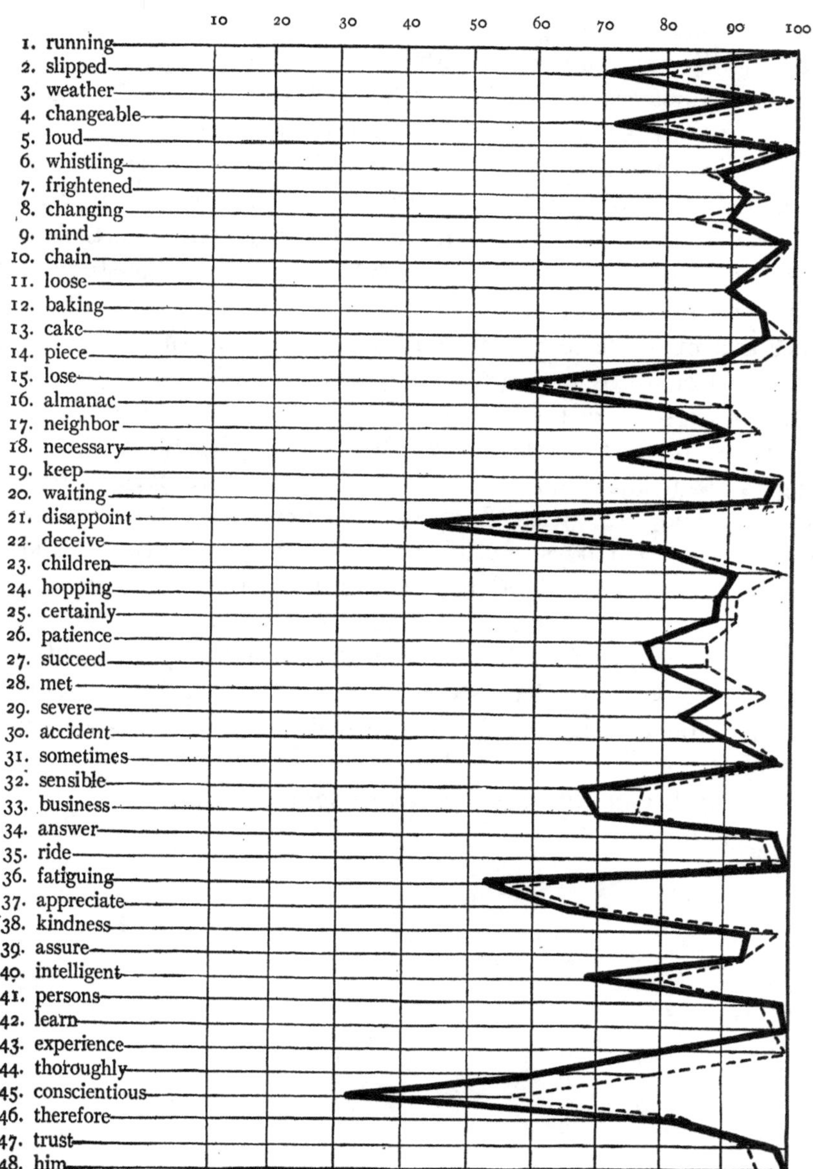


FIG. 13.—PART II—BOYS AND GIRLS, NOT SEPARATED

## CONCLUSIONS

The papers were generally well written. There was little variation in the number submitted in the different subjects, and the questionnaires were well answered, all of which goes to show the interest of both pupils and teachers in the examinations. The results indicate that the pupils from the "one teacher" rural schools knew more about the work covered than did those from the grade schools. The difference is not great but nevertheless there is a positive difference. In the beginning of this study it was assumed that the conditions were equal, and that any difference that might be found in the results could be attributed to the organization of the schools into grades. Later developments have shown some factors at work that could not be predetermined.

From the grade schools 114 boys and 97 girls handed in papers; from the "one teacher" schools there were papers from 57 boys and 112 girls. Expressed in percentage terms there were 54 per cent boys and 46 per cent girls in the graded, and 34 per cent boys and 66 per cent girls in the "one teacher" schools. It might be argued that since girls are better developed at that period of life, this preponderance of girls in the country schools would make the difference found in the returns. This was not found to be a sufficient explanation of the difference in the results, because when the boys were compared with the boys, and the girls with the girls, the same relation was present.

# MANUAL ACTIVITIES IN THE ELEMENTARY SCHOOL[1]

JESSE D. BURKS, PH.D.
Director of the Bureau of Municipal Research of Philadelphia

A distinguished New England theologian was once asked whether he considered Christianity to be a failure. He promptly replied: "I do not know, it has never yet been tried." Somewhat similarly, we might say that it is impossible to pass intelligent judgment upon manual activities in the elementary school for they have not been given a thorough and intelligent trial.

For thirty-five years educational leaders have had much to say concerning the need for manual activities in elementary education. During the latter part of this period the number of schools having manual training in their curricula has rapidly increased, until now one-half of the thirteen hundred organized local school systems in the United States have this subject in one or more of their elementary grades. In only one hundred and fifty of these cases, however, does handwork extend through all of the grades of the elementary schools, and of the six hundred school systems having manual training, three hundred give less than an hour a week to the subject, and only thirty-seven as much as half an hour a day.

These facts justify the statement that the country at large has not taken seriously the manual-training propaganda. Vastly more has been said than done and, with a few notable and gratifying exceptions, manual training remains in the main an isolated, abstract, and unprofitable fad; attached to, rather than incorporated in, the curriculum of the elementary school.

This means, of course, that, notwithstanding the notable advance in a few communities, the country as a whole has lost a

[1] Address delivered before the National Council of Education, on presentation of the report of the Committee on the Place of Industries in Public Education, J. D. Burks, chairman of the committee.

magnificent opportunity for educational achievement. Enough time, money, and energy have been expended upon manual training in elementary schools during the past twenty-five years to have demonstrated the claims of its advocates—to have convinced the entire country that manual activities are not only desirable, but indispensable, in elementary education. Tax-payers have waited for facts while educational leaders have furnished opinions.

An inquiry was recently made among one hundred and fifty superintendents of schools, in cities having elementary manual training, as to the available evidence concerning the value of manual training. These superintendents were asked to indicate what records they had of work done and results obtained that would show the effect of manual training upon (*a*) regularity of attendance; (*b*) continuance of pupils in school (elimination); (*c*) rate of progress of pupils (retardation); (*d*) progress of pupils in other school subjects; (*e*) physical welfare of pupils, and (*f*) successes in vocations. They were asked also as to the available evidence concerning (*g*) the most profitable time allowance; (*h*) the value of manual training as an index of specific mental and physical traits; (*i*) specific abilities developed by various types of handwork; (*j*) the relative importance of native abilities and special training in determining successes in various types of school work and vocations.

It is extremely significant that 67 per cent of these superintendents stated that they had no data whatever upon these points, and that only 15 per cent stated that they had evidence on as many as five out of the ten points in the list.

In the absence of concrete evidence, school boards and taxpayers naturally and properly have maintained a skeptical attitude toward manual training. If there were no other reason this would be sufficient to explain the weak grip that manual training now has on the educational practice of the country.

For there is another important explanation of the failure of manual training to win its way. The very term "manual training" suggests the now discredited "faculty psychology" with its will-o'-the-wisp of general discipline.

In the general movement toward social aims and social motives in education, manual training has to a very large extent lagged behind. Possibly it is no farther behind than other subjects in the curriculum; but by reason of its early promise much more was expected of this subject than of others in support of a social program for the elementary schools. It is this demand for a more concrete and more distinctly social program that explains the extraordinary transformation of manual training that is now in progress.

The remarkable interest in industrial education, which is now probably the dominant factor in the educational thought of the country, has all but eclipsed the interest in elementary manual training. It is significant that the program of the manual-training department at the present session of the National Education Association is given over almost entirely to the consideration of industrial education, and this has been true of the programs of this department for the last three or four years.

Other evidences of the rising tide of interest in the industrial as opposed to mere manual activities in the school are of course familiar. Laymen and professional leaders of education alike have deplored the social injustice of a school system which provides directly for the special needs of the 25 per cent of children who ultimately enter the commercial and professional pursuits, but ignore the requirements of the 75 per cent who enter industrial pursuits. National and state teachers' associations have devoted a large part of their programs to the discussion of this urgent issue; a new department of the National Education Association has been established for the study and promotion of technical education; state legislatures, special commissions, a national society for the promotion of industrial education, manufacturers' associations, the United States commissioner of education, the governors of many states, the President of the United States, the American Federation of Labor, and numerous other bodies and individuals have added the weight of many preambles and resolutions to the nation-wide demand that the schools draw nearer to human needs and equip our boys and girls for the struggle of modern industrial life. The educational and general press has given the subject a degree of publicity that is rarely accorded any similar matter. The whole country has repeatedly been astounded by the statement that, according to the report of the state commission on industrial education, twenty-five thousand children in Massachusetts between the ages of fourteen and sixteen were either idle or at work.

During these years, elementary manual training, with only a distant relationship to vocational pursuits, like Cinderella has remained demurely in the background, waiting for some fairy godmother to change her tattered rags into silken robes.

More important than these reasons for the failure of manual training to hold its own in the struggle for recognition and support, however, is the fact that educational leaders themselves have not yet found a consistent and defensible basis upon which to develop a program of handwork in the elementary school.

One of the most significant features of the report on the place of industries in public education is the fact that it definitely recognizes the place of industries in elementary education, and presents a program which it is hoped will hasten the metamorphosis of manual training. The report was originally projected "for the purpose of collecting data concerning the manual training work done throughout the country," and to suggest "courses adaptable to various conditions."

While the report in its general scope is somewhat larger and possibly somewhat different from that originally proposed, the committee believes that, in view of current tendencies in thought and practice, it has properly interpreted the spirit of the resolution under which it has carried on its work.

The report of the subcommittee on industries in the elementary school attempts to sum up and put into coherent and concise form the results of the best thought and practice of recent years. If this service has been acceptably rendered, the reports should furnish at least a provisional starting-point for a more intelligent program of manual activities in the elementary school than has heretofore been attempted. That such a platform is sorely needed is evidenced by the striking lack of agreement among educational leaders as to the significance of manual activities in the elementary school.

In the inquiry before referred to, the superintendents were asked to indicate the importance which they attach to each of eight suggested values of manual training in the elementary school. These eight suggested values were as follows: (*a*) general mental training—e.g., accuracy, honesty; (*b*) general manual skill—e.g., precision, dexterity; (*c*) industrial intelligence—e.g., ability to learn a trade quickly; (*d*) specific abilities—e.g., skill in a particular process; (*e*) vital motive for school work otherwise uninteresting; (*f*) makes stronger and more lasting the results of instruction; (*g*) intelligent appreciation of industrial life; (*h*) culture—enrichment of intellectual and social experience.

In order to summarize these estimates of value, I have counted the number of cases in which a superintendent placed each of the suggested values in the upper half of his own list, that is, first, second, third, or fourth in order of importance. Rated in this way the list stands as follows: general mental training, 65; industrial intelligence, 57; general manual skill, 55; vital motive for school work, 50; intelligent appreciation of industrial life, 45; strengthening the results of instruction, 40; culture, 40; development of specific abilities, 20.

General training is given first rank by 29; culture by 20; and general manual skill by 17.

It is instructive to note that while the great majority of the superintendents were perfectly frank in admitting the lack of concrete evidence as to the effect of manual training upon the mental and physical development of children, they had no hesitation whatever in making a definite rating of each of the suggested values for manual training.

One of the superintendents frankly states that he has not studied the question and gives no answers. One states that his estimates are guesswork; one feels much uncertainty beyond the first two or three; and one states that in his judgment the importance varies with the pupils. The others give definite estimates, in almost all cases assigning weight to each of the eight suggested effects.

These answers make it evident that there is no general agreement among our active leaders in education as to the place of manual training in the elementary school. Unless there can be a more widespread agreement, tentatively, at least, upon the place of industries in the elementary school, we cannot expect results during the coming decade to be more favorable than those of the past decade.

If the conclusions of the committee's report can command the confidence of educational leaders, and can be accepted as a point of departure, a tremendous step in advance will have been taken. In addition to this there should be a concerted effort to avoid one of the most serious mistakes of the past by providing for definite records of work undertaken and results accomplished, that will enable teachers, superintendents, members of boards of education, and citizens everywhere to read the story of achievement for any school or system of schools that has such a story to tell.

When educational leaders are in position to support their arguments by adequate records of work done and results accomplished, they will get not merely the uninformed and passive approval, but the active and intelligent co-operation of the communities whose educational interests they serve. With such co-operation under informed leadership in every community, we shall approach the time when sham and inefficiency will be eliminated from our system of education and 100 per cent of our children will get 100 per cent of the value that school training should represent.

# EDITORIAL NOTES

**Editorial Announcement**

The *Elementary School Teacher* has arranged with the Executive Committee of the Illinois Superintendents' and Principals' Association to print the reports prepared each year by the Committee of Seven of that association, and to print any announcements which the Executive Committee may wish to send out from month to month to members of the association.

**Value of Meetings Based on Prepared Reports**

The annual meetings of this association are unique among educational gatherings in that they take up for careful consideration a report prepared by the Committee of Seven, dealing with some phase of the course of study in the elementary school. The careful study of a local problem by those who are engaged in school work is significant for the members of the association and it is also important as an example to other associations. The *Elementary School Teacher* will profit by its connection with the association, because the chief function of this journal is to promote co-operative investigation of elementary school problems. If other associations would undertake in the same fashion to prepare exhaustive reports for discussion, this journal would welcome the opportunity of co-operating with them.

The following announcement prepared by the officers of the association is inserted as the first announcement of the association work. Hereafter space will be given to these announcements directly following the editorial page.

**The Committee of Seven**

The Committee of Seven of the Northern Illinois Superintendents' and Principals' Association, which has for several years been engaged in working out an Outline Course of Study on a Scientific Basis, hopes to complete its sixth annual report in a few weeks.

The members of the committee for 1910–11 are: Principal

D. A. Tear, Chicago, Professor O. W. Caldwell, The University of Chicago, Professor C. W. Whitten, State Normal School, De Kalb, and Superintendents M. G. Clark, Streator, R. G. Jones, Kewanee, J. L. Smith, Highland Park, and H. A. Bone, Batavia. The first meeting of the committee was held June 11, and an organization was effected by electing Dr. Tear chairman and Professor Whitten secretary.

The report this year will deal with the subject of elementary science. It is proposed to show the necessity of instruction in elementary science by a discussion of the "Relation of the Child to Nature." This will be followed by a discussion of the "Place and Purpose of Science in the School." It is the present plan of the committee to follow these discussions with a suggestive course of study. Recognizing the controlling influence of local conditions the committee scarcely hopes to be able to present a course suitable for adoption in all schools. It does hope, however, to illustrate in a concrete way the factors which must control in the selection of a course.

The committee has met monthly beginning with September. Messrs. Tear and Clark have reported on the psychological and pedagogical phases of the topic and this portion of the report is rapidly assuming permanent form. Tentative courses of study by Messrs. Jones, Bone, and Whitten have also been discussed by the committee.

Professor Ira B. Myers of the University of Chicago is co-operating with the committee and has rendered excellent service in the organization of the report thus far.

**The New Report of the Commissioner of Education**

There is a very widespread feeling of appreciation for the promptness with which the Commissioner of Education is getting out his reports. The value of these reports is much increased by their appearance at the close of the year.

The educational directory, for example, is of immediate value to everyone who has to do with other educators; and the descriptive material which appears in these volumes is not only of importance as history, but is of value for immediate use because of its prompt appearance.

**Contents of the Volume**

The Commissioner's introduction is of special interest in the 1910 volume. It gives a general view of important movements in all departments of education, and should be read by all teachers. Most teachers feel that these ponderous official volumes have little in them of immediate personal interest to those who are engaged in classroom work. A general survey of education such as the present tends to correct this impression, and to draw attention to the movement of American educational activities. A number of the special articles in the first volume of the report should be of very great interest to teachers. This is specially true of the articles on "Agricultural Education" and the "Prussian System of Vocational Schools." There is a very complete review of educational progress in other countries.

# BOOK REVIEWS

*A Bibliography of History for Schools and Libraries, with Descriptive and Critical Annotations.* By CHARLES M. ANDREWS, J. MONTGOMERY GAMBRILL, AND LIDA LEE TALL. Published under the auspices of the Association of History Teachers of the Middle States and Maryland. New York: Longmans, Green & Co., 1910. Pp. xiv+224, and 24 blank sheets. 60 cents.

This bibliography was begun by a committee of the Maryland History Teachers' Association appointed in 1908 to prepare reference lists upon American history and upon historical and biographical stories for children of elementary-school age. The lists were first published by the *Atlantic Educational Journal* and afterward enlarged and published under the auspices of the Association of History Teachers of the Middle States and Maryland.

The present form of the work includes the following subjects: The Study and Teaching of History and Historical Aids, World Histories, Ancient History, European History, English History, American History, Histories of Other Countries, Historical Stories for the Elementary Schools, and Stories for Children Preparatory to History. Out of its 204 pages, 104 are devoted to American history including the following subdivisions: bibliography; collection of documents; physiography; general histories; periods; constitutional, diplomatic, financial, industrial, economic, and political history; state histories; and biographies.

The authors believe that the book "will supply a real need of teachers both in elementary and secondary schools and will be useful to college instructors as well; that in the high school and college it may be used to advantage by students in connection with their regular work; and that it will prove serviceable to the general reader, to the student working alone, and in the public library."

Certainly there is a great demand for a work of this character from various classes of students and teachers. We have many bibliographies upon special periods of history and for advanced students but no single volume covering the whole field or giving annotated lists of books for children. These annotations describing critically the character and scope of each book should be of very great service. The lists of children's histories and stories are of especial importance for elementary teachers who have little time to investigate for themselves the merits of the numerous books now available for supplementary reading. The work was undertaken primarily for the assistance of elementary-school teachers and, although changed in plan, it has fulfilled remarkably well its original purpose. It will save much time and effort to find listed here the best material for teaching any period of history and even an estimate of the merits of the individual works.

This is one of the most important books recently published in the field of history and should contribute much toward improvement in the teaching of this subject.

E. J. R.

*A Primary History: Stories of Heroism.* By WILLIAM H. MACE, Professor of History in Syracuse University. Chicago: Rand, McNally & Co., 1910. Cloth. 8vo, pp. 396.

This book gives a simple and interesting story of American history by means of biographies, grouped according to periods. The purpose of the author has been "to bring before the mind of the pupils a series of great historical characters. These men do interesting things from the beginning to the end of life. Because their deeds are concrete and physical, they are easily pictured in imagination." The biographies are unusually well selected to give various types of heroism, emphasizing the services rendered to the country by overcoming great obstacles in its industrial development as well as by fighting its battles.

The author has wisely taken advantage of the charm always attached to biography. Children are not attracted by a brief, summarized treatment of events. It is the dramatic personal story that arouses interest. This is a principle well understood by teachers but rarely followed by writers of textbooks.

Professor Mace has not only written entertaining stories of the great men who made the nation but has also related these stories in such a way as to give a connected study of our history. Better still, each character is presented with some background of social environment which brings the child nearer to the understanding of historical problems than the mere story. However, the book covers too much ground to be entirely successful. The child's imagination cannot picture the social situation in any period without more detailed statements. For this reason it is doubtful if any one-volume textbook covering the whole of American history can ever be satisfactory. At least, such a textbook should be used in connection with supplementary reading offering fuller treatment of social life.

The style of this book is so vivid, simple, and clear that children of the fourth and fifth grades read it easily and enjoy it thoroughly. It is well illustrated with both pictures and maps.

E. J. R.

---

*Practical Agriculture.* By JOHN W. WILKINSON, A.M., Assistant State Superintendent of Oklahoma. Chicago: American Book Co., 1910.

This elementary and very much condensed treatise on agriculture, horticulture, forestry, stock-feeding, animal husbandry, and road-building forms a very interesting and instructive book for public-school use. Some historical matter concerning certain phases of agriculture is introduced, besides occasional statistical tables which are based on the most recent investigations by the government and state experiment stations. Every chapter contains valuable information and helpful suggestions, especially those dealing with fertilizers and the propagation and improvement of plant varieties. The criticism which may be applied to the whole book, namely, too superficial treatment, applies particularly to the chapters on horticulture with its subdivisions of vegetable, flower, and landscape gardening, and fruit growing. One finds himself wishing that the author had left out such subjects as "Civic Improvement," "Roads," and "Fuel and Light," which are so closely related to agriculture, and allowed more space for further development of some of the remaining topics. The book abounds in illustrations, most of them appropriate and well executed, especially those on the subject of animal industry.

C. F. PHIPPS

---

*Travels in History.* By MARK TWAIN. Selected from the works of Mark Twain by C. N. KENDALL, Superintendent of Schools in Indianapolis. New York: Harper & Bros., 1910. Pp. 170. 50 cents.

This volume, small in size but great in scope, contains well-chosen and carefully arranged selections from "The Prince and the Pauper," "A Connecticut Yankee in King Arthur's Court," and "The Personal Recollections of Joan of Arc." The book is timely, not only because of a general interest in the late "Mark Twain," but because these times demand literature that shall help to interpret, more directly, the spirit of our age to the growing young person. "In 'Mark Twain' we have the national spirit as seen with our own eyes," says Howells. In addition to the appeal mentioned, the selections have been admirably chosen so as to include adventure, pathos, much fun—in short, to present to pupils of the sixth, seventh, and eighth grades "Mark Twain" at his best.

JESSIE E. BLACK

---

*Stories of the King.* By JAMES BALDWIN. Chicago: American Book Co., 1910. Pp. 335. 50 cents.

In *Stories of the King,* James Baldwin has made a welcome addition to his already long list of supplementary readers for young people. These Arthurian tales, narrated as they are in twentieth-century English, make usable for immature readers some of the stories in Malory's *Morte D'Arthur,* adapted in content but too difficult in form for easy reading. The book may be used either as an introduction to a more serious study of the Arthurian legends, or to portray vividly to pupils in the intermediate grades what was noblest and most admirable in knighthood.

JESSIE E. BLACK

---

*Voice Training for School Children.* By FRANK R. RIX. New York: A. S. Barnes Co. Pp. 77.

In this book evolved from actual experience, we have a concise and clear statement of vocal method for use in schools. Mr. Rix explains the obstacles which arise in the effort to achieve good tone throughout the grades, and in simple, untechnical language gives ways and means of overcoming the difficulties. The text is arranged in paragraphs with headings in bold-faced type, facilitating the locating of special points. For teachers with or without professional training in the teaching of school music, this manual will be an inspiration to logical, intelligent work.

M. R. KERN

# BOOKS RECEIVED

## AMERICAN BOOK CO., NEW YORK

*Ernstes und Heiteres: Tales by Modern German Writers.* Edited by JOSEFA SCHRAKAMP. Cloth. Pp. 202. $0.35.

*Historical French Reader.* By FELIX WEILL. Cloth. Illustrated. Pp. 163. $0.40.

*Easy Standard French.* By VICTOR E. FRANÇOIS. Cloth. Pp. 171. $0.40.

*Sociology and Modern Social Problems.* By CHARLES A. ELLWOOD. Cloth. Pp. 331. $1.00.

*Art Songs for High Schools.* By WILL EARHART. Cloth. Pp. 283. $0.80.

*The Mastersinger.* By FRANK R. RIX. Cloth. Pp. 192. $0.65.

*Joan of Arc French Composition.* By H. A. GUERBER. Cloth. Pp. 68. $0.30.

## C. W. BARDEEN, SYRACUSE, N.Y.

*Plutarch on Education,* embracing the three treatises, "The Education of Boys," "How a Young Man Should Hear Lectures on Poetry," "The Right Way to Hear." By CHARLES WILLIAM SUPER. Cloth. Pp. 192. $1.00.

*Physical Training In and Out of School.* By WILLIAM TORREY HARRIS. Cloth. Pp. 35. $0.50.

## THE BOBBS-MERRILL CO., INDIANAPOLIS

*The Golden Hour. Stories and Poems for Opening Exercises in the School-Room.* By PRUDENCE LEWIS. Cloth. Pp. 360.

## CHARITIES PUBLICATION COMMITTEE, NEW YORK

*Wider Use of the School Plant.* By CLARENCE ARTHUR PERRY. Cloth. Illustrated. Pp. 404. $1.25.

## GINN & CO., BOSTON

*Leading Events of Maryland History.* By J. MONTGOMERY GAMBRILL. Cloth. Pp. 362. $0.90.

*Industrial Studies. United States.* By NELLIE B. ALLEN. Cloth. Illustrated. Pp. 335. $0.65.

## GOVERNMENT PRINTING OFFICE, WASHINGTON

*Statistics of State Universities and Other Institutions of Higher Education Partially Supported by the State.* Paper. Pp. 29.

*The Biological Stations of Europe.* By CHARLES ATWOOD KOFOID. Paper covers. Illustrated. Pp. 360.

## D. C. HEATH & CO., BOSTON

*Farm Friends and Farm Foes. A Textbook of Agricultural Science.* By CLARENCE M. WEED. Cloth. Illustrated. Pp. 134.

## HENRY HOLT & CO., NEW YORK

*The Silver Thread and Other Folk Plays for Young People.* By CONSTANCE D'ARCY MACKAY. Cloth. Pp. 239. $1.10.

HOUGHTON MIFFLIN CO., CAMBRIDGE

*American and English Classics for Grammar Grades.* Cloth. Illustrated. Pp. 136. $0.55.

*Selections from the Riverside Literature Series for Seventh Grade Reading.* Chosen by SUPERINTENDENT PEARSE and the Principals and Teachers of Milwaukee. Cloth. Illustrated. Pp. 256. $0.40.

*Selections from the Riverside Literature Series for Eighth Grade Reading.* Chosen by SUPERINTENDENT PEARSE and the Principals and Teachers of Milwaukee. Cloth. Illustrated. Pp. 255. $0.40.

*Children's Classics in Dramatic Form. Book Four.* By AUGUSTA STEVENSON. Cloth. Illustrated. Pp. 211. $0.50.

THE MACMILLAN CO., NEW YORK

*Elements of Business Arithmetic.* By ANSON H. BIGELOW AND W. A. ARNOLD. Cloth. Illustrated. Pp. 254. $0.70.

*Idealism in Education.* By HERMAN HARRELL HORNE. Cloth. Pp. 183. $1.25.

*A Text-Book in the Principles of Education.* By ERNEST NORTON HENDERSON. Cloth. Pp. 593. $1.75.

*Tillers of the Ground.* By MARION I. NEWBIGIN. Cloth. Illustrated. Pp. 224. $0.50.

*New Geographies.* Second Book. By RALPH S. TARR AND FRANK M. MCMURRY. Cloth. Illustrated. Pp. 440. $1.10.

CHARLES E. MERRILL CO., NEW YORK

*The Man without a Country, and My Double.* By EDWARD EVERETT HALE. Cloth. Pp. 100. $0.25.

THE NEALE PUBLISHING CO., NEW YORK

*Three Crimson Days.* By HARRISON PATTEN. Cloth. Pp. 67.

RAND, McNALLY & CO., CHICAGO

*Pilgrim Stories.* By MARGARET B. PUMPHREY. Illustrated by LUCY FITCH PERKINS. Cloth. Pp. 255. $0.45.

*Little Rhymes for Little Readers.* By WILHELMINA SEEGMILLER. Cloth. Illustrated. Pp. 87.

*Old Fashioned Fairy Tales.* Retold from the Poetic Version of Tom Hood by MARIAN FOSTER WASHBURNE. Cloth. Illustrated. Pp. 115. $0.45.

*Commercial Geography.* By EDWARD VAN DYKE ROBINSON. Cloth. Illustrated. Pp. 455.

ROW, PETERSON & CO., CHICAGO

*The Primer.* By HARRIETTE TAYLOR TREADWELL AND MARGARET FREE. Cloth. Illustrated. Pp. 120.

SILVER, BURDETT & CO., NEW YORK

*Literature in the School.* By JOHN S. WELCH. Cloth. Pp. 236. $1.25.

WORLD BOOK CO., YONKERS-ON-HUDSON, N.Y.

*New-World Speller, Grades One and Two.* By JULIA HELEN WOHLFARTH AND LILLIAN EMILY ROGERS. Cloth. Illustrated.

# CURRENT EDUCATIONAL LITERATURE IN THE PERIODICALS[1]

IRENE WARREN
Librarian, School of Education, The University of Chicago

ABBOTT, ALLAN. High school journalism. School R. 18:657–66. (D. '10.)

ADKINS, FRANK J. The compulsory evening school. Journ. of Educa. (Lond.) 42:789–91. (D.'10.)

ARMSTRONG, JAMES E. The high school lunch room. Educa. Bi-Mo. 5:154–58. (D. '10.)

BAGLEY, WILLIAM C. The Illinois educational commission. School R. 18:667–73. (D. '10.)

BAILEY, HENRY TURNER. Lest we forget drawing. Journ. of Educa. (Bost.) 72:651–52. (29 D. '10.)

BALDT, LAURA I. The relation of arithmetic to domestic art. Atlantic Educa. Journ. 6:7. (Ja. '11.)

BENNETT, CHARLES A. Visiting manual training schools in Europe. (7) Man. Train. Mag. 12:143–68. (D. '10.)

BENSON, ARTHUR C. The place of classics in secondary education. Liv. Age. 49:666–73. (D. '10.)

BERLE, A. A. Business men and education. Journ. of Educa. (Bost.) 72:653–54. (29 D. '10.)

BODINE, WILLIAM L. The value of compulsory education laws to school attendance. Educa. Bi-Mo. 5:140–42. (D. '10.)

BOLAND, GENEVIEVE. Taking a dare. Pedagog. Sem. 17:510–24. (D. '10.)

BROOKS, STRATTON D. Vocational guidance. School R. 19:42–50. (Ja. '11.)

BROWN, ELMER E. The lesson of the state universities. Educa. 31:280–88. (Ja. '11.)

BURNHAM, WILLIAM H. European investigations in school hygiene. Pedagog. Sem. 17:525–33. (D. '10.)

[1] Abbreviations.—Atlantic Educa. Journ., Atlantic Educational Journal; Col. Univ. Q., Columbia University Quarterly; Educa., Education; Educa. Bi-mo., Educational Bi-monthly; Educa. News, Educational News; Educa. R., Educational Review; Educa. T., Educational Times; El. School T., Elementary School Teacher; Journ. of Educa. (Bost.), Journal of Education (Boston); Jour. of Educa. (Lond.), Journal of Education (London); Liv. Age, Living Age; Man. Train. Mag., Manual Training Magazine; Pedagog. Sem., Pedagogical Seminary; Pop. Sci. Mo., Popular Science Monthly; Primary Educa., Primary Education; Relig. Educa., Religious Education; School R., School Review; School W., School World; Teach. College Rec., Teachers College Record.

CHAMBERLAIN, ARTHUR H. The vocational middle school. Man. Train. Mag. 12:105–13. (D. '10.)

CHARLES, FRED. Superannuation of teachers. School W. 12:441–43. (D. '10.)

CHASE, LEW ALLEN. Institutional history in the high schools. School R. 18:698–700. (D. '10.)

COE, GEORGE A. The education of ministers. Relig. Educa. 5:454–57. (D. '10.)

CONDON, RANDALL J. What the schools need. Educa. 31:313–34. (Ja. '11.)

COPE, HENRY F. College leadership and Sunday school efficiency. Relig. Educa. 5:493–500. (D. '10.)

CURTIS, JOHN B. Instruction of the blind in the Chicago public schools. Educa. Bi-Mo. 5:117–20. (D. '10.)

DENIO, HERBERT W. The founding of the University of Berlin. Educa. R. 40:473–87. (D. '10.)

DUNBAR, OLIVIA HOWARD. Three-cent luncheons for school children. Outlook 97:34–7. (7 Ja. '11.)

DYKEMA, PETER W. Music in public schools: rote singing (1). Atlantic Educa. Journ. 6:5–6. (Ja. '11.)

Education in Uruguay. School W. 12:453–54. (D. '10.)

FINDLAY, J. J. The dullness of school-masters. Educa. T. 63:480–82. (D. '10.)

Four years of progress in the public schools of St. Paul. Journ. of Educa. (Bost.) 72:654–55. (29 D. '10.)

HALL, G. STANLEY. The national child welfare conference: its work and its relations to child study. Pedagog. Sem. 17:497–504. (D. '10.)

———. Physical training. Pedagog. Sem. 17:491–96. (D. '10.)

HAMMOND, J. D. The education of ministers. Relig. Educa. 5:451–54. (D. '10.)

HANUS, PAUL H. The training of college bred teachers. Educa. 31:302–12. (Ja. '11.)

———. Vocational guidance and public education. School R. 19:51–6. (Ja. '11.)

HARVEY, LORENZO D. Training parents by school and church. Relig. Educa. 5:416–27. (D. '10.)

HILL, DAVID SPENCE. The child and the reading habit. Relig. Educa. 5:461–72. (D. '10.)

HITCH, RUFUS N. The value of the parental school to the community. Educa. Bi-Mo. 5:143–47. (D. '10.)

HODGE, RICHARD MORSE. The education of ministers. Relig. Educa. 5:458–61. (D. '10.)

JAGGAR, THOMAS AUGUSTUS. The duty of New England at the present time with reference to the endowed colleges and public schools. Educa. 31:289–301. (Ja. '11.)

JOHNSON, FRANKLIN W. The school party—its effects upon manners and morals. Educa. Bi-Mo. 5:165–68. (D. '10.)

———. A study of high school grades. School R. 19:13–24. (Ja. '11.)

JOHNSON, GEORGE R. Qualitative elimination from high schools. School R. 18:680–94. (D. '10.)

JOHNSON, MARY HANNAH. The School and the reading habit in children. Relig. Educa. 5:472–75. (D. '10.)

KELLOGG, KATE S. An experiment in practical civics. Educa. Bi-Mo. 5:174–84. (D. '10.)

KEPPEL, FREDERICK P. The occupations of college graduates as influenced by the undergraduate course. Educa. R. 40:433–39. (D. '10.)

KNOCKER, WINIFRED V. Play centres: their object and their needs. Educa. News 35:1,323. (23 D. '10.)

KRAUSKOPF, CHARLES E. The work for crippled children in the public schools of Chicago. Educa. Bi-Mo. 5:121–27. (D. '10.)

LEACH, A. F. The medieval education of women. Journ. of Educa. supplement (Lond.) 32:838–41. (D. '10.)

MCANDREW, WILLIAM, *Parens iratus:* his cause and cure. School R. 19:1–12. (Ja. '11.)

MCCOWEN, MARY. Types of deaf children and how they may be provided for in the public schools. Educa. Bi-Mo. 5:128–39. (D. '10.)

MCGOWN, W. E. Report on the hygienic and sanitary condition of a public school building. Pedagog. Sem. 17:480–90. (D. '10.)

MACMILLAN, D. P. The public education of exceptional children. Educa. Bi-Mo. 5:111–16. (D. '10.)

MACQUEARY, T. H. More concentration in history work. School R. 18:695–97. (D. '10.)

Mathematics in Austrian schools. School W. 12:454–55. (D. '10.)

MATTHEWS, BRANDER. University organization. Col. Univ. Q. 13:67–73. (D. '10.)

MEEK, CHARLES S. State and local taxation for public schools. Teach. College Rec. 11:43–54. (N. '10.)

MEYERS, IRA BENTON. The evolution of aim and method in the teaching of nature study in the common schools of the United States. El. School T. 11:205–13. (D. '10.)

MILES, WALTER R. A comparison of elementary and high school grades. Pedagog. Sem. 17:429–50. (D. '10.)

MILLER, H. L. A comparative study of the grades of the pupils from the different ward schools based upon the first year in high school. El. School T. 11:161–70. (D. '10.)

MONTAGUE, WILLIAM PEPPERELL. Philosophy in the college course. Educa. R. 40:488–98. (D. '10.)

MOULDEN, J. W. The teaching of letter writing. School W. 12:443–46. (D. '10.)

O'Shea, M. V. Readings in great educators: Education according to nature. Primary Educa. 19:5–6. (Ja. '11.)

Osborn, Henry F. Huxley on education. Col. Univ. Q. 13:25–38. (D.'10.)

Paton, Stewart. University reforms. Pop. Sci. Mo. 78:52–70. (Ja. '11.)

Phillips, Elizabeth W. British teachers for western Canada. School W. 12:448–51. (D. '10.)

Pressland, A. J. The English public school as a training school of citizenship. Educa. R. 40:499–511. (D. '10.)

Prosser, William C. Teachers' compulsory insurance. Teach. College Rec. 11:14–42. (N. '10.)

Rusk, Robert R. Experimental education. Journ. of Educa. supplement. (Lond.) 32:835–38. (D. '10.)

St. John, Edward Porter. Preparing the minister as an educator. Relig. Educa. 5:445–57. (D. '10.)

School education in Cape Colony. School W. 12:451–53. (D. '10.)

Shepherd, John Wilkes. The social spirit in the class room. Educa. Bi-Mo. 5:169–73. (D. '10.)

Simons, Sarah E. Imitative writing in the high school. Pedagog. Sem. 17:451–79. (D. '10.)

Snedden, David. The certification of high school teachers. Educa. 31:335–38. (Ja. '11.)

Stamper, Alva W. The financial administration of student organizations in secondary schools. School R. 19:25–33. (Ja. '11.)

Stillman, Bessie W. An experiment in teaching reading. Atlantic Educa. Journ. 6:7. (Ja. '11.)

Tirrell, Winthrop. Summer apprenticeship in the Boston high school of commerce. School R. 19:34–41. (Ja. '11.)

The value of a country education to every boy: a talk with the host of Craftsman farms. Craftsman 19:389–94. (Ja. '11.)

Wade, Frank B. On the ethical value of school athletics. Educa. Bi-Mo. 5:159–64. (D. '10.)

Wallin, J. E. W. A boy's exposition. Pedagog. Sem. 17:505–9. (D. '10.)

Watt, William E. Fresh air in the school and home. Educa. Bi-Mo. 5:148–53. (D. '10.)

Wiley, Frank L. The layman in school administration. Teach. College Rec. 11:2–13. (N. '10.)

Willson, Albert Clark. School administration and supervision in Connecticut. Teach. College Rec. 11:55–69. (N. '10.)

Works, George A. Suggestions for a practical course in high school botany. School R. 18:674–79. (D. '10.)

VOLUME XI NUMBER 7

# THE ELEMENTARY SCHOOL TEACHER

MARCH, 1911

## A GRADED COURSE IN SCHOOLROOM GYMNASTICS. III

JULIA ANNA NORRIS
School of Education, The University of Chicago

### GYMNASTICS BY COMMAND (*continued*)

It will be noticed that, beginning with the fourth lesson for the fifth grade (below, p. 353), and all higher grades, the introductory movement becomes a running in place with arm movements combined. This practice is introduced because at about the time of the year that this lesson would naturally be reached the weather becomes cold enough to complicate the ventilation question. Children who have been sitting quietly for some time may feel uncomfortably chilly if the windows are opened before they have had a chance to get the circulation started. If, however, a general vigorous exercise be taken first so that the skin is in a glow it will usually be safe immediately afterward to open the windows for the performance of the rest of the lesson.

Common-sense must, however, be used. It will often be better, instead of raising the windows at the bottom, to lower them at the top so that the wind will not blow directly on the children. The room may cool off so rapidly that it will be necessary to close the windows after only a few minutes, finishing the lesson under this condition. Care should be taken that children of low vitality do not stand close by open windows.

The arrangement of the class should be such as to facilitate observation of the children by the teacher and of the teacher by the children. The distribution within the rows, therefore, should be according to height, the shorter children in front. In the two upper grades it is well to have the boys and the girls stand in separate rows.

In the further interest of observation and especially of manual correction every third aisle should be vacant. This enables the teacher to come close to any child in the room by moving up and down the vacant aisles. The arrangement can usually be accomplished by having two rows rise on the right side of their chairs, the rest on the left, thus leaving one aisle free, and by assigning special places to the children occupying the other aisle to be vacated. In a full room it may be necessary that these special places shall be in front of the occupied aisles, but in many rooms a few vacant seats will help solve the difficulty.

A further change is sometimes found necessary for the jumping exercise in poorly constructed buildings, where a considerable jarring of the floor may be caused. All such difficulty is usually eliminated if the jumping is performed by half the class at a time along the two edges of the room where the ends of the floor beams are set in the walls.

In some school buildings the corridors are sufficiently wide, light, and airy to make it a decided advantage to take the gymnastics there. This affords greater freedom of movement, better opportunity to see and correct faults, and a chance to ventilate the schoolroom thoroughly during the absence of the class.

In the upper grades balance steps are introduced which combine the features of the leg, balance, and jump classes of movement. These three classes are omitted in lessons which include a balance step. The most convenient position for the hands during balance steps is the hips-firm position.

These movements resemble the balance class in calling for a fine adjustment of equilibrium and body control, but the conditions under which the control must be expressed are fluid rather than static. They resemble the jump class in their acceleration of heart and respiration, but here again the exercises are of a serial character rather than consisting of short, separate, vigorous efforts. Their rhythmic character and dancing grace appeal to the aesthetic side of the child, especially to the girl at this age when the conscious output of muscular energy may seem more or less of a burden.

Since they are less formal in nature than the rest of the lesson it is well to use them as the closing exercise, devoting to them somewhat more than their proportionate allowance of time. They require movement of the children around the room, and the best arrangement for this seems to be to have every other row face the back of the room and every two rows constitute a group. The children in each group then follow each other around the row of desks which stands in their midst. All the groups can work at the same time and there will be no such crowding as probably would occur if they were to form in a large circle around the walls of the room. There is an advantage also in the fact that no child will move very far from his own seat, so that when the exercise is over there will be comparatively little movement before sitting down.

It should never be forgotten that one of the prime objects of schoolroom gymnastics is good posture and carriage. With the lessening of conscious effort which is likely to attend rhythmic work, especially when accompanied by music, strength and beauty of posture are likely to suffer. The teacher should bear this in mind and require the same erect attitude as in the earlier part of the lesson.

Ease and grace of movement and lightness of foot work are the other chief considerations. If the step is at all difficult it should be analyzed and taught in place before trying it around the room.

Various devices may be resorted to for the musical accompaniment. Of course if there is a piano in the room that will solve the difficulty. If there is a piano in a hall it may be worth while to give up the whole lesson one day in the week to the practice of balance steps there.

In the absence of any piano at all it often works well to have the children make their own music, using popular airs. They may hum, or sing the syllable "loo," or whistle. The boys and girls may take turns supplying the music, the boys whistling and the girls humming. It is worth while to take some trouble to develop a good musical accompaniment, for its effect on the grace and rhythm and lightness of action is most valuable.

In teaching anything so military in character as gymnastics there is always danger of sacrificing the development of individual children to the perfecting of details which will improve the appearance of the class in mass action. While uniformity of action is important from the moral standpoint of good order and co-operation the teacher in working for it should not forget the fundamental physical purposes of the work, the development of strong posture, and performance of all gymnastic exercise with vigorous expenditure of energy and in strong attitudes.

In correcting the efforts of the children a higher stand should be taken than that of perfecting abstract form of movement. The children may be interested in the postural significance if that is the basis of the correction, or the hygienic if improvement of function is the object as in deep breathing, or the aesthetic as when beauty of form is to be developed by correct relations, or the social when individual taste needs to be subordinated to the uniform performance of the class.

In correcting postural faults the admonition "Shoulders back!" should never be used, since it results in an awkward, swayback posture. "Chest up!" "Head up!" "Stand tall!" are all good suggestions because they bring about an upward stretching of the whole body. If a child is found, however, whose best efforts are incapable of producing good posture the teacher should correct him manually by placing her hands on his shoulders, fingers in front, thumbs on shoulder blades, rolling the shoulders backward and off from the chest, at the same time forcing the chest upward and forward with her thumbs, which should press in on the wings formed by the shoulder blades. Gradually the child's muscle sense will be thus trained so that he will recognize the correct attitude and assume it voluntarily.

Praise heartily when you honestly can. A quick and generous recognition of an exercise well performed or of a conscientious striving toward it will stand out in gratifying relief against the background of stimulation and correction which must necessarily be a pretty constant accompaniment of the commands.

Improvement in the work is furthered by the judicious use of child critics in the lower grades and as high up as the practice interests the children. A child critic may be chosen for various reasons: because of unusually good effort, because of poor effort, because of having a special fault to be corrected, etc. He must invariably be a child, however, who can be trusted to stand before the class and carry out his part attentively and decorously. He should be told what to watch for, e.g., the row that is best in posture, or in quickness of response, or in strength of movement, or in a certain detail that needs improvement. Or he may be told to pick out the row which seems to him to be doing the best work in general, in which case he should give the reason for his choice. No child should be chosen for critic oftener than once in several weeks, and gradually all the children in the class may have a turn at it. Both the critic and the class benefit by this device if it is reasonably used.

Two weeks make a good unit of time to devote to one gymnastic lesson. The teacher may not be satisfied with the degree of perfection achieved by the end of that period, but if the children have worked in a thoroughgoing fashion they will be ready for the next lesson. It is better to go back and review an old lesson occasionally than to risk monotony by working too long on the same one. Such a review will usually show that marked improvement and power have been gained through the practice of the intervening lessons.

The new lesson should not be introduced all at once. It is better to give one or two new movements daily, introducing them in their proper order among the old ones.

It is good practice in all grades to substitute a game on one day of the week for the gymnastic lesson. Wednesday is the best day for this as it breaks the week into two equal, short periods. The game gives the teacher an opportunity to observe the children at a different angle from that of any of their studies and at a time when they are expressing themselves with freedom from strain or consciousness. There are many games in all grades which can be used in the ordinary schoolroom. In suitable weather and season it is of course better to play the games outdoors.

## GRADE I

### Keeping House

*Story*—The children are going to help the mother keep house today. They scrub the clothes clean and hang them on the line to dry. Then they sweep off the piazza and blow the dust from the railings and chairs. The baby begins to cry and they put him into his carriage and take him out for a ride. The mother then thanks them for helping her so nicely and sends them out to play.

*Exercises:*

1. Washing the clothes
   Purpose: Back and arm exercise.
   Signals: A. Take up the clothes.
   B. Rub them—down.
   Bend forward with straight spine and push arms out straight.
   C. Up.
   Return to erect position with arms bent.
2. Hanging the clothes on the line
   Purpose: Correction of chest and upper spine.
   Signals: A. Stand up on chairs.
   B. Pick up the clothing.
   Not a gymnastic movement, but part of the story.
   Children may suggest an article of clothing.
   C. Hang it on the line.
   Reach high up with both hands, look up, and clasp two fingers of one hand (clothes-pin) round one finger of the other.
3. Sweeping
   Purpose: Arm, shoulder, and trunk exercise.
   Signals: A. Take hold of the broom.
   B. Left.
   C. Right.
   Make a vigorous sweep in direction named, keeping feet flat on floor, swinging arms and twisting body.
4. Blowing dust
   Purpose: Full breathing.
   Signals: A. Breathe.
   Inhale through nose.

B. Blow.
Exhale forcibly through mouth, blowing at objects higher than the head.

5. Taking the baby out to ride
Purpose: Erect posture in walking.
Signals: A. Take hold of handle of carriage.
Bend hands up in front of shoulders.
B. Ready—walk.
Take 5–10 brisk steps forward rhythmically.
C. Turn.
D. Ready—walk.
With 5–10 brisk steps return to place.
E. Turn.

6. Running at play
Purpose: General exercise.
Signal: Ready—run.

*Miscellaneous Suggestions:*

The clothes line is very high so the children must stretch vigorously to reach it. Suggest objects to blow the dust from, always having the objects high, so that they will not blow in each other's faces. Only straight, strong children would be considered worthy to take the baby out to ride. The baby carriage is a full-size one, so the children have to reach up to the handle rather than to bend over.

## GRADE II

### The Snow Play

*Story*—The children reach up toward the clouds and try to pull the snow down out of them, scattering it on the ground in drifts. Then they gather it up, make it into snowballs, and throw them away. They try warming their hands by breathing on them and by swinging their arms across their bodies. They have a fine time coasting down hill on their sleds, and finally they run home again.

*Exercises:*

1. Making the snow fall
Purpose: Correction of chest and upper spine.
Signals: A. Reach.
Reach high with both hands, and look up.
B. Snowflakes.
Lower arms, letting hands and fingers suggest the falling snow.

2. Snowballing
Purpose: Back, leg, and arm exercise.

Signals: A. On left (right) knee—down.
Kneel on left (right) knee, at the same time bending forward and reaching out with hands to gather snow together.
B. Up.
Spring quickly to erect position, holding imaginary snow.
C. Press.
Press snowball into shape.
D. Ready.
Draw hand back ready to throw.
E. Throw.
Throw at some suggested target.

3. Warming hands with breath
Purpose: Full breathing.
Signals: A. Breathe.
Inhale while hands are held away from mouth.
B. Blow.
Blow into open palms.

4. Swinging arms for warmth
Purpose: Chest correction and arm exercise.
Signals: A. Arms up.
Raise stretched arms to shoulder height in side plane or a little back of it.
B. Slap.
Swing arms across quickly, letting hands touch opposite shoulders momentarily and then swinging them back again forcibly so as to expand chest.

5. Coasting
Purpose: Leg and back exercise.
Signals: A. Take hold of sled rope.
Clasp hands behind.
B. Climb hill—start.
Walk forward five steps, lifting knee high at each step.
C. Turn.
Face back of room quickly.
D. Ready—start.
Five more steps.
E. Boy fashion.
Children lie on their chairs, face downward, arms stretched out in front.
Or, Girl fashion.
Children sit on their chairs, arms and feet in front.

6. Running home
Purpose: General exercise.
Signal: Ready—run.

*Miscellaneous Suggestions:*

In coasting, there may be a race, in which case the children with the straightest backs win.

## GRADE I OR II

### Valentine's Day

*Story*—The children start out to give away their valentines. First they drop into the letter box those that are to go a long distance. Then they go to a friend's house and climb the steps very softly so as not to be heard. Suddenly someone opens the door and looks out. The children crouch instantly and hide, but as soon as the door closes they spring up again. Then they slip some valentines under the door, ring the bell, and run quickly home, when, being out of breath, they pant vigorously.

*Exercises:*

1. Climbing the steps
   Purpose: Leg exercise.
   Signals: A. Hands on hips.
   B. Ready—climb.
   Take a given number of steps forward, lifting the knees high, and counting softly.

2. Dropping valentines into letter box
   Purpose: Correction of chest and upper spine.
   Signals: A. Reach.
   Raise both arms high, look up, and stand on tiptoes.
   B. Down.
   Return to straight standing position.

3. Hiding
   Purpose: Trunk and leg exercise.
   Choose a child to represent the inmate of the house. He stands in a chair with his hands over his face (closed doors). Suddenly he parts his hands and looks out, whereupon the other children crouch quickly down on the floor. Presently he closes his hands again, and the children spring to straight standing position.

4. Slipping valentines under the door
   Purpose: Trunk and leg exercise.
   Signals: A. On left (right) knee—down.
   Kneel with back erect.
   B. Slip the valentine under.
   Slip hands forward just above floor.
   C. Stand.
   Spring up to straight standing position.

5. Running home
   Ring desk bell (door bell) for each row to run. Or the teacher may say "Ring" and the children respond by pressing an imaginary electric bell and saying "Ding," and running.
6. Breathing
   Signals: A. Breathe in.
   B. Breathe out.

*Miscellaneous Suggestions*:

Whose house shall we go to? How many steps are there to climb at that house? For whom shall we leave valentines? The choice of a child to open and close the imaginary doors may depend on good effort at taking the exercises well and holding good position.

## GRADE III

### Lesson III

1. Leg. *Hips—firm!* Foot placing forward with left (or right) foot, counting to eight—start! *Po—sition!*
   Foot placed forward on odd counts, replaced on even counts. Weight moves forward each time so as to be evenly borne by the two feet. No alternating.
2. Arch. Head forward—bend! Upward—raise!
   Head forward—bend! Neck relaxes and head drops forward on active chest.
   Upward—raise! Head is raised slowly and strongly with chin in and neck back; a deep full breath meanwhile raises chest vigorously.
3. Arm. Chest—firm! Po—sition!
   Each arm makes a horizontal shelf, elbow at height of shoulder in side plane, forearm bent forward, hand in front of chest, touching it, palm down. Hands are pulled as far apart as possible. Elbows are pulled well back.
4. Trunk. *Hips—firm! Feet sideways—place!* Trunk to left (right)—bend! Upward—raise! *Feet together—place! Po—sition!*
   Shoulders should be kept squarely to front. A deep inhalation should accompany the bending, an exhalation the raising.
5. General exercise. Mark time—march! Class—halt!
6. Breathing. Arm raising forward and upward—raise!—sink!
   Inhale while raising extended arms through the front plane to their full height above the head.

### Lesson IV

1. Leg. One step forward—march! One step backward—march!
   One step is taken in two counts, children counting, 1—2!
   1. Step forward or backward with left foot. 2. Bring right foot up to left foot with a click of heels.

2. Arch. *Shoulders—firm!* Head to left—twist! Forward—twist! To right, etc.
   The same in four counts—1!—2!—3!—4! *Po—sition!*
3. Arm. Neck—firm! Po—sition!
   Tips of fingers meet on back of neck, wrists straight, elbows back, neck pressed back against fingers.
4. Trunk. Trunk to left—twist! Forward—twist! To right, etc.
   Twist trunk and hips at least till shoulders are parallel with side wall, farther if possible. Keep shoulders at even height, feet flat on floor.
5. Jump. *Hips—firm! Heels—raise!* Jump, counting to ten—start! *Heels—sink! Po—sition!*
   Jump, keeping heels together and landing lightly on toes at each count. Teacher gives each count as a command at first; later the children count aloud and jump rhythmically.
6. Respiratory. *Arms forward—raise!* Arm moving sideways—1!—2! *Po—sition!*
   Arm moving sideways—1! Carry arms horizontally to side plane. 2! Return to front plane.
   After spending two weeks on each of the above four lessons spend two weeks in alternating the third and fourth.

## GRADE IV

### Lesson III

1. Introductory. Side step to left (or right)—march!
   Side step to left and right—march!
   Two side steps to left (or right)—march!
   Side step is taken in two counts. Left foot steps to left on "one," right heel is brought up to left with a click on "two."
2. Leg. *Hips—firm!* Foot placing forward with change of feet, counting to eight—start! *Po—sition!*
   See Grade III, Lesson III. Start with left foot and alternate.
3. Arch. Head forward—bend! Upward—raise!
   See Grade III, Lesson III.
4. Arm. Neck—firm! Po—sition!
   See Grade III, Lesson IV.
5. Trunk. *Hips—firm!* Trunk to left—twist! Forward—twist! To right, etc.
   See Grade III, Lesson IV.
6. Jump. *Hips—firm! Left foot forward—place! Heels—raise!* Jump with change of feet, counting to eight—start! *Heels—sink! Po—sition!*
   Land with right foot in front of left on odd numbers, left in front of right on even numbers.

7. Breathing. Arm raising forward and upward—raise!—sink!
See Grade III, Lesson III.

### Lesson IV

1. Introductory. Review the forward steps and the side steps.
2. Leg. *Hips—firm!* Foot closing and opening, counting to eight—start! *Po—sition!*
See Grade III, Lesson I.
3. Arch. *Head to left—twist!* Head twisting all the way—1!—2! *Forward—twist!*
4. Arm. Head—firm! Po—sition!
Tips of fingers meet on crown of head, wrist curved upward, elbows back.
5. Trunk. Neck—firm! Trunk forward—bend! Upward—raise! Po—sition!
The same in four counts—1!—2!—3!—4!
The same three times—go!
6. Jump. *Hips—firm! Left foot backward—raise!* Running in place, counting to eight—start! *Po—sition!*
Left foot backward—raise! Raise foot as high as knee. In the running movement throw the feet as high as the knees, and land on the toes. To facilitate finishing with both feet on the floor the word "down" may be substituted for the count "eight."
7. Breathing. Arm turning—1!—2!
Inhale while the arms are rotated outward until thumbs point backward, exhale while returning to starting position.

## GRADE V

### Lesson III

1. Introductory. Two steps forward—march! Two steps backward—march! Left about—face! Right about—face!
Two steps forward, etc. See Grade IV, Lesson II.
Left about—face! Same technique as in left facing, but the turn covers 180°.
2. Leg. *Hips—firm!* Alternate heel and toe raising, counting to ten—go! *Po—sition!*
Raise heels and lower toes on odd counts, raise toes and lower heels on even counts. Do not bend at hip joint.
3. Arch. *Hips—firm!* Head forward—bend! To left (right)—roll! Forward—twist! *Po—sition!*
To left—roll! Swing head in a quarter circle upward to left, at the same time turning it, so that child finishes with head erect, looking over left shoulder.

4. Arm. *Shoulders—firm!* Left arm sideways—stretch! Arms—change! Change! *Po—sition!*
See Grade VI, Lesson II.

5. Balance. *Hips—firm!* Left (right) knee upward—bend! Foot re—place! *Po—sition!*
Bend knee up in front plane till there is a right angle at hip joint and another at knee joint, with toe pointed downward.

6. Abdominal. *Hips—firm!* Trunk to left—twist! Forward—twist! To right, etc. *Po—sition!*
See Grade III, Lesson IV.

7. Back. *Hips—firm!* Trunk forward—bend! Neck—firm! Hips—firm! Neck—firm! Hips—firm! Trunk—raise! *Po—sition!*
The same in eight counts—go!
The counting should be in slow time.

8. Jump. *Hips—firm!* Jump in place—1!—2!—3, 4!—5!—6! *Po—sition!*
See Grade VI, Lesson II.

9. Respiratory. *Arms sideways—raise! Hands—turn!* Arm raising upward —raise!—sink! *Po—sition!*
Arm raising upward—raise! Raise arms to fully extended position above head. Sink! Lower them to height of shoulders in side plane.

## GRADE V

### Lesson IV

1. Introductory. *Hips—firm!* Running in place, counting to ten—go! *Po—sition!*
See Grade IV, Lesson IV.

2. Arch. *Hips—firm!* Neck backward—bend! Upward—raise! *Po—sition!*

3. Arm. Arm stretching upward and foot placing sideways—1!—2!
Position in two counts—1!—2!
1! Bring arms to shoulders-firm position and place left foot. 2! Stretch arms to full extension and place right foot.
Foot placing sideways. See Grade III, Lesson II.

4. Leg. *Hips—firm!* Foot placing forward and backward with change of feet—go! *Po—sition!*
Class counts to four twice. 1. Place left foot forward two foot-lengths' distance. 2. Replace it. 3. Place it backward a similar distance. 4. Replace it. 1, etc., Repeat with right foot.

5. Balance. *Hips—firm!* Left (right) leg backward—raise! Foot re—place! *Po—sition!*
Raise leg backward about 45° with knee straight and without tipping trunk forward.

6. Abdominal. Chest—raise! Re—turn!
See Grade VI, Lesson II.

7. Back. *Arms sideways stretch and feet sideways—place!* Trunk forward—bend! Arm turning—1!—2! Trunk—raise!
Or, Trunk bending forward and arm turning—go! *Po—sition!*
Arms sideways stretch, etc. Technique similar to that in Arm movement above, but children do the counting.
Arm turning—1! Rotate arms so that thumbs turn upward and backward.
Trunk bending, etc.—go! Taken in four counts. 1. Bend forward. 2. Rotate arms. 3. Rotate back again. 4. Raise trunk.

8. Jump. Jump with sideways flinging of arms—1!—2!—3, 4!—5!—6!
3, 4! The arms are flung sideways and returned to position while the child jumps upward and returns to landing position.

9. Respiratory. *Chest—firm!* Arm flinging sideways—1!—2! *Po—sition!*

## GRADE VI

### Lesson III

1. Introductory. Combination of one march step and one facing as:
One step forward and left about face—march! Left face and side step to left—march!
Make each step of facing complete.

2. Leg. Neck—firm! Heel raising and knee bending—1!—2!—3!—4! The same three times—go! *Po—sition!*
Bend knees to right angles only.

3. Arch. *Hips—firm!* Head to left—twist! To left—bend! Upward—raise! Forward—twist! To right, etc.
Head to left—twist! Twist head till chin is over shoulder. To left—bend! While inhaling deeply bend head toward back (following left ear), at the same time raising chest.

4. Arm. Arm stretching upward—1!—2! Stretching downward—1!—2!
Upward—2! as high above head as possible, elbows straight.

5. Balance. *Hips—firm!* Left knee upward—bend! Knee forward—stretch! Upward—bend! Re—place! Right knee, etc.
Knee upward—bend! See Grade V, Lesson III. Forward—stretch! Straighten the knee, lowering leg so that it forms angle of 45° with floor.

6. Abdominal. *Hips firm and feet—close!* Trunk to left—twist! Forward—twist! To right, etc.
Trunk to left—twist! See Grade III, Lesson IV.

7. Back. Trunk forward—bend! Arm raising sideways—raise!—sink! Trunk—raise!
Arms should be raised to shoulder height. In sinking they should move in a line parallel with axis of trunk.

8. Jump. Jump in place with the hips firm—1!—2!—3, 4!—5!—6!
   3, 4! As the children jump they change hands to hips-firm, and return them to fundamental position as they land.
9. Respiratory. *Hips—firm!* Arm pulling backward—1!—2! *Po—sition!*
   1! Inhale while pulling elbows backward vigorously. 2! Exhale while letting them slip forward passively.

## GRADE VI

### Lesson IV

1. Introductory. *Hips—firm!* Running in place, counting to ten (or twenty or thirty)—go! *Po—sition!*
   See Grade IV, Lesson IV.
2. Arch. *Hips—firm!* Chest—raise! Re—turn! *Po—sition!*
3. Arm. Left arm upward, right arm downward, stretching—1!—2! Arm changing—1!—2! Arm stretching downward—1!—2!
   1! Shoulders-firm position. 2! Arms extended in direction named.
4. Leg. *Hips—firm!* Foot placing diagonally forward and backward with change of feet—go! *Po—sition!*
5. Balance. *Hips—firm!* Left leg forward—raise! Feet—change! Feet—change! etc.
   Class counts 1—2! 1. Replace foot. 2. Lift the other.
6. Abdominal. *Left hip firm and right arm forward upward—fling!* Trunk to left—bend! Upward—raise! Arms—change! To right, etc. *Po—sition!*
   Fling! Both hands move at once. The right moves upward in front plane to highest point it can reach. Po—sition! Both hands move at once. The right moves down in front plane.
   Always bend trunk toward the side that has hand in hips-firm position.
7. Back. *Arms sideways stretch and feet sideways—place!* Trunk forward—bend! Arm rotation—1!—2! Trunk—raise! *In one count, po—sition!*
   See Grade V, Lesson IV.
8. Jump. Jump in place, flinging arms sideways—1!—2!—3, 4!—5!—6!
   3, 4! As children jump they fling stretched arms to height of shoulders in side plane. As they land they return arms to fundamental position.
9. Respiratory. *Shoulders—firm!* Slow arm stretching sideways—1!—2! *Po—sition!*

## GRADE VII

### Lesson III

1. Introductory. Combinations of one march step and two facings or two march steps and one facing, as:
   Two steps forward and left face—march!
   Left face, side step to left and left face—march!
   Make each step or facing complete.

2. Arch. *Neck—firm!* Chest—raise! Re—turn! *Po—sition!*
3. Arm. Left arm sideways, right arm upward stretching—1!—2! Arm changing—1!—2! Arm stretching downward—1!—2! 1! Shoulders-firm position.
4. Leg. *Hips—firm!* Foot placing forward, sideways, and backward with change of feet—go! *Po—sition!*
   Six counts with left foot, six with right. 1. Place foot forward. 2. Replace it. 3. Place foot sideways. 4. Replace it, etc.
5. Abdominal. *Left hip firm, right arm forward upward—fling!* Trunk to left—bend! Upward—raise! Arms—change! To right, etc. *Po—sition!*
   See Grade VI, Lesson IV.
6. Back. *Arms sideways stretch and feet sideways—place!* Trunk forward—bend! Arm rotation—1!—2! Trunk—raise! *In one count, po—sition!*
   See Grade V, Lesson IV.
7. Respiratory. Arm rotation and deep breathing—1!—2!
   See Grade IV, Lesson IV.
8. Balance Steps. *Hips—firm!* Four march steps and four slide steps alternating—go!
   Four march steps: four walking steps, beginning with left foot. Four slide steps: four slides forward with right foot, bringing left foot up behind each time.
   Development: A. (The line of march having been previously laid out.) March steps about the room in series—go! Class—halt! Halt is done as at same command after mark time—march!
   - B. Four slide steps forward with left, four with right—go!
   - C. Same as B in series, i.e., continuing until command, Class—halt! when class brings heels together on second count.
   - D. Four march steps and four slide steps alternating—go! March steps always start with left foot, slide steps with right.
   - E. Same as D in series.

## GRADE VII

### Lesson IV

1. Introductory. *Hips—firm!* Running in place, counting to ten (or twenty or thirty)—go! *Po—sition!*
   See Grade IV, Lesson IV.
2. Arch. *Hips—firm!* Head to left—twist! To left—bend! Upward—raise! Forward—twist! To right, etc. *Po—sition!*
   See Grade VI, Lesson III.

3. Arm. Arm stretching forward and backward—1!—2!—1!—2! Arm stretching downward—1!—2!
   1! Shoulders-firm position. 2! Stretch both arms in direction named.
4. Leg. *Hips—firm!* Heel raising and knee bending in series—go! Class—halt! *Po—sition!*
   Each movement is taken in four counts (see Lesson I), and this continues rhythmically till the command, class—halt! when the class stops in two counts.
5. Balance. *Hips—firm!* Left knee upward—bend! Knee forward—stretch! Knee—bend! Foot re—place! Right knee, etc.
   See Grade VI, Lesson III.
6. Abdominal. *Hips firm and left foot forward—place!* Trunk to left—twist! Forward—twist! Feet—change! Trunk to right, etc. *Po—sition!*
   Left foot forward—place! A two foot-lengths' placing, weight evenly divided. Feet—change! Taken in two counts: 1. Replace foot. 2. Place the other foot.
7. Back. *Hips—firm!* Left forward fall—out! Feet—change! Foot re—place! *Po—sition!*
8. Jump. *Hands for jump—place!* Jump over chairs—1!—2!—3, 4!—5!—6!
   Hands for jump—place! Turn so as to face chairs and place one hand on desk in front of chair and one on desk at rear.
   3, 4! Jump over chair landing softly in the farther aisle.
9. Respiratory. *Arms sideways—raise!* Arm rotation—1!—2! etc.

## GRADE VIII

### Lesson III

1. Introductory. Combinations of two march steps and two facings in one command, as:
   Right face, two side steps to right and right face—march!
   One step forward, right face, side step to right, and left face—march!
   Make each step or facing complete.
2. Arch. *Neck—firm!* Chest—raise! Re—turn! *Po—sition!*
3. Arm. Arm stretching sideways and upward—1!—2!—1!—2! Arm stretching downward—1!—2!
   1! Shoulders-firm position. 2! Straight arm extension in direction named.
4. Leg. *Hips—firm!* Foot placing forward, sideways, and backward with change of feet—go! *Po—sition!*
   See Grade VII, Lesson III.
5. Abdominal. *Left hip firm, right arm forward upward—fling!* Trunk to left—bend! Upward—raise! Arms—change! To right, etc. *Po—sition!*
   See Grade VI, Lesson IV.

6. Back. *Arms sideways stretch and feet sideways—place!* Trunk forward—bend! Arm rotation—1!—2! etc. Trunk—raise! *In one count. Po—sition!* See Grade V, Lesson IV.

7. Respiratory. *Chest—firm!* Arm flinging sideways—1!—2! etc. *Po—sition!*

8. Balance Steps. Waltz balance step, in three part time, preferably mazurka time. Performed with hips firm.

   Development:

   A. 1) Step to left with left foot.
      2) Step forward in front of left foot with right foot, lifting left foot from floor.
      3) Replace left foot on floor behind right, raising right from floor.
      4), 5), 6) Repeat to right.

   B. 1) Same as A 1).
      2) Same as A 2) except that right foot is slid forward instead of stepped forward.
      3) Same as A 3).

   C. 1) Same as B 1).
      2) Same as B 2) except that child rises on toes of both feet instead of lifting backward foot from floor.
      3) Heel of backward foot sinks to floor.

   D. Same as C except that some progress forward is made on the first count so that children gradually move up or down the aisles. Command "Class—halt" is signal for stopping, after the performance of one more step.

   N.B.—As the foot slides to left the body bends to right and vice versa.

## GRADE VIII

### Lesson IV

1. Introductory. *Hips—firm!* Running in place, counting to ten (or twenty or thirty)—go! *Po—sition!*
   See Grade IV, Lesson IV.

2. Arch. *Hips—firm!* Head to left—twist! To left—bend! Upward—raise! Forward—twist! To right, etc. *Po—sition!*

3. Arm. Arm stretching forward and backward—1!—2!—1!—2! Arm stretching downward—1!—2!

4. Leg. Neck firm and hips firm with heel raising and knee bending—go! The same three times—go!
   Taken in four counts: 1! Neck firm and heels raise. 2! Hips firm and knees bend. 3! Neck firm and knees stretch. 4! Po—sition!

5. Balance. *Hips—firm!* Leg swinging with left (right) leg—1!—2!—3! etc. *Po—sition!*

   1! Bend leg up with knee as nearly in side plane as possible and foot opposite other knee. 2! Straighten leg in side plane at angle of 45° with floor. 3! Replace foot.

6. Abdominal. *Hips firm and feet sideways—place!* Trunk to left—twist! Forward—twist! To right, etc. *In one count, Po—sition!*

7. Back. *Hips—firm!* Left forward fall—out! Feet—change! etc. Foot re—place! *Po—sition!*

8. Jump. *Hips—firm!* Jump with left facing twice—1!—2!—3, 4!—5, 6!—7!—8!

   3, 4! Jump facing left 90°. 5, 6! Jump facing left 90°.

9. Respiratory. *Hips—firm!* Arm pulling backward—1!—2! etc. *Po—sition!*

   See Grade VI, Lesson III.

# MEASUREMENT OF GROWTH AND EFFICIENCY IN ARITHMETIC (*Continued*)

S. A. COURTIS
Home and Day School, Detroit

Two of the abilities discussed in the analysis above—the ability to copy correctly, and the ability to "borrow and carry"—are not mentioned in the foregoing tables and graphs. The results of the tests of these abilities were obtained only by analysis of the mistakes made, and of the gross scores. In the case of the first of the two abilities, as the papers were corrected, the number of mistakes in copying made by each grade was noted and reduced, for purposes of comparison, to mistakes per hundred examples. The record is given in Table II. The total number of mistakes per hundred examples is also given, and the percentage one is of the other. Fig. 8 shows the last relation graphically.

TABLE II

MISTAKES IN COPYING

| Grade | Fundamentals | | | | | | Reasoning | | | | | |
|---|---|---|---|---|---|---|---|---|---|---|---|---|
| | September | | | June | | | September | | | June | | |
| | C* | T† | Percentage | C* | T† | Percentage | C* | T† | Percentage | C* | T† | Percentage |
| 4 | 0.0 | 41 | 0 | 2.8 | 30 | 9 | 8.3 | 80 | 10 | 4.0 | 50 | 8 |
| 5 | 7.7 | 28 | 28 | 4.2 | 38 | 11 | 3.4 | 49 | 7 | 4.5 | 36 | 13 |
| 6 | 7.7 | 26 | 30 | 3.4 | 36 | 9 | 11.0 | 45 | 24 | 3.9 | 48 | 8 |
| 7 | 11.5 | 29 | 40 | 1.8 | 14 | 11 | 7.1 | 42 | 17 | 1.6 | 23 | 7 |
| 8 | 3.9 | 15 | 26 | 5.6 | 21 | 27 | 4.6 | 29 | 16 | 1.9 | 24 | 8 |
| 9 | 8.0 | 30 | 26 | 8.0 | 34 | 24 | 2.7 | 26 | 10 | 4.7 | 26 | 18 |
| 10 | 4.6 | 26 | 18 | 6.1 | 33 | 18 | 3.9 | 27 | 14 | 4.0 | 19 | 21 |
| 11 | 7.2 | 20 | 36 | 4.8 | 39 | 12 | 1.7 | 28 | 6 | 5.7 | 24 | 24 |
| 12 | 6.0 | 24 | 25 | 6.2 | 25 | 25 | 1.4 | 25 | 6 | 4.5 | 21 | 21 |
| 13 | 3.3 | 17 | 19 | 5.8 | 24 | 24 | 2.8 | 25 | 11 | 2.3 | 24 | 10 |

* C—Mistakes in copying.
† T—Total mistakes.

The conclusions to be drawn from the table and figure are many. Chief among these are the facts that the ability in question is a determining factor in successful work, and that it may, or may not, be developed by the *general* work of the class-room. At the beginning of the year a special course was devised for Grade 7 to remedy the marked defect in this ability shown by the test of the previous year and confirmed by the September test under consideration. The success of these efforts is evident from the June results, more perhaps from the actual changes in the number of mistakes given in the table than from the relative values of the graph. On the other hand, Grades 5 and

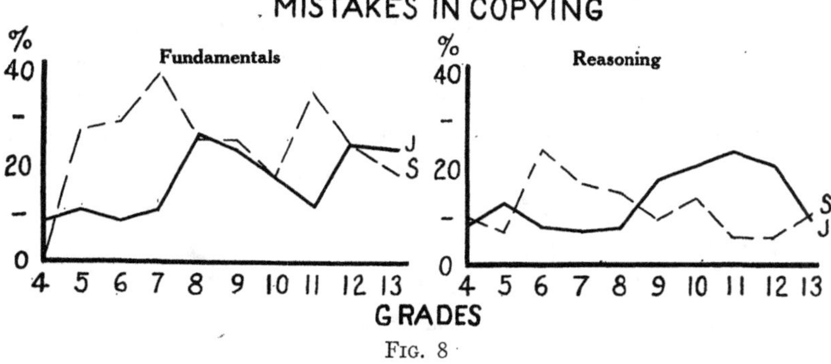


FIG. 8

6 improved during the year without special work, while Grade 8 has for abstract work, at least, suffered an actual loss.

Nothing is known in regard to the reason for the marked change in Grade 11, nor for the losses in the upper grades in the reasoning test. As these grades do not study arithmetic, any change in ability may be explained as transfer from other school work. Thus, the gain of Grade 11 may possibly be due to transfer from the work in geometry. The ability to pay close attention to the details of any work would seem to be a promising place for transfer to occur, so that the actual losses in one test and the small changes in the other are not easily explained.

In fundamentals, one-fifth of all the mistakes made, and in reasoning one-seventh, was due to pure carelessness in copying. The reasons for the smaller number of such mistakes in the reasoning test are probably (1) the greater attention that is given to the figures in the problems in order to grasp the meaning, and (2) the small proportion the copying is of the total work done. For both tests, however, the results seem to the writer to emphasize the need for cultivating the habit of constant checking. Such a habit would have increased the efficiency in these tests approximately 5 per cent without materially decreasing the amount of work done. Whether or not special exercises and special classroom attention will be generally helpful can be told only by actual trial.

The ability to "borrow and carry" proved more difficult to measure. For an individual finishing eight or more examples in the test on fundamentals, the effects of borrowing and carrying were shown in the larger number of mistakes in the second four examples involving carrying than in the first four in which no carrying was necessary. However, part of the increase was also due to the more difficult combinations involved, and the greater length of the examples. The results by totals are given in Table III.

TABLE III

TOTAL EXAMPLES ATTEMPTED AND RIGHT. PERCENTAGE RIGHT

| | Examples 1 to 4 | | | Examples 5 to 8 | | | Examples 9 to 12 | | |
|---|---|---|---|---|---|---|---|---|---|
| | At. | Rt. | Percentage | At. | Rt. | Percentage | At. | Rt. | Percentage |
| September | 943 | 807 | 85 | 837 | 601 | 72 | 347 | 214 | 62 |
| June | 903 | 775 | 86 | 834 | 574 | 69 | 498 | 269 | 54 |

DIFFERENCES IN PERCENTAGES OF EXAMPLES RIGHT

| | (Exs. 1–4) – (Exs. 5–8) | (Exs. 1–4) – (Exs. 9–12) | (Exs. 5–8) – (Exs. 9–12) |
|---|---|---|---|
| September | 85–72=13 | 85–62=23 | 72–62=10 |
| June | 86–69=17 | 86–54=32 | 69–54=15 |

The results by totals are certainly surprising, to say the least. That 15 per cent of the simple examples without carrying, examples so simple that the answers can easily be obtained mentally, should be worked incorrectly is disappointing from the point of view of the standards of the school. That examples of approximately the same length but involving carrying should be practically double the difficulty of the first is a new idea to the writer. That the increase in the length of Examples 9–12 over that of Examples 5–8 should again increase the difficulty by about the same amount was unsuspected. Finally, that the results in June should be less accurate than in September is simply incomprehensible.

In order to determine whether or not the results shown by the totals were general throughout the grades and in the various operations an analysis of the scores was undertaken. It is evident that in the comparison above, the individuals compared are not the same for all the examples. Nearly all the children finished the first four examples, while but a few were able to reach the twelfth. In the analysis comparison was made, example by example (that is, Examples 1 and 5, 2 and 6, etc.) for the first eight examples, and only the scores of those individuals in each grade were taken who succeeded in finishing both examples of each pair. Table IV gives, for each grade, the number of children that finished each pair of examples, the percentages the examples wrong are of those attempted for each example of the pair, and the difference between these percentages, or the effect of the borrowing and carrying. Fig. 9 gives the last results graphically.

The analysis at least makes plain what is happening through the school although there is little in the results to suggest an explanation. The effect of borrowing and carrying is least in substraction, but the results disclose an effect that was not foreseen. The four negative values in September and the six in June must mean that the procedure in subtraction is so uniform, that borrowing in subtraction becomes so habitual because most of the schoolwork demands it, that the habit persists in those cases in which no borrowing is necessary. That is, most of the classes actually solve the more difficult examples involving carrying more accurately than the simpler ones without it. The fact that the work of the year increased this effect would seem to confirm the explanation given.

For the other operations, the effects of borrowing and carrying in addition are apparently midway between those of subtraction and those of multiplication and division. For the last two operations, the grade variations are so extreme that a judgment of "equally difficult" is perhaps the best. From the average values, the effects in the case of multiplication would appear to be

TABLE IV

ABILITY TO CARRY

| Grade | Addition Examples 1 and 5 | | | | Subtraction Examples 2 and 6 | | | | Multiplication Examples 3 and 7 | | | | Division Examples 4 and 8 | | | |
|---|---|---|---|---|---|---|---|---|---|---|---|---|---|---|---|---|
| | No. Attempted | Percentage Wrong | | Difference | No. Attempted | Percentage Wrong | | Difference | No. Attempted | Percentage Wrong | | Difference | No. Attempted | Percentage Wrong | | Difference |
| September | | Ex. 1 | Ex. 5 | | | Ex. 2 | Ex. 6 | | | Ex. 3 | Ex. 7 | | | Ex. 4 | Ex. 8 | |
| 4 | 12 | 25 | 50 | 25 | .. | .. | .. | .... | .. | .. | .. | .. | .. | .. | .. | .. |
| 5 | 21 | 4 | 30 | 26 | 21 | 14 | 14 | 0 | 10 | 10 | 60 | 50 | .. | .. | .. | .. |
| 6 | 26 | 8 | 16 | 8 | 26 | 8 | 38 | 30 | 25 | 8 | 48 | 40 | 11 | 36 | 64 | 28 |
| 7 | 17 | 6 | 6 | 0 | 17 | 24 | 12 | −12 | 16 | 6 | 50 | 44 | 10 | 30 | 80 | 50 |
| 8 | 30 | 3 | 7 | 4 | 30 | 7 | 7 | 0 | 28 | 0 | 36 | 36 | 22 | 5 | 18 | 13 |
| 9 | 23 | 4 | 40 | 36 | 24 | 29 | 17 | −12 | 24 | 12 | 29 | 17 | 23 | 13 | 39 | 26 |
| 10 | 22 | 14 | 55 | 41 | 22 | 18 | 27 | 9 | 22 | 5 | 18 | 13 | 22 | 5 | 41 | 36 |
| 11 | 27 | 4 | 19 | 16 | 27 | 18 | 11 | −7 | 27 | 0 | 41 | 41 | 25 | 0 | 24 | 24 |
| 12 | 25 | 16 | 24 | 8 | 25 | 28 | 16 | −12 | 25 | 4 | 20 | 16 | 23 | 9 | 35 | 26 |
| 13 | 24 | 13 | 25 | 12 | 24 | 0 | 4 | 4 | 24 | 0 | 25 | 25 | 23 | 17 | 30 | 13 |
| Average | | | | 18 | | | | 0 | | | | 31 | | | | 27 |
| June | | | | | | | | | | | | | | | | |
| 4 | 10 | 0 | 60 | 60 | 6 | 16 | 0 | −16 | .. | .. | .. | .. | .. | .. | .. | .. |
| 5 | 22 | 9 | 27 | 16 | 22 | 9 | 23 | 14 | 21 | 0 | 48 | 48 | 13 | 54 | 70 | 16 |
| 6 | 23 | 5 | 48 | 43 | 23 | 22 | 9 | −13 | 23 | 0 | 61 | 61 | 19 | 58 | 80 | 22 |
| 7 | 16 | 0 | 6 | 6 | 16 | 0 | 6 | 6 | 16 | 0 | 12 | 12 | 15 | 7 | 40 | 33 |
| 8 | 27 | 4 | 7 | 3 | 27 | 15 | 11 | −4 | 26 | 4 | 19 | 15 | 25 | 4 | 16 | 12 |
| 9 | 26 | 10 | 35 | 15 | 26 | 19 | 12 | −7 | 26 | 4 | 50 | 46 | 24 | 25 | 38 | 13 |
| 10 | 20 | 5 | 20 | 15 | 20 | 15 | 15 | 0 | 20 | 0 | 30 | 30 | 20 | 5 | 50 | 45 |
| 11 | 24 | 17 | 33 | 16 | 25 | 12 | 20 | 8 | 25 | 0 | 36 | 36 | 24 | 16 | 54 | 38 |
| 12 | 24 | 8 | 25 | 17 | 24 | 25 | 4 | −21 | 24 | 8 | 37 | 29 | 24 | 8 | 42 | 34 |
| 13 | 24 | 8 | 25 | 17 | 24 | 21 | 8 | −13 | 24 | 8 | 33 | 25 | 24 | 8 | 46 | 38 |
| Average | | | | 21 | | | | −5 | | | | 34 | | | | 28 |

the greater, but from the values given in the table for Grades 9–13, grades which have finished their work in arithmetic, it would seem that the effects in the division are really slightly greater.

The inequality of the units of the tests, however, makes anything more than the most general conclusions of questionable value. Perhaps the only safe inference is that the data show the need for a very careful quantitative study of the various

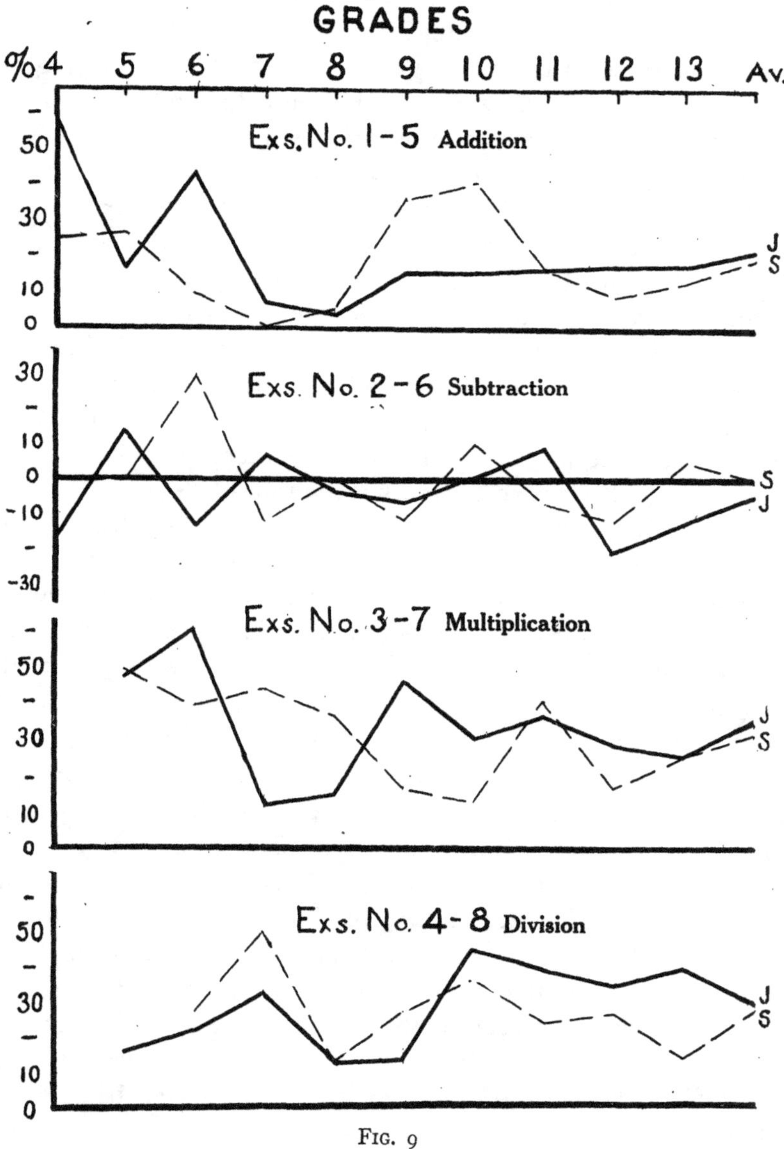


FIG. 9

factors in arithmetical work. If the mere introduction of borrowing and carrying into a multiplication example can cause an increase of 30 per cent in the number of examples missed, the ability under discussion becomes a factor of sufficient importance to receive direct classroom attention.

Perhaps the most striking fact shown by the data is the general increase in the effect of the borrowing and carrying at the end of the year's work. While for the grades actually studying arithmetic (except the erratic sixth) the year's work has, in general, produced some improvement, for most of the high-school grades, it has caused large losses. As the essential elements in borrowing and carrying are memory and attention, it would seem that a year's work in any subject should strengthen rather than weaken this ability and the writer is at a loss to account for the facts shown. In the case of Grade 6, the larger losses are probably due to the marked slump in ability; this grade will later be shown to have suffered near the close of the year (see p. 367) and it may be that something of the same kind took place in all the upper grades.

Although the general tests at the beginning and close of the year measure the total effects of the year's work throughout the school, the results of the special tests, given by the individual teachers in the various classrooms, are of interest as showing for certain grades just how the total effects were produced. The reliability of these results for purposes of comparison from grade to grade is not as great as that of the general tests which were given to the same grades at one time and by one person. However, the results for each grade are consistent with themselves and a comparison of final grade scores (the last week in June) with the previous classroom scores will show practically no difference in the results obtained. At the beginning of the school year, September, 1910, the same tests were again given in the various classrooms, and while at the time this article was commenced, they were not available, they are given here to show the loss during the summer vacation and to complete the story of the year's work. It must be remembered, however, that the last results are not strictly comparable with the others. The various classes change in membership each year, although the losses and gains form but a small fraction of the total enrolment of any grade.

TABLE V

YEAR'S GROWTH IN KNOWLEDGE OF TABLES. GRADE AVERAGES.

| Grade | Op. | Sept. 1909 | Nov. | Dec. | Jan. | Mar. | Mar. | April | | | | May | | | | | June | Sept. 1910 |
|---|---|---|---|---|---|---|---|---|---|---|---|---|---|---|---|---|---|---|
| | | | | | | | | 4 | 11 | 18 | 25 | 2 | 9 | 16 | 23 | 30 | | |
| 5 | + | 35 | 44 | 46 | 47 | 55 | 55 | 63 | 66 | 63 | 63 | .. | 65 | .. | 63 | 65 | 64 | 47 |
| | − | 30 | 40 | 46 | 45 | 50 | 50 | 48 | .. | 53 | 52 | 52 | 52 | .. | 54 | .. | 54 | 46 |
| | × | 24 | 32 | 39 | 40 | 45 | 46 | 43 | .. | 52 | .. | 50 | 52 | 52 | 55 | 52 | 56 | 34 |
| | ÷ | 19 | 30 | 36 | 38 | 41 | 44 | .. | .. | 51 | 50 | 51 | .. | 55 | .. | .. | 50 | 31 |
| 6 | + | 43 | 46 | 45 | 46 | 75 | 65 | 65 | 65 | 65 | 73 | .. | 66 | .. | 63 | 65 | 63 | 56 |
| | − | 33 | 42 | 43 | 47 | 50 | 51 | 51 | .. | 54 | 53 | 58 | 56 | .. | 55 | 49 | 53 | 53 |
| | × | 30 | 34 | 49 | 41 | 49 | 50 | 54 | 56 | .. | .. | 58 | 52 | .. | 56 | 56 | 47 | 42 |
| | ÷ | 26 | 31 | 36 | 36 | 50 | 54 | .. | 50 | .. | 49 | 54 | .. | 56 | 53 | 44 | 48 | 44 |
| 7 | + | 53 | 59 | 68 | 62 | 72 | 79 | 77 | 76 | 82 | 82 | .. | 80 | .. | 83 | 89 | 85 | 79 |
| | − | 36 | 48 | 54 | 50 | 54 | 60 | 57 | .. | 61 | 64 | 65 | 69 | .. | 69 | 66 | 64 | 59 |
| | × | 41 | 43 | 48 | 48 | 62 | 59 | 59 | .. | 72 | 70 | 68 | 74 | 72 | 77 | 77 | 74 | 64 |
| | ÷ | 34 | 43 | 48 | 48 | 59 | 59 | .. | 69 | .. | .. | 67 | .. | 70 | 74 | 74 | 70 | 62 |
| 8 | + | 56 | 65 | 68 | 66 | 73 | 76 | 82 | 83 | 84 | 84 | .. | 82 | .. | 85 | 84 | 84 | 79 |
| | − | 42 | 52 | 55 | 54 | 59 | 63 | 64 | .. | 67 | 69 | 69 | 70 | .. | 69 | 67 | 68 | 64 |
| | × | 49 | 55 | 60 | 56 | 62 | 68 | 67 | 68 | .. | .. | 71 | .. | 74 | 73 | 72 | 72 | 60 |
| | ÷ | 41 | 54 | 58 | 59 | 63 | 66 | .. | 65 | .. | 75 | 74 | 73 | .. | 76 | 70 | 77 | 67 |

From the graph, Fig. 10, it is evident at once that the story of the year's growth varies from grade to grade: Grade 5 shows a rapid gain during the first few weeks of school, a steady uniform growth in all operations during the rest of the year, and a large loss during the summer. Grade 6 shows less gain during the opening weeks, marked fluctuations both in the absolute and relative scores in the various operations during the rest of the year, a marked slump in ability the last six weeks of school, and the smallest loss of any class during the summer. Grade 7 shows the most rapid gain of the four classes, a gain quite uniform throughout. The loss during the summer is small and approximately the same for the various operations. The curve for Grade 8 shows rapid gain during the first weeks, a long "plateau," a marked gain in April, a gain that is held until the close of school, only to be followed by a large loss during the summer.

The cause of these variations is partly known. The writer has strong convictions as to the necessity, place, and amount of

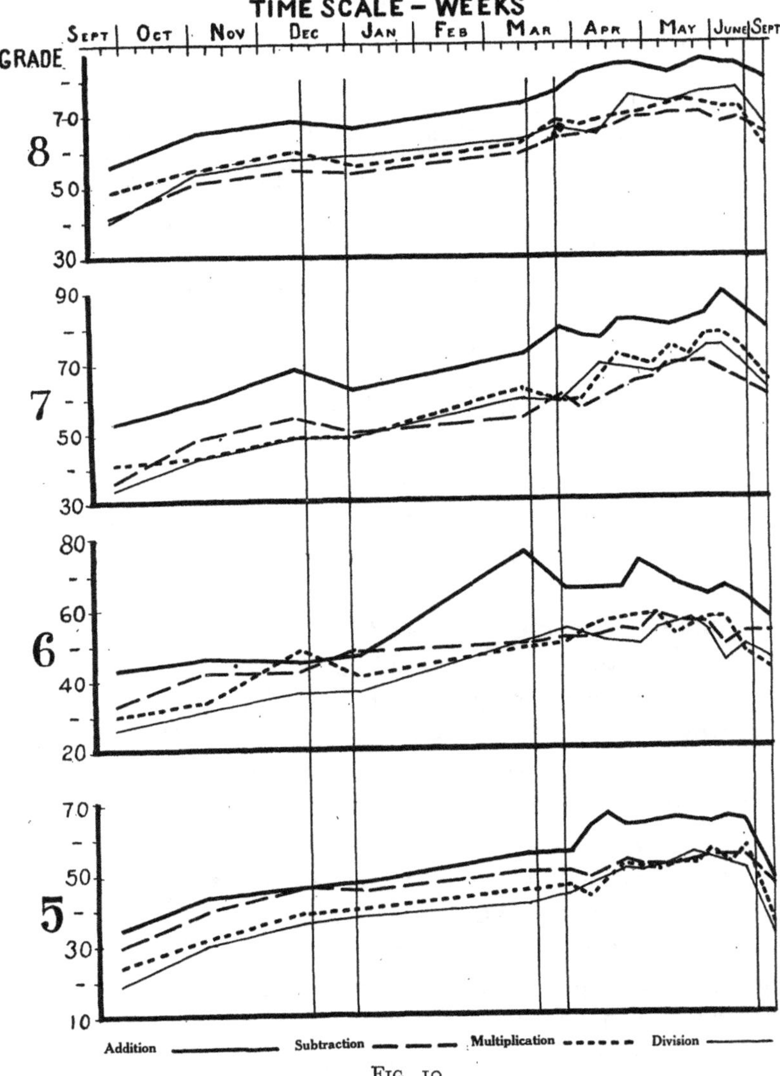


FIG. 10

drill required in elementary work, and in planning the work for the year it was decided to test out the various methods of drill used at different times in the school. In each of these four grades, the first five minutes of each class period (three per week) is devoted to drill work on the tables. In Grade 5 the spiral method was used, the same table, the same operation, or the same type of practice (visual, motor, oral, etc.) never being followed two days in succession. That is, if the table of 6's in multiplication was written one day, the table of 3's in addition might be practiced orally the next. In Grade 6, however, the drill on one operation was continued many weeks at a time, although the type of practice was frequently changed. In Grade 7 the method followed was a modification of the two extremes of the previous classes, the drill being on one topic for short periods with frequent changes of practice. Grade 8 was taught in three sections, each teacher following a different plan, and the effect as a whole is comparable with that of Grade 5. Unfortunately the press of other duties prevented a careful planning of the experiment and the making of complete records. Unfortunately, also, the observed peculiarities in the behavior of the different grades makes it impossible to say whether the results are due wholly to the methods used, or wholly to the stage of development of the children, or to the effects of one upon the other. The results are, therefore, chiefly valuable as showing the possibilities of such comparative tests.

So far as can be judged, within the limitation mentioned above, continuous drill produces immediate and marked growth followed by equally immediate and marked loss upon cessation of the drill. Note the rise in ability in multiplication in Grade 6 during six weeks in November and December to a position above that of all the other abilities, and the loss of half the gain in the following eighteen days of the Christmas vacation. The curve for addition shows the same effects during the winter term. Compare these ups and downs with the steady, continuous progress of Grade 5. If current opinion were true and "slow growth, sure growth," the method used with Grade 5 would be markedly superior to the others. The loss during the summer vacation, however, opens the whole question anew; for the actual loss that took place may be due to the method, or to the disorganization which, as noted above, makes its appearance regularly at this grade.

The coming year one method of drill will be used with all the grades, and by varying the method from year to year, the best method for each will eventually be determined. It is to be hoped, however, that some superintendent will undertake this same experiment on a larger scale. If the schools of the city were divided into districts of, say, ten schools each, and definite methods of drill assigned to each district, appropriate records of the work actually done being kept, comparative tests like those above would determine in a single year, with scientific exactness, the relative effectiveness of the various methods.

The results of Grade 6 have a bearing, also, upon the question of transfer discussed above. Note that the marked gain in multiplication is accompanied by but slight gain in division, while the curve for substraction is stationary and that for division actually depressed. In the same manner the loss in multiplication has equally little effect on division while the other two operations show recovery and slight gain. This, and other similar effects during the year, suggest some tendency toward equalization within the mind itself. If this proves to be in any degree true, it but serves, in connection with the tendency toward uniformity in relative rank of the various grades in September, to emphasize the importance for education generally of exact quantitative studies of the learning process.

# AGRICULTURAL EDUCATION: BOYS' AGRICULTURAL CLUBS

BENJAMIN MARSHALL DAVIS
Miami University

The actual introduction of agricultural subjects into the public schools has developed along two lines, one indirect and informal, the other direct and formal. They may be regarded as two stages of one development, for experience seems to indicate that creating an interest informally by means of boys' agricultural clubs is often, if not always, the most successful method of introducing the study of agriculture into the schools of a community.

Indeed, in many places where formal instruction has failed boys' clubs have been a great success. This is well illustrated in Louisiana. In that state, although the teaching of agriculture has been required since 1898, it has not received much serious attention in the elementary schools. But boys' clubs are being organized in every parish in the state, one parish school boys' club, for example, enrolling during the present year 555 members. This form of agricultural instruction is extending rapidly over the entire country, and is becoming a very important extension work in education as well as in agriculture. It tends to ally itself more and more with the public schools, until finally some more or less formal instruction becomes a regular part of the school work.

Thus in Ohio the state superintendent of agricultural extension work writes that most boys' and girls' club activities are now conducted as a part of the school work and that agricultural clubs as such are becoming a thing of the past, so that no separate records or statistics are now generally kept in the state (118, p. 12).[1]

Two good accounts of the agricultural club movement have been published by the United States Department of Agriculture,

[1] References by numbers are to the corresponding number in the bibliography at the end of this article, or in bibliographies following other articles of this series.

one tracing its development to 1904 (44), the other from 1904 to 1910 (118). The following discussion will therefore be confined chiefly to the present status of the movement with typical examples of successful work, and to the reaction of the agricultural clubs on rural education.

Various agencies have taken the initiative in starting this movement under particular local conditions, but the inspiration for state-wide activity in these lines has generally come from some individual or official source connected with the state department of education, the state agricultural college, or the United States Department of Agriculture. In the absence of such initiative the work has sometimes begun in the zeal and wisdom of some county officer or association, as the county superintendent of schools, the farmers' institute society, the county fair association, or teachers' association, the Grange organization, or the Young Men's Christian Association. Experience has shown that the work has always been most permanent and productive when it has resulted in a definite local organization, preferably under the leadership of the county school superintendent (118, p. 7).

Reference has already been made to the work of the state and college extension departments, of state departments of education, and of other agencies in the organization of these clubs (29, 32, 34, 44, 119).[2]

During the present year this work has been extended, and is becoming better organized. In 1909 there were clubs in twenty-eight states with a total membership of approximately 150,000. During the present year many new clubs have been formed, and the membership in many of those already organized has increased. An instance of the latter is found in the increase in membership of one club from 17 in 1909 to 555 in 1910. In the above estimate for 1909 several states that now have clubs are not included. For example, Kansas has one or more clubs in each county, with a total membership of more than 5,000. The eleven southern states that had a membership of about 13,000 in 1909 have this year nearly 50,000 enrolled. The total membership of 1910 for the entire country may conservatively be estimated at more than 300,000.

The most important recent development is that of the Boys' Corn Club work in the southern states. This work was under-

[2] This *Journal*, Vol. X, No. 6.

taken by representatives of the United States Bureau of Plant Industry through county superintendents of education four years ago. Three years ago it was extended in a few counties of the Gulf states where the boll weevil was damaging cotton crops. At the beginning of 1909 a systematic plan was undertaken to organize Boys' Corn Clubs in a few counties in each of the southern states. There were enrolled 12,400 boys. During 1910 in response to further demands the organizations have been extended into nearly 600 counties, with a total enrolment of 46,225 boys. Although no statistical summary of the work has been issued, a number of reports have been received by the department which show excellent work. In one county in Mississippi 48 boys averaged 92 bushels per acre; 20 boys in one county of South Carolina made 1,700 bushels of corn on 20 acres. Another club of 142 boys averaged 62 bushels to the acre, several going above 100, and two or three above 150 bushels.[3]

The Boys' Corn Club work is the Junior Department of the Government Demonstration Work now being carried on in all the southern states. The results of the boys' work have attracted the attention of the entire country. Considerable prominence was given to it by the public press in 1909, but much more to the results of 1910, particularly to the remarkable achievement of Jerry Moore of Winona, S.C., a boy not fifteen years old, who produced 228¾ bushels of corn on one acre of land, this being the second largest yield per acre in the history of corn production.[4]

The crowning event of the work of 1910 was a visit to Washington on December 12, 1910, of the prize winners from eleven southern states. They were awarded diplomas of merit by the Secretary of Agriculture, presented to the President of the United States, and personally conducted by O. B. Martin, assistant in charge of the Junior Demonstration Work, over the city of Washington, visiting all places of interest.

[3] The above facts were furnished in a letter from O. B. Martin, government assistant in charge of Boys' Demonstration Work.

[4] Results of 1909: *Youth's Companion*, April 10, 1910; Results of 1910: Associated Press account, *Chicago Record-Herald*, December 11 and 18, 1910.

The relation of this work to the schools is indicated by the following extracts from directions for organization and instruction sent out by the department:

Where this work is being introduced in a county, the county superintendent of education and teachers can reach the boys in all sections of the county more quickly and more effectively than any other agency. The superintendent can explain the plan to the teachers, and they can explain it to the boys and secure the names of all the boys who will agree to plant one acre of corn. . . . . Just as soon as the names of all the boys are assembled in the office of the county superintendent of education, duplicate lists should be sent to Dr. S. A. Knapp, Washington, D.C., who has charge of the Farmers' Co-operative Demonstration Work. These boys will from time to time receive circulars of instruction and information in regard to preparation, fertilization, cultivation, seed selection, etc. These circulars furnish excellent subject-matter for discussion at a club meeting, or for a lesson in school. They lead to further study of farmers' bulletins and books. A boy will profit much from such lessons, discussions, and books, because he is making practical application of the principles taught. He learns scientific agriculture because he needs it, and not because it is scientific. . . . . The object of the Boys' Demonstration Work is the same as that among men, namely, better methods of farming and greater yields at less cost. Many of the boys in the clubs who begin to study agriculture in this way will continue the study in agricultural colleges; others will continue such efforts on their farms, and all of them will make useful and more effective citizens.[5]

The organization of the clubs in various states differs somewhat in details, but in general there is a close co-operation between the state departments of education and the state agricultural college. A good example of a state organization is the Farm-Life Club Movement in Alabama:

The leading objects of the Farm-Life Club Movement are educational and for this reason it is our desire to make this movement have a close and vital connection with the work of the county superintendents of education, the teachers, and the schools of the state. There are many important educational problems in Alabama today, but the largest one is the question of better farming. In beginning the work in a county we first secure cooperation of the superintendent and through him interest the teachers. The work is discussed at a teachers' institute and later a letter is mailed requesting each teacher to interest the boys in his school and his community in this

[5] From mimeograph directions sent out by O. B. Martin, assistant in charge of Boys' Demonstration Work, June 1, 1910.

work. The names of the boys are sent to the county superintendent by the teachers.

This work furnishes the greatest opportunity yet launched for the county superintendents and teachers to be of invaluable service to the people in arousing interest in better farming and in improved agriculture.

The ultimate purpose of the work is to aid the great movement for better farming all along the lines, and to encourage the boy to get an education in agriculture and to remain on the farm.

The work in Alabama has been in progress scarcely a year and the results are very encouraging indeed. At present the work has been started in about 17 counties in the state. There is a total of approximately 2,000 boys listed in the work. There have been raised locally among merchants, bankers, and other public-spirited people over $2,000 in prizes. In addition to this the state fairs in Birmingham and Montgomery are offering a total of about $500 for the boys in the corn clubs. After making these exhibits at the state fairs the best of these will be carried to the National Corn Show.

It has been my pleasure during the last month to hold boys' meetings in several counties and to visit a large number of individual acres of corn. The yield in a great many cases is very remarkable. For example, one boy's acre of corn will yield at least 65 bushels of corn, and in addition to the corn there will be enough snap beans and corn middles to pay all the expenses for making the corn, including rent of land and interest on investment. I quote below from a letter recently received from a gentleman who lives in a community where a club has been organized: "Some of the boys are going to make 75 and 85 bushels per acre, and some are going to make as much as 100 bushels." Another letter from a business man will give some idea as to how the business men regard the work: "I think the boys' corn club has worked wonders in the cultivation of corn in this state. I have never seen as much enthusiasm among the old farmers as now prevails, and I feel certain that the Boys' Corn Club is largely responsible for it."

At a meeting held in northern Alabama I asked some of the boys to give me an idea as to the outlook of their corn crop. One, in making a report of his work, said: "Every farmer in a radius of two miles of my acre has visited my corn and said, If you make 35 bushels of corn on this acre we are going to follow your method." Prospects were good for a yield of more than 50 bushels on this acre. The father of this boy said, "I have a special acre myself and do not propose to have my boy beat me raising corn."

This movement is not a question of adding new duties to the county superintendent and teachers without additional pay, but a question of opportunity and service. No movement has yet been projected where superintendents of education and teachers may be of greater service to the people than in the organization of the Farm-Life clubs. This plan also furnishes the best method yet devised of bringing together in harmonious co-operation all the interests looking to better education and better farming. In this work the county superintendents, the teachers, the merchants, the newspapers, the State College of Agriculture, the State Department of Agriculture, and the State Department of Education can all work together for the common good.[6]

Another important phase of the agricultural-club idea is being developed by the Farmers' Institute specialist of the Office of Experiment Stations of the United States Department of Agriculture. It is known as Farmers' Institutes for Young People. The following statement in regard to these institutes will indicate the object and character of the work undertaken:

> In order, therefore, that opportunity to become acquainted with agricultural operations may be given to those who have left the public school and from whose ranks the future farmers and their wives must be supplied, the farmers' institutes in several states have organized and are now conducting what is known as "institutes for young people." The majority of these are not institutes in the sense in which the work of the farmers' institute has come to be defined. They are in reality boys' and girls' clubs conducted in the same manner as those operated by the public schools. . . . .
>
> Because of the fundamental difficulty in securing teachers capable of giving vocational training and instruction in agriculture in the rural schools, and from the fact that after the scholars leave school no provision has been made for giving them the opportunity to receive such instruction, the farmers' institute has undertaken the training in agriculture of rural children after leaving school. In doing this it has found it necessary to drop from its system of instruction the purely educational feature and to devote itself strictly to giving vocational instruction. Such studies and practice, therefore, as the institute utilizes have in view the perfecting of the individual in his vocation. The institute system, therefore, partakes more nearly than any other of the trade-school method, and is intended for youths above 14 years of age. It will become the connecting link between the agricultural-club movement on the one hand and the regular farmers' institutes for adults on the other (120).

In 1909, 20 states and territories are reported to have held institutes for young people. This system seems to be the best organized in Indiana, where about one-third of the counties have such institutes with an enrolment of over 12,000. The young people's institutes are held at the same time as the farm-

[6] From a letter written by L. N. Duncan, U.S. demonstrator for Alabama, and professor of school agriculture, Alabama State Agricultural College.

ers' institutes but in separate sessions. The public is interested as indicated by liberal contributions, one county appropriating in 1909 $1,000 for this work.

The extension department of the Kansas State Agricultural College is just introducing a correspondence school in connection with its young people's extension work. The object of this is similar to that of the young people's institute, being designed to help boys and girls who have been compelled to leave school.

The boys' clubs of Kansas, whose work thus far has been almost wholly confined to corn contests, are now being organized on a somewhat different basis. The plan follows that of the Boy Scouts of America and the clubs are known as the "Rural-Life Scouts." Although just started, considerable interest is being shown in these clubs. The leaders are generally principals of village schools or pastors of village churches. In counties where there is a Y.M.C.A. secretary, the organizations are affiliated with the Y.M.C.A. work.

The county superintendent of education and his teachers have been an important factor in making boys' clubs a success, whether under the auspices of the Government Demonstration Work, state agricultural colleges, or state departments of education. The work in large units, state or sectional, is really made possible by successful work carried out by county superintendents of schools or teachers in the various parts of the country. It may be of interest at this point to give somewhat in detail a concrete example of how a county superintendent of education went about organizing successful boys' agricultural clubs in his own county.

The county superintendent of Delaware County, Iowa, began to organize boys' clubs six years ago, holding township meetings where the boys brought corn selected from their fathers' seed corn. The meetings were addressed by an expert, on "What Constitutes Good Seed Corn." This was accompanied by demonstrations from samples of poor and good ears. The corn brought by the boys was then judged and commented upon by the expert. The superintendent then distributed seed corn which he had bought for this purpose. The year following the boys came together in a contest showing the results obtained from the corn distributed the year before. This work was continued through the next year, except that the boys selected their own seed corn from their fathers' corn. A short course in agriculture was held at Manchester, the county seat, where about sixty boys attended. The corn clubs continued to grow in interest from year to year until most of the boys were as good judges of corn as, or even better than, their fathers. Last year the work was varied by using oats instead of corn. The superintendent purchased forty bushels of Canadian oats, and distributed the seed among the boys of the county. At the close of the season a contest was held at which the results of the season's work were shown. The experiment was watched with much interest throughout the county, and the farmers were eager to purchase seed from the boys for their own farms. In one year the value of Canadian oats for Delaware County was demonstrated by the boys, and oat production in the county was greatly improved.

All this was extra school work, but the superintendent made good use of the interest thus aroused to help and improve the regular school work. Raising corn and oats became subjects of compositions, references to bulletins and books were used as reading lessons, and estimates of cost and yield furnished material for arithmetic. By means of printed instructions sent to teachers from time to time, the formal work of the schools became enlivened and strengthened by its practical application.

The work in Delaware County is a typical example of how the education of a county or township system may be redirected by means of boys' clubs. Springfield Township, Ohio (119), Keokuk (44) and Page (121) counties, Iowa, Natchitoches Parish, Louisiana, Winnebago County, Illinois (122, 123), Wexford County, Michigan, and many other places might be mentioned where boys' agricultural clubs have not only been the means of improving school conditions but by their success have led to similar work being introduced in other places.

Although not connected in any way with the public schools, the work of W. B. Otwell, editor of the *Otwell's Farmer Boy,*

Carlinville, Ill., deserves special mention. Mr. Otwell is chiefly responsible for the beginning of the state-wide development of boys' corn clubs in Illinois, and had charge of their exhibit at the St. Louis Exposition, where 1,250 boys' exhibits received awards. By means of his paper he is interesting a large number of boys of the Middle West. He is conducting at present a corn contest in which 25,000 boys are competing.[7] Another feature of his boys' club is an annual encampment for those who can attend, for the purpose of agricultural study.

In order to give description in sufficient detail, the foregoing discussion of boys' agricultural clubs has been limited to a few typical examples of what is now actually being accomplished. References have been made from time to time to the public interest in the clubs and to their influence upon the public schools.

It was the intention in preparation of this article to include a fuller discussion of the relation of this movement to rural education than space will now permit. Opinions have been gathered from a number of state superintendents, and from others interested in rural education as to the reaction of the agricultural club movement upon the rural schools. These opinions are well summed up in the following:

> Keeps boys in school longer; gives teacher greater influence and power; convinces farmers that school people want to and can be useful to the farming interests, and tends to make the school the center of community life; stirs farmers to greater endeavor and to better methods of farming, and increases general interest in agriculture and returns.

Perhaps the most important contribution that these clubs are now making to agricultural education in the public schools is in the recognition by the patrons of the direct value in dollars and cents that such instruction has, a recognition which will lead to better support and interest of the community in the schools.

## BIBLIOGRAPHY

The facts of the text have been gathered chiefly from correspondence with those interested in boys' agricultural clubs in various parts of the country. Only references indicated by number in the text are included in the following list.

[7] *Otwell's Farmer Boy*, Carlinville, Ill., December, 1910.

118. "Boys' and Girls' Agricultural Clubs," F. W. HOWE, U.S. Department of Agriculture, *Farmers' Bulletin No. 385* (1910), 23.

This bulletin contains history, plans, and recent development of these clubs under the following heads: Introductory Summary of Results; How Work Has Been Accomplished in Several States; Assistance Given by the Department of Agriculture; The Relation of Club Work to Rural Education; Suggestions for Organization; List of References; Statistics.

119. "Agricultural Clubs in Rural Schools," HOMER C. PRICE, *Ohio State University Bulletin*, Ser. 7, No. 10 (1904), 14.

The bulletin contains suggestions for organizing clubs in the rural schools of Ohio. These suggestions are the outgrowth of the previous year's experience of the first club formed in Ohio under the auspices of the students of the Agricultural Union. This bulletin is of special interest because it represents the beginning of organized effort to develop agricultural clubs in Ohio.

120. "Farmers' Institutes for Young People," JOHN HAMILTON, U.S. Department of Agriculture, Office of Experiment Stations, *Circular No. 99* (1910), 40.

This circular calls attention to "lack of adequate means for giving vocational training in agriculture to young people in rural districts after they leave the public school and before they enter upon their life occupations." Boys' and girls' clubs, farmers' institutes for young people, subjects for institute study, systematic course for contest work, boys' encampments, form of organization, season for meeting, states and territories in which young people's institutes are organized, model constitution for young people's institutes, order of topics for boys' institute, score cards for various products, are some of the subjects discussed.

121. *Boys' Agricultural Club Bulletin*, JESSIE FIELD, Office of County Superintendent of Schools, Clarinda, Iowa (1909), 14.

This bulletin gives an account of the boys' club of Page County, Iowa, including summary of results of 1908 and plans for 1909.

122. *The Winnebagoes*, O. J. KERN, Office of County Superintendent of Schools, Rockford, Ill. (1903). Pp. 64.

This is a report of the Winnebago County (Ill.) schools, with suggestions for their improvement. One chapter (pp. 39–49) is devoted to boys' and girls' clubs. An account is given of the Boys' Experimental Club organized in 1902. This was one of the first boys' agricultural clubs organized in the United States.

123. *Among Country Schools*, O. J. KERN, New York: Ginn & Co. (1906). Pp. 366.

This is one of the best contributions to rural education that has been written. One chapter is devoted to a Boys' Experiment Club (pp. 129–57).

# A BRIEF REPORT OF THE MOSCOW EXPERIMENTAL SCHOOL

N. KICITCHKO

A few of us who are interested in the newest methods of teaching determined to open a small experimental school, where we could put these methods to the test, and watch their effect upon the children's development. We also wished to prove to teachers that the new methods could be gradually ingrafted on the old school system, without entirely supplanting the latter. Moreover, we wished to show that special training for the teachers was not indispensable. This is an important point, because nowhere in Russia is special training for the new teaching obtainable. Therefore we were obliged to follow the usual program of the primary school, changing only the method of teaching. Our teachers had the same training as those of the usual public primary schools. There was among us a former teacher from one of these schools, who undertook the teaching in our school.

As we wished the school to be within reach of all, we fixed the school fee at 3 rubles yearly.

*The principles of the school.*—Our school is based on the following principles: the development of individuality, independence of character, and observation in the child, and the avoidance from the first of all mechanical routine. For developing the critical faculties of the children we depend largely upon frank criticism of the work of the class. Education by observation must be based on teaching the children to express their thoughts and impressions by manual work. Full scope must be given to their imagination and creative power.

*The program* is as follows: Scripture history, which is obligatory in all Russian schools, Russian, arithmetic, nature-study, manual work, and drawing. We do not use exclusively the phonetic method in teaching Russian, as phonetics make but slight impression on the memory, and our first object is to catch the eye and memory of the children. We have therefore prepared a special primer for use in our school. In teaching arithmetic we make a point of convincing the children of the value of counting in their own everyday lives. Then we gradually carry them on to more abstract calculations. We take care that they shall see each new problem worked out before them. In teaching nature-study to the youngest class we convey no new knowledge to the children, but make it our aim to adjust the impressions already gathered by them from familiar objects. Therefore we do not make nature-study a separate branch of instruction. Neither are manual work and drawing distinct branches; they form a necessary integral part of the study of Russian, arithmetic, and nature-study. Manual work and drawing are the means the children have of expressing their thoughts and fancies—their language, in fact. There are no special drawing-lessons, drawing serving simply as a means of illustrating the other subjects. Free play is given to the children's creative power. The teacher does not correct the drawings, but these are criticized by the whole class, and the ones which are approved are exhibited. This criticizing proves most useful.

*The idea of the school.*—The fundamental idea of the school is that reliance should be placed on the children themselves. It is they who have to keep the place in order; and discipline is maintained by the keen interest the children take in their lessons. The result of the children's criticizing each piece of work produced is that they all participate in it, and so learn to estimate the capacity of each child, and to be indulgent toward the less capable. The general interest thus awakened in the work makes for thoroughness, accord, and independence of character. Offenders are tried by their companions, to whose decision they have to submit. Thus the teacher is relieved from maintaining discipline, having rather to act as defender of the culprit, as his schoolmates are inclined to pass very severe sentences. Consequently the relations between teacher and pupils are most friendly, and the children love their school. This shows beyond all doubt that we are on the right track.

The whole school (25 children—boys and girls) is in the hands of a single teacher; the rest of us help her by criticisms, and aid in working out programs and methods.

Our experimental school has proved that it is possible to introduce drawing and manual work into elementary schools, and get the child to express in drawing what he sees and understands. In giving full liberty to the child's faculty of criticism we develop his independence of thought and individuality in work.

# EDITORIAL NOTES

There has just come from the press of the Macmillan Company Vol. I of a comprehensive educational treatise which is to contain in five volumes a general survey of all the topics which the teacher and the educational administrator discuss in their practical and technical conferences. Such psychological terms as "abstraction," "adolescence," and "attention" are treated. Such practical problems as "Air in the Schoolroom" and the "School System of Alabama" are taken up in this first volume. One finds here also all the higher institutions of learning, the chief persons who have figured in educational history, all the subjects of instruction, such as "architecture" and "agriculture."

**A Cyclopedia of Education**

The editor of this cyclopedia is Professor Paul Monroe, whose works on the history of education are universally known and appreciated. The list of departmental editors includes fifteen leading students of educational problems in this country and England.

**Editor**

This note is not intended as a review of the work; such an account will appear in the course of time and will take up fully the contents and character of the work. In the meantime it is worthy of comment that such a work has appeared in the English language. American teachers have been discussing for many years the possibility of developing a general body of educational doctrine which shall give unity to educational practice. In Germany they have had for some years a comprehensive work of the type now presented in English, in Rein's *Encyclopedia.* To be sure, the German work has not solved the problem of unifying German schools. Nor can any English work solve all our American problems. But both works serve in a very direct fashion to bring educational interests to a focus. There will be contradictions in the present work, there will be many posi-

**General Significance of the Book**

tions defended which will not stand in the years to come; but at all events we have now a common basis for discussions and for future formulations. This cyclopedia shows in definite form what has been achieved in America toward a definition of education, and it will promote further evolution by making clear what is past and by its statement of present practices and present aims.

This cyclopedia serves one purpose which has been the subject of editorial comment in earlier numbers of this journal.

**Educational Terminology**

We have here a common foundation on which to develop a technical educational terminology. There is no possibility of a general interest in educational science until teachers master some of the terms appropriate to their profession. The architect, the banker, the engineer, all find it necessary to master a technical terminology, and these specialists do not complain when books and articles addressed to them contain such special terms. Teachers have been less willing than members of other professions to master the terminology necessary in their special discussions. Indeed, there has been no good book to which the teacher could turn for explanation of these terms. Here is such a book of reference. When writers on education use technical words in the future, they can do it with some assurance that the reader who wishes to study education seriously has a reference work. All discussions will be made accessible by this work.

Finally, the book contains a great deal of material which will at once command universal acceptance. It is, therefore,

**Brings Together and Formulates Doctrines**

a strong influence in the direction of a central rational interpretation of American education. The articles present a body of scholarly material which will command respect from readers in other departments of science and letters. The intelligent general reader will also find here a broad view of school problems and educational doctrine. For what it contains, for what it codifies and makes available, and for what it promises, the book will be most heartily welcomed by all who are laboring to make American education scientific and systematic.

**The Committee of Seven of the Northern Illinois Superintendents' and Principals' Association**

The report of the Committee of Seven of the Northern Illinois Superintendents' and Principals' Association will appear in the April and May numbers of this journal. The complete report will be in the hands of members of the Association by April 10. The annual meeting will be held at DeKalb, as usual, on May 5 and 6. The special topic this year is "Elementary Science." The Committee of Seven has held a meeting in Chicago each month since September, and its report is now in the hands of a subcommittee for final writing.

# BOOK REVIEWS

*Richard of Jamestown, Mary of Plymouth, Ruth of Boston, Calvert of Maryland, Peter of New Amsterdam, Stephen of Philadelphia.* By JAMES OTIS. New York: American Book Co., 1910. Cloth, 12mo, about 165 pages each, with illustrations. 35 cents.

This series of six volumes is intended for supplementary history reading in the middle grades of the elementary schools. Its purpose as stated by the author is "to show the children the home life of the colonists" and "to give such homely facts as are not to be found in the real histories of our land." The stories are told "from the viewpoint of a child and purport to have been related by a child." They describe the life of the colonists in an intimate way, giving many details of the appearance of the country, the occupations of the people, the building and furnishing of their homes, their household life and comforts, and their hardships and privations in a new and strange land.

While "these books are not sent out as histories," they furnish exactly the kind of information necessary to make history a genuine study for children of ten and eleven years. Children at this time crave details which help them to feel at home in the life of the past. They get little satisfaction from the brief, abstract statements of the ordinary textbook. The details here chosen are well selected, often from the historical sources, and are given with much of the charm of the original narratives.

Many teachers will no doubt miss in these books the plot and continuous narrative of the ordinary story, but they will find the descriptions of colonial life and work as interesting as stories and more suggestive of problems that provoke thought and discussion on the part of the children. The books should be used as intended by the author in connection with works of "real history."

We have had much supplementary reading covering the events of our early history but no works treating in any adequate way of industrial and social life. Otis has given us books of a unique type, but a type that should become common for both elementary and secondary schools. This series treats of the very beginnings of colonial history and might well be followed by a series giving the later developments of colonial industries and the effects of these industries upon society. For instance, *Richard of Jamestown* ends just as tobacco becomes the leading product of Virginia, and a study of tobacco culture and its influence would be especially valuable.

The series is well planned to give studies of typical northern, southern, and middle colonies. The illustrations are attractive and in general well selected to explain the narrative.

E. J. R.

# BOOKS RECEIVED

## AMERICAN BOOK CO., NEW YORK

*A Language Series, Book I.* By ROBERT C. METCALF AND AUGUSTINE L. RAFTER. Cloth. Illustrated. Pp. 256. $0.40.

*A Language Series, Book II.* By ROBERT C. METCALF AND AUGUSTINE L. RAFTER. Cloth. Illustrated. Pp. 365. $0.60.

*Calvert of Maryland.* By JAMES OTIS. Cloth. Illustrated. Pp. 166. $0.35.

*Christmas Carols and Hymns for School and Choir.* Compiled by HOLLIS DANN. Cloth. Pp. 112. $0.45.

*Nature Study by Grades.* By HORACE H. CUMMINGS. Cloth. Illustrated. Pp. 274. $0.75.

*Practical Elementary Algebra.* By JOS. V. COLLINS. Cloth. Pp. 301. $0.85.

*Speaking and Writing: Book II.* By WILLIAM H. MAXWELL, EMMA L. JOHNSON, AND MADALENE D. BARNUM. Cloth. Illustrated. Pp. 128. $0.23.

*Stories of the King.* By JAMES BALDWIN. Cloth. Illustrated. Pp. 335. $0.50.

*The Story of Old France.* By H. A. GUERBER. Cloth. Illustrated. Pp. 374. $0.65.

## THOMAS Y. CROWELL & CO., NEW YORK

*The Land of Living Men.* By RALPH WALDO TRINE. Cloth. Pp. 302. $1.25.

## HARPER & BROS., NEW YORK

*Class Teaching and Management.* By WILLIAM ESTABROOK CHANCELLOR. Cloth. Illustrated. Pp. 343. $1.00.

*Harpers' Book of Little Plays.* By MARGARET SUTTON BRISCOE, JOHN KENDRICK BANGS, CAROLINE A. CREEVEY, MARGARET E. SANGSTER, AND OTHERS, with an introduction by MADALENE D. BARNUM. Cloth. Illustrated. Pp. 142. $0.75.

*The Children's Plutarch: Tales of the Romans.* By F. J. GOULD, with an introduction by W. D. HOWELLS. Cloth. Illustrated. Pp. 171. $0.50.

*The Children's Plutarch: Tales of the Greeks.* By F. J. GOULD, with an introduction by W. D. HOWELLS. Cloth. Illustrated. Pp. 167. $0.50.

*The Young Forester.* By ZANE GREY. Cloth. Illustrated. Pp. 224. $1.25.

*Travels in History by Mark Twain.* Selected from the works of Mark Twain by C. N. KENDALL. Cloth. Illustrated. Pp. 171. $0.50.

## LITTLE, BROWN & CO., BOSTON

*A Knight of Arthur's Court.* By JOHN HARRINGTON COX. Cloth. Illustrated. Pp. 95. $0.50.

*Beowulf the Anglo-Saxon Epic.* By JOHN HARRINGTON COX. Cloth. Illustrated. Pp. 91. $0.50.

*Fanciful Flower Tales Overheard in Fairyland.* By MADGE BIGHAM. Cloth. Illustrated. Pp. 162. $0.50.

*Grasshopper Green's Garden.* By Julia Augusta Schwartz. Cloth. Illustrated. Pp. 197. $0.60.

*Heroes of Chivalry and Their Deeds.* By Frances Nimmo Greene and Dolly Williams Kirk. Cloth. Illustrated. Pp. 199. $0.60.

*Smoky Day's Wigwam Evenings: Indian Stories Retold.* By Charles A. Eastman and Elaine Goodale Eastman. Cloth. Illustrated. Pp. 148. $0.60.

*Stories of British History.* By Tom Bevan. Cloth. Illustrated. Pp. 205. $0.50.

*The Children of History: Early Times.* By Mary S. Hancock. Cloth. Illustrated. Pp. 142. $0.50.

*The Children of History: Later Times.* By Mary S. Hancock. Cloth. Illustrated. Pp. 193. $0.50.

*The Louisa May Alcott Story Book.* Edited for schools by Jenny E. Coe. Cloth. Illustrated. Pp. 202. $0.50.

## THE MACMILLAN CO., NEW YORK

*A Modern Dictionary of the English Language.* Cloth. Pp. 765. $0.60.

*Child Problems.* By George B. Mangold. Cloth. Pp. 381. $1.25.

# CURRENT EDUCATIONAL LITERATURE IN THE PERIODICALS[1]

IRENE WARREN
Librarian, School of Education, The University of Chicago

ATWOOD, WALLACE W. The first-year science course in high school. School R. 19:119–23. (Fe. '11.)

AYRES, HARRY MORGAN. The degree of Master of Arts. Educa. R. 41:161–69. (Fe. '11.)

BAGLEY, WILLIAM C. Entrance requirements and "college domination" as sources of motivation in high-school work. School R. 19:73–84. (Fe. '11.)

BENNETT, CHARLES A. Visiting manual training schools in Europe (8). Man. Train. Mag. 12:247–70. (Fe. '11.)

BISHOP, E. S. Some new modifications of old experiments in physics. School R. 19:114–18. (Fe. '11.)

BOWEN, W. P. The classification of playground activities. Amer. Physical Educa. Rev. 16:44–50. (Ja. '11.)

BROWN, J. C. An investigation on the value of drill work in the fundamental operations of arithmetic. Journ. of Educa. Psychol. 2:81–88. (Fe. '11.)

BUTLER, NATHANIEL. Report of the joint committee on the relations between the University of Chicago and co-operating secondary schools. School R. 19:124–27. (Fe. '11.)

BUTLER, NICHOLAS MURRAY. The revolt of the unfit. Educa. R. 41:109–15. (Fe. '11.)

Colleges and high schools. Nation 92:30–31. (12 Ja. '11.)

Co-operative research work in school practice. Teach. College Rec. 12:2–4. (Ja. '11.)

CRAWSHAW, FRED. D. The relation between and the content in manual training and engineering shop courses (1). Man. Train. Mag. 12:209–17. (Fe. '11.)

DAVIS, BENJAMIN MARSHALL. Agricultural education: agricultural societies. El. School T. 11:266–74. (Ja. '11.)

[1] *Abbreviations.*—Amer. Phys. Educa. Rev., American Physical Education Review; Cent., Century; Educa. News, Educational News; Educa. R., Educational Review; El. School T., Elementary School Teacher; Journ. of Educa. (Bost.), Journal of Education (Boston); Journ. of Educa. (Lond.), Journal of Education (London); Journ. of Educa. Psychol., Journal of Educational Psychology; Man. Train. Mag., Manual Training Magazine; Pop. Sci. Mo., Popular Science Monthly; Primary Educa., Primary Education; School R., School Review; School W., School World; Sci. Amer. Sup., Scientific American Supplement; Teach. College Rec., Teachers College Record.

DAVIS, W. M. The disciplinary value of geography. Pop. Sci. Mo. 78:105–19. (Fe. '11.)

DEARBORN, GEORGE V. N. Attention: certain of its aspects and a few of its relations to physical education (3). Amer. Physical Educa. Rev. 16: 26–40. (Ja. '11.)

Experimental science teaching: some applications of Mariotte's bottle. Sci. Amer. Sup. 71:36. (21 Ja. '11.)

FOSTER, W. S. The effect of practice upon visualizing and upon the reproduction of visual impressions. Journ. of Educa. Psychol. 2:11–22. (Ja. '11.)

FRANKLIN, W. S. Physics from the college point of view. Educa. R. 41:82–89. (Ja. '11.)

FREUDENTHAL, WOLFF. Dry air in the schoolroom. Amer. Physical Educa. Rev. 16:23–25. (Ja. '11.)

GOETTSCH, CHARLES. A visit to the Frankfort *Musterschule*. School R. 19:103–13. (Fe. '11.)

HANEY, JAMES PARTON. Twenty-one years of manual training (1). Man. Train. Mag. 12:218–36. (Fe. '11.)

JASTROW, JOSEPH. An American academician. Educa. R. 41:27–33. (Ja. '11.)

JOHNSON, HARROLD. The basis of moral education: a lesson from France. Journ. of Educa. (Lond.) 42:19–22. (Ja. '11.)

KING, IRVING. The problem and content of a course in the social aspects of education. Journ. of Educa. Psychol. 2:23–34. (Ja. '11.)

LEAVITT, FRANK M. The relation of the movement for vocational and industrial training to the secondary schools. School R. 19:85–95. (Fe. '11.)

LINN, JAMES WEBER. What the university expects of high-school students in English. School R. 19:96–102. (Fe. '11.)

MCANDREW, WILLIAM. How to choose a public-school teacher. World's Work 21:13965–66. (Fe. '11.)

MACDONALD, WILLIAM. The interest of the public in the college curriculum. Educa. R. 41:60–70. (Ja. '11.)

MEYERS, IRA BENTON. The evolution of aim and method in the teaching of nature-study in the common schools of the United States (2). El. School T. 11:237–48. (Ja. '11.)

MONTMORENCY, J. E. G. DE. The medieval education of women. Journ. of Educa. (Lond.) 42:22–24. (Ja. '11.)

(The) more recent developments of education. School W. 13:15–17. (Ja. '11.)

(The) most notable school books of 1910. School W. 13:17–20. (Ja. '11.)

O'SHEA, M. V. Readings in great educators. Primary Educa. 19:65–66. (Fe. '11.)

PARKINSON, WILLIAM D. Sex and education. Educa. R. 41:42–59. (Ja. '11.)

RANCK, SAMUEL H. The use of the library lecture room. Lib. Journ. 36:9–14. (Ja. '11.)

Report on teaching technical grammar. Teach. College Rec. 12:5–22. (Ja. '11.)

RISLEY, JAMES H. The social service of public schools as indicated by the results of a study of a typical community. El. School T. 11:225–36. (Ja. '11.)

SALMON, LUCY M. The historical museum. Educa. R. 41:144–60. (Fe. '11.)

SAVAGE, WATSON L. Physiological and pathological effects of severe exertion (The Marathon race) (2). Amer. Physical Educa. Rev. 16:1–11 (Ja. '11.)

Secondary education in New Zealand. School W. 13:7–11. (Ja. '11.)

SHOWERMAN, GRANT. The Foxfielders at school. Educa. R. 41:1–26. (Ja. '11.)

SKINNER, M. M. Aspects of German teaching in America. Educa. R. 41:34–41. (Ja. '11.)

SMILEY, W. S. A comparative study of the results obtained in instruction in the "single teacher" rural schools and the graded town schools. El. School T. 11:249–65. (Ja. '11.)

SMYTH, HERBERT WEIR. Graecia capta. Educa. R. 41:116–26. (Fe. '11.)

STECHER, WILLIAM A. Philadelphia playgrounds. Amer. Physical Educa. Rev. 16:51–53. (Ja. '11.)

STEELE, ASA. The moving-picture show. World's Work 21:14018–32. (Fe. '11.)

STRAYER, GEORGE DRAYTON. Measuring results in education. Journ. of Educa. Psychol. 2:3–10. (Ja. '11.)

THORNDIKE, EDWARD L. Mental fatigue. Journ. of Educa. Psychol. 2:61–80. (Fe. '11.)

UPDEGRAFF, HARLAN. Improvement of the rural school. Educa. R. 41:135–43. (Fe. '11.)

VAILE, E. O. Reading for thought and its cultivation in school. Educa. R. 41:71–81. (Ja. '11.)

WELLS, AMOS R. Secret societies in high schools. Journ. of Educa. (Bost.) 73:5–9. (5 Ja. '11.)

WEST, ANDREW F. The proposed graduate college of Princeton. Cent. 81:600–12. (Fe. '11.)

WHITNEY, FRANK P. Differentiation of courses in the seventh and eighth grades. Educa. R. 41:127–34. (Fe. '11.)

WILLIAMS, J. E. The administration of justice in Dundee. Educa. News. 36:3–6 (6 Ja. '11.)

WOOLLATT, G. H. Handwork in relation to science teaching: the manipulative skill of the teacher. School W. 13:23–24. (Ja. '11.)

VOLUME XI NUMBER 8

# THE ELEMENTARY SCHOOL TEACHER

APRIL, 1911

## SUPERINTENDENTS' AND PRINCIPALS' ASSOCIATION OF NORTHERN ILLINOIS

DEKALB, ILLINOIS, MAY 5 AND 6, 1911

## REPORT OF COMMITTEE OF SEVEN ON AN OUTLINE COURSE OF STUDY ON A SCIENTIFIC BASIS

### SPECIAL SUBJECT—ELEMENTARY SCIENCE

*Committee of Seven*

DANIEL A. TEAR, Chicago, *Chairman*

H. A. BONE, Batavia
M. G. CLARK, Streator
R. G. JONES, Kewanee
IRA B. MEYERS, Chicago
JESSE L. SMITH, Highland Park
C. W. WHITTEN, DeKalb

### PROGRAM

*Friday, May 5*, 1:30 P.M.

REPORT OF THE COMMITTEE OF SEVEN, ON ELEMENTARY SCIENCE—
- General Statement: DANIEL A. TEAR.
- Fundamental Principles: M. G. CLARK.
- The Course of Study—
  - The Primary Period, including the Kindergarten: Discussion led by IRA B. MEYERS.

*Friday, May 5*, 7:30 P.M.

- The Course of Study (*continued*)—
  - The Intermediate Period: Discussion led by H. A. BONE AND JESSE L. SMITH.

*Saturday, May 6*, 8:30 A.M.

BUSINESS SESSION.
- The Course of Study (*continued*)—
  - The Adolescent Period: Discussion led by C. W. WHITTEN.

### OFFICERS OF THE ASSOCIATION

R. G. JONES, Kewanee........President
A. M. BLOOD, Park Ridge........Vice-President
L. A. HATCH, DeKalb........Secretary
W. W. COULTAS, Sycamore........Treasurer

EXECUTIVE COMMITTEE

Daniel A. Tear, Chicago..............................Term expires 1911
C. M. Bardwell, Aurora..............................Term expires 1912
Jesse L. Smith, Highland Park..............................Term expires 1913

## SCIENCE IN THE SCHOOL: ITS PLACE AND PURPOSE

Science finds its place in the school through the child's need of science information or science experience. It is probable that this need is not often consciously felt by the child, but whenever he is so conditioned in his relations with his environment—nature, social, industrial, etc.—that science information or science experience would enable him to react more intelligently to that environment and thus give him greater efficiency in meeting his problems, then we say that the child has a "need of science," a need that should be met at such a time and in such a way that it will prove most helpful to the child. In the early grades we can hardly, perhaps, call either the material of study "science" or the method of approach technically "scientific." Throughout the grades, however, the purpose of the science course should be so to meet these needs as to give to the child an experience of the various phases of his environment that will differentiate into those more technical and scientific investigations which his developing experiences, interests, and broadening opportunities will demand. If, in this way, we meet the child's needs of today we best prepare him for the larger, deeper needs of tomorrow.

Again, if the course of study in the lower grades is based upon the child's nature, social, and industrial environment, and has been planned to meet the child's developing needs; if this mass of thought-material and its motor expressions has been definitely worked out along the same lines and in accordance with the former reports of this committee; then nature-study and elementary science must constitute an important part of the subject-matter for these grades. The home life, the neighborhood life, and the industrial life of the community have furnished science material more abundantly than the school has been able to take advantage of. The child in the kitchen must experience the problem of boiling, freezing, and evaporating water, and there is constantly open to him something of the problem of home and community sanitation; the home garden introduces him to all the secrets of germinating, growing, flowering, and fruiting plants as well as to the various forms of insect and animal life that enter into the garden economy; his constantly expanding world experiences should lead him to the investigation of his geographical and elementary geological environments; the neighborhood brings its problems of scientific co-operation; and so one series of problems after another forces itself upon the child's attention and gives ample basis for the elementary science of the schools. It is not the "finding" of material but rather the "elimination" of material that becomes the serious problem of the teacher. The real work of the teacher in this field of the child's interests is so to direct the child's activities that he will be really appreciating, organizing, and controlling his more fundamental science experiences. At this stage there are no separate sciences. It is a study of the child's daily experiences. It is, in embryo, a study of all the sciences.

In the higher grades the problems gradually tend toward a specialization of the subject, but the danger is in specializing too rapidly rather than in continuing too long the unifications of the science material with the general subject-matter of the grade. We must never forget that the subject-matter of the grades, so far as it has an excuse for being at all, is a response to the needs of the expanding community life of the child and must find its interpretation in that life. All the departments of school activity demand an understanding of science facts and each of these, in turn, will suggest or require other facts which will keep the child constantly in touch with his science environment. It is not sufficient that the child talk about springs, wells, flood plains, or the general effect of frost and weather upon the rocks and soil. He should see these things, experience them in nature, and work them over in the classroom laboratory. Construct a spring in the sand pan, dig a well, disintegrate rocks, make drawings of all the observable phenomena and write up their history. Here again we should observe that the elementary-science course cannot be a formal statement of science facts to be taught in every school. To a great extent the course should depend upon the industries of the community and natural environment of the child. The children in the neighborhood of Highland Park, for example, have a nature environment that should enter largely into their science work, but such work would be without meaning to the children of Streator. Ottawa, LaSalle, and Peru have a natural means for geographical and elementary geological investigation which gives them a great advantage over the schools of many other parts of the state and should place them among the leaders in that line of science study. Streator and many other cities must depend more largely upon their industrial advantages, while the country schools have a rich field in their agricultural opportunities. If these varied opportunities were used by all schools, as they some time will be, we should find them affecting more largely the life-interests of their graduates. Highland Park should become the birthplace of naturalists, Ottawa of geologists, and Streator of captains of industry. It is to these needs that the course of study should give heed. If the course of study is scientifically planned the child is constantly thinking and investigating more deeply into his industrial and nature environment, his experiences are demanding a better and truer understanding of all these problems, and science will find the child, again and again, knocking at the door for necessary information. If the real needs of the various fields of activity are taken care of, the work of the earlier years will have built up a basis of science material and science experiences ready for organization that should double the value and efficiency of the later school work.

Little needs to be said of the science organizations of the high school more than that they should meet the industrial and economic demands of the community life first, and the demands of the higher institutions of learning second. The great majority of the high schools, if they are to serve their communities, must choose their science more from the standpoint of the needs of agriculture, horticulture, and the field of home industries and home economics than they have done in the past. The child feels but little or no need for botany, zoölogy, and chemistry as now taught in our high-school courses. He does need, because of his community environment, a scientific knowledge of elementary agriculture which should carry him into a far more intelligent scientific and economic study of plant and animal life. Here is the real high-school field for botany and zoölogy. Again, the pupil needs a chemical knowledge of soils and soil reactions and, in industrial communities, of clays, sands, minerals, and the means for their reduction and use. He needs to know the physics of heating and lighting plants, of gas manufacture, and of the practical appliances of the hundred and one things of the community life. In other words, the science courses of the high school should be organized about the community problems, and when this shall have been accomplished a course will have been organized that will form a practical basis for the more technical work of the college and university.

The public school, then, is not the place for the development of science "for science' sake" or from the more purely scientific standpoint. Its purpose is to give the child an understanding of his daily reactions and to give meaning and point to all his relations in the social and industrial world. If it does all this, and does it efficiently, it will at the same time, for those who are so situated that they can heed the call, so engage the interests of the pupil as to cause him to desire a more thorough and better organized scientific experience.

## THE CHILD AND NATURE

This report is based upon the work of the Committee of Seven for the preceding five years. It has been the purpose of the committee not to depart from the fundamental lines laid down in previous reports. It accepts the proposition that education is a process of adjustment; that conscious intellectual development and the higher aspirations and ideals of man, as well as the organized physical and social activities by which man accomplishes his ideals, are the outgrowth of fundamental necessities essential to all living beings. Out of the struggle to live there is born a conception of higher things; an appreciation of worth; a love of beauty; a demand for ethical living; a realization of a wider range of human interests and activities that mean vastly more in human life than the getting of food, clothing, and shelter. For the human soul, more and more, the struggle for a chance to live becomes the means merely to a fuller, freer, and better living.

Man lives in a given concrete environment. Advancement and appreciation are in exact proportion to the control which he exercises over that environment. Control comes through the adjustment of the individual to his environment, and through the adjustment of environment to the individual. Or, to speak more exactly, control is the adjusting, harmonizing, and getting command of one's total world of experience. There are not two worlds. One's whole objective world, including the bodily organism, is a projection of certain experiences into space: that is, experience compels each one of us to construct, as it were, a world in space. Just what that world is to each one of us depends absolutely upon what one's experience has been. My world is not your world, nor is yours mine. Yet there is a community of experience, an agreement both in our own successive experiences and in the experiences of different persons, that compels one to accept a certain persistence in existence and a certain regularity in its changes. We posit a world governed by general laws which is not dependent upon thinking, of which world of reality we are a part.

This whole objective world of experience is the world of nature, with its facts and laws and ever-changing complexity. Nature-study in its widest sense takes in all objective phenomena.

## ELEMENTARY SCIENCE

Science is variously defined as "knowledge"; as "comprehension and understanding of truth or facts"; as "that which is known"; and specifically, as "knowledge duly arranged and referred to general truths and principles on which it is founded and from which it is derived." Science, then, according to these definitions, covers the whole range of knowledge. Any field of human thought may be attacked in a scientific way. It is the attitude taken toward subject-matter that makes the procedure scientific. In selecting the title of this report, "Elementary Science," the committee would emphasize the scientific attitude in elementary education. While it has not been the purpose of this committee to investigate all phases of elementary education that should be approached in a scientific way, yet, the committee would have it understood that it would include under elementary science much more than is usually understood by the term "nature-study." The committee is of the opinion that not only so-called natural history, but also the industries, civic activities, social institutions, and any other phase of concrete environment are proper objects of study under elementary science.

The local environment furnishes from the beginning the means essential to the development of the individual. As a matter of convenience in classification, environment is spoken of as being made up of two phases: (1) a so-called nature phase, (2) a so-called social phase. This is an artificial division, since man is as much a product of nature, and his activities are as fully in accord with nature, as any other living organism. This course of study deals with both aspects in so far as these aspects are of a natural and normal nature, in contrast with what are known as purely artificial conditions.

An inspection of our nature environment, in its pure sense, shows it to be made up of:

1. Earth-forming materials and their surface contour.
2. Weather, climate—the atmosphere.

3. Plant life.

4. Animal life.

5. Change, motion, work, energy in the form of (*a*) physical changes; (*b*) chemical changes.

The "social" environment, as distinct from the nature environment, possesses certain characters. Among the most important of these are:

1. Social institutions; as the family, government, church, school, etc.

2. Industrial and commercial activities.

3. Civic activities, etc.

Particularly in the lower grades has this committee felt free to draw upon any field of the child's interests for subject-matter in science.

## GENERAL METHOD

First and primarily, the committee would place itself on record as standing for the scientific attitude in education; for the attitude, on the part of the child, of inquiry, of investigation, of experimentation; for the establishment of facts and principles through such intelligent investigation and the application of the results thus secured by the child to his own problems. This whole point of view conceives education to be a process of growth and organization arising out of the meeting and mastering of actual living problems. The problems which the child is to investigate and solve are those inherent in his own living. The function of the school is to emphasize the more fundamental of these problems, to assist the child in bringing to consciousness the more important ones and to provide him with suitable material and give him intelligent directions in solving them. It is recognized that only as the child himself comes to appreciate his problems and really works out his own solution is he being educated.

The problem of the teacher, then, is largely one of directing the activities of the child. Upon him lies the responsibility of determining largely the sort of problems in which the child shall be engaged, the general method of procedure in solving these problems, and the degree of clearness and efficiency that shall result.

As already indicated, the course of study outlined in this report includes not only what is usually given under nature-study, or natural history, but also much of social and, particularly, industrial activities. Especially in the lower grades is it necessary to include a wide range of activities. Life is a unity. One's activities and interest have their meaning in this life unity. Every act and every thought plays its part in the whole. With younger children the whole range of interests become subject-matter for educational purposes. The work of the school in these earlier years is, largely, the enriching, the orientation, and the organizing of the child's experiences. The only restriction should be that the child's activities are directed along the more fundamental lines of human interests. Certain interests do appeal to every normal child because they are fundamental and universal. As the pupil advances, his range of interests widens so that it is impossible to take up all lines that might be desirable. It becomes necessary to limit the range of study. The committee believes that the solution here is the selection of a few fundamental typical phases of life and the thorough mastery of them.

Following the outline of the preceding reports, this report discusses elementary science under three general divisions: the primary period, including the kindergarten and the work of the first, second, and third years; the intermediate period, covering the work done in the fourth, fifth, and sixth years; and, finally, the adolescent period, which outlines the work that might be done in the seventh to the tenth years, inclusive. Further, the committee has thought best to suggest the general character of the science work that, in its judgment, ought to be given in the last two years of the high school.

# THE COURSE OF STUDY

## KINDERGARTEN, FIRST, SECOND, AND THIRD GRADES

The following brief outline takes its genesis from the Second Yearbook of the Association and attempts to apply the principles therein outlined to the education of young children. The fundamental idea has been that of initiating a mode of procedure which develops and maintains that unity in the growth process exhibited in the individual child.

Some of the more fundamental "appetences" exhibited up to and including the kindergarten are: (1) acquiring control of the more massive body muscles; (2) functioning of the senses; (3) acquiring a greater or lesser number of stable feelings, or impressions, through sensuous experiences; (4) purposeful activity begins to dominate over impulsive activity; (5) acquirement of a fairly extensive acquaintance with the objects and phenomena of environment; (6) acquiring a fairly extensive noun vocabulary, especially class names.

The child is alive with an active, insatiable curiosity, exhibiting a tendency to pry about, to handle things, to test them out with several or all of his senses, and having sensed them to his satisfaction he casts them aside and goes on to something else. In following him up we find that no object fails to attract his attention, and from all he extracts something which determines his attitude toward each kind of object upon a second meeting. Now, if these sense-acquired materials stimulate organic growth and develop motor control, our procedure should be plain. (To this we may add the need of becoming accustomed and adapted to social co-operation.)

1. Rambles in yards, fields, woods, along shores and streams, on farm and in garden, and countless other places should furnish exercise, sense-experience, motor control.

2. Games, plays, gathering flowers, nuts, berries, building blockhouses, and a mass of other activities should include social assimilation.

3. Meeting real things instead of pictures and artificial things, touching them, handling them, smelling them, tasting them, under proper guidance of a mother or teacher, should give the normal and proper concrete feeling or reaction. To do these things and do them in abundance is the need of the kindergarten. In this generalized condition pupils enter the kindergarten.

### THE KINDERGARTEN

In addition, the instinct of imitation will still be strong, and the more dominant activities carried on by the people of their community, as observed in the home, on the farm, and along the roads and streets, will form nuclei, attracting their attention and stimulating imitation. Certain centralizing ideas, around which may be grouped a considerable range of materials and activities, offer good starting-points for the teacher.

### *The Fall*

The season plays considerable part in these activities, and in the fall the leading idea may be: that as Nature stores up for her rest-time, so must we provide for winter months.

GENERAL TOPICS

I. Nature's storehouses and provisions for winter.
II. Animals' storehouses and provisions for winter.
III. Man's storehouses and preparations for storing.
IV. Utilization of Nature's provisions by man.

*Topic I.* Nature's storehouses and provisions for winter.
- *a*) Seeds and seed coverings (fruits, flowers, weeds, and vegetables).
- *b*) Distribution of seeds.
- *c*) Leaf-buds on trees in relation to falling leaves.
- *d*) Flowers going to sleep and storing up seeds.
- *e*) Tubers, bulbs, etc.

*Topic II.* Animals' storehouses and provisions for winter.
- *a*) Caterpillars.
- *b*) Bees.
- *c*) Squirrels.

*Topic III.* Man's storehouses and preparation for storing.
- *a*) Jars, cans, jelly-glasses, jugs, etc.
- *b*) Barrels, boxes, pantries, barns, cellars.
- *c*) General harvesting.

*Topic IV.* Utilization of Nature's storehouses by man.
- *a*) Preserving of fruits and vegetables.
- *b*) Grinding of grains into flour and meal.
- *c*) Storing of nuts, pop-corn, and fruits.

(The whole accompanied by appropriate exercises, stories, games, and songs.)

### *Winter*

When shut up together so closely in houses the idea of social interdependence may lead, and general topics as indicated may be studied.

I. Home dependences and relationships.
II. Interdependence of the home and those in commercial life who come closest to the child.
III. Dependence and relationships existing between man and Nature.

*Topic I.* Home dependences and relationships.
1. Clothing.
   - *a*) Sewing.
   - *b*) Mending.
   - *c*) Washing and ironing.
2. Food.
   - *a*) Cooking.
   - *b*) Setting the table.
   - *c*) Washing dishes.

3. Shelter.
    a) By whom provided.
    b) Father's work.
4. Watchful care.
    a) By father.
    b) By mother.
    c) By older sisters, brothers, etc.

This should lead directly to a feeling of dependence and desire on the part of the children to offer some equivalent for the care bestowed upon them. With the co-operation of the parents much real, lasting good may be done in the direction of helpfulness in the home.

*Topic II.* Commercial interdependence.

1. Milkman, our dependence upon him and his dependence upon us and upon the cow.
2. Groceryman upon farmer.
3. Shoemaker and mender upon animal skins.
4. Newspaper-man.
5. Gas-man.
6. Mail-carrier, etc., etc.

Through this thought may be instilled into their minds the whole policy of honest commercial life. These contributors to our welfare receive a just compensation for their kind and helpful service, and our contentment should not be complete until a balance be adjusted between benefits bestowed and received. In all our plays and games play-money may be used and a just compensation for value received insisted upon.

*Topic III.* Relationship to Nature.

1. Clothing.
    a) Cotton = cotton plant.
    b) Wool = sheep.
    c) Leather = skin of different animals.
2. Heat.
    a) Coal = mines; freight cars for transportation.
    b) Wood = kindling-man; lumber yards; forests.
3. Shelter.
    a) Wood = wood-chopper; saw-mill; furniture store.
4. Water and where obtained.
    a) Faucets.
    b) Hydrants.
    c) Lake.
    d) Pond.
    e) River.
    f) Source of water = clouds, sunshine, moisture.
5. Food.
    a) Grocer, the medium between us and the farmer.
    b) Farmer, the medium between us and nature.
    c) Nature and her servants = earth, air, water, and sunshine.
6. Ice, ice-cutting and packing.

### *Spring*

The activities accompanying the awakening of spring may be enumerated as follows:

1. Changes that are gradual and temporary.
   *a*) Daily change of clothing to suit weather conditions.
   *b*) Cool mornings and evenings and warm middays.
   *c*) Changes in the weather: sunshine, cool and warm winds, rain, clouds, fogs, dews, frosts, etc.
   *d*) First green spots of grass, places first appearing.
   *e*) Flower beds and garden-making activities—hotbed and indoor box-seedlings.
2. The more gradual and permanent changes in Nature.
   *a*) Changes wrought by the gradually increasing temperature: swelling of buds early spring flowers.
   *b*) Changes wrought by rain.
   *c*) Changes wrought by sunshine.
   *d*) Changes wrought by wind.
   *e*) Changes from bare brown earth and trees to green covering.
   *f*) Return of birds, insects, and other animal life.
3. Changes going on in the schoolroom more or less under the control of children.
   *a*) Seedlings, bulbs, cuttings in window boxes and pots.
   *b*) Changes in frog, salamander, etc., eggs, taking place in aquarium.
   *c*) Changes taking place in cocoons collected in the previous fall.
   *d*) Changes going on with a pair of doves or pigeons, etc., in nest building, incubation, hatching and rearing brood: The whole used to stimulate observations on similar changes and activities out-of-doors.

#### PRIMARY PERIOD

*Characteristics.*—The general "appetences" of the earlier years are still present and maturing. Curiosity and its accompanying restless activity are still strong, but purposeful activities are beginning to dominate over impulsive activities. Children have acquired considerable ability to do definite bits of work in the form of study, observations, experimentation, making, etc., under the guidance of some simple idea. They are rapidly discovering their ability to do purposeful and useful things, and have a strong personal pride in doing things through their own initiative, and they expect attention from adults in describing or viewing the results. To the extent to which the teacher and the school afford the children opportunity and encouragement in doing independent work, to that extent the children will grow rapidly in power of self-reliance and individual initiative, and free the teacher from details; to the extent that the teacher and the school fail they induce dependence and load themselves with a mass of detail and drudgery.

*First grade.*—In this stage children begin to write short sentences and describe simple experiences; they have acquired considerable power in self-control and are able and anxious to perform a large number of simple activities guided by definite ideas or purposes of their own. Imitation is still strong and a simple suggestion and example may "set them off." In all, as a matter of economy, they need the guidance of the teacher, but never the dominance. Their daily life brings them into contact with many of the activities performed by people in their daily routine of life, activities pertaining to the house, the farm, the community. Types of work involving considerable action on the part of the children, yielding fairly striking results, and having ahead some definite purpose should be prominent. So far as relates to *learning* we may remain firm in the faith that "the amount of memory drill necessary to insure immediate interpretation is reduced in just the ratio in which practical and immediate contact with impression is increased." Direct handling and doing are the great means of training by which we may obviate the necessity of memory work and drill. The method of learning what things are, their properties, by using them, is so distinctly the modern method of learning that our schools should long since have been putting this type of work into practice, especially in the primary grades.

Activities pertaining to gathering and preserving fruits, gathering and storing seeds, finding out what people collect, prepare, and store away for winter; activities connected with home, farm, and community are rich in their educational possibilities when rightly treated.

The following brief outline relating to the food aspect is intended to illustrate the work involved:

STEPS IN EACH LESSON

1. Orientation—gathering the experiences of the children; what is already known. Formulation of the purpose, or end, if not already definite, and the problems, or difficulties, in the way of its realization.

2. Attempted realization of the end through the overcoming of the difficulties—gathering of material, investigation, experiment, and, finally, if successful, attainment of the end, which is the immediate "application" of the results of such investigation.

3. The wider application of the results to related experiences; some appreciation of the significance of these results in the child's life.

It is assumed that from the beginning the children are working under the direction, but not the dominance, of the teacher; and that the child is acquiring vocabulary, learning to read and to write and to care for the mechanics of expression.

*Lessons:*

1. List of foods eaten every day.
2. Source from which these foods are derived—plant, animal, etc.
3. Uses of foods.
4. Constituents of foods—test for starch with iodine.
5. Application of this knowledge to life—mastication, hygiene.
6. Test for albumens—coagulation.
7. Tests for carbon—burning.
8. Uses of carbon or charcoal.
9. Uses of water.

10. Sources of water. Purification of water—using carbon for filter, distillation.

11. Movements and organs concerned in ourselves and in animals in food getting.

Out of this series of exercises are gathered summaries of the work done, and the results, in the form of elementary composition and reading lessons, of which the following are examples:

LESSON I: What food do you eat every day?
I eat bread and butter.
I eat oatmeal.
I eat potato.
I eat meat.
I eat fruit.
I eat eggs.
I eat salt.
I drink water every day.
What foods do you eat most in summer?
What foods do you eat most in winter?

LESSON II: Where do we get our foods?
Most of it comes from plants.
Bread is made from wheat.
Oatmeal is made from oats.
Potatoes grow on a vine.
Fruits grow on trees and vines.
We get our meat from animals.
Most animals eat plant food.
The cow gives the milk we drink.
What does the cow eat?
The hens lay the eggs.
What do the hens eat?
Where do we get water and salt?

LESSON IV: (Constituents of foods—children write out the results which they obtained through their experiments.)
We had starch.
We put iodine on it.
It turned blue.
Then we put iodine on bread.
It turned blue.
I think there is starch in bread.

ARTHUR CULLUM

We had rice.
We put iodine on it.
It turned blue.
It had starch in it.

VERA MCFARLAND

We found starch in rice, bread, potato, and oatmeal.
They turned blue when we put iodine on them.

CARLTON DODD

Lesson VII: (Introduction to Carbon.)

One day we each had a piece of wood.
It was pine wood.
We tried to change it.
Some of us cut it.
Some of us broke it.
Some painted it.
It was still wood.
Then we burned it.
We saw a yellow flame.
We saw smoke.
We put it into a closed tin box.
There was something else left in the box.
It was black.
It was tasteless.
It would not dissolve in water.
We made an envelope for this black substance.
We put it away.

We burned wood, paper, and sugar.
We got carbon.
It is black.
It will not dissolve.

Luella Hopper

Lesson XI: (Impurities in Water, Uses of Carbon.)

We made a filter.
First we made a funnel of paper.
We put wood carbon in it.
We put quartz sand in it, too.
We filtered red water through it.
We filtered blue water through it.
We filtered muddy water through it.
The filtered water was clear.
We filter water at school.
We filter water at home.

Other topics may be treated in a similar manner, among which may be mentioned:

1. *Clothing:* (*a*) materials used for clothing, (*b*) sources from which these materials are derived, (*c*) steps and stages involved in securing these various materials and working them up into clothing, including gathering of materials, cleaning, spinning, dyeing, weaving, etc., (*d*) investigating the school area to find vegetable materials used for dyeing. The study may include wool, cotton, flax, furs, etc., along with a study of the various things made of each and the "why used" for special purposes.
2. *Animal covering:* materials which various animals have for protecting them and keeping them warm during the winter: (*a*) feathers, (*b*) fur and hair, (*c*) wool, etc. Which warmest? Animals having no covering and how they spend the

winter. How animals change their clothing from summer to winter—shedding, molting, thickened growth of fur, feathers, wool, etc.

3. *Fire making and other ways of keeping warm:* (*a*) various methods by which people make fire, (*b*) various ways or means by which buildings are heated, (*c*) various materials used for heating purposes, (*d*) various uses made of fire and heat other than keeping warm.

*Second grade.*—The children of the second grade should carry farther along uncompleted studies begun in the first grade. We have already noted in the first grade that by following a centralizing idea the work ramifies in all directions beyond what we can follow.

It is essential that we keep our work connected up all through the grades; that we take up the thread of the story in the second grade at the point at which we dropped it in the first grade. This is the stage to initiate nearly all of the fundamental ideas which children will deal with in their work in the succeeding grades. Two aspects of work lend themselves admirably to the needs of the grade: (1) A phase of work connected closely with human needs and human activities initiating the questions of a list of these needs and the way we meet them, and how other people meet them; (2) In passing to and fro children will meet many objects and phenomena and note many changes due to natural forces, as contrasted with changes induced by people.

Under the first type, as children in the first grade became familiar with foods used and some of their properties, so children in the second grade may investigate the methods by which people secure and prepare foods for use. The class names, as flour, fruits, meats, etc., become centers for investigation and study.

The following outline on the study of flour is a type of the successive steps that may be developed in the study of foods:

1. Collecting children's experiences on things used in making flour.

2. An examination of various flours, their physical differences, and the kind of bread made from each.

3. An examination of the bread-making constituents of flour. The constituents necessary to make real bread.

4. Making flour: (*a*) methods of crushing the grain until it is reduced to flour, (*b*) various ways people (especially primitive) ground their grains, (*c*) ways in which we make flour today.

5. Visit to flour mill, in which children trace out the processes through which the wheat passes from the time it enters the mill until stored in flour sacks and shipped; cleaning grain, scouring, breaks, sifting. Grades of flours, by-products, and uses made of them.

6. The chief bread-making grains of various countries and peoples; those using mostly rice, barley, rye, corn, wheat, millet, etc.

Similarly, the work of the first grade should be continued in a fuller investigation of the elementary processes involved in:

1. The making of clothing and textiles in general: (*a*) materials from which we get fibers—grass fibers, bark fibers, split wool fiber, bast fiber, cotton fiber, etc. Why we cannot spin all fibers, as hair, milkweed "cotton," etc.

2. The erection of shelter: (*a*) houses of various peoples, especially of primitive peoples as Esquimaux, Indians, Tree-Dwellers, etc., to our modern dwellings and their plan of construction.

NOTE.—The first part may have been started in first grade.

3. Methods of cooking: (*a*) making an out-door camp fire and cooking things according to primitive methods; cooking utensils; fireplaces to stoves and the evolution of the stove.

4. Methods of heating: (*a*) disadvantage, inconvenience, of camp fires in tent or cave, advantage of fireplace, advantage of stove, and evolution of heating of dwellings.

5. Lighting: (*a*) needs of lights, first lamps, disadvantage of burning brand, choice of pine knots, made fagots, and the elementary story of the evolution of lighting.

The full range selected for study should include all the more important primary individual needs of the race and should result in the children acquiring a fairly definite notion of man's dependence upon environment.

This, along with their native interests, should aid us in the next step: that of aiding children to take into account their own casual daily experiences, accumulating them, and seeing what they may get out of them.

A simple scheme, such as below, may aid the child in these first beginnings to observe and to record observations of interest and significance.

MONTH: OCTOBER

| Day | Date | Character of the Day | Observations |
|---|---|---|---|
| Monday........ | 3 | Cool, clear, n.w. wind, 52°. | Elm tree leaves beginning to fall. Oak tree leaves green. Flocks of sparrows in vacant lots. |
| Tuesday........ | 4 | Warm, hazy, s.w. wind, 67°. | Made painting showing landscape. Found caterpillar spinning cocoon. |

A couple of weeks' or a month's accumulation of data will yield material for a considerable range of problems, such as: significance of "elm leaves falling," of "caterpillar spinning a cocoon," etc., and a listing of observations indicating methods of preparing for winter: (1) list of ways in which animals prepare for winter; (2) list of ways, as observed, in which plants prepare for winter; (3) list of ways, as observed, in which people prepare for winter; (4) ways in which seeds are distributed.

In classifying and grouping these experiences there will always be a residue which will not group; observations of little worth, recorded, will, however, help the child to understand what gives an observation value. These same experiences may be summarized into a picture of the month.

OCTOBER

This is October.
The air is cool.
The sky is blue and clear.
There is frost in the morning.

The grass is brownish-green.
The leaves and nuts are falling.
We gather the aster seeds.
We gather the goldenrod seeds.
The wind gathers many seeds, too.
The maple leaves are yellow and red.
The oak leaves are brown and green.
The elm leaves are yellow.
The ash-leaf maple tree is bare.
We see the birds flying south.
We find the cocoons of the caterpillars.
We find the cocoons of the spiders.
We cannot find the caterpillars.
We cannot find the grasshoppers.
We cannot find the ants and earthworms.
Where are they?

If this work is adequately carried out, in range and quality, the children should, by the end of the year, have acquired a goodly number of definite ideas with reference to their environment and of man's relation to it and dependence upon it. They have also acquired ability to write, spell, experiment, observe, and work under direction. They should now be ready to take the greater mass of their minor and isolated experiences and group them around some fairly comprehensive idea or problem which would utilize all of their past experiences and make demand for a large range of additional experience. In this a study of the relation of the people of their local community with reference to the total activities carried on in that community, and of the way people came to settle in that region, affords opportunity for the type of study demanded by the grade. In a region like Chicago the history of its development is an excellent correlating center.

*Third grade.*—A study of the development of Chicago, as a type. The work of the fall is made up largely of various trips to different type areas with a view to gaining some familiarity with the physiographic character of the area. These type areas consist in the main of: (1) lake shore; (2) the sand-dune area; (3) the ridge-swamp area; (4) the flat plain; (5) the river valley and border; (6) the upland moraine, etc. Typical portions of these types are visited and examined with a view to determining: (1) the physical and scenic character of the area (painting or sketch usually made); (2) the character of mineral and soil materials found in each area; (3) the plant life common to the area; (4) the animal life common to the area; (5) uses, past and present, which man makes of the area.

On these trips data of the nature listed below are collected:

TRIP TO LAKE SHORE

1. Appearance of the country (see sketches made by class).

2. Location of area south end of Lake Michigan. (See Miller's Station on map of Chicago area.)

3. Mineral and soils. (See collection marked "Lake Shore at Miller's.")

4. Plant life.

| Name | Place Found Growing | Characteristics of the Plant, Stem, Roots, Foliage, Fruit, etc. | Influence on Area, Uses to Animal, Man, etc. |
|---|---|---|---|
| Sea-rocket... | On barren sand along beach and on dunes. | Low, oval, branching stalk with fleshy foliage. | A pioneer soil maker, hold sand, foliage used as greens. |
| Sand-cherry.. | Abundant along beach and along margins of dunes. | Low, five feet, spreading shrub of cherry type. | Fruit eaten by man and animals. |

5. Animal life.

| [Name | Place in Which Seen and Place It Makes Its Home | How It Lives and Food It Feeds Upon | Influences upon the Area and Uses to Man |
|---|---|---|---|
| Muskrat.... | Along Long Lake and swamps, lives in water. | Burrows in the earth, builds houses of mud and reeds, eats roots, clams. | Destroys plants, digs holes in earth, fur and flesh used by man. |

6. Ways in which man is making use of the area: (1) use made of land in way of crop raising; (2) use made of area as residences; (3) use made of any natural products: (*a*) of sand, gravel, etc., (*b*) of clay, of limestone.

7. Uses made of the area, in the past, as evidenced by the Indian remains found: (1) conditions attracting Indians: (*a*) wild life that inhabited lake, swamps, thickets, and prairie, (*b*) Indian life in relation to this original environment.

8. The coming of the white man and the story of the development of Chicago. In this Nature and man get so closely connected that science, industry, and history fuse. Old inhabitants are questioned, old books consulted, and every effort made to piece out the story of man in his relations to the region and how the region developed. The following extract from work of children will give some idea as to the tone and trend of the study.

"If you had been in Chicago years ago you would have seen many swamps on the South Side. A man lived here in 1830 and wrote to his friend telling him how the hunting was, and this is a portion of the letter: 'Vast quantities of water fowl were feeding on wild rice, seeds, and insects in the swamps. Swan, geese, brant, passing to and fro, kept up an incessant cackling. . . . . There were ducks of every kind, from the mallard and canvasback down to the tiny water witch and blue-winged teal, while hundreds of gulls hovered gracefully over the swamp.' "—L. L.

"Tall reeds, rushes, cattails, wild rice, and water lilies grow in the swamp. You will find dragonflies and fish and frogs there, too. The yellow-headed blackbird, and the red-winged blackbird are swamp birds which feed on the wild rice."—E. B.

"Wild rice grew on the banks of the Chicago River. The Indian squaws would go out and gather it in years gone by. They would paddle along in their canoes. When they came to a big patch they would bend the rice stalks over their canoes and beat them. They had a big mat on the bottom. They would empty the rice into a big basket. They gathered until their baskets were full. They used the rice for food."—E. W.

"The life and comfort of the Indians depended upon their skill and success in hunting. They needed the skins for clothing, for the wigwams, and the meat for food. The Indian had to learn the habits of animals in order to catch them."—F. Mc.

In this way they enter more and more into details in working out, with reference both to the present and to the past, man's intimate relations with and dependence upon his environment. In following up the idea of man's acquiring familiarity and control of environment they come to see how in early days man went out after the things which he needed, but that in later and present days he sits in his home, and things from the ends of the earth are brought to him, and the idea of the great importance of co-operative industry and commercial relations begins to acquire significance.

During the primary period the child has been interested in the facts and activities of the world about him mainly as facts and activities. His questions have been "What is it?" "What is it for?" and the replies to these questions have enabled him to orient himself to a greater or less degree. This attitude toward a new object is maintained through life, but other interests are added. The child of the intermediate period is not satisfied with knowing what an object is and what it is for; he goes a step farther and asks the question, "How does it work?" The world to him is not static. Results are accomplished through changing processes. He desires to get control over these processes. He wants to "make it work." This seems to point out what phases of Nature appeal most to the child of this period and the line to be followed in furthering his education. He is interested in how Nature supplies his needs and the needs of his home, and this interest widens so as to include the world. The course of study in science, then, should include the dynamic phases of Nature as it administers to human needs: a study of how the necessities of life are met. But Nature appeals to him in other ways than as merely supplying the necessities of life. His heart leaps up when he beholds the rainbow in the sky. Nature arouses his aesthetic instincts. Properly approached, the water-fowl, the chambered nautilus, the river, the mountain, and the waterfall become more to him than merely the means of supplying food, shelter, and clothing. They arouse and satisfy his aesthetic and spiritual instincts, and any study of Nature which does not carry the pupil through to a realization of these is falling short of its possibilities. But to the intermediate child, the utilitarian side of Nature appeals most strongly; and through a study of this phase he comes to a consciousness of the more refined aspects.

A careful study of the so-called "nature-study" movements in the nineteenth century reveals the fact that in almost every instance where a course of study in elementary science as science has been formulated, it has resulted in a formal study of science from a scientist's standpoint. Subject-matter in itself has become the basis of the course, and this subject-matter has been treated from an adult standpoint and more or less isolated from the mental attitude and interests of the child. It is thought best in this period not to differentiate science into separate subjects. In his study of the world about him as it ministers to his needs, he finds Nature is constantly at hand. The facts of bacteriology, physiography, geography, geology, astronomy, chemistry, physics, physiology, zoölogy, botany, entomology, domestic science, meteorology, mineralogy, and the whole round of sciences appear, but not in a differentiated form. They are applied sciences, but have not yet been precipitated and thought of as sciences. It may be desirable, and necessary at times, to devote a separate period to following up some phase of science that has come into the field in connection with some problem in the study of human needs. For instance, in the study of coal, a class may desire to give attention to the geologic ages related to coal formation, but not for the sake of studying geology. The primary problem is a different one. The period of differentiated science comes later, and it may be said that the school must see to it that attention be given later to gathering up the science material collected during the primary and intermediate grades into the form of organized groups, or into "the sciences."

TOPICS FOR STUDY

General Topic: Our needs.

What is needed every day in order to carry on life? How does your family supply these needs; that is, what is the occupation of your father?

Three methods of supplying: by physical labor, by mental labor, by mental and physical labor together.

A. Interests from the standpoint of physical needs.

I. A study of food interests.

Make a list of the foods used by your family. Which of them grow wild? Which were produced by yourselves? Which were produced in your locality? Which were produced in other parts of the world? Where were supplies not produced by the family secured?

*a*) People who collect and distribute our food.

1. The grocery.

Experiment: Visit the grocery.

Observe kinds of food found there, how they are wrapped or packed, methods of keeping clean, care to prevent waste, where secured, nature of the grocer's work from day to day, how he makes life more comfortable for us.

2. The meat market.

Experiment: Visit the meat market.

Observe kind of foods found there, how arranged in store. Safeguards against impurities, care to prevent waste, where supplies are secured, nature of owner's work from day to day, different cuts of meat, what makes some cuts more valuable than others, how the meat market is a convenience for us.

3. The bakery.

Experiment: Visit a bakery. Study in a similar way.

4. The dairy.

Experiment: Visit a dairy.

Note that the study of the source of food supply leads back to the farmer, the truck gardener, the fruit grower, and the fisherman.

*b*) The people who produce our food.

1. The farmer.

Experiment: Visit a farm.

Note the buildings and implements required, farm plants, farm animals, the work of the farmer from day to day and from season to season, how the farmer makes life more comfortable for us.

Farm plants.

*aa*) Corn.

Experiment: Plant corn at different depths in the school garden. Note results. What kind grows the best corn? kinds of corn, what kind of an ear is best, corn judging, elements in soil that produce best ear, kind that produces stalk, simple soil testing, part of the plant used for food, cross-fertilization, how the farmer plants, cultivates, and harvests his corn, different uses of the different parts of the plant, fodder, silo, ear and shelled corn, what he does with the surplus, food elements of corn, corn starch, corn oil, corn rubber.

Experiments: Test corn for starch; test corn for oil; pound up grains and bake the meal; visit mill where corn is ground; visit grain elevator, note how corn is dumped, shelled, put into cars.

Food value of corn and corn products.

Changes in the corn plant through cultivation.

Experiment: Visit Field Columbian Museum and note specimens of corn in a more primitive state.

Visit a field before husking time, note tassels with grains, note other irregularities which indicate a partial reversion to type.

The corn belt of Illinois: Where located, kind of soil, how soil was made, cities of corn belt, market for corn, Chicago. Make a map to show corn belt, cities, and lines of transportation.

Corn belt of United States. Chart.

Corn belts of the world. Chart.

Historical: The Indian of the prairie, and the corn plant, the coming of the pioneer to the prairie, route of coming, method of transportation, what he found, method of reducing the sod, oxen and horses, the buffalo, prairie fire, where early settlements were located, as along the streams, needs that gave the schoolhouse, the village with its store, blacksmith and wagon shop, orchards, roads, and bridges. The French in Illinois.

Study other corn areas of the world, make map to show principal cities, rivers, canals, and railroads. Account for location of principal cities.

*bb*) Wheat studied in same way.

*cc*) Other grains of the farm.

*dd*) Other plant products of the farm.

## SORGHUM

One day in May our teacher gave us some cane seeds to plant. The seeds were of a reddish-brown color and of an oval shape.

My father had the ground plowed and I took the rake and tried to rake out the lumps. Then he took the hoe and made a furrow across the garden, in which we dropped the seeds. Then we covered them with soil.

Sometimes I took a sprinkler and watered the ground where they had been planted. One day when I was out in the garden I saw some little green sprouts. It was the sorghum seed. It looked very much like grass only its leaves were broader.

The stalks grew to be from fifteen to sixteen feet high. They were jointed like corn, but the leaves were longer. The flowers were of a yellowish-green and bloomed in August. After the flowers disappeared the seeds could be seen. They grew in a cluster.

The first of October my father took a long corn knife and cut it down. He cut it near the ground because there is more juice in the bottom of the stalk. Then we stripped off the blades, cut off the tops, tied the stalks into a large bundle and took it to the schoolhouse.

One day all the pupils of our schoolroom went over to the laboratory of the high school. The boys had a clotheswringer to squeeze the juice out of the stalks, and a tub to catch the juice. We put the sorghum through the wringer twice to get all the juice. It had little pieces of stalk in it, which we strained out. Then we put the juice over the Bunsen burner.

It took it about three and one-half hours to boil down to syrup. As the impurities rose to the top they were skimmed off. The syrup was a reddish-brown color and we had about a pint and it tasted better than what we get in the store.

C. R., 5th Grade

Farm animals:

Experiment: Visit a farm.

Note the different farm animals, how the farmer cares for each, food of each, use the farmer makes of each, the benefit we get from them.

*aa*) The cattle industry.

Beef cattle: How cattle are fattened on the farm, how shipped to market, care in transit, corn-fed cattle and ranch-fed cattle, states where each method prevails, beef-producing states, make map to show beef-producing states and lines of transportation, which use corn-fed method, which use ranch-fed method, great stockyard cities, value of stockyards.

Experiment: Visit Union Stock Yards. Note area, method of handling cattle, follow through to cooling-room, how beef is marketed, use of refrigerators, care to preserve cleanliness, by-products, as hides, hair, gelatine, glue, oleo-oil, butterine, combs, buttons, knife-blades, jet trimming, fertilizers.

Ranch life, size of herds, methods of identifying, the round-up, early methods of marketing beef in the western states, why changed, why stockyards are built farther west.

Value of beef product in the United States, to what countries exported, nations which compete with the United States, locate them by making chart.

Kinds of beef cattle.

Historical.

John C. Fremont, Lewis and Clarke, Zebulon Pike, The Old Santa Fé Trail, The Oregon Trail.

Dairy Cattle.

Experiment: Secure milk, place in different places and let cream rise, note why it rises, where it rises the best, skim cream, churn sweet cream, let cream sour and churn, where the butter appears, prepare butter for the table.

### HOW WE MADE BUTTER

We bought two quart bottles of milk and a half-gallon bucketful. We put one bottle in the furnace room and we put the other bottle and the crock out on the fire escape. We let them stand until the next morning and found cream on the top. We let the cream stay on one bottle and took it off the other bottle in the furnace room and from the milk in the crock. The bottle in the basement did not have as much cream as the bottle out-doors. We put some of the sweet cream in a bottle and shook it hard for sixty-four minutes but it foamed and we could not get any butter, so we left the rest of the cream until the next day and shook it up good and got some butter in about eighteen minutes. Hildur said the butter would be sour, but it wasn't. Our teacher said the butter fat was wrapped up in little skins and the sour bacteria made the skins weak so when we shook it we let the butter out. The boys liked the buttermilk.

B. M., 4th Grade

Experiment: Visit a dairy farm.

Note arrangement of barn, feed suited to milch cattle, methods of handling and disposing of milk and cream, cream separator, precautions to insure cleanliness.

Experiment: Visit creamery.

Note testing of cream, means of removing impurities, churning, working and salting of butter, care of vessels and other precautions to insure cleanliness, methods of keeping fresh, preparations for market.

Make a map of the dairy section of the United States, why each section is devoted to dairying, difference in milk production in poor and high-grade cows, amount a good cow will produce, kinds of milch cattle, how cheese is made, milk-sugar, condensed milk, special methods of producing butter and cheese in Norway, Switzerland, and Holland, form in which butter is usually shipped to market, use of refrigerator cars, value of butter and cheese produced in the United States, what nations compete with us, locate other dairying nations and cities.

*bb*) The horse studied in the same way.

*cc*) The hog studied in the same way.

*dd*) Other farm animals.

*ee*) The poultry industry.

2. The truck gardener.

Experiment: Visit a truck farm.

Note the kinds of vegetables and berries he grows, equipment in way of hotbeds and labor-saving machines, nature of his work from day to day and season to season, how he makes life more comfortable for us.

*aa*) Cabbage.

Experiment: Plant cabbage seeds in different soils and note results.

Experiment: Make hotbed and grow plants, set out in school garden, cultivate, and market. Part of cabbage used for food, value as a food, how prepared for shipment, how served.

*bb*) Other products of the truck gardener.

The changes brought about through cultivation. The work of Mr. Burbank.

3. The fruit-grower.

The kinds of fruit grown in orchards—grapes, berries, apples, cherries, pears, peaches, oranges, grape fruit, figs, apricots.

Those grown in temperate regions, those in subtropical regions.

*aa*) The apple—the typical temperate climate fruit.

Experiment: Visit an apple orchard, note nature of trees, kinds of apples, season of ripening, how sorted and prepared for market.

Uses of apples: raw, cider, preserves, canned.

Part of plant used for food.

Time required for an apple orchard to come to bearing, insect enemies and friends, how enemies are held in check and friends encouraged, the grafting and budding of trees, rejuvenation of old orchards, the irrigated orchards of the West, orchards of Michigan and influence of Lake Michigan. Make map showing orchard sections, principal cities, etc.

Experiment: Visit Land Show at the Coliseum. Changes that have taken place under cultivation.

*bb*) Other fruit products of temperate climate. Make map.

*cc*) The orange, typical subtropical fruit.

*dd*) Other subtropical fruit.

Chart fruit areas, fruits as foods, methods of preserving: cold storage, drying, canning, preserving.

Experiments: Can peaches; dry apples; make preserves; the making of fruit butters and marmalade; a study of molds and ferments.

4. The fisherman.

What kinds of fish are found in your river; how caught; what kinds are best for food?

The equipment and work of the fisherman.

*aa*) The cod.

Study life-history and habits of the cod, regions frequented, how secured, uses made of it, how prepared for market. Make map.

*bb*) Other fish studied in same way.

*cc*) Oysters and other mollusks.

How does the fisherman make life more comfortable for us?

*c*) Water as related to food interests.

1. Directly.

Necessity for water on the part of plants and animals, where we get our water supply, ground water, wells.

Experiment: Collect soils of different natures, place in deep jar and pour some water over it. Note the kinds of soils that permit water to pass through most readily, which hold moisure longer. Study origin of springs, geysers, wells, cisterns, how water becomes purified, ways in which water may become contaminated, what finally becomes of ground water, how the farmer holds moisture in the ground, dry-farming.

Experiment: Visit the city water-plant, how the water is lifted, and how conveyed to homes.

2. As indirectly related to foods.

Sources of water, rain, snow.

Evaporation:

Experiment: Put water in different sized open vessels. What becomes of it? Does size of vessel have any relation to rapidity of evaporation? Does temperature? Wind? Other instances of evaporation.

Precipitation:

Pitcher of cold water on a warm day. What causes "sweating"? Other instances. Cause of precipitation: clouds, rain, frost, snow, sleet, hail, dew. The fair-weather cloud, the rain cloud, the storm cloud, the rainy areas. Make a chart. How are evaporation and precipitation of value in the production of food?

Running water:

Experiment: Notice the water that falls on the school yard during a rain. Note water partings, slopes, streams, pirating, meanders, wearing bank, building bank, oxbows, rapids, falls, the leveling work of a stream, how a river system is built up, how running water helps the people who produce our food.

*d*) Soil as related to food production.
Experiment: Examine different kinds of soil under the magnifier. What is found, how soil is formed, notice indication of weathering in various places, notice different soils as to color, fineness, sandy or gravelly, clay oı loam, where blackest, why. Test for humus.

*e*) Air as related to food production.
What plants and animals get from the air.
Experiments: Set a glass bell over a growing plant and watch results.
Experiment: Note feeling of lassitude when impure air is breathed for some time.
Air as it helps in evaporation and precipitation.

*f*) The use of foods.
Necessity of foods, how our bodies take up food through assimilation. Mastication and insalivation, digestion, assimilation, care of the teeth, need for different kinds of food elements, nutrients found in different foods, dietetics, effect of heat upon food materials.

II. A study of shelter interests.
Kinds of houses as to materials used, homes of primitive and arrested peoples.

*a*) People who contribute to the building of homes.

1. The carpenter, natuıe of work, tools used.
Experiment: Visit a house in process of building. Note kinds of lumber used, size of pieces, rough and dressed, difference in materials as to finish and durability.
Experiment: Work with different woods in shop, note difference in resistance. How the carpenter makes life more comfortable for us.
2. The mason. Studied in the same way.

MAKING CEMENT BLOCKS

We learned to make concrete blocks for building parts of Athens to illustrate our history work.

We had to have moulds so we found old boxes and boards down in the school workroom and made them. The moulds were three feet or more in length. We planed all the boards down till they were about a half-inch thick and very smooth. We put the boxes together with four-penny, wire finishing nails. When the moulds were done, the inside measurements were two inches wide, one inch deep. Then we measured on the side spaces one inch apart and sawed them across to the bottom board. While we were making the moulds, some of us boys were experimenting with the concrete. We tried two weeks before it satisfied us and these are the proportions: 1 qt. cement, 1 qt. sand, 1½ qts. crushed stone, very fine.

We sifted the sand and the crushed stone, and the more we sifted it the better concrete it made. We mixed it thoroughly while it was dry and then put water in it till it was thin enough to put in the mould. After it stayed an hour or two, we cut it with a sharp, thin knife into blocks. Next day we tipped out the blocks, which were soft, but grow harder every day.

P. P., 5th Grade

3. The plumber. Studied in the same way.
4. The electrician. Studied in the same way.
5. The painter and decorator. Studied in the same way.

*b*) Processes for making home more convenient, i.e., the mechanics of operating the home.

1. Light in the home.

   Primitive methods of lighting: kerosene, mechanics of the kerosene lamp, source of kerosene supply. Gas as a luminant, natural and manufactured gas.

   Experiment: Secure coal and clay pipe and make gas. Electric lights, simple principles of generating electricity by experiment in the laboratory.

   Experiment: Visit the city power-house.

   Gasoline and acetylene as illuminants.

   Experiment: Visit a building where these are used and study method of operating. Danger in the use of each kind of illuminant.

2. Heat in the home.

   Primitive and pioneer methods of heating.

   Kinds of material used for heating homes.

   *aa*) Coal.

   Study the two varieties, hard and soft coal, separately. How is each supposed to have been produced? Note difference. Location of hard coal and of soft coal mines of the United States, of Great Britain, of France, of Germany, of Austria, of Russia. The coal supply of other nations of the world. Number of square miles of hard coal regions in the United States. Coal mines are opened either by sinking a shaft to the vein, by tunneling to the vein horizontally, or, when the vein appears on the surface, by opening it. Method of mining hard coal. Life of the miner. His average weekly wages. The breaker boy. The door tender. The miner's helper. Use of the "breakers." Thickness of a vein of coal in the hard coal region. Depth to which the hard coal mines are sunk. Important uses of coal. How coal is taken to market. When owners of coal mines are also part owners of railroads that convey the coal to market, what harm may come? Square miles of soft coal regions in the United States. Annual value of soft coal product in the United States. Does the United States export coal, what kind and to what nations? Will this continue? Does the United States import coal and, if so, from what place and why? The relation of coal to manufacturing. Is the coal product of the United States likely to be soon exhausted? How is this in England? In France? Consumption of coal rapidly increasing. Reason. Burning smoke. Improvements in the methods of combustion and steam production. When was coal first used to any great extent in the United States? Make map to show coal areas.

   Experiment: Visit a coal mine. Note shaft, provision for ventilating, process of mining, coal props, danger of mining, how coal is elevated, means of lighting.

   Experiment: Fill bowl of clay pipe with pieces of "soft coal." Seal bowl with wet clay and fasten stem in clamp on ring stand. Heat bowl of pipe in Bunsen flame persistently for 15 minutes. When stream of smoke is seen issuing from stem, hold burning match to it. Result. This is illuminating gas. Let pipe cool, then break and examine contents of bowl. What is it? What by-product causes shiny appearance of parts of it? Is this process used in commerical preparation of the gas and by-products? What other method is also used?

Make map to show coal areas of the world.

*bb*) Other materials used for heating homes, studied in detail.

*cc*) Heating systems, fireplaces, stoves, hot air, hot water, steam, gas. The mechanics of heating studied by actual observation.

3. The water supply in the home. Mechanics of water supply. Precaution against impurities.
4. Sewage disposal. Methods in detail.
5. Rooms in the home, uses and arrangements of rooms to secure a maximum of comfort with a minimum of effort.
6. Principles of home decoration.

*c*) Materials used in the building of homes.

1. The lumber industry, lumber areas, a lumber camp, floating the logs to mill, the saw mill, plane and quarter sawed, the planing mill.
   Experiment: Visit planing mill.
2. Stone as a building material.
   Experiment: Visit a quarry. Study in detail. Kinds of stone and characteristics of each.
3. The brick and tile industry.

III. A study of clothing interests.

Clothing of primitive peoples. Where we get our clothing.

*a*) People who supply us with clothing.

The period of home manufacture, period of machine manufacture.

1. The dry goods and clothing store, kinds of cloth, arrangement of wares, nature of the work of the store-keeper, where he gets his supplies. How he makes life more comfortable for us.
2. The tailor.
3. The dressmaker.
4. The milliner.
5. The shoe store.

*b*) Materials used for clothing.

1. Wool.
   Experiment: Secure a fleece of wool, wash, comb, dye, spin, and weave; the sheep industry, areas of wool growing, the great woolen mills.
   Experiment: Visit a woolen mill. Note processes used. Methods of dyeing, materials used in dyeing.

OUR FLEECE OF WOOL

A few days ago we went down to the sheep sheds. While we were down there we bought a fleece of wool. It weighed 6 pounds and cost us 40 cents a pound. It was dirty and greasy, so we had to wash it out. It took us a long time to get it clean. Each one of us had a wad of it to wash. Some tried cold water and no soap, some tried warm water without soap, and some used soap and warm water. It was quite a job to find the best way to clean our wool. It was bad about getting knotted up into little balls, but when we got good soap and used hot soft water we got along all right. We borrowed some combs from some old ladies who used to make their own blankets, and combed it out as straight as we could. We looked at some under the magnifier and found that the wool hairs are rough and have little hooks on them. That is what makes the wool stick together. We tried spinning it into threads and found it was quite a job to do it like they used to by whirling a stick, but we got some yarn. We asked an old Swedish woman to come up and spin for us. We borrowed a spinning wheel and she came up and used it for us. She could work very fast and we tried it some, but we were too clumsy. We are trying to find out how to color our yarn now so it won't fade; but we haven't found a good way yet.

A. M., 5th Grade

2. Cotton.
3. Silk.
4. Flax.

OUR FLAX

Last May we thought we would raise some flax, so we got a pound of seed down at the drug store, and each one of us took home some to plant in our gardens. We had to ask a good many before we found how to plant it. Some of us thought it ought to be planted in hills, and some thought it ought to be planted in rows, and some thought it ought to be set out like tomato plants, but we found that it ought to be sowed like oats and raked over. Mine was a little slow about coming up and I thought it was weeds at first. I had to pull the grass and weeds out of it two or three times. It blossomed late in the summer. The flower was small and purple and the stems were about two feet high. After school commenced we began to talk about when we would harvest it. We read in a book that about three-fourths of the blossoms ought to be dead, so in October we cut it. Some of the children pulled theirs up by the roots, but I guess it is better to cut it close to the ground. We began studying how to get anything to weave. We tried breaking some of it up but could not get any threads. We put some out on the grass and left it for three weeks in the dew and rain, then brought it in and dried it. We found then that when we broke up the straw we could get the fibers. The part that is used for thread is under the bark and next to the wooly part of the stem. We found in the *Scientific American* how to make a flax brake and we boys made three in the shop. After we got it broken up we found it coarse, so made a hatchel out of a board and some nails. We combed the flax with this until we got the coarse stuff out of it. This coarse part is called tow and is used for stuffing couches and chairs. We made some threads of the finer part, but it was not very good. Our teacher got Mrs. L. to come up with her flax wheel and spin some thread for us. We borrowed some hand looms from the second grade and tried weaving. We are wanting to go down to Aurora and visit the cotton mills there and see how they do the work of spinning and weaving by machinery.

H. B., 5th Grade

5. Hemp.
6. Leather.
7. Rubber.
8. Other materials.

IV. Miscellaneous subjects not already treated. Tobacco, opium, medicinal herbs, beverages, condiments, gold, silver, lead, and other minerals.

If the study of each of the foregoing subjects has been carried out in detail, as intended, the child will have considerable knowledge of the facts of botany, zoölogy, physiology, geology, physics, chemistry, bacteriology, mineralogy, climatology, but not organized as science. It is thought that toward the close of the period he is ready to organize some of this into form as science, and earth science is taken as the first.

In his study of the source of the materials which satisfy his primal needs, he has visited every quarter of the globe and should have become familiar with the general facts of geography. He may now organize this knowledge into scientific form; he may take up earth science more as science and get the "why" of his facts, and the relation of these facts to each other and to human life in a more general way. The following outline is intended to view the facts from a somewhat different standpoint and to get them in a more organized form.

V. General Geography.

*a*) Globe studies, form of the earth, size, rotation, revolution, gravitation, day and night, changes of seasons, latitude, longitude, zones of temperature from the standpoint of latitude, atmospheric circulation due to unequal heating, origin of winds, zones of wind and belts of calm, causes for rain, altitude and climate, the ocean and ocean currents.

Make chart to show meridians, parallels of latitude, zones.

Make map to show wind belts.

Make map to show ocean currents.

SUGGESTED PROBLEMS AND EXERCISES

1. Locate the great mountain systems in each of the grand divisions of the earth.

2. Locate for January the northwest trade winds, the southeast trade winds, the three great belts of calms, the two belts of westerly winds, the Arctic and Antarctic winds.

3. Locate each of the chief ocean currents for December, as Gulf stream, Japanese current, Labrador current, etc.

4. Locate the same for July.

5. Draw the winter isotherm of 66° in the northern hemisphere and account for all the great bends in it.

6. Account for the heavy rainfall of the Amazon and Congo valleys.

7. Account for the following desert regions: Sahara, Persia, Gobi, interior of Australia, Utah.

8. Source of rainfall in Mississippi Valley. On the Atlantic slope.

9. Note the latitude of Montreal and of Venice and account for the difference of climate.

10. Suppose the Rocky Mountain system obliterated, how would it affect the climate of North America? Would it help United States if a mountain range extended along its northern boundary?

11. Suppose the Alps extended north from the Adriatic Sea to the Baltic. What changes in climate of Europe east of that line? West of that line?

12. Account for the frequent failure of the India wheat crop.

13. Why is the Orinoco Valley arid during a part of the year and drenched with rain at other times?

14. Where do most of the commercial rivers of Europe rise? Account for this.

15. Why has Spain less rainfall than France?

16. How is a vast amount of the vapor and heat of the equatorial regions transported to the temperate regions? Good of this?

17. Effect of large lakes and inland seas upon climate? Which shore of Lake Michigan is most affected? of Black Sea? of Mediterranean? Gulf of Mexico?

18. How do rivers determine the location of cities?

19. Explain the formation of rain, hail, snow, dew, frost.

20. Explain land and sea breezes.

*b*) Continental studies.

1. North America, with special reference to the United States.

*aa*) As a continent.

1. Location and relative size—extreme latitudes and longitudes, comparative latitudes, area compared with other continents, area as compared with land area of the earth, direction and distance from other continents.
2. Surface features—mountain areas, highlands, lowlands, the drainage basins, coast features.
3. Climate—tropical climate, inter-tropical climate, regions of constant rains, regions of rainy summers and dry winters, rainfall in the path of the trades, prevailing westerlies, mountain barriers in the path of the westerlies, temperate regions, frigid areas.
4. Life—effect upon vegetation, animal life, and man, of latitude, altitude, relief, climate, and all physiographic features. The ice areas, tundras, forest areas, grassy plains, agricultural areas, desert areas; vegetation of these areas; wild life on land and in water. Peoples, wild and civilized, and their characteristics, occupations, dress, habits of life, social institutions, distribution of population, etc.
5. Social organization—Dominion of Canada, United States, Mexico, Central American States, government of each. Subdivisions of United States. Principal cities.

*bb*) Divisions of the continent.

1. The Mississippi Valley—location and size, surface, climate, life, industry and commerce.
2. The great plateaus and the Pacific slope.
3. The Appalachian region.
4. Canada.
5. The Gulf coast.
6. Mexico and Central America.

2. Europe.

Studied first as a continent, then a study of local areas.

3. Asia.
4. Africa.
5. South America.

*c*) Study of world belts.

BELT OF 10° N. TO 10° S. AROUND THE WORLD

1. On outline map of the world trace the boundary lines of this belt. Name important countries of South America, of Africa, of East India Islands. Fill places on map as needed.

2. Prevailing winds in America, in Africa, in East Indies. Account for these winds. Which of the three sections has the most desirable climate? Why?

3. Compare, as to products and inhabitants and commercial use, the Amazon Valley and Congo Valley.

4. North and south of the forest regions found in answering No. 3 are treeless plains. Locate them, learn their names, and the reason for such plains.

5. Why is the climate of the islands of this belt so different from that of America and Africa in the same belt?

6. What are the important products of the islands in this belt? Three cities.

7. Account for great differences in the climate of the eastern and western coasts of South America in this belt. Name two cities on or near each coast.

8. What commercial products found on the Congo River? What does this valley promise for future development? Locate a city on each coast of Africa.

9. How is the Nile River dependent on what happens in this belt?

### BELT 10° N. TO 30° N. AROUND THE WORLD

1. On outline map of the world, trace the boundary lines of this belt. Name important countries included in America, in Africa, in Asia. Fill in all places called for below when needed.

2. Prevailing winds in America, in Africa, in Western Asia (summer winds and winter winds separately), Eastern Asia (summer and winter separately). Account for these winds.

3. Note the location of the highlands in relation to the prevailing winds and then tell about the rainfall in the different sections of this belt. (Three greatest desert regions and three regions of heavy rainfall.)

4. Locate cities of two hundred thousand or more: in America two, in Africa none, in Western Asia none, in British India eight, East India five. Reason for such a grouping of cities.

5. Character of the people compared with people of United States.

6. Compare temperature of different sections with that of City of Mexico or Manila. Account for contrasts.

7. What are important industries of the different sections?

8. What important nations are interested in the belt? Where is greatest progress now indicated?

9. What part of this section was in the Indies sought by Columbus? Would it be thought worth the effort today?

10. About what part of the population of the earth is in this belt and in what part of the belt? Is this belt a good one to live in? Reason. What races of men in this belt?

### BELT OF 30° N. TO 50° N. AROUND THE WORLD

1. On outline map of the world trace the boundary lines of this belt. Name important countries in America, Europe, Africa, Western Asia, Eastern Asia. Fill in places called for below as needed.

2. Prevailing winds in America, in Europe, in Africa, in Western Asia (in summer, in winter), in Eastern Asia (in summer, in winter). Account for these winds.

3. Note the location of the highlands in relation to the prevailing winds and then account for the rainfall in the different sections of this belt.

4. What important cities of United States in this section?

5. Note the desert and semi-arid regions of this belt, locate the northeast trade winds, and then account for the lack of rainfall in the different sections. Why the cities in Eastern Asia?

6. Give the great products of this belt. In the fertile regions, is it easy or difficult to raise these products? Is this good or bad for the people? Races found in this belt?

7. The great crops of United States grown in this belt? In what part is each produced?

8. About what part of the area of the United States in this belt?

9. Are the products you discovered in answering No. 8 largely manufactured in this region? Reason.

BELT NORTH OF 50° N.

1. Name important countries in this belt in America, in Europe, in Asia. Locate places on outline map of the world as needed.

2. Prevailing winds in winter and in summer in Southern Canada, in Southwestern Canada east of the Rocky Mountains, in British Columbia, in Alaska.

3. Locate the forest regions of America, of Siberia. Note the semi-arid region south of the forests of Siberia and explain why no such belt exists in America (Great Lakes and Gulf of Mexico).

4. Why is the influence of the Atlantic Ocean not large on the climate of Siberia? What prevents the Pacific Ocean from modifying the climate of most of Canada? Influence of Hudson Bay on Canada. Which has greater promise for the future, Canada or Siberia?

5. Locate the great river valleys in this belt. Compare, as to both area and usefulness, these rivers with those of the belt south of this. Reasons for your conclusions.

6. Contrast the climate of North America in this belt with that of Europe. Account for the difference. What section of North America (of Asia) has a climate similar to this belt of Europe south of 60° N.?

7. Locate all the large cities of this belt.

8. In the European section of this belt, excluding Norway, Sweden, and Russia, there are about two hundred million people. Compare with Texas, with California, with Brazil, with south half of China, as to value commercially, educationally, religiously.

(Belts of southern hemisphere studied in a similar way.)

VI. Commerical Geography.

Throughout this entire course, and especially in the study of food, clothing, and shelter interests, more or less attention is given to commercial activities. It is thought advisable, however, before taking up "physiography" to devote some time to a special study of commercial activities.

*a*) A review of the great agricultural areas; why they are such areas; what sort of products are grown in each; where each of these products are shipped (such as are not consumed at home); why people who receive such products do not grow them; principal collecting and distributing centers; what determines the location of such centers; chief routes of travel and why; methods of transportation and why.

*b*) A review of the chief mining areas; why so located; chief cities in each; what determines location; influence of such life on a people; methods of distribution; routes of travel, etc.

*c*) A review of the chief manufacturing centers; why given to manufacturing; influence of life on people; where products are sent and why; distribution; routes; etc.

*d*) A study of the development of transportation — steamship, railway; building of canals, harbors, terminals, tunnels, etc.

B. Science from the standpoint of aesthetic and general interests.

Space forbids a detailed outline of work in this phase of science, but such a treatment seems unnecessary here. With such excellent suggestions as are given by Holtz in his "Nature-Study" and by Hodge in "Nature-Study and Life" a mere suggestion here to show the recognition given by the committee to this phase of science seems sufficient.

I. Animal study.

*a*) Domestic animals and pets, a study of habits of these animals with such study of their structure as will explain their habits; care of these animals.

*b*) Wild animals.

1. Which have not disappeared with the coming of man, as the squirrel, the mink, chipmunk, birds, reptiles, insects, mollusks, coral, sponge, etc.
2. Big game.

The moose, bears, lions, wolves, seals, whales, the eagle, etc.

Note adaptation to climate and surroundings, protective coloration, food, methods of securing food, means of defense, means of attack, life habits. Some notice of classification. Protection and preservation of useful and interesting animals.

II. Bird-study.

The common birds studied out-of-doors in their native haunts: "a bowing acquaintance with the birds that nest in our gardens, or under the very eaves of our houses; that haunt our woodpiles; keep our fruit-trees free from slugs; waken us with their song, and enliven our walks along the roadside and through the woods." Attempt made to give the children a naturalist's point of view rather than that of the scientist.

A study of habits of birds such as mating, nesting, migration, manner of migration; calls, notes, coloration. Protection and preservation of birds, Audubon societies, Bird Day, methods of attracting birds.

III. Plant-study.

Germination of seeds, plant organs of the higher types of plants, names and characteristics of our common trees, care of tree, tree surgery, forest reserves, underground stems, buds, leaves, movements, distribution of plants, seed dispersal, Arbor Day.

## THE ADOLESCENT PERIOD

It is the belief of the committee that probably the most marked mental attitude accompanying the dawn of adolescence is an intensification of the child's interests in what may be termed the "world of adult activities" surrounding him. Moreover, it is believed that there are valid reasons, both psychological and practical, for the segregation of the sexes for their science work during at least a portion of this period. These beliefs are the justification of the committee for providing courses in household science for the girls during a part of the period and of courses in various phases of industrial science for the boys.

Some attempt has been made in the outlines that follow to provide a logical arrangement of topics. It should be understood, however, that it is not the thought of the committee that the order provided here must be strictly followed. Indeed, every topic should be approached, not as a topic in science, or in some particular branch of science, but as a vital problem in the life of the child; as an obstacle which comes between him and the rational mastery of his environment, the realization of his "larger self."

Again, while it is undoubtedly true that in the earlier high-school period we may venture somewhat farther from the child's immediate environment in our choice of topics, yet this only means that the "larger self" has come to include a greater portion of the world than formerly. The outlook has become broader and the child has appropriated the problems of, it may be, far distant peoples. We should remember, however, that it is still the real problem of real people that holds the attention and it is the thought of the committee that every topic studied should be approached with this fact clearly in view.

### Outline of a Course in Physiography for Last Half of the Seventh Grade

In this course as in all the other courses outlined in this report, it is the thought of the committee that the work should be accompanied at every step by, indeed should largely consist of, field studies and laboratory illustration and demonstration. No textbook nor teacher can take the place of actual observation.

A. The atmosphere.

- I. General conception.
- II. Constitution.
- III. The weather.
  - a) Careful and extended observations.
  - b) The factors of the weather.
    1. Temperature.
    2. Winds.
    3. Humidity.

- *c*) An experimental study of weather observation instruments.
  - 1. The thermometer.
    - *aa*) Experimental study of effects of heat.
  - 2. The barometer.
    - *aa*) An extended study of air pressure and its effects.
    - *bb*) Barometric changes due to convection currents.
      - (1) Experimental study of convection currents.
  - 3. The hygrometer.
    - *aa*) Studies in evaporation and accompanying heat effects.
    - *bb*) Full study of atmospheric moisture.
      - (1) Clouds, fogs, dew, frost, and the various precipitations.
- *d*) The general storm, or "low" or "cyclone."
  - 1. Its origin.
  - 2. Its characteristics.
  - 3. Why it brings stormy weather.
- *e*) An analysis of a large number of popular weather "signs" to determine whether or not they have scientific bases.
- *f*) Weather maps and weather forecasting.

IV. Climate.
- *a*) The various influences which affect it.

V. The work of the atmosphere.
- *a*) Mechanical.
- *b*) Chemical.

B. The hydrosphere.

I. The ocean studied as a whole.
- *a*) Sea-water.
  - 1. Its temperature in different localities.
  - 2. Its movements.
    - *aa*) Waves.
    - *bb*) Tides.
    - *cc*) Currents.
- *b*) Life in the ocean.
- *c*) The work of the ocean.

C. The lithosphere.

I. A more intensive study of the following topics.
- *a*) Relief features.
- *b*) Ground water.
- *c*) Running water.
- *d*) Snow and ice.
- *e*) Lakes and shores.
- *f*) Vulcanism.
- *g*) Crustal movements.

D. Influence of earth forms and features upon human life.

I. Rivers.
- *a*) As highways for migration and trade.
- *b*) As boundaries—ethnic and political.

II. Plains.
  a) Small and surrounded by barriers.
  b) Large and no barriers.
  c) Watered or arid.

III. Piedmont region.

IV. Mountains.
  a) As barriers.
  b) As habitations.
  c) Influence upon climate.

V. Islands.
  a) Continental and oceanic.
  b) As stepping-stones.
  c) As cradles.

VI. Oceans.
  a) As highways.
  b) As barriers.
  c) As sources of wealth.

VII. The coast—accessible from land and sea.
  a) Zone.
  b) Harbors.
  c) Contrast of coast and inland peoples.

### Course in Household Science for Girls, Eighth Year

The aim of this course is to make stronger, more perfect, more vigorous bodies, to decrease the number of attacks of preventable disease, to live more economically in regard to both money and energy, and at the same time to increase health and happiness; also to show that the manner of our living is not a haphazard affair nor regulated by tradition, but is based on scientific principles which are immutable.

Further, the course should arouse such an interest in the affairs of personal and household routine that they shall cease to be dull drudgery but shall appear, rather, as alive, as other, less commonplace, problems which require training and skill and are yet not so important for a healthy body and an efficient life.

To serve these purposes, the topics selected for study have been grouped about: A, the care of the individual; B, the care of the house; C, the care of the community.

This course, which is largely devoted to the more general principles, presupposes at least one year's work in cooking and one in sewing in the lower grades. In the absence of this, progress is slower, more application being necessary. And, to accomplish the best results, it should be accompanied by a thorough course in the actual preparation of food by way of application of the principles here worked out.

This course in the eighth or ninth grade will require an average of forty-five minutes per day in recitation and an equivalent period for preparation.

On three days of each week the two periods, recitation and study, should be combined and spent with the teacher in the laboratory.

The applications embodied in the course in cooking may be given on the two-period days, the recitation work being done on the one-period days and as it is called for by the subject-matter on laboratory days.

A. Needs of the individual.

I. Food.

*a*) To preserve it for future use.

Experiment I: To discover what makes food spoil.

*Method:*—Leave

1. Hard, smooth-skinned, whole fruit,
2. Hard fruit with broken skin,
3. Fruit with rough skin (orange, lemon),
4. Soft fruit with firm skin,
5. Tomato (acid),
6. Berries,
7. Fruits wrapped in paper,
8. Other foods, bread, eggs, meat, etc.,

in places where the following conditions may be investigated:

1. In barrel, box or basket, not separated.
2. Separated.
3. Temperature of 45 degrees. Refrigerator.
4. Temperature 75 to 85 degrees. Room.
5. Packed in sawdust, dry, clean sand, chaff.
6. Cool air, light, natural humidity.

Form conclusions as to:

1. What causes spoiling? (Molds)
2. Where does it come from?
3. Its growth as affected by:
   - *a*) Texture of fruit and skin.
   - *b*) Quiet air, darkness, contact.
   - *c*) Acidity.
   - *d*) Temperature.
   - *e*) Moisture.

Experiment II: To discover how molds injure foods.

*Method:*—

1. Study individual mold plants under the microscope.
   - *a*) Parts. Function of each.
   - *b*) Different kinds of molds.
2. Plant molds on fruit syrups and watch growth of all parts.
3. Smell molded food. Taste syrups prepared in (2).
4. Remove mold and boil. Effect on taste.

Experiment III: To preserve food from molds.

1. By drying.
   - *a*) Method of cutting.
   - *b*) Other conditions.

2. By heating to 180 degrees F. (temperature recommended for grape juice).
3. By heating to the boiling point.

Experiment IV: To determine the effects of yeasts upon fruit.

*Method:*—

1. Allow apple juice to stand for several days exposed to the air.
2. Put part of a yeast cake into apple juice and let stand. Compare results with (1). Examine under the microscope.
3. Boil some fruit juice from (2) after one day and leave open. Compare with the rest of (2) after several days.
4. Boil and seal.

Experiment V: To determine the effect of different temperatures upon the growth of yeast.

*Method:*—In fermentation tubes prepare solutions of sugar, add yeast, and keep at:

1. 125 degrees F.
2. 70 to 90 degrees F.
3. Use yeast which has been frozen before adding to the sugar solution.

NOTE.—Compare the rapidity of the evolution of gas in the various cases.

Experiment VI: To apply knowledge acquired in study of yeast:

1. To the making of bread.
2. To the keeping of yeast.
3. To fermented jelly, etc.

Experiment VII: To determine the cause of the spoiling of meat, milk, eggs, cereals, etc., and vegetables, not acid.

*Method:*—

1. Put samples into test tubes in water. Notice of decay—gas bubbles, odor. Compare odor with that resulting from mold and yeast activity. Is this caused by molds? Yeasts? Examine with microscope. See bacteria.

Experiment VIII: To determine methods for preserving foods from bacteria.

*Method:*—

1. Compare drying (Exp. III).
2. Antiseptics. Syrups, brine, spices, alcohol, vinegar, oils, each on appropriate foods.
3. Freeze once, seal, place in 70 to 80 degrees.
4. Boil samples for one minute, 5 min., 30 min. each, and seal.

Experiment IX: Application of heat to preserve fruit and vegetables indefinitely.

*Method:*—Work out from preceding experiments:

1. Advantages of three ways of canning.
2. Intermittent sterilization.

(Can fruits, vegetables, and make jelly.)

*b*) To preserve the wholesomeness of food for present use.

Experiment X: Bacteria in water.

1. Sources of water supply and chances of contamination.
2. Significance of bacteria in water.
3. Methods of purifying.
4. Methods of controlling contamination.

Experiment XI: Bacteria in milk.

1. Lactic acid bacteria. Make litmus tests.
   - *a*) Effects of temperatures: 50, 70, 90 degrees F.
   - *b*) Effects of pasteurizing by heating to 165 F. and cooling to 49 degrees, immediately.
   - *c*) Effect of heating to 165 degrees and maintaining that temperature 20 minutes.
   - *d*) Effect of boiling 1 min., 5 min., 30 min.
2. Other bacteria.
   - *a*) Source.
   - *b*) Effect on man.
   - *c*) Effect of heat and freezing.
   - *d*) What is good milk:
     As to chemical composition.
     As to bacterial contamination.

Experiment XII: Harmful organisms in meat.

1. Bacteria.
   - *a*) Kinds.
   - *b*) Sources.
   - *c*) Effect upon meat.
   - *d*). Effect upon person eating the meat.
   - *e*) How made harmless.
2. Parasites.
   - *a*) Kinds and sources.
   - *b*) Signs of.
   - *c*) Effects upon person.
   - *d*) How killed.

*c*) To make the food more palatable and nutritious.

NOTE.—The amplification of this topic is given in the accompanying outline on cooking. A laboratory and equipment are needed for it.

The preceding topics have been treated fully enough to suggest the method of treatment throughout. There follows a series of topics more briefly outlined. The same general experimental method of treatment should be observed in studying them.

The study of the bacterial contamination of foods studied in the preceding topics will lead to the following:

Experiment XIII: Sewage disposal.

1. Dangers from sewage.
2. Public and private methods of disposal.

Experiment XIV: Garbage and manure.

1. Dangers from.
2. Care to be taken of.
3. Disposal of.

Experiment XV: Flies and other insects.

1. Haunts.
2. Carrying ability.
   *a*) The feet.
   *b*) In their bodies. Tuberculosis bacilli in specks.

II. The freedom of the individual from disease.

*a*) A diseased individual as a spreader of disease.

1. Cause of an infectious disease.
2. Elimination of bacteria.
   *aa*) Mouth, nose, skin, eyes, genito-urinary tract.
3. Care of excretions to avoid possibility of their reaching another person while virile.
4. Disinfection of excretions.
5. Care of bedding, wash basins, bath tubs, toilets, drinking-cups, eating-utensils, handkerchiefs, soap, towels, combs, books (wetting fingers to turn leaves), etc.
6. Careless habits of breathing, coughing, talking, sneezing, kissing, playing halloween games, etc.

*b*) How an individual may take bacteria into the body.

1. By way of the mouth.
   *aa*) In food and drink.
      (1) How foods stuffs may become contaminated.
         Place where grown.
         Diseased animals.
         People handling them.
         Dust, flies, other insects.
         Persons in kitchen.
         Persons at table.
   *bb*) Fingers, pencils, handkerchiefs.
   *cc*) The nose.
      (1) Inhaled with dust.
   *dd*) The eyes.
   *ee*) Through the skin.
      (1) Through cuts or abrasions.
      (2) Rubbed through.
2. Precautions to prevent entrance of bacteria to body.

III. Personal hygiene.

*a*) Under this topic there should be presented enough biology to enable the children clearly to understand the meaning of a cell, a nerve, a muscle, a blood vessel, etc. There should be a study of plant and animal cells with a comparison of their structures and functions. There should also be given enough of the physiology of the digestive, circulatory, respiratory, excretory, muscular, and nervous systems to enable children to understand their hygiene.

*b*) The body's defenses against the multiplication of bacteria.

1. Air.
2. Food. Proper kinds and amounts, properly eaten.
3. Exercise.

4. Not over-fatigue. Study effects of work on muscles.
5. Not over-exposure. To extremes of hot and cold.
6. Increased number of leucocytes.

*c*) Elementary dietetics.

1. Comparative calorie values of different foods.
2. Simple dietetic principles and practices.

*d*) Emergencies.

1. Fainting, cuts, drowning, burns.

B. The care of the house.

I. Bacteriology and chemistry of:

*a*) Sweeping and dusting. (Also physical problems—settling.)

*b*) Scrubbing, laundering, dishwashing.

1. Soaps, washing powders, bluing, removal of spots and stains.

*c*) Cooking.

1. Use of fuels. Amounts necessary to produce definite results.
2. Comparison of different fuels.
3. Building a fire.
4. Conductivity of media.

*d*) Principles of artificial cooling.

*e*) Applications of the principles of cooking to the cooking of simple foods. This should both illustrate the principles of cooking and give skill in cooking all kinds of nutrients and food stuffs.

*f*) Lighting—natural and artificial.

*g*) Plumbing—the mechanism and care of.

*h*) Heating and ventilation.

C. The care of the community.

I. This will consist largely of a summary of previous work showing:

*a*) Individual's responsibility for welfare of the community.

*b*) Government's control of conditions affecting the welfare of the individual.

### The Course in Cooking

This course is to supply application in the household for the principles in the general science course for girls.

A. Heat and its use.

I. Temperature to be obtained in using water to conduct heat, and the phenomena observed in bringing it to a boiling point (applied to cooking fresh fruits).

II. Conditions affecting evaporation (applied to dried fruits). Cooling and freezing mixtures (applied to frozen dishes).

III. Conductivity of materials (freezers and fireless cookers).

B. Nutrients in foods.

I. Carbohydrates.

*a*) Sugars. Syrups and candies.

*b*) Starch. Corn starch.

*c*) Vegetables and fruits.

*d*) Cereals.

*e*) Flour.

1. Rôle of gluten in flour.
2. Leavening agents.
   *aa*) Physical.
   *bb*) Chemical.
   *cc*) Yeast.

(Applied to batters and doughs.)

II. Fats.
   *a*) Conductivity.
   *b*) Burning point.
   *c*) Emulsions.

(Use in frying, salad dressings.)

III. Proteins.
   *a*) Milk.
      1. Chemical composition.
      2. Effect of temperature.

(Cheese, junket pudding.)

   *b*) Eggs.
      1. Composition.
      2. Temperature.

(Eggs and custard.)

   *c*) Meat.
      1. Structure.
      2. Composition.
      3. Effect of temperature.
      4. Selection.

(Emphasis on use of cheap cuts.)

C. Planning and serving meals with reference to cost and balanced ration.

NOTE.—This is accompanied by elementary dietetics in the science course.

### SEWING. NINTH YEAR

The work of the second year is designed to supply:

A. A knowledge of the fabrics used in making cloths and of their manufacture into textiles to promote intelligent selection and buying of cloths.
   I. The tests for different fibers.

B. The principles of design as applied to color and form:
   I. In dress.
   II. In wearing the hair, etc.

C. Selection of materials with reference to their conductivity and hygroscopic qualities.
   I. Method of dressing with regard to conductivity.
      *a*) Purpose, money available, wearing qualities, etc.
      *b*) Thick layers as compared with a greater number of thinner layers holding air spaces.

D. Preparation of cloth for garments and care of cloth.
   I. Shrinking.
   II. Setting of colors.
   III. Removal of spots and stains.
   IV. Effects of washing chemicals and heating upon fibers and color.

E. The making of garments (underwear, waists, dresses).
  I. Principles of patterns, cutting, fitting, and sewing.

F. Calculation of cost of individual garments; also of outfits for girls of different environments and of different financial ability.

The last six weeks of the second year should be spent in a recapitulation of the principles involved in supplying the individual needs and in the care of the house and the community. Follow this with:

A. The evolution of the "shelter" into a "home."
  I. The primitive shelter. The purpose it served.
  II. Tribal, or group, shelter.
    a) Its disadvantages.
    b) Its advantages.
  III. The desire for better conditions for the working out of individual ideas led to a house apart for an individual and his companion, i.e., his wife.

B. Relations of husband and wife.
  I. What excites admiration.
    a) Physical, moral, and mental qualities.

C. Effects of various physical and moral conditions upon the home.
  I. Continuation of happiness.
  II. Health of husband and wife.
  III. Ability to hold the respect of the community.
  IV. Chance to do some share of the world's work.

D. Effect of these conditions upon children.
  I. Heredity.
    a) Reproduction.
    b) Inherited qualities—physical, mental, moral.
  II. Environment. Its influence.

E. The object of a home as ideally conceived.
  I. Preparation for making a home.
  II. The responsibility in undertaking to make a home.
  III. The ability to maintain a home.

## A Year's Work in Agriculture. Eighth Grade

The order of the following topics is determined by the assumption that the study will be taken up in the fall, September 1, and continued through the year.

It seems impracticable to make this outline either a textbook in agriculture or a laboratory manual. An attempt is made to suggest a series of topics suitable for attack by eighth-grade children, where the environment is of such a character as to warrant it. The importance of making the studies concrete at every step, of persistently studying things instead of "about" them, of laboratory illustration and investigation wherever possible cannot be too much emphasized.

A. The selection and storage of seed corn.
  I. Principles and rules governing the selection.
    a) Height of ear, angle, maturity, etc.

- II. Characteristics of different varieties of corn.
  - *a*) Three or four varieties raised in the neighborhood.
- III. Corn judging.
  - *a*) Rules of Illinois Corn Growers' Association.
  - *b*) Use of the score card.
- IV. Principles governing the storage of seed corn.
  - *a*) Conditions of temperature and moisture.

B. Harvesting and storing the summer and fall crops.
- I. The cereals.
  - *a*) Wheat, oats, corn.
    - 1. The machinery employed in harvesting and threshing, comparing with those of earlier days.
- II. Vegetables.
  - *a*) Potatoes, cabbage, turnips, etc.
- III. Fruits.
  - *a*) Peaches, pears, apples, etc.
- IV. Roughage for stock.
  - *a*) Hay.
    - 1. Timothy.
    - 2. The clovers, alfalfa.
    - 3. Other legumes.
  - *b*) Straw.
  - *c*) Corn fodder.
  - *d*) Ensilage.
    - 1. Construction and principle of the silo.

C. A study of fall weeds.
- I. Identify several varieties by leaf, stem, and seed.
  - *a*) Cocklebur, butter print, mustard, etc.
  - *b*) Make collections of seeds, place in bottles, and label.
- II. Provisions made for the survival of these weeds.
- III. Methods of eradicating.

D. The fall birds.
- I. Particularly the seed-eaters.
  Habits of feeding.
  Migration.

E. A study of farm animals.
- I. Characteristics and history of a few common breeds of:
  - *a*) Horses.
    - 1. Draft horses.
    - 2. Roadsters.
      - *aa*) Compare types of these two.
  - *b*) Cattle.
    - 1. Beef cattle.
      - *aa*) Two or three of the most common breeds.
      - *bb*) A study of stock dietaries.
      - *cc*) Plan balanced rations for beef cattle.

2. Dairy cattle.
   *aa*) The commonest breeds.
   *bb*) Compare with beef breeds.
   *cc*) Plan balanced ration for dairy cattle.

II. Detailed computations of the profits from stock.
   *a*) Profits from a work horse.
   *b*) Profits from breeding horses for sale.
   *c*) Profits in beef production.
   *d*) Profits from dairy cattle.

III. Similarly study sheep, hogs, poultry.

F. Make a more particular study of milk and butter.

I. Dairy methods to insure cleanliness.

II. Pasteurization and care of milk. Bacteria, etc.

III. Testing milk for butter fat.

IV. The cream separator.

G. Fall and winter phases of tree life.

I. Identification of trees in winter garb.

II. The cutting of trees.
   *a*) For lumber—poles, posts, boards, timbers, etc.
   *b*) For wood, i.e., firewood.

III. Compute the profit to the farmer of a "wood lot."
   *a*) How it can be had.
   *b*) Trees suitable to make quick growth.

H. A more extended study of general forestry.

I. Uses of forests.
   *a*) Firewood and lumber, as above.
   *b*) Conservation of moisture.
   *c*) Play spots for the people. Parks, reservations, etc.

II. Individual species of forest trees.
   *a*) Hard wood trees—oak, elm, walnut, etc.
      1. Uses, habitat, present supply and value, time required to reach maturity.
   *b*) Soft wood trees—the pines, etc.
      1. Same topics as above.

III. Conservation of forests.
   *a*) The government forest service.

K. The testing of seed corn.

I. The importance.
   *a*) Compute yield of an acre, having hills 3 ft. 8 in. apart each way, each yielding three 12-ounce ears.

II. Study the conditions necessary.
   *a*) Heat, moisture, air.

III. Study, also, the germination of other seeds.
   *a*) Better results will be obtained with large seeds.

L. Study and practice other methods of propagating plants.
  I. Make root grafts of apple trees.
  II. Make cuttings of willows or Carolina poplar.

M. An experimental study of the growth of plants.
  I. Effects of heat, light, moisture, gravity, etc.
  II. The significance of "leaf green."

N. Laboratory study of soil physics.
  I. Formation and physical composition of soils.
  II. Classification of soils according to texture.
  III. Moisture relations of soils. Experimental.
    *a*) As to percolation.
    *b*) As to capillarity.
    *c*) As to capacity for moisture.
    *d*) Moisture content as affected by tillage.
  IV. Physical effects of humus in the soil.
  V. Soil temperature as affected by color and drainage.
  VI. Improvement of physical condition of clays by addition of lime.

O. The experimental plot.
  I. Arrangement of the plot for experimental purposes.
    *a*) Plan a system of crop rotation and divide the plot in harmony with the plan.
  II. Studies in cultivation.
  III. Studies of fertilizers.
  IV. Preparation of the soil.
    *a*) Purposes.
      1. To render root penetration easy.
      2. To conserve moisture.
      3. To promote aeration.
  V. The planting of the plots.
  VI. The cultivation.
    *a*) To eradicate weeds.
    *b*) To conserve moisture.
    *c*) To promote aeration.
  VII. Animals as related to the experimental work.
    *a*) Earthworms and the soil.
    *b*) Gophers, mice, etc., in relation to the crop.
    *c*) Insect enemies of field and garden.
    *d*) Toads, frogs, etc., in relation to insects.
    *e*) Birds.
      1. Insect eaters.
      2. Weed-seed eaters.
      3. Vermin eaters.
  VIII. The weeds that bother and how to exterminate them.

R. Planting of trees and shrubs.
   I. Forest trees.
   II. Fruit trees.
      *a*) Pruning and care.
   III. Fruit-bearing shrubs.
      *a*) Currants, gooseberries, etc.
   IV. Ornamental shrubs.

### Industrial Science. Eighth or Ninth Year

The committee suggests for the work of the boys during the eighth and ninth years a series of topics in industrial science. The course in Agriculture outlined for the eighth year can be used where the interests are agricultural. In other communities, the community industries will largely suggest the character of the work. The following topics are suggested as suitable:

1. The elements of metallurgy.
2. Petroleum and its products.
3. Illuminating gas.
   Natural gas, coal gas, water gas.
   Study the coal-tar products in connection.
4. The lumber industry.
5. The meat-packing industry.
   Study soap-making industry.
6. Motive power.
   Animal, steam, electricity, gas, wind, water, etc.
7. Heating, lighting, plumbing of houses.

To suggest somewhat more definitely the possibilities implied in these topics, the committee has outlined the subtopics which may be studied in connection with one or two of them.

#### THE ELEMENTS OF METALLURGY: IRON

A. Get from the children a long list of the commercial forms of iron.
   I. Nails, pipes, tools, stoves, bolts, rods, castings, etc., etc. Extend this list until it is a *long* one.
   II. Have the children, from their general information, classify these forms into cast iron, wrought iron, and steel.
   III. Name the properties of these various forms and from these suggest the differences among cast iron, wrought iron, steel.

B. Study the properties of cast iron, wrought iron, and steel to be able to distinguish among them.
   I. Test samples of cast iron, wrought iron, and steel for:
      *a*) Malleability.
      *b*) Elasticity.
      *c*) Flexibility.
      *d*) Brittleness.
      *e*) Hardness.
   II. Name the uses of these various forms of iron as determined by their properties.
      *a*) Which kind likely to be used for the following, and why?
         1. Nails, stoves, water pipes, steam radiators, wagon tires, fence wire,

piano wire, springs, structural iron, cutting tools, railroad rails, iron roofing.

C. The manufacture of the different kinds of iron.
- I. Visit a blast furnace, if possible, and study the reduction of iron ore.
  - *a*) Study the construction of a blast furnace.
    - 1. Why called blast furnace?
  - *b*) The charge.
    - 1. The iron ore itself.
      - *aa*) Probably an oxide. Ferric oxide. $Fe_2O_3$.
    - 2. The reducing agent and fuel.
      - *aa*) Some form of carbon—coke or coal.
    - 3. The "flux."
      - *aa*) Limestone or sand.
        - (1) Dependent upon impurities in the ore.
  - *c*) The process.
  - *d*) The products.
    - 1. Cast iron—pig iron.
      - *aa*) White cast iron.
        - (1) Carbon largely in combination.
      - *bb*) Gray cast iron.
        - (1) Carbon largely crystallized out. Graphite.
- II. The chemistry of the reduction.
  - *a*) What determines the character of the flux used?
  - *b*) The fusion of the flux with the impurities to form "slag."
  - *c*) The reduction of the iron oxide. Formations of the oxides of carbon.
    - 1. Illustrate in laboratory with the reduction of cupric oxide.
  - *d*) Some carbon will inevitably be taken up by the iron.
    - 1. 2% to 5% the carbon content of cast iron.
  - *e*) Properties of cast iron.
    - 1. Brittle.
    - 2. Cannot be welded nor tempered.
    - 3. Strong, however, and durable if not subjected to shock.
- III. Study the history of iron-ore reduction.
- IV. Trace our ores to their sources.
- V. The making of steel.
  - *a*) Made from cast iron.
    - 1. By burning out part of the carbon.
      - *aa*) The open-hearth process.
      - *bb*) The Bessemer process.
      - *cc*) Crucible steel.
  - *b*) Properties of steel.
    - 1. Hard.
    - 2. Elastic.
    - 3. Can be tempered.
- VI. Wrought iron.
  - *a*) The puddling furnace.
  - *b*) Rolling mills.
  - *c*) Properties of wrought iron.

Having studied the metallurgy of iron, the metallurgy of other common metals can be taken up, it being only necessary to point out the differences among the processes. Several of the metals are combined with sulphur, in the form of sulphides, to form the ores. This is particularly true of zinc, lead, and mercury. The general rule is: Ores other than oxides are first roasted to change them to oxides. Then the process is very similar to that employed for the reduction of iron. Mercury, however, is an exception to the rule.

Again, in some cases there are valuable by-products. Thus, sulphuric acid is a valuable by-product of the zinc industry.

Aluminum will introduce the interesting processes of electrolysis.

The use of the "cyanide" process in the metallurgy of gold makes "pay dirt" of great masses of tailings formerly discarded.

Eight or ten common metals should be selected, their commercial forms listed, a study made of the location of the mines from which they come, the reduction of their ores investigated, and their properties and uses learned. A brief history of each will add interest to the work.

In addition, a considerable amount of actual work with the metals in the manual-training course accompanying this course would give far greater value to the knowledge sought in these lessons.

## Lighting and Heating of Dwellings

Note.—A book entitled *The Elements of Physical Science,* written and published by F. D. Barber, Normal, Illinois, contains a great deal of valuable information along the lines suggested by these topics.

A. The lighting of houses.
    I. History of fire—the first flame.
    II. Primitive lamps.
        *a*) The pine knot.
        *b*) Greek and Roman lamps.
        *c*) Present lamps of the Esquimaux.
    III. Candles.
        *a*) The burning of a candle.
    IV. Kerosene lamps.
        *a*) A study of petroleum and its products.
            1. Distillation. Fractional distillation.
    V. Gasoline. Its properties and uses.
        *a*) Gasoline lamps.
        *b*) Gasoline gas machines.
    VI. Illuminating gas.
        *a*) The coal gas industry.
    VII. Acetylene gas.
    VIII. Electric lighting.
        *a*) Incandescent lamps.
        *b*) Arc lamps.

B. The heating of houses.
    I. The historical aspect.

*a*) The open fireplace.
*b*) The first stoves.

II. The burning of wood and coal.
*a*) The chemistry of combustion.
1. The chemistry of the air.
*b*) The common heating-stove.

III. Kinds and compositions of common fuels.

IV. A study of furnaces.
*a*) Convection currents.
1. In water.
2. In air.
*b*) Drafts of chimneys.
*c*) Hot-air furnaces.
*d*) Hot-water furnaces.
*e*) Steam furnaces.

V. The open grate.
*a*) Importance in ventilation.

VI. Cooking-stoves and ranges.
*a*) Approach from the historical point of view.
*b*) Gasoline and gas stoves.
1. The manufacture of coal gas.
*c*) The fireless cooker.
1. The question of conductivity.
2. Questions of specific heat.

## PHYSIOLOGY AND HYGIENE. TENTH YEAR

In this as in the other courses it has not seemed practicable in every case to give details of experimental work. In so far as possible every principle taught should be rendered objective by laboratory illustration and demonstration.

A. The normal function of the human body.

I. Activity—the doing of useful work.
*a*) Physical work—muscular activity.
*b*) Mental work—nervous activity.
1. Both result in fatigue and final collapse, unless:
2. The store of energy be replenished in some way.

B. A study of "the cell" as the unit of structure of plant and animal tissues to give better understanding of the effects of activity.

I. A typical cell illustrated by California grape.
*a*) Wall.
*b*) Protoplasm.
*c*) Nucleus.

II. Study of cells.
*a*) In some tissues all of the same shape.
1. Skin of onion.
*b*) In some cases they show a variety of shapes.
1. Epidermis of lily—guard cells.
*c*) Some cells have special function as to product.
1. Starch cells of potato.

*d*) Plant and animal cells essentially alike.

1. Compare cells of onion skin with epithelial cells of the mouth.

III. Functions of cells.

*a*) Some cells able to do all the things any plant or animal can do.

1. Illustrated by pleurococcus and paramoecium.

*b*) As evolution progresses cells become highly specialized.

1. Nerve cells, muscle cells, fat cells, etc.

IV. Activity of the organs results in the breakdown of these cells.

*a*) The consequent necessity of replenishment.

C. Food. The new material necessary to promote cell growth and maintain the efficiency of the organs for activity.

I. Protoplasm, basic factor of cell composition, composed of:

*a*) Carbon, hydrogen, oxygen, nitrogen, sulphur, phosphorus.

1. Chemical study of these elements.

2. Study of their various compounds.

*aa*) Properties of the elements and of their compounds dissimilar.

(1) Compare hydrogen or oxygen with water.

(2) Compare carbon (charcoal) with butter.

(3) Compare nitrogen with white of egg.

(4) Compare sulphur with white of egg.

(5) Compare phosphorus with flesh of fish.

3. Except in the case of oxygen, these elements can be used by the body only in their compounds.

*b*) Uses made by the cells of these compounds of the elements.

1. Those rich in carbon for energy—heat, work.

*aa*) Study the oxidation of carbon and the products.

2. Those rich in nitrogen for building material and energy.

3. Study the chemical composition of starch, sugar, protein, and fats to determine their efficiency as foods.

4. Learn the chemical tests for these foods.

5. Classify by test a large number of common foods as to their use in the body.

*c*) A study of dietaries.

1. Necessity of knowing what foods furnish the desired elements in the right proportion.

2. The calorie values of foods.

*aa*) Chittenden, Voit, and Atwater tables.

*bb*) 100-calorie portions table. (Fisher.)

3. Plan balanced meals.

*aa*) As influenced by different occupations.

*bb*) To get highest nutrient value at lowest cost.

II. The preparation of foods.

*a*) Why foods are cooked.

1. To kill parasites and bacteria.

2. To conserve the nutrient factors.

3. To promote digestibility.

4. To render the food more palatable.

*b*) The importance of proper cooking to gain these ends.

III. The care of foods.

*a*) See outline of work in Eighth Grade (Household Science).

D. Digestion.
- I. In the mouth.
  - *a*) Mastication and insalivation.
    - 1. Structure, function, and care of the teeth.
      - *aa*) Comparative study of teeth.
        - (1) As suggestive of kind of food required.
    - 2. Structure, location, and function of the salivary glands.
      - *aa*) The saliva—ptyalin.
        - (1) Change of starch into a soluble compound.
    - 3. Importance of thorough mastication and insalivation.
      - *aa*) Apply starch and sugar tests to:
        - (1) Starch food (bread) not masticated.
        - (2) Starch food partially masticated.
        - (3) Starch food thoroughly masticated.
      - *bb*) Effects of acid fruits on action of ptyalin.
      - *cc*) Effects of cold water on action of ptyalin.
      - *dd*) Fletcherism—its significance.
- II. In the stomach.
  - *a*) The gastric digestion. Change of protein to peptone.
    - 1. Location, size, shape, anatomy of the stomach.
    - 2. Glands, juices, and motions of the stomach.
    - 3. Conditions which promote the normal progress of gastric digestion.
      - *aa*) Proper mastication and insalivation.
      - *bb*) Proper temperature of foods.
        - (1) Effects of ice-water and other cold foods.
      - *cc*) General good health.
      - *dd*) Normal appetite.
      - *ee*) Palatability of foods.
      - *ff*) Freedom from worry.
    - 4. Medicines as aids to digestion.
      - *aa*) Unnatural, showing abnormal condition.
- III. In the intestines.
  - *a*) Completion of other processes; emulsification of fats.
  - *b*) Importance to health of normal action here.
    - 1. Residues of food must be eliminated.
  - *c*) Form, structure, and function of the intestines.
  - *d*) The glands and fluids which contribute to intestinal digestion.
    - 1. The liver and the bile.
    - 2. The pancreatic juice.
  - *e*) Conditions which tend to clogging of the intestinal tract.
    - 1. Insufficient water as food.
    - 2. Insufficient exercise.
  - *f*) Remedial foods.
    - 1. Fruits. Entire grain cereals. Vegetables.
  - *g*) Auto-intoxication.
    - 1. Causes.
      - *aa*) Improper mastication.
      - *bb*) Inefficient peristaltic movement of intestines.
        - (1) Due to lack of salts in food.
      - *cc*) Unclean food.

2. Results.
   aa) Poisoning of various types.
      (1) Hives.
   bb) Indigestion.

IV. Absorption.
   a) What becomes of the digested food?
      1. The villi.
         aa) Osmosis.
            (1) Experimental study of.
      2. The lacteals.

V. Effect upon the digestive organs and processes of using contaminated foods.
   a) Diseases of the digestive tract.
      1. Dysentery, diarrhea, cholera infantum, typhoid fever, indigestion, appendicitis, etc.
         aa) Importance of sterilizing all discharges in bacterial diseases of the digestive tract.

E. The circulatory system.

I. Necessity for.
   a) Compare to river system carrying supplies to individuals and communities. (Cells.)
   b) How the digested food gets into the circulatory system.
      1. The portal circulation.

II. Circulation in frog's foot.

III. Structure and action of the heart.
   a) Work out the mechanics of the valves.

IV. Structure and uses of the blood tubes.
   a) Arteries.
   b) Capillaries.
   c) Veins.

V. The blood.
   a) Its composition and properties.
      1. The corpuscles and their function.
         aa) Number of corpuscles.
            (1) Anemia.
   b) Ability of cells to select needed materials from blood.

VI. The lymphatic circulation.

VII. Diseases of the circulatory organs and of the blood.
   a) Heart disease.
      1. Effects of overexertion.
      2. Influence of indigestion.
   b) Blood poisoning.
   c) Fevers, etc.
   d) Effects of alcohol.

VIII. The purification of the blood.

F. The respiratory system.

I. The organs of respiration.
   a) Nasal passages, larynx, trachea, lungs, bronchial tubes.
      1. Special study of structure of lungs.

II. The mechanics of respiration.
  a) Expansibility of air.
  b) Illustrate the mechanics of breathing.
  c) Lung capacity by use of simple apparatus.

III. The composition of "pure" air.

IV. The composition of exhaled air.
  a) Explain difference on basis of oxidation.

V. Importance of abundance of pure air.
  a) To maintain energy—heat.
  b) Amount of fresh air necessary for each individual.
    1. Ventilation.
      aa) Necessity and methods.
  c) Deep breathing.
    1. By chest expansion.
    2. Necessity of loose clothing.

VI. Diseases of the respiratory organs.
  a) Colds, bronchitis, catarrh, sore throat, adenoids, tonsilitis, pneumonia, diphtheria, tuberculosis.
  b) Illustrate bacterial character by means of culture plates.
  c) The resistant properties of tuberculosis bacilli.

TUBERCULOSIS

1. Graphic illustration to show prevalence.
   Estimate cost to the country.
2. Study of known characteristic case.
3. Cause and nature of disease.
   aa) Parts of body attacked.
   bb) Germs—thorough elementary study.
   cc) Contagion:
       Sputa.
       Dried sputa carried in dust.
       Spreads through use of water, drinking-cups, books, pencils, carried by flies and pests, found in milk of affected cows.
4. Means of prevention.
   Avoid promiscuous spitting.
   Keep body strong.
   Secure milk and food from sources known to be clean.
   Keep all avenues closed to germs so far as possible.
5. Treatment.
   Early attention.
   Live in the open.
   Complete rest.
   Climatic benefits.
   Nourishing food.
   Skilled medical attendance.
   Sanatariums.
   Avoid patent medicines.
   Avoid alcohol.

G. The skin and excretion.
- I. Structure and function of the skin.
  - *a*) The skin as a protection.
  - *b*) The elimination of waste products.
    - 1. The perspiratory system.
  - *c*) The regulation of the body temperature.
    - 1. The heat effects of evaporation.
- II. Hygiene of the skin.
  - *a*) Importance of bathing.
  - *b*) Care as to scratching and rubbing.
    - 1. Provides for entrance of bacteria.
  - *c*) Need of proper clothing for protection.
    - 1. Study "warmth" properties of clothing.
      - *aa*) Conductivity of such textiles as wool, cotton.
      - *bb*) Heat properties of various colors. (Experiment.)
- III. Structure and functions of the kidneys.
- IV. Diseases of the kidneys.
  - *a*) Bright's disease.

H. The skeletal system.
- I. Shapes of bones dependent upon their function.
- II. The uses of the bones.
  - *a*) For protection.
  - *b*) As levers for action of muscles.
    - 1. Study classes of levers and classify levers of body.

K. The muscles.
- I. The characteristic property of muscle.
  - *a*) Contractility.
- II. The relation of muscle to exercise.
- III. The limitations to the value of exercise.

L. The nervous system.
- I. The parts and their functions.
  - *a*) The brain, spinal cord, nerves, ganglia.
  - *b*) Illustrate with dissection of frog.
- II. The relations of the nerves to the other organs.
- III. Diseases of the nervous system.
  - *a*) Alcoholism.

M. The organs of special sense.
- I. The eye.
  - *a*) The elements of optics. Lenses.
  - *b*) The parts and functions.
  - *c*) The care of the eyes.
  - *d*) Glasses.
- II. The ear.
  - *a*) Its structure and function.
  - *b*) Care.
  - *c*) Diseases.
    - 1. Earache.

III. The sense of taste.
IV. The sense of smell.

N. Reproduction.
I. Reproduction in such plants as yeasts and bacteria.
II. Reproduction in higher plants.
III. Embryology of frog and chick.

## SUGGESTION FOR ELEVENTH AND TWELFTH YEARS

ELEVENTH YEAR, PHYSICAL AND CHEMICAL SCIENCES. TWELFTH YEAR, BIOLOGICAL SCIENCES

## BOOKS WHICH MAY BE OF AID IN THE SUGGESTED COURSE OF STUDY

### GENERAL GEOGRAPHICAL ASPECTS

Geographical Series, by Herbertson.
Geographical Series, by Carpenter.
Series of Food, Clothing, etc., by Chamberlain.
Place of Industry in Education, by Dopp.

### GENERAL HOUSEHOLD, BIOLOGICAL AND AGRICULTURAL, ETC.

Bulletins of Our Illinois State Laboratory. Bulletins of the U.S. Department of Agriculture and Bulletins of the Various State and College Experiment Stations.
Conn, Bacteria, Yeast, Molds.
———, Bacteria in Relation to Country Life.
Duggar, Plant Diseases.
Coulter, Plant Life and Plant Relations.
Jordon, Animal Life.

### TECHNOLOGICAL: LUMBER, TEXTILES, METALLURGY, DYEING, CLAYS, ETC., ETC.

Cassell & Co., Technical Series.
Wiley & Co., Technical Series.
George Bell & Sons, Technical Handbooks.
Matthews' Books on Textiles (Wiley & Co.).

### PHYSIOLOGY, HYGIENE, ETC.

Gulick's recent books.
Hoag, Health Studies.
Hough & Sedgwick, The Human Mechanism.
Prudden, Water and Ice.
———, Dust and Its Dangers.
Elliott, Household Hygiene.
———, Household Bacteriology.
Millard, The Wonderful House That Jack Has.
Allen, Civics and Health.
Millikan and Gale, First Course in Physics.
Harrison, Lessons on Sanitation.
Price, Handbook on Sanitation.
Cotton, Care of Children.
Pope, Home Care of the Sick.
Ravenhill, Practical Hygiene.
Cornell College, Bulletins of Farmers' Wives' Reading Courses.

# EDITORIAL NOTES

**Co-operative Tests in Arithmetic**

The *Elementary School Teacher* is glad to give as wide publicity as possible to an announcement made by Mr. S. A. Courtis of the Home and Day School, Detroit, Michigan. Mr. Courtis has put his arithmetic tests, which will be familiar to readers of this journal, into such form that they may readily be utilized by supervisors or principals. He is now planning to make a general investigation covering as many schools as he can reach. He wishes to announce that he will distribute 10,000 sets of his standard tests, together with the necessary instructions for the use of these tests, to schools. Up to this number he intends to distribute the material free of charge. He is also prepared to furnish the same material at cost to any workers who may be willing to co-operate on this basis in their schools. He has had the tests plated, so that the preparation of reproductions will be very simple and economical. The actual working time required for a grade is twenty-four minutes. The instructions to the children on taking up the papers will, however, consume some time, and Mr. Courtis recommends that the test be tried in two sections, one part each day. He has prepared record sheets for the compilation and stating of results. He finds that the time required for scoring, entering, and computing the average grades and variability of groups of fifty children does not exceed two hours.

**Valid Method for Such Tests**

The project which Mr. Courtis has undertaken is somewhat novel. We are familiar with tests that have been made by individual students in various departments, but an effort to secure the co-operation of a large number of superintendents or teachers for the use of a carefully prepared series of tests promises much for our educational system, if it can be successfully carried out. The difficulties which arise in attempting to compare the results of tests of this sort are well known to educational investigators

If the tests are not conducted in uniform manner at different centers, and if the results are not computed in exactly the same way, comparisons are misleading. The value of the method, therefore, is one of the chief considerations. Mr. Courtis has given this question of method much attention. He has a large array of careful workers who are prepared to stand sponsors for the efficiency of his method. The *Elementary School Teacher* has published three of Mr. Courtis' articles, and the present writer has examined carefully the tests which he has prepared, and we believe there should be the largest confidence for these tests.

C. H. J.

**Report of Committee of Seven**

This number of the *Elementary School Teacher* carries out the arrangement with the Northern Illinois Superintendents' and Principals' Association, which was announced in February. The full report of the Committee of Seven is presented. This report will be discussed at the May meeting.

**Enthusiasm for Nature-Study**

The subject of the report is one which is commanding a great deal of attention in the educational world at the present time. A generation ago the suggestion came from Germany that concrete material should be more freely used in the schools. This suggestion was received with enthusiasm by a few elementary school teachers and supervisors. In the meantime in our higher institutions of learning science was beginning to gain a foothold. Physics, chemistry, and biology were seen to be productive for practical life and suitable for mental discipline. Spencer's *Essays on Education* set forth in vigorous terms the advantages of studying science, and the enthusiasm which had been fostered by discussions of concrete education was increased in intensity and taken up by a larger circle of teachers. Finally, the practical world with its dependence on science for its new mechanical devices and for the principles underlying its development began to make a demand on the schools for the training of children in these lines. This demand gave a new impetus to the movement, and the introduction of nature-study was undertaken as one of the most promising educational innovations of the day.

**Criticism of Nature-Study**

The experiment has been under way for some time, and the enthusiasm with which many teachers took up the work has waned, if not disappeared entirely. Several systems of nature-study have had their day, and dropped out of sight. Several guiding principles of selection have been advocated, accepted, tried, discarded, and finally forgotten, except by the student of educational history. We have now reached the period of serious reconsideration. The enthusiasm of extreme youth is gone; there is a frank recognition of serious difficulties, and on the whole a better and safer attitude of conservative study of the problem.

**Social Interests of Young Children**

It is perhaps pretentious for the writer to attempt to add, by way of editorial comment, to the discussion of the committee, but there is one consideration which is significant and so likely to be overlooked by the specialist that it may be worth setting down as a part of the debate. It is not true that a child's strongest impulse is in the direction of attention to natural objects. A child is absorbed in people more than in things. A child's interest in color always attaches itself to some person. Children want the things that they see other children have. Social observation is very keen, at least as early as observation of objects. When observation of objects begins, it is superficial. It is guided by accidental motives, not by any principles of scientific analysis. For these reasons young children will not study objects in the lower grades with the devotion which they can be induced to show in the pursuits of the social arts, such as reading and writing. Sometimes conservative teachers have bewailed the competition between the newer subjects and the fundamental social arts. There is no need of anxiety. The fundamental arts of reading, writing, and number have demonstrated their vitality so fully that they can be relied on to outlive any excess of enthusiasm in other directions. The fundamental fact of human nature is that social interests are the most potent interests. Indeed, science is the formulation of certain principles of the relation between the external world and the scientific thinker. Science does not come from without. It is cultivated from within. There is some danger that the advocates of nature-study will forget this dependence of science upon inner motives. They forget that the child cannot get science from things. Science is the best and most productive thought of man. Science deals with things, but it is not made by things nor dictated by things. Things have always been in the world, but science is very young; it came through co-operative human thinking. The present writer believes that such considerations show the necessity of much training in language as a means of scientific progress. He would look for a check in the nature-study movement so long as that movement over-emphasizes things.

C. H. J.

# CURRENT EDUCATIONAL LITERATURE IN THE PERIODICALS[1]

IRENE WARREN
Librarian, School of Education, The University of Chicago

ANGELL, JAMES R. William James. Educa. Bi-mo. 5:189–92. (Fe. '11.)

ARNOLD, FRANK R. College stagecraft. Educa. 31:466–71. (Mr. '11.)

BAGLEY, W. C. The present status of moral education in institutions for the training of teachers. Relig. Educa. 5:612–40. (Fe. '11.)

BAKER, MARGARET. Teaching English to foreign students at Oxford. Educa. Bi-mo. 5:205–14. (Fe. '11.)

BAUR, EVA E. VON. Trade education in Germany: its value to the laborer. Craftsman 19:598–607. (Mr. '11.)

BLACK, JESSIE ELIZABETH. Practice in literary form in advanced grades. Educa. Bi-mo. 5:237–41. (Fe. '11.)

BLOCK, LOUIS JAMES. The study of English literature in the secondary schools. Educa. Bi-mo. 5:215–19. (Fe. '11.)

BROADUS, ELEANOR HAMMOND. An experiment in education. Educa. Bi-mo. 5:242–48. (Fe. '11.)

CABOT, ELLA LYMAN. Moral instruction and training in the schools of Massachusetts. Relig. Educa. 5:663–70. (Fe. '11.)

CARROLL, CLARENCE F. Moral instruction and training in the public schools of New York. Relig. Educa. 5:640–44. (Fe. '11.)

CASSIDY, MASSILLON ALEXANDER. A Kentucky experiment. Relig. Educa. 5:702–4. (Fe. '11.)

COLEMAN, NORMAN F. Moral instruction and training in the state of Washington. Relig. Educa. 5:689–93. (Fe. '11.)

Curriculum of training colleges. School W. 13:41–43. (Fe. '11.)

DE BEY, CORNELIA B. A pedagogic thought from Darwin. Educa. Bi-mo. 5:229–36. (Fe. '11.)

The evils of overteaching. Educa. R. 41:232–37. (Mr. '11.)

FITE, WARNER. The case of the college professor. Pop. Sci. Mo. 78:273–82. (Mr. '11.)

[1] *Abbreviations.*—Educa., Education; Educa. Bi-mo., Educational Bi-monthly; Educa. R., Educational Review; El. School T., Elementary School Teacher; Harper, Harper's Magazine; Journ. of Educa. (Bost.), Journal of Education (Boston); Journ. of Educa. Psychol., Journal of Educational Psychology; Liv. Age, Living Age; Pop. Sci. Mo., Popular Science Monthly; Print. Art, Printing Art; Psychol. Clinic, Psychological Clinic; Relig. Educa., Religious Education; School W., School World; Teach. College Rec., Teachers College Record; Univ. of Chic. Mag., University of Chicago Magazine.

FitzGerald, Ellen. The schoolmaster as a writer. Educa. Bi-mo. 5:220–28. (Fe. '11.)

Fitzwilliam, Sarah E. Raymond. An educational reminiscence. Educa. Bi-mo. 5:193–200. (Fe. '11.)

Gordy, Wilbur F. Influence of local conditions upon the moral aim dominant in the state schools. Relig. Educa. 709–14. (Fe. '11.)

Gray, David. A modern temple of education: New York's new public library. Harper 122:562–76. (Mr. '11.)

Greenwood, J. M. The home and school life. Educa. 31:390–96. (Fe. '11.)

Haney, James Parton. Industrial education. Educa. 31:436–43. (Mr. '11.)

Harper, Charles F. How can the high school serve more effectively the interests of the community? Educa. 31:355–69. (Fe. '11.)

Hayes, Carlton Huntley. History in the college course. Educa. R. 41:217–31. (Mr. '11.)

Hicks, Vinnie Crandall. A study of a subnormal child. El. School T. 11:296–307. (Fe. '11.)

Hill, Albert Ross. Some successes and failures of the American college. Univ. of Chic. Mag. 3:127–37. (Ja. '11.)

Hodgson, Geraldine. Education in citizenship. School W. 13:47–49. (Fe. '11.)

Hosic, James Fleming. Recent educational conferences. Educa. Bi-mo. 5:201–4. (Fe. '11.)

Johnson, Franklin W. Significant experiments in the state of Illinois. Relig. Educa. 5:696–702. (Fe. '11.)

Johnson, Harrold. Moral education in schools: an international problem. Relig. Educa. 5:704–8. (Fe. '11.)

Kent, Ernest B. Manual training and local industry, a course of study for boys of the two upper grades. Educa. 31:374–83. (Fe. '11.)

Laird, Raymond G. The commercial high-school curriculum. Educa. 31:456–65. (Mr. '11.)

Murray, E. R. A short history of infant schools and kindergartens in England (1). Child Life 13:7–10. (Ja. '11.)

Pegram, George B. The attitude of the newer physics toward the mechanical view of nature. Educa. R. 41:290–302. (Mr. '11.)

Perkins, Henry A. The educational system of France. Educa. R. 41:245–60. (Mr. '11.)

Platt, S. The meaning and value of co-education. Child Life 13:11–15. (Ja. '11.)

Professor S. H. Butcher. Educa. R. 41:280–89. (Mr. '11.)

Pyle, W. H., and Snyder, J. C. The most economical unit for committing to memory. Journ. of Educa. Psychol. 2:121–32. (Mr. '11.)

Ranck, Clayton H. Self-help among college students. Educa. 31:444–48. (Mr. '11.)

RAVENHILL, ALICE. The play-interests of English elementary-school children. Child 1:217–26. (D. '10.)

ROUSE, W. H. D. The place of classics in secondary education: a reply. Liv. Age 50:103–6. (14 Ja. '11.)

RUGH, C. E. Moral instruction and training in the schools of California. Relig. Educa. 5:644–63. (Fe. '11.)

SANDIFORD, PETER. Day training colleges in England. School W. 13:52–54. (Fe. '11.)

SEASHORE, C. E. The consulting psychologist. Pop. Sci. Mo. 78:283–90. (Mr. '11.)

SHARP, FRANK CHAPMAN. Moral instruction in certain high schools and normal schools of Wisconsin. Relig. Educa. 5:693–95. (Fe. '11.)

SHOW, ARLEY BARTHLOW. Historical significance of the religious problem in the German schools. Educa. 31:423–36. (Mr. '11.)

SISSON, EDWARD O. Can virtue be taught? Educa. R. 41:261–79. (Mr. '11.)

SMILEY, W. S. A comparative study of the results obtained in instruction in the "single-teacher" rural schools and the graded town schools (2). El. School T. 11:308–22. (Fe. '11.)

Stage children. Dial 50:145–47. (Mr. '11.)

STERN, WILLIAM. The supernormal child (1). Journ. of Educa. Psychol. 2:143–48. (Mr. '11.)

STRAYER, GEORGE D. The legal aspect of moral education. Relig. Educa. 5:599–611. (Fe. '11.)

SUZZALLO, HENRY. The teaching of primary arithmetic. Teach. College Rec. 12:5–70. (Mr. '11.)

TAYLOR, CHARLES KEEN. Boys' backs. Psychol. Clinic 4:274–76. (Fe. '11.)

TAYLOR, J. MADISON. Motor education for the child. Pop. Sci. Mo. 78:268–72. (Mr. '11.)

Teacher's salary report. Journ. of Educa. (Bost.) 73:117–19. (2 Fe. '11.)

THOMAS, CHARLES SWAIN. New England association of teachers of English. Educa. 31:384–89. (Fe. '11.)

University training for printers. Print. Art 16:448. (Fe. '11.)

UPTON, HENRY L. The problem of public education. Educa. 31:397–403. (Fe. '11.)

WALLIN, J. E. W. The new clinical psychology and the psycho-clinicist (1). Journ. of Educa. Psychol. 2:121–32. (Mr '11.)

WEISSE, H. V. The educational ladder. School W. 13:45–47. (Fe. '11.)

WELSH, CHARLES. The outlook in teaching history. Educa. 31:370–73. (Fe. '11.)

WILSON, M. C. Some defects in our public school system. Educa. R. 41:238–44. (Mr. '11.)

WITMER, LIGHTNER. Courses in psychology at the summer school of the University of Pennsylvania. Psychol. Clinic 4:245–73. (Fe. '11.)

VOLUME XI NUMBER 9

THE ELEMENTARY SCHOOL TEACHER

MAY, 1911

# A STUDY OF RETARDATION IN THE SCHOOLS OF MINNESOTA

FREEMAN E. LURTON
Superintendent City Schools, Anoka, Minnesota

*The materials.*—The statistics brought together in this paper were gathered, for the most part, in two separate investigations. One, relating principally to retardation in all its aspects, was conducted under the auspices of the Minnesota Psychological Conference. The other, concerning itself mainly with the first year of retardation, or with repeaters, was made at the request of the Associated School Boards of Minnesota.

Part of the data collected was laid before these bodies at their respective 1910 meetings. Both reports have been combined, condensed, rewritten, and several sets of other interesting statistics introduced for comparative purposes.

*The schools studied.*—The schools contributing the data on retardation proper are fifty-five of the smaller systems of the state. They each maintain high schools known in Minnesota as "state high schools," owing to the fact that they are carefully inspected and listed with the State High School Board for a large yearly special grant direct from the state treasury. They are, therefore, schools which are kept at a high state of efficiency.

*Only grade pupils considered.*—Only the pupils in the grades below the high school are considered, for several reasons. First, the high-school students are invariably promoted by subjects, hence accurate statistics as to retardation among them, in the usual sense of the term, cannot be had. Then, again, with the eighth grade once passed, and often earlier, the most retarded pupils, being safely beyond the compelling influence of the truancy law, or of social opinion, quickly drop out of school and the problem of retardation becomes so confused with the problem of elimination as to make the figures of doubtful value.

*A state-wide study.*—The schools studied were well distributed over the state so as to embrace every variety of size, location, and environing conditions, and to make the study fairly representative of the entire state, and the results are believed to be an index to the prevailing conditions throughout the state.

*The Ayres standard for retardation.*—In the Ayres investigations, published by the Russell Sage Foundation, children in the first grade are considered normal if they are under eight years of age. In the second grade ages under nine are normal, and so on through the grades. The reasons for thus allowing an extra year are not given. The text asserts that these are the ages allotted to the grades "by common consent." But certainly it is not in accord with the actual practice in administering schools in Minnesota, and I doubt if it is anywhere. Its effect is to conceal one year's retardation for every child during his progress through the grades, provided he entered at six years of age, and last year only 441 children in the schools under consideration entered later than six, while very many entered earlier, as they are usually admitted if they are six by the middle of the year.

A child entering the first grade at six should be in the second grade at seven, the third at eight, and so on. Now suppose he fails to "make grade" while in the second grade and remains there two years, repeating and retarded, yet his age, when he enters the third grade, would be only nine. By the Ayres method that would be considered normal, and yet he is retarded. By that method it is possible then for every child in a school system to be retarded one year after entrance and yet for the system to appear absolutely free from retarded pupils.

*The Minnesota standard for retardation.*—In every school system covered by this investigation the children are admitted at six years of age or younger. We have reckoned the entering age of six. Further, in every one of these schools, promotions are made only once a year, in June. Each grade by its very conception means a year's work. Therefore, the child who enters the first grade at six should enter the second at seven, the third at eight, and so on, grade by grade. And further, from the administrative point of view, the state expects to provide the child with only eight years of grade schooling, which is to begin at the age of six. From this point of view the child who waits till he is seven before entering is already behind the schedule. He will get out later and have one year less of economically productive working life, and that is what the state has in view in the education of its children.

*The tabulated statistics.*—The complete results of the investigation are given in Table I. This gives the grade-age status of 17,279 grade children in fifty-five cities and villages of Minnesota. They were gathered in the fall and account for children actually enrolled. This makes the showing favorable to the schools, for some children who failed to win promotion no doubt dropped out during the summer.

TABLE I

SHOWS, GRADE BY GRADE, AND BY SEX, THE AMOUNT OF RETARDATION

| Numbers | | | | Percentages | | | | | |
|---|---|---|---|---|---|---|---|---|---|
| Grade | Total | Boys | Girls | Retarded | | Normal | | Advance | |
| | | | | Boys | Girls | Boys | Girls | Boys | Girls |
| 1...... | 2,691 | 1,436 | 1,255 | 38.7 | 33.6 | 63.8 | 59.0 | 7.5 | 7.4 |
| 2...... | 2,065 | 1,096 | 969 | 54.0 | 41.1 | 37.8 | 47.2 | 8.2 | 11.7 |
| 3...... | 2,164 | 1,134 | 1,030 | 61.1 | 57.7 | 33.1 | 40.9 | 5.8 | 7.4 |
| 4...... | 2,268 | 1,134 | 1,134 | 65.9 | 56.1 | 28.2 | 35.5 | 5.9 | 8.4 |
| 5...... | 2,129 | 1,109 | 1,020 | 68.8 | 63.2 | 25.2 | 29.8 | 6.0 | 7.0 |
| 6...... | 1,944 | 977 | 967 | 73.7 | 67.7 | 21.0 | 25.0 | 5.3 | 8.0 |
| 7...... | 1,862 | 929 | 933 | 70.4 | 65.9 | 24.3 | 27.1 | 5.3 | 7.0 |
| 8...... | 2,007 | 886 | 1,121 | 74.0 | 67.0 | 30.5 | 26.4 | 5.8 | 6.6 |
| Total 17, 279 | | | Averages: 58.9 | | | 34.2 | | 7.1 | |

Retardation is computed upon the Minnesota basis of entering at six, and spending a single year, and no more, in each grade.

In studying this table four facts will be noted, all, probably.

contrary to popular belief. First, the boys equal or exceed the girls in number in every grade up to the seventh where they fall only four behind. It is in, or at the close of, the seventh grade, then, that the boy meets his decisive defeat. Second, the workings of the process of elimination can most clearly be seen in the last three grades. The normally placed child would enter the sixth grade at eleven; the retarded ones would be older. But discouragement, economic pressure in the homes, and the non-applicability or the non-enforcement of the truancy law permit them to drop out. Third, the retardation begins heavily in the very first grade and steadily increases grade by grade through the eighth grade with the exception of the downward drop of the curve in the seventh grade, due probably to the working of the law of elimination. Also, fourth, the retardation of the boys is greater than that of the girls from the start and remains so, grade by grade, varying from an excess of 5.1 in the first grade to 7 per cent in the eighth grade.

The average percentage of retardation officially reported to exist in these schools, under their own standard of requirements, is 58.7. As I have said elsewhere, when the course of study makes requirements such that only 41.3 per cent of the pupils can and do meet them, we have a curious state of affairs resulting, where to be abnormal is the usual or normal state of affairs.

*Reduced to the Ayres standard.*—The Ayres method of computing retardation would be incorrect according to the conditions governing the school systems under consideration. But for the sake of comparison, the data on hand have been computed by that method also and the results are shown in Table II.

There the average percentage of retardation is 30.9 per cent. And that is serious enough. This, however, is only 52.6 per cent of that amount known to exist in these schools. The balance is concealed by the allowance of an extra year in the grades for possible late entrance, when such entrances are so few as to warrant no such allowance.

The Ayres figures for thirty-one important cities give an average of 33.7 per cent of retarded children, varying from 7.5

in Medford, Mass., to 75.8 per cent among the colored children of Memphis, Tenn.

TABLE II

THIS IS TABLE I REDUCED TO THE AYRES STANDARD FOR RETARDATION

| Numbers | | | | Percentages | | | | | |
|---|---|---|---|---|---|---|---|---|---|
| | | | | Retarded | | Normal | | Advanced | |
| Grade | Total | Boys | Girls | Boys | Girls | Boys | Girls | Boys | Girls |
| 1...... | 2,691 | 1,436 | 1,255 | 14.6 | 9.1 | 77.9 | 83.5 | 7.5 | 7.4 |
| 2...... | 2,065 | 1,096 | 969 | 22.5 | 17.3 | 69.3 | 71.0 | 8.2 | 11.7 |
| 3...... | 2,164 | 1,134 | 1,030 | 30.6 | 20.8 | 63.6 | 71.8 | 5.8 | 7.4 |
| 4...... | 2,268 | 1,134 | 1,134 | 38.2 | 27.7 | 55.9 | 63.9 | 5.9 | 8.4 |
| 5...... | 2,129 | 1,109 | 1,020 | 44.2 | 34.8 | 49.8 | 58.2 | 6.0 | 7.0 |
| 6...... | 1,944 | 977 | 967 | 47.4 | 38.5 | 47.3 | 53.5 | 5.3 | 8.0 |
| 7...... | 1,862 | 929 | 933 | 44.2 | 36.3 | 50.5 | 56.4 | 5.3 | 7.0 |
| 8...... | 2,007 | 886 | 1,121 | 45.3 | 39.5 | 49.2 | 53.9 | 5.5 | 6.6 |
| Total...... 17,279 | | | Average 30.9 | | | 62.0 | | 7.1 | |

TABLE III

SOME STATISTICS FOR PURPOSES OF COMPARISON

| | Minnesota | Ayres |
|---|---|---|
| 1. Children in grades of the fifty-five systems ................ | 58.7 | 30.9 |
| 2. Children in grades of the forty-one graded-school systems.. | 64.6 | 33.9 |
| 3. Children in grades of the four special systems............ | 66.5 | 33.7 |
| 4. Children in grades of the St. Paul system..................... | | 56.5 |
| 5. Children in grades of the Fargo, N.D. system.............. | 55.6 | 24.9 |

The forty-one schools given in item two are what are termed "graded schools" in Minnesota. They are small, but inspected, schools ranking below systems having high schools. They are mostly small, with four to five teachers. They enrol 5,340 grade pupils in all.

The four "special" cities are large systems whose figures are not included with the fifty-five cities given above. They are conceded to be among the best in the state. They enrol 3,753 grade pupils in all.

There are 2,087 children in the Fargo contingent.

The St. Paul enrolment in round numbers was........................23,000
The other 101 cities and villages enrol..............................28,459
Table III carries this total.........................................51,459

*Repeaters.*—Possibly one of the best ways to get at the real loss in a school system is to compute it from the number of repeaters. Here no confusion results over the question of their age at entrance nor the age limits proper for each grade. Elimination works confusion here as well as by the first method tried. And we must bear in mind that repeaters are only one year's contribution to the full army of retarded children. Financially it is only during the time he repeats that the retarded child costs the taxpayer anything.

In order to ascertain at first hand the amount of repeating in the schools of Minnesota, I recently sent out a printed questionnaire to all the superintendents in the state. Ninety-six, which is nearly half, replied promptly with well-arranged data.

The figures given include a total of 40,710 grade children and 8,302 high-school students. To this number we might add about 28,000 pupils in the grade and high schools of St. Paul which are not included in the main results. That makes a total of 77,012 children investigated as to the repeating among them.

The number of children repeating the work of their grade for this year was found to be as follows:

GRADES

| First | Second | Third | Fourth | Fifth | Sixth | Seventh | Eighth | |
|---|---|---|---|---|---|---|---|---|
| 664 | 309 | 296 | 374 | 396 | 330 | 318 | 443 | Total 3,130 |

Also, 168 others are repeating the work for the second time.

And in the high schools 981 are repeating one subject; 335, two subjects; 108, three subjects; and 60, all four subjects. That is equal to a total of 2,214 in single subjects, or, dividing by four, the number of subjects usually carried by a high-school student, we have the equivalent of 553 high-school students repeating full work.

This is 7.4 per cent of the total enrolment in the 96 systems. But this does not adequately measure the ground lost last year in these schools for two reasons. First, the statistics being gathered in the fall from the actual enrolment of the schools and not compiled from office records does not account for the number of students who dropped out during the summer, and the number thus eliminated must be considered. Second, and this is an important factor never alluded to so far as I have discovered in the literature of the subject, there is a practice, almost uniform among superintendents, of promoting a child at the end of two years in a given grade, whether his work merits it or not. This practice conceals a considerable amount of the very worst sort of repeating, and likewise, by forcing the child on through the grades whether deserving or not, reduces the apparent amount of retardation. Akin to this practice is another which has the same effect, namely, the practice of promoting "on trial" children who do not fully meet the requirements but for one reason or another are permitted to continue on with the class. And need it be added that when once a child has been allowed to go on with the class he is rarely reduced to the grade below, no matter how poor his work?

The data shows 1,612 children promoted on trial; there are no figures for the number arbitrarily promoted at the end of the second year in the grade. It is certain that these two practices reduce the actual number of repeating and retarded children considerably.

*Compared with Ayres' results.*—While my figures show a considerably larger percentage of retarded children, those of Ayres, curiously enough, show in the fifty-five leading cities given in his tabulated report, that the average percentage of repeaters is 15.4. That is due, I think, to the fact that his method conceals part of the retardation but not of the repeating. Repeating is high in the large cities. If repeating is high, retardation should be.

Having carefully studied the laggards in our Minnesota schools from two standpoints, it is interesting to note how strikingly the results agree. We found the percentage of retardation to be 58.9 and that of repeaters to be 7.4. Now, bearing in mind that the number of repeaters is merely one year's quota of retarded ones, and multiplying 7.4 by eight, the number of years in the grade course, we have 59.2 as the calculated number of laggards. The ascertained number is only 0.3 of 1 per cent less than this.

*The money cost of the laggards.*—School administrators and the public generally would consider the gist of the whole problem to be its fearful money cost. Money spent on doing the same work twice over is money wasted.

Minnesota spends annually for her schools about $15,000,000 and if 7.4 per cent of this is spent on repeaters then the cost is $1,110,000.

It is estimated that the nation similarly loses from fifty-seven to eighty million dollars from the same cause.

We justly boast of our great school fund in Minnesota of about $27,000,000, but here is for the United States as a whole a sum two or three times as great wasted yearly because of loss and waste in our management of the public schools along this one line alone.

*The true loss.*—The true loss, however, is the spiritual one which refuses to submit to statistical investigation. The retarded pupils personally lose that fine spirit of initiative, of progress, of growth, of self-reliance, and of eagerness to achieve, which constitutes the chief glory of youth, and which sends him from school into life an effective member of society. By allowing him to become retarded that birthright of the American boy is traded for the pottage of idleness, failure, and self-distrust.

# THE EIGHTH-GRADE VOCABULARY

JEAN SHERWOOD RANKIN
Minneapolis, Minn.

Whether the relationship be that of cause to effect, of effect to cause, or of mixed cause and effect, the fact is very evident that broad scholarship, and even mere general culture, is always accompanied by the mastery of a wide vocabulary. This fact seems not to have entered the consciousness of the makers of our common-school courses of study, for such courses are usually constructed wholly without reference to this or other basic facts of language acquirement.

It would seem that inductive reasoning might long ago have cleared up finally the problem of language teaching; but inductive reasoning seems to have done little in a practical way, and theories rather than facts confront us on every side. For this reason, it may be wise to seek a solution for our problem deductively, and this article is a frank attempt to present facts which may help us to infer a few fundamental principles.

That there is a language problem, no one can deny. Our schools still turn out a product which is weakest on the side of language-use and of literary comprehension. It is even doubtful whether the tremendous question of truancy will not largely be solved when the language-training problem is solved. When one visits a school made up of so-called "incorrigibles," and finds that every one of the hapless lot is so unskilled in reading, writing, and spelling as to be hopelessly behind grade, he begins to get light on the relationship between so-called "incorrigibility" and two of the three R's. But this is aside from our main discussion.

As yet, the essential relationship between vocabulary and general education is not recognized in textbooks or in courses of study. With more light on the subject we shall have new methods. The prevailing ignorance and misconceptions are so absurd as to be almost appalling. Partly to be blamed for this is the fictitious tradition sprung upon a gullible public by Dean Alvord of otherwise revered memory. This worthy but most credulous gentleman stated that the working men of his acquaintance used scarcely two hundred words in all. Now if the dean had but followed up one of his working friends with pencil and pad in hand, he would soon have found out what a poor guesser he himself had been. Unluckily for posterity, the dean's poor guess has become almost a classic among famous errors.

The extreme ignorance prevailing upon the subject of vocabulary, even among well-educated persons, is shown by the statement of a well-known American educational writer who boldly claimed that a man may converse very well with a vocabulary of only seventy-five words. Ridiculous as is such a statement, the ever-unscientific public gulps it down with avidity and sighs comfortably in the assurance that it has seventy-five usable ideas all tagged with their proper word-signs. It does not occur to the public—who prefer ideas and clothes both ready-to-wear—that the baby of eighteen months is usually in good command of more than seventy-five words, yet is not able to "converse very well."

Some light is shed on this subject by the fact that the average primer presents about three hundred fifty words for the six-year-old to learn to recognize. The most ambitious primer offers about one thousand, but this is exceptional. No one has had the enterprise as yet to ascertain how many words are actually necessary to a comprehension of first-grade subjects, of those in the second grade, in the third grade, and so on. But these facts will some day become known, and in that day the mechanics who tinker theoretical courses of study will begin to recognize the essential relation between general scholarship and mastery of the vernacular.

As one small contribution to the almost unknown field of language-fact which we are bound to explore if American school children shall come into their heritage of literary appreciation, I offer here one collection of data. In order to help determine approximately the necessary vocabulary of the successful eighth-grade pupil, I have compiled—with no small pains, be assured—the actual vocabulary used in a popular and excellent modern textbook in United States history. (I do not name the text, but will do so by letter upon request.)

TABLE SHOWING UNDER EACH LETTER OF THE ALPHABET (*a*) the TWO FIRST AND THE TWO LAST WORDS USED IN A POPULAR TEXT IN UNITED STATES HISTORY AND (*b*) THE WHOLE NUMBER OF SUCH WORDS

| |  |  |
|---|---|---|
| A. | abandon, abdication . . . . awful, awkward | 343 |
| B. | baby, bachelors . . . . by, byway | 280 |
| C. | cabal, cabbage . . . . cutlery, cylinder | 507 |
| D. | daguerreotype, daily . . . . dwelt, dying | 293 |
| E. | each, eager . . . . extravagant, extreme | 215 |
| F. | fabrics, face . . . . fury, future | 269 |
| G. | gag, gain . . . . gunpowder, gymnastics | 123 |
| H. | habits, habitual . . . . huzzahs, hymn | 184 |
| I. | ice, idea . . . . isthmus, itself | 190 |
| J. | jackets, jail . . . . justice, justify | 32 |
| K. | keenly, keep . . . . known, know-nothings | 29 |
| L. | labor, labor-saving . . . . lumbering, luxury | 139 |
| M. | machines, machinery . . . . mutually, mysterious | 207 |
| N. | navigation, navigators . . . . nurses, nut | 95 |
| O. | oak, oar . . . . owners, ox | 124 |
| P. | paces, pacific . . . . push, put | 341 |
| Q. | quaint, Quaker . . . . quit-rent, quorum | 24 |
| R. | rabble, raccoon . . . . runner, rush | 319 |
| S. | Sabbath, sachem . . . . system, systematic | 655 |
| T. | tables, tablet . . . . tyranny, tyrant | 359 |
| U. | ugly, unable . . . . utmost, utter | 96 |
| V. | vacate, vacancies . . . . vote, voyages | 50 |
| W. | wading, wage-earners . . . . wrong, wrote | 163 |
| Y. | yards, yarn . . . . your, yours | 16 |
| Z. | zeal, zigzag, zone | 3 |
| | Total | 5,036 |
| | Proper names not counted above | 909 |
| | Final total | 5,965 |

To the 5,036 words in the lists are added 909 proper names also used. Many words were used as two or three different parts of speech, and hence were counted more than once. The total is 5,965. So many words must the eighth-grader know who studies intelligently the book in question.

But the eighth-grade child must know far more than the words of his textbook in history. There is a special vocabulary attached to each of his other studies, including many words not contained in the history text, and he recites in geography, grammar, writing, arithmetic, music, physical culture, drawing, cooking, sewing, and perhaps gardening. How shall we estimate the contribution to his usable ideas gained through each of these subjects?

The question may be attacked from another side. A certain Minnesota superintendent kindly consented to test the vocabulary of a few eighth-grade pupils. These went through their small high-school dictionaries, counting word by word all that they felt sure they knew and might have used. Of four pupils who made the test, three claimed between nine and ten thousand words, exclusive of proper names, and one, a very strong student of excellent Scotch parentage, estimated for himself nearly fifteen thousand words. These figures tally well with the reports upon vocabularies published by the one or two lone explorers in the field of high-school vocabularies, and lead us to the conclusion that the eighth-grade student who completes his work successfully must possess from ten to fifteen thousand words.

Will the reader ponder on the question where and how pupils are to learn this matter of six thousand words which they will need when they come to study history? Are they to wrestle with both the history and a new vocabulary and be thereby handicapped, or does the course of study afford opportunity for the pleasant and gradual absorption of a wide vocabulary? If not, why not?

# AGRICULTURAL EDUCATION: ELEMENTARY AND SECONDARY SCHOOLS

BENJAMIN MARSHALL DAVIS
Miami University

One of the most important recent tendencies in education is the redirection of schools of a community in terms of the daily welfare of its people. For a rural community such redirection must be largely in terms of agriculture and of other country-life interests. It is for this reason that so much emphasis is placed upon agriculture as a means of increasing the efficiency of rural schools.

When this idea began to express itself in practice in rural communities the elementary school was the first to receive attention. But age of pupils, many grades in one room, lack of properly qualified teachers, and various other limitations have led many to doubt the wisdom of this selection. The results of introducing agriculture as a school subject into the elementary schools have thus far not been entirely satisfactory. Nevertheless adjustments are taking place, so that agriculture, not as a systematized subject of instruction but in certain of its nature-study aspects, will no doubt find an important place. About all that may reasonably be expected of agriculture in the elementary schools is to interest the children in country-life subjects so that they may know the common birds, insects, trees, weeds; the meaning of some of the best farm practices, such as selecting and testing seed, how the soil holds water and means of preventing its loss, care of milk and value of its fat content, etc.; and through such studies to lead the children to appreciate the fact that there is something worth while in the immediate world in which they live.

The rural high school is now being recognized as the best place below the college for instruction in agriculture. Such a high school is closely related to rural education in two ways:

one in the adjustment of its own work to the industrial and social needs of its community, the other in giving its graduates who expect to teach in rural elementary schools some preparation for teaching country-life subjects.

## ELEMENTARY SCHOOLS

The introduction of agricultural subjects into elementary schools has proceeded mainly along two lines—one as a result of legislation, the other as a natural outgrowth of boys' agricultural clubs.

In many places in states where agriculture is a required subject for instruction in rural schools no such legislation was really needed, for the subject was already being introduced in a sane and effective way, and was being made use of as far as the experience of the teacher and conditions of the school environment would permit.

The results of compulsory teaching of agriculture in the elementary schools have been twofold: first, in stimulating those in charge of the administration to provide helps to those teachers who are expected to carry out the provisions of the law; second, in the production and use of textbooks on elementary agriculture. The first has been done through bulletins, teachers' leaflets, institute instruction, summer normal schools, and in various other ways. Some agricultural colleges have been called upon to give attention to elementary education sooner than they otherwise would. They have been forced to study the rural-school situation and devise means for improving it. The work of state offices of education and of agricultural colleges in promoting agricultural education in rural communities has already been considered somewhat in detail in previous articles of this series.[1] But the contributions of these two agencies to agricultural education in elementary schools must not be ascribed wholly to legislation, for in several states having no requirements as to teaching of agriculture both state departments of education and agricultural colleges have done excellent service

[1] This journal, Vol. X, Nos. 3, 4, and 6.

in providing helps for teachers wishing to introduce the subject in their schools.

The second result has been less satisfactory. Indeed, in some instances it has proved a positive detriment to agricultural education. It has in effect added another textbook subject to an already crowded rural-school curriculum, for many teachers, in spite of whatever suggestions they may receive from leaflets or institute instruction, know of no other way to teach except by means of a textbook. It has put undue emphasis on the agricultural textbook. More than a score of elementary textbooks have appeared within a decade. Publishers have been very active in securing the use of their books in the rural schools.[2] While the value of a good textbook must be conceded, it is apt to be the means of substituting agricultural information for real agricultural instruction. The kind of agricultural instruction best adapted for the elementary schools cannot be given merely by means of recitations from a textbook.

There may be some justification in making the teaching of a subject compulsory on the ground that otherwise it would never be taught. On the other hand it may seriously be questioned, since the whole burden of such a measure falls upon the teachers, whether efficient teaching of any subject may be secured by mandatory legislation. The length of teaching service of the average rural teacher is very short, perhaps less than three years. As a result rural teachers are constantly being recruited from the young graduates of grammar and high schools. It is claimed by some that whatever preparation these inexperienced teachers may make is largely determined by what they are expected to teach. If they must teach agriculture they will make some effort to prepare themselves to teach this subject. It is probably on this theory that so many states have tried this plan of introducing agriculture into the rural schools. At least sixteen states have tried this plan, and in several other states bills providing for such instruction are being considered by

[2] The subject of textbooks on agriculture will be considered in the next article of this series.

legislatures now in session. Doubtless some of these bills will become laws.

The second line of development of agricultural education in elementary schools has produced a much better type of instruction than the former or mandatory method. This is partly because the results of boys' clubs have shown the value of agriculture as a school subject, and have thus secured for it public approval and support, and partly because experience in managing these clubs has given the teachers some insight into methods of adapting the subject to the needs of the school, and of making it an effective part of the regular school work.

Teachers who have been the most successful are those who have selected agricultural subjects of special interest to the school community, and who have used methods calling for self-activity on the part of the pupils—having the pupils learn by doing rather than by reciting. The following is a list of various kinds of work reported to be successfully adapted to rural schools (124)[3]: experimental plots for plant breeding, soil inoculation, and other soil experiments; ear-to-row method of improving corn, and use of acre plots; seed germinating including tests of viability; collection of economic plants, weeds, weed-seed, and insects; budding, grafting, pruning, and spraying fruit trees; milk testing with Babcock milk tester.

The importance attached by pupils and patrons to such work is well illustrated by the following report. In one county in Iowa it is the practice for each school to have in the spring a germinating test for corn. One teacher says of this work:

> My boys who would not go across the road for a song book went two miles in the snow to get some sawdust for a germinating box. When the corn had germinated, the farmers came to the schoolhouse to see how their corn had turned out, and incidentally saw the work of the school. Why, farmers came who couldn't remember when they had been inside the schoolhouse before! (125, p. 18).

The rural school is badly in need of redirection, but it will take more than the teaching of agriculture to bring this about.

[3] References by number are to corresponding numbers in the bibliography at the end of this article, or in bibliographies appended to other articles of this series.

However, some sort of nature-study agriculture that has elements of interest to pupils and parents alike may do much toward putting the rural school in the way of redirection. Here and there are promises of the fulfilment of L. H. Bailey's vision of a rural school living up to its possibilities. Referring to the kind of agricultural studies suggested in the above report, he says:

All such teaching as this will call for a new purpose in the school building. The present country-school building is a structure in which children sit to study books and recite from them. It should also be a place in which the children can work with their hands. Every school building should have a laboratory room, in which there may be a few plants growing in the windows, and perhaps an aquarium and terrarium. Here the children will bring flowers and insects and samples of soil, and varieties of corn or cotton in their season, and other objects that interest them, and here they may perform their simple work with tools. Even if the teacher cannot teach these subjects, the room itself will teach. The mere bringing of such objects would have a tremendous influence on children: patrons would ask what the room is for; in time a teacher would be found who could handle the subject pedagogically. Now we see children carrying only books to school; some day they will also carry twigs and potatoes and animals and tools and contrivances and other personal objects (102).

## SECONDARY SCHOOLS

Previous to 1906 there were but few high schools (excepting agricultural high schools) giving instruction in agriculture; in 1906–7 there were 75–80; in 1907–8, 240–50; in 1908–9, over 500; in 1909–10, probably 1,000; in 1910–11, incomplete data indicate as many as 1,500. The number of agricultural high schools (those giving two or more years of agricultural instruction) in 1909 was 125; in 1910, 144. Of these there were receiving local support, in 1909, 24; in 1910, 33; receiving state aid in 1909, 29; in 1910, 39; technical schools giving agricultural instruction in 1909, 37; in 1910, 47; connected with agricultural colleges in 1909, 34; in 1910, 35.[4]

Secondary agricultural education has developed along several lines, giving rise to as many as eight more or less distinct types, viz., (*a*) agricultural-college, (*b*) district, (*c*) country,

[4] The above data were taken from a manuscript article on "Agriculture in High Schools," written by C. H. Robinson and soon to appear as one of the Columbia University publications.

(*d*) village-township, (*e*) city, (*f*) state aid, (*g*) technical, (*h*) normal.[5]

The agricultural-college type is well illustrated by the School of Agriculture of the University of Minnesota. This school has the distinction of being one of the first secondary schools of agriculture. It was

organized in 1888 with the object of giving practical education to young men and women who are unable to pursue the full college course in agriculture. It offers a practical course of study designed to fit young men and women for successful farm life, and aims to give its students the necessary preparation for useful citizenship (127, p. 8).

The district type is found in Alabama, Arkansas, Georgia, Oklahoma, and Virginia. The districts in each of these states except Oklahoma correspond to the several congressional districts. The objects of all these schools are similar and are summed up in the following statement concerning the Alabama District Agricultural Schools which were the first of this type of schools to be established:

To turn out young men well grounded in the underlying principles of scientific and practical agriculture, that they may make successful planters and advance the farming interests of the state.

To give such instruction and training as will fix in the minds of the young men high ideals of country-life education, as is done in the best agricultural high schools under the name of "agriculture and home economics."

To educate and fully equip young men and women for efficient teaching in the public schools of the state.

To prepare those who desire to enter higher institutions of learning (128, p. 15).[6]

The establishment of county agricultural high schools is now authorized in at least twenty-one states. In many of these states such schools receive state aid. The county schools of Wisconsin are the oldest and best known. In the Wisconsin schools

the courses are two years in length and include subjects of general agriculture; biology and physical subjects; laboratory and field and shop work;

[5] The first four types of this classification are suggested by G. A. Bricker in his *Teaching of Agriculture in the High School*, chap. ii (126).

[6] See *Georgia District Agricultural Schools*, 129.

domestic science, home economy, and hygiene; sewing and millinery; farm management and accounts, besides courses in English, history, civics, and other branches of the usual high-school type (126, p. 23).

The Baltimore County (Md.) Agricultural High School presents some features that deserve special mention:

The school is meant especially to meet the needs of a rural community. It presents all the usual subjects taught in high schools, except foreign languages, and in addition teaches agriculture, domestic science, and manual training. It is thus planned that students graduating from this school will, in addition to a good general or academic education, have some industrial or vocational training to fit them to take their places in the world (130, p. 1).

The principal, who is a specialist in agriculture, devotes the entire year to the school, spending the usual summer vacation in the interests of the school, inspecting and directing the work of the pupils who are carrying out in a practical way experiments and problems outlined during the school year. In this manner the principles of agriculture taught in the school are carried over into practice under normal farming conditions. In addition to offering excellent instruction in agriculture and in other subjects, the school further serves the community by giving courses for farmers and their wives, and to rural-school teachers, and by furnishing a center for religious service and literary and social activities for the young people (131).

Most of the high schools giving instruction in agriculture are of the village-township type. The work of two of these high schools which were among the first to make agriculture a subject of instruction has already been referred to in a previous article of this series.[7] The motive for reorganizing rural village and township high schools on the basis of country-life interests is well expressed in an account of the New Holland (Ohio) High School:

The larger percentage of the boys and girls who are enrolled in the village and township high schools of this state will spend their lives either in the rural districts or villages where farm life and agricultural industries are the leading interests. They will be either farmers or farmers' wives, or they will be engaged in business very intimately connected with agriculture. In

[7] This journal, Vol. X, No. 6.

view of this condition the Board of Education at New Holland, Ohio, has placed agriculture in the curriculum of the high school (132, p. 3).

Another of the earlier schools of this type whose success has attracted considerable attention is the John Swaney School, Putnam County, Illinois (133).

High schools of cities surrounded by agricultural communities enrol a large number of pupils from the country. The special needs of such pupils have recently been recognized by a few city high schools. Thus in the Stockton (Cal.) High School a department of agriculture was organized at the beginning of the present school year. A director, who is an agricultural-college graduate, has charge. He is not expected to teach more than one-third of his time; the rest of his time is to be devoted to the "study of agricultural problems at first hand throughout the farm area tributary to Stockton." He is to take up any agricultural problem at any time, go to the farm, and help find a solution. By this means the farmer is reached directly and made to feel that our school director and teachers are willing and able to educate boys and girls for profitable farm life and to cope with economic problems troublesome and burdensome to them. Short courses are also offered to farmers and those interested in agriculture who cannot take the full course. A course is offered to students who expect to be teachers with a view of providing the rural schools with teachers having a knowledge of, and an interest in, farm life. Further aid is given the rural schools by a series of teachers' meetings and conferences with the director in charge (134).

The Gardena High School of Los Angeles has been offering courses in agriculture with particular reference to horticulture, gardening, and poultry raising which are the dominant interests of the community (135). The San Diego (Cal.) High School has also recently established a department of agriculture somewhat after the Stockton plan.

Agriculture in city high schools located in farming regions offers a very promising field for further development. These schools have advantages that compensate somewhat for their immediate non-rural surroundings. Their laboratory facilities are usually very good, and they are able by means of high salaries to secure experienced and well-equipped teachers.

In order to encourage the introduction of agriculture into rural high schools some states have offered the inducement of state aid to a limited number of schools undertaking this work. For example Minnesota is now giving for this purpose $2,500 to each of ten high schools. Ten more are soon to be added to this number. This method has some advantages over entire local support, for it not only makes possible the securing of good teachers but provides for a higher standard of efficiency than is likely to be secured by a purely local management.

The Hinckley State High School which is a good example of this type of high school organized in Minnesota offers the following courses: literary course, four years; agricultural-industrial course, four years; special agricultural course, two years; short course for institutes for farmers; normal course for rural teachers, one year (136).

A somewhat different plan of state aid to high schools giving instruction in agriculture, mechanic arts, and home-making is being worked out in New York. The following extract from the educational law of 1901 will indicate the scope of the New York plan:

> The Commissioner of Education in the annual apportionment of the state school moneys shall apportion therefrom to each city and union free school district the sum of $500 for each independently organized general industrial school, trade school, or school of agriculture, mechanic arts and home-making, maintained therein for 38 weeks during the school year and employing one teacher whose work is devoted exclusively to such school, and having an enrolment of at least 25 pupils, and maintaining a course of study approved by him. The Commissioner shall also make an additional appropriation to each city or union free school district of $200 for each additional teacher employed exclusively in such schools for 38 weeks during the school year (137, p. 3).

In order to secure successful operation of this law, the organization and general oversight of all schools receiving state aid for teaching agriculture are under the direction of the State Department of Agricultural Education. The State Department of Education has also prepared a very complete series of syllabi of courses in agriculture for high schools. From this series it is possible for a school to select subjects adapted to the particular agricultural interests of the community (138).

Agriculture in the technical type of secondary schools receives much the same attention as in the district type, the chief difference being that the latter offers no courses in mechanic arts. These schools seem to be patterned after state agricultural and mechanical colleges, but offering only instruction of secondary grade. A good example of this type is the California Polytechnic School, which was opened in 1903 at San Luis Obispo. This institution is supported by the state, and is intended "to furnish to the young people of both sexes mental and manual training in arts and sciences, including agriculture, mechanical engineering, business methods, domestic economy, and such other branches as will fit students for non-professional walks of life" (12, p. 22).

Agricultural education in State Normal Schools has already been discussed in a previous article of this series.[8] Instruction in agriculture in these schools is usually of secondary grade but with the special aim of preparing teachers. In some of these schools considerable emphasis is placed upon agriculture, and work corresponding to some of the best agricultural high schools is offered. For example, the Cape Girardeau (Mo.) State Normal School has a department of agriculture not only for teachers but for furnishing "young men from the farm an opportunity of obtaining the equivalent of a good high-school education of such a nature as will fit them to carry on the business of farming according to the most approved farm methods" (139, p. 63).

The development of secondary agricultural instruction has proceeded along two lines, one by employing existing high schools, the other in organizing separate agricultural high schools. The recent tendency as indicated by the statistical summary introducing this discussion seems strongly in the direction of the former. No doubt there is much to be said in favor of separate agricultural high schools to meet conditions in certain localities, but taking the country as a whole the natural tendency,

[8] This journal, Vol. X, No. 8.

as above indicated, of maintaining the unity of our present school organization presents obvious advantages which the public has already begun to realize.

Attention should be given, in this connection, to the fact that much misapprehension and undue concern exists as to the plan of organization of the agricultural high school. A careful analysis of the course of study of the average agricultural high school will show less divergence from the plan of the ordinary high school than many suppose. It will be found that the courses of study are essentially the same in many particulars, the chief difference being the substitution of agricultural and household arts subjects for the foreign languages, with perhaps more emphasis on the practical side of the sciences and less emphasis on certain phases of mathematics[4] (140).

One real difficulty in making the most of agriculture as a school subject lies in the fact that there is little opportunity for agricultural practice corresponding to shop practice in mechanic arts. The most active season of agricultural work is during the summer vacation. This difficulty may be met in the way already referred to in the account of the Baltimore County (Md.) Agricultural High School, where the teacher of agriculture devotes the usual summer vacation period to looking after experiments being conducted by the pupils. This matter has been carefully studied by a special agent of the Massachusetts State Board of Education and conclusions submitted to the legislature in the form of a *Report of the Board of Education on Agricultural Education* (141). Provision for proper farm practice as recommended in this report is secured by part-time work in agriculture which may utilize "home land, equipment, and time, outside school hours, for practical training supervised by the school." The scheme is worked out in considerable detail by means of concrete examples of various "farming projects" that may be undertaken. Among the major projects suggested are caring for a kitchen garden, keeping a pen of poultry, caring for a selected part of an orchard, raising a specified crop of potatoes, caring for one cow. Each major project is broken up into minor projects. For example, keeping a pen of poultry would include as minor projects building a poultry house according to plans and specifications worked out at school. This in turn is divided into such subordinate minor projects as are necessary for successful completion, such as selecting a site for the house, taking into consideration: soil as related to poultry culture, underdrainage, conditions of sunlight and shade, convenience of access, etc. It seems likely that the legislation proposed by this report will be passed by the legislature now in session. If the proposed plan goes into effect, its results should be carefully studied by all who are interested in secondary agricultural education.

The rapid introduction of agriculture in high schools is responsible, in part at least, for two interesting educational reactions. One is the changed attitude of colleges toward agriculture as an entrance unit. A few years ago most colleges refused to give any credit for work done in this subject in high schools. Now 36 colleges actually recognize the subject and 27 express a willingness to do so when it is offered as an entrance unit, and several other colleges are considering the matter (142).

The other reaction is upon the method of presenting secondary science. There is now a growing tendency to relate science instruction more and more to the practical affairs of life (143). Recent experiments seem to justify this method of approach to a science even when judged from the point of view of pure science (144, 145).

Agricultural colleges are now well established, and their problems are largely matters of detail and of research. The problems of agricultural education are now being shifted to the secondary schools offering agricultural instruction. There is a great diversity, not only in respect to types of schools, but also as to methods, time devoted to the subject, equipment, qualification of teachers, and in other respects. But of the widespread interest there can be no doubt. The results on the whole promise much for the development of rural education and redirection of rural schools.

## BIBLIOGRAPHY

Only titles cited by number in text are included in the following list:

124. "What Constitutes Successful Work in Agriculture in Rural Schools?" B. M. Davis, *Proceedings of the National Education Association for 1908,* 1189–94.

This discussion is based on a study of replies to a questionnaire addressed to teachers and others interested in agricultural education.

125. "The District Schools in a County as Educational and Social Centers," Jessie Field, National Society for the Study of Education, *Tenth Yearbook,* Part II (1911), 17–19.

In the county system described agricultural studies are an important means for bringing the school and community into a closer relation. The subjects are not uniform in the various schools of the county but are chosen primarily because of some dominant community interest.

126. *The Teaching of Agriculture in the High School,* G. A. Bricker. New York: Macmillan (1911), XXV, 202.

The subject is considered from a teaching standpoint in the following chapters: "Nature of Secondary Agriculture"; "Rise and Development of Secondary Education in Agriculture in the United States"; "Social Results"; "As a Separate Science"; "Psychological Determination of Sequence"; "Seasonal Determination of Sequence"; "Organization of the Course"; "Aims and Methods of Presentation"; "Organization of the Laboratory and Field Work"; "Illustrative List of Classified Exercises"; "Educational Aims, Values, and Ideals." This is the first attempt to present in detail the problems of secondary agriculture from the point of view of instruction.

127. "The School of Agriculture," *University of Minnesota Bulletin,* XIII, No. 10 (1910), 66.

Annual announcement of the School of Agriculture connected with the University of Minnesota.

128. *Secondary Agricultural Education in Alabama,* C. J. Owens, United States Department of Agriculture, Office of Experiment Stations, Bulletin 220 (1909), 30.

This bulletin contains "concrete information as to methods of organizing, courses of study, needed equipment, and cost of secondary agricultural schools."

129. *First Annual Report of the Congressional District Agricultural Schools of Georgia,* Georgia State College of Agriculture, Bulletin for December, 1909.

A complete account of the organization of these schools is given.

130. *Agricultural High School,* B. H. Crocheron, Philopolis, Md. Prospectus of the Baltimore (Md.) Agricultural High School (1909).

A brief account of the foundation, purpose, entrance requirements, courses of study, and equipment of this school.

131. "Community Work in the Agricultural High School," B. H. CROCHERON, National Society for the Study of Education, *Tenth Yearbook*, Part II (1911), 9–16.

A detailed description of the community work undertaken by the Baltimore (Md.) County Agricultural High School. It includes an account of the school, its organization, and work among the farmers, farmers' wives, and young people of the community. This paper shows the great possibilities of a rural high school in its service to an entire community, children and adults as well.

132. "Elementary Agriculture in the New Holland (Ohio) High School," G. A. BRICKER, *Ohio Agricultural College Extension Bulletin*, III, No. 7 (1908), 6.

A brief description of the organization of work in agriculture with concrete examples of some of the things actually accomplished.

133. "The John Swaney School," V. C. KAYS, *Nature-Study Review*, IV, No. 9 (1908), 271–75.

An account of the history and of the first two years' experience of this school. It is in the country, "planned and built by country people for the education of country children."

134. *Opportunity for the California High School: Industrial and Agricultural Education*, EDWARD HIATT, California State Department of Education, Special Bulletin (July, 1910), 21.

This bulletin describes the plans for introducing agriculture in the high school of the city of Stockton, Cal.

135. "Agriculture in the Secondary Schools of California," E. B. BABCOCK, *Nature-Study Review*, V (1909), 210–18.

The work of several high schools giving instruction in agriculture is described. The article includes extracts from a report of F. H. Bolster of the Gardena (Los Angeles City) High School. This is of particular interest as it is claimed that the Gardena High School is the first city high school to "offer agriculture as the one principal purpose of the school."

136. "The State High School," A. E. PICKARD, *Hinckley* (Minn.) *High School Bulletin* (1910), 23.

A full account of this school is given, including courses of study, general information as to admission, expenses, certificates, scope and purposes of courses, etc., detailed description of work offered in agriculture, manual training, domestic science, and normal work. This school is one of the ten high schools of Minnesota receiving state aid. All of these schools are similar in organization to this one.

137. *Schools of Agriculture, Mechanic Arts, and Home Making*, F. W. HOWE, New York State Department of Education, Special Circular (November 1, 1910).

This circular contains a "general statement in reference to the relations of this type of school to the so-called "trade schools," and the responsibility of the Division of Trade Schools in respect to it, and the text of the law relating to these schools, notes on this law, brief descriptions of some typical schools teaching agriculture, mechanic arts, and home-making, a list of books, periodicals, and national and state publications dealing with agriculture, farm mechanics, and household economy.

138. "Syllabus for Secondary Schools: Agriculture," *ibid.*, Annual Report (1910), III, 1–102.

This syllabus includes apple growing, general fruit growing, cereal and forage crops, potato growing, dairy husbandry, animal husbandry, poultry husbandry. Each subject is presented as a series of exercises, giving the object of the exercise, materials, and directions for study.

139. Department of Agriculture, E. A. COKEFAIR, Cape Giradeau, Mo.: *The Missouri State Normal School Bulletin,* Catalogue Number (1909), 63–67.

A description of objects of work offered and detailed outline of course of study. It is of particular interest because provision is made for giving instruction to farmers as well as to teachers.

140. "The Curriculum of the Agricultural High School," STUART G. NOBLE, *The Mississippi School Journal,* XV (1911), 7–11.

The writer presents the results of a detailed study of the curricula of the agricultural high schools of Alabama, Georgia, and Mississippi.

141. *Report of the Board of Education on Agricultural Education,* R. W. STIMSON, *et al.,* Massachusetts State Department of Education, Special Report (1911), 104.

This report was prepared for the state legislature which requested that an investigation be made as to the advisability of establishing a system of agricultural education throughout the commonwealth. The matter presented in this report is a valuable contribution to the literature of agricultural education because it outlines some plans not hitherto undertaken in agricultural instruction.

142. "Report of Committee on Encouraging College-Entrance Credit in High-School Agriculture," A. B. GRAHAM, *Proceedings of the National Education Association for 1910,* 480–83.

This report is the result of an investigation of a committee appointed the previous year by the Department of Rural and Agricultural Education of the N.E.A.

143. "Practical Aspects of Science in Secondary Education," W. R. HART, *et al., ibid.,* 446–80.

This general topic was discussed at a joint session of the departments of secondary, of science, and of rural and agricultural education. Following the presentation of the pedagogical and scientific viewpoints are brief discussions of the subject as related to the various sciences usually taught in high schools.

144. "An Experiment of Methods of Teaching Zoölogy," J. P. GILBERT, *Journal of Educational Psychology* (June, 1910), 321–32.

This paper is a preliminary report of a series of investigations "to determine the relative merits of the pure-science and applied-science methods of approach in teaching secondary science."

145. *Ibid., School Science and Mathematics,* XI, No. 3 (March, 1911), 205–15.

A further report of the experiment referred to in 144. The following significant statement occurs among the conclusions of the author: "In former discussions those who advocated applied science have been forced to take the defensive. While the data here obtained do not finally settle the question of the relative merits of the pure-science and applied-science approach to secondary-school zoölogy, they do shift the burden of proof to those who advocate the cultural approach."

# A GRADED COURSE IN SCHOOLROOM GYMNASTICS. IV

JULIA ANNA NORRIS
School of Education, The University of Chicago.

## GRADE I

### Birds Learning to Fly

(Adapted from *Gymnastic Stories and Plays* by Rebecca Stoneroad, M.D. D. C. Heath & Co.)

*Story*—One fine spring morning the mother bird says it is time she gave the little birds a lesson in flying. First they try their wings and legs to see if they are strong, and they look over the edge of the nest to see what is on the ground below them, and they do a little hopping on the branches. Then after a long flight they return to their nests and take a singing lesson.

*Exercises:*

1. Trying strength of wings
   Purpose: Correction of chest and upper spine.
   Straight sitting position on desks with feet in chairs.
   Signals: A. Make your wings.
   Bend elbows and bring hands up to outer surface of shoulders.
   B. Up.
   Lift elbows at the side, each time a little higher, till after three or four times the hands touch each other behind the neck.
   C. Down.
   Return to position of "make your wings."

2. Looking over the edge of the nest
   Purpose: Trunk exercise.
   Straight sitting position.
   Signals: A. Hands on hips.
   B. To left (right)—look over.
   Bend over as far as possible without losing balance and look down, keeping chest active.
   C. Straight up.
   Return quickly to straight sitting position.

3. Trying strength of legs
   Purpose: Leg exercise.
   Straight standing position.

Signals: A. Spread your wings.
Raise stretched arms to height of shoulders in side plane.
B. Bend.
Bend knees, trunk erect, lower arms to sides.
C. Straighten.
Straighten knees, and raise arms again.

4. Hopping on the branches
Purpose: Balance.
Signals: A. Hands on hips.
B. Up on toes.
C. Hop. (Count for each hop.)
Hop forward on toes, both feet at a time.
Later children may count and hop rhythmically.

5. Flying
Purpose: General exercise.
Signal: Fly.
Run round room, raising and lowering stretched arms as if flying, and finish by climbing up into chairs.

6. Singing lesson
Purpose: Respiratory.
Signals: A. Breathe.
B. Sing.
Children exhale slowly, singing the syllable "Loo."

## GRADE II

### The Fire Fighters

*Story*—The fire bell rings a number that the children know and the fire chief gallops on ahead of the other firemen to the fire. The firemen play water on the flames till they have quenched them, and then they climb up the ladders to rescue people or valuable articles in case the fire should break out again. Their lungs then are full of smoke which they must get rid of, and finally they drive back to the engine house with their galloping horses.

*Exercises:*

1. Driving horses to the fire
Two children who did the story play especially well the day before gallop round the room, one driving the other.

2. Playing water on flames
Purpose: Practice in straight standing position.
Signals: A. Hands on hose.
Hands raised in front grasping imaginary large-sized hose.

B. Left.
Step to left and point hose to left. A soft hissing sound may be made with mouth.

C. Right.
Step to right and point hose to right.

3. Climbing ladder to upper windows
Purpose: Leg and arm exercise.
Signals: A. Turn.
Children face their chairs.
B. One, two, etc., to ten.
Left hand and foot raised at "one"; right hand and foot, at "two." At "nine" step on to chair with left foot; at "ten," with right foot.

4. Descending ladder
Purpose: Leg exercise.
Arms remain held over head but do not take part in movement.
Signals: One, two, etc., to ten.
At "one" bend right knee and lower left foot a few inches from chair; replace foot on chair. At "two" bend left knee and lower right foot; replace foot on chair. At "nine" step on floor with left foot; at "ten," with right foot.

5. Getting rid of smoke in lungs
Purpose: Respiratory.
Signals: A. Breathe in.
B. Breathe out.

6. Driving horses home
Purpose: General exercise.
Signal: Ready—gallop.

## GRADE III

### Lesson V

1. Introductory. Two steps forward—march! Two steps backward—march!
Taken in three counts, children counting. 1. Step forward with left foot. 2. Step forward with right foot, passing beyond left. 3. Bring left heel up to right with a click.

2. Arch. Shoulders—firm! Head to left—bend! Upward—raise! To right, etc. The same in four counts —1!—2!—3!—4! Po—sition!

3. Arm. Head—firm! Po—sition!
Finger tips are placed on crown of head, wrists elevated as high as possible, elbows back.

4. Trunk. Hips—firm! Trunk forward—bend! Upward—raise! etc.

5. Jump. Hips—firm! Heels—raise! Spring jump with feet apart and together counting to ten—go! Po—sition!
Jump, landing on toes with feet two foot lengths' distance apart on every odd count and together on every even count. On the last count heels come to the floor softly.

6. Respiratory. Arms sideways—raise! Hands—turn! Arm raising with deep breathing—raise!—sink! etc.
Inhale while arms pass from horizontal to upward stretched position. Exhale while they return to horizontal position.

## GRADE III

### Lesson VI

1. Introductory. Side step to left—march! Side step to right—march!
Taken in two counts, children counting. 1. Step left two foot lengths' distance with left foot. 2. Bring right foot to left with a click.
2. Arch. Shoulders—firm! Head forward—bend! Upward—raise! etc.
3. Arm. Hips—firm! Arm pulling backward—1!—2! etc. Po—sition!
Arm pulling backward. 1! Pull elbows back as far as possible without causing a sway back. 2! Relax and let elbows return to original position.
4. Trunk. Hips—firm! Trunk to left—bend! Upward—raise! To right, etc.
5. Jump. Hips—firm! Left foot forward—place! Heels—raise! Jump, changing feet counting to ten—go! etc.
Jump, landing on toes with right foot in front on every odd count, left foot on every even count. Let heels come softly to floor on last count.
6. Respiratory. Arms forward—raise! Arm raising upward—1!—2! etc.

## GRADE IV

### Lesson V

1. Introductory. Left facing—1!—2! Right facing—1!—2!
See Grade V, Lesson II, for technique. The teacher will keep the counting in her own hands in this lesson. Making four facings in the same direction in succession, thus completing a circle, helps the children to understand the degree of each facing.
2. Leg. Hips—firm! Foot placing backward with change of feet—go! etc.
Taken in four counts, children counting. 1. Place left foot backward. 2. Replace it. 3. Place right foot backward. 4. Replace it.
3. Arch. Hips—firm! Head to left—bend! Head bending all the way—1! —2! etc. Upward—raise! Po—sition!
1! Bend head from left to right.
2! Bend head from right to left.

4. Arm. Shoulders—firm! Arm flinging sideways with palms up—1!—2! etc. Po—sition!
   1! Fling arms to horizontal position, palms up. 2! Return to shoulders-firm position.
5. Trunk. Neck—firm! Trunk to left—bend! Upward—raise! To right, etc.
6. Jump. Hips—firm! Left leg sideways—raise! Jump, changing feet counting to ten—go! etc. Po—sition!
   Land on toes at each jump, on odd counts with left foot on floor and right raised sideways, on even counts right foot on floor and left raised sideways. On tenth count replace the raised foot without raising the other, thus finishing with both feet on floor, heels down.
7. Respiratory. Arms forward—raise! Arm moving sideways—1!—2! etc. Po—sition!
   1! Move straight arms horizontally from front into side plane. 2! Return to front plane!

## GRADE IV

### Lesson VI

1. Introductory. Left—face! Right—face!
   Let children do the counting.
2. Leg. Hips—firm! Alternate heel and toe raising counting to four (eight or twelve)—go! etc. Po—sition!
   Children count. 1. Raise heels. 2. Lower them. 3. Raise toes. 4. Lower them.
3. Arch. Shoulders—firm! Head forward—bend! Upward—raise! etc.
4. Arm. Chest—firm! Arm flinging sideways—1!—2! etc. Po—sition!
   1! Fling arms to stretched horizontal position in side plane. 2! Return to chest-firm position.
5. Trunk. Neck—firm! Trunk to left—twist! Forward—twist! To right, etc. Po—sition.
6. Jump. Hips—firm! Left leg forward—raise! Jump—changing feet counting to ten—go! etc. Po—sition!
   On odd counts land on left foot with right raised forward, on even counts, vice versa.
7. Respiratory. Neck firm with deep breathing—1!—2!
   1! Slowly raise arms to neck-firm position while inhaling. 2! Slowly return to fundamental position while exhaling.

## GRADE V

### Lesson V

1. Introductory. Hips—firm! Running in place, changing to neck-firm, counting to ten (twenty or thirty)—go! etc. Po—sition!
   See Grade V, Lesson IV. The only change is that hands are flung from hips-firm to neck-firm position on every other count.

2. Arch. Hips—firm! Head to left—twist! To left—bend! Upward—raise! Forward—twist! etc. Po—sition!
   See Grade VI, Lesson III.
3. Arm. Neck—firm! Arm flinging sideways—1!—2! etc. Po—sition!
   1! Fling arms to horizontal position in side plane. 2! Return to neck-firm position.
4. Leg. Hips—firm! Foot placing sideways with heel raising and change of feet—go! etc. Po—sition!
   Taken in eight counts, children counting. 1. Place left foot two foot lengths' distance to left. 2. Raise both heels. 3. Lower heels. 4. Replace foot. 5–8. Repeat movement on right side.
5. Balance. Shoulders—firm! Left knee upward—bend! Foot—replace! etc.
   Left knee upward—bend! Raise bent knee in front plane to height of hip, forming right angle at hip, right angle at knee, and pointing toe downward.
6. Abdominal. Left hip right neck—firm! Trunk to left—bend! Upward—raise! etc. Arms—change! To right—bend! etc.
7. Back. Shoulders—firm! Trunk forward—bend! Arm flinging sideways—1!—2!—1!—2! Trunk—raise! Po—sition! The same in eight counts—go!
   Arm flinging sideways—1! Fling arms to stretched horizontal position, palms up.
   2! Return to shoulders-firm position.
8. Jump. Hips—firm! Jump in six counts changing to neck-firm—1!—2!—3, 4!—5!—6! etc.
   3, 4! Jump upward flinging hands to neck-firm position and quickly back to hips-firm position.
9. Respiratory. Arm raising sideways upward—raise!—sink!
   Carry straight arms up in side plane to upward stretched position, turning palm gradually as arms go up. Return in same plane.

## GRADE V

### Lesson VI

1. Introductory. See Lesson V.
2. Arch. Shoulders—firm! Neck backward—bend! Upward—raise! etc. Po—sition!
   See Grade VI, Lesson I.
3. Arch. Arm stretching upward—1!—2! Stretching downward—1!—2!
   1! Shoulders-firm position. 2! Arm stretched in straight position in direction indicated.
4. Leg. Shoulders firm and heel raising in series—go! Class—halt!
   Children count silently until commanded to halt. On odd counts take

shoulders-firm position and raise heels. On even counts return to fundamental position. The word "halt!" should be given on an even count, and two more counts should then be performed before stopping the movement.

5. Balance. Hips—firm! Left leg sideways—raise! Foot—replace! etc. Raise leg with knee straight about 45°.
6. Abdominal. Right hip left chest—firm! Trunk twisting to left with left arm flinging sideways—1!—2! etc. Arms—change! To right, etc.
   1! Trunk twist forcibly to left, at the same time flinging left arm to side plane. 2! Trunk twist forward and return arm to chest-firm position.
7. Back. Arms sideways—raise! Trunk forward—bend! Arm sinking—1! —2! etc. Trunk—raise! Po—sition!
   1! Lower straight arms in plane parallel with axis of trunk. 2! Raise again.
8. Jump. Jump with sideways flinging of arms—1!—2!—3, 4!—5!—6!
   3, 4! Jump and fling straight arms up to height of shoulders in side plane, and immediately down again so that they are in fundamental position when toes touch floor.
9. Respiratory. Arm circling—1!—2!
   1! Inhale while raising arms through front plane to full extension. 2! Exhale while lowering arms through side plane to fundamental position.

## GRADE VI

### Lesson V

1. Introductory. Hips—firm! Left foot backward—raise! Running in place, counting to ten (twenty or thirty), changing hands to neck firm—go! See Grade V, Lesson V.
2. Arch. Shoulders—firm! Chest—raise! Re—turn! Po—sition!
3. Arm. Arms sideways—raise! Arm swimming—1!—2!—3! etc. Po—sition.
   1! Chest-firm position. 2! Shoot arms out in front at height of shoulders, palms down, index fingers touching. 3! Turn hands back to back and swing arms out to side plane, thumbs down, little fingers up.
4. Leg. Heels raise and hips—firm! Knees bend and neck—firm! Knees stretch and hips—firm! Po—sition! The same in four counts—go!
5. Balance. Neck—firm! Heels—raise! Knees deep—bend! Knees—stretch! Po—sition!
6. Abdominal. Right hip and left chest—firm! Arm flinging and trunk twisting to left—1!—2! etc. Arms—change! To right, etc. See Grade V, Lesson VI.
7. Back. Arms sideways—raise! Hands—turn! Trunk forward—bend! Arms raising upward—1!—2!—1!—2! Trunk—raise! Po—sition!

8. Jump. Hips—firm! Jump forward—1!—2!—3, 4!—5!—6!
3, 4! Jump forward clearing about a foot of floor.
9. Respiratory. Arm raising sideways and heel raising—raise!—sink!

## GRADE VI

### Lesson VI

1. Introductory. Like Lesson V.
2. Arch. Chest—firm! Chest—raise! Re—turn! Po—sition!
3. Arm. Arm stretching sideways and upward—1!—2!—1!—2! Arm stretching downward—1!—2!
1! Shoulders-firm position. 2! Both arms stretched in direction indicated!
4. Leg. Hips—firm! Foot placing forward, sideways, and backward with change of feet—go!
Taken in six counts. 1. Place left foot forward. 2. Replace it. 3. Place it sideways. 4. Replace it. 5. Place it backward. 6. Replace it. 1–6. Repeat with right foot.
5. Balance. Hips—firm! Left knee upward—bend! Knee backward—stretch! Foot—replace! etc.
Knee backward—stretch! Straighten knee backward at angle of about 45° with the floor.
6. Abdominal. Neck—firm! Trunk to left—bend! Upward—raise! To right, etc.
7. Back. Hips—firm! Left foot long step forward—place! Left knee—bend! Knee—stretch! etc. Feet—change! Right knee, etc.
When left knee is bent, right should be straight and trunk should incline sufficiently forward to maintain a straight line from backward heel up to head.
8. Jump. Hips—firm! Jump with sideways flinging of feet—1!—2!—3, 4!—5!—6!
3, 4! Jump upward, flinging feet apart and bringing them together so that the landing position is with heels together.
9. Respiratory. Arm raising forward upward with heel raising—raise!—sink!

## GRADE VII

### Lesson V

1. Introductory. Hips—firm! Left foot backward—raise! Running in place, counting to ten (twenty or thirty), changing hands to neck firm—go!
See Grade V, Lesson V.
2. Arch. Neck firm and feet sideways—place! Chest—raise! Re—turn! In one count. Po—sition!
Neck firm and feet sideways—place! Taken in one count with a jump.

3. Arm. Left arm forward, right arm upward stretching—1!—2! Arm changing—1!—2! Arm stretching downward—1!—2!
4. Abdominal. Sitting on desks—place! Neck—firm! Trunk to left—twist! Forward—twist! To right, etc. Standing position—place!
5. Back. Arm sideways—raise! Trunk forward—bend! Arm swimming—1! —2!—3! etc. Trunk—raise! Po—sition!
   See Grade VI, Lesson V, arm movement.
6. Respiratory. Arm raising sideways and heel raising—raise!—sink!
7. Balance Step. Hands—place! Polka step forward—go!
   Time. Two-part time. One, two, three, hold.
   Development:
   A. Soft stamping in place—left, right, left, hold; right, left, right, hold; etc.
   B. Same on toes.
   C. Same as B stepping forward on one.
   D. Same as C prefacing the first count by a little hop.

## GRADE VII

### Lesson VI

1. Introductory. Like Lesson V.
2. Arch. Hips—firm! Neck backward—bend! Head circling to left (right) —1!—2!—3!—4! Upward—raise!
   1! Quarter circle to left both bending and twisting neck. 2! Quarter circle bringing to head-forward-bend position. 3! Quarter circle to right. 4! Quarter circle bringing head to neck-backward-bend position.
3. Arm. Arm stretching sideways, upward, and downward—1!—2!—1!—2! —1!—2!
   Any three directions may be substituted for these three.
4. Leg. Hips—firm! Kneeling on left (right) knee—1!—2! Standing position —1!—2! The same in four counts—go!
   Kneeling position—1! Touch left toe to floor behind as far as it can stretch with trunk erect. 2! Kneel softly on left knee. 3! Rise, leaving left foot touching floor behind. 4! Replace left foot.
5. Balance. Hips—firm! Heels—raise! Knees deep—bend! Knees— —stretch! Heels—sink! Po—sition!
6. Abdominal. Hips firm and left foot forward—place! Trunk to left— bend! Upward—raise! etc. Feet—change! To right, etc.
7. Back. Hips firm and left (right) forward fall—out! Neck—firm! Hips— firm! Neck—firm! Hips—firm! Po—sition! The same in six counts— go!

8. Jump. Jump forward with one start step—1, 2!—3!—4!
   1, 2! Taking one running step with left foot and jump forward landing with heels together on toes with knees bent. 3! Stretch knees. 4! Lower heels.
9. Respiratory. Shoulders—firm! Slow arm stretching sideways with palms up—stretch!—bend!

## GRADE VIII

### Lesson V

1. Introductory. Hips—firm! Left foot backward—raise! Running in place, changing between neck and hips firm, counting to ten (twenty or thirty) —go!
   See Grade V, Lesson V.
2. Arch. Neck firm and feet sideways—place! Chest—raise! Re—turn! Po—sition!
3. Arm. Arm stretching sideways, upward and downward—1!—2!—1!—2! —1!—2! Arm stretching downward—1!—2!
   Any three directions may be substituted for these three.
4. Abdominal. Sitting on desks—place! Hips—firm! Trunk backward—bend! Upward—raise! etc. Standing position—place!
5. Back. Hips firm and left (right) backward fall—out! Neck—firm! Hips—firm! Neck—firm! Hips—firm! Po—sition! The same in six counts—go!
6. Respiratory. With palms up, arms sideways—raise!
   Arm raising and heel raising—raise!—sink!
7. Balance step. Two slides forward and two waltz balance steps in place—go!
   Waltz time. Each step occupies four measures.
   First measure. Slide forward with left foot, bringing right up behind on third beat.
   Second measure. Same as first.
   Third measure. Waltz balance step starting with left foot.
   Fourth measure. Waltz balance step starting with right foot.

## GRADE VIII

### Lesson VI

1. Introductory. Like Lesson V.
2. Arch. Chest—firm! Neck—firm and chest—raise! Chest—firm and re—turn! The same—1!—2! etc. Po—sition!
3. Arm. Hands on desks—place! Foot placing backward—1!—2! In one count, po—sition!
   Hands—place! Rest each hand on the desk at its side. Foot placing

backward. 1! Place left foot backward, at same time letting other knee and both arms bend. 2! Place right foot backward beside left. Po—sition! Spring back to fundamental position, hands at sides.

The spine should be kept straight in this movement and the shoulder blades flat. The length of the step backward should depend on the ability of child to keep shoulder blades flat.

4. Leg. Hips—firm! Foot placing forward and backward with heel raising and change of feet—go!

   Taken in eight counts with each foot. 1. Place left foot forward. 2. Raise heels. 3. Lower heels. 4. Replace foot. 5–8. The same backward.

5. Balance. Hips—firm! Left (right) knee upward—bend! Knee backward—stretch! Knee upward—bend! Foot—replace!

   Knee backward—stretch! Straighten knee backward to an angle of about 45° with floor.

6. Abdominal. Neck firm and left foot forward—place! Trunk to left—twist! Forward—twist! etc. Feet—change! To right, etc.

7. Back. Arms forward upward fling and feet sideways—place! Trunk forward—bend! Arm parting—1!—2!—1!—2! Trunk—raise! Po—sition! The same in eight counts—go!

   The foot placing is taking in one count; also the return to fundamental position.

8. Jump. Hips—firm! Jump forward with one start step—1, 2!—3!—4!

   1, 2! Take one running step with left foot and jump forward, landing with heels together, heels raised and knees bent.

   3! Stretch knees. 4! Lower heels.

9. Respiratory. Arm circling and heel raising—raise!—sink!

   Raise! Raise heels and raise arms forward upward—sink! Lower heels and lower arms sideways downward.

## EDITORIAL NOTES

At the meeting of the Department of Superintendence at Mobile, there was passed a resolution adopting the so-called scientific alphabet. This alphabet, if actually used in books, would change the spelling and appearance of many common words. It would increase, in the end, the ease of pronouncing new words on the part of one who had mastered the new alphabet. It would meet in many details the difficulties which now arise from the fact that units or articulation are not paralleled by units of visual symbolization. It is only one of a number of alphabets proposed for the solution of these problems by associations which are interested, and it is by no means evident that the alphabet submitted to the department is the best which has been suggested.

**The Alphabet Adopted at Mobile**

There are two lines of thought which are stimulated by the action at Mobile. The first relates to English spelling and its difficulties. One is reminded that we are still using the alphabet which arose in Asia Minor centuries ago to represent the relatively simple sounds of a more primitive language. One thinks of the many sources from which our present sounds are drawn, and of the long history through which letters have passed in their migrations from the shores of the eastern Mediterranean to our western world. One thinks of his own struggles with the complexities of the English spelling, and of the struggles which children of this generation are having. Such thoughts as these make one very hospitable to the idea that some kind of a change should be made.

**English Spelling**

The second line of thought which is suggested by the action at Mobile relates to the organization which passed the resolution. Gathered in the auditorium where the vote was taken were about a thousand people, more or less. Let us admit that these were the most representative educational people in Mobile at the time. Let us go further and admit that these people had a right to consider themselves representative of the educational interests of the whole country. They divided so nearly half and half on the votes that it was evident to a casual observer that the educational world had not made up its mind in this matter. Furthermore, it is the belief of the present writer that no great impersonal problem can possibly be settled at such a meeting. There were none of the appearances of a dispassionate calm consideration which one thinks of as desirable in the solution of a problem of this type. The observer did not have confidence after the vote was taken that the great majority of the voters had any well-established convictions in the matter.

**How Such Votes Are Taken**

When one goes over the largest contributions which have been made by the N.E.A. to educational thinking, he finds that it is not the votes of that body which have been most influential. The reports of certain committees have had great weight in the thoughts of teachers, because these reports carried conviction. A report which influences people because it contains great truths will have influence when it is published, even if it is not sanctioned by an auditorium full of people. A plan which does not attract to itself the confidence of people can be passed annually or semiannually for several decades, and remain a lifeless and useless incumbrance on the pages of the educational statute books. It is a mistake in the light of N.E.A. history to try to legislate alphabets or other reforms into existence. The plan of N.E.A. influence is the educational plan. We all like to be educated into the use of new alphabets and new courses of study and new hygienic devices, but we are likely to rebel against votes passed anywhere by the members of any meeting. The frank fact is that such a vote at such a time is the weakest possible way of promoting a great interest.

**How the N.E.A. Has Influenced Education**

So emphatically do these considerations about the organization assert themselves in one's thinking that he is likely to forget the earlier considerations about the alphabet.

**The Alphabet Cannot Be Legislated into Use**

The alphabet ought to be thought of, and doubtless will be some day when the educational method of changing it has been worked out. The present method of pushing this particular alphabet is likely to keep the alphabet in the background.

C. H. J.

# BOOK REVIEWS

*Principles of Education.* By FREDERICK E. BOLTON, PH.D. New York: Scribner, 1910.

This work makes accessible for beginners the latest results of the scientific study of education mainly from the biological-psychological point of view. The child is treated as the central figure and the crowning product of an evolution that has not yet ceased, but at every point are also skilfully woven in the effects that society has had in shaping the individual consciousness.

The author first outlines the adaptation of functions in the development from unicellular life, showing that there is no evidence of purposive reactions in the lower orders, and tracing the development of the nervous system in man. He then treats the theory of "recapitulation," concluding with Spencer that "education must accord in mode and arrangement with that of man considered historically." But while he holds that the development of the ascending forms of life may throw light on that of the individual, he repudiates all Herbartian attempts to prescribe for the various periods of child development. Yet he finds that the order of development of movements and structure in the race, "from fundamental to accessory," should be better observed in educational method than at present. Instincts, he shows, are the results of the conservation of habits through heredity, but may be modified through environment, and should be developed or atrophied by education. While heredity is the great factor, education should not be neglected, but be made wiser through the study of individual capacities and differences. He next deals with the "psycho-physical parallelism" and the importance to education of a better understanding of the close relations of mind and body. This leads to a discussion of fatigue and school hygiene, and of individual variations in mental qualities as well as physical structures. Memory is then demonstrated to be primarily a physical phenomenon, requiring health for its best functioning. Similarly, imitation, observation, motor expression, emotional life, and other phases are treated from the standpoint of their physical bases and the consequent educational implications. Interspersed are some excellent chapters on the higher aspects of mental life—imagination, the nature of thinking, induction and deduction, interest, volition and morality, and general discipline, which exhibit a careful assimilation of late psychological investigations and a constant effort to apply the results to educational theory and practice.

Dr. Bolton seems to the reviewer to have erected a monument to his patient industry as a student of psychology and scientific pedagogy. This book is clearly his *magnum opus,* and gives us the results of many years of study, thinking, and practice. Its strong points are fundamental and obvious. (1) Education is viewed in the broadest way. From the beginning of the treatise that process is seen to be far larger than book facts, drill, and formal discipline; its means includes not only the school and college, but the home, all social institutions, the farm, play, and even chance environment. The connotation is almost as wide as life itself. (2) The biological foundation is consistently adhered to throughout. Hints at this procedure are growing in popularity, but seldom has so thoroughgoing an attempt been made in stating educational principles. (3) The work is a great storehouse of well-digested material upon nearly every conceivable topic of discussion in educational psychology. What others have undertaken to do by means of syllabi and references to a library of works, Dr. Bolton has concentrated under one cover.

With so extensive a scope, it is inevitable that certain defects should creep in. To a large extent they are correlated with the merits themselves. (1) The very breadth of the author occasionally leads him into matters rather remote from education, and he is sometimes obliged to narrow down before striking "pay dirt." This appears in his "liver fluke," the evidences in the Lamarck-Weismann controversy, and other interesting but elaborate discussions. At times, too, his psychology seems to contain flaws in consistency or recency. For example, he leans toward Titchener's or Sully's theory of the emotions, but finds the James-Lange theory (which he does not reconstruct according to Dewey, Baldwin, and others) to be more interesting and suggestive pedagogically. Likewise, he holds that we have "memories rather than memory," but refers to memory variously as a "power," a "conservation," and a "record," and exhorts the "training of memory." His discussion of formal discipline is excellent, but fails to take full account of the modifications of the Thorndike position worked out lately by Judd, Pillsbury, Angell, and Winch. (2) A biologist would hold that Dr. Bolton is too dogmatic. For the most part he gives an accurate statement of the various theories and in the light of them makes a reasonable interpretation of his facts, but he tends to treat as settled many theories that are still on trial, or even to select one out of several hypotheses as the only explanation. For example, he accepts Fiske's "prolonged infancy" completely, and he explains instincts by inherited memories rather than by any physiological operation of the nerve tracts. He also fails to note that at present there seems to be no conclusive experimental evidence for either Lamarck or Weismann, and that scientists have agreed to stop discussing the question until more evidence comes in. Sometimes he uses a theory that has marked limitations, like that of "nascent periods," as an absolute interpretation of his facts. A more serious matter, however, is his emphasis of heredity to the extent of refusing to recognize any difference of environment between the Jukes and the Edwards family. (3) In the inclusiveness of his material, Dr. Bolton has fallen into occasional repetitions both of facts and illustrations, and the book lacks considerably in organization. The preface disclaims all thought of a "comprehensive system," but more order might possibly have been introduced without hardening into a "logic chopper."

Other superficial criticisms might be made on the style and occasional use of words, but even what has already been said seems gratuitous in view of the undoubted merit of the work. Such a book has long been needed. It will not only afford an excellent introduction to the subject and a handbook for the student, young teacher, and parent, but will prove interesting and suggestive to the specialist and investigator. The treatise is a valuable résumé of modern educational theory, and will meet with speedy recognition.

Frank P. Graves

The Ohio State University

*Mental Discipline and Educational Values.* By W. H. Heck. New York: John Lane & Co., 1909. Pp. 147.

The aim of this book is to bring together and critically discuss the evidence for and against the doctrine of formal discipline and to put his conclusions in such form that they may be brought to bear on school practice. In spite of the disclaimer of any finality in the conclusions which is made in the introduction the author comes to rather positive conclusions such as the following: "The theories of localization [of brain function] now accepted are sufficient in themselves to disprove the doctrine of formal discipline" (p. 88). On the basis of his theoretic conclusions the author holds that educational values are entirely intrinsic and utilitarian.

The earlier part of the book gives a very excellent summary of the observations and experiments which have a bearing on the question of formal discipline and brings out the factors which must be borne in mind in considering the significance of these experiments and facts. For example, apparent transfer may be due to native difference in mental ability or to natural advancement in maturity. This summary lays the experimental facts before the reader in a clear manner and enables him if he so desires to pursue the matter in more detail by consulting the sources.

The next chapter discusses the localization of brain function and reaches the conclusion already indicated. The process of reasoning from data to conclusion is not entirely clear, however. The fact established is that the centers governing the movement of restricted groups of muscles are localized in well-defined areas of the brain. But when this small item of knowledge is compared with our wide ignorance of brain functions—for example, in the so-called association areas—it would seem that we are as much if not more justified in inferring from the mental to the physiological as the reverse.

While denying the validity of the notion of formal discipline the author admits a certain kind of transfer or extension of practice effects. This takes place only through the formation of a "concept of method." Practice may go on without effecting this formation, in which case it is merely a special ability that is trained. Or the "understanding of methods" is often gained at school without ability to use them. The degree of general effect then varies with the manner in which the material is utilized. Specifically the material is to be treated according to the manner of the five "formal steps."

Some of the discussion in this section is rather obscure, as, for example, the sentence which is quoted with approval from Hoose, "Form in mental activity means that peculiar activity which the mind exerts when it does any particular thing, or thinks any particular thought or word." This sounds like the type of psychological discussion one had thought past. The question may in general be raised whether discussions of this subject do not fail to reach common ground because of the obscurity of the expression "formal discipline" and of differences in the notion of what transference refers to, e.g., transference from one mental process to another or from one sort of material to another.

If this contribution to the subject does not clear up all the difficulties in it, it may be recommended as setting forth the various aspects of the problem in for the most part clear fashion and is therefore to be recommended for class reference or individual reading.

Frank N. Freeman

*Manual of Mental and Physical Tests.* By G. M. Whipple. Baltimore: Warwick & York, 1910. Pp. xix+534.

This first systematic book on tests consists of a detailed description of the method of procedure and a presentation of the results which have been obtained from fifty-one specialized tests and three test series. Though some well-known tests have been omitted most of them are included. There is a selection among different methods of testing the same processes, but little selection of the kind of test based on its proven usefulness. A good share of the inconclusive results of some of the tests, the author attributes to lack of uniformity in method, and he aims to supply such uniformity as will standardize further tests. He has worked out the details of method with care, and in this respect the book performs substantial service.

There is much variety among the tests themselves in respect to the process or characteristic tested and to the aim. There are physical and mental tests, tests of function and of information, tests of simple and of complex processes. The aim is now to determine the bodily normality or abnormality, now to determine special or general mental capacity, and now to determine the degree of mental maturity or retardation. What each test is suited to is to be decided by an examination of the test itself, and the results of previous investigations with it. It is difficult to determine what the results in general are, since the conclusions of various investigators are presented with little criticism. For example, the difference between the cephalic index of American and South German children is presented without suggesting the explanation of a racial difference. Hence it would be difficult to use the book as a guide as to what tests offer reasonable prospect of success for any particular purpose.

In the introductory chapter the author gives a summary of the statistical methods for the interpretation of data obtained from the application of tests. This description goes far enough to enable one unacquainted with such methods to apply the formulae but does not give their mathematical derivation. For this one may consult the sources to which reference is made.

The notion of what constitutes a test seems to the reviewer to be vague and to require more precise definition. It seems to differ very little in some cases from the mere psychological investigation of a particular process. It usually includes also, it is true, the problem of individual psychology, that is, the correlation of different mental processes or mental and physical processes. But there is still a purpose implied in tests but scarcely differentiated from the one just mentioned, and that is individual diagnosis. A general, average correlation of .81 may be established, for example, between pitch discrimination and certain fundamental processes indicating intelligence. But this was found after making a correction of the original "raw" correlation of .59. Such correction can only be made on the results from a group of subjects. It would not, therefore, apply to individual diagnosis. This is one of the highest correlations found in the tests. It is obvious, therefore, that many of these tests contribute nothing to the solution of the problem of the individual diagnosis. They have a theoretical interest as bearing on the general problem of the correlation of mental functions, but would not serve as a means of grading or judging children. The book then has its chief value for the experimental psychologist, but would not well serve as a practical guide for the educator.

FRANK N. FREEMAN

# CURRENT EDUCATIONAL LITERATURE IN THE PERIODICALS[1]

IRENE WARREN
Librarian, School of Education, The University of Chicago

BILLINGS, JOHN S. The New York Public Library. Cent. 81:839–52. (Ap. '11.)

Boys and the theater. Out. 97:722–23. (1 Ap. '11.)

BURNHAM, WILLIAM H. Arithmetic and school hygiene. Pedagog. Sem. 18:54–73. (Mr. '11.)

BUSHNELL, HENRY DAVIS. Educational efficiency. Atlan. 107:498–501. (Ap. '11.)

CAMPION, ANNA COOPER. Problems of the social worker. Psychol. Clinic 5:1–12. (15 Mr. '11.)

CHUBB, PERCIVAL. Reading of high school boys and girls. Pub. Lib. 16:134–38. (Ap. '11.)

CUMMINGS, EDWARD P. Elimination and retention of pupils. Psychol. Clinic 5:20–23. (15 Mr. '11.)

CUTTING, STARR WILLARD. The teaching of German literature in high schools and academies. School R. 19:217–24. (Ap. '11.)

DUNBAR, OLIVIA HOWARD. Defective children in school. R. of Rs. 43:449–59. (Ap. '11.)

FABER, CHARLOTTE. Value of a library in teaching history. Pub. Lib. 16: 139–41. (Ap. '11.)

FOSTER, WILLIAM T. The spelling of college students. Journ. of Educa. Psychol. 2:211–15. (Ap. '11.)

HARD, ANNE. The younger generation: an apologia. Atlan. 107:538–47. (Ap. '11.)

HARTSON, LOUIS D. A study of voluntary associations, educational and social, in Europe during the period from 1100–1700. Pedagog. Sem. 18:10–30. (Mr. '11.)

JOHNSTON, W. DAWSON. The library as a reinforcement of the school. Pub. Lib. 16:131–34. (Ap. '11.)

KELSEY, FRANCIS W. The sixteenth Michigan classical conference. School R. 19:196–201. (Mr. '11.)

[1] *Abbreviations.*—Atlan., Atlantic; Cent., Century; El. School T., Elementary School Teacher; Journ. of Educa. Psychol., Journal of Educational Psychology; Man. Train. Mag., Manual Training Magazine; Out., Outlook; Pedagog. Sem., Pedagogical Seminary; Psychol. Clinic, Psychological Clinic; Pub. Lib., Public Libraries; R. of Rs., Review of Reviews; School R., School Review.

KERSCHENSTEINER, GEORG. The fundamental principles of continuation schools. School R. 19:162–77. (Mr. '11.)

———. The organization of the continuation school in Munich. School R. 19:225–37. (Ap. '11.)

KICITCHKO, N. A brief report of the Moscow experimental school. El. School T. 11:381–83. (Mr. '11.)

KOOPMAN, HARRY LYMAN. A basic educational delusion. Pedagog. Sem. 18:44–46. (Mr. '11.)

LURTON, FREEMAN E. Retardation statistics from the smaller Minnesota towns. Psychol. Clinic 5:13–19. (15 Mr. '11.)

MACLAURIN, RICHARD C. The outlook for research. Pedagog. Sem. 18:1–9. (Mr. '11.)

MCMURRY, OSCAR L., and EGGERS, GEORGE W. Bookbinding in the school (3). Man. Train. Mag. 12:356–71. (Ap. '11.)

MAYER, MARY JOSEPHINE. The vital question of school lunches. R. of Rs. 43:455–59. (Ap. '11.)

MORGAN, WALTER P. Conditional promotions in the University high school. School R. 19:238–47. (Ap. '11.)

MUZZEY, DAVID SAVILLE. State, church, and school in France. The public school in France (1). School R. 19:178–95. (Mr. '11.)

———. State, church, and school in France. The campaign for lay education (2). School R. 19:248–65. (Ap. '11.)

OGDEN, R. M. Knowing and expressing. Pedagog. Sem. 18:47–53. (Mr. '11.)

RADOSAVLJEVICH, PAUL R. What is education? Pedagog. Sem. 18:31–43. (Mr. '11.)

SHOWERMAN, GRANT. The American idea. School R. 19:145–61. (Mr. '11.)

STERN, WILLIAM. The supernormal child. Journ. of Educa. Psychol. 2:181–90. (Ap. '11.)

STOCKBRIDGE, FRANK PARKER. Half time at school and half time at work. World's Work 21:14265–75. (Ap. '11.)

TERMAN, LEWIS M. A school where girls are taught home-making. Craftsman 20:63–68. (Ap. '11.)

VAN DEUSEN, CLINTON S. Co-operative plan for woodwork in rural schools. Man. Train. Mag. 12:315–25. (Ap. '11.)

WALLIN, J. E. WALLACE. Human efficiency. Pedagog. Sem. 18:74–84. (Mr. '11.)

———. The new clinical psychology and the psycho-clinist. The psychological clinic and the public schools (2). Journ. of Educa. Psychol. 2:181–90. (Ap. '11.)

WILLIAMS, T. A. Intellectual precocity. Comparison between John Stuart Mill and the son of Dr. Boris Sidis. Pedagog. Sem. 18:85–103. (Mr. '11.)

VOLUME XI NUMBER 10

THE ELEMENTARY SCHOOL TEACHER

JUNE, 1911

# A GRADED COURSE IN SCHOOLROOM GYMNASTICS. V

JULIA ANNA NORRIS
School of Education, The University of Chicago

## GRADE I

### THE ORGAN GRINDER

*Story*—The hand-organ man goes pushing his organ up one street and down another until he stops before the house of some child. Here he grinds out tunes for the children, who give pennies to his monkey. The monkey politely bows in acknowledgment of each gift. The children dance merrily to the music and stop out of breath.

*Exercises:*

1. Pushing the organ.
   Purpose: Good carriage and rhythm.
   Signals: A. Hands on handle.
   Hold hands up in front of shoulders, well apart.
   B. Ready—go!
   Children march round room briskly, with erect posture, pretending to push (full-sized) organ.
2. Playing the organ.
   Purpose: Arm muscles, chest correction, rhythm.
   Signals: A. With left (or right) hand take hold of crank.
   Hold hand up at side, elbow bent.
   B. Ready—play!
   Arm describes the largest circle the child can make, moving first upward then backward, then downward, then forward. This may well be done in time to some popular air which the children may hum.
3. Giving pennies to the monkey.
   Purpose: Back and leg exercise.
   Signals: A. Down. Reach down with left (or right) hand, bending knees, and bending forward at hip joint with back straight.
   B. Up. Quickly spring to straight standing position.

4. Bowing of the monkey.
   Purpose: Practice in straight standing position.
   Signals: A. Hand on cap.
   Raise right hand to head.
   B. Bow.
   Nod head quickly, and make quick motion of arm as if pulling off and replacing cap.
   Repeat bowing as many times as there were pennies given to the monkey.
5. Dancing of the children.
   Purpose: General exercise.
   Signal: Ready—skip!
   Children join hands by rows, and each row skips sideways about the room.
6. Panting.
   Purpose: Full breathing.
   Signals: A. Breath in.
   B. Breath out.

## GRADE II

### Soldiers at Drill

*Story*—The soldiers march about the parade ground saluting their officer as they pass him. They raise the flag and give it a hearty cheer, and then go through with their rifle practice. At the end of the drill the bugle is blown and they march from the parade ground in double quick time.

*Exercises:*

1. Marching about the parade ground.
   Purpose: Good carriage and rhythm.
   Signals: A. Left (or right) shoulder—arms!
   Bend hand up at side, arm held close to body, hand at shoulder height.
   B. Forward—march!
   March briskly about room with erect posture.
   One child may stand in a chair as officer of the day; in passing him each child will salute by raising the free hand to the forehead and dropping it again immediately. It is best to arrange the march so that the free hand will be on the side toward the officer.
   C. Stack arms. Pretend to lean rifles against desks after the marching.
2. Raising the flag.
   Purpose: Correction of chest, and arm exercise.

Signals: A. Hands on rope.
Hands in front of body, one above the other.
B. Pull. Bring the upper hand *strongly* down till it rests on the lower one.
C. Reach. Remove the lower hand and reach high up with it.

3. Three cheers for the flag.
Purpose: Correction of chest, arm exercise.
Signals: A. With left (or right) hand take caps or handkerchiefs.
Boys remove imaginary caps from heads, girls hold up imaginary handkerchiefs.
B. One! Two! Three!
At each count wave hand in *large* circle and shout, "Hurrah!" in a stage whisper.

4. Target Practice.
Purpose: Trunk and leg exercise.
Signals: A. Right shoulder—arms!
As before.
B. On left (or right) knee—down!
Kneel with back erect and hands holding rifle out in front.
C. Aim!
Bend forward at hip joint and take aim by sighting along bore of gun.
D. Fire!
Quickly spring back to erect kneeling position, pulling right hand back (pulling trigger) and saying, "Bang!" Repeat Aim! and Fire!
E. Stand—up! Spring to standing position with gun at "Right shoulder arms."

5. Bugle call.
Purpose: Full breathing.
Signals: A. Take bugle in left (or right) hand.
Hold half-closed hand up in front to represent bugle.
B. Breathe.
C. Blow.
Holding bugle to mouth sing some simple bugle call with the syllable, "loo," using only one breath for entire call. "I can't get 'em up," though inappropriate in sentiment, is good because short.

6. Running.
Purpose: General exercise.
Signals: A. Right shoulder—arms!
B. Double quick—march!
Children run around room to seats.

## GRADE III

### Lesson VII

1. Introductory. One step forward and backward—march!
One step backward and forward—march!
Class counts 1, 2! 1, 2! in responding to each command. Introductory exercises from previous lessons may also be used at random in order to exact alert attention from the children.
2. Arch. *Hips—firm! Head to left—twist!* Head twisting all the way—1! —2! *Head forward—twist! Po—sition!*
1. Twist head from left to right. 2. From right to left.
3. Arm. Shoulders—firm! Arm flinging sideways—1!—2! Po—sition! The same in four counts—go!
1. Shoulders—firm position. 2. Fling arms sideways with palms up and elbows straight at shoulder height. 3. Shoulders—firm position. 4. Fundamental standing position.
4. Trunk. *Hips—firm!* Trunk to left—twist! Forward—twist! To right, etc. *Po—sition.*
5. Jump. *Hips—firm! Left foot backward—raise!* Running in place, ten counts—go! *Po—sition!*
See Grade IV, Lesson IV.
6. Respiratory. Arm raising sideways upward—raise!—sink!
Arms move in side plane, rotating smoothly while moving so that palms face each other when arms are up.

## GRADE III

### Lesson VIII

1. Introductory. Two steps forward and backward (or backward and forward) —march!
Children count 1, 2, 3! 1, 2, 3! Use introductory exercises from previous lessons at random in order to exact alert attention from children.
2. Arch. *Hips—firm!* Neck backward—bend! Upward—raise! *Po—sition!*
Bend neck backward till face looks toward ceiling. In raising head arch the neck strongly so as to set it far back between shoulders; push neck back against collar and pull chin in.
3. Arm. *Chest—firm!* Arm flinging sideways—1!—2! *Po—sition!* See Grade IV, Lesson VI.
4. Trunk. Shoulders—firm! Trunk forward—bend! Upward—raise! Po—sition! The same in four counts—go!
In responding to the last command the children should count aloud.
5. Jump. *Hips—firm! Left leg sideways—raise!* Jump changing feet counting to ten—go! *Po—sition!* See Grade IV, Lesson V.

6. Respiratory. *Arms sideways—raise! Hands—turn!* Arm raising upward with deep breathing—1!—2! *Po—sition!*
   1! Inhale while raising arms to full height. 2! Exhale while lowering them to height of shoulders.

## GRADE IV

### Lesson VII

1. Introductory. Review left and right facings and the march steps given in previous lessons, and require alert attention of the children by varying the commands instead of repeating the same exercise.
2. Arch. *Hips—firm!* Neck backward—bend! Upward—raise! *Po—sition!* See Grade III, Lesson VIII.
3. Arm. *Neck—firm!* Arm flinging sideways—1!—2! Etc. *Po—sition!*
   1! Fling arms sideways to horizontal plane, thumbs up. 2! Neck-firm position.
4. Leg. *Hips—firm!* Foot placing sideways with heel raising and change of feet—go! *Po—sition!* Children count to eight. 1. Place left foot sideways. 2. Raise heels high. 3. Lower heels. 4. Replace foot. 5–8. Same with right foot.
5. Trunk. Hips—firm! Trunk forward—bend! Neck—firm! Hips—firm! Trunk—raise! Po—sition!
   The same in six counts—go!
6. Jump. *Hips—firm! Left foot backward—raise!* Running in place with extra hop ten counts—go! *Po—sition!*
   Children count 1, and, 2, and, etc. 1. Left foot goes down and right foot up behind. And. Hop on left foot. 2. Right foot goes down and left foot up behind. And. Hop on right foot, etc.
7. Respiratory. *Arms sideways—raise! Hands—turn!* Arm raising upward —1!—2! *Po—sition!*
   1. Inhale while raising arms to full height. 2. Exhale while lowering them to shoulder height.

## GRADE IV

### Lesson VIII

1. Introductory. Left about—face! Right about—face!
   Technique is the same as in left and right facing, but the turn is 180° instead of 90°.
2. Arch. *Hips—firm!* Head to left—twist! To left—bend! Upward—raise! Forward—twist! To right, etc. To left—bend! With head held sharply twisted take a deep breath and bend head and neck over toward back of body without bending shoulders backward. This is called to-left—bend because the head bends toward its own left side.

3. Arm. *Head—firm!* Arm flinging to star position—1!—2! *Po—sition!* Star position. Arms extended diagonally upward from shoulders in side plane.
4. Leg. *Hips—firm!* Foot placing forward and backward with change of feet—go! *Po—sition!* Children count to eight. 1. Place left foot forward. 2. Replace it. 3. Place it backward. 4. Replace it. 5–8. The same with right foot.
5. Trunk. *Left hip, right neck—firm!* Trunk to left—bend! Upward—raise! etc. *Arms—change!* Trunk to right, etc.
6. Jump. Hips—firm! Left leg sideways—raise! Jump changing feet with extra hop counting to ten—go!
   Put the extra hop in as in Lesson VII.
7. Respiratory. Arm turning—1!—2!
   See Lesson IV.

## GRADE V

### Lesson VII

1. Introductory. Mark time—march! Class—halt!
   Bend knee well up in front and land, toes first, at each count. Brisk time. At the command "Class—halt!" the class takes two more steps and halts.
2. Arch. Chest—raise! Return! See Grade VI, Lesson II.
3. Arm. *Left arm sideways, right arm upward stretching—1!—2!* Arm changing—1!—2! *Arm stretching downward—1!—2!*
   Arm changing—1! Shoulders-firm position. 2! Stretch arms in opposite direction.
4. Leg. *Hips—firm!* Heel raising and knee bending three times (or more)—go! *Po—sition!*
   To be taken in 4 counts. 1. Raise heels. 2. Bend knees. 3. Stretch knees. 4. Lower heel.
5. Balance. *Neck—firm! Left leg backward—raise!* In two counts feet—change. *Po—sition!*
   Foot changing. 1. Replace raised foot on floor. 2. Raise other foot.
6. Abdominal. *Head firm and feet—close!* Trunk to left (or right)—bend! Upward—raise! *Po—sition!*
   Head—firm! Tips of fingers meet on crown of head, wrist curved upward, elbows back.
7. Back. *Chest—firm! Trunk forward—bend!* Arm flinging sideways—1!—2! *Trunk—raise! Po—sition!*
   In flinging the arms they should be carried up over the shoulders rather than backward.
8. Jump. Jump with left (or right) facing—1!—2!—3, 4!—5!—6!
   3, 4! Make a quarter circle turn in the jump.
9. Arm raising sideways and heel raising—raise!—sink!
   Raise arms to height of shoulders.

## GRADE V

### Lesson VIII

1. Introductory. Mark time—mark! Forward—march! Class—halt! At command "forward—march" the children step forward on the next count after the word "march," and march lightly round the room until they hear the next command, which may be either "Class—halt" or "Mark time—mark." If the former, they come to a halt in two counts; if the latter, they immediately begin to mark time in place until another command is given.

2. Arch. *Hips firm and feet sideways—place!* Chest—raise! Re—turn! *Po—sition!*
   Children jump to feet-sideways-place position in one count.

3. Arm. Arm stretching forward—1!—2! Arm stretching downward—1!—2!
   This stretching may be done in any one of five directions at will: forward, backward, upward, sideways, or downward. In the backward stretching the arms are extended as far back of the fundamental position as can be done without tipping the body forward.

4. Leg. *Hips—firm!* Foot placing forward with heel raising and change of feet. *Po—sition!*
   Children count to 8. 1. Place left foot forward. 2. Raise heels high. 3. Lower heels. 4. Replace foot. 5–8. Same with right foot.

5. Balance. *Hips—firm! Left knee upward—bend!* In one count feet—change. *Po—sition!*
   Change feet in one count with a little jump, and hold new position steadily.

6. Abdominal. *Arms forward upward fling and feet—close!* Trunk to left (or right)—twist! Forward—twist! *Po—sition!*
   Arms forward upward fling. Arms are swung through the forward plane up to their greatest height and are held strongly stretched during the movement.

7. Back. *Arms sideways—raise! Hands—turn! Trunk forward—bend!* Arm flinging upward—1!—2! *Trunk—raise! Po—sition!*
   In the arm flinging note three points: trunk must be kept down, head must be kept up, and arms flung so far up that the child cannot see his own hands.

8. Jump. *Hips—firm!* Jump forward—1!—2!—3, 4!—5!—6! *Po—sition!*
   3, 4! Jump forward clearing about a foot of floor space.

9. Respiratory. Arm raising forward upward and sinking sideways downward—Raise!—Sink!
   Raise! Inhale while raising arms through the forward plane to their greatest height, palms facing each other. Sink! Exhale while lowering arms in side plane turning palms as they descend.

## GRADE VI

### Lesson VII

1. Introductory. Stretching exercises, three times each—go!
   This movement consists of three vigorous stretches with the arms in the side plane at height of shoulders, three vigorous stretches to the greatest height the arms can reach accompanied by heel raising, three extreme forward bendings of the trunk touching the floor with finger tips if possible, and three deep squats with extreme bending of knees and back erect. The counts may be 1, (stretch arms sideways), And, (relax), 2, And, 3, And, (raise arms high above head); 1, (stretch arms up and raise heels), And, (relax arms slightly and lower heels), 2, And, 3, And; 1, (bend trunk forward downward in necessarily slower rhythm), And, (raise trunk to erect position with arms over head), 2, And, 3, And, (raise trunk to erect position and drop arms at sides); 1, (deep squat), And, (erect standing position), 2, And, 3, And, (erect standing position should be held in military fashion).
   This exercise takes the place in warmer weather of the running exercise which was done in the winter.
2. Arch. *Shoulders—firm!* Head to left—twist! to left—bend! upward—raise! forward—twist! to right, etc.
   See Lesson III.
3. Arm. Arm stretching forward—1!—2! Arm stretching downward—1!—2!
   This stretching may be done in any one of five directions at will: forward, backward, upward, sideways, and downward. In the backward stretching the arms are extended as far back of the fundamental position as can be done without tipping the body forward.
4. Leg. *Hips—firm!* Kneeling position on left (or right) knee—1!—2! Standing position—1!—2! The same in four counts—go! *Po—sition!*
   1. Stretch left leg backward and touch toe to the floor as far back as possible without tipping the body forward.
   2. Kneel on left knee with back erect.
   3. Rise retaining backward stretched position of left leg.
   4. Replace foot.
5. *Hips—firm! Left leg sideways—raise!* By jumping, feet—change! *Po—sition!*
   Hold position steadily after each change.
6. Abdominal. *Neck firm and feet—close!* Trunk to left (or right)—twist! Forward—twist! *Po—sition!*
7. Back. *Shoulders—firm! Trunk forward—bend!* Arm stretching upward—1!—2! *Trunk—raise! Po—sition!*
   Note three points to be observed during arm stretching: trunk should be kept down, head up, and arms stretched so far upward and backward that child cannot see his own hands.

8. Jump. *Hips—firm!* Jump with left (or right) facing—1!—2!—3, 4!—5! —6!
   3, 4! make a quarter circle turn while jumping.
9. Respiratory. *Arms sideways—raise! Hands—turn!* Arm raising and heel raising—raise!—sink! *Po—sition!*
   Lower arms to horizontal position at the word "sink."

## GRADE VI

### Lesson VIII

1. Introductory. Stretching exercises three times each—go!
   See Lesson VII.
2. Arch. *Neck—firm!* Chest—raise! Re—turn! *Po—sition!*
3. Arm. *Left arm backward, right arm upward stretching*—1!—2!
   Arm changing—1!—2!
   The direction in which arms are to be stretched may be changed at will of teacher, who may choose any two of the five possible directions.
4. Leg. Shoulders firm and heels—raise! Arms sideways stretch and knees —bend. Shoulders firm and knees—stretch! Po—sition! The same in 4 counts—go!
5. Balance. *Hips—firm!* Left knee (or right) upward—bend! Knee sideways—move! Forward—move! Foot re—place! *Po—sition!*
   Knee sideways—move! Keeping knee at height of hip move it toward the side without twisting shoulders.
6. Abdominal. *Hips—firm! Double kneeling position—1!—2!*
   Trunk backward—bend! Upward—raise! *Standing position!—1!—2! Po—sition!*
   Double kneeling position—1! Kneel on left knee—2! Kneel on both. Standing position—1! Place left foot forward on floor—2! Rise to standing position.
   The bending should be done in the knee joint; the spine should go back as one straight section with chest up and head back. Be especially careful that chest does not grow hollow and that hip joint does not bend.
7. Back. *Arms sideways—raise! Trunk forward—bend!* Arm swimming—1!—2!—3!
   For arm swimming see Lesson V.
8. Jump. Jump forward with forward flinging of arms—1!—2!—3, 4!—5!—6!
   3, 4! Jump forward clearing about a foot of floor space and assist the jump by swinging the arms forward in jumping and lowering them to the sides in landing.
9. Respiratory. Arms circling and heel raising—raise!—sink!
   Raise! Inhale and swing arms forward upward to their full height and raise heels.
   Sink! Exhale and lower arms sideways downward and lower heels.

## GRADE VII

### Lesson VII

1. Introductory. Stretching exercises, three times each—go!
   See Grade VI, Lesson VII.
2. Arch. *Hips firm and left foot forward—place!* Chest—raise! Re—turn! *Feet—change!* Chest, etc.
   During the raising of chest keep weight well forward.
3. Arm. *Left arm backward, right arm upward stretching*—1!—2! Arm changing—1!—2! *Arm stretching downward*—1!—2!
   Any two directions may be chosen out of the five possible ones: forward, backward, upward, sideways, or downward. Backward: the arms are extended as far back of the fundamental position as can be done without tipping body forward.
4. Abdominal. *Left hip firm and right arm forward upward—fling!* Trunk to left—bend! Upward!—raise! *Arms—change!* Trunk to right, etc. *Po—sition!*
5. Back. *Shoulders firm and feet sideways—place! Trunk forward—bend!* Arm stretching upward—1!—2!—1!—2! *Upward—raise! Po—sition!*
   The same in eight counts—go!
   For special points see Grade V, Lesson VIII.
6. Respiratory. *Arms forward—raise!* Arm raising upward and heel raising—raise!—sink! *Po—sition!*
   Sink! To shoulder height.
7. Balance Steps. Combine four forward slides with two forward polka steps. Four slides beginning with left foot, polka step beginning right, polka step beginning left, four slides beginning with right foot, polka beginning with left, polka beginning with right.

## GRADE VII

### Lesson VIII

1. Introductory. Stretching exercises, three times each—go!
2. Arch. *Chest—firm!* Neck firm and chest raising—1!—2! *Po—sition!* 1. Neck firm and chest raise. 2. Chest firm and return.
3. Arm. Arm stretching forward, upward and downward—1!—2!—1!—2!—1!—2!
   Any three directions may be used at will of teacher, requiring alert attention of children.
4. Leg. *Shoulders—firm!* Foot placing forward and backward with heel raising and change of feet—go! *Po—sition!*
   Children count to eight twice. 1. Place left foot forward. 2. Raise heels. 3. Lower heels. 4. Replace foot. 5–8. The same backward. 1–8. The same with right foot.
5. Balance. *Hips—firm! Heels—raise!* Knees deep—bend! Neck—firm! Hips—firm! Knees—stretch! Heels—sink! *Po—sition!*

6. Abdominal. *Sitting on desks—place! Hips—firm!* Trunk to left—twist! To left—bend! Upward—raise! Forward—twist! Trunk to right, etc. *Standing position—place!*
   To left—bend! Keeping trunk vigorously twisted add a side bend, lowering left shoulder and raising right.
7. Back. Arms upward fling and left (or right) backward fall—out! Po—sition!
   The left-backward-fall-out position is the same as the right-forward-fall-out position, described in Lesson II for Grade VII. At the same time that the left foot goes backward the arms are flung forcibly above head.
8. Jump. Hands for jump—place! Jump over chairs—1!—2!—3, 4!—5!—6! Left about—face! etc.
   See Lesson IV.
9. Respiratory. *Arms sideways—raise!* Arm turning and heel raising—1!—2! *Po—sition!*

## GRADE VIII

### Lesson VII

1. Introductory. Stretching exercises, three times each—go!
   See Grade VI, Lesson VII.
2. Arch. Arm rotation and chest raising—1!—2!
   1! Raise chest and turn palms outward. 2! Return.
3. Arm. Arm stretching forward, backward, upward and downward—1!—2!—1!—2!—1!—2!—1!—2!
   Any four directions may be used at will of teacher, requiring alert attention of children. If the children are taking this exercise with good strength they may be allowed to go through the eight counts without a separate command for each count; the command would then end with "and downward—go!"
4. Leg and Abdominal. *Hips—firm! Left sideways fall—out!* Feet—change! *Po—sition!*
   Left sideways fall—out! Long lunging step to left with left knee bent to right angles, trunk bent to left so as to make a straight line from right foot to right shoulder, face to front, right foot flat on floor.
   Feet—change! Two counts. 1. Resume erect standing position with a spring. 2. Fall out to right.
5. Back. *Arms sideways—bend!* Trunk forward—bend! Arm stretching upward—1!—2! Trunk—raise! *Po—sition!*
   Arms sideways—bend! Swing arms up to a position resembling the letter E on its back with the child's head representing the middle stroke; the arms are extended horizontally sideways to elbow, which is bent at right angles, forearms and hands pointing upward. In the arm stretching upward note three points: trunk must be kept down, head up, and arms stretched so far upward and backward that child cannot see his hands.

6. Respiratory. Arm raising forward upward with heel raising—raise!—sink!
7. Balance Step. Two step-hops and two waltz balance steps. Mazurka time.
   First measure. Step on left foot (2 counts), hop on left swinging right freely out in front (3d count).
   Second measure. Step on right foot, hop on right swinging left in front.
   Third and fourth measures. Two waltz balance steps.
   Fifth measure. Repeat first measure, and so on.

## GRADE VIII

### Lesson VIII

1. Introductory. Stretching exercises, three times each—go!
2. Arch. *Arms forward—bend!* Chest raising and arm rotation—1!—2! *Po—sition!*
   Arms forward—bend! Like arms-sideways-bend position (Lesson VII) except that forearms are horizontal, pointing forward from elbow joint.
   1! Raise chest and rotate forearms upward, pivoting on elbow until arms-sideways-bend position is reached. 2! Relax chest and return to arms-forward-bend position.
3. Arm. *Left arm forward upward—fling!* By flinging arms—change! *Po—sition!*
   Hold shoulders and trunk very steady while arms exchange positions by cutting the air with a straight arm swing in forward plane.
4. Leg. Arm stretching sideways with heel raising and knee bending in counts—go! The same three times—go!
   1. Shoulders firm and heels raise. 2. Arms sideways stretch and knees bend. 3. Shoulders firm and knees stretch. 4. Arms downward stretch and heels sink.
5. Balance and Back. *Hips firm and left forward fall—out!* Heels—raise! Heels—sink! *Feet—change!* Heels, etc. Maintain fall-out position carefully while raising heels.
6. Abdominal. *Sitting on desks—place! Shoulders—firm!* Trunk to left—twist! To left—bend! Upward—raise! Forward—twist! Trunk to right, etc. Standing position—place!
   See Grade VII, Lesson VIII.
7. Jump. Hips—firm! Jump with left about facing (or right about facing) twice—1!—2!—3, 4!—5, 6!—7!—8!
   3, 4! Jump facing 180° while in air. 5, 6! Another similar jump. Completing circle.
8. Respiratory. *Arms sideways—raise! Hands—turn!* Arm raising and heel raising—raise!—sink! *Po—sition!*
   Lower arms to horizontal position at the word "sink!"

# AGRICULTURAL EDUCATION: TEXTBOOKS

BENJAMIN MARSHALL DAVIS
Miami University

One striking evidence of the growing interest in agricultural education in elementary and secondary schools is the number of textbooks on agriculture that have appeared in recent years.[1] Of the seventy-five or more textbooks on this subject nearly forty have been published since 1900.

An excellent account of the textbooks of agriculture, including historical aspects, was written by L. H. Bailey in 1903 (146).[2] The present discussion will therefore be confined chiefly to the textbooks published since 1903. In this period of seven years at least twenty-seven textbooks of various kinds have been written. Emphasis should be put on *various,* for the diversity of plan and treatment of the subject in these books makes it difficult to find a basis of classification. They will be considered in this discussion as three types: for elementary schools, for secondary schools, and for teachers.

Most elementary textbooks are informational in character. The subject is generally presented in clear and simple language easily within the grasp of the pupil. It is assumed that the pupil has had sufficient concrete experiences with agricultural matters, and that the text will help him to interpret these experiences. There is a minimum of effort required of the pupil to find out things for himself. Questions are often given at

[1] It is possible that this statement should be qualified, for the number of books published does not indicate the number in actual use. A quotation from a private letter written by the editor of one of the largest publishing companies of agricultural books is significant: "Outside of one textbook published by a Boston house, I do not believe there is another manual of agriculture or agricultural textbook that has paid the publishers anything beyond mere cost, and some have not even paid cost." This was written in 1909. Since then conditions may have changed for there has been a great development of interest in the subject. Besides, thirteen books have been written during and since 1909. It seems likely that the small demand for certain textbooks may be due to the quality of the books themselves.

[2] References by number are to corresponding numbers in the bibliography at the end of this article, or in bibliographies appended to other articles of this series.

the end of each chapter, but they are usually merely a summary of the text, and test the memory rather than ability to interpret. Sometimes experiments are introduced, either in the text or at the end of chapters. But conclusions to be drawn from these experiments are either so implied in the text or are so obvious that the suggested experiments become merely concrete examples or illustrations of discussion in the text. Books of this kind are easily adapted to the prevailing recitation method and consequently are in extensive use (147). Several books have appeared in which the experiment predominates. Here problems and some suggestions as to procedure are given. The pupil is expected to find answers by means of his own investigations. He is supposed to learn to find out things for himself. However, even in otherwise admirable books, induction is often "ready-made for the pupil" (148). This method of teaching by means of experiment does not fit in very well with prevailing methods of teaching Many of the teachers themselves have not had the benefit of laboratory training, and hence know very little of any other than the textbook method of learning or teaching.

Another kind is the one in which agriculture is correlated with arithmetic. Problems for demonstration of the various arithmetical principles relate to agricultural affairs. In the preface of one book occurs the statement, "The pupil will unconsciously absorb and retain many valuable facts and principles relating to agricultural practice"; in the preface of another, the statement, "We trust that this little book, by combining the subjects of arithmetic and agriculture, will be of material assistance to teachers in their efforts to do effective work in both branches" (152, 168).

Perhaps one reason for the number of elementary agricultural textbooks lies in the nature of the subject itself.

Considered as an industry, agriculture is manufacturing, buying, and selling. It is business. But unlike most other businesses, the operator is producer of the raw material as well as dealer in the products. In order to produce his wares to the best advantage he must know much of the principles in accordance with which the most successful production must proceed. In other words, he must know much of the sciences on which agriculture is based, as physics, chemistry, botany, and other sciences. But he should never forget that the practice of agriculture is an art and not a science.

These remarks will suggest why it is that there is such a bewildering diversity in plan in the various textbooks of agriculture. One reason why these textbooks have not been more successful in accomplishing the missions for which they are designed is the fact that they look upon agriculture from the academic point of view rather than from the agricultural. Another reason is the attempt to make them "practical" by inserting specific directions for the performing of accustomed farm operations; for these directions must necessarily be of local and temporary application, whereas principles are general and abiding (146, p. 690).

Considered from the standpoint of scientific accuracy most of these textbooks are good, but in some there are inaccurate data, or statements at variance with well-established facts. Considered from the standpoint of pedagogy most of these texts are lacking. The matter is often presented with little or no reference to this important aspect of a textbook. Indeed, some are barely more than abridged encyclopaedias of agricultural information. This general defect may possibly be accounted for when we consider the fact that the authors of all these books, with a few exceptions, are college professors, whose chief interest is in the subject-matter with apparently little interest in organizing material from a teaching standpoint, and giving no recognition to the social possibilities of their subject.

It is probable that the most useful book, at least for the present, will be one that attempts at the same time to awaken an interest in country life and to set the pupil at the working out of specific problems. Mere problems are too "dry" to attract pupils, except now and then under the inspiration of an extra-good teacher. On the other hand, mere information-giving has little teaching value and is not likely to arouse any important enthusiasm for the open country and the farm. On account of the diversity of interests to be served, no single textbook of agriculture can hope to have great leadership in all parts of the country. The thoroughly satisfactory text is apparently yet to be written (102).

The purpose of an agricultural textbook for secondary schools is well expressed in the preface of a recent book of this grade: "to make the teaching of agriculture in existing high schools comparable in extent and thoroughness with the teaching of physics, mathematics, history, and literature." Although some of the elementary textbooks already referred to are being used to some extent in high schools there are only five books known to the writer that measure up to the standard just quoted. No two of these follow the same plan of treatment. In one laboratory work largely predominates; in another good laboratory exercises follow each chapter; in another some experiments are suggested in the text and among the questions at the end of the chapters; in two no laboratory exercises are suggested except in a general way in the text (151, 165, 170, 172, 175). These are all well written, and where one is used as a textbook the others could be used to advantage as reference books. For a detailed comparison of these textbooks the bibliography should be consulted.

There are three other books which properly belong among secondary textbooks of agriculture but which do not cover the entire subject. "There are those who believe that when agriculture is fully introduced as a secondary subject, it will consist, as in college, not of one but of several courses, each with its distinct and separate text." One of these is a laboratory manual dealing with soils and crops (173); the other two are textbooks, one dealing with fertility of the soil, the other with plant and animal improvement (159, 171).

A third type includes books for teachers. These books deal with the subject from the standpoint of teaching. Five are for teachers in elementary schools (160, 162, 164, 169, 174), and one is for teachers in secondary schools (126). Not much attention has yet been given to the teaching problems of the subject of agriculture, but they are quite as important as the subject-matter.

Referring to elementary agricultural textbooks, L. H. Bailey says: "Efforts enough have been made, but they have fallen short of anticipations. Before textbooks we need teachers; and we must appeal to the child through his interest in nature rather than technically in the farm" (146, p. 696). Elementary textbooks are not nearly so important as elementary teachers. It is to the new teachers who are to have at least a high-school education that we must look to carry agricultural education into the rural elementary schools. It is for this reason that additional importance is to be attached to instruction in agriculture and country-life subjects in rural high schools. A good textbook with well-selected experiments, although alone not sufficient, is, nevertheless, quite essential to any general introduction and efficient instruction in these high schools.

As this discussion of textbooks of agriculture is really supplementary to one already made by L. H. Bailey (146), his plan of chronological bibliography, with annotations as to contents, will be followed. The two articles will thus bring the subject up to date.

## BIBLIOGRAPHY

The references included in this bibliography are of two kinds: one general, the other, of textbooks published since 1903. One textbook, published in 1902 but not mentioned by L. H. Bailey, is also included.

146. "Development of the Textbook of Agriculture in North America," L. H. BAILEY, U.S. Department of Agriculture, Office of Experiment Stations, *Annual Report for 1903*, 689–712.

This article is based on a similar contribution to *Book Reviews*, VII (1899), No. 2, 43–53, but is greatly extended. An abridged discussion of this subject by the same author is found in the *Cyclopedia of American Agriculture*, IV (1909), 379–85.

A historical account of the development of the textbook of agriculture in North America is given, and is followed by an annotated chronological bibliography of forty-five titles, including the first textbook (1824) and all others known to the writer at the time of publication (1903).

147. "Textbooks of Agriculture," B. M. DAVIS, *Nature-Study Review*, V (1909), No. 9, 244–48.

Four types of textbooks are briefly discussed. These are illustrated by reviews of seven textbooks.

148. "Some Textbooks for Secondary-School Agriculture," C. H. ROBISON, *Nature-Study Review*, III (1907), No. 6, 180–85.

The article is introduced by a general discussion of the movement for agricultural education, and is followed by a detailed account and criticism of three well-known textbooks representing three distinct types.

149. *The School and Farm*, CHARLES A. EGGERT, Chicago: W. M. Welch & Co. (1902), 279.

The book is divided into six parts: Basis and Conditions of Farming; Field Crops; Animals on the Farm; Forest; Science and Agriculture; Rural Scenery. Each part is divided into chapters, e.g., Part II into Raising and Rotation of Field Crops; Grain Crops, Corn; Grass, Clover, and Hay; Root Crops, Potatoes; Value of Different Fertilizers; Silos and Ensilage.

150. *First Principles of Agriculture,* EMMETT S. GOFF and D. D. MAYNE, New York: American Book Co. (1904), 248.

"The first part is based on experiments which may be performed in the school or at home. A summary entitled 'What We Have Learned' has been placed at the close of each chapter. These summaries furnish definite statements for pupils to learn, and may be used by the teacher as a basis for drill work."

There are forty chapters: Dead and Living Matter; Soil and Soil Water; Plant and Water; How Plants Grow; Ideal Soil; Soil Fertility; Humus; Clover; Rotation; Saving Soil Moisture; Plant Parasites; Seeds and Soil Water; Air and Germination; Seed Testing; How Seeds Come Up; Value of Large Seeds; Budding; Transplanting; Plant Improvement; The Flower; Crop and Weeds; Garden Orchard; Insect Destroyers; Animal Husbandry; Dairy Breeds; Beef Breeds; Feeding; Horses; Sheep; Swine; Poultry; Bee-Keeping; Home and School Grounds. There is an Appendix of fifteen pages, including various tables, and also directions for Babcock milk-testing.

151. *Agriculture through the Laboratory and School Garden,* C. R. JACKSON and MRS. L. S. DAUGHERTY, New York: Orange Judd Co. (1905), x+403.

The author's aim is to "present actual experimental work in every phase of the subject possible." Contents: Nature and Formation of the Soil; Classification and Physical Properties of Soils; Soil Moisture and Preparation of the Soil; The Soil as Related to Plants; Leguminous Plants; Principles of Feeding; Rotation of Crops; Milk and Its Care; Propagation of Plants; Improvement of Plants; Enemies of Plants; Ornamentation of Grounds. General References, Agricultural Publications, List of Experiment Stations, Publishing Houses, and Glossary follow. For critical summary of this book see 148.

152. *Elementary Agriculture with Practical Arithmetic,* K. L. HATCH and J. A. HASELWOOD, Chicago: Row, Peterson & Co. (1905), 198.

Each chapter is followed by a set of practical farm problems to be used as exercises for arithmetic class. Contents: Growth of Plants; Plant Water; Plant Foods; Soil; Soil and Crops; Wearing the Soil; Legumes; Drainage; The Crop; Insects; Weeds; Farm Stock; Feeding; The Three C's; Dairy; Poultry; Special Crops; Farm Buildings; Accounts; Forestry; Grounds; School Gardening; Home Gardening; Barn Plan and Ventilation.

153. *Elements of Agriculture,* J. H. SHEPPERD and J. C. MCDOWELL, St. Paul: Webb Publishing Co. (1905), 254.

This book is intended especially for use in the Northwestern states. "The course of study follows the seasons: the work on farm crops coming in the fall, that on domestic animals in the winter, and the work on soils and the beautifying of the home and school grounds forms a large part of the course during the spring months."

154. *The First Book of Farming,* CHARLES L. GOODRICH, New York: Doubleday, Page & Co. (1905), xx+259.

The subject is developed by means of experiments as follows: Roots; Soils; Relation of Soils to Water; Forms of Soil Water; Loss of Soil

Water; Soil Temperature; Plant Food in the Soil; Seeds; Seed Planting; Spading and Plowing; Harrowing and Rolling; Leaves; Stems; Flowers; A Fertile Soil; Soil Water; After Cultivation of Crops; Farm Manures; Commercial Fertilizers; Rotation of Crops; Farm Drainage.

155. *Agriculture: Its Fundamental Principles,* ANDREW M. SOULE and EDNA LEE TURPIN, Richmond, Va.: B. F. Johnson Pub. Co. (1907), 320.

"The aim of this book is so to state the scientific facts and principles which underlie the processes of agriculture that they will be intelligible and interesting to young people." Contents: The Soil; The Plant; Soil Improvement; Field, Orchard and Garden Crops; Crop Enemies and Friends; Domestic Animals; Miscellaneous, Including Trees, Tools, Roads, School Gardens, etc. An Appendix giving tables, references, etc., is included.

156. *Rural School Agriculture,* CHARLES W. DAVIS, New York: Orange Judd Co. (1907), vii+267.

"This book is a manual of exercises covering many phases of agriculture" as follows: Plants; Soils and Fertilizers; Corn; Wheat and Oats; Cotton; Feeds and Feeding; Milk; Fruits; Home Grounds; Insects; Spraying. There is a Glossary and an Appendix of useful tables.

157. *Agriculture for Southern Schools,* J. F. DUGGAR, New York: Macmillan (1908), 355.

As the title indicates, this book is intended especially for southern schools, the adaptation being the use of the best practices and materials of southern agriculture for illustration.

The first part of the book deals with plant growth, including the plant's relation to the soil. The second part deals with crops, including enemies (the cotton boll-weevil receiving particular attention), animal husbandry, farm machinery. Important reference tables are arranged in an Appendix.

158. *Elements of Agriculture,* W. C. WELBORN, New York: Macmillan (1908), xvi+359.

This book is prepared for use in southern and western elementary schools. Three phases of the subject are taken up as follows: Crop Production, including the plant and its environment, characteristics of various field crops, soil fertility, etc.; Special Crops, in which the management of each crop is described in detail; Animal Production, including feeding and ration, care of animals, various kinds of farm animals in detail. An Appendix gives a classification of the most common economic plants, plant diseases, and insect enemies of plants and their remedies, score cards for judging, and a Glossary.

159. *First Principles of Soil Fertility,* ALFRED VIVIAN, New York: Orange Judd Co. (1908), 265.

The book is intended for home reading as well as for school use. It is divided into four parts: Plant Food, Its Nature and Source; Making Potential Plant Food Available; Barnyard Manure; Commercial Fertilizers.

160. *Manual of Agriculture for the Common Schools of Illinois,* D. O. BARTO, New York: Appleton & Co. (1908), 52.

"The writer has tried to outline in this little guide sets of studies and exercises in agriculture on topics of general importance and interest to farmers in all sections of Illinois." The "sets of exercises" are as follows: What Is a Soil? Water; Demands on Water Supply of the Soil; Saving the Soil Water; Effect of Color on Temperature of Soils; Plant and Essentials of Plant Production; Seed; Testing the Seed; Importance of Fine Tilth; Seed Planting; Roots; Root Tubercles; Inoculating the Soil; Plot Experiments; How Necessary Fertilizers Can Be Obtained; Care of Plot Experiments in Vacation; Studies in Corn; Pollination. Two pages of references are given.

161. *One Hundred Lessons in Elementary Agriculture,* A. W. NOLAN, Morgantown, W.Va.: Acme Publishing Co. (1908).

The wide range of topics included in the hundred lessons touches all important phases of agricultural problems. Soils, seeds, gardens, trees, crops, insects, weeds, poultry, foods, birds, machinery, rural civics, and economics—these suggested by titles of prominent lessons—indicate the scope of the book. Much of it is nature-study with agricultural materials and some of it is strictly the technical aspect of the science of agriculture.

162. *Teachers' Manual of Elementary Agriculture, Nature-Study, and Domestic Science,* F. E. THOMPSON, T. S. PARSONS, *et al.*, Boston: Ginn & Co. (1908).

This manual was prepared under the direction of the Colorado Teachers' Association. After an introduction dealing with the educational aspects of the subject follow chapters on Soils, Plant Life, School Gardening and Improving School Grounds, Field Crops, Insects and Birds, Live Stock, and Domestic Science. Five pages are devoted to a Bibliography for agriculture and nature-study work.

163. *Agriculture for Common Schools,* MARTIN L. FISHER and FASSETT A. COTTON, New York: Scribner (1909), xxiii+381.

The book is divided into five sections as follows: I, Soils; II, Farm Crops; III, Horticulture; IV, Animal Husbandry; V, Dairying. There are several appendices. One of these deals with the teaching of the subject with special reference to correlation with reading, arithmetic, geography, etc.

164. *Agriculture in the Public Schools,* LESTER S. IVINS, Lebanon, O.: March Bros. (1909), 156.

This is a handbook for teachers. It includes suggestions for organization of rural schools, teaching of nature-study and agriculture in rural schools, plans for conducting parents' meetings, public displays of school work, corn, potato, and vegetable growing contests, home, rural, and city-school flower gardens, and other valuable information that is intended to be helpful to the teacher.

165. *Elements of Agriculture,* G. F. WARREN, New York: Macmillan (1909), xxiv+434.

"This book is intended for use in high schools, academies, and normal schools, and in colleges when only a short time can be given to the subject." The author has attempted to carry out the suggestions of the Committee on Instruction in Agriculture of the Association of American Colleges and Experiment Stations. All important phases of agriculture are discussed in the eighteen chapters that make up the body of the book. The text of each chapter is followed by questions, laboratory exercises, and collateral reading. A summary of chap. v, "The Soil," will illustrate the method of treatment which is typical of each chapter: What Soil Is; Rock Particles of the Soil; Soil Water, Including Irrigation and Drainage; Soil Air; Organic Matter of the Soil; Life in the Soil. The chapter is reviewed by means of twenty-four questions. The following is typical: "Where does a fence post rot most rapidly? Why?" Fifteen excellent laboratory and field exercises give concreteness to the text. Ten references are given in the collateral reading. There are twenty pages of appendix containing information useful to teacher and pupil.

166. *Elementary Principles of Agriculture,* A. M. Ferguson and L. L. Lewis, Sherman, Tex.: Ferguson Publishing Co. (1909), xvi+318.

The aim of the book is perhaps best expressed by the authors: "Our own ideas are that the primary object of a text on agriculture, intended for the common schools, is to satisfy the natural interest of all children about the *whys* of common farm conditions."

The book is in three parts: Part I deals with the plant, soil diseases of plants, injurious insects, etc.; Part II, with animals, including dairying; Part III is devoted to special topics, such as home lot, school gardens, forestry, etc. There is an Appendix of nine parts, including references, formulae for sprays, tables of nutrients, rainfall, etc.

167. *Practical Agriculture,* John W. Wilkinson, New York: American Book Co. (1909), 383.

This is a "brief treatise on agriculture, horticulture, forestry, stock feeding, animal husbandry, and road building." These subjects are discussed in forty-five chapters. In the Appendix of twenty-two pages are found useful tables and references, and a list of apparatus needed for conducting laboratory courses in agriculture.

168. *A Practical Arithmetic,* F. L. Stevens, Tait, Butler, and Mrs. F. L. Stevens, New York: Scribner (1909), ix+386.

In addition to the usual aims sought in arithmetic tests, the authors have included "teaching valuable facts by basing the problems of the book upon problems of real life." The book contains a good collection of interesting and valuable applications of arithmetic to the affairs of farm life. Instead of the hypothetical problems concerning what A and B did, occur such problems as, "If kainit contains 12½ per cent potash and muriate of potash contains 50 per cent potash, how many pounds of kainit will it take to supply as much potash as 40 pounds of murate of potash?"

169. *Practical Nature-Study and Elementary Agriculture,* John M. Coulter, John G. Coulter, and Alice Jean Patterson, New York: Appleton & Co. (1909), ix+354.

This is a manual for use of teachers and normal students. It is divided into four parts. The first part considers the educational aspects of nature-study and agriculture; the second, "a detailed topical outline by grades and seasons of the materials used in nature-study in the training school at the

Illinois State Normal University"; the third, "a shorter outline for work in the lower grades arranged according to seasons, and leading more directly to agricultural studies of the seventh and eighth grades"; the fourth "comprises certain chapters upon general topics; material which has been found serviceable for teachers whose general science training has been slight or lacking entirely."

170. *Agriculture for Schools of the Pacific Slope,* E. W. HILGARD and W. J. OSTERHOUT, New York: Macmillan (1910), xix+428.

This book contains twenty-three chapters devoted to plants and their cultivation. Five chapters are devoted to animals. This emphasis on plants is doubtless due to the fact that horticulture is one of the chief agricultural industries of the Pacific Slope. The living plant in all its relations receives more attention than is usual in an agricultural textbook. The book could very well be used as a textbook of botany. It is illustrated by 209 good illustrations.

171. *Domesticated Animals and Plants,* F. DAVENPORT, Boston: Ginn & Co. (1910), xiv+321.

This is a brief treatise upon the origin and development of domestic races with special reference to the methods of improvement. It is in two parts, one "constituting a brief course covering the essential principles that are fundamental to an understanding of hereditary transmission and of the business of plant and animal improvement"; the other deals with the origin of domesticated races.

172. *Farm Development,* WILLETT M. HAYES, New York: Orange Judd Co. (1910), xii+391.

This is "an introductory book in agriculture, including a discussion of soils, selecting and planning farms, subduing the fields, drainage, irrigation, roads, fences, together with introductory chapters concerning farm business, and the relations of the general science of agriculture."

173. *Manual of Agriculture: Soils and Crops,* D. O. BARTO, Boston: D. C. Heath & Co. (1911), xi+492.

This manual is a series of laboratory and field experiments in two parts, one relating to soils; the other to crops. The work included is considered sufficient to cover one year of the high-school course in agriculture, and is intended to "offer training in science comparable to that furnished by the other science courses in good high schools."

174. *Outlines of Agriculture for Rural Schools,* C. M. EVANS, Chicago: W. M. Welch Mfg. Co. (1910), 31.

A year's work is outlined for rural schools with one lesson each week.

175. *Fundamentals of Agriculture,* JAMES EDWARD HALLIGAN, Boston: D. C. Heath & Co. (1911), xi+492.

"Every subject in this book is written by an expert in his line. This idea was carried out in order to furnish the student with the best information that could be obtained. The editor thought it would be better to have authorities treat of the various topics rather than write the book alone, as there are very few men competent enough to warrant their writing the best book on agriculture." Thirty-three experts in various fields of agriculture have contributed.

176. *An Introduction to Agriculture,* A. A. UPHAM, New York: Appleton & Co. (1911), xi+270.

The aim of the book is "to touch those matters which would be most useful to the pupils in our rural schools, and especially to give the underlying theory for many farm processes and practices." There are twenty-one chapters and an Appendix. All of the usual subjects of agriculture are covered in these chapters, and the Appendix contains references and a number of useful tables.

# MEASUREMENT OF GROWTH AND EFFICIENCY IN ARITHMETIC (*Concluded*)

S. A. COURTIS
Home and Day School, Detroit

Of equal importance with the question of the amount of growth produced by a year's work is that of the permanence of the growth. Table VI gives for Grades 4 to 9 the average scores in the speed tests in September, 1909, the highest scores made at any time during the year, and the scores of the same classes the following September after the long summer vacation. From these the gains during the year, the losses during the summer can easily be computed. The last two columns show the differences between the September tests and the percentage of improvement.

The results are striking and suggestive. The large gains of the fifth and sixth grades are offset by the large losses during vacation, while the growth of the seventh and eighth grades is seen to be relatively permanent. If these results are confirmed by future work, the seventh and eighth grades would seem to be the place in the course where rigid drill on the combinations would be most effective.

At the beginning of the year it was felt by all concerned that there was one question that the year's work must settle, and settle very definitely. Do such short, simple, comparative tests yield reliable results, or would repeated tests give very different relative standings? There is not space here to marshal all the evidence that proves the grade averages reliable measures of grade abilities, but an examination of the results in Table V[1] from this point of view will show how consistently grade after grade has obtained the same score in successive tests. It is to be remembered that all these grades were subject to constant practice in their daily work and drill, so that it is only the before-and-after-vacation scores, or successive scores during a

[1] See *Elementary School Teacher* (March, 1911), 367.

"plateau" that can be expected to be constant. Such scores are, however, remarkably constant. Extended practice, as has been shown, does produce a rise in score, yet but a part of this is permanent, and the abilities in question, slowly built up by hours

TABLE VI

GAINS AND LOSSES

| Grade | Operation | Score | | Maximum Gain | Score | September 1910 (Loss during Summer Vacation) | Gain 1910 over 1909 | Percentage |
|---|---|---|---|---|---|---|---|---|
| | | September 1909 | Highest | | September 1910 | | | |
| | + | 23 | 39 | 16 | 37 | 2 | 14 | |
| | − | 19 | 37 | 16 | 33 | 4 | 14 | |
| 4 | × | 6 | 22 | 16 | 17 | 5 | 11 | |
| | ÷ | 7 | 25 | 18 | 17 | 8 | 10 | |
| | Average | 13.7 | .. | 16.5 | .. | 4.7 | 12.2 | 89 |
| | + | 35 | 66 | 31 | 47 | 19 | 12 | |
| | − | 30 | 54 | 24 | 46 | 18 | 16 | |
| 5 | × | 24 | 56 | 32 | 34 | 22 | 10 | |
| | ÷ | 19 | 55 | 36 | 31 | 24 | 12 | |
| | Average | 27 | .. | 30.7 | .. | 20.7 | 12.5 | 46 |
| | + | 43 | 73 | 30 | 56 | 17 | 13 | |
| | − | 33 | 58 | 25 | 54 | 5 | 20 | |
| 6 | × | 30 | 58 | 28 | 42 | 16 | 12 | |
| | ÷ | 26 | 56 | 30 | 44 | 12 | 18 | |
| | Average | 33 | .. | 30.7 | .. | 12.5 | 14.7 | 44 |
| | + | 53 | 89 | 36 | 79 | 10 | 26 | |
| | − | 36 | 69 | 33 | 59 | 10 | 23 | |
| 7 | × | 41 | 77 | 36 | 64 | 13 | 23 | |
| | ÷ | 34 | 74 | 40 | 62 | 12 | 28 | |
| | Average | 41 | .. | 36.2 | .. | 11.2 | 25 | 61 |
| | + | 56 | 85 | 29 | 79 | 6 | 23 | |
| | − | 42 | 70 | 28 | 64 | 6 | 22 | |
| 8 | × | 49 | 74 | 25 | 60 | 14 | 21 | |
| | ÷ | 41 | 77 | 36 | 67 | 10 | 26 | |
| | Average | 47 | .. | 29.5 | .. | 9 | 23 | 49 |
| | + | 67 | 81 | 24 | 71 | 10 | 4 | |
| | − | 45 | 64 | 19 | 63 | 1 | 18 | |
| 9 | × | 56 | 69 | 13 | 68 | 1 | 12 | |
| | ÷ | 46 | 64 | 18 | 61 | 3 | 15 | |
| | Average | 53.5 | .. | 18.5 | .. | 4 | 12.2 | 22 |

of study and drill, must be considered relatively stable quantities. The constancy of very many grade and individual scores in repeated tests proves conclusively that the results obtained from even a single test carefully conducted are reliable measures of grade ability.

On the other hand it is important to state that this is not true of the scores of the individuals composing the grade. Even when the grade average is perfectly constant, individual scores are found to vary. This is shown clearly in Table VII, the individual records in the addition speed test of 23 of the 31 members of the eighth grade. The records omitted are those in which through absence the series was not complete. The graph

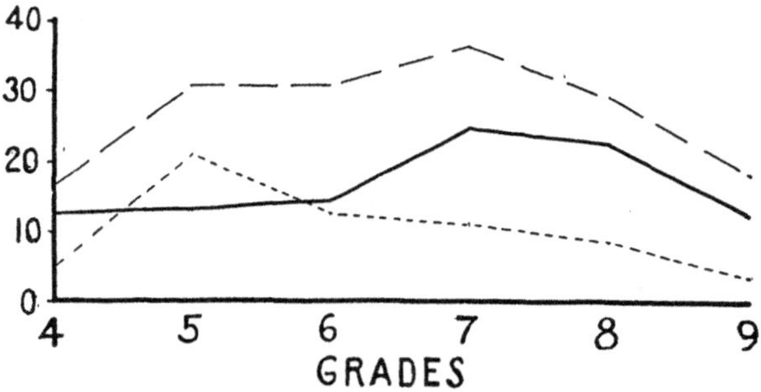


FIG. 11.—Gains and losses for the year. Broken line shows maximum gain—from September, 1909, to highest point reached at any time during year. Dotted line shows effect of summer vacation—loss from highest point reached to September, 1910. Full line shows net gain for year, September, 1910, over September, 1909.

(Fig. 12) makes possible the rapid visual comparison of the changes in the individual scores with those of the grade average, the heavy central line. It will be seen that at such times as the grade average is constant, the constancy is due to the fact that the variations of certain individuals in one direction are offset by the variations of others in the opposite direction. For the individual, therefore, repeated tests are needed to determine his most frequent score and the range of his variation from it.

By far the most important fact to be gained from a study of Table VII is the wide range of ability within the grade. The score of the best girl is on the average twice that of the poorest girl, in spite of the fact that the individuals in this class represent the survivals of eight years of "passing" on a 70 per cent basis. The graph shows plainly that the grade average is really representative of very few scores, and that a measure of the range of variation is needed in addition to the measure of the average performance. The writer has chosen the average devia-

TABLE VII

SCORES IN ADDITION SPEED TEST OF TWENTY-THREE INDIVIDUALS OF EIGHTH GRADE

| Rank | September 1909 | November | December | January | March 1–18 | March 18–30 | April | | | | May | | | | | June | September 1910 | Rank |
|---|---|---|---|---|---|---|---|---|---|---|---|---|---|---|---|---|---|---|
| | | | | | | | 4 | 11 | 18 | 25 | 2 | 9 | 16 | 23 | 30 | 6 | | |
| 1 | 89 | 85 | .. | .. | 86 | 91 | 97 | 98 | 98 | 102 | .. | 86 | .. | 105 | 120 | 100 | 88 | 7 |
| 2 | 77 | 78 | 80 | 70 | 78 | 57 | 83 | 81 | 77 | 82 | .. | 85 | .. | 84 | 91 | 83 | .. | 10 |
| 3 | 69 | 81 | 87 | 91 | 90 | 107 | 107 | 116 | 111 | .. | .. | 98 | .. | 115 | 120 | 109 | 104 | 1 |
| 4 | 68 | 81 | 83 | 85 | 90 | 91 | 93 | 94 | 101 | 107 | .. | 97 | .. | 104 | 116 | 99 | 92 | 4 |
| 5 | 65 | 82 | 77 | 79 | 83 | 84 | 85 | 91 | 85 | 98 | .. | 90 | .. | 104 | 100 | 97 | .. | 5 |
| 6 | 64 | 83 | 87 | 94 | 84 | 100 | 100 | 110 | 105 | 107 | .. | 100 | .. | 108 | 120 | 106 | 97 | 2 |
| 7 | 62 | 55 | 60 | 58 | 64 | .. | 66 | 74 | 70 | 70 | .. | 73 | .. | 73 | 77 | 79 | 74 | 14 |
| 8 | 58 | 63 | 68 | 64 | 77 | 72 | 80 | 80 | 73 | 84 | .. | 80 | .. | 80 | 88 | 83 | 80 | 11 |
| 9 | 57 | 77 | 72 | 76 | 75 | 79 | 83 | 80 | 84 | 90 | .. | 81 | .. | 90 | 96 | 86 | 83 | 8 |
| 10 | 56 | 77 | 80 | 78 | 80 | 76 | 86 | 85 | 97 | 102 | .. | 94 | .. | 105 | 110 | 88 | 90 | 6 |
| 11 | 55 | 69 | 75 | 74 | 77 | 82 | 83 | 84 | 87 | 87 | .. | 85 | .. | 84 | 83 | 90 | 83 | 9 |
| 12 | 52 | 69 | 71 | 77 | 84 | 86 | 90 | 99 | 90 | 94 | .. | 90 | .. | 92 | 92 | 100 | 97 | 3 |
| 13 | 52 | 60 | 51 | 57 | .. | 80 | 83 | 80 | 82 | 86 | .. | 79 | .. | 80 | 70 | 81 | 72 | 16 |
| 14 | 52 | 53 | 75 | 50 | 68 | 60 | 78 | 80 | 82 | 71 | .. | 66 | .. | 67 | 77 | 80 | 76 | 12 |
| 15 | 51 | 65 | 55 | 62 | 68 | 63 | 73 | 69 | 76 | 77 | .. | 78 | .. | 83 | 88 | 82 | .. | 17 |
| 16 | 46 | 51 | 54 | 47 | 57 | 59 | 55 | 64 | 60 | 66 | .. | 69 | .. | 62 | 73 | 69 | .. | 18 |
| 17 | 46 | 40 | 39 | 43 | 48 | 47 | 55 | 54 | 60 | 61 | .. | 62 | .. | 66 | 71 | 67 | .. | 19 |
| 18 | 44 | 65 | .. | 60 | 68 | .. | 72 | 71 | 80 | 80 | .. | 80 | .. | 80 | 78 | 83 | 73 | 15 |
| 19 | 44 | 58 | 68 | 70 | 67 | 72 | 77 | .. | 75 | 74 | .. | 82 | .. | 75 | 85 | 80 | 76 | 13 |
| 20 | 43 | 30 | 50 | 56 | 60 | 59 | 59 | 61 | 55 | 61 | .. | 58 | .. | 55 | 52 | 64 | 59 | 20 |
| 21 | 35 | 43 | 50 | 27 | 52 | 40 | 53 | 51 | 42 | .. | .. | 42 | .. | 55 | 57 | 51 | 48 | 23 |
| 22 | 31 | 30 | .. | 39 | 42 | .. | 49 | 57 | 61 | 55 | .. | 52 | .. | 54 | 50 | 53 | 49 | 22 |
| 23 | 30 | 40 | 45 | 47 | 48 | 58 | 55 | 54 | 50 | 57 | .. | 57 | .. | 56 | 55 | 59 | .. | 21 |
| Aver. | 54 | 62 | 66 | 64 | 70 | 73 | 77 | 79 | 79 | 81 | .. | 78 | .. | 82 | 85 | 82 | 79 | .. |
| A.D. | 10.8 | 14.3 | 12.2 | 14.2 | 11.9 | 14.5 | 13.2 | 14.1 | 14.3 | 13.6 | .. | 12.2 | .. | 15.8 | 17.3 | 12 | 12.3 | . |
| Var. | 20 | 23 | 19 | 22 | 17 | 20 | 17 | 18 | 18 | 18 | .. | 16 | .. | 19 | 22 | 15 | 16 | .. |

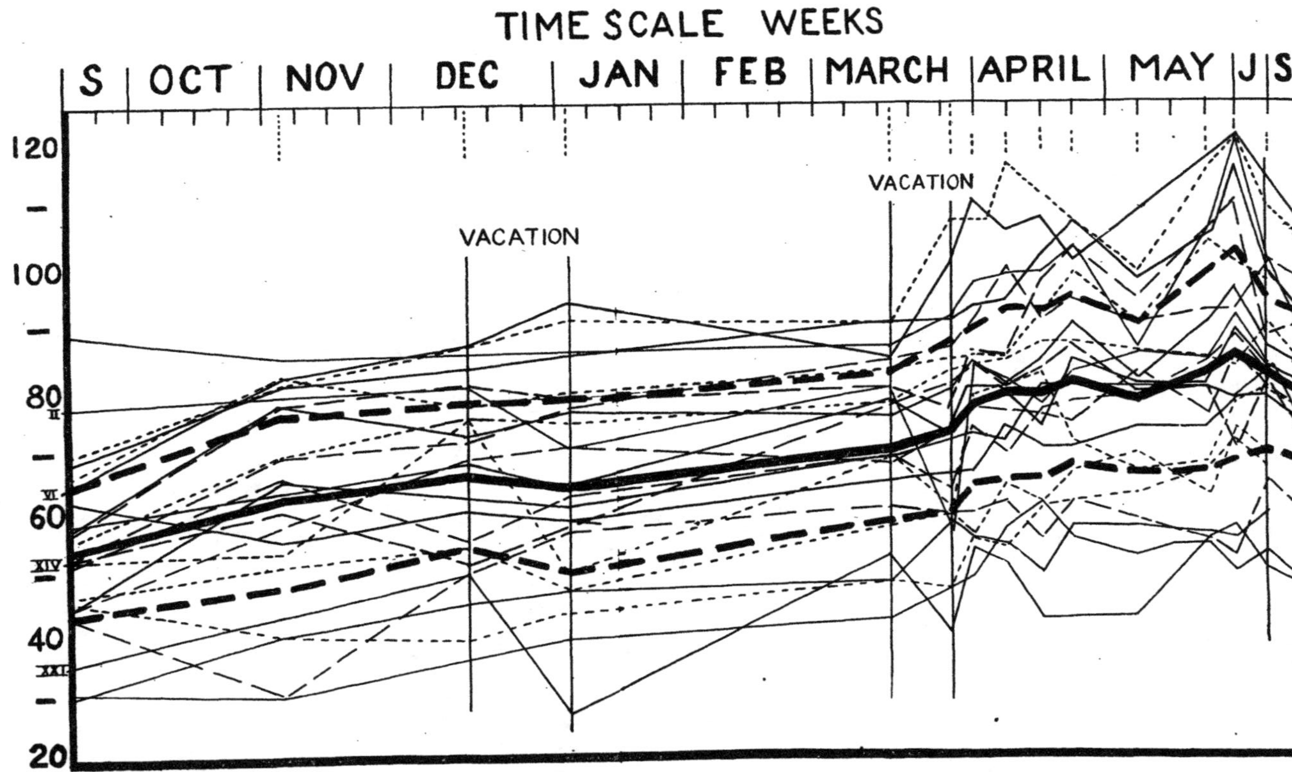


FIG. 12.—Records of twenty-three individuals of the eighth grade in fifteen trials of the speed test in addition from September, 1909, to September, 1910. Full, heavy line shows the average score. Heavy broken lines are at a distance from the average equal to the average deviation. The zone bounded by the two broken lines corresponds to a variability of 18 per cent.

tion, the average difference of the individual score from the grade average, as the measure of variability, and for purposes of comparison the average deviations will be expressed as percentages of their respective averages. The significance of the measure is shown graphically in the plot. On each side of the heavy line representing the grade average, there has been drawn a heavy broken line at a distance from the average equal to that of the average deviation. Between the two broken lines will be found roughly 50 per cent of the class. That is, the exceptionally weak and the exceptionally able have been excluded, and the upper and lower limits of ability of the remainder of the class are given by the broken lines. Because of this wide individual range, therefore, the ability of a class is better thought of as a "zone" than as a single average score. A narrow zone indicates a compact well-graded class, the product of an efficient system of promotion. Unfortunately the zones from the present tests are wide, wider at least than would seem to the writer to be expected in any school that prides itself on its standards, and he would hesitate to publish such results did not returns from other schools using the same tests under the same conditions show zones of the same or greater width. It seems probable that the condition is general in education at the present time. Within the school other tests and measurements make comparisons possible. The variability of the same 23 individual girls whose scores in addition were given in Table VII, and whose variability was there shown to be 18 per cent, was 3 per cent in age, 7 per cent in handwriting (samples measured by Thorndike's scales), 15 per cent in formal English grammar, 26 per cent in height, 30 per cent in memory of important dates and men, 60 per cent in ability to reproduce after 24 hours the main points of a historical passage read once in class.

No one result of the testing work has proved more disturbing to the writer, more startling in its implications, than this extreme variability found in all the grades. Its full significance can be appreciated only by one who has made a careful study of the individual records and then noted the behavior of the same individuals in the classroom. The writer believes weakness and inefficiency are due more to failure to secure complete, all-around development in the fundamental abilities of a subject, and standard growths in each grade, than to any other one cause. Just how inefficient the present conditions are is shown in the case of knowledge of the multiplication tables by the results in Table VIII and Fig. 13. The table gives the average and the average deviation for each of the four grades in all the

TABLE VIII

COMPARATIVE RECORD OF GRADE ABILITY IN MULTIPLICATION SPEED TESTS THROUGHOUT THE YEAR

| Grade | | Sept. 1909 | Nov. | Dec. | Jan. | Mar. | Mar. | April 4 | April 11 | April 18 | April 25 | May 2 | May 9 | May 16 | May 23 | May 30 | June 6 | Sept. 1910 |
|---|---|---|---|---|---|---|---|---|---|---|---|---|---|---|---|---|---|---|
| 5 | Av. | 24 | 32 | 39 | 40 | 45 | 46 | 43 | 52 | 50 | 52 | .. | 52 | .. | 55 | 52 | 55 | 34 |
| | A.D. | 8 | 9 | 10 | 11 | 12 | 12 | 12 | 13 | 12 | 17 | .. | 14 | .. | 12 | 11 | 15 | 9 |
| | Var. | 35 | 29 | 26 | 28 | 26 | 25 | 28 | 25 | 25 | 33 | .. | 27 | .. | 21 | 21 | 28 | 27 |
| 6 | Av. | 30 | 34 | 49 | 41 | 49 | 50 | 55 | 56 | .. | .. | 58 | 52 | 54 | 56 | 56 | 47 | 42 |
| | A.D. | 10 | 9 | 12 | 15 | 11 | 14 | 15 | 13 | .. | .. | 13 | 12 | 17 | 14 | 14 | 14 | 13 |
| | Var. | 35 | 27 | 25 | 37 | 22 | 28 | 28 | 23 | .. | .. | 22 | 24 | 31 | 24 | 24 | 29 | 31 |
| 7 | Av. | 41 | 43 | 48 | 48 | 62 | 59 | 59 | .. | 72 | 70 | 68 | 74 | 72 | 77 | 77 | 74 | 64 |
| | A.D. | 12 | 12 | 11 | 12 | 14 | 14 | 14 | .. | 15 | 17 | 14 | 14 | 11 | 12 | 16 | 11 | 15 |
| | Var. | 29 | 28 | 22 | 25 | 22 | 23 | 23 | .. | 20 | 24 | 21 | 18 | 16 | 16 | 21 | 15 | 23 |
| 8 | Av. | 49 | 55 | 60 | 56 | 62 | 68 | 67 | 68 | .. | .. | 71 | .. | 74 | 73 | 72 | 72 | 60 |
| | A.D. | 11 | 9 | 11 | 12 | 10 | 12 | 11 | 12 | .. | .. | 12 | .. | 15 | 10 | 14 | 12 | 13 |
| | Var. | 22 | 18 | 18 | 21 | 17 | 18 | 17 | 18 | .. | .. | 18 | .. | 20 | 13 | 19 | 17 | 21 |

multiplication tests of the year. The graph shows the zone of ability of each grade shaded in such a way that ground common to two or more grades can be detected at once. The overlapping of grade upon grade is such that for two-thirds of the year a part of the territory is common to *all four grades,* while a large part of it is at all times common to three grades. The table and figure together make very plain the complete breakdown of the *grade* idea. For it is to be remembered that the zones do not include the extremes, but the central core of the class only. In other words, the variations of individual ability within the grade are far greater than the increase of knowledge or ability from grade to grade. It will be seen, therefore, that just so far as these conditions are truly general, the problem of the degree of variability that can be permitted within a grade is a vital one for graded systems.

The cause of such breakdown of grade standards is to be

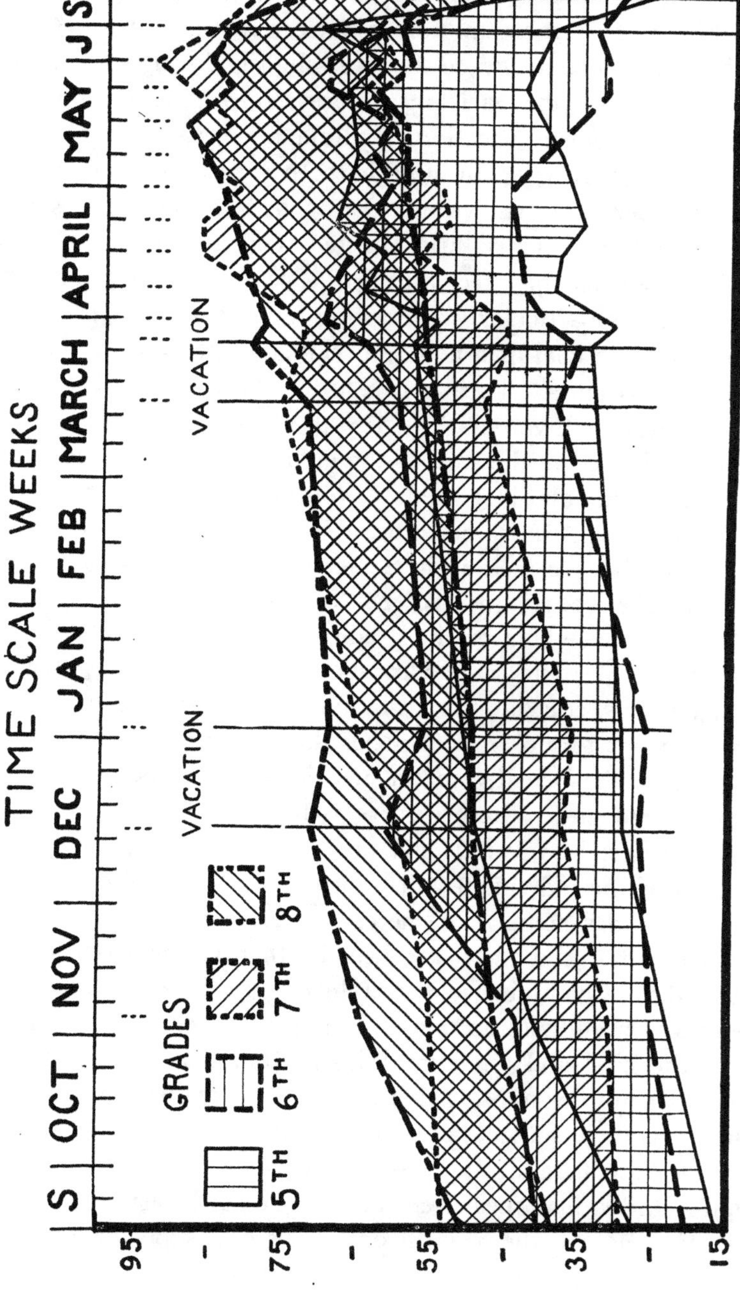


FIG. 13.—Record of year's tests in the multiplication tables for Grades 5–8, showing the extent to which the abilities of the grades overlap. The "zone" of ability for each grade is determined by the grade average and the average deviation from it. Within a zone, therefore, are included merely the abilities of the central core of a class; roughly, the half of the class nearest the grade average.

found in the inherent differences in individual children. Consider the effect of vacation, for instance. In Fig. 12 it will be seen that as a whole the grade score fell slightly during the Christmas vacation and the variability increased, while the opposite was true of the spring vacation. Individuals 2, 14, and 21, however, are consistently demoralized by both vacations. Individual 6, on the other hand, shows just the opposite effect, while some of the others are very slightly affected if at all. One looks in vain for *any* constant effect during the year. The test the last week in May is particularly interesting as bearing on this point. It represents the trial of a new test, similar to the old but better balanced as to units. To many children it proved much easier, but there were individuals in every grade to whom it seemed more difficult, and in the case of the eighth grade the variability was correspondingly increased. From the point of view of the year's growth the same thing is evident. The grade work that enabled No. 12 in rank in September, 1909, to become No. 4 in September, 1910, and No. 18 No. 12, changed the relative rank of other members of the grade very little, while there are a few whose absolute score also shows but little improvement. In other words, education is an individual matter, and no grade instruction nor group work can possibly be devised to minister adequately and efficiently to the widely differing needs of any group selected under the present system.

The writer, however, is not one of those who believe that the needs of the individual will bring about the abolition of our present graded system. The necessity for handling large numbers of children and the many benefits that accrue from group work make its continuance a certainty. At the same time the differences in individuals make it imperative that each child receive the kind and amount of instruction that his particular mental makeup demands. These two conditions can be met by having for each subject and each grade standard scores and standard growths in all those component abilities that are fundamental. Individual measurement by standard tests and constant checking of the results of classwork, supplemented by individual prescriptions of study and work, would insure the attainment of any desired degree of minimum ability, and still leave room in the nonessentials of the subject for all those permissible individual variations which make for personality. If education is to become either scientific or efficient, more attention must be given to accurate determinations of both the material to be acted upon, and the effects produced. In the future it may well be that a testing department will be a vital part of every well-organized school system.

One other question will briefly be discussed, the correlation between the elemental abilities and the complexes of which they form a part. The question of how far drill on the multiplication tables, for instance, must be carried in order that a child may be able to multiply correctly in the solution of problems is one of some importance. Although in all discussions based upon the present tests the defects of the tests themselves and the consequent possible unreliability of the results must be kept in mind, two correlations attempted seem to yield results of value.

The first is the relation between rate of motor activity and total score in the speed tests. It seemed reasonable to suppose that a child able to copy figures more rapidly than another would obtain higher scores in writing the combination, even though the two children really had equal knowledge of the tables. To test this point the June scores of 182 individuals of all grades above the third were thrown into one large group and distributed on the basis of their scores in copying figures. The average total score in each of these smaller groups was then determined. Figure 14 shows the results graphically. It is evident from the curve that there is a very close connection between the two types of scores up to a certain point, but that beyond this point the ability to copy figures with extreme rapidity does not carry with it the corresponding ability to obtain a high score in the other speed tests. This critical score, therefore, approximately 115 figures in a minute, has been taken by the writer as the standard to be reached before the work in arithmetic is completed. Standard scores, graded down from this maximum, have been set for the other classes below the eighth, and the attempt is being made by classwork and by

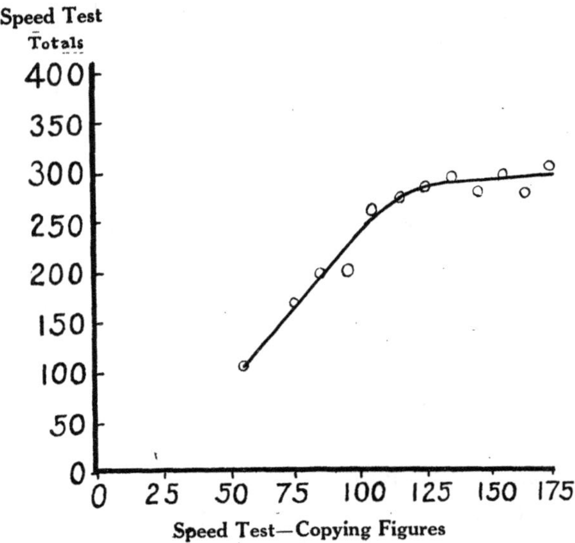


FIG. 14.—Correlation between speed in copying figures and total scores in the speed tests.

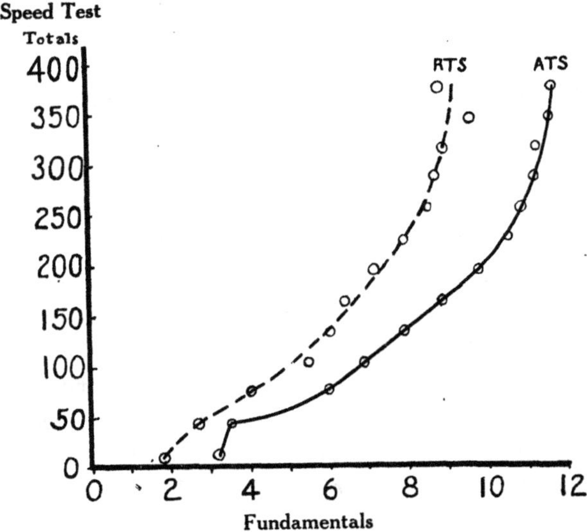


FIG. 15.—Correlation between total scores in the speed tests and the number of examples attempted and right in the test on fundamentals.

extra special individual work to bring the score of every individual up to the score for her grade. By thus securing a standard growth in each grade, the final maximum ability will be insured.

A second correlation of some importance is the relation between total scores in the speed tests and the scores in the tests on abstract examples. Figure 15 gives the results both for examples attempted and for examples right. The general form of the curves is the same. That is, there is probably a critical degree of knowledge of the tables to be attained by drill beyond which an increase in score does not carry with it an increase in ability to work examples. The determination of the proper balance between these fundamental abilities of a subject affords a large number of important problems for experimental work.

No general summary of the points made in the foregoing discussions will be attempted. The writer feels, however, that the work of the year has proved conclusively the necessity of measurements of individual needs and individual growth, as well as the great possibilities of comparative tests from the standpoint of intelligent determination of courses and methods. It has also made possible the construction of tests composed of units of known values, so that future measurements will be free from this source of error. The immediate work of the future is, therefore, the determination of standards for each grade and of standard growths. It must also settle the question of whether or not the teacher will be able, by use of the knowledge gained from the tests, to bring individuals up to standard scores. It is with these questions that the experimental work of the school during the coming year is to deal.

# THE HANDWRITING OF SCHOOL CHILDREN

SUPERINTENDENT G. M. WILSON
Connersville, Indiana

Last fall an attempt was made to secure samples of the *ordinary* writing of all pupils and teachers in the Connersville (Ind.) schools. About 1,200 samples were secured under conditions that gave, for the most part, the *ordinary* writing. These samples were then graded according to the Thorndike Scale A,

TABLE I

| Grade | Speed (Letters per Minute) | | Quality (Thorndike Scale A) |
|---|---|---|---|
| | Median | Range | |
| 1B | 22 | 8– 26 | 9.2 |
| 1A | 9 | 5– 19 | 9.5 |
| 2B | 17 | 7– 45 | 10.1 |
| 2A | 14 | 7– 30 | 10.4 |
| 3B | 20 | 10– 54 | 9.9 |
| 3A | 36 | 9– 66 | 10.3 |
| 4B | 48 | 14– 86 | 10.2 |
| 4A | 60 | 29–131 | 10. |
| 5B | 51 | 30– 84 | 10.2 |
| 5A | 52 | 28– 84 | 10.3 |
| 6B | 71 | 43–100 | 11.4 |
| 6A | 60 | 43– 87 | 11.7 |
| 7B | 58 | 22– 91 | 11.4 |
| 7A | 55 | 31– 95 | 11.7 |
| 8B | 86 | 54–108 | 11.2 |
| 8A | 74 | 26– 96 | 11. |
| 9th year | 81 | 48–119 | 11.7 |
| 10th year | 91 | 69–120 | 11.8 |
| 11th year | 100 | 91–211 | 11.5 |
| 12th year | 108 | 78–150 | 11.8 |
| Teachers | 98 | 76–126 | 12.9 |

for Handwriting. The speed per minute was noted. The work was graded by three judges. A full exhibit by building and judges would be interesting, but space will permit only a brief summary.

This study showed us the actual conditions existing in our writing work. It showed what was being done. The questions naturally arose, Is this as it should be? What is the correct standard for each grade in our schools? Accordingly a table was constructed indicating a *tentative* standard for each grade as follows:

TABLE II

| Grade | Speed (per Min.) | Quality (Scale A) |
|---|---|---|
| 1A | 12– 16 | 8–10 |
| 2B | 15– 20 | 8–12 |
| 2A | 15– 25 | 9–12 |
| 3B | 15– 30 | 9–12 |
| 3A | 25– 40 | 9.5–13 |
| 4B | 30– 55 | 10–13.3 |
| 4A | 40– 65 | 10–13.6 |
| 5th | 45– 65 | 10–14 |
| 6th | 50– 70 | 11–14 |
| 7th | 50– 75 | 11–14.5 |
| 8th | 55– 75 | 12–15 |
| 9th year | 55– 85 | 12–16 |
| 10th year | 60– 85 | 12–16 |
| 11th and 12th years | 65–100 | 12–16 |
| Commercial H.S | 65–100 | 13–18 |

The teachers were asked to co-operate with the writing supervisor in testing the standards indicated. The quality last fall (Table I) was practically the same in all grades. The question arose, May we not expect to reach a higher quality in upper grades? The low speed in the lower grades indicated a slow *drawing* of the letters and a *finger* movement which greatly sacrificed speed. Question, Should we not increase the speed in lower grades? A fact not showing in the general summary but which did show in the detail of rooms and buildings was that a grade here and there stood out far in advance of the same grades in other buildings or of the grade above or below in the same building. Did this not indicate that it would be possible to secure and maintain a higher standard of writing both as to speed and quality by giving more attention to it?

In attempting to answer the above questions and prove the correctness of our tentative standards as shown in Table II tests were made in grades 3A, 4A, 5A, 6B, and 6A. In each instance the work was graded by three judges, one of the judges being different in each grade. As the work proceeded, the chief question came to be, *How is quality affected by speed?* The results in the 6A grade are representative.

| | | Average Speed (Letters per Min.) | Average Quality (Scale A) |
|---|---|---|---|
| Speed and quality in Writing, 6A Grade | Slow writing....... | $46\frac{17}{21}$ | $14\frac{38}{40}$ |
| | Natural writing.... | $73\frac{3}{21}$ | $14\frac{28}{42}$ |
| | Rapid writing...... | $82\frac{7}{21}$ | $14\frac{5}{42}$ |

The tests point strongly to the conclusion that *speed may be secured without any sacrifice of quality,* at least in intermediate grades.

This conclusion is borne out by an experience extending over five years in the St. Louis public schools, where speed by the muscular movement is a main object. Supervisor H. C. Walker writes me:

> We have but one rate of speed in all the grades. In the primary grades the pupils practice oval exercises at the rate of about 180 revolutions a minute. This sets the standard of speed that is used in the writing and while the letter formation is sacrificed to some extent we notice that the pupil's control improves as he passes through the grades.
>
> We place as much stress on the manner in which the writing is done as we do upon the immediate result in the formation of exercise or letter. We have been following this plan very successfully for about five years and at present have a number of second-grade rooms where the pupils write as freely and almost as accurately as we are able to find in the intermediate rooms.

In the light of this experience and our own tests, it appears that our tentative standards (Table II) were much too low as to speed in the lower grades. A minimum of 60 or 70 letters per minute for all lower grades and a minimum of 80 to 100 letters per minute for the upper grades and high school appears to be nearer the correct standards.

It further appears that in order to prevent constant dropping to lower standards, the writing work must be reinforced at every point in the school work and not left entirely to the writing period and the writing supervisor. Good writing should not be confined to the writing period. The teacher should expect good writing in all lines of school work and should accept no work in which the writing falls below the minimum standard. This will require that the teacher provide sufficient time for written work in order that the writing may be good, and this will doubtless mean less written work on the part of pupils. It will mean avoiding the rush and hurry incident to much of our school work. It goes without saying that the board work of teachers should show the correct form combined with a high quality of excellence.

In conclusion, we must continue our study. We have at least indicated a *method* of investigation, and that is worth more than the energy in time and effort expended on our study. Let us continue to collect evidence until we have enough evidence to justify an opinion.

# EDITORIAL NOTES

The withdrawal of Dr. Elmer E. Brown from the Commissionership of Education may very properly be made the occasion of comment on both the office and the man. Dr. Brown has done much to make the reports issued by the Bureau of Education more valuable to all who seek information on educational matters. The reports of the Commissioner have appeared very promptly at the opening of the year. The tables have been modified in such a way as to make the facts more accessible. Digests of the statistics have been prepared which set forth the meaning of the technical matter in easily comprehensible form. A series of separates covering vital interests has been issued from time to time by well-qualified specialists. The library of the Bureau has made its material more than ever available to students. For all this steady and helpful improvement of the Bureau, the educational world owes much to Dr. Brown.

**Dr. Brown's Resignation**

Discouragements have arisen because of the attitude of Congress. Dr. Brown launched a campaign for more research funds. His plans were comprehensive and contemplated work on the part of the federal government in the investigation of schools and other social institutions which contribute to education. The need of investigations of this type was not regarded by Congress as sufficiently imperative to warrant appropriations. The number of people who are directly affected by educational legislation is comparatively small as contrasted with those affected by the work done by the federal government in agriculture. Yet it is difficult for this smaller group of professional educators to see how the country at large can fail to demand some more highly organized educational investigations. Dr. Brown has done a large service in interpreting his office as responsible for investigation. The Bureau must be aggressive in its collection of information. It has been

**Need of Educational Research**

more aggressive than ever before under Dr. Brown. It is to be hoped that the next commissioner will follow this part of Dr. Brown's program with vigor.

**Educators Must Co-operate with the Bureau**

The call of a single institution was strong enough to take an officer from a government bureau. New York University is to be congratulated on securing the services of a man of national reputation and high scholarly attainments and standing. The Bureau of Education ought to be a place of such influence and dignity that no one could find a larger sphere of influence than the headship of this Bureau. The frank fact is that the Commissioner of Education does not have at the present time a position of the dignity and influence which he should command. For this state of affairs, those who have charge of schools are responsible. Superintendents and teachers should make it clear to their representatives that there is a desire—a widespread demand—for educational investigations. There is at the present time too little interest on the part of teachers in the service which the Bureau renders. A representative at Washington of a district where the publications of the Bureau are little used is not likely to initiate a movement for the enlargement of the Bureau. The educators of the country must make known in unequivocal fashion their demand for the enlargement of the Bureau. Dr. Brown undoubtedly saw before him at New York University a more congenial opportunity. The lesson to be learned from his resignation by all who are interested in the Bureau is not obscure. It is to be hoped that the Bureau may soon receive the support which will make it what it should be.

# BOOK REVIEWS

*Problems in Wood-Turning.* By Fred D. Crawshaw. Peoria, Ill.: Manual Arts Press. Pp. 35 and 25 plates. $0.80.

Written as a textbook for students, this volume is also an excellent reference book for teachers of wood-turning. The author has succeeded in giving a series of lucid descriptions of the manipulation of wood-turning tools, in arranging progressively the several processes, in illustrating interesting applications of these processes to useful articles, and in setting forth logically such principles of design as are inherent in this relatively inartistic or non-artistic branch of woodworking.

The accuracy tests and puzzle rings are ingenious and interesting and the useful models shown are exceptionally well designed and suggestive of development by the individual pupil.

As to the book itself the arrangement is good, the illustrations are well drawn and illuminating, and the plates are unusually good examples of well-dimensioned working drawings.

Frank M. Leavitt

---

*What to Do at Recess.* By George E. Johnson. Boston: Ginn & Co., 1910. 12mo, cloth; 33 pages; illustrated. 25 cents.

This practical little book is rich in profitable suggestions for making good use of play periods. It is addressed to teachers, but will also prove an excellent first handbook for people who have charge of recreation centers anywhere. The needs and enjoyments of children of primary, intermediate, and grammar age are taken up separately. Brief explanations of many games are given and simple forms of playground apparatus are discussed. The book is easily read and will commend itself to those busy people who wish to get this kind of information in condensed form.

J. Anna Norris

---

*The Building and Care of the Body.* By C. N. Millard. New York: Macmillan, 1910. $0.40.

This book emphasizes primarily hygiene and hygienic habits of life in discussions that are simple and clear and easily applicable to the daily experiences of children in the fourth, fifth, and sixth grades, for whom it is especially intended. In addition to sections on the various aspects of personal hygiene, food, air, exercise, care of special sense organs, etc., there is a good chapter on the care of younger children, and one on the simplest elements of first aid to the injured.

A small amount of anatomy is incorporated where it will aid in clearness of discussion. In this connection it may be regretted that in so useful a book a few technical errors have crept in, as the repeated use of the term "expansion" of the diaphragm when "contraction" is plainly intended. Also the drinking of water with meals is categorically condemned although there is much authority for the opposite contention.

J. A. N.

---

*The Reasoning Ability of Children of the Fourth, Fifth, and Sixth School Grades.* By FREDERICK G. BONSER. New York: Teachers College, Columbia University, 1910. Pp. 133.

This monograph gives the results of an experimental study of the abilities of 757 fourth-, fifth-, and sixth-grade children of Passaic, N.J., to use what the author regards as the "most fundamental four phases of reasoning activity," namely, "controlled association, mathematical judgment, selective judgment, and the complex analysis and synthesis found in literary interpretation."

For the test of mathematical judgment fifteen easy problems involving knowledge to be expected of the children were given: for controlled association, (1) a list of twenty sentences requiring that appropriate words be substituted where blanks occurred, (2) twenty sentences requiring the choice of a right or wrong word to make proper sense in each, and (3) sixty words requiring opposites; for selective judgment, (1) the choice of the right reasons from a variety of reasons why certain things are so, and (2) the selection of good definitions from a number of definitions of objects; for literary interpretation, the telling or giving the meaning of two stanzas of poetry.

The author reaches the conclusion that the above tests are valid tests of native reasoning ability, as there is a "progressive development through the grades," as the younger children of a grade are uniformly superior to the older, and as there are "substantial percentages of the lowest grades represented in the highest quartile of ability of all." Mr. Bonser says that the conclusion which is of the greatest pragmatic value is the one drawn from the last two results stated above—that "the worst type of retardation is that which withholds appropriate promotion from those who are the most gifted, therefore of most significance as social capital."

The tests show careful preparation, the conditions under which they were given were kept uniform, and the presentation is thorough and clear. Were the results given in percentages as well as in terms of median abilities the comparison of the tests with each other could be more readily noted. However, the table of correlations brings this out fairly well. Mr. Bonser's results certainly make clear that there is a wide variation in ability in each grade and force the conclusion that the teaching and management of the schools are not meeting the conditions.

Whether the tests employed by the author are adequate for determining the status of reasoning ability is a different question. Can we say that mathematical and selective judgment, controlled association, and the analysis and synthesis found in literary interpretation are the "four fundamental phases of reasoning ability"? Are not the formulation and testing of hypotheses, the establishment of general conclusions, and their verification quite as fundamental?

The motive for reasoning, implicit or explicit, is found in a problematical situation which confronts the individual. Mr. Bonser's tests do not afford this except in a highly artificial and static form. The very fact that the time taken by the first pupil in the room to complete the exercise was made the time limit for all pupils vitiates the value of the test as one for reasoning and makes it rather a test for knowledge and habits that have become automatized. Mr. Bonser comments upon this but does not think that the value of the test for reasoning is lessened thereby. Certainly there must be a stock of knowledge and ability to control associations before reasoning in a given situation can take place, but the mere recall of knowledge through associations is not necessarily a test of reasoning ability, nor does it follow that the associations were built up as a result of reasoning.

The selective judgment and literary interpretation tests are better adapted to call forth reasoning than the controlled association and mathematical judgment tests, but the same objections to the imposed time limit and the lack of a problematic situation apply here also.

The author draws the conclusion that since the younger children in each grade score more points than the older, and since a good percentage of the lower grade children reach the highest quartile of all, the tests are of native as well as of acquired ability. In Test III for controlled association there is such a small gain from grade to grade, and for the younger over the older that it is barely noticeable. This may indicate that the knowledge required by the test was acquired early and had reached a high degree of automatization in the lowest grade. On the other hand, Test IV for controlled association shows a marked gain from year to year and for the younger over the older, and may be interpreted as meaning simply that the information necessary for the solution of this test had not yet been acquired as habit in the lower grades. The fact that there is a marked gain in Grade 5B over 4A for both younger and older children may mean that this information was a part of the teaching of Grade 5B.

There is only from four to six months' difference between the average age of the younger 25 per cent of Grade 4A and that of Grade 5A, and three months between the older groups of the same grades. Despite the small difference in age Test IV shows an appreciable difference in ability between these two grades, being about the same for the younger as for the older groups. This would seem to indicate that the difference is due largely to school training.

Perhaps the effects of retardation have not sufficiently entered into the author's conclusions. Making the very liberal allowance of three years to a grade, eight to eleven years for Grade 4, and so on, from 30 to 40 per cent of the children are above age. Taking the ages nine to ten for Grade 4, ten to eleven for Grade 5, and eleven to twelve for Grade 6, out of 757 children only 20 are below the normal age. Hence the younger 25 per cent represents the normal-age group, while the older 25 per cent consists of very much retarded children. The difference in ability found between the younger and older groups does not necessarily indicate that these tests are of native reasoning ability; they may be interpreted as simply indicating that the normal-age or younger group was able to automatize acquired knowledge more quickly than the older, retarded group.

In a study of this kind information in regard to when and where the children received definite training along the lines of knowledge required by the tests might throw some light upon the interpretation of the results in terms of native and acquired ability.

The conditions under which the author worked seem to the reviewer to be too complicated for obtaining valid information concerning the reasoning ability of children. Children should be studied in groups of the same age and ability. Individual records should be kept. A suitable situation should confront the children involving a problem known to be new to them and for the solution of which they have an adequate stock of old knowledge. The reasoning process itself must be studied as well as the results of learning, for the learning may or may not have involved reasoning.

M. A. Grupe

The University of Chicago

# CURRENT EDUCATIONAL LITERATURE IN THE PERIODICALS[1]

IRENE WARREN
Librarian, School of Education, The University of Chicago

ADDISON, J. T. Young China in the classroom. Out. 97:787–91. (8 Ap. '11.)

ANDREWS, CHARLES. Education: the next phase. Educa. 31:512–18. (Ap. '11.)

BENSON, HARRIET. A girl at Heidelberg. Out. 97:782–87. (8 Ap. '11.)

BOSTWICK, A. E. The social work of the library. Pub. Lib. 16:192–95. (My. '11.)

BOYNTON, F. D. Children's reading. Amer. Educa. 14:352–54. (Ap. '11.)

BRICKER, G. A. Agriculture in the public schools. Educa. R. 41:395–403. (Ap. '11.)

BURNITE, CAROLINE. The standard of selection of children's books. Lib. J. 36:161–66. (Ap. '11.)

BUTLER, NICHOLAS MURRAY. University administration in the United States. Educa. R. 41:325–44. (Ap. '11.)

DANA, JOHN COTTON. The country church and the library. Out. 98:34–35. (6 My. '11.)

DAVIS, BENJAMIN MARSHALL. Agricultural education: elementary and secondary. El. School T. 11:469–84. (My. '11.)

DAY, CLIVE. A new course of study in Yale college. Educa. R. 41:371–81. (Ap. '11.)

DEW, LOUISE E. Open-air schools for abnormal children. World To-day 20:557–64. (My. '11.)

DYER, F. B. Industrial education in Cincinnati. School R. 19:289–94. (My. '11.)

ENDRES, ERNEST A. H. America's school social centers. Pop. Educator 28:453–55. (My. '11.)

FARR, HARRY. Library work with children. Lib. J. 36:166–71. (Ap. '11.)

FELMLEY, DAVID. The normal schools and vocational education. West. Journ. of Educa. 4:154–60. (Ap. '11.)

[1] *Abbreviations.*—Amer. Educa., American Education; Educa., Education; Educa. R., Educational Review; El. School T., Elementary School Teacher; Harp. W., Harper's Weekly; Journ. of Educa. Psychol., Journal of Educational Psychology; Journ. of Home Econ., Journal of Home Economics; Lib. J., Library Journal; Lit. D., Literary Digest; Liv. Age, Living Age; Out., Outlook; Pop. Educator, Popular Educator; Pop. Sci. Mo., Popular Science Monthly; Psychol. Clinic, Psychological Clinic; Pub. Lib., Public Libraries; School R., School Review; Sci. Amer., Scientific American; West. Journ. of Educa., Western Journal of Education.

GAUSS, CHESTER A. A college student's view of educational methods. Educa. R. 41:404–11. (Ap. '11.)

GENUNG, JOHN FRANKLIN. My lowly teacher. Harper 122:842–46. (My. '11.)

GREENMAN, EDWARD DOUGLAS. The bibliographic work of the library of the United States Bureau of Education. Lib. J. 36:180–81. (Ap. '11.)

HARDING, B. F. A secondary school curriculum. Educa. 31:499–511. (Ap. '11.)

HARDY, CARRIE A. The evolution of the American high school (1). West. Journ. of Educa. 4:169–75. (Ap. '11.)

HARDY, E. Yorkshire schools. Liv. Age 51:218–20. (22 Ap. '11.)

HOLMES, ARTHUR. Classification of clinic cases. Psychol. Clinic 5:36–53. (Ap. '11.)

Idols of education. Dial 50:333–35. (1 My. '11.)

JASTROW, JOSEPH. Problems of modern education. Dial 50:341–44. (1 My. '11.)

JOSEPHSON, AKSEL G. S. Schools for social workers. World To-day 20:617–19. (My. '11.)

KENNAN, GEORGE. Student disorders in Russia. Out. 97:968–74. (29 Ap. '11.)

KERSCHENSTEINER, GEORG. The technical day trade schools in Germany. School R. 19:295–317. (My. '11.)

KIRKLAND, JAMES H. What it is to be a college president. Educa. R. 41:412. (Ap. '11.)

LARSSON, GUSTAF. To what extent should vocational training be recognized in our elementary schools? Educa. 31:527–28. (Ap. '11.)

LEARNED, WILLIAM S. An American teacher's year in a Prussian gymnasium. Educa. R. 41:345–70. (Ap. '11.)

LELAND, C. G. Classroom libraries in New York. Lib. J. 36:178–79. (Ap. '11.)

LIPMANN, OTTO. Pedagogical psychology of report. Journ. of Educa. Psychol. 2:253–61. (My. '11.)

LURTON, FREEMAN E. A study of retardation in the schools of Minnesota. El. School T. 11:457–64. (My. '11.)

MCGAUFLIN, ISABELLE. Vocational training for girls. Educa. 31:523–26. (Ap. '11.)

MAYO, EARL. The conservation of the child. Out. 97:892–903. (22 Ap. '11.)

Meeting of superintendents' and principals' association of northern Illinois: report of Committee of Seven on an outline course of study on a scientific basis. El. School T. 11:393–449. (Ap. '11.)

MOORE, CHARLES LEONARD. The educational system of the elder Mr. Weller. Dial 50:335–37. (1 My. '11.)

MUZZEY, DAVID SAVILLE. State, church, and school in France. The separation of church and school (3). School R. 19:318–32. (My. '11.)

O'Shea, M. V. A great educational reference work. Dial 50:349–52. (1 My. '11.)

Parsons, William W. The housing question in the state normal school. West. Journ. of Educa. 4:145–53. (Ap. '11.)

Pearson, Edmund L. The evil that books do. Pub. Lib. 16:188–91. (My. '11.)

Pearson, Henry C. The scientific study of the teaching of spelling. Journ. of Educa. Psychol. 2:241–52. (My. '11.)

Ralph, Georgia G. Child welfare exhibit in retrospect. Lib. J. 36:157–61. (Ap. '11.)

Rankin, Jean Sherwood. The eighth-grade vocabulary. El. School T. 11: 465–68. (My. '11.)

Rankin, Julia T. Story hour in the Carnegie library of Atlanta. Lib. J. 36:181. (Ap. '11.)

Ravenhill, Alice. The educational value of play in childhood. Amer. Educa. 14:348–51. (Ap. '11.)

Richards, Ellen H. The social significance of the home economics movement. Journ. of Home Econ. 3:117–25. (Ap. '11.)

Robison, C. H. The present status of agricultural education in public secondary schools of the United States. School R. 19:333–44. (My. '11.)

Roosevelt, Theodore. Education: how old the new. Out. 97:791–92. (8 Ap. '11.)

Russell, Isaac. Is our public school system behind the times? Craftsman 20:140–45. (My. '11.)

Scharlieb, Mary A. D. Recreational activities of girls during adolescence. Child 1:571–86. (Ap. '11.)

Splendors of the Morgan library. Lit. D. 42:680–81. (8 Ap. '11.)

Stearns, Wallace N. The college and the rural districts. Educa. 31:529–35. (Ap. '11.)

Taylor, Charles Keen. Educational aspects of Christian Science. Psychol. Clinic 5:29–35. (Ap. '11.)

———. Moral training of private school boys. Educa. 31:541–47. (Ap. '11.)

Thorndike, Edward L. G. Stanley Hall. Sci. Amer. 104:399. (22 Ap. '11.)

(The) training of college students. Harp. W. 55:23. (15 Ap. '11.)

Upton, Clifford Brewster. The training of teachers of mathematics in professional schools of collegiate grade. Educa. R. 41:382–94. (Ap. '11.)

Walsh, James J. Science at the medieval universities. Pop. Sci. Mo. 78: 445–59. (My. '11.)

Wilson, Louis N. Some new fields of library activity. Pub. Lib. 16:183–88. (My. '11.)

# The Elementary School Teacher

June, 1911

Vol. XI, No. 10

THE UNIVERSITY OF CHICAGO PRESS
CHICAGO, ILLINOIS, U.S.A.

AGENTS
CAMBRIDGE UNIVERSITY PRESS, LONDON AND EDINBURGH
TH. STAUFFER, LEIPZIG

# The Elementary School Teacher

PUBLISHED MONTHLY EXCEPT IN JULY AND AUGUST

EDITED BY

THE FACULTY OF THE SCHOOL OF EDUCATION

WITH THE CO-OPERATION OF

THE FACULTY OF THE FRANCIS W. PARKER SCHOOL

---

Vol. XI CONTENTS FOR JUNE, 1911 No. 10



---

**The Elementary School Teacher** is published monthly from September to June. ¶The subscription price is $1.50 per year; the price of single copies is 20 cents. ¶Postage is prepaid by the publishers on all orders from the United States, Mexico, Cuba, Porto Rico, Panama Canal Zone, Republic of Panama, Hawaiian Islands, Philippine Islands, Guam, Tutuila (Samoa), Shanghai. ¶Postage is charged extra as follows: For Canada, 30 cents on annual subscriptions (total $1.80), on single copies, 3 cents (total 23 cents); for all other countries in the Postal Union, 46 cents on annual subscriptions (total $1.96), on single copies, 6 cents (total 26 cents). ¶Remittances should be made payable to The University of Chicago Press, and should be in Chicago or New York exchange, postal or express money order. If local check is used, 10 cents must be added for collection.

**The following agents** have been appointed and are authorized to quote the prices indicated:

For the British Empire: Cambridge University Press, Fetter Lane, London, E.C., England. Yearly subscriptions, including postage, 8*s.* each; single copies, including postage, 1*s.* each.

For the Continent of Europe: Th. Stauffer, Universitätsstrasse 26, Leipzig, Germany. Yearly subscriptions, including postage, M. 8.25 each; single copies, including postage, M. 1.10 each.

**Claims for missing numbers** should be made within the month following the regular month of publication. The publishers expect to supply missing numbers free only when they have been lost in transit.

**Business correspondence** should be addressed to The University of Chicago Press, Chicago, Ill.

**Communications for the editors** should be addressed to them at The University of Chicago, Chicago, Ill.

Entered October 12, 1903, at the Post-Office at Chicago, Ill., as second-class matter, under Act of Congress March 3, 1879

vose

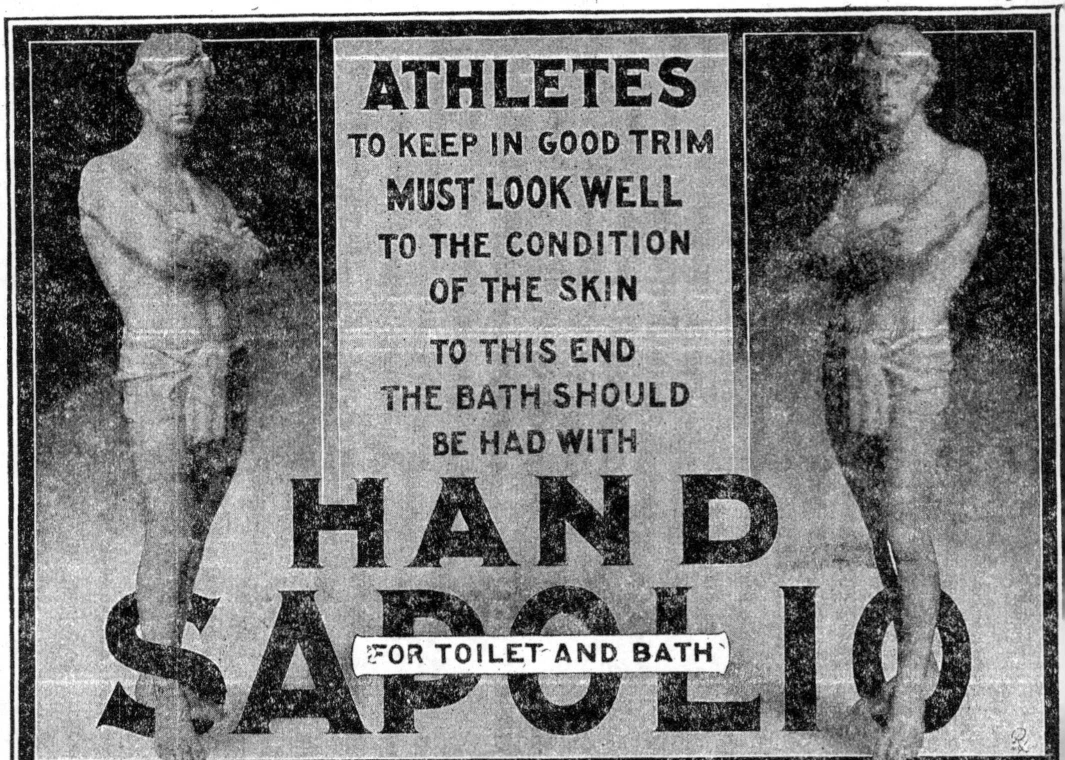

www.ingramcontent.com/pod-product-compliance
Lightning Source LLC
LaVergne TN
LVHW010521100826
845148LV00001B/58